Sociological Theory

Titles of Related Interest from Pine Forge Press

Sociology for a New Century, by York W. Bradshaw, Joseph F. Healey, and Rebecca Smith

Adventures in Social Research: Data Analysis Using SPSS for Windows 95/98®, by Earl Babbie, Fred Halley, and Jeanne Zaino

Taking It Big: Developing Sociological Consciousness in Postmodern Times, by Steve P. Dandaneau

Illuminating Social Life: Classical and Contemporary Theory Revisited, Second Edition, edited by Peter Kivisto

Key Ideas in Sociology, by Peter Kivisto

Multiculturalism in the United States: Current Issues, Contemporary Voices, by Peter Kivisto and Georganne Rundblad

Social Prisms: Reflections on Everyday Myths and Paradoxes, by Jodi O'Brien

The Production of Reality: Essays and Readings on Social Interaction, Third Edition, by Jodi O'Brien and Peter Kollock

The Social Worlds of Higher Education: Handbook for Teaching in a New Century, edited by Bernice Pescosolido and Ronald Aminzade

The McDonaldization of Society, New Century Edition, by George Ritzer

Worlds Apart: Social Inequalities in a New Century, by Scott Sernau

Of Crime and Criminality: The Use of Theory in Everyday Life, edited by Sally S. Simpson

Sociology for a New Century: A Pine Forge Press Series

EDITED BY CHARLES RAGIN, WENDY GRISWOLD, AND WALTER W. POWELL

An Invitation to Environmental Sociology, by Michael M. Bell

Global Inequalities, by York W. Bradshaw and Michael Wallace

Schools and Societies, by Steven Brint

Economy/Society, by Bruce Carruthers and Sarah Babb

How Societies Change, by Daniel Chirot

Ethnicity and Race: Making Identities in a Changing World, by Stephen Cornell and Doug Hartmann

The Sociology of Childhood, by William A. Corsaro

Cultures and Societies in a Changing World, by Wendy Griswold

Crime and Disrepute, by John Hagan

Gods in the Global Village: The World's Religions in Sociological Perspective, by Lester R. Kurtz

Waves of Democracy: Social Movements and Political Change, by John Markoff

Development and Social Change: A Global Perspective, Second Edition, by Philip McMichael

Aging, Social Inequality, and Public Policy, by Fred C. Pampel

Constructing Social Research, by Charles C. Ragin

Women and Men at Work, by Barbara Reskin and Irene Pakavic

Making Societies: The Historical Construction of Our World, by William G. Roy

Cities in a World Economy, Second Edition, by Saskia Sassen

Gender, Family, and Social Movements, by Suzanne Staggenborg

Law/Society: Origins, Interactions, and Change, by John R. Sutton

Sociological Theory

Bert N. Adams

University of Wisconsin

R. A. Sydie

University of Alberta

Pine Forge Press

Thousand Oaks, California | London | New Delhi

For information:

 Pine Forge Press
A Sage Publications Company
2455 Teller Road
Thousand Oaks, California 91320
(805) 499-4224
E-mail: order@pfp.sagepub.com

Sage Publications Ltd.
6 Bonhill Street
London EC2A 4PU
United Kingdom

Sage Publications India Pvt. Ltd.
M-32 Market
Greater Kailash I
New Delhi 110 048 India

Printed in the United States of America

Library of Congress Cataloging-in-Publication Data
Adams, Bert N.
     Sociological theory / Bert N. Adams and R. A. Sydie.
          p.   cm.
     Includes bibliographical references and index.
          ISBN 0-7619-8557-3
     1. Sociology.   I. Sydie, R. A. (Rosalind Ann), 1940–   II. Title.
          HM585 .A33   2001
          301'.01—dc21

                                        00-012704

This book is printed on acid-free paper.

01   02   03   04   05   06   10   9   8   7   6   5   4   3   2   1

Publisher: *Stephen D. Rutter*
Assistant to the Publisher: *Ann Makarias*
Production Management: *Scratchgravel Publishing Services*
Copy Editor: *Margaret C. Tropp*
Typesetter: *Scratchgravel Publishing Services*
Indexer: *James Minkin*
Cover Designer: *Ravi Balasuriya*

About the Authors

Bert N. Adams (Ph.D., University of North Carolina) has taught sociological theory extensively, both in East Africa and at the University of Wisconsin–Madison. He has published on consensus and coercion theories and on the importance of classical theory to a degree in sociology. He also teaches and writes on the sociology of the family. He and his co-author, R. A. Sydie, have written a paper on C. P. Gilman and Beatrice Webb, which was published in *Sociological Origins* in October 2000.

R. A. Sydie has been professor of sociology at the University of Alberta in Edmonton for the past 30 years and is the current chair of the department of sociology. Her research interests include sociological theory, art and culture, and gender studies. Professor Sydie is the author of *Natural Women, Cultured Men*. Her latest research project involves a historical examination of sociological work on love and eroticism.

About the Publisher

Pine Forge Press is a new educational publisher, dedicated to publishing innovative books and software throughout the social sciences. On this and any other of our publications, we welcome your comments.

Please write to:

> **Pine Forge Press**
> A Sage Publications Company
> 31 St. James Ave., Suite 510
> Boston, MA 02116
> (617) 753-7512
> E-mail: info@pfp.sagepub.com
>
> *Visit our World Wide Web site, your direct link to*
> *a multitude of online resources:*
>
> www.pineforge.com

To Diane and Campbell

Brief Contents

Detailed Contents

SECTION IV

Sociological Theories of Complexity and Form   167

7   Social Action and Social Complexity   169
Max Weber and Marianne Weber

8   The Sociology of Form and Content   197
Simmel

SECTION VII

Twentieth-Century Functionalism and Beyond   343

14   Twentieth-Century Functionalism   345
Parsons and Merton

Preface

There are many sociological theory texts currently available. So why produce another? What makes this text unique? How will the student reader benefit from it?

Rediscovery

Robert K. Merton once referred to the importance of giving "credit where credit was due" (1967:26). Sociological theory has not done that. By 1950, male scholarship had either ignored or marginalized women theorists and many others, excluding them from the history of social thought. However, in recent decades, increasing numbers of theorists and theory instructors have recognized that the "dead white male" approach to the history of social thought is at least incomplete, if not insidious.

In Chapter 2 of this text, Harriet Martineau is introduced as one of the founders of sociology. Throughout the book, the views of women theorists and others are represented in far more than token fashion. Thus, rediscovery means hearing the voices of important theorists such as W. E. B. Du Bois, Marianne Weber, Charlotte P. Gilman, and Rosa Luxemburg. It also means becoming acquainted with Joseph Schumpeter, V. I. Lenin, and—more recently—Niklas Luhmann, Theda Skocpol, contemporary Marxist Erik Olin Wright, the evolutionist Elman Service, Arlie Hochschild, Dorothy Smith, Patricia Hill Collins, and Immanuel Wallerstein.

This text, then, pays attention to the questions asked and the answers given by more than the "usual suspects." Such rediscovery is intellectually exciting and challenging.

Organization

With the wealth of information covered, our aim is for readers always to be aware, chronologically and intellectually, of where they have been, where they are headed, and how the many different parts of their reading "journey" relate to one another. To accomplish this goal, we have organized the book as follows.

Classical and Contemporary Theories   The first two chapters sketch the history of social thought until the mid-nineteenth century. Chapters 3–13 and 14–23 are divided at about 1930. This division is approximate because quite a few of the writers in Chapters 3–13 lived and wrote beyond 1930. For example, Sigmund Freud lived to 1939, Beatrice Webb to 1943, Schumpeter to 1950, and Du Bois to 1963. However, the chapter division reflects the early and the later generations of sociological theorists. In a somewhat arbitrary fashion, Talcott

Parsons and Robert Merton in Chapter 14 may be viewed as the beginning point for contemporary theory.[1]

Schools of Thought   A key organizing principle of this text is to trace the following major schools of thought as they appear and reappear from chapter to chapter.

1. *Functionalism,* from Herbert Spencer through Durkheim, Parsons, and Merton, to Luhmann.

2. *Evolutionism,* from Spencer through W. G. Sumner to Service. Together these two sociological theories have generally been supportive of the status quo. Thus, they are treated as baseline theories to which many others have reacted.

3. The anticapitalist *revolutionary and conflict perspective* begins in the work of Karl Marx and Friedrich Engels, and we trace it through Lenin and Luxemburg to Raya Dunayevskaya, Nicos Poulantzas, and Erik Olin Wright.

4. A closely allied brand of theorizing is *critical of capitalism* but is less optimistic about curing its ills. This is traced from Thorstein Veblen and Du Bois, through the pre–World War II Frankfurt School, to Wallerstein and Michel Foucault.

5. The *complexities* of history and social action are found in the works of Max Weber and Georg Simmel, theorists who should not be pigeonholed within a single theoretical school.

6. Reactions to the *political and economic aspects* of Marxism can be seen in the writings of Vilfredo Pareto and Robert Michels as well as Veblen and Schumpeter.

7. An important theoretical perspective in this book concerns gender or *feminism.* In this book we introduce the works of Gilman, Dunayevskaya, Smith, and Collins, among others.

8. The *micro*-perspectives on society theorize about the self and interaction. They are traced from C. H. Cooley, G. H. Mead, and Freud to Erving Goffman and Hochschild.

While these are among the major theoretical schools introduced, other branches of the sociological "tree" also appear throughout the chapters.

Consistent Organization Within Chapters   Readers new to sociological theory often face the "forest and trees" problem—that is, they become immersed in the details of one theory after another and are unable to compare or relate them. This problem becomes particularly difficult in texts that do not provide consistent means for making connections. We address this problem by fol-

---

[1] It is worth noting that we also plan to divide this text into two brief volumes, so that those who teach separate courses on classical or contemporary theory will be able to use the appropriate brief text, along with appropriate supporting materials.

lowing a consistent organizational scheme within the chapters. After covering the setting and background of a particular theorist or school of thought, each chapter follows a pattern of presentation that includes:

Central Theories and Methods

Nature of Society, Humans, and Change

Class, Gender, and Race

Other Theories and Theorists

Critiques and Conclusions

Final Thoughts

The section entitled "Nature of Society, Humans, and Change" examines a theorist's fundamental assumptions underpinning his or her theoretical views, often leading to a consideration of the theorist's ideology—what that individual thought was good or bad, right or wrong, better or worse about society and human nature. Each chapter includes a "Class, Gender, and Race" section, with one or more of these topics sometimes being the primary focus of a particular thinker. For example, Wright focuses on class, Gilman and Smith on gender, and Collins on race and gender. We devote a section of each chapter to these topics—despite the fact that not every theorist treats them thoroughly—because the broad theme of *inequality* is an important one in this textbook.

An important section of each chapter is "Other Theories and Theorists." This section presents theoretical issues less central to the writer, but nevertheless noteworthy. For example, in the "Other Theories" section of Chapter 14, we introduce Merton's "self-fulfilling prophecy." In this section we also connect the theorist under consideration to others who are directly referred to in the theorist's work but who have not yet been discussed in that chapter; at times we also relate the theorist to others whose ideas have some connections. The "Critiques and Conclusions" section summarizes the ideas of the theorist or theorists considered in that chapter and presents criticisms of each theorist from critics of their own day as well as critics of today. Each chapter closes with "Final Thoughts," sometimes poignant, sometimes ironic, and sometimes offering a broader view.

Important Themes in Sociological Theory That Cut Across Chapters

We also seek to help students recognize connections across social theories by noting additional key *themes* beyond those included in the chapter headings, themes that recur as theoretical topics. These consistent themes include the following:

The characteristics of modern societies

Attitudes toward capitalism

Power and inequality in society

Relationship of the individual to society

As these themes appear and reappear throughout the chapters, the terms are *italicized* so that students can more easily make connections across chapters.

Additional Learning and Teaching Features

In addition to the content, organization, and thematic innovations of this book, several other learning and teaching features are worth noting. First, a *Timeline* in a four-panel fold-out in the back of the book places all the theorists clearly into their historical periods. The theorist's life span, and the chapter in which she or he appears in this book, are superimposed on important world events occurring during that time. The birth and death dates of each theorist help readers relate the theorists to one another. Students can also see and remember which theorists are alive in the year 2001.

Each of the nine major sections in this book begins with a *section introduction* that ties the individual chapters to each other in groupings, usually focusing on a school of thought and helping the student look both backward and forward.

Key terms are **boldfaced** in the text when they are first defined and discussed, and they are also boldfaced in the index.

The *References* at the end of each chapter include both the original publication date and the republication date, if any, of the edition referred to or quoted in this volume.

Brevity

A central goal of this text is to be as concise as possible while also doing justice to a wide variety of theorists. The text may seem long, but the table of contents shows that the theorists and breadth of theoretical issues covered are also quite extensive. Instead of covering 4 to 12 theorists, we give substantial treatment of some 45 thinkers. Our intention has been to cast the net widely enough to capture diversity both within and between theoretical viewpoints or schools of thought. Thus, given the range of ideas, historical contexts, and theorists covered, we believe this book is indeed brief.

Limitations of This Book

This text covers a large number of theories and theorists as cogently as possible. There are, however, two limitations. First, we have not introduced the important non-Western views of society. Confucius produced a philosophical and theoretical basis for understanding Chinese society. Ibn Khaldun, in the fourteenth century, explained society from a North African perspective. Recently, Kwame Gyekye (1987, 1997), a Ghanaian thinker, has written about the nature of society as viewed from within his culture. A compendium of world sociological ideas needs to be attempted, but this volume is not it. We believe it is enough to rediscover the women theorists and others, such as Du Bois, and to bring them into the corpus of Western sociological theory.

A second limitation is that, despite covering more than 40 major thinkers, we may have included a theorist considered by one instructor to be superfluous and left out another's favorite classical or contemporary thinker. One might question why we have included Service on evolutionary thought, Wright on contemporary Marxism, or Hochschild on symbolic interactionism. The justification for each of them is that each does an outstanding job of bringing together and contributing to the issues in his or her theoretical specialty. After expending considerable effort sorting through contemporary theorists, we decided that the ones included are the best for both creative and summary purposes. No one knows, of course, whether Luhmann, Poulantzas, or Coleman will be considered an important theorist 25 years from now.

If we have omitted one of your favorite theorists, you can introduce that particular thinker through supplementary materials. We optimistically think this will be necessary in only a very limited number of cases.

We hope you and your students will find the pages that follow to be as worthwhile and exciting to read as we have found them to write during these past five years. We welcome your criticisms and suggestions as well as those of your students. Please write to us in care of Pine Forge Press, or email us at adams@ssc.wisc.edu.

Bert N. Adams
R. A. Sydie

References

Gyekye, Kwame. 1987. *An Essay on African Philosophical Thought: The Akan Conceptual Scheme.* Cambridge: Cambridge University Press.

———. 1997. *Tradition and Modernity: Philosophical Reflections on the African Experience.* New York: Oxford University Press.

Merton, Robert K. 1967/1996. *On Social Structure and Science* (Peter Sztompka, ed.). Chicago: University of Chicago Press.

Acknowledgments

This book has required the efforts and dedication of many people. First and foremost is Steve Rutter, the Publisher of Pine Forge Press. His enthusiasm, encouragement, and insights have kept us going throughout the project. Rebecca Smith's knowledge of students and of editorial style helped make the entire manuscript more "reader friendly." Anne Draus at Scratchgravel Publishing Services competently oversaw the process of copy editing and typesetting.

At the Pine Forge office, Sherith Pankratz encouraged us at the early stages, and Ann Makarias kept track of details and deadlines in the later stages. Jillaine Tyson designed and rendered the Timeline. University of Wisconsin–Madison colleague Mary Campbell reviewed the literature and references included in some chapters. Janet Donlin and Sandy Ramer of U.W.–Madison computerized portions of the work and worked on permissions.

We are grateful to the publishers who gave us permission to use lengthy quotes from their materials. We also thank the reviewers who read and criticized portions of the book at the early stages:

Joan Alway, University of Miami
Kevin Anderson, Northern Illinois University
James J. Chriss, Kansas Newman College
Harry Dahms, Florida State University

Anne F. Eisenberg, State University of New York, Geneseo
Kate Hausbeck, University of Nevada, Las Vegas
Peter Kivisto, Augustana College
Steven Lybrand, College of St. Thomas
Neil McLaughlin, McMaster University
Chris Prendergast, Illinois Wesleyan University
Robert E. L. Roberts, California State University, San Marcos
Kathleen Slobin, North Dakota State University
Dana Vannoy, formerly of the University of Cincinnati

These reviewers were absolutely essential to the final product, although, of course, they are not responsible for any lingering errors or misinterpretations.

Finally, the authors' spouses, Diane Adams and Campbell Sydie, have both encouraged and tolerated this multiyear endeavor. Without their good humor, patience, and suggestions, this project might never have seen the light of day.

A Note to Students

—●—

You as Theorist

Are you already a social theorist? Think about the following questions: Do some people have the cards stacked in their favor, while others have them stacked against, or do we all get pretty much what we deserve? Do you act the same way at a basketball game, in a bar, in a grocery store, and at a religious service, or do you behave differently as you move from place to place? Why are people in one country always fighting, while in another they seem so peaceful? Are they peaceful because they like one another or because some keep others under control?

Are men and women actually pretty much the same, except for their roles in childbearing? As my friend Steve says, "Well, you know how women are." As Maureen jokes, "Why is it men won't ever ask for directions?" Just what is it that women, or men, really want? And why? Why do politicians change their message "at the drop of a hat" to suit their audience? Do they really believe in anything? "The more things change, the more they stay the same"—how could that be, and what does it mean?

"What is good for General Motors (or Toyota) is good for the country"—is that true? Why does the head of General Motors make a seven-figure salary, a doctor six figures, a school teacher five, and a day care provider four? Does the salary correspond to how hard they work, or how long they went to school, or how smart they are? Is the world actually run by money? If so, what does it mean to "run the world"?

Whenever you make any of these comments, or ask or answer any of these questions, you are a social theorist. You theorize whenever you try to make sense of, understand, or explain your social world. This book introduces you to insightful and interesting answers that have been proposed over the years to these and other such questions. It does not tell you what to think, but helps you clarify your own thoughts, relate your various views of society to each other and to the views of others.

How can the study of sociological theory help you understand your world? An example, addressed in this text, may help answer that question. In our society many believe that success or failure is basically an individual matter, that no one should be allowed to stand in the way of your success, and that wealth is the best measure of success. However, not all societies have these as central values. In fact, in some societies the individual is expected to subordinate herself or himself to the good of the family or community. Such societies deemphasize the unique personality and may also limit worldly gain. Theorists have explained how such societies got that way and why such societies make sense to those who live in them. The study of different sorts of societies is not intended to make an individual less committed to his or her own society and its values, but such a study may at least broaden the individual's perspective on, and comprehension of, the varieties of workable human societies.

How This Book Is Organized

One organizing principle of this book is its division of theorists into thinkers of the *pre- and post-1930* periods, with the first 13 chapters covering the earlier time. Although some writers in the first 13 chapters lived beyond 1930, those in Chapters 14–23 did all their writing from 1930 on. Answers to the kinds of questions raised at the beginning of this Note to Students tend to be joined together into *schools of thought*. For example, those who believe people get what they deserve are apt also to believe that society exists because people like one another and like where they live. Such clusters or schools of thought are presented in most of the groupings of chapters in sections of this text. For example, you will find in Chapters 3, 4, and 14 the thoughts of those who believe that the various parts of society work together for the good of the whole and satisfy those living within it. Likewise, Chapters 5, 6, and 17 examine the theories of those who believe society is oppressive and is run by a small number of individuals who keep the others under control. Most chapters focus on one or more individuals who represent a particular school of thought.

Internally, chapters are organized consistently according to the following topics:

1. Central Theories and Methods
2. The Nature of Humans, Society, and Change
3. Class, Gender, and Race
4. Other Theories and Theorists
5. Critiques and Conclusions
6. Final Thoughts

The consistency of chapter organization makes it easier to compare, contrast, and relate the issues raised by one theorist with those raised by another. Another way we have tried to ease your way through this book is the introduction of *themes* that run through the volume. Some of the headings listed above, such as change, class, gender, and race, are also themes. Other important themes include how individual theorists have thought about the characteristics of modern society, what their attitudes are concerning capitalism, their views on power and inequality in society and on how individuals and society affect each other.

You have glimpsed the great variety of issues—some of which you already have an opinion about and some of which you may never have thought about before. Putting your views of society into this larger context is an adventure in learning and understanding. So let us begin the journey together.

Sociological Theory

SECTION I

The European Roots of Sociological Theory

To understand what sociological theory is, we must distinguish it from other explanations of social life. For example, religious explanations point to faith and revelation to justify their assertions. In contrast, sociological theory or explanation relies on evidence from the senses and from the social world itself to arrive at its conclusions. A shooting or bombing in a suburban school might be explained religiously as a result of original sin or as the devil's work. A sociological explanation, however, might point to the influence of the media, lack of parental supervision, and the accessibility of weapons.

Another important distinction is between sociological theory and ideology. Ideology, a central issue in this book, involves value judgments about what is good or bad, right or wrong, better or worse. Looking at the issue of school violence, one's ideology might simply say that life in the suburbs today is bad. It might even draw the comparative judgment that life is worse now than in the old days, when most people lived and worked on farms. But that is only one point of view. When you read in the newspaper that, say, an international trade agreement is economically advantageous or disadvantageous, you will draw your own conclusion about it. But you will also find yourself trying to decipher what the writer believes about how society operates, and about what he or she considers good or bad.

As you will see in this book, many theorists also have ideologies, although they may not state them explicitly. General categories of social ideology, as in politics and other aspects of social life, include liberal, conservative, and radical. A theorist who argues, for example, that society is held together by agreement on the rules and by our mutual need for one another is very likely basing her or his theory on the conservative ideology that "what is, is good."

The first two chapters of this book will introduce you to three topics: (1) the nature of sociological theory; (2) the history of theory prior to the nineteenth century; and (3) three early nineteenth-century "parents" of sociology. Chapter

1

1 describes social philosophies in Europe in the seventeenth- and eighteenth-century ages of enlightenment, reason, and revolution. In that time period, social thinkers began to question the age-old seeking of truth by religious revelation and church authority. Instead, they argued that truth is best discovered by reason—by the use of the human mind. The debate between reason and revelation has never been settled, but the latter has been on the defensive for at least two centuries.

The age of revolution in the eighteenth and nineteenth centuries involved the French Revolution, the American Revolution, and the industrial revolution. Many of the intellectual issues you will be exposed to in the pages ahead are firmly linked to either the French or industrial revolution. Sociological theories are still grappling with the character and effects of industrialization—along with its companion developments of urbanization, bureaucratization, and market capitalism. These issues are important themes throughout the book.

As you will discover in Chapter 1, philosophers writing in the seventeenth and eighteenth centuries addressed the roles of science and reason in efforts to build a better world. Later, after the French Revolution, other prominent theorists wrote from a conservative ideological position, wanting either to "conserve" the status quo or to bring back the "good old days" of prerevolutionary France. Besides such radicals and conservatives, in Chapter 1 you will meet philosophers concerned with social ethics. The chapter will conclude with several of the key issues confronting European thinkers at the beginning of the nineteenth century.

Chapter 2 is where the history of sociological theory, as distinct from social philosophy, begins. You will meet three important figures from the early nineteenth century: Henri de Saint-Simon, Auguste Comte, and Harriet Martineau. Comte is generally credited with being the "father of sociology," and with having coined the term *sociology*. However, all three, but especially Comte and Martineau, are among sociology's "parents." All three believed that scientific principles could be utilized to understand society.

By the time you finish reading the first two chapters, you will be aware of different types of theories, and of the ideologies that are intertwined with them. In the remainder of the book, we will put each theory's "best foot forward," while also meeting its critics. You will find your sympathies inclining toward some of these theories or ideologies more than others. You will also find that much current public—even political—discussion in the media revolves around these same basic ideas. And so your journey through Western theories of society begins. We believe you will find it both interesting and valuable.

Chapter 1

The Origins of Sociological Theory

Sociological theory is the aspect of sociology that students often find the least compelling. Compared, for example, to the interesting discussions of crime and deviance, or sex and gender, or popular culture students encounter in other sociology courses, theory seems to be a dry, abstract enterprise unconnected with "real" social interactions. Furthermore, even when theory does seem to have some connection to the everyday, it is often explained in complex and esoteric language.

Although some sociological theory can be accused of unnecessary complexity and abstraction, it is theory that underpins the "interesting" sociological discussions. In essence, theory is nothing more than sociologists' generalizations about "real" social interactions and the everyday practices of social life. For example, the fact that women rather than men do the bulk of housework and child care in our society is explained, in part, by the concept of patriarchy, meaning the rule of the father or oldest male, and the cultural assumption that housework is not real work. Taken together, the concept and the assumption provide a basis for a theory about gender relations.

Theorizing is and always has been a part of everyone's way of thinking. Every time you try to guess why a group of people act in a particular way, you are theorizing about a social phenomenon on the basis of your own knowledge of reality. Sociologists do much the same thing, with a bit more formality.

In this chapter you will learn what sociological theory is and what it is not. At the core of the chapter is an account of how, beginning in the 1600s and extending into the early 1800s, European intellectuals struggled to understand the dramatic transformations taking place around them. They produced explanations, from various perspectives, that helped them make sense of their world and the changes they experienced in their daily lives. The work of these intellectuals, although not strictly sociological, was the basis for the later development of the new discipline. More important, their theories are the touchstone for many of those who today work to help us understand and improve the social world. The chapter ends with an explanation of how the rest of the book is organized.

The Contours of Sociological Theory

All human beings attempt to make sense of their world and their place in that world. In other words, we do not simply *react* to our situations in the world, we *theorize* about them. We reflect upon, interpret, and most important, represent symbolically our actions and interactions. As Karl Marx (1887:178) pointed out, bees construct complex dwellings, but what distinguishes the "poorest architect" from the "best of bees" is that the architect constructs the building in his/her imagination before constructing it in reality. In contrast to the bee, the architect's construction is present from the beginning, from its conception, in the "imagination of the worker, in its ideal form." The architect is able to *theoretically* create a building and then represent the theory abstractly and symbolically with drawings, blueprints, and models. Furthermore, in contrast to the programmed responses of the bee, which do not allow for reflective modifications, the architect is able to modify or reject in response to some new idea or new factor that had not been foreseen in the initial plans.

Sociologists use theory as architects do. Sociological **theory**[1] is an abstract, symbolic representation of, and explanation of, social reality. But when we talk about sociological theory, we are talking about guidelines for thinking in a disciplined manner about the social world.

Deductive and Inductive Reasoning

The sociological theorist is often like the architect who is in the planning stages. The sociological theorist may start with an idea, or theory, about the nature of society and social behavior and proceed to construct in relatively abstract, symbolic terms some sort of model that can explain social life. That is, the sociologist may theorize **deductively**, proceeding from the general to the particular. Alternatively, the sociologist may observe some interesting but puzzling feature of social life and, examining the social context of the puzzling feature, derive a general explanation, or theory, about this particular social puzzle. The theory formulated by this procedure is arrived at **inductively**.

Whether theorizing deductively or inductively, the sociological theorist is attempting to provide a comprehensive yet simple and elegant explanation of society and the causes of social behaviors. But given the complexity of society and the human failings of sociologists, no theory is ever a perfect explanation. The sociological theorist may modify or even reject a theory if it fails to provide a plausible, coherent explanation of the social world. The search is then on for a better theory, one that will explain more about the social world. This search, in

---

[1]Key terms appear in boldface throughout this text.

turn, will produce new problems in need of theoretical explanation and interpretation. Obviously this process takes time—perhaps decades or, if more than one theorist is drawn into the search, centuries. And as the search continues, sociologists' understandings of the problems and the explanations continuously evolve.

Ideology and Objectivity

In their attempt to explain and interpret the social world, theorists have asked some basic questions: Who and what are human beings, where are they and why, and what might the future hold? Only relatively recently, however, have we attempted to answer these questions sociologically. In the past, and still for some in the present, these questions have been answered by invoking myth, legend, folklore, or more often, religion.

For example, Filipino culture has an interesting mythical explanation about the origin of different races. When the gods decided to make human beings, they shaped the clay and placed it in an oven to bake so as to make the clay warm and alive. When the gods pulled out the clay figure the first time, they looked at it and said, "This is not done, it is too pale." So they tossed it over their shoulders, and it landed way up north in the cold and snow. Then they said, "A mistake is a mistake, we must try again." They put another shape in the oven and left it a long time. But when they pulled it out, it was burned, and they dropped it along the equator in front of them. So the gods said, "We will try once more." This time, after putting the clay in the oven, they kept watch over it, and when it was nice and brown and just right, they took the figure out and put it down in the Philippines.

This story explains something about human origins, and it also interprets the observation that different people have different complexions. But it is *not* a theory. The explanation provides no possibility of proof either for or against its assertions. But what it may provide, as all myths and legends may, is a basis for ideological judgments.

Ideology is commonly thought of as a set of ideas that justifies judgments about good/bad, superior/inferior, better/worse. Furthermore, when applied to individuals or groups, ideology is thought to assert or legitimize the power of some group over another. But we all make ideological judgments in our everyday lives, and not all of these judgments are deliberate attempts to assert or maintain power over others in a direct, confrontational, prejudicial manner.

Karl Mannheim (1929) characterized the difference between these two aspects of ideology as the difference between particular and total ideologies. **Particular ideologies** involve systems of knowledge that deform or conceal facts. For example, the assertion by the major tobacco companies that smoking does not affect health is an example of a particular ideology—a more or less deliberate distortion of facts to advantage the companies. **Total ideologies** are systems of knowledge tied to the social/historical place and time of the individuals who espouse them, irrespective of good or bad intentions. The belief in the inherent superiority of a particular race as the basis for the organization of social relations is an example of a total ideology.

Whether particular or total, ideology is *not* theory. However, as a knowledge system, an ideology can present problems for sociological theory. Sociologists, like anyone else, may not be aware that their views are based on the biases or the ideologies of their time and place. Sociologists—like politicians, pundits, and ordinary citizens—tend to espouse views that are conservative, liberal, or radical. Separating sociological knowledge from personal ideological positions is a problem that you will confront in reading about many of the theorists discussed in this book.

Ideological content does not necessarily make a theory wrong. When the ideological content can be disentangled from the theory, the theory may still have some merit as an explanation. In addition, sociologists are well aware of the dangers of ideological content and will usually adopt some procedure to either eliminate or at least minimize the difficulties ideology presents.

The problem of ideologies within sociology is, according to Ralf Dahrendorf (1968), endemic to the sociological project. From the beginning, sociology had "two intentions." It was supposed to help us to understand society by using objective, "scientific" methods; at the same time, it was supposed to help individuals achieve "freedom and self-fulfillment" (1968:58–59). Dahrendorf suggests that sociology has often paid for the scientific ambition to be objective by ignoring its intention to help people. In doing so, it becomes a "thoroughly inhuman, amoral science" (1968:59). Dahrendorf's judgment on scientific objectivity is rather overdrawn, but sociologists must keep in mind that statistical data, for example, always need theoretical interpretation to make them relevant to nonsociologists. At the same time, sociologists must recognize that the second intention, to emancipate human beings, requires empirical data to justify theoretical and ethical claims and recommendations.

Sociological Subjects

In the debate over the role of ideology in sociology, Max Weber (1864–1920) stated that objectivity was an "impossible obligation" but one that sociologists must assume. Chapter 7 expands on Weber's methodological position. But let's examine here the relationship between this "impossible obligation" and the subject matter of sociology. The problem is in good part a result of the fact that sociologists themselves are both subjects and objects of sociology. As subjects (sociological theorists), they aspire to a detached or objective view of society; as objects (human beings), they are rooted in a particular society and have personal beliefs about it.

The subjects and objects of sociological scrutiny are never static and may well undergo changes as a result of sociological interest. For example, if the human "objects" of sociological interest know that they are being observed, then they are likely to adapt their behavior to fit what they assume the observer is interested in. More generally, as you will see, historical time and place as well as race, class, and gender have influenced how sociologists have theorized about society. The things investigated by researchers in the natural sciences are similarly changeable, but the natural scientist is generally not both the subject and the object of the investigation.

Many sociologists mitigate the subject/object dilemma by taking the position that, as far as possible, they must declare their evaluative stance on the issues or situations being investigated. More recently, some sociologists have taken the position that trying to remain objective is not only impossible but also undesirable (Sica, 1997:3). From the very beginning, sociologists have sought "to participate in social change, not merely to record it in a 'scientific fashion'" (Sica, 1997:3). Even in the most rigorously scientific sociological circles, the investigators' ethical viewpoints have always been a factor.

Research Traditions

Sociological research traditions make assumptions about how the social world is organized and how it operates and how human beings can know that world. Generally, sociologists can be classified as positivists, idealists, or critical theorists. In practice, however, aspects of two or three research traditions may be combined in the work of any particular theorist.

Positivism   Early in the development of sociology, some theorists assumed that the social world could be studied in the same manner as the natural world and that social laws could be formulated much like the laws formulated in natural science to describe the behavior of physical phenomena. This approach is usually called **positivism.** Positivists seek to find social laws that will enable them to make predictions about social behavior, just as the laws of the natural sciences can be used to make predictions in physics, chemistry, and biology.

In the search for social laws, positivists look for the determining causes of events or phenomena. For example, why do some teens engage in violent acts? Or why do some people join cults? As sociological scientists, positivists dismiss anything that is not accessible to observation as peripheral to the subject matter of sociology.

The problem with the positivist tradition is that it ignores questions relating to such intangibles as values and beliefs. With a certain degree of success, however, some positivist sociologists have managed to study nonobservable entities by treating them as though they were observable. For example, in dealing with attitudes and beliefs about racial minorities, the sociologist might construct a scale to measure the nature of prejudice.

Generally, positivists subscribe to the position that there are observable, stable relationships in the social world that can be accurately observed, described, and explained in causal terms. Furthermore, positivists believe that the sociologist can objectively investigate the "facts" in the external social world with no preconceived value judgments. Positivism therefore claims to be the most scientific, objective research tradition in sociology.

Idealism   The positivist tradition is often contrasted with **idealism**. The idealist is less concerned with searching for universal laws than with understanding or interpreting meaning. In addition, the idealist assumes that meaning is not an immutable law but is historically changeable.

The sociologist working in the idealist tradition attempts to explain behaviors and events in terms of the meaning they have for the participants. Explanation is therefore sought in the motivations, or the beliefs and values, of the subjects under investigation.

The sociologist does not stand apart from the data but is engaged with the subjects under investigation in order to see and understand the world from the their point of view. The sociologist is thus a subjective interpreter rather than an objective experimenter in this research tradition.

The distinction between positivism and idealism is not as clear-cut as this description might suggest. Like idealists, positivists must eventually interpret the data, which requires some subjective knowledge of the abstract rules of symbolic communication.

Critical Theory   The third tradition, critical theory, is far more antagonistic to positivism than to idealism. **Critical theory** rejects altogether the idea that knowledge can be objective—that is, abstracted from human interests and practices. Whereas positivism can reveal how to reach certain goals but is morally indifferent to the goals themselves, critical theory aims to reveal what those goals should be and how they can produce a better society.

Although critical theory is opposed to the presumed objectivity of positivism, it does have in common with positivism the search for causal explanations. However, cause is sought not in an external, separate social reality but in the underlying structures and forms that underpin the observable phenomena and relations, or everyday sense impressions, of the social world. This level of reality is discovered by "thinking away" the details in order to reveal the real causal relations that the details may obscure. For example, instead of seeing the behavior of homeless youth as evidence of deviant or criminal tendencies, the critical theorist would ask why the youth are homeless in the first place and why they are automatically associated with deviance and criminality.

Critical theory assumes that human beings are knowledgeable about or conscious of their social practices and institutions. But because these practices and institutions exist prior to the participation of any particular individual, the participants unconsciously reproduce, or accept as given, the structures and relations that seem to govern them. Critical reflection, however, can emancipate people from the structural conditions that constrain their behavior to produce freedom.

The goal of critical theory is social change. As one of the major critical theorists noted, "The philosophers have only *interpreted* the world differently, the point is, to *change* it" (Marx & Engels, 1845:199). Some of the philosophers Marx was referring to are the ones you will now meet.

The Philosophical Precursors of Sociology

Recognition of the dual role of sociologists resulted from the idea that society itself could be the subject of scientific scrutiny. This idea had its origins in the eighteenth century and led, in the nineteenth century, to the establishment of sociology—a term coined by Auguste Comte (1798–1857).

You will learn more about Comte in Chapter 2. But first you should realize that explaining and interpreting social events and experiences is not necessarily a sociological enterprise. As we have seen, religious and even magical explanations have been offered. Natural scientists, philosophers, economists, and political scientists have also offered explanations of the social world, and their accounts have played an important role in the development of sociological theory.

Here we will look at the ideas of several nonsociologists whose work was nevertheless important to the subsequent development of sociology. Where sociology differed from these other accounts was in recognizing that society is a separate, discrete entity, that it is amenable to scientific investigation, and further, that it is an entity constructed by human beings and therefore subject to variations and change.

At the onset of Western modernity, various intellectuals promoted the positivist idea that the social world could be understood in the same terms as the physical world of nature because of the human capacity of reason. Understanding the social world through the exercise of human reason, they assumed, would reveal the social laws to be followed to achieve social progress and human perfectibility.

These intellectual developments were connected with various transformations of the traditional social world to a modern world, which became particularly evident in Western societies starting in the eighteenth century. In essence, sociology emerged as a way of explaining and dealing with the problems and dislocations accompanying the gradual transformation to modernity in Western society. Social observers were particularly concerned with such characteristics of modernity as capitalism, industrialization, bureaucratization, the division of labor, urbanization, nationalism, imperialism, democracy, and individual rights and freedom.

Whether modernity was considered good, bad, or mixed depended on the theorist's ideology regarding social transformation. **Liberals** generally believe that humans beings are rational and perfectible and thus society can be improved. **Conservatives** have generally preferred to avoid tinkering with society. **Status quo conservatives** call for the protection of things as they are, whereas **reactionary conservatives** seek to bring back tradition and the "good old days." **Radicals** are similar to reactionary conservatives, but in the opposite direction. They want to overthrow the status quo in favor of a better future. These underlying attitudes toward social change characterize not only sociology's philosophical precursors but the classical sociological theorists and contemporary "postmodern" sociological theorists as well.

Tradition and Modernity

In the Western medieval, feudal world, the interconnections of material, human, and divine existence were expressed in the idea of the Great Chain of Being. This idea, endorsed and promoted by the Church, ranked the physical, the human, and the divine in a hierarchy, with rocks at the bottom, God at the top, and "man" occupying the space just below the angels. This ordering of the material and divine universe remained an important idea until the late eighteenth century (Lovejoy, 1936). The Great Chain illustrated the ultimate subservience of all objects and beings to a universal God.

The first tentative changes in this view began in the Renaissance of the fifteenth century, with a shift from the idea of God as the supreme creator of nature to the idea of God expressed in the laws of nature. Many intellectuals came to believe that these laws could be discovered by human beings through mathematics. This idea had profound implications for science as well as art.

The artist and inventor Leonardo da Vinci (1452–1519) formulated the idea of exact science with his insistence that "Reason is the immanent, unbreakable law governing nature" (quoted in Cassirer, 1964:156). He believed that human beings cannot *know* nature's secrets through the senses alone; only the "principle of sufficient reason," which is the "principle of mathematical explanation," can reveal these secrets. On this point the experimental scientist and astronomer Galileo (1564–1642) agreed. For Galileo, nature "does not so much 'have' necessity, but rather *is* necessity" (Cassirer, 1964:156). Thus, the scientist and the artist were in agreement. Human beings could discover the laws of the universe. The scientist discovers the "empirical truth of things" through understanding, and the artist does the same thing through imagination.

René Descartes (1596–1650) was one of the first to examine systematically the idea that science and mathematics, not religious dogma, are the basis for control over the physical world. However, the idea of natural laws accessible through reason—especially through the certainty of mathematical reason—did not immediately displace the authority of God. On the contrary, intellectuals began searching for natural laws in order to reveal God's purpose for human beings and produce a godly realm on earth. But the idea that human reason could reveal the "nature of nature" was a significant departure from the theological authoritarianism of the medieval period. In the thirteenth century, the key words for discussing the universe would have been "God, sin, grace, salvation, heaven," but by the eighteenth century the more meaningful words were "nature, natural law, first cause, reason, sentiment, humanity, perfectibility" (Becker, 1932:47). The Church resisted these challenges to its authority, but the seed was sown for the idea that human reason could, and should, replace revelation as the foundation for organizing social life.

The claims of the Catholic Church were also undermined by the challenge of Protestantism. The challenge was not simply to religious dogma and ritual but also to traditional ideas about community, labor, and individual autonomy. The Protestant believer required no priestly intermediary in her or his relationship with God. Every believer had an individual responsibility to live a virtuous, industrious life in society, rather than in monastic retreat, in order to help establish a community of saints on earth. As you will see in Chapter 7, Max Weber's *The Protestant Ethic and the Spirit of Capitalism* elaborated this point.

Skepticism about theological explanations of the nature of society was reinforced by the economic and political changes that were gradually transforming social life. The transformation of many European societies from primarily agricultural, rural societies to industrial, urban societies upset the traditional hierarchies of authority and status that were exemplified in the Great Chain of Being. The relatively static and contained communities of traditional societies gave way to rapidly changing, urban conglomerates. The traditional status rankings, with kings and bishops at the top, were gradually replaced by economic or class rankings, with merchants and bankers at the top. And the traditional patterns of deference that governed social life—characterized by master-servant, patron-client relationships—changed when people began thinking of human beings as rational, autonomous individuals.

These social, economic, and political transformations were connected with the expansion of trade on a global scale. One of the most important factors in the early establishment of capitalism in Britain and in other western European countries was world trade (Braudel, 1984, vol. 2). As Western traders, explorers, and conquerors traveled the globe, they brought back stories of different cultures and different social practices that reinforced ideas about the variable nature of society. Ironically, however, many Europeans saw the cultural differences as confirmation of the superiority of Western society, which in turn justified Western imperialist activities, including, as you will see in Chapter 2, the imperialist claims of Western sociology.

But a group of eighteenth-century Enlightenment thinkers known as the *philosophes* used this new wealth of comparative data on societies to construct a theoretical basis for a decisive challenge to traditional socioreligious theory and ideology. As a twentieth-century observer noted, "The advance of knowledge, whether devout Christians liked it or not, meant the advance of reason" (Gay, 1969:27).

The Philosophes *and the Enlightenment*

Enlightenment thinkers put society and social relations under intense scrutiny. Their central interest was the attainment of human and social perfectibility in the here and now rather than in some heavenly future. They considered rational education and scientific understanding of self and society the routes to all human and social progress. Such progress was assured because all human beings have the faculty of reason. Reason need only be educated and exercised without any arbitrary restraint, whether of tradition, religion, or sovereign power. As you will see later, however, some human beings were still excluded as less rational than others and therefore in need of control. The excluded were generally women, nonwhites, children, and the lower orders or classes. Nevertheless, the *philosophes* claimed that educated individuals would exercise their critical reason for their own happiness and, by extension, the happiness and welfare of society as a whole.

For this reason, the *philosophes* placed a great deal of emphasis on practical knowledge—how to farm, how to construct bridges and dams, how to relate to fellow citizens. A systematic and exhaustive compilation of practical and theoretical knowledge was found in the *Encyclopédie*, the great work by Denis Diderot and Jean Le Ron d'Alembert. The first volume of the *Encyclopédie* was published in 1751 and the last in 1765.

The assumption behind the work was that education in known facts and scientifically proven truths was the key to human and social progress. Diderot maintained that "nature has not made us evil; it is bad education, bad models, bad legislation that corrupt us" (quoted in Gay, 1969:170). In other words, reason was an acquisition. The *philosophes* rejected the idea that reason was the storehouse of "innate ideas," like a "treasury of the mind in which truth like a minted coin lies stored" (Cassirer, 1951:13). Rather, reason enabled the discovery of truth. Central to the discovery of truth was rational, scientific education.

Critical to the discovery of truth as well was the scientific method, exemplified in Isaac Newton's (1642–1727) work. Newton's discovery of regularities and relationships in the physical world rested on observation rather than simply abstract, theoretical reasoning. This was the approach that Enlightenment thinkers applied to the investigation of society. Just as order was observable in the physical world, so order, they assumed, could be discovered in the social world through careful observation and comparison of the facts of that world.

Political Revolutions

Enlightenment social and political thought paved the way for revolutionary ruptures in traditional social relations. From the Renaissance on, western European societies acquired modern characteristics, but Enlightenment ideas and the American, French, and Industrial revolutions ushered in some of the definitive characteristics of modern capitalist society. The profound upheaval of the French Revolution, in particular, highlighted some of the problems and issues of concern to prerevolutionary Enlightenment thinkers. These became the problems and issues of the "new science," sociology, at the beginning of the nineteenth century.

Thomas Jefferson's preamble to the Declaration of Independence, a prime example of Enlightenment thinking, assumed that all "rational" individuals would agree with the "self-evident truths" that "all men are created equal" and endowed with "inalienable rights" of "life, liberty, and the pursuit of happiness." These rights justified the rejection of an unjust, tyrannical authority. Indeed, it was the duty of reasonable people to resist and reject such a government. This appeal to reason and "natural" rights as justification for resistance to traditional, religiously sanctioned authority was a profound challenge to the political status quo, especially in combination with the idea that government was a form of contract between the ruler and the ruled. If the ruler did not fulfill the terms of the contract, then the subject had the right to reject the ruler and institute a new form of government.

The American Revolution obviously had considerable impact on Great Britain, but citizenship claims against traditional authority had the most important consequences in France. Many eighteenth-century French considered America the ideal society embodying the admired qualities of "innocence, rugged directness and freedom" (Schama, 1989:27–28).[2] As a result of the American Revolution, the term *democracy* took on its modern reference of government by the

---

[2]Schama (1989:43–44) also suggests that Benjamin Franklin was aware of the idealization of America as a "place of natural innocence, candor and freedom" and that while he was in Paris, Franklin "milked the stereotype for all it was worth." Franklin's "peculiar beaver cap" and his "undressed hanks of white hair and his ostentatious brown coat, deliberately worn at court audiences, were expressly affected with public sensation in mind and they succeeded brilliantly."

people. In Great Britain the term had been used in connection with "mob rule," and democrats were usually regarded as "dangerous and subversive mob agitators" (Williams, 1963:14).

Democracy involved a new relationship between individuals and society, or the state, which later became a fundamental issue for several key sociological theorists. Democracy raised important questions as to the rights and responsibilities of free, rational, and autonomous *citizens*—who were no longer *subjects* of the state—and how those rights and responsibilities might be guaranteed.

These questions had been asked prior to the political revolutions in France and America in the hope of providing a blueprint for the harmonious, orderly, good society. The questions became more urgent in the aftermath of the revolutions, however, most especially in the violent aftermath and subsequent Napoleonic imperialism of the French Revolution. Jean-Jacques Rousseau's claim in his *Social Contract* (1762a) that "Man is born free; and everywhere he is in chains" was an inspiration to many of the participants in the French Revolution of 1789. But some of those same participants, such as the republicans Robespierre and Saint-Just, were also responsible for "the Terror," a decidedly chaotic and distressing response to change (Fox-Genovese, 1987:267).[3] The considerable initial optimism about the revolution was voiced by William Wordsworth (1809).

> Bliss was it in that dawn to be alive
> But to be young was very heaven!

But such enthusiasm was quickly abandoned in the bloody aftermath of the revolution and the beheading of the king, Louis XVI, in January 1793.

Subjects and Citizens

Both the American and the French revolutions were possible in part because subjects had gradually been transformed into citizens. In traditional societies, all members are **subjects** of the ruler, who derives authority from custom and tradition, usually divine custom and tradition. Resistance to any particular ruler is difficult because power resides in the institution of rulership. Consider the phrase "The King is dead, long live the King."

Resistance to traditional authority became more possible with the dissemination of the ideas of Thomas Hobbes, John Locke, Montesquieu, Jean Jacques Rousseau, and Mary Wollstonecraft. Their work contributed to the gradual transformation of subjects into self-governing **citizens**.

Thomas Hobbes (1588–1679)   Thomas Hobbes's contribution was the suggestion that the social order was made by human beings and therefore could be

---

[3]Beginning in 1793, the republican government in France set about exterminating any French who opposed the revolution and the establishment of the Republic. The military were instructed to "pacify" areas that resisted, or were thought to resist, the Republic. The area of the Vendée was particularly targeted, and in a tactic that unfortunately has modern echoes, on January 23, 1794, "two hundred old people, along with mothers and children" were forced to kneel before a "large pit they had dug" and were "then shot so as to tumble into their own grave" (Schama, 1989:791).

changed by human beings. This theory marks an important beginning in the transformation of subjects into citizens.

In Hobbes's view, human beings are governed by a selfish and "perpetual and restless desire for power after power" (1651:49). This lust for individual power continues until death. Anarchy—"every man against every man"—is curbed only by the fact that men fear death. As all men are rational, they may be convinced to adopt "convenient Articles of Peace" in order to avoid social anarchy and death (1651:66):

> The final cause, end, or design of men, who naturally love liberty, and dominion over others, in the introduction of that restraint upon themselves, in which we see them live in commonwealths, is the foresight of their own preservation, and of a more contented life thereby. (1651:109)

Even under authoritarian rule, in Hobbes's account, authority is given by the subjects themselves. The consent that subjects give to the sovereign power can therefore be withdrawn, presumably for justifiable reasons. Hobbes wrote during a period of revolutionary upheaval in England. By the end of the English Civil War and the restoration of Charles II to the throne in 1660, the monarch's power had been profoundly curtailed. The event marked a watershed in the way ordinary people regarded the power of the monarch. The state became an impersonal body—the Leviathan theorized by Hobbes as "Mortall God" (Corrigan & Sayer, 1985:79). As Jefferson stated in America some years later, "Kings are the servants, not the proprietors, of the people." The withdrawal of consent to sovereign power in the American case was justified by the battle cry "No taxation without representation." Representation transforms subjects into free citizens.

Hobbes derived his version of competitive, calculating subjects who make social order to ensure their own happiness from what he believed to be an objective assessment of human psychology. Hobbes's account seemed to contain no preconceived moral judgment on either human nature or political order, which was an important innovation in political theory. He "objectively" presented human nature and reached the conclusion that the only way to avoid chaos is to combine with others to curb innate desires and create order in civil society. Hobbes's focus on the individual, along with that of John Locke, was later echoed in the work of British social theorists such as John Stuart Mill and Jeremy Bentham and the sociologist Herbert Spencer, all of whom based their analyses on what they perceived to be the nature of individual human beings (Levine, 1995:150).

John Locke (1632–1704)   John Locke also formulated a theory about the nature of human beings in the original state of nature. In contrast to Hobbes's notion of asocial, competitive individuals, however, Locke believed that human beings were originally social, cooperative beings. Like Hobbes, Locke based his theory on the rights of individuals and the need to curtail the powers of the sovereign. But Locke did not subscribe to Hobbes's defense of the political absolutism the Leviathan involved (Levine, 1995:130).

Locke postulated that individuals were in a "State of perfect Freedom" and a "State also of Equality" before the formation of the state (1711:25). This free and equal state was not a "State of Licence" because it was governed by the law of nature as embodied in reason. The law of nature, or reason, "teaches all Mankind . . . that being all equal and independent, no one ought to harm another in his Life, Health, Liberty, or Possessions" (1711/1988:25).

Because all were free and equal in the original state of nature, "no one can be put out of this Estate, and subjected to the Political Power of another, without his own Consent."

> The only way whereby any one divests himself of his Natural Liberty, and *puts on the bonds of Civil society* is by agreeing with other Men to joyn and unite into a Community, for their comfortable, safe, and peaceable living one amongst another, in a secure Enjoyment of their Properties, and a greater Security against any that are not of it. . . . When any number of Men have so *consented to make a Community* or Government, they are thereby presently incorporated, and make *one Body Politick*, herein the *Majority* have a Right to act and conclude the rest. (1711:28)

Making a contract with others means that individuals "give up Equality, Liberty, and Executive Power they had in the State of Nature, into the hands of Society, to be so far disposed of by the Legislative, as the good of the Society shall require." But individuals do not change "their condition with an intention to be worse." It is because they are rational and wish to preserve their own "Liberty and Property" that they relinquish their powers. The major task of the state is the "Preservation of . . . Property" and the "Peace, Safety, and publick good of the People" (1711:30).

The social contract theories of Hobbes and Locke were influential with both American and French revolutionaries. Jefferson, for example, thought that Locke was one of the great men of history. But their ideas were criticized by others, most notably the French theorist Montesquieu.

Charles Louis de Secondat, Baron de la Brede et de Montesquieu (1689–1775)   Montesquieu argued that all human beings are social beings and that to seek the origins of society in the presocial dispositions of human beings, as Hobbes and Locke had done was futile. To understand society, one must observe the facts of society, just as the natural scientist observes the facts of the physical world. Through observation, social theorists could find the law-like patterns of social relations, similar to the laws of cause and effect discovered by natural scientists. In his preface to his *De l'esprit des lois*, Montesquieu remarked, "I have not drawn my principles from my prejudices, but from the nature of things" (1748:170).

In *De l'esprit des lois*, Montesquieu discussed the types of government he had observed and the form of social organization arising from each particular type. Relating types of government to the study of social organization was an innovative contribution to the eventual development of sociology (Aron, 1970:22).

Montesquieu distinguished three types of government—republic, monarchy, and despotism—on the basis of his observations and comparisons of various

Exhibit 1.1   Montesquieu's Three Types of Government

Type of Government	Nature	Principle
Republic	The people have sovereign power.	Civic virtue is the prevailing sentiment that legitimates the government.
Monarchy	A single person has sovereignty in accordance with established laws and conventions.	Honor is the prevailing sentiment that legitimates the government.
Despotism	A single person, unhampered by laws and ruling by his or her own will, has sovereignty.	Fear is the prevailing sentiment that legitimates the government.

societies. As Exhibit 1.1 shows, each type of government had a characteristic nature and a principle or prevailing sentiment that legitimated the government. In a republic, individuals are citizens and are therefore equal. In a monarchy, the principle of honor produces hierarchies of rank and status among the subjects. A despotism promotes equality among the subjects, but it is an equality of fear and impotence.

The types of government outlined by Montesquieu are generalized, abstract constructions that Montesquieu recognized would vary in their particulars according to the time and place in which they appeared. This idea was another important contribution to sociological theory (Aron, 1970:27). It suggested that government is not a universal, divinely ordained form but rather a human construction that is culturally and historically relative.

Montesquieu claimed to base his ideas on the "facts," without personal prejudice, but he did not always succeed. For instance, in analyzing despotism he noted dispassionately that it appeared most often in vast empires and hot climates (Gay, 1969:331). But he could not resist calling it a "monstrous" form of government. Similar value judgments creep into many of his writings, but in this respect Montesquieu is like other sociologists. It is one thing to objectively describe conditions and practices that characterize remote societies that the researcher might find personally repugnant (Aron, 1970:40). It is quite another problem to remain objective when analyzing one's own society or historical period. How can sociologists suggest the reform of repugnant conditions and practices they find around them if they admit that such conditions and practices are an inevitable part of the human condition (Aron, 1970:40)? This question has generated some of the most significant and contentious ideological, theoretical, and methodological debates among sociologists, as you will see in this book.

Montesquieu, whose methodology was historical and comparative, is considered a **cultural relativist**. He suggested that the laws of nature apply to all, but that they take on different forms and expressions according to the form of government—as well as according to climate, soil, the geographical size of the country, the number of inhabitants, and the social factors of religion, customs, and the economy. The laws that govern a nation are therefore an expression of the general "spirit" of the nation; they define the "originality and unity of a given collectivity" (Aron, 1970:45).

Emile Durkheim, one of the early-nineteenth-century sociologists and a continuing influence in the field (see Chapter 4), regarded Montesquieu as one of the most significant precursors of sociology. Durkheim pointed to Montesquieu's recognition that human societies could be compared not only in terms of their political structures but also in terms of "morality, religion, economic life, the family," which are the "actual stuff of life and consequently the subject-matter of social science" (Durkheim, 1892:9).

Jean-Jacques Rousseau (1712–1778) Durkheim regarded Jean-Jacques Rousseau as another significant precursor of sociology. Like Montesquieu, Rousseau criticized Hobbes's view of human beings as independent individuals in society, but he did agree with Hobbes that society was an artificial construction. Furthermore, like Locke, Rousseau thought that society was formed as a result of a contract among individuals.

Rousseau's focus was on the possibility of drastic social change. Montesquieu's political philosophy was liberal, exemplified in his idea that social order could be found in the equilibrium of the people and their rulers. Rousseau's ideas were more radical. He believed that man's original nature was corrupted by society, and that the only way man could become a virtuous, moral being was to totally transform society.

Rousseau suggested that the Hobbesian state of war among individuals was a social phenomenon, not an innate quality of human beings. He cautioned that we must "beware concluding with Hobbes, that man, as having no idea of goodness, must be naturally bad" (1762a:191). Society, with its invention of private property, produced the misery and oppression afflicting man. According to Rousseau (1762a:202),

> The first man, who, after enclosing a piece of ground, took it into his head to say, "This is mine," and found people simple enough to believe him, was the true founder of civil society. How many crimes, how many wars, how many murders . . . would that man have saved the human species, who pulling up the stakes or filling up the ditches should have cried to his fellows: Be sure not to listen to this imposter; you are lost, if you forget that the fruits of the earth belong equally to us all, and the earth itself to nobody!

Rousseau claimed that private property brought about war, conflict, and thus the need for a civil state, noting "there is scarcely any inequality among men in the state of nature." The inequality "that we now behold owes its force and its growth to the development of our faculties and the improvement of our understanding, and at last becomes permanent and lawful by the establishment of property and laws" (1762a:233).

Rousseau's prescription for the rejuvenation of the individual and society was not a return to the original state of nature. Indeed, the concept of the state of nature was for Rousseau "merely a hypothetical and conditional" form of reasoning, more to "illustrate the nature of things than to show their true origin" (1762a:169). That is, the concept is a methodological device used to uncover the basic social principles for the reform of society. Rousseau believed that reform of society would only be possible if all members shared equally in the construction of laws for their common happiness. That is, sovereign authority must reside in the General Will. All individual rights would be surrendered to the community in return for civil liberty and protection of property. The basic principle was that the individual "giving himself to all, gives himself to nobody." The good society was a "society of free men, served rather than dominated by their government, freely obeying the laws that they themselves have made" (Gay, 1969:549).

Rousseau's political theory was important because it demonstrated that the presumed innate properties of human nature were in fact social products. In addition, it suggested a blueprint for a harmonious, democratic society of free and equal citizens.

But Rousseau's free, equal, and virtuous citizen was essentially a male citizen. In the *Social Contract* (1762a) Rousseau stated that in the savage state there was a sort of parity between men and women, and their "coupling" did not arouse any family feeling or feelings of affection. It was only with evolutionary "developments of the heart" that the "sweetest sentiments the human species is acquainted with, conjugal love and paternal love," arose (1762a:206). It was at this point that "Every family became a little society . . . and it was now that the sexes, whose way of life had been hitherto the same, began to adopt different manners and customs." The women became "more sedentary" and stayed at home to care for the children, while the men roamed in search of sustenance for their families. Rousseau's point was that biological sex differences were the "natural" basis for socially constituted distinctions and, more important, for ideal gender relations.

Rousseau explored gender relations in *Emile* (1762b), which described the ideal education of a young boy to produce a good and virtuous citizen. Rousseau believed that the early education of the child shaped the moral nature of the adult. Because children cannot reason, an education has to be devised that will build on the child's natural inclinations, such as his feelings of affection and love of play. Rousseau stressed two important requirements at the outset of the child's life: a mother who performs her duty by caring for and nursing the child, and a father who instructs the child as he grows up.[4]

Rousseau's emphasis on maternal care, especially breast-feeding the child instead of sending the child to a wet nurse, became the hallmark for the enlightened mother in the later eighteenth century. But in fact only upper-class women could afford to implement the demands of Rousseau's new concept of

---

[4]Rousseau himself was a less than ideal father. As Fox-Genovese (1987:267) reveals, Rousseau lived with a servant, Therese, "on whom he apparently depended emotionally, but to whom he never appears to have granted the adoring love he bestowed on various more aristocratic women. For Rousseau, women, sex, and love presented insoluble problems. So did fatherhood. He turned all four of his and Therese's children over to a foundling home."

motherhood. Because of the need for their paid labor, working-class mothers continued to rely on the services of wet nurses, who were usually peasant women.

As Emile matures, he requires a female companion, so Rousseau introduces Sophie, whose education has been as "natural" as that of Emile, but with a different content and form suited to the different "nature" of women compared to men. In essence, Sophie's education was designed to make her the perfect companion for Emile. She was to be weak and passive to his strength and activity. Emile's physical training was for the "development of strength," whereas Sophie's was designed for the development of grace. Sophie's education was "planned in relation to man. To be pleasing in his sight, to win his respect and love, to train him in childhood, to tend him in manhood, to counsel and console, to make his life pleasant and happy, these are the duties of women for all time, and this is what she should be taught while she is young" (1762b:328). Sophie's education was entirely practical, because the "search for abstract and speculative truths, for principles and axioms in science, . . . is beyond a woman's grasp" (1762b:349). The virtuous male citizen was thus to be complemented by the devoted, dutiful, and selfless wife who would be "always . . . in subjection to a man, or to a man's restraints" (1762b:333).

This sort of gender differentiation is an important subtext in many of the sociological accounts in this book, but some early social theorists did make note of the hypocrisy inherent in seeking to free some human beings from control while prescribing subjection for others. Rousseau's ideas did not go unchallenged by his contemporaries, among them Mary Wollstonecraft.

Mary Wollstonecraft (1759–1797)   Mary Wollstonecraft produced a rebuttal to Rousseau that was based on the standard Enlightenment philosopher's contention that *all* human beings have reason and that when reason is educated, all human beings can become good and virtuous citizens.

Wollstonecraft opened *A Vindication of the Rights of Woman* (1792) with the statement that she would consider women "in the grand light of human creatures, who, in common with men, are placed on this earth to unfold their faculties" (1792:33). Both men and women have the faculty of reason, and if women's reason were not cultivated alongside men's, women would "stop the progress of knowledge and virtue" (1792:24).

What Wollstonecraft had discovered was that in the revolutionary promise of liberty, equality, and fraternity, fraternity had to be taken literally as not including women. This revelation is one that numerous revolutionary women comrades have discovered in retrospect. For example, the resolution of the "woman question" that Marxist revolutionaries promised would be addressed after the revolution usually failed to materialize. Certainly in the postrevolutionary Soviet Union as well as in China, gender equality was never adequately addressed.

Wollstonecraft called Rousseau's portrait of Sophie "grossly unnatural." She pointed out that "Liberty is the mother of virtue, and if women be, by their very constitution, slaves, and not allowed to breathe the sharp invigorating air of freedom, they must ever languish like exotics, and be reckoned beautiful flaws in nature" (1792:72–73). Wollstonecraft also accused Rousseau of being "unphilosophical" when he claimed that women had a "natural"—that is, innate—love of dress and adornment because they are naturally flirts.

> The absurdity . . . of supposing that a girl is naturally a coquette, and that a
> desire connected with the impulse of nature to propagate the species
> should appear even before an improper education has, by heating the
> imagination, called it forth prematurely, is so unphilosophical, that such a
> sagacious observer as Rousseau would not have adopted it, if he had not
> been accustomed to make reason give way to his desire of singularity, and
> truth to a favourite paradox. (1792:80)

Wollstonecraft followed with the point that "to give a sex to mind was not very consistent with the principles of a man who argued so warmly . . . for the immortality of the soul. But what a weak barrier is truth when it stands in the way of an hypothesis! Rousseau respected—almost adored virtue—and yet he allowed himself to love with sensual fondness" (1792:80).

Rousseau's reflections on the "natural," and complementary, differences between Emile and Sophie were bound up with the problem that sexual passion represented to an orderly society. The assumption was that women not only inflamed men's passions but also that women's own emotions and desires were inherently unstable. Many eighteenth-century theorists forged "a strong symbolic link between female rebellion and political upheaval" (Browne, 1987:19). Women therefore needed control and containment if social order was to be maintained.

In *Vindication* Wollstonecraft insisted that, within marriage, reason was necessary in order to "teach passion to submit to necessity." The ideal was an enlightened bourgeois family in which the sober pursuit of duty was not jeopardized by passion or sensuality (1792:65).

For many eighteenth-century social theorists, the family remained the critical institution for the maintenance of public order—in large part because the old political "family" exemplified by the patriarchal authority of a monarch was no longer appropriate. But if the sexes are equal, then there is no foundation for authority and hierarchy within the family. By stressing the special nature of the maternal role, social theorists could maintain inequality in the somewhat disguised form of "separate but equal."

In subsequent work Wollstonecraft took a somewhat different stance. She suggested that sexual passion and maternal feelings could be the ethical touchstone for control of the irrationality demonstrated in men's political and economic actions. Specifically, the world of commerce was irrational and did violence to men by estranging them from their feelings and emotions and, consequently, from their humanity. "Rational" capitalists were, in Wollstonecraft's view, incapable of virtuous actions. The rational, enlightened male citizen was a misnomer because, devoid of that humanity that resided in attention to the "passions," devoid of the sensibility activated through the imagination, a man could not be entirely rational. As she claimed, imagination is "the true fire, stolen from heaven, to animate this cold creature of clay" (Wardle, 1979:263). In short, reason *and* passion were necessary in the virtuous citizen, and women, in Wollstonecraft's view, were best able to demonstrate this combination.

Capitalism and Industrial Revolution

For Wollstonecraft and others of her era, political revolution made debates over social order, gender relations, and the nature of citizenship vitally important. But from the late eighteenth century on, social thinkers began to notice that the political revolutions that transformed subjects into citizens took place in the midst of industrial transformations that were just as revolutionary.

The industrial transformations were fueled by earlier capitalist developments, beginning in the sixteenth century, and together they generated new social and political arrangements. The urban middle classes were becoming a significant social force, and "free" wage workers were becoming the standard in a competitive, largely unregulated marketplace. By 1780, the industrial revolution had appeared in Great Britain (Hill, 1969:282). France, the United States, and later Germany also underwent industrial transformation in the early nineteenth century.

For a long time, the word *industry* had been used to refer only to a skill or ability. Then Adam Smith, in *The Wealth of Nations* (1776), used the word to refer to manufacturing institutions. Williams notes that "*Industry*, with a capital letter is thought of as a thing in itself—an institution, a body of activities—rather than simply a human attribute." Consequently, by the early nineteenth century, the term *industry* became a commonly used "collective word" for manufacturing and productive institutions (Williams, 1963:13–14).

French writers of the 1820s coined the term *Industrial Revolution*, drawing a parallel with the French Revolution of 1789: "As that had transformed France, so this has transformed England; the means of change are different, but the change is comparable in kind; it has produced . . . a new society" (Williams, 1963:13–14).

The "new society" that industrialism produced was not an overnight phenomenon, but it marked the definitive end of ideas about the Great Chain of Being and the social order that such ideas represented. Class relations replaced hierarchies of rank and status in importance, and the wealth acquired from industry and trade became as significant as land and title to claims of power and authority. Most important, the middle classes became more numerous and more important in the political control and direction of the state.

An important impetus for the transition to industrial society was an earlier agricultural revolution. The agricultural changes that made food production more efficient resulted in the dispossession of large numbers of rural workers. They moved to the towns and eventually became a source of cheap labor in the new factories.

One significant factor in the dispossession of rural workers was the progressive enclosure, or fencing, of common land. Most landowners, although motivated by an interest in personal profit, evicted rural tenants as a means of improving agriculture and thus the wealth of the nation—which, it was assumed, would eventually benefit everyone. However, enclosure deprived the rural peasantry of a crucial cushion against the seasonal unemployment and general underemployment that characterized agricultural life. As long as peasants had access to some small plot of land on which to grow some food or to pasture an animal, they could avoid complete destitution when work was scarce. But with the loss of access to land, peasants were forced into the cities—or even further afield. The dispossessed and destitute were often the ones searching for a new life in America, "prepared to face the risks of drowning in the Atlantic or starving in a New England winter, in the hope of ultimately winning free land and a regular source of livelihood" (Hill, 1969:71).

The forced migration to the cities and wage labor in factories permanently changed lifestyles. In an agrarian society, household production and agricultural work generally involved all members of the family, including children. When men, women, and children went to work in the factories, however, the family livelihood was no longer a collective enterprise. Each member of the family was employed and paid as an individual worker. The situation was particularly difficult for women, who had been able to make adjustments in their household activities in an agrarian setting to accommodate child care but could not in the factory context. But everyone resented the loss of independence, a resentment increased by the overwhelming power that capitalist employers had gained over employees (Hill, 1969:264).

Nevertheless, industrial development proceeded, pushed along by a number of scientific and technological advances. Improvements in agricultural practice were matched by landowners' more aggressive exploitation of mineral wealth, especially coal, lead, and iron. The commercial development of this wealth was further assisted by the increasing interest in science, especially practical scientific inventions, after the mid-seventeenth century.[5] A long list of critical inventions (for example, see Exhibit 1.2) enabled the development of large-scale manufacturing and mining industries over a relatively short period.

Among those critical inventions were the steam engine and the spinning mill, which required a new system of production and thus new work habits (Beaud, 1983:66). Most important, workers no longer had control over the rhythm and timing of their work; they were ruled by the clock and the machine. Nor did they have control over the product of their labor. This alienation of productive activities from the products of such activities became a central issue for sociologists, most especially for Karl Marx and Friedrich Engels (see Chapter 5).

Great Britain's early development of industrialization was linked to its dominance of world trade. By the end of the eighteenth century England was the "premier merchant power," an accomplishment that facilitated colonial expansion (Beaud, 1983:97). Furthermore, the slave trade was one of the most profitable commercial endeavors in the eighteenth century (Hill, 1969:228). Tracing direct connections between the "spectacularly large sums" that British business interests realized from the slave trade and especially from the "organized looting

---

[5]Hill (1969:251) suggests that it was a "great piece of good fortune for England that after 1600 the nonconformist middle class was excluded from Oxford and Cambridge, where they would have learnt to despise science." The connection between scientific inventions and religious dissent was close. Many of the British radicals believed that scientific knowledge, like religious knowledge, should be available to all. Just as "Any man or woman who had the spirit of God might preach better than a university-divine who lacked the spirit," so science should be a pursuit freely available to all who were interested (Hill, 1985:298).

Exhibit 1.2   Inventions Facilitating the Industrial Revolution

1764	Spinning jenny (weaving)
1776	Iron rails
1779	Mule jenny (weaving)
1779	Iron bridge
1783	"Double-effect" steam engine (Watt)
1785	Spinning mill run by steam engines

Source: Adapted from Beaud, 1983:66.

of India" is impossible, but colonial and imperial markets were clearly critical to the consolidation of industrial capitalism (Hill, 1969:245).

In combination, these social, technological, and economic transformations produced a new social world—of competitive individualism, of faith in the "invisible hand" of the marketplace, and, with the decline of family farms and household production, of increasing demarcations between women's work and men's work. Family relations in general were transformed. It was an increasingly comfortable world, with material prosperity and conspicuous consumption for the old landed gentry and the aristocracy as well as for the upper middle classes. But for great numbers of the working class it was also a world of precarious employment in dangerous and demoralizing jobs that could provide only poverty wages.

These class differences were evident in the physical layout of the growing cities. Engels described early-nineteenth-century London as an "immense tangle of streets" in which "there are hundreds and thousands of alleys and courts lined with houses too bad for anyone to live in" found in close proximity to the "splendid houses of the rich" (1892:63). The problems of rapid urbanization, and the poverty and crime of the large metropolis, became critical issues for sociologists. Their ethical concern for the improvement of urban society prompted the collection of statistical facts, an important component of sociological work. Sociologists hoped that this objective demonstration of the nature and extent of urban problems would point to the need for social change and provide a basis for implementing such changes.

Order and Change

In the midst of the profound social and economic transitions of the industrial revolution, the American and French political revolutions occurred. Many social theorists had initially welcomed these upheavals of the traditional social order, but their zeal for change was tempered by sober analysis of the disruptions that accompany revolution. It is not surprising, then, that the early enthusiasm for the French Revolution registered by some social theorists—for example, Wollstonecraft—was not general.[6]

---

[6]Wollstonecraft had witnessed Louis XVI being taken to prison when she was living in Paris in 1792, and initially hailed the Revolution as a triumph of men's natural, inalienable rights as rational creatures. Like many others, however, her early enthusiasm was quickly tempered by the Terror.

Conservative reactions to revolution produced some of the most important ideas of sociological theory, especially the ideas dealing with social order (Nisbet, 1966). Whereas liberal and radical thinkers had focused on individualism, democratic equality, class, and secular perspectives, conservatives began exploring issues of community, authority, status, and the sacred. The alienation, or estrangement, of individuals from society as a whole was the only idea common to both groups.

The theorists discussed so far in this chapter had promoted liberal or radical notions of social change. The Enlightenment *philosophes* all wanted to see the end of arbitrary, despotic government and the institution of rational regimes based on law reflecting empirically established social facts. For example, Rousseau had proposed a more revolutionary solution than Montesquieu, but both thinkers were convinced that enlightened reason could produce a good society of free, rational, cooperative citizens.

The work of Edmund Burke in England and Louis de Bonald and Joseph de Maistre of France stands in conservative contrast to these theorists. For the reactionary conservatives in particular, the society that the revolutions had ushered in represented the triumph of mob rule and the destruction of social order and social harmony. The conservative rejection of Enlightenment ideals became more pronounced as the ills and problems of the industrial revolution became increasingly apparent. Reactionary conservative theorists sought a solution to these problems in the restoration of traditional society, advocating "community, kinship, hierarchy, authority, and religion" (Nisbet, 1966:11). They had come to believe that the forces of liberalism and radicalism would produce social chaos.

Edmund Burke (1729–1797)   As a privileged Englishman, Edmund Burke wanted no revolution in Britain. He considered tradition, custom, hierarchy, and subservience the basis of good government. He believed that any reform, or change of any sort, was not to be undertaken lightly. Like Montesquieu, Burke believed that political authority must be tailored to the particular social and historical circumstances and that any changes must be slow and carefully worked out. Politically, Burke considered prudence the "primary virtue of civil government" (Williams, 1963:25). Burke (1790) described his reactions to the French Revolution as "alternate contempt and indignation; alternate laughter and tears; alternate scorn and horror" (p. 158). His *Reflection on the Revolution in France* (1790) explicitly rejected radical change in favor of the preservation of traditional hierarchy and customary authority.

According to Burke, the "science of government" required experience, "even more experience than any person can gain in his whole life." Therefore, great caution must be exercised by anyone who would venture "pulling down an edifice, which has answered in any tolerable degree for ages the common purposes of society" (1790:209). The leaders of the French Revolution were, in Burke's view, "so taken up with their theories about the rights of man, they have totally forgotten his nature." That "nature" required a civil society that provided for human "wants," one of which was "sufficient restraint upon their passions" (1790:208). Such restraint can only be exercised by "a power out of themselves" (1790:208). In essence, he considered restraint upon citizens as much a right as liberty.[7]

"Society is indeed a contract," wrote Burke, but it is not a contract on the same order as an "agreement in a trade of pepper and coffee, calico and to-bacco":

> It is to be looked on with other reverence; because it is not a partnership in things subservient only to gross animal existence of a temporary and perishable nature. It is a partnership in all science; a partnership in all art; a partnership in every virtue, and in all perfection. (1790:244)

Furthermore, society is a partnership between the *present* as well as the *past* and for the *future,* so that "each contract of each particular state is but a clause in the great primeval contract of eternal society." Society is a "fixed compact sanctioned by inviolable oath which holds all physical and moral natures, each in their appointed place" (1790:245).

Burke also theorized that society is a reality set apart from its participants. He stated that society is not a collection of self-interested individuals, but a unified, organic whole—an idea important to many of the classical sociologists. But Burke's conception of the organic society was being challenged in his own lifetime, not only by the political revolutions he despised but also by industrialization and the aggressive, capitalist individualism that were defining features of nineteenth-century Western modernity. Instead of cohering, society was developing even stronger divisions between political and socioeconomic classes.

Louis de Bonald (1754–1850) and Joseph de Maistre (1754–1821)   Like Burke, Louis de Bonald and Joseph de Maistre viewed the French Revolution as a disaster and viewed social, political, and economic relationships in the aftermath of the Revolution as destructive to social order and harmony. De Bonald and de Maistre's conservatism was, however, different from that of Burke. Whereas Burke wanted to conserve the status quo, de Bonald and de Maistre, living in postrevolutionary France, wanted to bring back the "good old days" of monarchy and religious authority. De Bonald believed that the development of modern industry and capitalism had undermined the divine social order, and he regarded medieval society as the ideal society. Both de Bonald and de Maistre saw modern life as especially destructive of the traditional—that is, patriarchal—family, which they believed formed the cornerstone of a stable, ordered state. De Bonald was opposed to what he regarded as the anarchic individualism

---

[7]Mary Wollstonecraft criticized Burke's conservative position in her *A Vindication of the Rights of Men* (1790), a work that preceded *A Vindication of the Rights of Woman,* published in 1792. Wollstonecraft was part of a circle of English radicals that included the artist William Blake, the writer William Godwin (who later became her husband), and Thomas Paine. Thomas Paine (1737–1809) was a radical republican who emigrated to America and became a supporter of American independence. Paine returned to Europe in 1787 and wrote *The Rights of Man* (1791), which was a defense of the French Revolution against Burke's conservative reaction. Because of his dispute with Burke, Paine was exiled from England. He went to France and became a French citizen in 1792 and then returned to America in 1802.

of his time, and he was especially opposed to the views of Rousseau and Montesquieu.

De Bonald and de Maistre considered that society was made by God not men. The divine link and the long historical chain of tradition and custom had established the superiority of society over the individual. The basic social institutions of the Church, the state, and the patriarchal family were all based on God's will, and therefore the individual should subordinate self to these institutions and to the traditions associated with them (Zeitlin, 1997:56).

As society is the expression of the will of God, so the purpose of society is the conservation of that "general will." Note, however, that this notion of general will is not Rousseau's General Will (that is, the sum of individual wills), but rather the divine will.

De Maistre was perhaps the more conservative of the two. He insisted that the origins of society could be found in a historical document, the Old Testament, in the story of Genesis. In addition, he rejected the idea that savages were closer to the state of nature than were modern Europeans. In his view, human beings could not make society because it is society that makes them human. As Burke (1790:246) had claimed, "without . . . civil society man could not by any possibility arrive at the perfection of which his nature is capable. . . . They conceive that He who gave our nature to be perfected by our virtue, willed also the necessary means of its perfection—He willed therefore the state." Consequently, the social arrangements of savages are not a true society. The notion of the "noble savage" was nonsense, and savagery was a sign of degeneracy. This idea—that some people, or more specifically some races, are degenerate—appears later in some of the sociological discussions of race.

Science and Ethics

Conservative reactions to the momentous changes in social life were in large part reactions to the perceived absence of traditional moral standards in society. The secularization of society, conjoined with a faith in science and objectivity, did produce a problem for intellectuals: how to secure an ethical basis that could guide practical actions (Levine, 1995:100). Key issues for classical sociologists were determining the basis for notions of the "good society" and determining the essence of human nature that prompts individuals to act ethically.

Efforts by philosophers Immanuel Kant and Georg Wilhelm Friedrich Hegel to deal with these questions form an important background to the work of early sociologists. Their theories also inform contemporary debates about the sociology of knowledge.

Immanuel Kant (1724–1804) How the rational, autonomous individual could be a moral being without appealing to some external divine connection was addressed by the philosopher Immanuel Kant. He was influenced by Rousseau but disagreed with Rousseau's idea that the essence of human nature could be discovered in the presocial state of nature. Human nature, in Kant's view, is defined by the ability to transcend and oppose nature through the exercise of both reason *and* moral standards.

The man of reason and morality becomes a sovereign subject and is free, Kant believed, whereas "natural" man is an object determined by sensory experience and is unfree. As he stated in his essay "Was ist Aufklaäring?" ("What Is Enlightenment?"), "All that is required for this enlightenment is *freedom*; and particularly the least harmful of all that may be called freedom, namely the freedom for man to make *public use* of his reason in all matters"(1784:134). As both natural beings and rational subjects, human beings are therefore free to be immoral or moral. Although society may encourage moral action, it cannot determine or guarantee such action, because human beings have free will.

Nor are individuals passive receivers of sensory knowledge. They are active subjects who use their reason to organize the chaos of sensory data. Human beings do not have immediate knowledge of things or nature. Sensory data are sorted into a priori, or preexisting, categories of the mind such as time or space. Kant noted that human beings use the a priori categories to give meaning to sensory reality. Human beings cannot know "things-in-themselves"; they can only know through reason, which organizes the chaos of sensory data.

Like Rousseau, Kant's perspective is individualistic, in that the autonomous moral being is the subject of his analysis. But Kant wondered how such autonomous subjects could form a moral community. How is the free will of the individual reconciled with the collective need for integration and order? The issue is particularly difficult because Kant saw conflict as the driving force of history. The "unsocial sociability" or mutual antagonism of human beings is what encouraged the development of human potential toward freedom and rationality.

This problem becomes particularly important in a capitalist, industrial society, which relies for order on self-interested, autonomous subjects. Kant concluded that only in an altruistic community can people's selfish goals be satisfied and social order and harmony be maintained. And although natural impulses may encourage people to act selfishly, ethical human beings transcend or oppose nature through practical reason. Consequently, an altruistic community is achieved by human beings motivated by a sense of duty (Levine, 1995:183).

Georg Wilhelm Friedrich Hegel (1770–1831)   Hegel attempted to overcome the contradiction between Kant's notions of the rational, autonomous individual and of collective morality. Hegel perceived that Kant had become stuck by focusing on the moral individual instead of the moral community.

Hegel agreed with Kant that social history was a history of conflicts, the purpose of which was "the progressive realization of humanity's capacity for reason and freedom" (Levine, 1995:190). He also agreed that reason and freedom were attained by the individual's pursuit of "selfish interests and social strife" rather than moral intentions. But he disagreed with Kant's idea that morality and the a priori categories for sorting sensory data were innate and ahistorical. Hegel believed that rationality and morality evolve as a collective project as individuals attempt to understand their society and their history. That is, human beings do not simply interpret their world—they also critically reflect upon that world. The a priori categories used to sort sensory data change as human beings become more aware of how their understanding is shaped by the social-historical world. In turn, this awareness changes their moral standards, and consequently, the social world.

Hegel recognized that under modern conditions individuals do experience themselves as autonomous and self-interested, and they correctly identify the social world as a network of impersonal exchange relationships. This is the nature of a capitalist civil society. But because civil society is an individualistic, alienating place, the role of the state is vitally important. In contrast to Kant or Rousseau, Hegel saw the state as standing apart from the contractual relations of individuals. The state promotes the collective good by helping individualistic citizens to be altruistic and to undertake their duties to their fellows. The state—not the individual—is the progressive embodiment of pure reason and the arbiter of collective morality. Therefore, the state is the means for each individual to realize personal freedom.

Individual progress toward pure reason and absolute freedom is accomplished **dialectically,** in Hegel's view. That is, as individuals reflect upon themselves and their situation, they are able to contradict and go beyond what has been acceptable in the past and thus reach a new level of understanding. More important, in the pursuit of freedom or emancipation, individuals achieve an understanding that demands social change. Because of this dialectical process of give and take, a person's ethics come to reflect those of the larger society and, at the same time, shape society's ethics (Levine, 1995).

Hegel also embraced the duality of human nature that Kant theorized. But Hegel did not reject as problematic the sensual, passionate part of human nature. Like Wollstonecraft, Hegel considered the senses (or the imagination) just as vital as reason to understanding and moral progress.

Hegel's idealism was an important corrective to the belief that the social world could be understood scientifically in the same manner as the natural world. Reason to him was not an impersonal, ahistorical force but an historically situated product of human reflection. His legacy for sociology was the idea that society and human beings cannot be studied as objects like the objects of natural science. Sociologists need to understand the subjective meaning of social actions, bearing in mind that sociologists bring their own a priori understandings to the inquiry. That is, sociologists cannot help but have evaluative or normative stances regarding the topics they study; they cannot avoid ideology.

Another important idea for later sociological analyses was Hegel's distinction between understanding and reason. Understanding is knowledge that looks for causal connections between sense impressions. Reason involves reflecting on how that understanding is achieved and recognizes that it is human beings who develop the categories of understanding. Thus, reason is concerned not only with what is but also with what might be or should be.

Hegel extends Kant's notion of practical reason with the notion of critical reason. But both philosophers go beyond the positivist claim that knowledge is obtained only through sense impressions and that the goal is to establish causal relations among things. Knowledge must have an ethical component that indicates not simply how social ends can be achieved but why they should be achieved.

Final Thoughts on the Philosophical Precursors

According to both reactionary conservatives seeking to bring back the "good old days" and radicals wanting to overthrow the status quo in favor of a better future, the revolutions of the eighteenth century had introduced a host of problems into the social world: disorder, alienation, insecurity. However, other social theorists were more sanguine about the revolutions, believing that they had brought scientific rationalism and autonomous individualism, which were the bases for individual freedom and the construction of an equitable society. The status quo conservatives believed that this postrevolutionary, modern society was self-corrective; the liberals believed that it was good but could be improved through conscious effort.

Sociology emerged out of these theoretical and ideological debates as a science that could explain modern social life. In fact, the Enlightenment discovery of "society" as an independent, scientifically understood entity with a reality apart from its individual members was the fundamental concept that led to the development of the specialization that Comte called sociology. However, the impulse to resolve the ethical problems produced by modern life has not been easily satisfied by the sociological enterprise, as you will find in reading the rest of this book (Dahrendorf, 1968).

We hope you will find the story told in the following chapters to be an interesting one. Our goal in writing this book was to help you understand how theories about the nature of society have developed in Western culture in the past 200 years. But although the theorists featured in this book are presented in roughly chronological order, we do not want you to think that this book is a dry history of sociological theory. Diverse voices, women's and men's, have contributed to sometimes heated debates on matters that are relevant even today, both to our social world and to sociology as a discipline.

References

Aron, Raymond. 1970. *Main Currents in Sociological Thought* (2 vols.). New York: Anchor Books.

Beaud, Michel. 1983. *A History of Capitalism, 1500–1980*. New York: Monthly Review Press.

Becker, Carl L. 1932/1960. *The Heavenly City of the Eighteenth-Century Philosophers.* New Haven, CT. Yale University Press.

Bonald, Louis de. 1840. *Oeuvres*. Paris: Libraire d'Adrien le Clerc et C.

Braudel, Ferdinand. 1984. *Civilization and Capitalism, 15th–18th Century* (Sian Reynolds, Trans.) (3 vols.). London: Collins.

Browne, Alice. 1987. *The Eighteenth-Century Feminist Mind*. Sussex: Harvester Press.

Burke, Edmund. 1790/1909. *Reflections on the French Revolution*. New York: Collier & Son.

Cassirer, Ernst. 1951. *The Philosophy of the Enlightenment*. Princeton, NJ: Princeton University Press.

———. 1964. *The Individual and the Cosmos in Renaissance Philosophy*. New York: Harper and Row.

Corrigan, Philip, and Derek Sayer. 1985. *The Great Arch: English State Formation as Cultural Revolution*. Oxford: Basil Blackwell.

Dahrendorf, Ralf. 1968. *Homo Sociologicus*. London: Routledge and Kegan Paul.

Durkheim, Emile. 1892/1960. *Montesquieu and Rousseau*. Ann Arbor: University of Michigan Press.

Engels, Friedrich. 1892/1977. *The Condition of the Working-Class in England*. Moscow: Progress Publishers.

Fox-Genovese, Elizabeth. 1987. "Women and Enlightenment." In Renate Bridenthal, Claudia Koonz, and Susan Stuard (Eds.), *Becoming Visible: Women in European History* (pp. 251–277). Boston: Houghton Mifflin.

Gay, Peter. 1969. *The Enlightenment: An Interpretation*. New York: W.W. Norton & Company.

Godwin, William. 1798/1928. *Memoirs of Mary Wollstonecraft*. London: Constable & Co.

Hegel, Georg Wilhelm Friedrich. 1896/1956. *Lectures on the Philosophy of History* (J. Sibtree, Trans.). New York: Dover.

Hill, Christopher. 1969. *Reformation to Industrial Revolution*. Harmondsworth, England: Penguin.

———. 1985. *The Collected Essays* (vol.1). Amherst: University of Massachusetts Press.

Hobbes, Thomas. 1651/n.d. *Leviathan*. London: J. M. Dent & Sons.

Kant, Immanuel. 1784/1977. "What Is Enlightenment?" In Carl Friedrich (Ed.), *The Philosophy of Kant* (pp. 132–139). New York: Modern Library.

Krause, Richard, W. 1982. "Patriarchal Liberalism and Beyond: From John Stuart Mill to Harriet Taylor." In Jean Bethke Elshtain (Ed.), *The Family in Political Thought*. Amherst: University of Massachusetts Press.

Levine, Donald. 1995. *Visions of the Sociological Tradition*. Chicago: University of Chicago Press.

Locke, John. 1711/1988. *Two Treatises of Government* (Peter Laslet, Ed.). Cambridge: Cambridge University Press.

Lovejoy, Arthur. 1936. *The Great Chain of Being*. Cambridge, MA: Harvard University Press.

Maistre, Joseph de. 1884–1886. *Oeuvres complètes*. Lyon: Vitte et Perrussel.

Mannheim, Karl. 1929/1960. *Ideology and Utopia*. London: Routledge and Kegan Paul.

Marx, Karl. 1887/1967. *Capital* (vol. 1) (Friedrich Engels, Ed.). New York: International Publishers.

Marx, Karl, and Friedrich Engels. 1845/1947. *The German Ideology*. New York: International Publishers.

Montesquieu, Charles. 1748/1977. Preface to *De l'Esprit des Lois [The Spirit of the Laws]*. In Melvin Richter, *The Political Theory of Montesquieu*. Cambridge: Cambridge University Press.

Nisbet, Robert A. 1966. *The Sociological Tradition*. New York: Basic Books.

Randall, Willard Sterne. 1993. *Thomas Jefferson: A Life*. New York: Henry Holt & Co.

Rousseau, Jean-Jacques. 1762a/1910. *The Social Contract: A Discourse upon the Origin and the Foundation of Inequality among Mankind*. New York: P. F. Collier & Son.

———. 1762b/1986. *Emile* (Barbar Foxley, Trans.). London: Dent.

Schama, Simon. 1989. *Citizens: A Chronicle of the French Revolution*. New York: Alfred A. Knopf.

Sica, Alan. 1997. "Back to 'Ethical Culture.'" *Perspectives: The ASA Theory Section Newsletter, 19*(1).

Smith, Adam. 1776/1976. *An Inquiry into the Nature and Causes of the Wealth of Nations* (E. Cannan, Ed.). 2 Vols. Chicago: University of Chicago Press.

Sydie, R. A. 1992. "From Liberal to Radical: The Work and Life of Mary Wollstone-craft." *Atlantis, 17*(1): 36–51.

Tomalin, Claire. 1974. *The Life and Death of Mary Wollstonecraft*. London: Wiedenfeld and Nicholson.

Wardle, Ralph. 1979. *The Collected Letters of Mary Wollstonecraft*. Ithaca: Cornell University Press.

Weber, Max. 1903–1917/1949. *The Methodology of the Social Sciences*. Glencoe, IL: Free Press.

Williams, Raymond. 1963. *Culture and Society, 1780–1950*. Harmondsworth, England: Penguin.

Wollstonecraft, Mary. 1790/1996. *A Vindication of the Rights of Men*. Amherst, NY: Prometheus Books.

———. 1792/1967. *A Vindication of the Rights of Woman*. New York: W. W. Norton.

Wordsworth, William. 1809/1952. "French Revolution." In *The Poetical Works of Wordsworth* (E. deSelincourt, Ed.). Oxford: The Clarendon Press.

Zeitlin, Irving. 1997. *Ideology and the Development of Sociological Theory* (6th ed.). Upper Saddle River, NJ: Prentice-Hall.

Chapter 2

Theorizing After the Revolution
Saint-Simon, Comte, and Martineau

The French Revolution was predicated on the idea that social harmony and order were tied to the freedom of the rational individual. Ordinary citizens, rather than kings or bishops, were rightfully in charge of society and would create a better world. The actual aftermath of revolution was, however, often messy, unfair, and even dangerous. The revolutionary spirit seemed to give rise as much to anarchy as it did to orderly progress toward a good society.

Not everyone liberated by the Revolution seemed capable of making rational decisions that benefited society. Many social theorists blamed the continuing social problems on the lack of education. A scientific education was seen as the answer. Educating people to think logically and objectively, as scientists were trained to do, would elevate the thinking and impulses of the citizens. These educated citizens were to usher in an enlightened, harmonious society.

Auguste Comte was one of the social theorists who developed a theory of the good society built around the idea of subjecting society itself to scientific scrutiny. In Comte's view, scientific objectivity applied to the social world would produce order and progress. The linking of the seemingly contradictory principles of order and progress remain important catchwords to this day for many politicians and social engineers attempting to chart their visions of social transformation. In this chapter you will discover the basis for the appeal of the Comtean emphasis on order and progress. In the process, you will also witness the birth of sociology itself.

Introductory sociology books often describe Comte as the "father of sociology" (Stewart and Glynn, 1971:15). Comte did indeed coin the term *sociology*, and his support helped to spread the idea that society could be described by scientific knowledge of social laws. But his work was anticipated by others, most notably by his mentor Henri Saint-Simon. And Comte's English translator, Harriet Martineau, did much to flesh out the ideas often credited to Comte. We might say, then, that sociology had parents of both sexes.

Claude-Henri, Comte de Saint-Simon (1760–1825)

Saint-Simon was a minor noble who led a fascinating life during the upheavals of the French Revolution and its aftermath. The democratic revolutionary Assemblies gave way in 1795 to the oligarchic Directories, in 1799 to the military dictatorship of Napoleon, and eventually, in 1814, to the restoration of the Bourbon monarchy. All of these changes were accompanied by social and economic disruptions, as well as religious controversy, and all these internal conflicts were made worse by foreign wars. Saint-Simon therefore lived during times of profound upheaval, which had an effect on his ideas about the nature of society and how it might be changed.

As a young man Saint-Simon joined the army, and in 1779 he went to join Lafayette in America fighting in the American War of Independence. When Saint-Simon returned to France, he participated in revolutionary activities and associated with various radical circles in Paris. At the same time, he amassed and lost several fortunes in land speculations.

By 1789 Saint-Simon was no longer a financier, and in 1790 he renounced his title. He became instead a philosopher and prophet, writing extensively on social and political matters. In 1817 Saint-Simon took on Auguste Comte as secretary and collaborator.

Saint-Simon's Central Theories and Methods

Saint-Simon's central idea was that society, at least Western society, had reached a critical point. Science would replace religion as the important unifying institution. Furthermore, Saint-Simon suggested that the "social sciences would become positive by being reduced to physics" (Markham, 1952:xxii). Note this explicitly positivist point of view, in which the study of society is likened to the study of the natural world. For Saint-Simon, the ultimate goal of any science was symbolized by the Newtonian law of gravitation, which represented the "unity of all knowledge in its most perfect, deductive, *a priori* form" (Markham, 1952:xxiii). The analogy with physics is something that continued to be an important issue in sociological debates well into the twentieth century.

Above all else, Saint-Simon theorized that the study of society must be based on **empirical** observations of the facts gathered either from experience or experiment. He also considered society a suitable subject for study using physiological concepts because it is an **organic** phenomenon, undergoing growth and development like a living thing. In society's case, he believed, development is in the direction of increasing rationality and scientific knowledge.

Saint-Simon's and Comte's ideas on the importance of a scientific method for the study of society were very similar. Although Saint-Simon was the first to enunciate them, Comte often gets the credit (Dondo, 1955:176; Ionescu, 1976:20). To be precise, like many of his seventeenth- and eighteenth-century peers, Saint-Simon believed that a truly logical system of knowledge, specifically mathematics, could be applied to the natural and social sciences alike. Consequently, Saint-Simon sought a universal concept, similar to the law of gravitation, that would unify the social sciences. Social science should be autonomous and have its own laws (Markham, 1952:xxxvi).

Still, no less a figure than Emile Durkheim, as well as others, sought to give Saint-Simon his due: "It is to him that one must, in full justice, award the honor currently given to Comte" (Durkheim, 1897:142). Some have suggested that Comte might have been designated the father of sociology only because Saint-Simon was not just a theorist of society but also a socialist (Gouldner, 1962:12, fn. 5). Acknowledging Comte is "less professionally damaging" than accepting that "blacksheep brother," socialism, and reinforcing the lay assumption that socialism and sociology are similar.

Nature of Society, Humans, and Change

For Saint-Simon, the development of industrial society was the culmination of social change since the feudal era. The American and French revolutions marked the transition point. But industrial society demanded new forms of social relationships and social structures. Society, which had become rigid and inflexible prior to the revolutions, would be restored to an organic state through science and industry. As Saint-Simon remarked in a letter to an American friend, "Where shall we find ideas which can provide this necessary and organic social bond? In the idea of industry; only there shall we find our safety and the end of revolution" (Markham, 1952:69).

Furthermore, Saint-Simon believed that all social change was the result of the development of human knowledge and beliefs: "Institutions are only ideas in action" (quoted in Durkheim, 1897:129). The development of an industrial society therefore demanded a new form of knowledge—namely, science—which would replace the religious and metaphysical knowledge of the previous era.

Here again, Saint-Simon's focus on organic change helped him to understand the phenomena he studied. Observing history, he noted progressive changes in religious ideas as well as in science. He also pointed to the gradual development of science itself, beginning with astronomy and proceeding through physics, chemistry, and biology to reach, in the modern era, society. From there it was but a short hop to the argument that the "human sciences have to be constructed in imitation of the other natural sciences, for man is only one part of nature." And since it is the positive method that "allows us to know the inorganic world, it follows that it alone is suited to the human world also" (Durkheim, 1897:135).

Generally, Saint-Simon argued that societies progress through stages. He posited three:

- Polytheistic, primitive stage
- Theological, feudal stage
- Modern stage of science and industry

He believed that Western society was entering the third stage. "When the French Revolution broke out, it was no longer a question of modifying the feudal and theological system, which had already lost almost all its real force. It was a question of organizing the industrial and scientific system, summoned by the level of civilization to replace it" (Taylor, 1975:228).

Saint-Simon agreed with the reactionary conservatives Louis de Bonald and Joseph de Maistre (see Chapter 1) that medieval society, corresponding to his second stage, was the ideal unified, organic whole. But unlike them, he believed that it was futile to want to restore medieval society (Markham, 1952; Taylor, 1975; Zeitlin, 1997).

Similarly, Saint-Simon agreed with de Bonald's emphasis on "systematic unity" as the basis for scientific studies, but he did not agree with de Bonald's "enthusiasm for Deism" (Markham, 1952:18). Science, as the "new religion," had the same ability as religion to offer a coherent explanation of the world and the whole of human existence. In addition, science and industry had made any return to the old theological forms impossible; only through scientific laws could the unity of the spiritual and temporal be restored. Nevertheless, Saint-Simon recognized that an ethical basis for society was necessary, and he later developed what he called a New Christianity.

Despite his acceptance of religion's role, Saint-Simon thought that in the new society that industrialization produced, the members most useful for social order and progress would be scientists, industrialists, and artists. The political division of labor was to be "spiritual power in the hands of the scientists; the temporal power in the hands of the property owners; the power to nominate those who should perform the functions of leaders of humanity in the hands of all; the reward of the rulers, esteem" (Markham, 1952:11). More specifically, it was the "work of the scientists, artists, and industrialists" that would "in discovery and application, contribute most to national prosperity" (Markham, 1952:78).

Politics would be transformed in the new society to become the *"science of production* that is to say, that science whose object is the creation of an order of things most favourable to every kind of production" (Ionescu, 1976:108). Governments would therefore "no longer command men; their functions will be limited to ensuring that useful work is not hindered" (Taylor, 1975:165). Government, in other words, would simply administer "things." And the administrators would be technocrats—the scientists and managers of industrial production.

Saint-Simon extended his discussion of future political organization with a plan titled "Reorganization of European Society" (1814). In medieval society, the Church had been an international organization ensuring order and stability. Although no church could perform that task in the modern era, Saint-Simon theorized that some new international organization, based on scientific, positivist principles, must take its place:

> Europe would have the best possible organization if all the nations composing it were to be governed by parliaments, recognizing the supremacy of a common parliament set above all national governments and invested with the power of judging their disputes. (Markham, 1952:46)

The present-day European Union may not be precisely what Saint-Simon had in mind, but perhaps if some semblance of his ideas had been adopted earlier, two of the most devastating wars of the twentieth century might have been averted.

Class, Gender, and Race

Saint-Simon had little to say about gender and race, but he was concerned with social class. The basic class division, in Saint-Simon's view, was between producers and consumers. Industrial entrepreneurs, industrial workers, scientists, and artists composed the productive class, in contrast to aristocrats, churchmen, courtiers, and rentiers, who composed the consuming class. Class conflict was between the producing class and the parasitic, nonproducing classes. Social order would only be established when society had eliminated the nonproducing classes.

Understandably, Saint-Simon was interested in promoting the development of industry:

> All society rests on industry. Industry is the only guaranty of its existence. . . . The most favorable state of affairs for industry is, for this reason, the most favorable to society. (quoted in Durkheim, 1897:173–174)

Saint-Simon understood the term *industry* as including all activities that benefited society as a whole. Consequently, it could include the activities of scientists and artists as well as industrial workers. Nonetheless, the class of industrialists was the most important to society, in Saint-Simon's view. It did not need other classes to produce, but other classes needed industrialists.

Saint-Simon predicted that in the new industrial society, inequality would be eliminated. For Saint-Simon, **equality** meant that the individual draws "benefits from society in exact proportion to his social outlay, . . . to the beneficent use he makes of his abilities. And this equality is the natural foundation of industrial society" (quoted in Durkheim, 1897:192). Therefore, managers of industry are not superior to workers but simply perform a different, but necessary, function for the benefit of all. In the new society, government would also be transformed into a purely administrative entity: "Politics is the science of production" (quoted in Durkheim, 1897:179).

The new industrial society could not be fully established in isolation from other societies. Saint-Simon understood that industrialization demanded an international stage. Nationalism would be replaced by more "global" organizations, starting with the European nations. Industry does not distinguish between nations, and all industrial producers are "united by the general interests of production" and are "therefore essentially friends." Consequently, "Nothing stands in the way of their uniting, and the coalition of their efforts is the indispensable condition if industry is to attain the ascendancy it can and should enjoy" (quoted in Durkheim, 1897:214).

Saint-Simon's version of a classless, international community of industrial producers has survived to this day. For instance, investors and stockbrokers in present-day financial markets have international or global loyalties apart from national boundaries and interests that Saint-Simon postulated two centuries ago.

Other Theories and Theorists

Saint-Simon's celebration of exact science as the guiding principle for society was balanced by his conviction that the Christian injunction to "love one another" as brothers should become the controlling principle for social progress. Saint-Simon pointed out that the "similarity of positive moral ideas is the single bond which can unite men into society" (quoted in Durkheim, 1897:128). The other-worldly focus of this Christian idea was rejected in favor of "an earthly and practical morality" (quoted in Durkheim, 1897:204). This was necessary because the political and industrial transformation of society encouraged egoism. Religion had curbed egoism in the past, but in the absence of religion, egoism makes "frightening progress" and "all is tending to isolation" (quoted in Durkheim, 1897:205).

Saint-Simon recognized that "without charity, mutual obligation, and philanthropy, the social order—and still more the human order—was impossible" (Durkheim, 1897:227). Economic unity must be balanced by spiritual unity if social progress is to be achieved. Private charity must be transformed into public welfare.

> The most direct means to accomplish the moral and physical amelioration of the majority of the population consists in considering as primary expenses of the State, those required to procure work for all able-bodied men in order to ensure their physical existence; and those which seek to spread acquired knowledge as fast as possible to the proletariat class; and finally those which guarantee individuals composing this class pleasures and gratifications appropriate to the development of their spirit. (quoted in Durkheim, 1897:209)

These three state responsibilities—public works, free education, and uplifting recreation—are the cornerstones of twentieth-century welfare states.

Saint-Simon's new society was not a cold technocracy governed by scientists and industrialists; it was a new Jerusalem that brought the Christian ideal into the practical, everyday world. The need for moral unity in a positivist social context is also a central concern for the sociologists who followed Saint-Simon—most notably, Comte and Emile Durkheim.

Critique and Conclusions

Saint-Simon was an aristocrat who realized that the society that gave him this privileged status was finished and that a new social order was rapidly developing in Europe. His focus was on the development of a scientific, positivist approach that would produce an ordered, unified society in which the well-being of all could be assured. His essential optimism is embodied in his prediction that "the Golden Age of the human race is not behind us but before us; it lies in the perfection of the social order" (1814:136).

Saint-Simon's most influential contributions were the idea that knowledge progresses through historical stages,[1] his positivist analysis of human society,

---

[1]Markham (1952:xxv, fn. 3) insists that Saint-Simon was the first to outline the positivist understanding of stages of historical evolution and that the Law of Three Stages "pompously announced by Comte as an original discovery, is merely a precise formulation of St.-Simon's argument." Durkheim (1897:144) also pointed out that in Saint-Simon's work the "entire program of positive philosophy and positive sociology" is sketched out.

and even his later ideas about a "new Christianity," or a new set of moral ideas, to underpin and consolidate the application of the scientifically validated laws of social order and development. All these ideas were incorporated in various ways into other sociologists' theories—most especially, as you will see, those of his secretary, Auguste Comte.

Auguste Comte (1798–1857)

Auguste Comte's life was characterized by conflict and contradictions. He had been a brilliant student in school, and in 1814 he entered the newly created École Polytechnique in Paris. This school, which had been created in 1794, became a renowned center for scientific research. However, the school was the creation of France's postrevolutionary government and was therefore subject to the upheavals that accompanied the postrevolutionary period. After the school was closed and reorganized in 1816, Comte did not return.

He lived a marginal life in Paris, tutoring in mathematics until 1817, when he met Saint-Simon and became his secretary and collaborator. The collaboration lasted until 1824, when a rather acrimonious dispute over authorship of a book of essays led to Comte's departure. Comte was once more thrust into a marginal existence, tutoring and attempting to arouse interest in his ideas in a series of public lectures.

Comte married Caroline Massin, a bookseller, in 1825, but the marriage was a stormy affair. In 1826 Comte became ill and was treated for "mania." He attempted suicide twice, but his rescue on the second attempt convinced him that he had been saved in order to complete his life's work—the elaboration of a positivist philosophy. It should be noted that Caroline stood by him during this difficult time.

During the years 1830–1842, Comte wrote his masterwork, *Cours de philosophie positive*. By 1838, however, Comte decided for reasons of "cerebral hygiene" that he would no longer read any more scientific work, and in his last years the only book he read "over and over again" was the *Imitation of Christ* (Coser, 1977:18). Throughout this period he continued to have financial difficulties. He had a series of low-paid, marginal academic jobs, such as appointments as an external examiner at the École Polytechnique and as a mathematics teacher at a private school. Comte's attempts to get a regular academic appointment were futile, and in 1844 his appointment as an external examiner at the École was not renewed (Coser, 1977:18). In addition, his marriage deteriorated, and Caroline left him just after the completion of the *Cours*.[2]

---

[2]In discussions of Comte's life and work, many authors observe that although Caroline Massin was a bookseller when Comte married her, she had formerly been a prostitute. The basis for this allegation is the "Secret Addition" that Comte added to his *Testament* many years after their separation. Pickering (1993:373–380) suggests that there are good grounds to dispute Comte's version, given his paranoia by the time the *Testament* was written and the bitterness of the separation. Pickering (1993:40–41) indicates that the accusation was doubly duplicitous because it was Massin who had "helped establish the positivist periodical, the *Revue de la Philosophie Positive*" and who did the "most to solidify Comte's reputation" after his death.

Comte's life became more bearable in 1844 when he met the young Clotilde de Vaux and fell in love. Madame de Vaux's husband was a minor official who had embezzled government funds and disappeared, leaving his wife in serious difficulties. Clotilde suffered from consumption, and two years after meeting Comte she died. Comte vowed to devote the rest of his life to his "saint" and credited Clotilde with providing, through her love, the inspiration for his last major work, the organization of a Religion of Humanity.[3]

Comte's Central Theories and Methods

Comte, like most French intellectuals, and European intellectuals in general, framed his ideas in response to the crises and conflicts that marked the aftermath of the French Revolution.

In addition, like Saint-Simon, Comte proceeded from positivism to secular religion. Comte's positivism was a synthesis of many ideas, most especially those of his former mentor. Like Saint-Simon, he believed that a new science was both timely and necessary and that ideas or knowledge had reached a stage when the search for invariable social laws was possible—that is, society was entering a positivist stage. "Now that the human mind has grasped celes-tial and terrestrial physics . . . there remains one science, to fill up the series of sciences of observation,—social physics" (Comte, 1853:30). Comte coined the term *sociology* after discovering that the term *social physics* had already been used by the statistician Adolphe Quetelet to describe a quite different form of social investigation.

For Comte, sociology was at the apex of a hierarchy of sciences: "MATH-EMATICS, ASTRONOMY, PHYSICS, CHEMISTRY, PHYSIOLOGY, SOCIAL PHYSICS" (1853:50ff). The hierarchy moved from the study of the "most general, simple, abstract and remote phenomena known to us, and those that affect all others without being affected by them" (mathematics) to the "most particular, compound, concrete phenomena, and those which are the most interesting to Man" (social physics, or sociology) (1853:46). Later, when Comte settled on "love" as the basic principle of existence, he added morals as the last, most "positive" of the sciences.

Each science in Comte's hierarchy builds on the science that precedes it, so that sociology is a distinct science but "closely connected, from first to last, with biology," or physiology (1853:448). Sociology and biology are closely connected because they are **synthetic sciences**—that is, they examine the parts of any phenomenon in relation to the whole. In contrast, the **analytical sciences** at the base of the hierarchy focus on isolated phenomena.

As it was for Saint-Simon, for Comte society was an **organic** phenomenon. A major "scientific principle" was that "there must always be a spontaneous

---

[3]Pickering (1993:376) suggests that Clotilde, who refused to have sex with Comte, became his "angel in the Religion of Humanity" and Caroline then became the antithesis, the fallen woman, who as a "threat to the family and patriarchal society, represented the ultimate symbol of evil in the positive system." Comte's devotion to his "angel" was steadfast, and he visited Clotilde's grave in Père Lachaise cemetery every week until his final illness and death in 1857.

harmony between the whole and the parts of the social system," and the only task of any "political system . . . temporal or spiritual" was to guide the social system "towards its determinate ends" (1853:459–460). This task could now be accomplished because the new science, sociology, could reveal the invariant laws of social development.

Comte advocated that sociology be concerned with the discovery of the most general, most fundamental social laws. Such laws would indicate the ways in which society could be changed. That is, sociology could determine what *is*, what *will be*, and what *should be*, because it discovers what conforms to human nature. Comte believed that the time had come to "complete the vast intellectual operation begun by Bacon, Descartes, and Galileo, by constructing a system of general ideas which must henceforth prevail among the human race" and in this way "put an end to the revolutionary crisis which is tormenting the civilized nations of the world" (1975:37).[4]

Never a modest theorist, Comte claimed that his sociology solved the former antagonisms between the "theological and positive spirit, owing to their assumptions of the opposite points of view," as well as solving the "struggles of mathematical philosophy with expiring theology and metaphysics, up to the present hour." When the "positive spirit" is extended to "moral and social speculation," then the "fatal antagonism by which intellectual progress appeared to be contradictory to moral progress" disappears (1975:796). The sociologist is simultaneously the prophet of the new order and a scientist employing an objective methodology.

Comte's debt to Saint-Simon is fairly clear. But Comte comes into his own in his codification of a methodology for the sociological enterprise. As a science that rejects metaphysical concerns with "essential nature" or any search for "first causes" and concentrates on the discovery of invariable laws, sociology should rely on four methods for learning about social phenomena:

Observation. The sociologist observes social "facts." But most important, observation is "first directed, and finally interpreted, by some theory" (1853:474). Any isolated, empirical observation is "idle" unless it is connected "at least hypothetically, with some law" (1853:475). In a statement that would be echoed in Durkheim's work (see Chapter 4), Comte stated that "No social fact can have any scientific meaning till it is connected with some other social fact." Until the connections are made through theory, information is anecdotal, having no "rational utility" (1853:476).

Experiment. Comte believed that experiments similar to physical science experiments were difficult, although not impossible, for sociology. But he distinguished between two types of experiment: direct and indirect. Comte recognized that, as in biology, direct experiments are difficult on such a complex and changeable organism as society. But the indirect experiment is possible for both biology and sociology. The analysis of a pathology—

---

[4]Although Comte suggested that all "civilized nations" were approaching the positivist stage, he believed that France would lead the way because it was there that the "revolutionary state had been most conspicuous" and it was "better prepared . . . than any other, for true reorganization" (1853:401).

biological or social—involves the investigation of cases in which the "natural laws, either of harmony or succession, are disturbed by any causes, special or general, accidental or transient" (1853:477). Thus, social disturbances are "analogous to diseases in the individual organism." The study of physical and social suffering discloses the "real laws of our nature, individual or social"—that is, they disclose what is normal and right (1853:477).

Comparison. Three forms of comparison are possible in sociology: comparison of human and animal societies, comparison of all existing human societies, and comparison of societies at different stages of development. The first form of comparison has "scientific utility" in illustrating the "elementary laws of social interconnection, by exhibiting their action in the most imperfect state of society" (1853:479). The second comparison illustrates the different evolutionary stages of all societies. But it is the third form, historical comparison, that is the "chief scientific device" for sociology.

Historical Analysis. The historical method "verifies and applies . . . that chief quality of sociological science,—its proceeding from the whole to the parts" (1853:481). The method is critical because no "examination of facts can explain our existing state to us, if we have not ascertained, by historical study, the value of the elements at work" and comparison cannot be "decisive unless it embraces to whole of the past" (1853:483).

Comte formulated his theories through an exhaustive study of the philosophy and social theory of the past. He was convinced that this course of study had led inevitably to his discovery of sociology.

Comte's first lectures and publications were well received by many prominent intellectuals in France, as well as in England and America, and by a few Germans. One admirer was the English philosopher John Stuart Mill, who organized a subscription fund among other English supporters to tide Comte over some of his financial difficulties.

But Comte's views changed in the early 1850s, when he began to formulate his Religion of Humanity, with himself as high priest. His church did attract some believers, but they were few. Former enthusiasts for his positivist sociology were dismayed by his reversion to religion, especially one modeled on the medieval Catholic Church. The majority of his former admirers eventually repudiated him.[5] Still, many of Comte's ideas have great staying power.

Nature of Society, Humans, and Change

The key to Comte's new science was the idea that society has a "real" existence with properties separate from, and different from, those of individuals. In fact, individual human beings are absent from Comte's sociology; he is almost entirely concerned with society (Marcuse, 1954:359).

---

[5]Not everyone abandoned Comte, and interestingly some of his American admirers remained steadfast, hoping to establish the Religion of Humanity in the United States. For a discussion of Comte's reception in the United States, see Hawkins, 1936, 1938.

The idea of society as the primary object of analysis was itself proof that the time was ripe for sociology, because it demonstrated that society had reached the third stage in what Comte called the **Law of Human Progress**. This law refers to both social and intellectual development: "The human mind, by its nature, employs in its progress three methods of philosophizing, the character of which is essentially different, and even radically opposed" (1853:25).

Comte theorized that knowledge "passes successively" through the following theoretical conditions (1853:25):

1. **Theological or fictitious stage**. The focus of society and intellectual effort is the search for origins and for the essential nature and purpose of all things. The basic assumption is that all phenomena are produced by "supernatural beings," and the highest point of this stage is reached when the "providential action of a single Being" replaces the former proliferation of gods.

2. **Metaphysical or abstract stage.** This stage is a "modification of the first," in which society as a whole and intellectuals replace supernatural beings with abstract, even mysterious, forces that are "inherent in all beings." The high point for this stage is when human thought substitutes "one great entity (Nature)" for the "multitudes of entities" as the cause of all phenomena.

3. **Scientific or positive stage.** In this final stage of societal development, the "mind has given over the vain search after Absolute notions, the origin and destination of the universe, and the causes of phenomena, and applies itself to the study of their laws—that is, their invariable relations of succession and resemblance." The "first characteristic of Positive Philosophy" is to regard "all phenomena as subject to invariable natural *Laws*" (1853:28, emphasis in the original). Intellectuals use reason and observation to study the world and base their explanations on "facts" and the "establishment of a connection between a single phenomenon and some general facts." Like Saint-Simon, Comte retained a Newtonian model of scientific perfection. The "ultimate perfection of the Positive system" would be achieved when all phenomena could be represented as "particular aspects of a single general fact—such as Gravitation, for instance."

These three stages were interconnected, each leading into the other. Each stage was characteristic of the development of individual minds as well as of societies and science. According to Comte, the individual mind is "an indirect evidence of . . . the general mind" and of human progress because "each of us is aware . . . that he was a theologian in his childhood, a metaphysician in his youth, and a natural philosopher in his manhood" (1853:27). Comte believed that in his day the nations of western Europe, under the leadership of France, were entering the positive stage and were therefore at the forefront of progress, although this progress would in time be "extended beyond the white races, as the outlying groups of humanity become fitted to enter the system" (1853:772).

Comte claimed to have used historical comparison in matching types of societies to stages in the Law of Human Progress. Societies were distinguished in terms of their contributions to **order** and **progress**:

- Theological stage: Military men and priests dominate, and the major social unit is the family. This stage offers order but no progress.
- Metaphysical stage: The priests' dominance is challenged by lawyers, and the major social unit is the state. This stage offers progress, usually of the revolutionary kind, but no order and often anarchy.
- Positive stage: Order and progress are reconciled under the guidance of scientists and industrialists, who act on behalf of the major social unit—humanity.

Comte suggested that although order and progress had been seen as irreconcilable in the past, their union was the major feature of positivist social science. Order and progress were, in "Social Physics, as rigorously inseparable as the idea of Organization and Life in Biology" (1853:401).

In line with this biological analogy, Comte thought of sociology as the study of two aspects of society: social statics and social dynamics. This analytical distinction was not a "real separation of the science into two parts," but a distinction corresponding to the "double conception of order and progress" (1853:457):

- **Social statics**—social structure in more current sociological terminology—was concerned with investigating the "laws of action and reaction in the different parts of the social system" and their contribution to the order and stability of that system (1853:457). The sociological unit of study was not the individual but the interconnections between structures, because the "scientific spirit forbids us to regard society as composed of individuals" (1853:502). Social structures can only be understood in terms of other social structures, but this understanding provides the basic foundation for the necessary control of individual desires and the development of moral instincts. The family, the "true social unit," embodies the "true germ of the various characteristics of the social organism" because it is the intermediate structure between the individual and society.

- **Social dynamics**, or social change, was exemplified in Comte's application of the Law of Human Progress to the historical progression of societies. The "master-thought of continuous progress, or rather, of the gradual development of humanity" was the key (1853:463). Social dynamics studied the "laws of succession," or the changes over time in all social structures. It was this revolutionary characteristic that distinguished sociology from biology. Comte believed that his principle of social development afforded a "perfect interpretation of past society" and was the basis for the systematic prediction of future human and social progress (1853:541). Not surprisingly, he believed that the study of social dynamics was more interesting sociological work than the study of social statics.

Statics reveals the diversity of a particular society out of which the principles of social order can be discovered. Dynamics reveals the successive and necessary laws of progress for human beings and societies. But the two are vitally connected: Order is the basic condition for progress, and progress tends to consolidate social order. Thus Comte theorized that social change is **dialectical**. That is, each stage prepares the ground for the transition to the next, higher stage. As he confidently asserted, "if we want to conceive of the rights of the sociological spirit to supremacy, we have only to regard all our conceptions . . . as so many necessary results of a series of determinate phases, proper to our mental evolution, personal and collective, taking place according to invariable laws, statical and dynamical, which rational observation is competent to disclose" (1853:793).

Class, Gender, and Race

Comte had little to say on the issue of class. On the issue of race, he believed that the French most especially, and Europeans generally, were superior, although others might, in time, advance to the same level of development.

Comte was, however, centrally concerned with gender. As indicated earlier, he considered the family, not the individual, the basic social unit. It was the place where individuals learned how to be social beings by controlling their egoism in favor of altruism.

The family was also the place in which the "fundamental principle" of the "natural subordination of women" was demonstrated (1975:268). This "natural subordination," Comte maintained, had "reappeared under all forms of marriage, in all ages" and was confirmed by biological observations (1975:268). Throughout the animal world, "radical differences, physical and moral, distinguish the sexes." In the human species especially, the female was "constitutionally in a permanent state of infancy" and was therefore "more remote, in all important respects, from the ideal type of race" (1975:268–269). Consequently, Comte claimed, "Sociology will prove that the equality of the sexes, of which so much is said, is incompatible with all social existence" (1975:269).

Throughout history, at every stage in the development of society, Comte maintained, "women's life is essentially domestic, public life being confined to men" (1975:374). But women were still critical to the reorganization of social life because they were the repository and representation of the moral principle of positivism, which was altruism (love). Women were superior to men in the "spontaneous expansion of sympathy and sociality, as they are inferior to men in understanding and reason" (1853:505). Consequently, women's task was to modify the "cold and rough reason" of men by the exercise of their "social and personal vocation" of love (1853:505–506).

As civilization advanced, Comte argued,

> the law of social progression, as regards the sexes . . . consists in disengaging women more and more from all employment that is foreign to their domestic functions; so that . . . we shall hereafter reject, as disgraceful to Man, in all ranks, . . . the practice of subjecting women to laborious occupations; whereas they should be universally, and more and more exclusively, set apart for their characteristic offices of wife and mother. (1853:628)

Although during Comte's era some women had begun to claim the right to full citizenship and to the vote, in his view women were quite clearly unfitted for political power. He noted that "some visionaries have claimed for women" political power, but insisted this claim was made on behalf of women "without their consent" (1975:373).

In sum, a woman was unfit for mental labor "either from an intrinsic weakness of her reason or from her more lively moral and physical sensibility, which are hostile to scientific abstraction and concentration" (1853:505). Obviously, women could not hope to become sociologists. One can only speculate what Harriet Martineau, Comte's very capable translator and contributor to sociological theory in her own right, made of these opinions!

After Comte met Clotilde, he began to opine that women, as the repository of love, would become the hope for the transformation of humanity. Women's mission in Comte's ideal world was to ensure that men's activities were always guided by "universal love" or the "subjection of self-interest to social feeling" (1975:373). In fulfilling this task, women would always merit the "loving veneration" of men who recognized that women embody the "purest and simplest impersonation of humanity" (1975:377).

Other Theories and Theorists

Comte was firmly convinced that the initial converts to his new Religion of Humanity, outlined in his *System of Positive Polity*, published between 1851 and 1854, were most likely to be women because of their "natural" altruistic disposition. He consistently exhorted his followers to concentrate on recruiting women to the church. Ironically, the positivist who promoted the science of society proclaimed himself Pope of the new religion.

Comte worked out in intricate detail the organization and functions of the new church, including rituals, prayers, holy days, priestly training, and even the robes to be worn by priests. The center of the church was Paris. Like Saint-Simon, Comte believed that old religious organizations, such as the Roman Catholic Church, were based on outdated theology. What was needed in the positivist stage of society was a secular religion that worshiped the "great being of humanity."

Comte's turn to religion was an extension of his earlier observation that some common system of moral belief was an indispensable basis for any government. He pointed out that society was an organic phenomenon and the separation of individuals in the modern industrial division of labor made the new, positive religion a necessity for social unity and order. To order and progress, Comte now added love. The egoism of the modern age was to be countered by the altruism of the Religion of Humanity.

Critique and Conclusions

The French Revolution was regarded by both Saint-Simon and Comte as marking the point at which abstract speculations about human happiness and society could be replaced by scientific certainty, which would guarantee social order and social happiness. Saint-Simon looked to the forces of industrialization, under the guidance of scientists, artists, and industrialists, to steer society in the right direction. Comte also considered scientists and industrialists to be the leaders of the future. The leaders of society would base their actions on the scientific discovery of invariant social laws equivalent to the laws that govern the natural world.

Saint-Simon's work has had continued relevance largely in regard to the history of socialism, whereas Comte's work has often been neglected. Many authors have been quite critical of Comte's work, with one going so far as to suggest that the "majority of Comte's ideas ought to be forgotten" (Ritzer, 1996:87). Comte's contemporaries were equally critical after his turn to religion. His former supporter John Stuart Mill described his religious views as "the most complete system of spiritual and temporal despotism that ever issued from the brain of any human being" (quoted in Zeitlin, 1997:88).

But Comte should not be and cannot be "forgotten," if only because he invented the term *sociology*. Comte also set out a theoretical blueprint for sociology, with his conception of society as a "real" phenomenon, his division of society into statics and dynamics, his recognition of the interconnections of structures, and his insistence on the importance of theory to the observation of social "facts."

Comte's program for sociological investigation has been an important foundation for many other sociologists, but it too has come in for criticism. Most especially, some sociologists have criticized Comte's empirical, scientific approach, or what some have called the "physics envy" that positivism has often produced. Saint-Simon's and Comte's vision of sociology as an exact science is suspect because it may enable us to see "what is" but not "what should be" (Marcuse, 1954:345). The certainty that scientific observation provides simultaneously eliminates the freedom of the rational, enlightened, autonomous individual.

Others have suggested that the contemporary version of positivism as a "reductive, quantifiable approach to human knowledge" is a travesty of Comte's ideas. Comte was not a "naïve advocate of scientism"; he sought to balance the "needs of the heart and those of the mind, order and progress, rationalism and empiricism, materialism and idealism, the spiritual power and the temporal power, religion and science, objectivity and subjectivity" (Pickering, 1993:35). Comte, Saint-Simon, and, as you will see, Martineau all sought to cure the ills of modern society by *using* science for the benefit of human beings.

Harriet Martineau (1802–1876)

Harriet Martineau is best known as Comte's translator, but she herself was a prolific writer on a multitude of social, political, economic, and religious issues. Some critics have undervalued her work, seeing it as simply representative of the moral earnestness and belief in social engineering characteristic of mid- and late-nineteenth-century middle-class reformers. Until recently, most sociologists have taken Martineau's astonishing output of critical essays, commentaries, novels, and general journalistic contributions as evidence of her lightweight intellectual status. But two things should be said in her defense. First, her output was dictated by economic necessity. Writing represented one of the few occupational opportunities available to "distressed middle-class women" of her era—at least if they wished to retain some vestige of middle-class "respectability." Second, and more important, Martineau was an excellent synthesizer and popularizer of difficult material. This was no small achievement, especially with respect to the often arcane material, such as Comte's, that she reworked for popular consumption.[6]

Martineau began to go deaf at an early age and had various other handicaps—she could not taste or smell—that made her life difficult. Books and ideas were a sanctuary, especially as most of her family was less than sympathetic to her handicaps. During the 1820s, she began to write short pieces on religious issues that were published in a Unitarian publication, the *Monthly Repository*. In 1829 the family manufacturing business, which had supported Martineau and her family after the death of her father in 1826, failed. Suddenly her writing became an economic necessity.

Fortunately Martineau's work met with great success, and the "little deaf woman from Norwich" became "one of the most prolific and influential intellectuals of her time."[7] Of particular significance were her *Illustrations of Political Economy*, which began to appear in 1832. These were a series of didactic stories illustrating the ideas of Adam Smith, David Ricardo, Thomas Malthus, and James Mill. These stories remained popular through the mid-nineteenth century and were read by many of the first generation of American sociologists in their youth.

The basis for Martineau's development as a sociologist lay in her religious and social background. Harriet Martineau and her family were Unitarians and therefore dissenters from the established Anglican Church of England. Unitarians looked to the Bible for guidance but were far from fundamentalists, believing that the Bible was not the word of God as such but a record kept by those who had been privy to God's revelations. Thus there was room for flexibility in their religious beliefs. According to some commentators, this flexibility allowed Unitarians to accommodate the challenge of nineteenth-century science within their religious beliefs more easily than other denominations. The necessarian doctrine they espoused was a case in point.

Necessarianism derived from John Locke's claim that two kinds of knowledge exist: knowledge of God as a result of revelation, and knowledge that is the product of experience. This duality enabled Locke to envisage an empirical-causal universe while preserving the idea of a transcendent deity. This "uneasy accommodation between radicalism and biblicism" was intellectually inconsistent, but it did allow Martineau, along with other coreligionists, a way of combining her scientific convictions and reformist interests with her faith (Pichanick, 1980:26).

Necessarianism denied free will, claiming that everything was the result of what had preceded it. Therefore, "man's freedom of choice is circumscribed and even predictable" (Pichanick, 1980:25). The escape from such absolute determinism was through the education of reason, which allowed individuals to understand the forces that determine behavior and, by understanding, to take measures to change and improve the world. As a result, Martineau could quite

---

[6]For a comprehensive examination of Martineau's life and work, see Hoecker-Drysdale, 1992.

[7]The comment was made by a Lord Brougham and is quoted in Hoecker-Drysdale, 1992:16.

confidently state, "The great impediment to the true understanding of the purposes of human life is the prevalent ignorance or error respecting the primary laws of sensation and thought," and this ignorance perpetuated "great social evils" (1837:120). In other words, empirical study of the social world would give human beings the means to change oppressive conditions.

Martineau's Central Theories and Methods

The contradiction involved in the necessarian doctrine did not impede Martineau's attempts to objectively describe the social world. In an 1829 review of a book, *Natural Theology*, Martineau observed:

> A world of truth is before us. We cannot help desiring to explore it; and we know of no interdiction which need exclude us from any part of it. We ought, therefore, to disregard the mistaken advice and impotent threats which would deter us, and press forward to the limits of science, determined to ascertain for ourselves where we must stop, and heed no prohibition but that of Nature, or of Him who constituted Nature. (Martineau, 1836, 2:267)

In 1830 Martineau was introduced to the ideas of Saint-Simon, and she became enthusiastic about French positivism. Saint-Simon's idea on the evolution of society, "the positivist basis for knowledge and social reorganization, and the organic nature of society" began to appear in her work (Hoecker-Drysdale, 1992:28).

Armed with her scientific certainty and faith in the regularity of God's laws in the social and natural worlds, Martineau set sail for America in 1834. She intended to observe the social consequences of constitutional democracy in action. There was considerable fascination with America after the 1776 Revolution, and many Europeans traveled to America in the guise of explorers of an uncharted social as well as geographical territory. Alexis de Tocqueville is among the better-known travelers. His *Democracy in America* is a reflection on both postrevolutionary America and the postrevolutionary anarchy and despotism in France.[8] Martineau's work is likewise a commentary on American society as well as on English society.

While on board ship, Martineau wrote the methodological treatise *How to Observe Manners and Morals*, eventually published in 1838. The ideas Martineau advanced in this work represent an embryonic sociology that was put into practice in her subsequent works, *Society in America* (1837) and *Retrospect of Western Travel* (1838b). In these books, she set out the ethical principles that should govern sociological inquiry, as well as the methods to pursue such an inquiry.

Ethical Principles   In observing "modes of conduct," Martineau stated, two principles are at play. The first principle must be that "the law of nature is the

---

[8]For a comparison of Martineau's and de Tocqueville's American experiences and comments, see Lipset, 1968.

only one by which mankind at large can be judged" (Martineau, 1838a:27). Rational, universal principles of cause and effect operated in the social as well as the natural world, and the discovery of these social laws was possible through empirical observation of the regularities and uniformities of social life.

The second principle was that "every prevalent virtue and vice is the result of the particular circumstances amid which the society exists" (1838a:27). The divine law of nature does not prevent vice. Vicious behavior can, however, be overcome and brought into line with the law of nature through education. In fact, the human capacity for reason is what made the probability of reform possible. The other side of the coin is that, for Martineau, intellectual disorder was a cause of social disorder which could only be alleviated with clear, "factual" knowledge of society.

Sociological Methods   Martineau opened her methodological treatise, *How to Observe Manners and Morals*, with the insistence that, although everyone assumed that traveling and observing the inhabitants and the environment provided a sufficient basis for judgment on the manners and morals of a people, in fact such methods were insufficient. The "powers of observation must be trained, and the habits of method in arranging the materials presented to the eye must be acquired, before the student possesses the requisites for understanding what he contemplates" (1838a:6). Martineau recognized that when we train our eyes on the social world, our gaze is not innocent or unbiased.

Furthermore, surface evidence can be misleading, and the conclusions reached about what is seen can promote or reinforce error. For example, if you see an unkempt individual slumped in the gutter, you may assume that he or she is drunk or on drugs. This ready assumption does not provide any information about the person as a social being and, furthermore, may be incorrect. The fall may have been the result of a heart attack. Simple observation does not allow certain knowledge about people or their condition. Martineau recognized that sociologists need to acquire methodological skills that enable them to question the obvious and discover the social conditions surrounding events and behaviors.

The study of society was therefore as much a scientific enterprise as botany, and "intellectual preparation" was necessary for both. "Natural philosophers do not dream of generalizing with any such speed as that used by observers of men"—even though natural philosophers might, in Martineau's view, do it "with more safety, at the risk of incalculably smaller mischief" (1838a:6).

Systematic observation was a preferred basis for scientific certainty because it could reveal the connections between phenomena rather than simply their "essence" or "final cause." Observation in conjunction with experimentation and comparison—the central Comtean methodological prescriptions—were already prefigured in Martineau's account. Furthermore, Martineau pointed out, not all observations are equal. It was essential that observation be guided by theory.

Martineau's basic framework for her theoretical approach was a utilitarian one of "the greatest happiness" of the majority (1838a:13). "It is not enough for the traveler to have an active understanding, equal to an accurate perception of individual facts in themselves; he must also be in possession of principles which may serve as a rallying point for his observations, and without which he cannot determine their bearings, or be secure in putting the right interpretation upon them" (1838a:15). This evaluative framework was the basis for her studies.

In the American case, Martineau's intention was to examine the practical consequences of the democratic ideal of social equality enshrined in the U.S. Constitution. She made it quite clear in *Society in America* that the **manners** (social interactions) and **morals** (cultural values and beliefs) of the society would be evaluated according to the egalitarian promise set forth in the Declaration of Independence.

At the same time, Martineau used the American situation to point to equity problems in English society. For example, the status of women in the postrevolutionary United States contradicted that nation's legitimated, constitutional prescription for equality and democracy. But American women—that is, white women—were still in a better position than English women to mount a protest because their position was clearly a contradiction. "Instead of a constitution, the English had law and tradition, and most people never realized that women have 'never actually or virtually assented' to those laws that govern their lives." Therefore, any change in the English case would be far more difficult to effect (Walters, 1976:333).

Martineau believed that an evaluative framework was essential if the traveler was to observe from the perspective of "Humanity" and not from some "narrow sectarian view." But the mind of the observer was nonetheless an "instrument—a rational, objective means for the description and analysis of manners and morals" (1838a:17). Martineau did not advocate absolute value neutrality for the sociological observer, but insisted that the observer articulate the value basis for the observation and analysis. She was conscious of the difficulties involved in this process and cautioned that the observer, "to be perfectly accurate, should be himself perfect." But as one cannot "wait to be perfect" before traveling and observing, the observer must be content with the clear articulation of his/her standpoint (1838a:17).

Martineau also set out the nuts and bolts of the observation process: how data should be collected and sources checked, how interviews should be conducted, and how sampling should be done. She also explained the necessity of a comparative/historical perspective in evaluating the data.

Martineau suggested that, although social interaction was the principal interest, the observer should first gather preliminary data from records and an analysis of institutional structures. As she pointed out, it is best to begin "with the study of THINGS, using the DISCOURSE OF PERSONS as a commentary upon them" (1838a:63). In fact, the "eloquence of Institutions and Records" was, in her view, "more comprehensive and more faithful than any variety of individual voices" (1838a:64).

The objective analysis of records and institutions was an invaluable basis for analysis, but the heart of any inquiry, she believed, was participant observation. From a purely positivist perspective, observation should be conducted so that personal interference is reduced to a minimum and only the "facts" are recorded. Complete objectivity is, however, difficult to achieve, as Martineau recognized. So she advised the observer to have "untrammeled and unreserved" sympathy, because an observer who could not find his or her "way to hearts and minds" would be "liable to deception at every turn" (1838a:45).

This advice was particularly important if "morals" were to be understood. As Martineau said, manners "cease to have meaning" when separated from morals. And, when examining manners, Martineau advocated examining those that conformed as well as those that deviated from the morals, or cultural values and beliefs, of the society.

Martineau believed that nothing should be overlooked in pursuit of a rounded picture of a society. Consequently, she recommended that the observer might gather data best by "diverging from the high road as much as possible" (1838a:57). In *Society in America* and *Retrospect of Western Travel*, it is clear that Martineau followed her own advice. Despite her handicaps, which included reliance on an ear trumpet because of her deafness, Martineau's travels took her from Niagara to New Orleans, from Boston to Kentucky, and she often experienced considerable discomfort as well as danger. Martineau was an adventurous, and always observant, traveler.

Martineau recommended that data be sought in unexpected places. A good place to study morals, she suggested, was cemeteries. Tombstone inscriptions could teach "more than the longest discourse of the living." When one knows how death is commonly regarded, then the observer will have "penetrated into the interior of their morals," because all epitaphs conform to the injunction "De mortuis nil bonum" (Do not speak ill of the dead). It follows that such epitaphs "must everywhere indicate what is there considered good" (1838a:107).

Other sources of information that would not ordinarily be on the itinerary of the nineteenth-century traveler, but which Martineau considered essential to any understanding of a society, were prisons. Her idea that the treatment of the criminal was an "all-important index to the moral notions of a society" anticipated Emile Durkheim's later discussion of how forms of justice indicate forms of social organization (see Chapter 4). Martineau cautioned that the examination of the legal system must be treated with care, however, because "societies of civilized countries are in a state of transition from the old vindictiveness to a purer moral philosophy." Excessive reliance on brute force in the treatment of the guilty, as in "savage lands, and also in countries under despotism," can only reflect the "morals of the rulers" and the "degree of political subservience of the people" (1838a:124). Martineau's remarks here predate not only Durkheim's discussion of penal practices but also that of Michel Foucault (see Chapter 23) in the mid-twentieth century!

In more advanced societies, Martineau supposed that property offenses and offenses that arose "out of domestic miseries" would be more prevalent than violent crimes. Furthermore, she suggested that "where there are fewest assaults occasioned by conjugal injuries and domestic troubles, the state of morals is purest" (1838a:131).

Again anticipating Durkheim, Martineau recommended that the observer also take account of suicides. She pointed out that a lot could be learned from the nature and number of suicides, "both as to the notions on morals which prevail, and the religious sentiment which animates to or controls the act" (1838a:96). She developed a typology of suicides that Durkheim's typology would later echo:

suicides occasioned by shame (Durkheim's fatalistic suicide), those occasioned by complete devotion to others (Durkheim's altruistic suicide), and those occasioned by withdrawal from duty and others' expectations (Durkheim's anomic suicide). She also recognized what Durkheim would call "collective representations" in the nature of suicides:

> Suicide is one thing to a man who is certain of entering immediately upon purgatory; and to another whose first step is to be upon the necks of his enemies; and to a third who believes that he is to lie conscious in his grave for some thousands of years. It is because countries "share in differences like these, according to the prevalent religious sentiment" that suicide provides an important index of the nature of both manners and morals. (1838a:96–97)

Interviews were, of course, indispensable to rounding out the "classes of national facts the traveler has observed" (1838a:221). But Martineau also recognized a problem of bias in using interviews. "The chief reason why the discourse of individuals, apart from the observation of classes of facts, is almost purely deceptive as to morals, is that the traveler can see no more than one in fifty thousand of people and he has no security that those he meets are a sample of the whole" (1838a:226). In an effort to guard against this problem, she recommended using a wide-ranging interview pool so that some randomness could be introduced into the procedure. The observer must seek "intercourse with all classes of society he visits, not only the rich and the poor, but those who may be classed by professions, pursuit, habits of mind, and term of manners. He must converse with young men and maidens, old men and children, beggars and savants, postillions and potentates" (1838a:222). In all cases the interviews must be checked against the evidence from records and institutions.

Martineau recognized the problem that interaction presented in the collection of data, especially in the case of participant observation. The "traveler who has the air of taking notes in the midst of conversation, is in danger of bringing away information imperfect as far as it goes, and much restricted in quantity in comparison with what it would be if he allowed it to be forgotten that he was a foreigner seeking information" (1838a:232). If the observer can simply allow the "conversation to flow on naturally," then more information will be obtained. Finally, the observer must keep track of the observations and interviews. Here Martineau established her sociological credentials. She recommended that notes be made after interviews. To maintain the focus of inquiry, the next day's work should be outlined the evening before, so that a "glance in the morning at his list of queries may suggest inquiries which he might not otherwise remember to make; and they will help him afterwards to arrange the knowledge he has gained" (1838a:232).

Examination of suicide rates and types, conversations with criminals, and examination of tombstones were not standard fare for early-nineteenth-century travelers, especially female travelers. Nor was Martineau's recommendation that useful information could be had from an analysis of popular songs, as an "index of popular morals" and a representation of living culture (1838a:134). Martineau's practical advice to the student of society was a comprehensive and exhaustive list of what constitutes sociological data and how those data could be obtained and recorded. In this respect, *How to Observe Manners and Morals* is a remarkable book. It is the first methodological text for sociology. Comte's *Cours* might claim first place as a comprehensive theoretical exposition, although here again Martineau might be considered to have a prior claim, but in terms of methodological advice that has continued relevance for sociology today, Martineau's work must be accorded first place.

Nature of Society, Humans, and Change

Martineau approached the study of society as a comparative, historical exercise. Her concern was identifying the character of society through observation of its institutional structures and its moral beliefs and values. This concern was always animated by a belief in the progressive improvement of society as the key to understanding history; a belief in human perfectibility; and a "faith" in science as the means to understand and thus improve society. "It is my deliberate opinion that the one essential requisite of human welfare in all ways is scientific knowledge of human nature" (Martineau, 1869, 2:332).

These views contributed to Martineau's innovative analyses of some of the central issues of the nineteenth century: women's rights, slavery, industrialization, and democratic reform. Martineau believed that her reservations about the negative effects of industrial development could be answered by "objective" sociological analysis. Women's rights and slavery were, in her view, connected with democratic reform.

Class, Gender, and Race

Martineau visited America to see democracy in action and also to see two impediments to full democratic equality: women's subjection and slavery. She indicated in her methodological book that one of the most significant institutions for observation was marriage. Special attention should be paid to the professed ideals and the actual practices involved in marital and domestic relations. "The degree of the degradation of women is as good a test as the moralist can adopt for ascertaining the estate of domestic morals in any country" (1838a:174). Martineau's position echoes that of Mary Wollstonecraft (discussed in Chapter 1). Human reason could not be confined to men, and human rights must, by definition, include women.

Martineau's position on women's rights was also extended to the rights of slaves. She was an abolitionist before she went to America. In her *Society in America*, she attacked the widespread assumption that blacks would not know what to do with freedom and needed the "care" and "protection" of whites. This attitude, she said, was a denial of the fundamental principles of the new republic. Furthermore, she observed that by oppressing blacks, white society oppressed itself. The ever-present fear of the potential threat that blacks represented to white masters and their families was evidence of this mutual unfreedom. Martineau was particularly clear about the contradictions inherent in slave/master relations. Those masters whose sexual exploitation of female slaves gave them offspring, which they then proceeded to sell, were the same ones who accused the Northern abolitionists of advocating miscegenation.

Martineau's feminism and anti-slavery position, as well as her scientific perspective on these issues, is summed up in her letter to the American Women's Rights Convention in 1851. In the letter, she thanked the organizers for their invitation to attend the convention and assured them of her "warm and unrestricted sympathy." She then went on:

> I have said it till my listeners and readers are probably tired of hearing it—
> that there can be but one true method in the treatment of each human
> being of either sex, of any colour, and under any outward circumstances—
> to ascertain what are the powers of that being, to cultivate them to the
> utmost, and then to see what action they will find for themselves. . . . This
> has probably never been done for men, unless in some rare individual
> cases. It has certainly never been done for women; and, till it is done, all
> debating about what women's intellect is . . . is mere beating of air. A priori
> conceptions have long been found worthless in physical science, and
> nothing was really effected till the experimental method was clearly made
> out and strictly applied in practice, and the same principle holds most
> certainly through the range of Moral Science. Whether we regard the
> physical fact of what women are able to do, or the moral fact of what
> women ought to do, it is equally necessary to abstain from making any
> decision prior to experiment. (quoted in Yates, 1985:75)

Martineau's letter was written after she had rejected religion in favor of a purely positivistic, scientific approach to the study of society.

Other Theories and Theorists

By 1851, Martineau had endorsed the view that for raising "human hope and human effort to the highest attainable point," the best recourse was the "pursuit of Positive Philosophy." In her earlier work, she had pursued a positivist approach despite her religious faith. But in 1851 Martineau published, with coauthor Henry Atkinson, *Letters on the Laws of Man's Nature and Development*. In this book, her rejection of religion as the premise for explaining social and moral life was made public. Martineau recorded that, after the publication of *Laws*, she had "got out of the prison of my own self," which had been captive to the "gleams and shadows and faint colours" of the imagination. She had also learned that "to form any true notion whatever of the affairs of the universe, we must take our stand in the external world, regarding man as one of the products and subjects of everlasting laws of the universe and not as a favourite of its Maker"(1869, 2:333–334).[9] A more distinct personal statement of the transition from the metaphysical to the positivist stage that Comte had envisioned could not be devised.

---

[9]With the publication of *Laws*, many of Martineau's critics, including her own brother, James—a Unitarian minister—leveled the charge of atheism against Martineau and Atkinson. Many of her Unitarian friends, as well as her brother, rejected her. Brother and sister never reconciled.

Not surprisingly, Martineau enthusiastically read Comte in 1851. Her prior work set the stage for her free translation and condensation of the six volumes of Comte's *Cours* into two volumes. In the process, Martineau came to fully embrace positivism, rejecting religion in favor of science. She stated in her *Autobiography* that "science (or the knowledge of fact inducing the discovery of laws) is the sole and eternal basis of wisdom,—and therefore human morality and peace" (1869, 2:332).

Martineau's translation of Comte's work was favorably received by most English positivists, and both Herbert Spencer and T. H. Huxley thought her translation and condensation admirable. More important, Comte himself thought the work well done and wished to have it retranslated into French.

The attraction of Comte's work for Martineau was the systematization of a scientific approach to the study of social and moral issues. As she stated in the Preface to her translation,

> We find ourselves living, not under capricious and arbitrary conditions, unconnected with the constitution and movements of the whole, but under great, general, invariable laws, which operate on us as part of the whole. Certainly I can conceive of no instruction so favourable to aspiration as that which shows us how great are our faculties, how small our knowledge, how sublime the heights which we may hope to attain, and how boundless an infinity may be assumed to spread beyond. (Comte, 1853:xiv)

Note that *How to Observe Manners and Morals* was published partway through Comte's publication of his six-volume *Cours de philosophie positive*, which appeared successively between 1830 and 1842. Although Comte's work was known to a few English philosophers and intellectuals in the English-speaking world prior to Martineau's translation and abridgement in 1853, it had a marginal status in discussions of a "moral science" of society.

The translation of *Cours* and Martineau's enthusiasm for it must be distinguished from her opinion of Comte's later work. She would not countenance his theological positivism. Many of Comte's other views, such as the superiority of the white race and the inferiority of women, as well as his hierarchical view of the world as ideally governed by a technocratic elite (which became translated into the priesthood of all humanity), were in sharp contrast to Martineau's views (Thomas, 1985:74).

Critique and Conclusions

Some critics have suggested that her early enthusiasm for Comte demonstrates Martineau's "lack of critical ability" (Thomas, 1985:74; see also Webb, 1960). But another interpretation is that Martineau considered Comte's later ideas aberrations, especially the idea of a "doctrine built upon a scaffold of ecclesiastical authority" (Pichanick, 1980:197). She, along with John Stuart Mill and others, rejected Comte's secular religion but "seized hold of the main elements: that humankind should seek to understand only the phenomena of the knowable; that the West should be liberated from anachronistic theologians and anarchic metaphysicians in order to constitute a 'true sociocracy'; and that society should assume the responsibility for its own education" (Pichanick, 1980:197).

Several authors have also wondered about Martineau's reactions to the misogynist opinions in the *Cours*. Harriet Taylor Mill and John Stuart Mill were upset with Martineau "not so much for having translated Comte's work as for having been taken in, apparently, by some of his ideas" (Zeitlin, 1997:129). But once again Martineau may have embraced Comte's scientific perspective but rejected those opinions on women that were offensive to her.

In other words, Martineau was not as naïve as her critics have suggested. Furthermore, we must remember that her translation and condensation of Comte's work was not intended to be a critical version but rather a popular synthesis for the promotion of positivism.

In any case, Martineau's *Society in America* is "among the most thorough sociological studies of a society in the nineteenth century" (Hoecker-Drysdale, 1992:57). In this work, she investigated government, politics, the economy, and other social institutions; she described how each institution was structured and how each functioned. Martineau's sociological account can be contrasted with Comte's purely theoretical account and the "little actual sociology" offered in the *Cours* (Ritzer, 1996:110).

Martineau remarked in her *Autobiography* that "the science of Human Nature, in all of its departments is yet in its infancy" but that "science or the knowledge of fact inducing the discovery of laws" was the "eternal basis of wisdom, and therefore of human morality and peace" (1869, 2:335). Until recently, Martineau had disappeared from the sociological canon. Yet clearly she was a sociologist before Comte coined the term. Her methodological prescriptions remain up-to-date, and the sociology that issued from these prescriptions remains significant; for example, her discussions of slavery and gender relations in the Middle East (1848) clearly merit more attention. Martineau had been "preaching sociology without the name" for years (Webb, 1960:308). Thus, she too should be considered a founder of sociology, alongside Saint-Simon and Comte.

Final Thoughts

The three theorists discussed in this chapter were all concerned with the problems that *modern capitalist* societies produced. Their central concern was to provide a method by which the problems and social changes could be definitively identified and, therefore, changed for the greater benefit of human beings.

Ideologically, these three theorists run the gamut from *conservatism* to *radicalism*. Comte's position on the reconstitution of society is more conservative than the radical, socialist position of Saint-Simon. Martineau is more of a liberal in her perspectives. However, all three theorists would have rejected any ideological label. The scientific objectivity that positivism endorsed was supposed to eliminate any of the ideological problems that may have troubled previous analyses of social conditions.

In Chapter 3 you will again be confronted with the ideological issue, but from a conservative point of view. Herbert Spencer and William Graham Sumner both believed that the scientific analysis of social evolution revealed the law of "survival of the fittest" in social as well as biological life.

References

Comte, Auguste. 1853. *The Positive Philosophy of Auguste Comte* (freely translated and condensed by Harriet Martineau). New York: Calvin Blanchard.

———. 1875/1976. *System of Positive Politics* (4 vols.) (John Henry Bridges, Trans.). New York: Burt Franklin.

———. 1975. *Auguste Comte and Positivism: The Essential Writings* (Gertrude Lenzer, Ed.). Chicago: University of Chicago Press.

Coser, Lewis, A. 1977. *Masters of Sociological Thought*. New York: Harcourt Brace Jovanovich.

Dondo, Mathurin. 1955. *The French Faust: Henri de Saint-Simon*. New York; Philosophical Library.

Durkheim, Emile. 1897/1962. *Socialism* (Alvin W. Gouldner, Ed.). New York: Collier Books.

Gouldner, Alvin W. 1962. Introduction. In Emile Durkheim, *Socialism*. New York: Collier Books.

Hawkins, Richard Laurin. 1936. *Auguste Comte and the United States, 1816–1853*. Cambridge: Cambridge University Press.

———. 1938. *Positivism in the United States, 1853–1861*. Cambridge: Cambridge University Press.

Hoecker-Drysdale, Susan. 1992. *Harriet Martineau: First Woman Sociologist*. Oxford: Berg Publishers.

Ionescu, Ghita. 1976. *The Political Thought of Saint-Simon*. Oxford: Oxford University Press.

Lipset, Seymour Martin. 1968. "Harriet Martineau: A Pioneer Comparative Sociologist." In Seymour Martin Lipset, *Revolution and Counterrevolution*. New York: Basic Books.

Marcuse, Herbert. 1954. *Reason and Revolution*. Boston: Beacon Press.

Markham, F. M. H. 1952. *Henri Comte de Saint-Simon: Selected Writings*. Oxford: Basil Blackwell.

———. 1964. *Henri de Saint-Simon: Social Organization and the Science of Man*. New York: Harper & Row.

Martineau, Harriet. 1836/1975. *Miscellanies* (2 vols.). Boston: Hilliard, Gray and Company.

———. 1837. *Society in America* (2 vols.). London and New York: Saunders and Otley.

———. 1838a. *How to Observe Manners and Morals*. London: Charles Knight.

———. 1838b *Retrospect of Western Travel* (2 vols.). London: Saunders and Otley.

———. 1848. *Eastern Life: Present and Past* (3 vols.). London: Edward Moxon.

———. 1851. *Letters on the Laws of Man's Nature and Development* (with Henry G. Atkinson). London: John Chapman.

———. 1869/1983. *Autobiography* (2 vols.). London: Virago Press.

Pichanick, Valerie Kossew. 1980. *Harriet Martineau: The Woman and Her Work, 1802–1876*. Ann Arbor: University of Michigan Press.

Pickering, Mary. 1993. *Auguste Comte: An Intellectual Biography*. Cambridge: Cambridge University Press.

Postlethwaite, Diana. 1984. *Making It Whole*. Columbus: Ohio State University Press.

Ritzer, George. 1996. *Classical Sociological Theory* (2nd ed.). New York: McGraw-Hill.

Rossi, Alice S. 1973. "The First Woman Sociologist: Harriet Martineau (1802–1876)." In Alice S. Rossi, *The Feminist Papers: From Adams to de Beauvior*. New York: Columbia University Press.

Saint-Simon, Henri. 1814. "The Reorganization of European Society." In F. M. H.

Markham (Ed.), *Henri Comte de Saint-Simon: Selected Writings* (pp. 28–68). Oxford: Basil Blackwell.

Stewart, Elbert W., and James A. Glynn. 1971. *Introduction to Sociology*. New York: McGraw-Hill.

Taylor, Keith (Ed.). 1975. *Henri Saint-Simon: 1760–1825*. London: Croom Helm.

Thomas, Gillian. 1985. *Harriet Martineau*. Boston: Twayne Publishers.

Walters, Margaret. 1976. "The Rights and Wrongs of Women: Mary Wollstonecraft, Harriet Martineau, Simone de Beauvior." In Juliet Mitchell and Ann Oakley (Eds.), *The Rights and Wrongs of Women*. Harmondsworth, England: Penguin.

Webb, R. K. 1960. *Harriet Martineau: A Radical Victorian*. London: Heinemann.

Yates, Gayle Graham. 1985. *Harriet Martineau on Women*. New Brunswick, NJ: Rutgers University Press.

Zeitlin, Irving M. 1997. *Ideology and the Development of Sociological Theory*. Englewood Cliffs, NJ: Prentice-Hall.

SECTION II

Conservative Theories

In Section I, you learned that fundamental social changes prompted many Western thinkers to examine the nature of society. From diverse viewpoints, theorists we would classify as reactionary conservatives, liberals, and radicals all saw industrial capitalism as imperfect and in need of change. However, others considered capitalism an exciting and appropriate new form of social organization. Chapters 3 and 4 explain how these status quo conservative ideas developed in the late 1800s and early 1900s.

We introduce conservative theories and ideology first because this was the dominant viewpoint to which most other theorists were reacting. We will begin by emphasizing again the covertly conservative nature of positivism and then focus on two primary varieties of status quo conservatism: evolutionism and functionalism. Thus, the three types of nineteenth-century theory that supported capitalism were (1) positivism, which argued that society is orderly and rational, and that our job is to understand it scientifically as it is; (2) evolutionism, which argued that society changes slowly and is self-corrective in the process; and (3) functionalism, which described society as similar to an organism, with interrelated structures that meet needs and perform functions. All three can be labeled status quo conservative, because they either implicitly accepted or overtly championed capitalist society.

You have already met the positivist Auguste Comte, who accepted the results of the French Revolution and argued that those who study society should seek to understand objectively the way things are, rather than try to change them. In accepting things the way they were, he and other positivists covertly supported the status quo.

In his book *Reflections on the Revolution in France* (1790), Edmund Burke, an Englishman, argued that society is an organism that has evolved slowly to its present state. Therefore, no group, such as the French revolutionaries and their philosophers, had the right to decide what to destroy and what new forms to introduce. Burke cherished the rights he had inherited and could see only terror and disorganization in postrevolutionary France, where Comte saw a new and better society.

Burke's ideas were followed in the nineteenth century by the evolutionary thought of Herbert Spencer and William Graham Sumner—the subjects of Chapter 3. As in the biological world, they believed that conditions sometimes give rise to disintegration rather than integration, but that the entire process is self-corrective and progressive. Spencer did not advocate doing nothing to change society, but he advocated postponing action until we have an adequate understanding of structure and causation. In his view, reformers, and especially revolutionaries, tend to rush in and act without sufficient understanding.

Sumner's evolutionary thinking was even more conservative. He argued that inequities in society result from the "survival of the fittest," and benefit society as a whole. The laissez-faire individualism and societal competition characterizing Spencer's and Sumner's view dominated Western thought at the turn of the twentieth century.

In addition to being evolutionists, Spencer and Burke were also functionalists. They believed that each of society's parts, like those of a biological organism, exists to meet certain physiological, psychological, or social needs. Burke, as we said, saw society as an organism that had evolved slowly. Spencer expanded this organic analogy at great length in *The Study of Sociology* (1873). As a thoroughgoing functionalist, he explained his view thus: "There can be no true conception of a structure without a true conception of its function. To understand how an organization originated and developed, it is requisite to understand the need subserved at the outset and afterwards" (Spencer, 1896:151). So, this third form of status quo conservative theory and ideology argued that society is a functioning whole, with diverse but integrated parts.

Chapter 4 continues the discussion of functionalism and evolution, focusing directly on the theories of Emile Durkheim, a towering figure in sociology. Durkheim argued that society had evolved into a complex organism, with a division of labor among its parts, all working for the common good. He believed that modern capitalism had made progress through an orderly, gradual evolution. Durkheim did have liberal tendencies, however, adding that it was necessary to "tinker" with society to make it work better—but not to overthrow it.

The main thrust of Chapters 3 and 4, then, is to add to positivism the twin status quo conservative views: evolutionism and functionalism. Their unifying idea is that society is evolving and corrects itself when allowed to. It is to be studied and understood as a functioning organism. The dominant ideology concerning the industrial capitalist world, as propounded by Spencer, Sumner, and Durkheim in this section, is that what exists in nineteenth-century Europe is good.

References

Burke, Edmund. 1790/1960. *Reflections on the Revolution in France*. New York: E. P. Dutton.

Spencer, Herbert. 1873. *The Study of Sociology*. London: Kegan Paul, Trench.

———. 1896/1969. *The Principles of Sociology* (vol. I). London: Archon Books.

Chapter 3

Evolutionism and Functionalism
Spencer and Sumner

Some call it evolution,
And others call it God.
　—W. H. Carruth, 1908

Despite the poet's belief, creationists and evolutionary scientists would not agree that biblical and scientific explanations of the world are interchangeable. Creationists assert that God created the earth and human beings in perfect form at a definite time; evolutionists assert that form naturally changes over time, gradually perfecting itself.

This chapter introduces two evolutionists in the realm of sociological theory. Herbert Spencer and William Graham Sumner applied evolutionary theory to the social world they saw around them in the latter half of the nineteenth century, and rejected religious explanations about its origins and structure. In this sense, they were thoroughly modern.

Spencer and Sumner adopted the scientific, positivist viewpoint in another way as well: They likened society to a living organism and assumed that each element in its structure served a purpose. Thus they were also functionalists.

These two philosophical positions—evolutionism and functionalism—do have something in common with religious explanations of the social world. Their ideology is inherently conservative. However, evolutionists and functionalists are status quo conservatives. They do not wish to return to traditional religious conceptions of the ideal social structure but rather wish to preserve the structures that developed with industrial capitalism in the modern era.

Herbert Spencer (1820–1903)

Twenty years after Herbert Spencer's death, economist Crane Brinton (1933: 226) asked, "Who now reads Spencer?" A few years later, sociologist Talcott Parsons (1937:3) pronounced that "Spencer is dead" as a significant influence

on sociology. Parsons's pronouncement was premature, although in the years immediately after Spencer's death it did seem that his work had been forgotten by the sociological community. But Spencer's neglect is surprising. We know today that his work was influential in early American sociology and British social anthropology and, at the turn of the century, in British social reform circles. More important, Spencer's functionalist perspective and his evolutionary theories of social change have consistently been appropriated by subsequent sociologists, who have often failed to acknowledge their debt to him.

Spencer was born in England, the oldest of nine children and the only one to survive infancy. His parents, like Harriet Martineau's, were Dissenters who espoused religious freedom and social and political egalitarianism.

Spencer attended school for about three months, after which he was educated at home by his schoolmaster father and later by his clergyman uncle. His uncle was a dissenting Protestant minister with radical sympathies. Spencer later rejected the formal religious atmosphere of his youth. When he was twenty, his father drew his attention to "religious questions and appealed to religious feelings," but Spencer indicated that for him the "acquisition of scientific knowledge, especially physical, had cooperated with the natural tendency thus shown (a dislike for authority and ritual); and had practically excluded the ordinary idea of the supernatural" (Spencer, 1904, 1:152–153). Spencer was educated largely in science and mathematics, accompanied by religious, social, and political radicalism. He had little training in English, history, or languages. Although his family would have liked him to attend university, Spencer, perhaps recognizing the narrowness of his educational background, did not feel that university would be beneficial.

In 1837 Spencer took a position as an engineer for the London and Birmingham Railway and later for the Birmingham and Gloucester Railway. This engineering background was important to his subsequent sociology, as you will see in his initial definitions of the process of social evolution and his insistence that the instrumental logic of the physical and natural sciences could also be applied to the social sciences.

The construction work for the railways uncovered numerous fossil remains, which sparked Spencer's interest in geology and paleontology and, in turn, led to an interest in evolution. To find out more about fossils, he read Charles Lyell's *Principles of Geology*, which contained a rebuttal to the ideas of Jean-Baptiste Lamarck on the origin of species. Lamarck had suggested that acquired traits, such as shyness or bravado, could be genetically transmitted and thus influence evolution. Spencer was not convinced by Lyell's critique. Instead, the work produced in him "a decided leaning" toward Lamarck's evolutionary idea that the "human race has been developed from some lower race" and toward the idea that acquired characteristics could be inherited. Spencer remarked that his inclination to accept Lamarck's idea of evolution as true "in spite of Lyell's adverse criticism, was, doubtless, chiefly due to its harmony with that general idea of the order of Nature which I had, throughout life, been growing" (1904, 1:176).

Lamarck's idea about acquired traits ran counter to Charles Darwin's later idea about **natural selection**, which suggested that individuals born with advantageous genetic traits were the ones that survived to reproduce and contrib-

ute to the evolution of the species. Spencer believed, however, that Lamarckian adaptation and Darwinian natural selection proceeded together and, with the elimination of traits no longer useful to society, human beings and society progressively improved.

Spencer was also influenced by the work of political economists such as Adam Smith and the population theorist Thomas Malthus. Spencer's reading habits were always selective. He did not read many books but rather *"picked up most of his facts"* from periodicals and newspapers, and as a friend of "all the leading savants" he was able to pick their brains and extract "all that they knew" (Collier, 1904:208–209). This jackdaw approach, in combination with sociological materials obtained for him by his assistants, gave him all the "facts" to support his conception of social evolution. All these influences, along with his own agnostic but moral social conscience, are combined in his version of a science of sociology.

When the railway work was completed in 1841, Spencer was discharged. Until 1848, when he became a subeditor for the London *Economist*, he subsisted on writing for various radical and dissenting journals and on performing occasional engineering work. In 1842 he published a series of twelve letters on "The Proper Sphere of Government" in the journal *The Nonconformist*, and these were later expanded into his first book, *Social Statics*, published in 1850.

In 1853 Spencer's clergyman uncle died and left him a legacy, which enabled Spencer to take on the life of a private scholar. In 1854 he published *The Principles of Psychology*.

Soon after, Spencer suffered his first nervous breakdown, which left him unable to concentrate for any length of time on reading or writing or to tolerate social contacts. After a year or so he recovered, but he was to suffer periodic relapses throughout his life. He became somewhat obsessive about his health. Beatrice Webb, his close friend and, in her early years, disciple, remarked on his hypochondria and the rather sad life he lived in his last years: "Poisoned by morphia and self-absorption, and contorted by that strangely crude vision of human life as a series of hard bargains," he seemed "in his last years to be stumbling in total darkness, hurting himself and then crying aloud in his lonely distress, clinging to his dogmas but without confident faith—with an almost despairing and defiant pride of intellect" (Webb, 1946:32). But Webb predicted that all of these defects, which were "like an ugly and distorted setting to a small but brilliant stone," would be forgotten after his death, and he would be judged "among the elect."

After his partial recovery from the first breakdown, Spencer continued to write voluminously and became a well-known and successful author. But he complained that his first, and in his view his weakest, work, *Social Statics*, was more critically acclaimed than any of his subsequent, more important works. In the last years of his life, Spencer continued to write on issues of the day. But increasingly his individualism and his assumptions about evolutionary necessity—which led him to conclude, for example, that any welfare provisions for the poor and deprived interfered with "natural" social progress—reduced public interest in his work. The exception was North America, where his free-enterprise, laissez-faire doctrines remained influential for some time.

Spencer's Central Theories and Methods

Spencer's conservatism held particular appeal for the self-confident middle classes of mid-nineteenth-century Britain.[1] Britain was for a short period the workshop of the world, and its economic and industrial supremacy was matched by an imperial political reach that extended around the globe. Emblematic of Britain's confidence was the 1851 Crystal Palace Exhibition, where all the latest manufacturing, scientific, and industrial advances were celebrated. Despite the persistence of poverty and urban social problems, many British of the time believed that industrialization and free market economic practices, unfettered by excessive state controls, demonstrated evolutionary progress toward peace and prosperity. Spencer's writings supported these views.

By the last quarter of the nineteenth century, Britain's position as a preeminent world power was in decline. Sociologists, as well as some politicians, were expressing considerable skepticism about unfettered laissez-faire capitalism. Political and economic relations were being transformed by the extension of voting rights, the development of trade unions, and greater state control over a wide range of social life. Nevertheless, Spencer continued to endorse social evolution and to advocate conservative political positions in line with what he believed to be evolutionarily inevitable. His position was summed up in a series of what he believed to be scientific laws.

Social Laws   Spencer's individualism was expressed in his **law of right social relationships**, which stated that *"Everyman has freedom to do all that he wills, provided he infringes not the equal freedom of any other man"* (Spencer, 1850:55). Spencer considered democracy compatible with this law. In his view, a genuine democrat "loves liberty as a miser loves gold, for its own sake and quite irrespective of its apparent advantages" (1850:105). The law of right social relationships was an invariant law and just as unchangeable as the invariant laws of the physical universe.

Spencer maintained that the same evolutionary principle governed the social world as well as the natural, physical world. However, unlike the physical world, evolutionary progress in the social world incorporated a moral evolution. "Progress is not an accident but a necessity"; human beings *must* become perfect because "evil and immorality" *must* disappear (1850:32).

Another of Spencer's social laws was the **law of individuation**. He asserted that the "different kinds of organization that society takes on, in progressing from its lowest to its highest phase of development, are similar in principle to the different kinds of animal organization" (1850:268). The progression in both the social and the natural world is a "tendency to individuation." In other

---

[1]Spencer started out as a middle-class radical in the early stages of his career. He opposed the privileges of the aristocracy and government regulations that fettered individual enterprise. But as members of the middle classes became successful industrialists and politicians, they tended to become the proponents of government regulation to protect their interests. Consequently, Spencer's continued adherence to the principles of limited government, individualism, and property rights put him on the conservative side in the latter part of the nineteenth century.

words, society becomes a separate entity as people take on specialized roles to fulfill social needs:

> This union of many men into one community—this increasing mutual dependence of units which were originally independent—this gradual segregation of citizens into separate bodies with reciprocally-subservient functions—this formation of a whole consisting of unlike parts—this growth of an organism, of which one portion cannot be injured without the rest feeling it—may well be generalized under the law of individuation. The development of society, as well as the development of life generally, may be described as a tendency to individuate—*to become a thing*. And rightly interpreted, the manifold forms of progress going on around us, are uniformly significant of this tendency. (1850:272).

As Spencer indicated in a footnote to the revised, abridged edition of *Social Statics*, the process of individuation was the "primary process of Evolution." It was "not a trait of living things alone, but is a trait of all evolving things," including inorganic things (1892:256).

Spencer considered the tendency to individuate to be functional. That is, the emergence of specialized parts was meant to ensure survival of the whole. The **law of organization** dictated a "function to each organ and each organ to its own function" in both the social and the natural world (1850:121). This functional differentiation was a progressive, evolutionary feature. Spencer concluded that the evolutionary process of individuation inevitably produced the moral axiom that individuals should be as free as possible from externally imposed restraints, especially the restraints of government.

In *Social Statics*, Spencer described the process of individuation and the principle of freedom from restraints as gender neutral. Spencer claimed that when society became civilized and "women shall have attained to a clear perception of what is due to them, and men to a nobility of feeling which shall make them concede to women the freedom which they themselves claim," there would be an "equality of rights between the sexes" (1850:78). As you will see, this liberal position was rather drastically reversed in his later work.

Spencer considered civilization indispensable for the complete manifestation of everyone's individuality: "To be that which he naturally is—to do just what he would spontaneously do—is essential to the full happiness of each, and therefore to the greatest happiness of all." Consequently, Spencer proposed the **law of adaptation**. Social progress "must be towards a state in which this entire satisfaction of every desire, or perfect fulfillment of individual life, becomes possible" (1850:253). The only duty of the state was to protect each citizen from the "trespasses of his neighbours" and to defend society "against foreign aggression." All other interactions were to be left to contractual agreements among free individuals (1850:117). In an advanced society, any other form of state intervention would create distortion and risk a reversion to an earlier, less civilized form of existence. Many of today's political conservatives would endorse Spencer's preference for limited government intervention in everyday life.

They would also endorse Spencer's views on government social welfare measures. He considered them an "injurious" check on the "process of adaptation" and argued that philanthropic activities only produced "greater misery on future generations":

> Blind to the fact that under the natural order of things society is constantly excreting its unhealthy, imbecile, slow, vacillating, faithless members, these unthinking, though well-meaning, men advocate an interference which not only stops the purifying process, but even increases the vitiation— absolutely encourages the multiplication of the reckless and incompetent by offering them an unfailing provision, and *dis*courages the multiplication of the competent and provident by heightening the difficulty of maintaining a family. (1850:151)

The words may be somewhat florid, but the same sentiment is found in some current conservative positions on the issue of welfare. Spencer, like many present-day conservatives, did not object to "helping men help themselves," but he did object to the careless use of charity that "fostered into perfection a system of organized begging" (1850:152).

The individualism and laissez-faire sentiments expressed in *Social Statics* reappeared in Spencer's subsequent work. But his fulminations against philanthropy also presage some sociologically more significant concepts that were developed in his *Principles of Psychology* (1854) and in his multivolume *Synthetic Philosophy*, the first volume of which, *First Principles*, was published in 1862. In these works Spencer developed his concept of evolution and refined the organic analogy, in addition to promoting the science of sociology.

In the *Principles of Psychology*, Spencer developed an all-encompassing theory of the universal principles of social structure and social change, concentrating on society as a whole. He used "social facts," or examples, when they were appropriate and could be fitted into his evolutionary scheme. Spencer sought to produce a philosophy that would reveal general "truths which unify concrete phenomenon belonging to all divisions of Nature" (1902:277). These general truths, or laws, were, he maintained, the same for the physical, organic, and social worlds. Sociology was therefore the "study of Evolution in its most complex form" (1891:350). Furthermore, sociology was a necessary science because evolution was, in Spencer's view, progressing at a faster pace than ever before.

Methodological Insights   Spencer was also directly concerned with methodological issues, responding to the critique that sociology was an inexact science. Spencer pointed out that only mathematics and physics could be called exact sciences, because they expressed relationships quantitatively. But for most of the other physical sciences, only small parts could be called "exact." In geology, biology, and psychology, most of the relations are expressed qualitatively, but these relations are still regarded as scientific (1891:40). Consequently, although the generalizations offered by sociology are subject to wide variations and are often not quantifiable, to the extent that there can be generalization "there can be a science." Furthermore, when people express political opinions on the order of "such and such public arrangements will be beneficial or detrimental," they acknowledge a belief in social science because they acknowledge that "there is a natural sequence among social actions, and that as the sequence is natural results may be foreseen"(1891:40).

Spencer's sociology was focused on explaining what was empirically knowable, but he was aware of the difficulties this focus presented. The nature of social facts and the nature of human observers of social facts were "impediments in the way of Sociology . . . greater than those in the way of any other science" (1891:65). He listed three impediments:

- Sociology was "hindered by the nature of its subject-matter," because sociological phenomenon are not directly perceptible.

- All sociological observers have some feeling or opinion about the phenomena under investigation and, although "emotion is a perturbing intruder in every field of inquiry," it is particularly strong with regard to sociology.

- Emotional involvement is compounded by the fact that the sociologist investigates the properties of phenomena in which "he is himself included" (1891:66–67).

> To cut himself off in thought from all his relationships of race, and country, and citizenship—to get rid of all those interests, prejudices, likings, superstitions, generated in him by the life of his own society and his own time—to look on all the changes societies have undergone and are undergoing, without reference to nationality, or creed, or personal welfare; is what the average man cannot do at all, and what the exceptional man can do very imperfectly. (1891:67)

Thus Spencer was one of the first to recognize the nature and sources of **bias** in sociological investigation (although, as you will see, like most of his contemporaries and some present-day "objective" sociologists, he did not identify his own gender bias). Among the important sources of bias, Spencer identified education, patriotism, class, politics, and theology.

Educational bias, for example, was the result of the unquestioned acceptance of cultural beliefs regarded as functional for a particular society. For example, the bias against warfare in an industrial society serves the needs of that society by helping to maintain and develop its material resources. In militant societies, warfare is functional—that is, it fulfills a need to expand control or territory. Spencer also recognized that various actions abhorrent to the observer might well, in the past, have been necessary, functional contributions to social evolution:

> Shudder as we must at the cannibalism which all over the world in early days was a sequence of war—shrink as we may from the thought of those immolations of prisoners which have, tens of thousands of times, followed battles between wild tribes—read as we do with horror of the pyramids of heads and the whitening of bones of slain peoples left by barbarian invaders . . . we must not let our feelings blind us to the proofs that inter-social conflicts have furthered the development of social structures. (1899, 2:232)[2]

---

[2]The genocidal conflicts and various military barbarities of presumably "evolved" societies of the twentieth century suggest that warfare remains functional for industrial, capitalist societies or, alternatively, that such societies have not evolved to the extent supposed by Spencer.

The patriotic bias, exemplified in the phrase "My country, right or wrong," Spencer believed would be gradually eliminated as comparative, historical sociological methods developed. Generally, sociological analysis and evolutionary progress would ensure the elimination of any bias—although bias can "diminish only as fast as Society advances" (1891:265).

Compounding the sociologist's difficulties was the problem of data collection. Again, Spencer's comments are instructive, although today this work rarely receives the recognition it deserves. Spencer pointed to the possible unreliability of respondents, or witnesses, because of "carelessness, or fanaticism, or self-interest" and because of the problem of sorting out significant social data from trivial facts—the "curious things which serve for gossip" that hide the "vital connections and the vital actions underneath." He also pointed out that sociological observations cannot be reliably drawn from singular objects or acts but require "registration and comparison of many objects and facts," a process complicated by the "distribution of social phenomena in Space" and over time (1899, 2:87, 232, 352).

Spencer also characterized sociology as both a **deductive** and an **inductive** process. Sociology deductively applies general principles to particular cases and inductively uses particular cases to construct general rules. Using the general law of evolution, for example, Spencer deduced the nature of social evolution; he then supported this deduction with inductive evidence from ethnographic observations and historical data. Together, these two methods gave him the basis to establish sequences of cause and effect.

The need for inductive evidence for his theories prompted Spencer to produce *Descriptive Sociology* (1874), which catalogued a wealth of ethnographic data on diverse societies. This collection of ethnographic "facts" was intended to make the task of comparing societies easier. Just as the biologist could make little progress without a "systematic description of different kinds of organisms," making possible comparison of "connexions, and forms, and actions, and modes of origin, of their parts," so must the sociologist have a similar classification of social facts before sociological generalizations could be made (1874:3).

Some have suggested that Spencer's *Descriptive Sociology* has been unjustly neglected; if Spencer's "strategy had been followed, sociology and anthropology would have a much better data base for conducting cross-cultural research" (Turner, 1985:95). The closest approximation to Spencer's intentions may be the Human Relations Area Files compiled by George Murdock and others (1961).[3] The significance of an exhaustive classification of social facts will become apparent in our discussion of Spencer's descriptions of social evolution, in which he used the comparative data to construct models, or types, of historical societies.

Nature of Society, Humans, and Change

Although some societies might fail to progress and others might backslide, Spencer believed that, generally speaking, societies would evolve just as the natural

---

[3]Turner (1985:86, fn.1) points out that the Human Relations Area Files have a connection to Spencer. Sumner, who introduced Spencer's work to North American academia, and another Spencerian, Albert Keller Galloway, were George Murdock's teachers.

world and human beings evolve. Consequently, "There can be no rational apprehension of the truths of Sociology until there has been reached a rational apprehension of the truths of Biology" (1891:305). Spencer used an organic analogy as a basis for understanding the evolution of society and for classifying societal types based on his observations.

The Organic Analogy   Spencer used an **organic analogy** to describe the workings of society. In the *Principles of Sociology* (1899, 1:22ff), he explained the similarities between societies and biological organisms:

- As living organisms, societies continuously grow. Societies, "like living bodies, begin as germs—originate from masses which are extremely minute in comparison with the masses some of them eventually achieve."
- As societies grow, **structure**, or organization, increases, and "parts become unlike."
- As the organizational structure increases and differentiation arises, the **functions**, or activities, of the parts become more specialized. But these different activities are interdependent—that is, they are "so related as to make one another possible." In other words, the parts of a society, like the parts of an organism, function to maintain the structure of the whole.
- Although the parts are differentiated, they form coherent wholes in themselves at the same time that they remain parts of a larger whole. (For example, societies are made up of discrete individuals.)
- The "life" of the parts can continue for some time after the demise of the whole, and the whole has a "life" that "exceeds in duration the life of its units."

Although societies are like any other organic system, they are also **superorganic**, with some critical differences from biological organisms:

- Biological entities are a fixed, observable "concrete whole," whereas the "parts of a society form a whole which is discrete" from those parts.
- The parts of a biological entity are physically tied to one another, but the parts of a society are "free." That is, they are not in direct contact but are more or less widely dispersed.
- The interdependent parts of biological entities cannot move around relative to each other, but the mobility of the parts or individuals in society is not curtailed.
- In biological entities, "consciousness is concentrated in one small part" of the whole, whereas in society all of the parts possess consciousness. That is, they all "possess the capacity for happiness or misery."
- Unlike biological entities, societies have no "social sensorium." The welfare of the whole does not take precedence over the welfare of the parts because "society exists for the benefit of the members, not its members for the benefit of society."

Having illustrated the similarities and differences between biological and social organisms, Spencer then asserted that these analogies were only a "scaffolding to help in building up a coherent body of sociological inductions," or a body of data about real societies. The scaffolding could be taken away because the "inductions will stand by themselves." These inductions constituted "in rude outline an Empirical Sociology" (1899:150–151).

Evolutionary Change   Spencer first applied the term *evolution* to human society in his essay "Progress: Its Law and Cause," published in the *Westminister Review* of 1857. However, as early as 1852 Spencer had already expressed support for a theory of biological evolution (Carneiro, 1967:xviii), and he referred to it thereafter in his writings and conversations with other thinkers. In his *Principles of Psychology* (1854), he stated that life had evolved from the "lowest and simplest beginnings." In any case, his explicit endorsement of evolution preceded that of Darwin, whose *Origin of Species* appeared in 1859.

What Darwin's work contributed to Spencer's theories was a satisfactory mechanism—natural selection—to explain organic evolution (Carneiro, 1967: xx). In 1864, in his *Principles of Biology*, Spencer proposed that the phrase **survival of the fittest** was equivalent to Darwin's concept of natural selection, and apparently Darwin agreed with the suggestion.[4] Darwin's term, *natural selection*, suggested an intelligent agent—Nature—doing the selecting for humanity's benefit. In contrast, Spencer's term was a "plain expression of the fact," because nature does not select so much as it eliminates the "unfavourable" variations (Carneiro, 1967:xx).

In fact, however, Spencer's term went beyond Darwin. Darwin focused on the process of transformation for each species, whereas Spencer focused on both the biological and the social processes, and on the end result—the survival of the fittest (Peel, 1972:142). Darwin himself recognized that his explanation of organic evolution had been expanded in Spencer's account to include human society, and he suggested that in the future Spencer would be acknowledged as "by far the greatest living philosopher in England; perhaps equal to any that have lived" (quoted in Carneiro, 1967:ix).[5]

Spencer outlined his ideas about evolution in *First Principles* (1862:307). The universal principle of "integration of Matter and the dissipation of Motion" was seen as the key to the development of a synthetic philosophy and the basis for the claim that sociology was a **synthetic** science that examines the parts in relation to the whole. "There can be no complete acceptance of sociology as a science, so long as the belief in a social order not conforming to natural laws, survives" (1891:394). Conformity to natural law was illustrated by the fact that, organic or inorganic, natural or social, evolution was progress from the "homogeneous to the heterogeneous, it is change from the indefinite to the definite . . . an advance

---

[4]Coser (1977:108) points out that Malthus's *Essay on Population* was most influential in Spencer's development of the idea of the survival of the fittest, just as Malthus was important to Darwin's *Origin of Species*.

[5]Despite this praise, Darwin was not entirely positive about Spencer's work and remarked, "If he had trained himself to observe more, even at the expense of . . . some loss of thinking power, he would have been a wonderful man"(quoted in Ritzer, 1996:117).

from simplicity to complexity . . . [and] an advance from confusion to order" (1862:361).

Having said this, Spencer acknowledged that evolution did not imply a "latent tendency to improve, everywhere in operation" or that evolution was "inevitable in each particular society, or even probable" (1899, 1:95–96). Social change occurred in response to specific physical and social conditions. Evolution was not a series of inevitable stages but a process of **adaptation**, and disintegration was as likely as integration:

> During the earlier part of the cycle of changes, the integration predominates—there goes on what we call growth. The middle part of the cycle is usually characterized, not by equilibrium between the integrating and disintegrating processes, but by alternate excesses of them. And the cycle closes with a period in which the disintegration, beginning to predominate, eventually puts a stop to integration, and undoes what integration had originally done. (1862, 1:287)

In sum, the evolution of societies is accompanied by a growth in size and complexity that results in specialization, differentiation, and a corresponding need for integration of the parts.

Social Types and Constitutions   Spencer identified three types of functional systems within societies:

- **Sustaining system**: productive activities required by an organism or a society to maintain and develop itself.
- **Regulating system**: governing structures of the organism or society.
- **Distributing system**: means by which the sustaining and regulating systems are linked together. This system is critical to the maintenance of relationships between the interdependent parts of both biological and social organisms. In a society, the distributing system involves communication channels, transportation means, and the circulation of goods and people.

As societies grow and develop, all of these functional systems increase in **structural complexity**, with elements of the systems combining. Furthermore, what Spencer called the "dissipation of motion and integration of matter" occurs. That is, the integration of the specialized parts is always accompanied by **structural differentiation,** or increased specialization of structures.

In organic and superorganic systems alike, growth is the result of compounding and recompounding. That is, smaller units join together (compound) to form ever larger, more structurally and functionally complex units. Spencer determined that societies compound as follows:

- **Simple societies** are characterized as "headless" because they form a "single working whole unsubjected to any other," and the "parts co-operate with or without a regulating centre, for certain public ends" (1899:111).
- **Compound societies** result from the merger, either peaceful or because of war, of two or more simple societies under the regulation of a supreme chief (1899:113). They are usually more settled agricultural societies with some basic division of labor and permanent residences.

- **Doubly compound societies** have more complex political structures, more "rigid and complex" ecclesiastical forms, and a formal legal system, and they "demonstrate considerable progress in knowledge and the arts" (1899:113). Generally, compound societies become doubly compound only after the parts have consolidated under a single head, whether "by conquest or by federation in war" (1899:115).

- **Trebly compound societies** are the "great civilized nations" of the past and the present. These are the societies in which the complexity of structures and the increased mutual dependence is most apparent.

In all cases, the stages must be passed through in succession. "No tribe becomes a nation by simple growth," and "no great society is formed by the direct union of the smallest societies" (1899:5).

The evolution of structural complexity is similar for all societies. In contrast, **organizational purpose** varies. Spencer outlined two contrasting organizational purposes:

- **Industrial**: the social whole exists for the benefit of its member parts. Consequently, industrial societies are based on the "principle of voluntary co-operation."

- **Militant**: The member parts are subordinate to the wishes of the commanding center or whole. The principle governing militant societies is "compulsory co-operation."

These two types, in their extreme forms, are "diametrically opposed" to each other, and "the contrasts between their traits are among the most important which Sociology has to deal" (1899:134).

These organizational purposes cross-cut the structural divisions. For example, a simple society can be either a militant or an industrial type. Additionally, the purpose of a society can change over the course of its existence.

The militant and industrial social types are ideal types. That is, they are representations of the basic components of societies, not descriptions of any particular society. They enable the sociologist to categorize the beliefs and ideals of a society as a whole or of any component of a society, and to estimate how well the parts of a society are in accord.

In a militant society, the "army is the nation mobilized" and the nation is the "quiescent army." Control is highly centralized, with a military chief usually assuming supreme political control. In this type of society, all of the "units," or individuals, are "coerced into their various combined actions," and the "will of the citizen in all transactions, private and public" is "overruled by that of the government," so that cooperation is compulsory (1899:124). In a militant type society, the regulating system dominates the sustaining system.

In industrial societies, the sustaining system assumes more significance. Co-operation is voluntary in all relationships. State regulative power is minimal and functions only to protect individual rights and property. The "will of the citizens is supreme and the governing agent exists merely to carry out their will" (1899:128). In this type of society, moreover, it is the citizen's duty to "resist irresponsible government." In all relationships, at all levels of society, "the mutual rendering of services is unforced," and no individual should be subordinated to another (1899:128–129).

Although Spencer foresaw a general evolutionary trend toward the establishment of industrial societies, he also recognized that reversions to the militant type could occur. In addition, he pointed out that war was a necessary precondition to the establishment of industrial societies. War brings about "social aggregation," without which a developed industrial state cannot exist. "Industrial habits . . . and habits of subordination to social requirements" are, indirectly, the result of warfare (1891:176–177).

But the advantages of militancy eventually become disadvantages, not only for industrial development but also for the "higher intellectual developments that aid industry and are aided by it." The effects of the "discipline of war" on the moral and mental status of the subjects become detrimental "after a certain stage of progress is reached" (1891:179). Thus, like other nineteenth-century observers, Spencer thought that industrialism was compatible only with laissez-faire capitalism and was therefore unlikely to flourish under conditions of warfare. What Spencer did not take into account was the possibility that industrial capitalism could flourish during war by retooling and producing goods for the war effort.

Spencer was initially hopeful that Western societies had at last reached the industrial stage and would be unlikely to revert to militancy. But in 1898 he was less sanguine and predicted that "There is a bad time coming, and civilized mankind will (morally) be uncivilized before civilization can again advance." However, resistance was futile in the face of the coming "wave of barbarism," in which the "white savages of Europe are overrunning the dark savages everywhere . . . now that we have entered upon an era of social cannibalism in which the strong nations are devouring the weaker" (1898:259).[6]

This pessimistic outlook, prescient in the light of the wars and incursions of the twentieth century, was later modified. Spencer foresaw a time when inferior social forms and barbarous actions would be eliminated and the world would "progress towards that equilibrium between constitution and conditions—between inner faculties and outer requirements—implied in the final stage of human evolution." At this point the "ultimate man will be one whose private requirements coincide with public ones. He will be that manner of man who, in spontaneously fulfilling his own nature, incidentally performs the functions of the social unit; and yet is only enabled so to fulfill his own nature by all others doing the like" (1899, 3:331). In other words, the "fittest" or the "higher types" of men and societies would prevail and introduce a state of "equilibrium between constitution and conditions"—as long as there was no human interference in the evolutionary process. "Progress," according to Spencer, "is not an accident, but a necessity" (1850:65).

---

[6]This observation was made in a letter to an M. D. Conway in response to Conway's proposal, made at the time of the Spanish-American War, for a "supreme court of civilization"—a sort of early United Nations idea—to prevent war and aggression.

Class, Gender, and Race

Spencer did not have much to say about class, but his views on gender and race were quite controversial. They were consistent, however, with his functionalist, evolutionist perspective.

Gender   In 1850 in *Social Statics*, Spencer was in favor of equal rights for women. He argued that the evolutionary process of individuation, which produced the moral axiom that individuals should be as free as possible from externally imposed restraints, should also apply to women. He advocated that women be freed from external restraints in their domestic as well as political lives. "Equality knows no difference of sex. In its vocabulary the word *man* must be understood in a generic, and not in a specific sense" (1850:155).

Not too long afterward, however, he repudiated this position. The reason for Spencer's about-face on the question of gender equity may have been his own personal relations with women rather than any objective, philosophical reflection (Gray, 1984:228). Spencer had a relationship with Marion Evans (the novelist George Eliot). He found her intellectually stimulating, but although it seemed that Evans was "utterly besotted with Spencer" (Gray, 1984:223), Spencer liked feminine women, and Evans appeared somewhat masculine. In Spencer's early years in London there was speculation among their friends and acquaintances that the two were romantically involved, but in his autobiography Spencer claimed that he never had any intention of marrying her (Wiltshire, 1978:54). Spencer had equally close friendships throughout his life with a number of other women, such as Beatrice Webb and her mother, who were as independent as Marion Evans and certainly did not embody the subservient domestic "angel of the home" that Spencer later suggested was the appropriate, "functional" role for women.

The commitment that marriage demanded seemed to frighten Spencer, despite his lifelong position that celibacy was, in general, not a desirable state. Spencer told of meeting Comte, who advised Spencer to marry to cure his nervous problems. This advice seems a bit ironic given Comte's own marital problems (see Chapter 2). Nonetheless, Spencer's inhibitions and anxieties about his own "physical and mental adequacy" may have precipitated his reversal with regard to gender equity (Gray, 1984:228). In his later writings Spencer maintained that women "neither deserved nor needed the vote." Perhaps the notion that women had failed him personally led to the notion that women had failed society (Gray, 1984:228).

In 1891 Spencer asserted that to regard men and women as "mentally alike, is as untrue as that they are alike bodily. Just as certainly as they have physical differences which are related to the respective parts they play in the maintenance of the race, so certainly they have psychical differences, similarly related to their respective shares in the rearing and protecting of offspring." To assume that different parental activities did not mean differences in mental abilities was to "suppose that here alone in all Nature, there is no adjustment of special powers to special functions" (1891:340–341). In short, gender differences, both physical and mental, were the inevitable result of evolution and were functional for the stability of industrial societies.

Spencer's views on gender were part of his broader concern with kinship. He believed that kinship was one of the first social institutions, being necessary for the management of that basic need of all organisms—reproduction. Spencer suggested that from the earliest times there was a need to regulate sexual relations and provide for the care and protection of children. Survival of the fittest meant that general promiscuity must have been short-lived, because the "rearing of more numerous and stronger offspring must have been favoured by more regular sexual relations" (1899, 1:652).

Spencer believed the regulation of sexual relations evolved in stages. **Polyandry** (in which a woman has several husbands, often brothers) was an evolution from promiscuity but was, according to Spencer, an inferior form to **polygyny** (in which the husband had a plurality of wives). Polygyny was more suitable to militant societies, because multiple wives could produce more warriors more quickly. It was also an advance because it promoted patrilineal descent and social stability resulting from a clear line of succession. Spencer seems to ignore the fact that descent, and therefore succession, can be clearly charted in matrilineal cases as well. He should have known this from his exhaustive collection of ethnographic data, where matrilineal descent patterns would have been evident in some societies.

As industrial societies evolve, **monogamy** (one husband and one wife) becomes prevalent. Spencer suggested that monogamy improves the status of women; most notably, they are not treated as cruelly as was usually the case in polygynous militant societies. Industrial societies are more stable than militant societies because monogamy creates a "permanent, deep sense of aesthetic interest" in the marital relationship, through the sentiments of love and romance. Thus men are less likely to be brutal with their wives. But some of the spousal abuse statistics in current "civilized" industrial nations qualify this optimistic view.

The problem with Spencer's evolutionary scheme is that it actually contradicts some of the key evolutionary features of social structures as he himself outlined them. He had predicted evolution in the direction of greater complexity and interdependence of parts. However, monogamy is a less complex form than polygyny or polyandry. In addition, monogamy is not dependent for its development on the supposed prior form, polygyny.

The evolution of kinship and marriage was matched, in Spencer's view, by an evolution in the physical and psychological natures of men and women. The differences were primarily connected with women's special reproductive function. He posited an earlier arrest of "individual evolution in women than in men" in order to reserve the "vital power to meet the cost of reproduction" (1891:341). Women's arrested development meant that, compared to men, they were less capable of "abstract reasoning and that most abstract of emotions, the sentiment of justice—the sentiment which regulates conduct irrespective of personal attachments and the likes and dislikes felt for individuals." Women have "special aptitudes for dealing with infantine life" in contrast to men, whose "instinct" is not specific to infants but is a "more generalized relation to all the relatively-weak who are dependent upon him" (1891:342).

Women, in Spencer's view, remain more simple ("natural") as men become more complex (cultured).[7]

Spencer maintained that gender differences were the result of the struggles of primitive peoples to survive. The primitive tribes that survived were the ones in which the men were "not only powerful and courageous, but aggressive, unscrupulous, intensely egoistic." The men of these "conquering races" had predominantly "brutal characteristics," and women, "unable by strength to hold their own" with such men, had to develop the "ability to please" in order to survive. Women's survival also rested on their ability to disguise their feelings. Women "who betrayed the state of antagonism produced in them by ill-treatment, would be less likely to survive and leave offspring than those who concealed their antagonism" (1891:343). Their survival also depended on the ability to quickly detect the emotional state of others:

> In barbarous times a woman who could from a movement, tone of voice, or expression of face, instantly detect in her savage husband the passion that was rising, would be likely to escape dangers run into by a woman less skilled in interpreting the natural language of feeling. Hence, from the perpetual exercise of this power, and the survival of those having the most of it, we may infer its establishment as a feminine faculty. (1891:343)

It should be noted that the gender-specific attributes that Spencer assigned to women are, in fact, the attributes likely to be displayed by any subordinate, especially when the possibility of physical danger is present.

Spencer suggested that women themselves actively promoted the very danger they fear by preferring stronger, more brutal men. Women, he suggested, "who were fascinated by power, bodily or mental, and who married men able to protect them and their children, were more likely to survive in posterity than women to whom weaker men were pleasing, and whose children were both less efficiently guarded and less capable of self-preservation if they reached maturity." This "admiration for power" continued into modern civilized life, as demonstrated by the fact that women more often "continue attached to men who use them ill . . . than they . . . continue attached to weaker men who use them well" (1891:344). The bully who kicks sand in the face of the weakling will always triumph in Spencer's world. He does not consider the possibility that fear, or the lack of any viable alternatives, might account for the attachment of the weaker to the stronger, largely because of his commitment to the evolutionary idea of the "survival of the fittest." Current sociobiological accounts of gender relations echo Spencer's account, as you will see in Chapter 20.

The gender differences that Spencer elaborated had important consequences for the political organization of a society. Because women had a reverence for

---

[7]The view that mental and physical differences between men and women were an inevitable result of evolution is also found in the work of many of the classical theorists. As you will see in Chapter 4, Durkheim's analysis of gender differences and their structural and functional significance is almost identical to that of Spencer. In addition, Freud also believed that women were deficient in the sense of morality and justice.

power, he believed they were less likely to promote individual freedom and more likely to seek strong, controlling government. In addition, "family values" should not be the basis for state organization, because they were based on compassion for the weak and a focus on immediate needs rather than on future welfare. Social progress depended on rewarding the strong and resisting government control in the interest of future growth and progress.

Although Spencer believed that family values should not be the basis for political institutions, he nevertheless considered the monogamous, patriarchal family to be the most advanced family form and women to have the function of maintaining it. Consequently, nineteenth-century feminist arguments for improving women's education and opening up the professions to women were, in Spencer's view, evolutionarily regressive. He believed that over time there might be a "diminution of the political and domestic disabilities of women" but that these changes would not alter the essential, natural differences, which were tied to women's biology and fitted them primarily for family life. Any educational changes for women "made with the view of fitting them for business and professions, would be mischievous." Moreover, he observed, the demand for political rights and careers for women was the result of an abnormal excess in the numbers of women. Many women were temporarily excluded from their "natural careers in which they are dependent upon men for subsistence" because warfare was depleting the male population (1899, 1:767).

Spencer assumed that in the future extrafamilial relations in industrial societies would become more cooperative, which would spill over into marital relations. The result would be more equal partnerships, in which "affection" rather than legal rights would take precedence. Men would increasingly have sympathy for the "weaker sex," which would compensate women for such disadvantages as their exclusion from voting.

If women themselves understood "all that is contained in the domestic sphere, they would ask no other," especially as "absolute or relative infertility was generally produced in women by mental labour carried to excess" (1899, 2:486). Spencer was particularly concerned about "upper-class girls" and their "deficiency of reproductive power," which he attributed to the "overtaxing of their brains." The problem with educating women was particularly demonstrated, he contended, by the inability of educated women to "suckle their infants"; he noted that most "flat-chested girls who survive their high-pressure education, are incompetent to do this" (1899, 2:486).

The Lamarckian evolutionary view that acquired characteristics could be inherited prompted Spencer to conclude that the most important contribution a woman could make to racial evolution was a beautiful, healthy physique—in contrast to the man's contribution of a "fully developed brain." Because men's attraction to women was physical rather than intellectual, a "cultivated intelligence based on a bad physique is of little worth, seeing that its descendents will die out in a generation or two" (quoted in Paxton, 1991:33).

Spencer's description of the evolution of gender relations contains a serious inconsistency that illuminates the problem he has in reconciling his organic analogy with his individualism. The evolution of women is toward a more collective orientation for the preservation of the patriarchal family, whereas the evolution of men is increasingly individualistic—although their individualistic freedom rests on the bedrock of patriarchal family authority.

Spencer's treatment of women and the family is perhaps understandable given his status as a Victorian bachelor (Andreski, 1969:xvi). He does not seem to have looked beyond the standard, idealized family pattern of Victorian England, forgetting his own methodological advice about preconceptions and emotions—"that rigidity of conception produced in us by experiences of our own social life in our own time." He abandons the intellectual "plasticity that can receive with ease, and accept as natural, the countless combinations of social phenomena utterly unlike, and sometimes exactly opposite to, those we are familiar with" (1891:132).

Race   Although Spencer's views on gender relations are sociologically unreflective, his views on race are less so. His idea of the "survival of the fittest" has often been misinterpreted as a promotion of the racial superiority of white Europeans. However, Spencer's Lamarckism must be taken into account (Peel, 1972:143). To Spencer, evolution was not simply a natural, inevitable process; it was also a process governed by the "biological law of adaptation," which applied equally to the natural and the social worlds. Given the nature of physical and mental adaptation, "the intellectual and emotional natures required for high civilization" transposed to a less civilized society would simply result in the latter's "gradual decay and death, rather than adaptation" (1891:319).

Spencer did not use this concept to create a hierarchy of races. The "different forms of society presented by savage and civilized races all over the globe" are not simply "different stages in the evolution of one form." Rather they are "like types of individual organisms"; they do not "form a series, but are classifiable only in divergent and re-divergent groups" (1891:329). This perspective does not justify regarding some races as superior to others. The only thing that can be said it that some societies or some individuals have not progressed as far or as fast, or in the same manner, as some others.

In addition, any missionary or colonizing efforts on the part of those who suppose themselves superior are misguided because they would interfere with the evolutionary process. However, the "evolution of a society cannot be in any essential way diverted from its general course" (1899:132). Furthermore, when interest in the colonized or conquered people is really about trade, there is a distinct possibility that a "brutality will come out which the discipline of civilized life kept under" among the so-called superior race in their dealings with "inferiors."

Although Spencer was critical of colonizing efforts fueled by racist assumptions, he did suggest that a society formed by "nearly-allied peoples" for whom racial differences were small, so that the "conquering eventually mixes with the conquered," would be "well fitted for progress." In those situations in which the two races were "widely unlike . . . no progeny can arise." If by chance they did combine, they would likely produce a "mule incapable of propagating" (1899: 132–133). Spencer maintained that the result of "inter-marriages of human races," as of the "inter-breeding of animals," was *"invariably a bad one"*—as evidenced by the "Eurasians in India, and the half-breeds in America" (1898:256).

It was because of the special constitutional adaptation of a race to a particular way of life that racial intermarriages were to be avoided: "If you mix the constitutions of two widely divergent modes of life, you get a constitution which is adapted to a mode of life of neither—a constitution which will not work properly." Therefore, in Spencer's view, it was best to *"keep other races at arm's length as much as possible"* (1898:257).

Thus Spencer was not a racist in the sense that he believed in the invariable superiority of one race over another. But his evolutionary concept of "survival of the fittest" was an idea that supported the racist arguments of others, who then claimed a debt to Spencer's work. For Spencer, the evolutionary point was actually that "Every age, every nation, every climate, exhibits a modified form of humanity," and to mix these differences together would be a mistake because "All evil results from the non-adaptation of constitution to conditions" (1898:7–8).

Other Theories and Theorists

As you will see in Chapter 4, Emile Durkheim used an organic analogy similar to Spencer's. But where Spencer's organic analogy supported his belief in individualism, Durkheim's was more collectivist. Durkheim maintained that the parts of the social organism, namely its individual members, should be subordinate to the welfare of the whole society. In *The Division of Labor in Society*, Durkheim criticized Spencer's individualistic position.

Spencer explicitly stated that "society exists for the benefit of the members, not its members for the benefit of society" (1899:22). He needed to make that last point to reconcile his political individualism and laissez-faire economic position with the idea of society as an organism:

> It is well that the lives of all parts of an animal should be merged in the life of the whole; because the whole has a corporate consciousness capable of happiness or misery. But it is not so with society; since its living units do not and cannot lose individual consciousness. And this is an everlasting reason why the welfare of citizens cannot rightly be sacrificed to some supposed benefit of the State; but why . . . the State is to be maintained solely for the benefit of citizens. (1898:60)

Spencer did remark that his organic analogy was similar to Auguste Comte's ideas. But he insisted that Comte had made a critical error in assuming that social institutions were an "artificial arrangement" that could be "re-organized in conformity with the principles of his 'Positive Philosophy'" (1899:149–150).

In the early years, Spencer was often compared to Comte, and some commentators suggested he was a disciple of Comte. Spencer took exception to this view. In his autobiography, he pointed out that when he first began to discuss the parallels between the structure and evolution of society and of biological organisms in his first work, *Social Statics*, he had not read Comte. Furthermore, his methodological approach was different from that of Comte.

Later Spencer wrote a short essay, *Reasons for Dissenting from the Philosophy of M. Comte* (1864b), in which he acknowledged his debt to Comte for the terms *sociology* and *social consensus*. But otherwise Spencer disagreed with Comte on a number of fundamental points, most notably Comte's emphasis on the evolution of mental states as being more important than the evolution of social structure. Spencer claimed that Comte's emphasis was subjective, whereas his own focus on social structure was objective. In addition, Spencer's individualistic "political creed" was profoundly different from Comte's collectivist position, and Comte's later adoption of a Religion of Humanity was something that Spencer found incomprehensible.

Spencer praised Comte for "familiarizing men with the idea of social science, based on other sciences," but he dissented from the "positive philosophy" outlined by Comte, which Spencer insisted was not what he and others "currently" understood by positive philosophy (1864b:25). Spencer was like Comte in his formulation of a grand theory of evolution. But whereas Comte regarded all evolution as linear, Spencer regarded evolution, whether organic or inorganic, as fluctuating, even cyclical.

Critique and Conclusions

The point has been made that "Modern British sociology was built . . . as a defense against Spencer" (Abrams, 1968:67). This reaction to Spencer was largely caused by the political conclusion he drew from the idea of survival of the fittest: that it is the motor of social evolution. Spencer insisted that any legislative efforts designed to improve social conditions were useless—or even actively dysfunctional. Spencer had in fact made such claims early in his career, but spent his later years "modifying or disavowing them" (Abrams, 1968:73). However, by then it was too late to alter others' opinions about his work.

Perhaps the most bitter pill for Spencer was repudiation by his friend and colleague Thomas Huxley, who promoted Darwin's work. In his autobiography, Spencer claimed that after their first meeting in 1852, he and Huxley had frequent conversations about the idea of evolution (Carneiro, 1967:xvii–xix). However, Huxley explicitly rejected Spencer's ideas in his 1893 *Evolution and Ethics*. Over a period of thirty years, their ideas had gradually diverged, especially over issues of "the law of progress, the perfectibility of man, laissez-faire social policy, radical individualism, and utilitarian ethics" (Paradis and Williams, 1989:45–46).

Spencer maintained that he had not intended survival of the fittest to be interpreted as a "philosophy of inaction." Rather, he advocated the postponement of action "until it could be derived from a sociologically adequate analysis of social structure and social causation" (Abrams, 1968:74). Sociological analysis was necessary to counteract the dangerous tendency to rush in and "do something" about perceived problems. But this position did not alter Spencer's basic belief in the truth of evolution and the survival of the fittest.

Despite the British reaction to Spencer, *The Study of Sociology* may have been the most successful textbook of general sociology ever produced in Britain, and many of the ideas retain significance in modern sociological theory (Abrams, 1968:72). More recently, Turner (1985) has championed Spencer's revival, suggesting that Spencer's sociological contributions were as significant as those of many other classical theorists and that his problematic political and moral positions can be separated from his sociological ideas. In fact, Turner maintains that there are "far fewer ideological tracks" in Spencer's work than in Durkheim's, Weber's, or Marx's (1985:13).

However, although Spencer has been neglected, his ideological positions cannot be separated from his theoretical sociology—any more than they can for any other theorist. Spencer himself did not separate his political and moral convictions from his sociology: "My ultimate purpose . . . has been that of finding for the principles of right and wrong in conduct at large, a scientific basis. Now that moral injunctions are losing the authority given by their supposed sacred origin, the secularization of morals is becoming imperative" (1879, 1:v–vi).

Spencer's important legacy was his functionalist perspective, which became the dominant theoretical perspective in mid-twentieth-century sociology, as well as an important perspective in anthropology.[8] *Descriptive Sociology* was also significant, being the inspiration, as indicated above, for Murdock's categorization of ethnographic data in the Human Relations Area Files. Spencer's stage model of evolution has also been an enduring concept in sociology. His **synthetic philosophy**, which stressed the common principles governing the operation and growth of all social, biological, and material reality, was the first approach to systems theory. His methodological ideas are also an important legacy and are probably more accessible than Durkheim's celebrated work, *The Rules of Sociological Method* (Turner, 1985:18). More important, Durkheim's own work was created as a "sustained critical confrontation with the work of Spencer" (Coser, 1977:126–127). Although Durkheim disputed some of Spencer's main assumptions, his attention to Spencer's work kept some of Spencer's insights alive. Spencer's work was particularly influential in the early years of American sociology; Charles H. Cooley, the founder of sociology at the University of Michigan, remarked that initially his own generation of sociologists "were all Spencerians."

The neglect of Spencer had a lot to do with the Social Darwinism that many of his followers promoted, most notably his American admirers. They tended to exaggerate the conservative moral and political implications of his idea of the survival of the fittest. We turn now to a brief examination of the work of William Graham Sumner, an American disciple who endorsed a rigid interpretation of the evolutionary idea and who thus, ironically, contributed to Spencer's subsequent neglect.

William Graham Sumner (1840–1910)

In 1882 Spencer visited the United States, where he was greeted enthusiastically by various intellectuals as well as business tycoons such as Andrew Carnegie and John D. Rockefeller. In the first edition of *The Social Science Review*, established in 1865 by the New York–based Society for the Advancement of Social Science, an unsigned article asserted that Spencer's *Social Statics* represented the birth of "modern Social Science" and that Spencer himself was "one of the

---

[8]See, for example, A. R. Radcliffe-Brown, 1935.

most influential thinkers in the world" (quoted in Bernard and Bernard, 1965:469). Spencer's success in the United States was largely due to the theoretical justification he provided for a free enterprise system (Hofstadter, 1965: 46). One of the most enthusiastic supporters of Spencer and untrammeled free enterprise was William Graham Sumner.

Sumner was born in Paterson, New Jersey, and after 1845 lived in Hartford, Connecticut. Both of his parents had emigrated from England. Sumner's mother died when he was eight years old. His father was a self-educated, working-class man, and Sumner, who attended Yale in 1859, was the first in his family to attend university. After university, Sumner went to Europe and studied in Geneva, Göttingen, and Oxford.

In 1866 he returned to become a tutor at Yale, but resigned this position in 1869 to become assistant to the rector of the Calvary Church in New York. Sumner had been ordained a deacon in the Protestant Episcopal Church in 1867. In 1870 he became rector of the Church of the Redeemer in Morristown, New Jersey. However, Sumner was beginning to have religious doubts. These were resolved in 1872 by his election as Professor of Political and Social Science at Yale, which enabled him to leave the ministry.

Although Sumner repudiated his religious beliefs, the central Protestant virtues of hard work, thrift, and duty remained important to him. In his view, no one could "ever be emancipated from the necessity of industry, prudence, continence and temperance if they are to pass their lives prosperously" (1963:38). When he was young, Sumner read Harriet Martineau's *Illustrations of Political Economy*, which popularized the ideas of Malthus and the economist Ricardo. He later stated that "my main conceptions of capital, labor, money and trade were all formed by those books I read in my boyhood" (Persons, 1963:1).

Sumner taught the first course in North America to be called "sociology." He was one of the founders of the American Sociological Society and its second president.[9]

Sumner's Central Theories and Methods

Sumner's approach was an elaboration of Spencer's work, applied to the conditions of the expanding industrial and capitalist society of the United States. After 1872 he abandoned religion for an uncompromising form of social evolutionism and became a major spokesman for the doctrine that was labeled **Social Darwinism** to indicate its application of Darwinian ideas (actually an elaboration of Spencer's ideas about "survival of the fittest") to the social world.

Sumner himself regarded his work as scientific sociology and maintained that "sociology is the science of life in society" (1963:9). As a science, sociology had a "practical utility" in being able to derive the "rules of right social living from the facts and laws which prevail by nature in the constitution and functions of society"(1963:10). He likened sociology to the natural sciences, particularly biology: "Sociology is a science which deals with one range of phenomena produced by the struggle for existence, while biology deals with another. The

---

[9]The first president was Lester F. Ward, elected in 1906. Ward was also a Spencerian.

forces are the same, acting on different fields and under different conditions," but the two sciences are "truly cognate" (1963:14). Both sociology and biology, he noted, deal with the consequences of the "survival of the fittest." This conclusion places Sumner firmly in the conservative tradition.

The practical, objective nature of sociology meant that it would invariably "come into collision with all other theories of right living which are founded on authority, tradition, arbitrary intervention, or poetic imagination" (1963:10). Consequently, "utopians and socialists" as well as "reformers and philanthropists," who "never contribute much to the improvement of society in any actual detail," make "easy work of the complicated phenomena with which sociology has to deal" (1963:10–11). Sumner noted that these well-meaning—but misguided—individuals often rejected sociology as unnecessary or characterized it as simply stating the obvious, a complaint that is still occasionally leveled against sociology.

The complicated nature of sociological data meant that sociology required a "special method." The first methodological requirement, according to Sumner, was to develop a theoretical framework, a "classification," in order to "take up the facts in a certain order." The goal was to prevent the sociologist from being "overwhelmed in the mass of his material" (1963:12). In his view, statistics was one of the most objective and useful tools for sociology. The sociologist must remember that "pessimism and optimism are alike impertinent," that values have no place in the scientific sociological enterprise because they involve "passing judgement on what is inevitably fixed" and on which the "approval or condemnation of man can produce no effects" (1963:24–25).

Sumner demonstrated the use of a classification scheme for organizing facts about society in his best-known work, *Folkways and Mores*, in which he used ethnographic data to illustrate Social Darwinism. *Folkways* was similar to Spencer's *Descriptive Sociology* but conceptually richer, a broadly useful, comprehensive classification of cultural variability that introduced several important sociological concepts: folkways, mores, we-group and they-group, in-group and out-group, and ethnocentrism. These concepts are Sumner's enduring legacy.

Sumner pointed out in *Folkways* that "Competition and combination are two forms of life association which alternate through the whole organic and superorganic domains" (1907:18). In the latter case—that is, in society—they occur in response to the four "great motives" of human action: hunger, love, vanity, and fear. These motives underlie the constant effort to sustain and improve social life and result in "mass phenomena" such as "currents of similarity, concurrence, and mutual contribution" (1907:18–19).

These mass phenomena, in turn, produce **folkways**—the practical guides to conduct that develop in society. Folkways are the "most fundamental, and the most important ways" in which social groups survive and evolve. As the "life of society consists in making folkways and applying them," the "science of society might be construed as the study of them" (1907:34). The origin of folkways is "unconscious, spontaneous, uncoordinated," but always in tune with the evolutionary stage of the group or society (1907:18–19).

> All the practical and direct element in folkways seems to be due to common sense, natural reason, intuition, or some other original mental endowment.

It seems rational (or rationalistic) and utilitarian. Often in the mythologies
this ultimate rational element was ascribed to the teaching of a god or
a culture hero. In modern mythology it is accounted for as "natural."
(1907:28)

Folkways become **mores** when they become associated with "philosophical
and ethical generalizations as to societal welfare." Mores are coercive and constraining and cover "usage in dress, language, behavior, manners etc., with the
mandate of current custom, and give it regulation and limits within which it becomes unquestionable" (1907:521). Deviation from folkways might be criticized, but deviation from mores brings more severe sanctions because mores ensure the welfare of the group or society. Moreover, as the society's or group's
folkways and mores are considered the only "right" ones, they contribute to the
solidarity of we-groups and in-groups. Mores do change slowly over time, but it
would be futile, in Sumner's view, to legislate against mores.

Mores that absolutely prohibit certain acts are **taboos**. Taboos can be either
protective or destructive. For example, "Women are subject to some taboos
which are directed against them as sources of possible harm or danger to men,
and they are subject to other taboos which put them outside of the duties or
risks of men" (1907:30–31).

Sumner acknowledged that folkways, mores, and taboos vary from society
to society. Consequently, they illustrate the cultural relativity of presumed
"natural," unalterable, and morally right customs and traditions. Not only are
there differences between societies, but within societies some mores are common to the whole society whereas others are specific to social classes, professions, religious and philosophical sects, and "all other subdivisions of society."
Sumner noted that different "life conditions" produce "societal states of complete and distinctive individuality (ethos)" (1907:39).

Mores, Sumner stated, are the "regulators of the political, social, and religious behavior of the individual," and as they are "faiths," they are not affected
by "scientific facts" (1907:59, 98). Nevertheless, the task of the sociologist is to
dispel "illusions about what society is and may be" and to give "knowledge of
the facts which are the basis of intelligent effort by man to make the best of his
circumstances on earth" (1963:24–25). What the sociologist must do is present a
"colorless report of the facts." But like his mentor, Spencer, Sumner was not
neutral or colorless about the nature and purpose of society.

Nature of Society, Humans, and Change

Sumner may have renounced his formal identification with religion after reading Spencer, but vestiges remained in his sociology. He equated the Protestant
ideal of hard work and temperate appetites with fitness for social survival
(Hofstadter, 1965:51). For example, in his article "The Abolition of Poverty"
Sumner stated, "Let every man be sober, industrious, prudent, and wise, and
bring up his children to be so likewise, and poverty will be abolished in a few
generations" (1887, 1:109).

Generally, Sumner held that a stable, harmonious society was an evolutionary inevitability if only governments and tenderhearted do-gooders would cease to intervene in the process. Because the law of survival of the fittest was not a man-made law, any attempt by men to alter it would only produce "survival of the unfittest." Therefore, "socialists and sentimentalists" were wrong in their proposals for the alleviation of poverty and other social ills (1963:17). The only civil function that government should perform was the protection of property, not the redistribution of wealth.

As in Spencer's case, Malthus's ideas about population were the basis of Sumner's evolutionary perspective. Malthus had suggested that the ratio of population to land was what controlled the "possibilities of human development," and that social progress was the result of man's constant struggle over nature. In the struggle for land, "Nature is entirely neutral" and will "submit to him who most energetically and resolutely assails her. She grants her rewards to the fittest." However, Sumner concluded that when there is an "abundance of land and few men to share it," then "men will be equal," but when land is scarce, "earth hunger" develops and with it war, colonization, and conflict (1963:25).

Conflict is the natural response to competition over scarce resources, but Sumner also recognized a response he called **antagonistic cooperation**. This form of cooperation occurs when people or groups combine to "satisfy a great common interest while minor antagonisms of interest which exist between them are suppressed" (1907:18). In other words, conflict and cooperation are not necessarily opposed but may be intertwined in some cases.

Yet Sumner by no means recommended government interference to resolve conflict among individuals. In his essay "Socialism," Sumner asserted that "If you want equality you must not look forward for it on the path of advancing civilization. You may look back to the mode of life of the American Indian, and, although you will not then reach equality, you will escape those glaring inequalities of wealth and poverty by coming down to a comparative equality, that is, to a state in which all are equally miserable." Social inequality is more "natural," and capitalist profits are the "fruit of prudence and self-denial." Consequently, anything that makes it "uncertain whether the industrious man can dispose of the fruits of his industry for his own interest exclusively" is likely to produce "violence, bloodshed, poverty, and misery" (1963:88, 95–97).

Sumner went so far as to link survival of the fittest in the social world with an advantage in biological evolution. "Millionaires are the product of natural selection," he said, just like "great statesmen, or scientific men, or military men" (1963:157). Because of intense competition for their positions in the social order, only the fittest assume these coveted roles.

The fact that millionaires are selected through a natural mechanism explains how "wealth—both their own and that intrusted to them—aggregates under their hands." To him that has, shall be given! Although the rich may live in luxury and obtain great rewards, the "bargain is a good one for society." Competitors learn from the successful. The result is "discipline and the correction of arrogance and masterfulness" as well as social progress (1963:157). This idea of the benevolence of capital in furthering social progress may be compared to a questionable contemporary conservative idea that tax breaks for the rich will produce the desire to invest in job creation, which will result in improving the lot of the unemployed and destitute.

Sumner produced a great many essays commenting on the state of society and the remedies that in his view were sociologically validated, which meant they could restore the "natural" equilibrium needed to ensure evolutionary progress. These essays remain interesting, especially in light of some of the current neoconservative ideas about social problems and their solutions. But contemporary sociologists have generally dismissed Sumner—although continuing to draw on the concepts introduced in *Folkways*—because of his uncompromising evolutionism.

Class, Gender, and Race

Social Darwinism and Sumner's work were influential in the United States in the last years of the nineteenth century, largely because considerable numbers of Americans saw their own society mirrored in the idea of survival of the fittest. The idea of competition was heavily promoted by industrialists, politicians, and the media (Hofstadter, 1965:201). This orientation had an impact in the United States on popular views of social class, gender, and race.

Sumner believed that socialist schemes to alleviate the distress of the working classes were as impossible as a "plan of changing the physical order." The socialist who attempted to rescue the victims of poverty and misery, like the philanthropist, "is only cultivating the distress which he pretends to cure" (1963:97). For Sumner, the "only two things which really tell on the welfare of man on earth are hard work and self-denial (in technical language, labor and capital)" (1963:24). Social class divisions are inevitable results of economic competition and human interests. Any interference in the natural evolution of the market place results, in Sumner's view, in the survival of the "unfittest."

Any interference in monogamous, patriarchal gender relations would be equally foolhardy. Like Spencer, Sumner believed that women's reproductive capacities produced "special disabilities" in the struggle with nature and that these "disabilities grow greater and last longer as civilization advances." In fact, the one thing "which the student of history and sociology can affirm with confidence" was that "social institutions have made 'progress' or grown 'better'" because of the advent of patriarchal monogamy. All the evidence, he believed, pointed to the "fact" that "monogamy, pure and strict, is the relation which conduces most to the vigor and intelligence of the race" (1963:71).

Although the laissez-faire individualism of Spencer and his disciple Sumner came under increasing criticism after the turn of the century, it was often the basis for racist formulations (Hofstadter, 1965:202). For instance, the law of evolutionary progress and the idea of survival of the fittest were used to justify the "manifest destiny" of the white races to triumph over "lesser breeds." Another offshoot of Social Darwinism was the eugenics movement, which sought to improve the human race by preventing "inferior" individuals from breeding.

Its consequences included the Holocaust and still reverberated well into the 1970s in the forced sterilization of selected populations in Sweden, Canada, and Switzerland.

Other Theories and Theorists

Folkways was Sumner's legacy, and his in-group/out-group concepts have been particularly important. He pointed out that the peace, harmony, and comradeship of the in-group is correlated with the hostility and aggression directed to the out-group. Like Georg Simmel (see Chapter 8), Sumner recognized that conflict could be a source of social solidarity: "The exigencies of war with outsiders are what makes peace inside" (1907:12).

Related to Sumner's observations on in-groups and out-groups is the concept of ethnocentrism. Ethnocentrism represents the tendency of any group to see itself as the "center of everything, and all others as scaled and rated with reference to it" (1907:13). The belief in the superiority of the group applies to family or kin groups, neighborhoods, school cliques, and close friends as well as to whole societies or whole nations. Ethnocentrism can provide the solidarity needed in conflict, just as it can fuel the same conflict

Critique and Conclusions

Sumner's work and the uncompromising Social Darwinism it embodied were passé among sociologists by the end of the First World War. But the evolutionary idea of survival of the fittest has had a long afterlife. Just consider some of the current neo-Nazi movements and the advocacy of a return to "traditional," patriarchal gender relations. Many mainstream conservative measures can also be traced back to Sumner's ideas, such as the effort to get welfare mothers working so that they can simultaneously contribute to society and provide a model of the work ethic for their children.

The sociologist Albion Small characterized Sumner's work as a "mixed blessing" (Hofstadter, 1965:202). His *Folkways* was an admirable sociological contribution, but his polemical essays contradicted the objectivity sociology sought to convey. Sumner's central belief was that "Society needs first of all to be free from meddlers—that is, to be let alone," and he poured forth passionate defenses of free enterprise and competitive individualism to support that belief (1883:120).

Final Thoughts

Both Spencer and Sumner offer a couple of interesting contradictions. Ideologically they were status quo conservatives, although their ideas about the nature of society, humans, and social change emerged from the radical Enlightenment faith in human reason and progress. Both endorsed equality of rights and equality of opportunity, although they also recognized that those with greater abilities or those who worked more diligently would be more handsomely rewarded. They considered this inequality of outcome socially progressive, however, because the wealth of the "fittest" would contribute to the wealth of society as a whole.

Capitalism and *industrialism,* unfettered by government interference, were the motors of social progress in their view. According to Spencer, in seeking gratification of desires, individuals' "private activities and their spontaneous cooperations, have done much more towards social developments than those which have worked through government agencies." In fact, "Perpetually, governments have thwarted and deranged . . . growth" (1891:100).

Spencer's and Sumner's ideas had a great initial impact on sociology, but limited staying power. Their sociology was superceded by the realization among sociologists that the "decisive factors in social relations" were psychological not biological (Hofstadter, 1965:202). With the expansion of sociology and the exposure of sociologists to other perspectives, most notably those proposed by other European sociologists, both Sumner and Spencer fell out of favor.

However, Spencer and Sumner have had an undeniable influence on sociological theory. Among those who read Spencer and responded to his work was Emile Durkheim. In one of his first books, *The Division of Labor in Society,* Durkheim explicitly contradicted the Spencerian and Sumnerian belief that the state should confine itself to protecting individual rights and maintaining military defense. In Durkheim's view, as you will see in Chapter 4, the state has a vital role to play in the maintenance of the "good society."

References

Abrams, Philip. 1968. *The Origins of British Sociology, 1834–1914.* Chicago: University of Chicago Press.

Andreski, Stanislav. 1969. Introduction. In Herbert Spencer, *The Principles of Sociology* (3 vols.). New York: Macmillan.

Bernard, L. L., and Jessie Bernard. 1965. *The Origins of American Sociology.* New York: Russell & Russell.

Brinton, Crane. 1933. *English Political Thought in the Nineteenth Century.* London: Ernest Benn.

Carneiro, Robert L. (Ed.). 1967. *The Evolution of Society: Selections from Herbert Spencer's Principles of Sociology.* Chicago: University of Chicago Press.

Carruth, W. H. 1908/1953. *Each in His Own Tongue and Other Poems.* In *The Oxford Dictionary of Quotations.* Oxford: Oxford University Press, p. 131.

Collier, James. 1904. "Personal Reminiscence." In Josiah Royce, *Herbert Spencer: An Estimate and Review.* New York: Fox, Duffield & Co.

Coser, Lewis. 1977. *Masters of Sociological Thought* (2nd ed.). New York: Harcourt Brace Jovanovich.

Gray, T. S. 1984. "Herbert Spencer on Women: A Study in Personal and Political Disillusionment." *International Journal of Women's Studies,* 7(3).

Hofstadter, Richard. 1965. *Social Darwinism in American Thought.* Boston: Beacon Press.

Galloway, Albert Keller, and Maurice R. Davie. (Eds.). 1969. "Autobiographical Sketch of William Graham Sumner." In *Essays of William Graham Sumner.* New Haven, CT: Yale University Press.

Murdock, George P., et al. 1961. *Outline of Culture Materials*. New Haven, CT: Human Relations Area Files.

Paradis, James, and George C. Williams. 1989. *Evolution and Ethics*. Princeton, NJ: Princeton University Press.

Parsons, Talcott. 1937. *The Structure of Social Action*. New York: McGraw-Hill.

Paxton, Nancy L. 1991. *George Eliot and Herbert Spencer: Feminism, Evolutionism and the Reconstruction of Gender*. Princeton, NJ: Princeton University Press.

Peel, J. D. Y. 1972. *Herbert Spencer: The Evolution of a Sociologist*. New York: Basic Books.

Persons, Stow. 1963. Introduction. In William Graham Sumner, *Social Darwinisms: Selected Essays*. Englewood Cliffs, NJ: Prentice-Hall.

Radcliffe-Brown, A. R. 1935. "On the Concept of Function in Social Science." *American Anthropology, 32*, 390–402.

Ritzer, George. 1996. *Classical Sociological Theory*. New York: McGraw-Hill.

Spencer, Herbert. 1850/1910. *Social Statics Together with Man and the State*. New York: D. Appleton & Co.

———. 1854/1895. *The Principles of Psychology* (2 vols.). New York: D. Appleton.

———. 1862/1901. *First Principles*. New York: P. F. Collier & Son.

———. 1864a/1913. *The Challenge of Facts and Other Essays*. New Haven, CT: Yale University Press.

———. 1864b/1968. *Reasons for Dissenting from the Philosophy of M. Comte and Other Essays*. Berkeley, CA: Glendessary Press.

———. 1874. *Descriptive Sociology; or Groups of Sociological Facts*. London: Williams and Norgate.

———. 1879. *The Principles of Ethics* (2 vols.). London: Williams and Norgate.

———. 1891. *The Study of Sociology*. New York: Appleton.

———. 1892. *Social Statics Together with the Man Versus the State, Abridged and Revised*. London: Williams and Norgate.

———. 1898/1971. *On Social Evolution: Selected Writings* (J. D. Y. Peel, Ed.). Chicago: University of Chicago Press.

———. 1899/1969. *The Principles of Sociology* (3 vols.) (Stanislav Andreski, Ed.). New York: Macmillan.

———. 1902. *Facts and Comments*. New York: Books for Libraries Press.

———. 1904/1926. *An Autobiography* (2 vols.). New York: Appleton.

Sumner, William Graham. 1863/1969. "Autobiographical Sketch of William Graham Sumner." In Albert Keller Galloway and Maurice R. Davie. (Eds.), *Essays of William Graham Sumner* (pp. 3–105). New Haven, CT: Yale University Press.

———. 1883. *What Social Classes Owe Each Other*. New York: Harper.

———. 1887/1969. "The Abolition of Poverty." In Albert Keller Galloway and Maurice R. Davie. (Eds.), *Essays of William Graham Sumner*. New Haven, CT: Yale University Press.

———. 1907/1979. *Folkways and Mores* (Edward Sagarin, Ed.). New York: Schoken Books.

———. 1963. *Social Darwinisms: Selected Essays* (Stow Persons, Ed.). Englewood Cliffs, NJ: Prentice-Hall.

Turner, Jonathan H. 1985. *Herbert Spencer: A Renewed Appreciation*. Beverly Hills, CA: Sage.

Webb, Beatrice. 1946. *My Apprenticeship*. London: Longmans, Green & Co.

Wiltshire, David. 1978. *The Social and Political Thought of Herbert Spencer*. Oxford: Oxford University Press.

Chapter 4

Society as *Sui Generis*
Durkheim

Emile Durkheim is one of the classical theorists whose work has enduring significance for sociological theorizing. Sociologists continue to focus on the questions Durkheim raised and "to plunder the Aladdin's cave of concepts he bequeathed" (Parkin, 1992:1).

Durkheim's underlying ideology is similar to that of Herbert Spencer, featured in Chapter 3, who has far less influence today than Durkheim. Both compared society to an organism, both distinguished between structure and function in the operation of society, and both had an evolutionary perspective on social change. However, Durkheim and Spencer differed in one important respect: Although, like Spencer, Durkheim was convinced that modern industrial society produced pathologies, Durkheim did not see the solution as lying in less government or less social regulation. Rather, Durkheim believed that society itself was the key influence on individuals. "We should not, as does Spencer, present social life as the mere resultant of individual natures alone, since, on the contrary, it is rather the latter that emerge from the former" (Durkheim, 1893:286).

In *The Division of Labour in Society* Durkheim asked, "How does it come about that the individual, whilst becoming more autonomous, depends ever more closely upon society?" (1893:xxx). Durkheim's sociological theory is largely concerned with providing the answer to this question.

Throughout Durkheim's writings, he consistently focused on the problem that his predecessors had also identified: reconciling freedom and morality, or individualism and social cohesion, in modern society. As you will see, however, Durkheim took a path different from that of either the radicals or the reactionary conservatives. He recognized the inevitability, indeed the desirability, of social change, but not at the expense of a cohesive society buttressed by ethical norms. He was concerned with morality because he believed that civilized society was, in his time, suffering from a "state of deep disturbance" (Durkheim, 1897b:391). The science of sociology was the means, in his view, to discover the ways in which modern society could become moral and harmonious.

Emile Durkheim (1858–1917)

Although Auguste Comte (introduced in Chapter 2) coined the term *sociology*, he was never able to obtain the academic recognition he so desired for "his" theory. The first sociologist in France to hold an academic post was Emile Durkheim.

Durkheim's background was religious and intellectual. He was descended from a long line of rabbis, and in his youth he studied Hebrew and the Talmud as well as attending secular schools. Initially he intended to follow the family tradition and become a rabbi, but in his adolescent years he became an agnostic. As you will see, however, he maintained a lifelong sociological interest in religious phenomena.

Durkheim was a brilliant student, and in 1879 he was admitted to the prestigious École Normale Supérieure. Durkheim was not, however, entirely happy with the literary and philosophical thrust of the school, being more interested in scientific and social issues (Coser, 1977; Thompson, 1982; Ritzer, 1992; Lukes, 1973). He was interested in sociology at an early stage but bemoaned the fact that sociology, although French in origin, had become a "German science" (Jones, 1994:4).

On leaving the École in 1882, Durkheim taught philosophy at a number of schools in the Paris area. In 1885 he was offered a scholarship to study in Germany for a year. One reason for the scholarship was Durkheim's views supporting the French republic and his advocacy of a "secular morality based on science" (Clark, 1968).

Another reason, in a sense, was France's defeat in the Franco-Prussian War of 1870. Many French policymakers believed that France's outdated educational institutions had been "a major factor in the French defeat" (Clark, 1968:44). A result of that defeat was a program to reform the educational system from top to bottom, focusing on secularization. Reforms at the university level took German universities as the model; Durkheim, along with other young scholars, was sent to Germany to investigate the secular, scientific nature of education at German universities.

At university in Germany, Durkheim was impressed by the scientific psychology of Wilhelm Wundt. Durkheim found especially significant Wundt's contention that moral phenomena had to be treated as "facts of social existence, *sui generis*"—that is, as facts irreducible in "origin and operation to individual acts" (Thompson, 1982:36). On his return from Germany in 1887, Durkheim obtained a position at the University of Bordeaux. This first position was with the Department of Philosophy. It was not until 1896 that he was appointed a full professor of Social Science, the first such position in any French university. There he wrote three of his most important sociological works: *The*

Division of Labour in Society (1893), *The Rules of Sociological Method* (1895), and *Suicide* (1897b).

In addition to the books, in 1898 Durkheim founded a new journal, *L'Année Sociologique*. The journal was a yearly review of sociological works and works of related interest in the other social sciences, such as law, history, ethics, economics, geography, and in later years, religion. The journal attracted a number of like-minded collaborators who, in their association with Durkheim, formed a "school" that has been described as "the most brilliant" group of sociologists "ever gathered in the history of the discipline" (Coser, 1977:165). Their interests and contributions included anthropology, history, law, and economic sociology, as well as general sociology. The collaboration lasted until the First World War, but even after Durkheim's death, the journal retained its significance for a range of social science disciplines.

Durkheim had introduced a course in sociology at the University of Bordeaux, and he held the Chair of Social Science there from 1896 to 1902. In 1902 Durkheim moved to the Sorbonne in Paris, where he remained until his death. He was appointed Professor of the Science of Education; only in 1913 was the title changed to Science of Education and Sociology.

Despite the success of the journal and the positive reception of Durkheim's own work, for many tradition-bound academics sociology was still a suspect intellectual upstart (Giddens, 1978:15). From the outset of his academic career, Durkheim had set out to promote sociology as a legitimate and significant academic discipline. He believed that the promotion of sociology as a legitimate discipline was imperative because philosophy and psychology claimed to cover the subjects that sociology claimed for itself. But "for sociology to be possible, it must above all have an object all its own" (Durkheim, 1897b:38). He intended his work as proof that sociology did indeed deal with subjects that other disciplines did not cover and thus could claim a legitimate place in the academy. It was in order to begin this task that *L'Année Sociologique* was founded.

Moreover, Durkheim believed that French intellectuals had a special role to play in the discipline of sociology. In 1915 he wrote, "To set forth the role which belongs to France in the establishment and development of sociology is almost tantamount to writing the history of this science; for it was born among us, and although there is not a country today where it is not being cultivated, it nevertheless remains an essentially French science" (1915:381).

Durkheim's promotion of sociology was not simply academic and theoretical; he also stressed its practical importance. As he remarked in his first book, *The Division of Labour*, although sociology aims to study reality, it does not follow that "we should give up the idea of improving it." On the contrary, "we would esteem our research not worth the labour of a single hour if its interest were merely speculative" (1893:xxvi). Nonetheless, Durkheim recognized that sociology was often accused of simply observing "what exists" without supplying "rules for future conduct" (1893:xxvi). Durkheim wanted to remedy this state of affairs. He believed that the ideal to be sought could only be distilled from the scientific observation of reality, not from some idealist "aspiration of the heart" (1893:xxvii).

Durkheim's Central Theories and Methods

As you have seen in previous chapters, *modern industrial* society was regarded by many as responsible for excessive *individualism*, which was thought to produce disruptive, even anarchic, effects. More specifically, specialization and *division of labor* encouraged autonomous individualism, which in turn threatened social harmony and cohesion. Durkheim shared these views. "If public opinion recognises the rule of the division of labour, it is not without some anxiety and hesitation" (1893:5). In modern society, specialization and the division of labor is a "duty," and the traditional, humanist ideal of the "perfect man" as one "capable of being interested in everything, but attaching himself exclusively to nothing" now appears to be a "flabby, lax form of discipline" (1893:3–4). The new emphasis on specialization did not, however, mean that social cohesion must be forfeit. On the contrary, the greater the individual autonomy and specialization, the greater the individual's dependence on society.

The central question in *The Division of Labour in Society* was, therefore, how can the individual "whilst becoming more autonomous" depend "ever more closely upon society?" (1893:xxx). Durkheim's general answer was that **social solidarity**, or social cohesiveness and harmony, itself is transformed by the division of labor. That is, in modern society the division of labor becomes the "source—if not the sole, at least the main one—of social solidarity" (1893:23). As people fulfill specific roles within modern, capitalist, industrial society—mechanic, doctor, merchant, street sweeper, student, and so on—they become more dependent on others within society for the goods and services that they themselves do not have the time or the means to produce.

Durkheim identified **collective consciousness,** or the "totality of beliefs and sentiments common to the average members of a society," as the basis for social solidarity (1893:38–39).[1] This totality of beliefs and sentiments forms a "determinate system with a life of its own" (1893:39). Collective consciousness varies from one society to another because it varies according to the nature of the division of labor.

In *The Division of Labour in Society*, Durkheim demonstrated how the division of labor and the development of autonomous individuality affect social solidarity. The argument proceeds in three parts: a determination of the function of the division of labor—that is, "the social need to which it corresponds"; a determination of "the causes and conditions upon which it depends"; and a description of "normal" and "abnormal" forms of the division of labor (1893:6–7).

Social Solidarity and the Division of Labor   Durkheim identified two types of social solidarity: **mechanical** and **organic.** In using the term *mechanical*, Durkheim was making an analogy with inanimate objects, the parts of which (analogous to the individuals in a society) cannot operate independently if the harmony and cohesion of the whole are to be maintained. For example, a clock

---

[1] The collective conscience is a translation of Durkheim's term *conscience collective*. It should be noted that the French term "conscience" translates as "consciousness" in English, although consciousness obviously affects the English-sense word "conscience."

cannot work if one of its parts malfunctions. The term *organic* is an analogy with a living body, in which harmony and cohesion are produced by the interdependent operation of the parts. For example, the loss of a limb is a misfortune but not life-threatening. Durkheim used these two terms to describe the function of the division of labor in a society, but they are purely conceptual. That is, they do not refer to any actual or specific society.

Mechanical solidarity is characteristic of more primitive societies, in which the division of labor is minimal and "individuality is zero" (1893:84). The individual "does not belong to himself" but is "literally a thing at the disposal of society" (1893:85). The common consciousness in this type of society is primarily religious. Religion "pervades the whole of social life," which is made up "almost entirely of common beliefs and practices" (1893:130). In such societies, **communism**—in this context meaning simply common ownership of the society's property—is evidence of the "cohesion that swallows up the individual within the group." The "collective personality" is the only one, and therefore "property itself is inevitably collective" (1893:130). Property can only become private property when the individual frees herself or himself from the mass and becomes a "personal, distinctive being," as is the case in modern organic societies.

The organic type of society is characterized by specialization and individuality. The resemblance between individuals is replaced by difference between them, and the individual personality, as opposed to the collective, asserts itself. The collective consciousness "leaves uncovered a part of the individual consciousness, so that there may be established in it those special functions that it cannot regulate" (1893:85). As the division of labor increases and each individual becomes more specialized, each individual must rely more on others. The division of labor itself thus produces social solidarity: "each of us depends more intimately upon society the more labour is divided up" (1893:85). The function of the division of labor in this type of society is therefore social cohesion and harmony.

One of Durkheim's chief concerns, as mentioned earlier, was morality in modern society. He noted that the collective consciousness becomes more secular in organic society, moving toward the "cult of the individual," and that such morality is "more human, and consequently more rational" than that found in mechanical solidarity (1893:338). Organic collective consciousness requires us to be "charitable and just towards our fellow-men, to fulfill our tasks well," and to work "towards a state where everyone is called to fulfill the function he performs best and will receive a just reward for his efforts" (1893:338). The cult of the individual is not about "hedonistic license" but the "worth and dignity of 'man' in the abstract" (Jones and Kibee, 1993:11). For Durkheim, then, it was "wrong to oppose a society that derives from a community of beliefs to one whose foundation is cooperation, by granting the first a moral character, and seeing in the latter only an economic grouping," because the sort of cooperation that characterizes organic society also has its own "intrinsic morality" (1893:173–174). The celebration of medieval society as the ideal, as in the work of de Maistre and other conservatives, was therefore misguided in Durkheim's view.

A society's transition from mechanical to organic solidarity is a consequence of dynamic density—that is, an increase in the number of people that, in turn, produces an increase in social interactions and in the division of labor. Greater density also makes the "struggle for existence more strenuous," but this struggle is a "gentle *denouement*" because "rivals are not obliged to eliminate one another completely, but can coexist side by side" (1893:213).

To demonstrate the transition from mechanical to organic solidarity, Durkheim needed an external index of change. Solidarity is a moral phenomenon and thus cannot be subjected to "exact observation and especially not to measurement" (1893:24). The external index Durkheim used was the law. He pointed out that social life "cannot enlarge its scope without legal activity simultaneously increasing in proportion" (1893:25). Consequently, law reflects all the "essential varieties of social solidarity" (1893:65).

Legal sanctions that enforced moral codes thus provided evidence of the nature of social solidarity. Legal sanctions represent society's reaction to the "outrage to morality" resulting from a criminal act (1893:47). A criminal act does not shock "the common consciousness because it is criminal," but "it is criminal because it offends that consciousness" (1893:40).

Durkheim identified two types of legal sanctions:

- **Repressive sanctions,** which are characteristic of mechanical solidarity, are embodied in penal law. These sanctions consist of "some injury, or at least some disadvantage" imposed on the criminal with the intention of doing harm to him through "his fortune, his honour, his life, his liberty or to deprive him of some object whose possession he enjoys" (1893:29). The moral outrage expressed in mechanical society to criminal acts is more intense than in organic society because of the greater unity and strength of collectively held moral sentiments (1893:58). Inflicting pain and suffering on the criminal serves to reaffirm the common consciousness and restore social solidarity.

- **Restitutive sanctions** are embodied in civil law, commercial law, procedural law, and administrative and constitutional law. They do not necessarily produce suffering for the criminal but consist in "restoring the previous state of affairs" (1893:29). Organic solidarity relies on this type of sanction because of the need to regulate relations between individuals. Some repressive sanctions might carry over into organic society—for example, the retention of the death penalty for certain crimes—but restitutive law, administered by special agencies, is more common.

Although the direct effects of the common consciousness are muted in organic society as a result of individualism, it makes itself felt in the ties that connect, or bind, individuals. The best example of the common consciousness at work in organic solidarity was to be found, according to Durkheim, in contract law.

Contract law is the expression of the need for individuals to cooperate. But for harmonious cooperation "it is not enough that they should enter into a relationship, nor even be aware of the state of mutual interdependence in which they find themselves" (1893:160). If the contract is to be binding, the obligations involved have to be more than moral obligations particular to the parties to the contract; they have to be sanctioned by society. All contracts therefore assume that "behind the parties who bind each other, society is there, quite prepared to intervene and enforce respect" for the contractual arrangements. Even the most private contract is only binding because "society . . . confers that force" (1893:71).

Because of contract law and other social sanctions, the "cult of the individual" characteristic of organic solidarity does not normally give rise to unregulated, egoistic individuals. On the contrary, egoism is an abnormal feature of organic solidarity (1893:173). However, Durkheim perceived, as did others, that in the real world, as opposed to the conceptual world he described in *The Division of Labour in Society*, modern organic solidarity was in a pathological state—as suicide rates attested. In investigating this sign of social pathology, Durkheim established sociology's credentials as a legitimate science of society.

Methodological Issues   Durkheim believed that by focusing on society itself, the pressing issues of modern society could be unearthed and, hopefully, mitigated. In his essay "Sociology and Its Scientific Field," Durkheim pointed out that history, political economy, statistics, and demography study "what occurs in society, not society itself" (1900:355). Without sociology it is impossible to know the origins, progress, or social context of the subject matter of those disciplines (1900:381). The "most urgent reform" was therefore to "bring sociology and these other special techniques" together and in doing so "give sociology the data it lacked, and inversely, to bring the sociological idea down into these disciplines in such a manner as to make true social sciences of them" (1900:381).

In *The Rules of Sociological Method* (1895), Durkheim demonstrated the legitimacy of sociology as a scientific discipline. He carefully outlined *what* sociology studied and *how* it was studied. Durkheim defined **sociology** as the "science of institutions, of their genesis and of their functioning" (1895:lvii). He noted that society has a reality sui generis—that is, an objective reality apart from the individuals within it.

> It is upon this principle . . . that all sociology has been built. This science, indeed, could be brought into existence only with the realization that social phenomena, although immaterial, are nevertheless real things, the proper objects of scientific study. (1895:lvii)

Durkheim also noted that institutions comprise "all the beliefs and all the modes of conduct instituted by the collectivity" (1895:lvi). In other words, institutions contain all the **social facts** that sociology studies.

Social facts are not "factual," they are "things"—objective, even measurable things. Social facts can be of three general types:

- Material facts, such as the nature of society itself, social structures, and morphological facts such as population size and density and geographical location

- Communication links or nonmaterial facts, such as norms and values, or collective representations and the collective consciousness

- Social currents—"the great movements of enthusiasm, indignation, and pity in a crowd"—which do not arise in any one individual consciousness (1895:lvi).

Durkheim defined social facts as "ways of acting, thinking, and feeling, *external* to the individual and endowed with the power of *coercion*, by reason of which they control him" (1895:3). For example, Durkheim pointed out that in the fulfillment of "obligations as brother, husband, or citizen" the individual performs duties and roles that are defined externally to himself, and that constrain his interpretation and fulfillment of those roles (1895:1–2). It is the exteriority and the constraint of social facts that make them visible to the sociologist. Because they are independent of any individual, social facts can only be explained in terms of other social facts, not in terms of "states of individual consciousness" (1895:110).

Durkheim clearly distinguished between causal and functional explanations of social facts: "When, then, the explanation of a social phenomenon is undertaken, we must seek separately the efficient cause which produces it and the function it fulfills" (1895:95). Durkheim used the term *function* rather than *end* or *purpose* because social phenomena do not have intentions or purposes in the way that human beings do. **Function** refers to the "correspondence between the fact under consideration and the general needs of the social organism," and this correspondence has an existence apart from whether it was intentional or not. In fact, Durkheim stated, "All these questions of intention are too subjective to allow of scientific treatment" (1895:95).

The function of a social fact is to produce "socially useful effects"; if it also "serves the individual," this is a bonus. But the correspondence with human needs is not the "immediate cause" of the function, because the *"function of a social fact ought always to be sought in its relation to some social end"* (1895:111). The *"determining cause of a social fact should be sought among the social facts preceding it and not among the states of individual consciousness"* (1895:110).

In observing any social fact, Durkheim enjoined sociologists to examine it without any preconceptions, look for empirical evidence of the phenomenon, and determine whether it is "normal" or "pathological"—that is, whether the social fact is in conformity with the "conditions which determined this generality in the past" and whether the conditions still apply. If the conditions have changed, then the continued existence of the social fact is evidence of the pathology of this particular phenomenon.

Finally, sociological explanations of social facts must address causation, but as "social phenomena evidently escape the control of the experimenter, the comparative method is the only one suited to sociology" (1895:125). The comparison could involve social facts at two different times in a given society, or simultaneously in two different societies.

If sociologists use the comparative method scientifically—"i.e., by conforming to the principle of causality as it occurs in science itself"—then the basis for comparisons must be the proposition *"A given effect has always a single corresponding cause"* (1895:128). The example Durkheim used in making this point was suicide. He pointed out that "if suicide depends on more than one cause, it is because, in reality, there are several kinds of suicide" (1895:129). We now turn to the work that Durkheim believed would "demonstrate the possibility of sociology better than any dialectical argument": *Suicide* (1897b).[2]

The Methodology Demonstrated: Suicide European scholars had been particularly interested in the problem of suicide since the eighteenth century.

---

[2]Durkheim also noted that the same was true of criminal acts.

Many believed that the increasing suicide rates of modern societies were a sign of social instability occasioned by the "cult of the individual" and by the decline of traditional, hierarchical, religious society. They blamed modern civilization for the rise in suicide rates; Durkheim himself referred to suicide as the "ransom money" of civilization (1897b:367).

Durkheim's interest in suicide may have been prompted in part by the suicide of a close friend at the École (Lukes, 1973:191). But it was also a demonstration of Durkheim's claim that sociology had an "object all its own" in the examination of "a reality which is not in the domain of other sciences" (1897b:38). Examining what was popularly assumed to be the most individual and private act, and therefore more amenable to psychological than sociological explanation, was an audacious move on Durkheim's part.

In his examination of suicide, Durkheim first looked at explanations offered by previous investigators. He demonstrated that these explanations—based on such factors as insanity, imitation, race, and cosmic factors—were inadequate. Durkheim then pointed out that looking at suicide as an individual phenomenon must involve a psychological explanation, but that **suicide rates** were also a collective phenomena. Thus they must be explained sociologically. When suicides "committed in a given society during a given period of time" are examined as a whole, this "total is not simply a sum of independent units . . . but is itself a new fact *sui generis*, with its own unity, individuality and consequently its own nature—a nature dominantly social" (1897b:46).

The social character of suicide rates is demonstrated, Durkheim pointed out, by their variation in relation to the degree of solidarity in society. Each society "has a collective inclination for the act, quite its own, and the source of all individual inclination, rather than their result." This collective inclination is determined by the "currents of egoism, altruism or anomy running through the society under consideration" (1897b:299). Egoism, altruism, and anomie are each a measure of the social cohesion or integration in the society, and suicide therefore "varies inversely with the degree of integration of the social groups of which the individual forms a part" (1897b:209).

Egoistic suicide occurs when the cohesion and solidarity of the group or community has declined to such an extent that the individual cannot rely upon it for any support. The individual "depends only on himself and recognizes no other rules of conduct than what are founded on his private interests" (1897b: 209). The individual is isolated and potentially suicidal because the "ties uniting him with others are slackened or broken" because of the "weakening of the social fabric" (1897b:281). The cause of egoistic suicide is, therefore, "excessive individualism," which modern, industrial society tended to encourage. Egoistic suicide may be characteristic of society as a whole or of particular, less integrated groups within a society, such as urban dwellers, industrial workers, Protestants, and unmarried men.

Altruistic suicide is the obverse of egoistic suicide. It is the result of the excessive integration of the individual into the group. Suicide occurs because the "ego is not its own property" (1897b:221). The suicidal individual who is completely absorbed by the group feels it is his or her duty to commit suicide in order to benefit the group or collectivity. Although Durkheim thought that "lower" or less civilized societies were the "theatre par excellence of altruistic suicide," he noted that this form of suicide affected one group in modern societies—the army. In the army, individuality is discouraged in the interests of the welfare of the whole. Durkheim suggested that the frequent suicides of French Revolutionary men were "at least partly due to an altruistic state of mind"; in that period of civil strife, the individual personality was discounted and the "interest of country or party outweighed everything" (1897b:228, fn.34). Egoistic suicide occurs because "society allows the individual to escape it," whereas altruistic suicide occurs because "society holds him in too strict tutelage" (1897b:221).

Anomic suicide is a result of the breakdown of the moral community and the resulting disturbance of social equilibrium. According to Durkheim, it is "man's nature to be eternally dissatisfied" and to have unlimited desires (1897b:257). Unlike animals, there is nothing in man's "organic nor in his psychological constitution which sets a limit" on his desire for "well-being, comfort or luxury." But unlimited desires are "insatiable by definition and insatiability is rightly considered a sign of morbidity" (1897b:247). Consequently, the "passions must be limited," and only society, as the "moral power superior to the individual," has the authority to set limits (1897b:249). Man accepts the restraint of society as a "conscience superior to his own." But when this conscience is disturbed, it cannot exercise restraint, and the result is "sudden rises in the curve of suicides" (1897b:252).

Anomic suicide was particularly prevalent in modern society, especially in the economic world where "it has most victims" (1897b:257). Durkheim pointed out that "for a whole century, economic progress has mainly consisted in freeing industrial relations from all regulation." Consequently, economic success, instead of being seen as a means to an end had become an end in itself, and "the appetites thus excited have become freed of any limiting authority" (1897b:255). Therefore, it was not surprising that the industrial, commercial occupations and the liberal professions, with their "unregulated consciences which elevate to a rule the lack of rule," are the ones that "furnish the greater number of suicides" (1897b:257).

Durkheim identified a fourth type of suicide as well. Just as altruistic suicide was the opposite of egoistic suicide, Durkheim found **fatalistic suicide** to be the opposite of anomic suicide. His discussion of fatalistic suicide was very brief, however, and he accorded it little significance in the whole sociological account of the nature of suicide. Fatalistic suicide was the result of excessive social regulation, of "persons with futures pitilessly blocked and passions violently choked by oppressive discipline" (1897b:276, fn.25). Historically, the suicides of slaves and those subject to "excessive physical and moral despotism" were examples of this form of suicide. In modern society, fatalistic suicide occurred among very young husbands and childless married women, but Durkheim insisted that in general it had "little contemporary importance and examples are hard to find" (1897b:276, fn.25).

Egoistic and anomic suicide are similar as both are the result of "society's insufficient presence in individuals" or too little regulation (1897b:258). In egoistic suicide, the deficit is in "truly collective activity, thus depriving the latter of object and meaning"; in anomic suicide, society's influence is deficient in controlling "individual passions, thus leaving them without a check-rein" (1897b:258). Ego-istic suicide is the consequence of too little **integration,** and anomic suicide is the consequence of too little **regulation**.[3] In contrast, altruistic suicide is the result of overattachment to society, and fatalistic suicide the result of overregulation.

The effects of social integration and regulation on suicide have interesting gender consequences in Durkheim's account. Religious ties and stable family and political structures protect the individual from egoistic suicide. But Durkheim found that the protective integration of the family has different consequences for women and men, as evidenced by the fact that married women in his era had much higher suicide rates than unmarried women in any age group. Married women also had much higher rates than married men, especially when divorce was unavailable. Where divorce was available, more men committed suicide than women. In addition, the suicide rate was much lower for single women between the ages of 20 and 45 years than for single men in the same age group.

From these findings Durkheim concluded that *"From the standpoint of suicide marriage is more favorable to the wife the more widely practiced divorce is; and vice versa"* (1897b:269). Marriage does women "less service than it does a man" (1897b:275). Men need marriage, especially indissoluble marriage. Unlike women, who are "instinctive creatures" and are "more effectively restrained by biological imperatives than by intellectual preoccupations," men require the so-cial regulation and restraint of their desires. For men, "love is a far more mental than organic fact." When a man is forced "to attach himself forever to the same woman," then "his passion is forbidden to stray" and "its fixed object [the wife] is forbidden to fail him" (1897b:270). Monogamy is a restraint "without any great advantages" for a woman, but for men it is a positive protection, especially as "custom . . . grants him certain privileges which allow him in some measure to lessen the strictness of the regime" (1897b:272). Generally speaking, then, married women's suicides, especially in regions where divorce is prohibited, are fatalistic suicides occasioned by excessive sexual regulation.

Marriage protects men not only from egoistic suicide but also from anomic suicide. Because sexual passion no longer has the "regular, automatic periodic-ity it displays in animals" but is complicated by "aesthetic and moral feelings," it requires social regulation (1897b:270). The mental rather than the physical im-petus to passion is, however, more characteristic of men than women. A woman's "sexual needs have less of a mental character, because generally speaking, her mental life is less developed," so that the discipline of marriage that provides "moral calmness and tranquility" for men is without "any great advantages" to women (1897b:272). Marriage is, in fact, a source of restraint for women. In contrast, unmarried men can constantly seek new pleasures and partners. But in the search, "new hopes constantly awake, only to be deceived, leaving a trail of weariness and disillusionment behind"(1897b:271). The result

---

[3]In a test of Durkheim's thesis that suicide varies in relation to social integration, Breault (1986) found that for the period 1933–1980 in 216 counties in 50 states in the United States, levels of family and religious integration were indeed related to suicide rates; the relationship with political integration was not so clear-cut, however. Overall, Durkheim's thesis was supported.

is likely to be a "state of disturbance, agitation and discontent which inevitably increases the possibilities of suicide" (1897b:271). The bachelor's anomic state is potentially that of the married man where divorce is readily available.

In his review of the statistics on marriage, divorce, and suicide, Durkheim concluded that, contrary to the usual assumptions in his era, marriage is good for men but bad for women. Monogamy, which is "often represented as a sacrifice made by man of his polygamous instincts, to raise and improve women's condition," is in fact a sacrifice that women make, and the supposed liberty that men renounce turns out to be a "source of torment to him" (1897b:275). This finding seems to apply today if the greater readiness of men to remarry after divorce or widowhood is any guide.

Despite these findings, Durkheim proposed that marriage be made even more restrictive by eliminating divorce. This proposal was offered as a temporary solution to the current pathology. As he pointed out, all societies had a "greater or lesser aptitude for suicide," and a certain level of suicide must be regarded as normal. But "all proofs combine . . . to make us consider the enormous increase in the number of voluntary deaths within a century as a pathological phenomenon becoming daily a greater menace" (1897b:370). Eliminating divorce would reduce the pathological levels of suicide among married men—although Durkheim recognized that "what makes the problem especially disturbing and lends it an almost dramatic interest is that the suicides of husbands cannot be diminished in this way without increasing those of wives." The result is an "antimony which is insoluble" (1897b:384).

Durkheim asked, "Must one of the sexes necessarily be sacrificed, and is the solution only to choose the lesser of two evils?" It seemed that the answer was yes to both questions. The lesser evil was to make marriage more indissoluble until men and women became "creatures of the same nature," although women would never be able to "fulfill the same functions in society as man" (1897b:384–385). In the meantime, to try to alleviate the suicidal tendencies of married women, Durkheim suggested that wives might assume more of the aesthetic functions of social life and thus free men to pursue the "functions of utility." In this way the sexes would "approximate each other by their very differences." How this problematic state of affairs between men and women originated will be examined in the next section.

Nature of Society, Humans, and Change

Under "normal" conditions, in Durkheim's view, the progression of societies from mechanical to organic solidarity was a progression from homogeneity to heterogeneity, or from similarity to difference, at all social levels and for all individuals. Just as tasks, or functions, become more specialized as societies move toward the organic, so individuals become more specialized. Social change was inevitable, although it could lead to problems for social stability and human development. This view of social change fueled Durkheim's analyses of the nature of society.

Durkheim's overriding sociological task was the development of a "positive science of moral acts" (Durkheim, 1904:127). To this end, he suggested that each society at any given moment in its history has a "moral discipline appropriate to it." Morality is not some abstract universal, but a set of "diverse moral standards" linked with institutions that vary over time and place (Nandan, 1980:129). In fact, there can be no society without moral regulation; "man is man only because he lives in society. Take away from man all that has a social origin and nothing is left but an animal on a par with other animals" (Durkheim, 1992:60).

Moral standards may vary, but they are always under the jurisdiction of the collectivity. In modern society, that collectivity is the **state**. The "fundamental duty of the State" is to call the individual to a "moral way of life" (1992:69). Consequently, "moral individuality, far from being antagonistic to the State, has on the contrary been a product of it. It is the State that sets it free" (1992:68–69). The state does not tyrannize over the individual, but rather "redeems the individual from society"(1992:69). Through the state, the cult of individuality takes the place of "religious cults of former times"; it is "just as simple for men to draw together to work for the greatness of man as it is to work for the glory of Zeus or Jehovah or Athena" (1992:69–70).

The state may act in place of religion in modern society, but it obtains its legitimacy in this role by its emergence from religion. In fact, religion is fundamental to the nature of society.

Not until 1895, according to Durkheim, did he achieve a "clear view of the essential role played by religion in social life" and begin to tackle religion sociologically (Lukes, 1973:237). Durkheim became convinced that religion "contains in itself from the very beginning . . . all the elements which . . . have given rise to the various manifestations of collective life" (Durkheim, 1896–1897:350–351). He hoped that by understanding how religion, as the essence of collective solidarity, functioned in more primitive societies he could discover how egoism and anomie, which demonstrate the absence of collective solidarity, could be alleviated in modern society.

Society and Religion   In looking for the essence of religion, Durkheim's primary empirical referent was the society of the Arunta aborigines of Australia. This society, and other primitive societies, he believed, offered "privileged cases . . . because they are simple cases" in which "life is reduced to its essential traits"; they are therefore "less easily misunderstood" (1912:18–19).

Durkheim first looked at previous explanations and theories of religion and rejected them. For example, he rejected the idea that religion arose out of primitive man's need to explain cosmic, often catastrophic, natural events. "Even supposing that this sensation of being 'overwhelmed' were really able to suggest religious ideas, it could not produce this effect on the primitive, for he does not have it. He is in no way conscious that cosmic forces are so superior to his own . . . he attributes to himself an empire over things which he really does not have, but the illusion of which is enough to prevent his feeling dominated by them" (1912:105). Religion was not an "illusion" or an "inexplicable hallucination," but a truth. It expressed the "eternal truth that outside of us there exists something greater than us, with which we enter into communion." Religion is the means by which individuals "represent to themselves the society of which they are members" (1912:257).

Durkheim defined **religion** as *"a unified system of beliefs and practices relating to sacred things, that is to say, things set apart and forbidden—beliefs and practices which unite into one single moral community called a Church, all those who adhere to them"* (1912:62).

The essence of religion is to be found in beliefs and practices. The common denominators for all religions are found in the beliefs that divide the world into sacred and profane, along with prescriptions of particular ways of behaving toward the sacred. Animals, plants, places, or people can be designated as sacred; the key is that **sacred** things are set apart and dealt with in ritualized ways. Most particularly, the sacred thing is *"par excellence* that which the profane should not touch, and cannot touch with impunity"* (1912:55). As a result, any individual moving from the **profane**, or secular, world into the world of the sacred must undergo purification rituals.

The sacred is not an intrinsic property of the object or thing; it is something that is added. The addition of the sacred designation explains why it is that when an object is broken up, each of the parts "is equal to the whole." For example, the "debris of the relic," exemplified in the medieval trade in pieces of the "true cross," has the same virtue as the whole (1912:261–262).

Once the sacred attribution has been conferred, the object or thing becomes a symbol or totem of the group's identity. The **totem** is the "outward symbol and visible form" of the "totemic principle or god." It is therefore the "source of the moral life" of the group or clan (1912:219, 236). The totemic principle or god is "nothing else than the clan itself, personified and represented to the imagination under the visible form of the animal or vegetable which serves as totem" (1912:236). Durkheim noted that some Australian totems included the kangaroo, crow, sun, moon, plants, or even "some particular organ of the animal . . . such as the tail or stomach of an opossum, the fat of the kangaroo" (1912:125). The totem is a collective moral force that acts upon and is incorporated into the individual consciousness of each clan member. Worship of the totem is therefore worship of the clan.

The moral force of the clan is impressed upon the individual consciousness through collective rituals and ceremonies. **Positive rituals** are those that maintain the sanctity of the sacred, whereas **negative rituals** protect the sacred or purify the individual to enter into contact with the sacred. These rituals and ceremonies may produce exalted states in which the individual feels "dominated and carried away by some sort of external power which makes him think and act differently than in normal times" so that it "seems to him he has become a new being" (1912:249). The loss of self in the collective experience may release such powerful passions that individuals feel themselves transported out of themselves. These experiences are in contrast to daily life, which "drags wearily along." It is in these exalted moments that the "religious idea seems to be born" (1912:251).

Exaltation and loss of self-control are especially important for the affirmation of group identity and solidarity. All individuals want to belong to the collectivity; they want social solidarity; they want to be moral beings. It is through participation in religion and ritual that their belonging and their moral solidarity are confirmed. Religion is therefore "true," because it symbolizes group or social solidarity, and the sacred is simply "society transfigured and personified" (1912:388).

Durkheim came to the conclusion that religion is nothing less than the worship of society. The "universal and eternal objective cause" of religious sensations is society. Thus, the believer is "not deceived when he believes in the existence of a moral power upon which he depends and from which he receives all that is best in himself: this power exists, it is society" (1912:257).

Because religion is society personified, it is therefore the source of all knowledge, supplying the "fundamental categories of thought"—such as "ideas of time, space, class, number, cause, substance, personality"—that form a "solid frame" for all thought (1912:21–22). Until recently, Durkheim noted, "all moral and legal rules have been indistinguishable from ritual prescriptions." Thus, it can be said that "nearly all the great social institutions have been born in religion," including science (1912:466). Although religion was generally understood as the "mortal enemy" of science, Durkheim did not dismiss or reject religion; instead, he appropriated it to prove the existence of society sui generis (Lehmann, 1993:206). Religion has "given birth to all that is essential in society" because the "idea of society is the soul of religion" (Durkheim, 1912:466).

Durkheim considered religion the prime source of solidarity in both mechanical and organic societies. But in modern, organic society he saw a need for some secular re-creation of the format and elements of religion. The critical institution for the re-creation of solidarity and moral equilibrium, replacing religion, was education. Education was essential for molding human nature for organic solidarity.

Education and Morality   In the mechanical type of society, the moral code is pervasive, authoritarian, and taken for granted. In the organic type, moral codes are subject to scrutiny and critique, which introduces the possibility of a "pathological loosening of moral authority upon the lives of individuals" (Nisbet, 1974:192). Durkheim thought that the egoism and anomie of modern life illustrated the lack of moral authority. The institution critical for the prevention of such pathologies was, in Durkheim's view, education.

Whether education should be subject to religious or secular control was a controversial issue in late nineteenth-century France (Giddens, 1978:72). Durkheim firmly believed that a secular, state-controlled education system, rather than a religious or family-based one, was necessary. His conviction attracted the Director of Higher Education's attention and furthered his career, as with the scholarship to Germany.

In his opening series of lectures at the Sorbonne in 1902, Durkheim laid out his position on the nature of education in modern society. In these lectures, Durkheim introduced a secular morality founded on the social valuation of individualism. This individualism was not an egoistic hedonism, but a collectively agreed upon moral stance that emphasized respect for the personal dignity of the individual (Marske, 1987:3). This collective moral stance, according to Durkheim, should be the central focus of the education process.

Education was to include both moral socialization and vocational training. The three basics of moral education were devotion to society or collective ideals, discipline, and autonomy. To counter the potential pathological individualism of modern life, the young must first be taught the value of abstract moral beliefs—such as justice, peace, and individual dignity—and only later taught the skills required for specialized occupational roles. This priority was important because human beings are egoists as well as moral beings; in the young, the unstable urges of egoism predominate.

Discipline of children, then, must consist of restraint over the passions, rather than any physical, corporal form of punishment. If "one of the chief aims of moral education is to inspire in the child a feeling for the dignity of man," then corporal punishment is a "continual offence to this sentiment" (1925:183).

According to Durkheim, the young should be taught that "to be free is not to do what one pleases; it is to be master of oneself, to know how to act with reason and accomplish one's duty" (1925:21). Inculcating this philosophy should be easy because the young are suggestible. The teacher therefore becomes the "interpreter of the great moral ideas of his time and country" who molds future citizens (1925:155).

Such a secular, humanist education would produce enlightened consent to collective moral ideals and an individual capacity to restrain passion and desire. An education of this type was necessary because, unlike in previous periods, "Morality no longer consists in merely behaving, even intentionally behaving, in certain required ways. Beyond this, the rule prescribing such behaviour must be freely desired, . . . freely accepted; and this willing acceptance is nothing less than enlightened assent" (1925:120). The result would be the ideal, moral citizen—an autonomous individual who understood and freely accepted the reasons for, and necessity of, moral behavior.[4]

Once the foundations of morality are laid, then vocational education can commence. Vocational education was to be tailored to the "specific milieu" for which the individual was "specifically destined." According to Durkheim, individuals are "destined to fulfill a special function in the social organism" and must learn in advance how to play their role. This did not mean that the "child should be brought up prematurely for a particular occupation, but he should be induced to like limited tasks and well-defined horizons" (1893:341, fn.3). Again, the key feature of vocational education was the regulation of desire and the tempering of expectations. However, to prevent this sort of constraint from becoming too onerous, the occupational role must be matched to the individual's natural talents and abilities. If these educational goals could be met, the pathology of the "forced division of labour" would be eliminated. The result would be that "social inequalities exactly express precisely natural inequalities" (1893:313).

Durkheim seems oblivious in this prescription to the possibility that education might restrict an individual's life chances, or that it might perpetuate racial and gender hierarchies (Lukes, 1973:133). Perhaps his blindness to these issues is related to his generally functionalist stance, which focuses on how human

---

[4]Durkheim's debt to Rousseau seems clear. The acceptance of traditional, usually religious, ideals without reflection was anathema to both. For both, modern individualism demanded enlightened, freely chosen assent to collective ideals.

beings should adapt to society rather than on how individuals adapt society to their own ends (Zeitlin, 1997:357).

The Duality of Human Nature   In *The Elementary Forms of Religious Life*, Durkheim indicated that all religious beliefs propound the idea of a sacred soul separate from, but located in, the profane body. He concluded that all individuals are "really made up of two beings facing in different and almost contradictory directions, one of whom exercises a real pre-eminence over the other. Such is the profound meaning of antithesis which all men have more or less clearly conceived between the body and the soul, the material and the spiritual beings who coexist within us" (1912:298). In short, human nature is dual. This duality of human nature he saw also reflected in two forms of intelligence: "On the one hand, are sensation and sensory tendencies, on the other, conceptual thought and moral activity." These tendencies are not only distinct, they are also "opposed to one another" (1914:327).

Man is thus both an "angel" and a "beast," not exclusively one or the other (1914:329). The "beast" is egotistical and sensual, whereas the "angel" is moral and altruistic. The result of this dichotomy is that "we cannot pursue moral ends without causing a split within ourselves, without offending the instincts and penchants that are most deeply rooted in our bodies" (1914:328).

How does this duality arise? How is it that the human being is a "monster of contradictions" that can never be satisfied? The answer, Durkheim indicated, was to be found originally in religion. Sacred things are collective ideals that originate in the group but come to have ascendancy over the group. "When these ideals move our wills, we feel that we are being led, directed, and carried along by singular energies that manifestly, do not come from us but are imposed on us from outside" (1914:335). The result is that man not only "feels himself to be double"; he actually is double (1914:337).

All human beings experience this duality as conflict between sensory appetites and intellectual and moral tendencies. For individuals to be social beings, they must constantly "do violence to certain . . . strongest inclinations" and appetites (1914:339). The conflict is less obvious or important in mechanical societies, but it becomes significant in organic societies as individuals become aware of their autonomy. Durkheim predicted that the "struggle between the two beings within us" would increase with the progress of civilization. Collective bodies would need to progress as well in order to curb sensory tendencies and control the psychological conflict.

Durkheim suggested that men experience and understand the dualism and the conflict it represents but that women, because they are firmly fixed in their biology, experience it very little and understand it even less. Women's sensibility is "rudimentary rather than highly developed," with the result that "society is less necessary to her because she is less impregnated with sociability" (1897b: 215). Durkheim believed that "civilized" women evolved in such a way that they were "naturally" subject to sensory passions and appetites, to the virtual exclusion of moral and intellectual tendencies. For example, because they are guided by their passions and appetites, women could "endure life in isolation more easily than men" as the case of old, unmarried women demonstrates. As

Durkheim saw it, "With a few devotional practices and some animals to care for, the old unmarried woman's life is full" (1897b:215). Men in contrast are "more complex," and their moral balance is more easily upset. They could only maintain their "equilibrium . . . by finding points of support outside" themselves (1897b:216). For this reason Durkheim recommended that marital bonds be strengthened, despite the problems that might result, including a higher suicide rate among wives.

The duality of human nature was thus mirrored in gender duality. Durkheim saw the difference between men and women in modern society as the difference between the "primitive, physical, amoral, profane, inferior—the relatively non-human—and the modern, mental, moral, sacred, superior—the absolutely human" (Lehmann, 1995:576).

Class, Gender, and Race

Durkheim had little to say about race. Although he did not address the issue of class directly, his discussion of modern industrial society has relevance for the question of social class. His comments on gender are numerous and scattered throughout his work.

Class   As you have seen, Durkheim believed that individualism and specialized state institutions develop together. The function of the state is to ensure the freedom and dignity of each individual by coordinating the interests and needs of all individuals. Using an organic analogy, the state is society's "brain" or consciousness (1992:89).

Durkheim maintained that, except for some abnormal cases, the "stronger the State, the more the individual is respected" (1992:96). In modern society, however, the state was too remote to provide daily moral guidance; furthermore, a state that was too strong might oppress the individual. For these reasons, Durkheim saw a need for "secondary cadres to interpose between the individual and the State" (1992:96). He thought two groups might qualify as these "secondary cadres": regional districts and professional groups. Regional districts were less important than professional or occupational groups, because with a mobile population ties among the members were too easily broken. The professional or occupational group, however, was "omnipresent" and "ubiquitous" and exerted control over the major part of any individual's life. An occupational group "follows the workers wherever they go"; workers find it "enveloping them, recalling them to their duties, supporting them at need" (1897b:379).

Durkheim believed that the organization of occupational groups within specialized industrial corporations could act as the primary source of social solidarity in modern society. Similar to medieval guilds, the occupational or professional groups would counter the anomie and egoism of modern life. In addition, these groups would eliminate the issue of social class, because no longer would rich and poor be opposed "as if the only possible solution consisted of diminishing the portion of one in order to augment that of the other" (1897a:246). Individuals would be assigned to functions that matched their natural abilities, and these functions would be rewarded according to their value to the collectivity.

The decisions as to value and reward would be determined by elected assemblies of representatives of the employer, or managers, as well as of the workers. Consequently, the occupational or professional group would curb the "appetites" of both employer and worker and "set a limit to the state of disarrangement, excitement, frenzied agitation"—the anomie and egoism—characteristic of modern society (1897a:247).

As a basis for political representation, the establishment of such groups would not require, in Durkheim's view, a wholesale transformation of society. In addition, these arrangements would eliminate any reason for the implementation of socialism or even communism.

Durkheim was interested in and sympathetic to socialist ideas. He defined **socialism** as "every doctrine which demands the connection of all economic functions, or of certain among them, which are at the present time diffuse, to the directing and conscious centres of society" (1897a:54). He emphasized the idea of "connection, not subordination" because socialism involves the integration of government and industrial and commercial life. However, Durkheim opposed some aspects of socialism as articulated by others, such as class war and social change that might benefit only one part of society (1897a:34).

Durkheim distinguished socialism from communism, even though their mutual rejection of capitalism gave them a "certain family resemblance" (1897a:75). Communism, in Durkheim's view, was a primitive solution, an abstract philosophical conception produced by "secluded men" dealing with "problems of general morality while enclosed in study rooms" (1897a:73). Socialism was at least the work of "men of action." It was a response to the progress of industrialization and capitalism and was more practical and relevant. However, he considered both socialism and communism to be simplistic and flawed, because both saw society as simply an economic system rather than a moral entity.

Durkheim's solution to the anomie and egoism of modern life was thus the development of social solidarity within occupational or professional groups. Note, however, that this is essentially a solution to male anomie and egoism. Durkheim assumed that the inevitable progression of specialization and division of labor differentiated not only functions or tasks but also men and women. Men and women were becoming quite different species with different but complementary functions, and only men were likely to inhabit a workplace amenable to the development of a supportive occupational group.

Gender   Durkheim, like many other late-nineteenth- and early-twentieth-century commentators, believed that modern society produced pathological gender relations. The accepted wisdom was that there were fundamental physical and mental differences between the sexes and that these natural, or biologically based, differences meant that women and men were suited to quite different tasks, or functions, in social life. Problems arose when disruptions to the traditional gender divisions distorted the "natural" abilities of the sexes.

For Durkheim, the gender issue and the associated disruptions and distortions were particularly serious because they affected the harmony and stability of society. As you have seen in his discussions of suicide, disruptions to the "natural" roles played by the sexes could have, in his view, profound negative social consequences. These negative consequences were especially evident with respect to marriage and the family.[5]

Durkheim made a critical distinction between marriage and family relations in connection with the division of labor and in connection with social solidarity.

Regarding the division of labor, Durkheim noted that the various functions performed by the family were at first "undivided and confounded with one another" but became, over time, "separated . . . apportioned among relatives according to sex, age, relations of dependence, in a way to make each of them a special functionary of domestic society" (1893:124). With modernization, specialized, differentiated social structures gradually expanded and took over functions originally performed by the family, such as medical care, education, and occupational training (Mauss, cited in Simpson, 1965:532, fn.15). The progressive division of labor in the family was accompanied by the progressive contraction of family relations and the increasing political and legal regulation of marriage by society. The modern conjugal family came to be defined as "the husband, the wife, and minor and unmarried children."

Durkheim suggested that the first family group was the homogeneous clan united around a sacred totem. He claimed that the Iroquois represented "an almost wholly pure model" of such an unspecialized family group. Among the Iroquois, he suggested, "adults of both sexes are equal to one another" and "kinship itself is not organized, for the term cannot be applied to the fact that the mass of the people is distributed in various generation layers." Among the Iroquois, "all persons of the same age were linked to one another in the same degree of kinship."[6] Although there were some "special ties of obligation joining the child to his maternal relatives," these ties did not "appreciably differ from those he maintained with other members of society" (1893:127).

As societies move from mechanical to organic solidarity, the undifferentiated clan organization gradually gives way to patriarchal families dominated by the father and then to modern conjugal families. In primitive, mechanical society the maternal ties are more important than ties with the father and his family, and the "natural supremacy of the husband is held in check." But as society develops, and a "stronger governmental organization and a more active life" is required, the patriarchal family emerges (Durkheim, 1904:179).

In Durkheim's view, the transition from clan to patriarchal family to conjugal family is connected to the fact that family solidarity rests on both persons and things: "We are attached to our family because we are attached to the people who compose it. But we are attached to it also because we cannot do without material things, and under the regime of family communism it is the family that possesses these things." But as the family contracts in size and

---

[5]Nandan (1980:115) points out that Durkheim considered religion and the family as the most important "institutional elements of social structure" and that there were more reviews of family texts than any other subject in *L'Année Sociologique*.

[6]The accuracy of Durkheim's assumptions about the Iroquois social organization are somewhat questionable, but he was relying on L. H. Morgan's work, *Ancient Society*, for his information. Interestingly, Friedrich Engels also relied on Morgan for his account of early family relations in *The Origins of the Family, Private Property and the State*.

functions, family communism ceases and material things no longer serve as a significant source of solidarity. In the conjugal family, "family solidarity becomes completely personal. We are attached to our family only because we are attached to the persons of our father, our mother, our wife, our children" (Simpson, 1965:533).

Modern conjugal family solidarity is structured and maintained in two different ways—by the marital relationship and by the family group. For the husband and wife, the family includes "1. the wife or husband; 2. the children," although these two associations do not have the "same origin, nor the same nature, nor consequently . . . the same effects." The first association originates with contract and "elective affinity," the second from the natural phenomenon of consanguinity; the first unites "members of the same generation," the second unites "one generation to the next"; the first was "organized at a relatively late date," whereas the second was as "old as humanity" (Durkheim, 1897b:185). The two associations have different functions and are regulated in different ways by society.

As society progresses, the state increasingly intervenes on the children's behalf, taking them "under its protection" and ensuring that kinship ties are indissoluble. At the same time, the conjugal family has a "less common life" than the earlier patriarchal family and is "less powerfully integrated" because "all children sooner or later depart from the (paternal) homestead" (Simpson, 1965:530–531). The restricted time frame and small size of the conjugal family meant that "common sentiments and memories cannot be very intense; for there are not enough consciences in which they can be represented and reinforced by sharing them. . . . Small families are also invariably short-lived; and without duration no society can be stable" (Durkheim,1897b:202). The only way in which egoism was averted in the context of the modern conjugal family was through the need to work for the children's inheritance. Durkheim himself advocated the abolition of inheritance, but he recognized that if the "capacity to enrich the domestic patrimony" were eliminated, then the "attachment to work" and the powerful "moral stimulant" it entailed would be removed (Simpson, 1965:534). The conjugal family was thus a potentially unstable unit and left some of its members susceptible to anomie and egoism that sometimes resulted in suicide.

Durkheim believed that because family life was weakened in organic society, marriage should be strengthened. Monogamous marriage should become the norm, in contrast to former times when there was no such thing as marriage and sexual relations were rather casual affairs, "made and unmade at will, the partners being bound by no legal tie" (1893:19). However, Durkheim doubted that the conjugal relation could ever replace the family as the basis for moral action and solidarity: "conjugal society by itself is too ephemeral"—it is "dissolved by death in each generation"—and therefore a spouse "cannot be strong enough reason to make the other sacrifice momentary pleasures" (Simpson, 1965:555).

Although marriage was not sufficiently powerful protection against egoism and anomie in modern society, it remained important if only because of the children. Irregular sexual unions produced an "immoral society," and children reared in such an environment would show "many moral defects." For organic solidarity, juridical regulation of marriage was essential: "A child cannot have a moral upbringing unless he lives in a society whose every member feels his obligations towards every other member. For outside such a society there is no morality" (Simpson, 1965:536).

Ideally, for Durkheim, marriage should be indissoluble. In his examination of suicide, Durkheim regarded the prevention of divorce as the "lesser of two evils" even though it would increase the suicide rates of married women. There is a real sociological contradiction in the fact that the family provides a positive, integrative experience for men, who find in it an antidote to the anomie of public life, but that women who spend, or are supposed to spend, their life within its protective custody are immune to its positive effects. In explaining this contradiction, Durkheim, like so many of his contemporaries, resorted to a biological argument, suggesting that men are "almost entirely a product of society" whereas women are "to a far greater extent the product of nature" (Durkheim, 1897b:385). For Durkheim, biological evolution and progressive specialization of the sexes made modern women "asocial" and thus different from and inferior to men (Lehmann, 1995:924).

Gender Differentiation   Durkheim saw the strengthening of the marriage bond at the expense of extended family ties as a result of the increasing differences between men and women. In a society in which the "two sexes are only slightly differentiated," physiologically, psychologically, and socially, the marriage tie is very weak (1893:20). Such a marital state was characteristic of early mechanical society, in which the woman "was not at all the weak creature she has become as morality has progressed" (1893:18). In fact, the female form was the "close image of what was originally that single, common type from which the male sex has gradually become distinct" (1893:18). In drawing this conclusion, Durkheim relied upon travelers' reports and a scientific study of male and female brains undertaken by a Dr. Lebon. Dr. Lebon claimed to have established with "mathematical precision" that the sexes in more primitive societies were similar with regard to that "pre-eminent organ of physical and mental life, the brain" (1893:18). Over time, however, with the "advance of civilization," the brain size and "consequently the intelligence" came to exhibit "considerable differences in favour of the man" (1893:18).

The progressive differentiation of anatomy was paralleled by progressive differentiation of personality, intellect, and economic and political functions. Durkheim stated that "even now there is still a very large number of savage peoples where the woman takes part in political life" and may even accompany men to war (1893:19). Generally, in more primitive societies, women participate "in the life of man in countless ways." One of the "distinctive attributes of woman today, that of gentleness, does not originally appear to have been characteristic of her" (1893:19).

In the light of Dr. Lebon's finding that the brains of men and women had become more differentiated with the progress of civilization, Durkheim concluded that in modern society women should take care of the affective or emotional functions and men the intellectual functions. Physiological differences were matched with functional role differences, which were, in turn, functional for social solidarity.

Marriage was an important example of the solidarity that the sexual division of labor produced. As Durkheim pointed out, sexual attraction is based on similarity and love that "presumes a certain harmony of thought and feeling," but the real energy and character of sexual attraction is difference. It is "because men and women differ from one another that they seek out one other with such passion" (1893:17). It is thus "the sexual division of labor which is the source of conjugal solidarity" (1893:18).

The progressive division of labor is also evidence for Durkheim of the progress of civilization. Thus there can be no reason "to suppose that woman may ever be able to fulfill the same functions in society as man" (1897b:385). In fact, male and female roles would presumably become even more differentiated. Woman's domestic role was "natural" and functional in the logic of progressive specialization, as well as being important to the moral health of society.

> The moral importance of the wife's role increased to the degree that domestic life had a greater place in the context of life in general; the conjugal association became more strongly organized. For the family is unexcelled as a territory for feminine activity. But . . . it is inevitable that, at least at a given moment in history, the matrimonial bond cannot become tightly constricting and the family cannot hold together without a resulting legal subordination of the wife to her husband. For this subordination is the necessary condition of family unity. (Durkheim, 1904:209)

Durkheim considered social solidarity to be a social fact that was external to the individual and exercised coercive power over the individual. Resistance to social pressure was thus futile, if not immoral. The fact that the specialized, domestic roles of women were necessary for the moral health of men but detrimental to women was seen as an unfortunate stage in social development. It might in the future be rectified, when women would be allowed to play "more active and important" roles in society. Such roles would, however, be "peculiarly her own" as "determined by her aptitudes" and would certainly not be similar to those played by men. On the contrary, women's roles would be even more differentiated from men's, but they would be of "greater social use than in the past" (1897b:385).

In *Suicide*, Durkheim suggested that the alleviation of women's distress in marriage might be accomplished by allowing women to take over the aesthetic functions of social life, so that men could concentrate on the instrumental functions. He saw this functional division as a division between sensual, impulsive nature and rational, regulated culture.

Durkheim understood aesthetic activities as unregulated or seemingly "freed of all control and limitation" (1972:239). But if activity is to be moral, then it must be regulated. Aesthetic activity in particular needs regulation because it could encourage the expenditure of "too much energy on the superfluous." Concentrating on the imagination means that "obligatory tasks are necessarily neglected" and "all discipline appears intolerable." As a result, "too great an artistic sensibility is a sickly phenomenon which cannot become general without danger to society" (1972: 239–240). In fact, those involved in the "domain of the unreal, of the imaginary" risk losing all contact with reality when they "fully experience aesthetic feeling" (1972:110).

The point at which aesthetic activity becomes a danger to society will vary with the developmental stage reached by that society, or the individual.

The limit beyond which excess begins is, of course, variable, according to the people or the social environment. It begins much sooner as society is less advanced, or the environment less cultivated. The workingman, if he is in harmony with his conditions of existence, is and must be closed to pleasures normal to the man of letters, and it is the same with the savage in relation to civilized man. (1972:240)

This distinction between the savage and the civilized man is echoed in the distinction between modern men and women. According to Durkheim, "Woman has had less part than man in the moment of civilization," and she "recalls . . . certain characteristics of primitive natures" (1893:247). Consequently, if women are to take on the aesthetic functions in organic society, they run a risk in respect to their moral development because they are governed by their natural, sensual, or organic constitutions rather than their intelligence.

The danger of aesthetic activity is that it is individualistic, abstract, imaginative work undertaken at the expense of collective, practical, moral action in the world. The danger is increased when aesthetic activity takes morality as its subject matter. When this occurs, "art makes us live an existence on the level of ideas which, save that it is fictional and imaginary, has the external characteristics of a truly moral life." The danger with these preoccupations is that we will come to believe, for example, that we are dutiful "because we are capable of eloquently praising duty or because we receive pleasure from hearing others offer such eloquent praise" (1972:111). How much more dangerous must such activities be to women who are already less amenable to moral restraint. Nonetheless, Durkheim assigned to these "more primitive" beings modern society's aesthetic functions in combination with its domestic functions.

In the interests of theoretical symmetry, although of doubtful gender accuracy, the aesthetic sphere of sensations and imagination is the counterpart, in Durkheim's account, to the rational, intellectual realm of economic and political activities, and each is gender specific. Durkheim was not alone is assuming that civilization was dependent upon "natural" (that is, biologically determined) female functions and that the mark of social progress was the control of nature—which, by definition, included the control of "natural" women by men.

To maintain these contradictory assertions, Durkheim used a classic nineteenth-century idea (which retains considerable currency today): the notion of "different but equal." Woman must "seek for equality in the functions which are commensurate with her nature," and in modern society these functions were essentially domestic. Any alteration of this functional division of labor would contribute to the "weakening of the organic unity of the family and of marriage," which "must inevitably dry up the source of woman's rise to higher status." The feelings of "respect that have directed her way . . . originate, in large part, in the religious respect inspired by hearth and home."[7] In fact, the evolution of the

---

[7] Durkheim made these comments in his review of Marianne Weber's *Ehenfrau und Mutter in der Rechsentwicklung* (Tübingen: Mohre, 1907). His review was critical of Weber's call for easier divorce laws and for the complete equality of sexes before the law. He suggested that she had failed to grasp the "complexity of the problem" because her basic premise was that the patriarchal family demanded women's complete subservience, which Durkheim felt was "wide open to question."

patriarchal family, he suggested, produced a more intense and important family life in which the "woman's role, which is precisely to preside over life indoors, has . . . assumed more importance, and the moral scope of the wife and mother has increased" (1910:288). At the same time, the marital relationship was closer because the "centre of gravity in the life of the male has ceased to be sidetracked away from the home as much as in the past." As family matters increasingly "intervene to occupy a man's mind, the more he falls out of the habit of regarding his wife as an inferior" (1910:288). Consequently, turn-of-the-century feminist demands for greater equality, less stringent divorce laws, and the greater participation of women in public life would lead, Durkheim maintained, to a diminished domestic stature. The "gains she will settle for with the acquisition of rights claimed in her behalf will be offset by important losses" (1910:288–289). Durkheim considered feminism to be based on the false assumption that men and women are similar and equal (Lehmann, 1993:11).

Like so many of the classical sociologists, Durkheim's sociological imagination seems to have deserted him when it came to the question of gender. The moral health of modern society was the matter of paramount importance to Durkheim, and he regarded feminist demands at the turn of the century as jeopardizing social harmony and stability—just as they are regarded by some observers today.

Other Theories and Theorists

Durkheim was passionately engaged with the new discipline of sociology, and his early training introduced him to sociology's French predecessors. His doctoral thesis (written in Latin) was on Montesquieu's *De l'esprit des lois*. Although Durkheim was critical of Montesquieu, he did appreciate Montesquieu's recognition of the need for a discipline such as sociology. He admired Montesquieu's identification of diverse societal types, his "refusal to deduce 'rules valid for all peoples' from artificial first principles" and his "explanation of the *esprit* of each societal type as the natural consequence of structural features" (Jones, 1994:33). Durkheim also agreed with Montesquieu's refusal to explain law in terms of human nature or original covenants with God.

Although Montesquieu understood society as a reality apart from the individual, Jean-Jacques Rousseau's elaboration of this idea had a greater influence on Durkheim. Rousseau's idea of society as a separate, moral phenomenon, combined with his idea of a general will as the expression of social solidarity, contributed to Durkheim's ideas about moral education, collective consciousness, and social order.

These ideas also made Saint-Simon's work appealing to Durkheim. You may recall from Chapter 2 that Saint-Simon equated socialism with science. In his review of Saint-Simon's work, however, Durkheim concluded that socialism was not a science. He noted that "even the strongest work—the most sympathetic, the richest in ideas—that this school has produced: Marx's *Capital*" was not scientific. By the same token, *laissez-faire* capitalist theories were equally unscientific. Socialism was not a "sociology in miniature—it is a cry of grief, sometimes of anger, uttered by men who feel most keenly our collective *malaise*. Socialism is to the facts which produce it what the groans of a sick man are to the illness with which he is afflicted. . . . But what would one say of a doctor who accepted the replies and desires of his patient as scientific truths?" (1897a:41). But as socialist and capitalist economic theories are social facts, they can be the objects of scientific sociological study (1897a:41–42).

Durkheim recognized that Saint-Simon had grasped the significance of industrialization, which was "no small accomplishment" (1897a:245). However, Saint-Simon had made the mistake of assuming that change required that "industry should be organized without subordinating it to anything," which meant that he proposed as "a remedy, an aggravation of the evil" (1897a:245). Durkheim pointed out that individuals are not "naturally inclined to . . . use self-restraint," and if they "follow no rule except that of clear self-interests, in the occupations that take up nearly the whole of our time, how should we acquire a taste for any disinterestedness, or selflessness or sacrifice?" Unrestrained "unleashing of economic interests" would be accompanied by the "debasing of public morality" (1897a:12). Durkheim concluded that socialism was a process of "economic concentration and centralization" and that a socialist state would still be afflicted with "wretched people and inequalities of every kind" (1897a:90).

Durkheim called Saint-Simon sociology's harbinger, but Comte its "father." Comte gave sociology the "beginnings of its existence"; he "defined its method and established its framework" (1893:377). The important ideas that Durkheim took from Comte were (1) that in the discovery of social laws, facts must be governed by theory; (2) that the methods of sociology were observation, experimentation, comparison, and historical analysis; (3) that the division of labor could be a source of social solidarity; and (4) that sociology was a distinct science, irreducible to any other science, just as biology was irreducible to physics or chemistry.

Despite the importance he accorded to Comte's work, for Durkheim it remained at the level of "philosophical generalities." In the search for the "law" that dominates social evolution in general, "sociology was reduced to a single problem in Comte's work. Comte believed that he had "not only founded sociology but had also completed it at the same time" (1893:379–380). Durkheim's position was that sociology could only become a positive science when it "renounced its initial and over-all claim upon the totality of social reality" and introduced analysis that distinguished among "parts, elements and different aspects which could serve as subject matters for specific problems" (1964:380). Indeed, Durkheim's own sociological work concentrated on just such specific problems within society (Hughes, 1977:282).

Critique and Conclusions

Durkheim's work—whether concerned with gender, education, occupations, socialism, crime, or religion—was always framed by a concern about what he, as well as others, saw as the crisis of French culture, and modern European culture in general. This crisis, which characterizes many societies today, revolved around the pathologies of modern industrial society, including increased suicide rates, family and marital disruptions, economic dislocations and conflicts, and social injustice.

Durkheim considered socialism and even communism to be expressions of concern about this social malaise, but not solutions. They were not solutions because they either demanded an overwhelming state power (socialism) or eliminated any institution, such as the state, that could ensure the moral solidarity of the society (communism).

Sociology, in contrast, was part of the solution to the malaise. Sociology examined society scientifically. In doing so, it was able to pinpoint social pathologies as well as offer solutions to policymakers and politicians. Thus, Durkheim's sociology was functional as well as ethical.

Durkheim understood society as an objective reality in which specialized functions contributed to the stability and harmony of the whole. In a *modern, industrial, capitalist society,* stability and order were essential. However, harmony could only be attained with the protection of individual rights. Consequently, any solutions to the disruptions facing such a society could not be simply functional—as in a restoration of order—but must also address the need for radical reforms.

Despite the *conservative* label that has been attached to Durkheim, his analyses of the profound changes affecting modern societies have a *radical* cast. This radical element in Durkheim's work is often overlooked, especially in the work of twentieth-century functionalists. Although much of the functionalist work, especially in American sociology, claims descent from Durkheim, it is generally purged of Durkheim's "critical analysis of modern social pathology" (Gane, 1992:5).

We have discussed Durkheim's work in some detail largely because it has been a central referent for much of twentieth-century Western sociology. It was particularly important to the mid-twentieth-century structural-functionalist school, as you will see in Chapter 14. His influence also extends beyond sociology into anthropology, history, criminology, and linguistics.

Final Thoughts

Durkheim's four most important contributions to sociological theory are:

- His conception of the discipline of sociology as the scientific study of society, which he understood as an objective reality standing apart from the individual

- His insistence that social phenomena must be understood in terms of their social function, or their contribution to the whole

- His methodological prescriptions

- His conception of social evolution and the nature of modernity

Throughout his work, Durkheim attempted to reconcile freedom with morality and individualism with solidarity (although this attempt fell short when it came to the question of gender differences).

The ethical stands that Durkheim took on the crises facing Western societies in the twentieth century complicated his positivist methodological position. Social phenomena may be "things," but they also carry meanings and therefore cannot be approached in quite the same manner as the objects of the natural world.

What is remarkable, however, is that many of the social "pathologies" Durkheim identified are still prevalent, and his analysis of their origins and consequences remains salient to sociology at the beginning of the twenty-first century. Durkheim's overriding concern was the moral disintegration of society as a result of the inevitable and progressive division of labor in modern society. His various discussions of suicide, crime, family, religion, and, of course, gender relations are all infused with his need to find a way to reestablish a harmonious, moral social order. This is what made Durkheim more than a status quo conservative. But although he wished to change society, Durkheim was not a radical. He wished to promote and protect individual autonomy without resorting to profound, revolutionary transformations. In that regard, he was quite unlike the subjects of the next section: Karl Marx, Friedrich Engels, V. I. Lenin, and Rosa Luxemburg.

References

Braudel, Fernand. 1972. "Personal Testimony." *Journal of Modern History,* 44.

Breault, K. D. 1986. "Suicide in America: A Test of Durkheim's Theory of Religious and Family Integration, 1933–1980." *American Journal of Sociology,* 92, 628–656.

Clark, Terry. 1968. "Emile Durkheim and the Institutionalization of Sociology in the French University System." *European Journal of Sociology,* 9, 37–87.

Coser, Lewis, A. 1977. *Masters of Sociological Thought.* New York: Harcourt Brace Jovanovich.

———. 1984. "Introduction." In Emile Durkheim, *The Division of Labour in Society* (W. D. Halls, Trans.). London: Macmillan.

Durkheim, Emile. 1892/1960. *Montesquieu and Rousseau.* Ann Arbor: University of Michigan Press.

———. 1893/1984. *The Division of Labour in Society* (W. D. Halls, Trans.). London: Macmillan.

———. 1895/1938. *The Rules of Sociological Method* (Sarah A. Solovay and John H. Mueller, Trans.; George G. Catlin, Ed.). New York: Free Press.

———. 1896–1897, 1897–1898/1964. "Prefaces to *L'Année Sociologique.*" In Kurt W. Wolff (Ed.), *Essays in Sociology and Philosophy* (pp. 341–353). New York: Harper Torchbook.

. 1897a/1962. *Socialism* (Alvin W. Gouldner, Ed.). New York: Collier Books,

———. 1897b/1951. *Suicide: A Study in Sociology* (John A. Spaulding and George Simpson, Trans.; George Dimpson, Ed.). New York: Free Press.

———. 1900/1964. "Sociology and Its Scientific Field." In Kurt H. Wolff (Ed.), *Essays in Sociology and Philosophy* (pp. 354–375). New York: Harper & Row.

———. 1904/1980. Review of "La Morale et la Science des Moeurs" by Lucien Lévy-Bruhl. In Yash Nandan (Ed.), *Emile Durkheim: Contributions to L'Année Sociologique* (pp. 127–130). New York: Free Press.

———. 1910. Review of "Ehefrau und Mutter in der Rechtsentwicklund: Eine Einfrunbrung" by Marianne Weber. In Yash Nandan (Ed.), *Emile Durkheim: Contributions to L'Année Sociologique* (pp. 285–289). New York: Free Press.

———. 1912/1961a. *The Elementary Forms of Religious Life* (Joseph Ward Swain, Trans.). New York: Collier Books.

———. 1914/1964. *Essays on Sociology and Philosophy* (Kurt H. Wolff, Ed.). New York: Harper and Row.

———. 1915/1964. "Sociology." In Kurt H. Wolff (Ed.), *Essays on Sociology and Philosophy* (pp. 376–385). New York: Harper & Row.

———. 1922/1956. *Education and Sociology* (S. D. Fox, Trans.). Glencoe, IL: Free Press.

———. 1925/1961b. *Moral Education*. Glencoe, IL: Free Press.

———. 1972. *Selected Writings* (Anthony Giddens, Ed. and Trans.). Cambridge: Cambridge University Press.

———. 1992. *Professional Ethics and Civic Morals* (Cornelia Brookfield, Trans.). London: Routledge.

Fenton, Steve, with Robert Reiner and Ian Hammett. 1984. *Durkheim and Modern Sociology*. Cambridge: Cambridge University Press.

Gane, Mike (Ed.). 1992. *The Radical Sociology of Durkheim and Mauss*. London: Routledge.

———. 1994. "A Fresh Look at Durkheim's Sociological Method." In W. S. Pickering and H. Martines (Eds.), *Debating Durkheim*. London: Routledge.

Giddens, Anthony. 1978. *Durkheim*. London: Fontana.

Gross, Neil. 1997. "Durkheim's Pragmatism Lectures: A Contextual Interpretation." *Sociological Theory, 15,* 126–149.

Hughes, H. Stuart. 1977. *Consciousness and Society*. New York: Vintage Books.

Jones, Robert Alun. 1994. "Ambivalent Cartesians: Durkheim, Montesquieu, and Method." *American Journal of Sociology, 100.*

Jones, Robert Alun, and Douglas A. Kibee. 1993. "Durkheim, Language and History: A Pragmatic Perspective." *Sociological Theory, 11*(2), 152–170.

Lehmann, Jennifer M. 1993. *Deconstructing Durkheim: A Post-post-structuralist Critique*. London: Routledge.

———. 1995. "Durkheim's Theories of Deviance and Suicide: A Feminist Reconsideration." *American Journal of Sociology, 100,* 904–930.

Lukes, Steven. 1973. *Emile Durkheim: His Life and Work*. London: Allen Lane, Penguin Press.

Marske, Charles E. 1987. "Durkheim's 'Cult of the Individual' and the Moral Reconstitution of Society." *Sociological Theory, 5,* 1–14.

Mestovic, Stjepan G. 1991. *The Coming Fin de Siècle*, London: Routledge.

Miller, W. Watts. 1994. "Durkheim: The Modern Era and Revolutionary Ethics." In W. H. Pickering and H. Martines (Eds.), *Debating Durkheim*. London: Routledge.

Nandan, Yash. (Ed.). 1980. *Emile Durkheim: Contributions to L'Année Sociologique*. New York: Free Press.

Nisbet, Robert. 1974. *The Sociology of Emile Durkheim*. New York: Oxford University Press.

Ritzer, George. 1992. *Classical Sociological Theory* (2nd ed.). New York: McGraw-Hill.

Parkin, Frank. 1992. *Durkheim*. Oxford: Oxford University Press.

Simpson, George. 1965. "A Durkheim Fragment: The Conjugal Family." *American Journal of Sociology, 70,* 527–536.

Thompson, Kenneth. 1982. *Emile Durkheim*. London: Tavistock Publications.

Turner, Bryan S. 1992. "Preface." In Emile Durkheim, *Professional Ethics and Civic Morals* (Cornelia Brookfield, Trans.). London: Routledge.

Zeitlin, Irving. 1997. *Ideology and the Development of Sociological Theory*. Englewood Cliffs, NJ: Prentice-Hall.

SECTION III

Radical Theory

As you learned in Section II, positivist, evolutionary, and functionalist theories contributed the following ideas to sociological theory: (1) society is understandable, and deserves scientific attention; (2) society evolves slowly and corrects its own problems, if given time; and (3) society is like an organism, with the various parts accepting the rules, being interrelated, and meeting needs or performing functions. In addition, Durkheim and others within this tradition argued that, although society is generally functional, it can be made better by creative change within the rules—a liberal viewpoint.

We come now to a theoretical stance that views capitalist society as negative and problem-producing, as oppressive instead of functional, and as needing to be completely overthrown and replaced. The early radical theorists you will encounter in this section—Karl Marx and Friedrich Engels in Chapter 5 and V. I. Lenin and Rosa Luxemburg in Chapter 6—are explicitly anticapitalist.

Against the view that consensus or a social contract formed the "good" society and stopped the war of all against all, an idea articulated by Thomas Hobbes in the 1600s, the radicals often viewed human nature as intrinsically good and industrial capitalist society as evil. Against the conservative position that capitalism signifies freedom and opportunity, Marx and his followers argued that the nature of capitalist society is coercive, with little freedom or opportunity except for the rulers or leaders of society. Against the idea that capitalist competition benefits the entire society, even those at the bottom (an idea that may remind you of "trickle-down" economics), the radicals claimed that capitalists live off the labor and at the expense of those who work for them. Against the smooth-running, efficient, and organism-like division of labor, the radicals argued that such specialization eliminates the meaning of work for the worker. Against the idea of slow, self-corrective change, the radicals asserted the need to overthrow capitalism.

Thus, by the time you finish reading Chapters 5 and 6, you will have been exposed to two opposing views of and explanations for the modern world.

Much of the rest of the book will add to one side or the other of this argument. Chapters 14 and 18 expand on the conservative themes, and Chapters 16 and 17 present twentieth-century versions of radical theory. In addition, radical feminist critiques are found throughout the book, but especially in Chapters 11 and 22.

Before reading Chapters 5 and 6, you should note that conservative and radical ideologies need not be society-specific. This means that in an avowedly Marxist society, the status quo conservative position would be Marxist, not capitalist, and the radical position would be held by those seeking to overthrow the Marxist status quo. But as we have already noted, this book focuses on Western societies, most of which are at least ideologically capitalist, if not so in all their characteristics.

We turn now to Marx, his colleague Engels, and the second-generation Marxists, Lenin and Luxemburg.

Chapter 5

Radical Anticapitalism
Marx and Engels

When a group of shareholders in Royal Dutch/Shell Group, led by the Worldwide Fund for Nature, presented a resolution this year at the annual meeting demanding that the largest Western oil company become a better corporate citizen on environmental and human-rights issues, they didn't stand a chance. The proposal was defeated by an overwhelming majority. It's not that Shell investors don't care about such matters. Rather, it's that they own the stock to make money, not to clean up the planet. (de Aenlle, 1997)

If there is one thing that the anticapitalist Karl Marx and the conservative capitalist commentator agree on, it is this: the capitalist businessperson or investor is motivated by the desire to make money. Over the past two centuries, some thinkers have argued that behavior based on this motivation is the way life in the capitalist industrial world should be, while others have argued that it is what is wrong with our world.

In the early nineteenth century, Britain, and to a lesser extent Germany and France, were industrializing—ushering in the age of machines. This made for a rapid rise in productivity, but also made for difficult conditions for the workers. As France reconstructed after its Revolution, some, such as Auguste Comte, were very enthusiastic about the outcome and the future, including anti-monarchy and pro-capitalist developments. In the previous chapters you were introduced to the views of theorists, such as Comte, Spencer, and Durkheim, who saw in capitalism the solution to Europe's problems.

We come now to two thinkers, Karl Marx and Friedrich Engels, who, early in their lives, concluded that industrial capitalism was not the solution to, but the source of, the modern world's problems. Moreover, they took it upon themselves to promote radical change in their society by aggressively exposing its flaws. Marx, at the age of 26, described his role as follows: "We realize all the more clearly what we have to accomplish in the present—I am speaking of a *ruthless criticism of everything existing*—ruthless in two senses: The criticism must not be afraid of its own conclusions, nor of conflict with the powers that be" (Tucker, 1978:13).

Marx and Engels were collaborators for some 40 years. Given the closeness of their working relationship, we will not attempt to separate them, but will interweave their histories and ideas, noting when a viewpoint originated with one or the other.

Karl Marx (1818–1883) and Friedrich Engels (1820–1895)

Carl Heinrich Marx was born in the Rhenish city of Trier. He was one of nine children, and the only male among the four who lived to be 40. Just before Carl's birth, his Jewish father was baptized as a Christian, because of legislative pressure from the Prussian government. In the mid-1820s Carl—later called Karl—his sisters, and eventually his mother, were also baptized. Some commentators perceive in Karl a certain amount of insecurity and mental discomfort, resulting from his family's equivocal status. However, another suggests, "The young Karl was a strong character—we must not picture him shrinking from his school-fellows, holding his head in shame, or crying with frustration at the fact that he was different. His sisters, later in life, recalled that he bullied them mercilessly, but made up for everything by reading them wonderful stories" (Kamenka, 1983:xv).

Having begun the study of law at Bonn, Marx transferred to the University of Berlin, where the influence of the philosopher G. W. F. Hegel was still dominant five years after his death. There Marx identified himself with the leftist Young Hegelians,[1] becoming an atheist, a democrat, and a radical critic of the Prussian state—and of everything else. In 1842 he became editor of a liberal newspaper, the *Rheinische Zeitung*, from which he resigned in 1843, just before marrying Jenny von Westphalen, who was from a middle-class German family. Karl's liberal—often radical—ideas caused the young couple to leave Germany, which they would seldom visit again (Kamenka, 1983:xvi). And, we should add, they began a lifelong struggle with hardship and poverty.

They settled first in Paris, which at the time had in its population socialists such as Henri Saint-Simon (see Chapter 2). In Paris Marx met a young German from Wuppertal, Friedrich Engels, the son of an industrialist. Engels was educated with a view to entering his father's enterprise. While attending lectures on Hegel in Berlin, Engels—who had not yet met Marx—became a spokesman for the Young Hegelians. In 1843 he was apprenticed to the Manchester, England, branch of his father's firm, Ermen and Engels.

---

[1]The Young Hegelians were students of Hegel's philosophy during the early 1800s. However, they rejected Hegel's metaphysical and religious interpretations of reality and truth, arguing that the way for human beings to be genuinely free is to give up the mythological and superstitious elements of Christianity and religion.

In Manchester Engels made the acquaintance of young Mary Burns, a factory worker who was involved in the English workers' movement. Burns remained Engels's companion until her death in 1863. When Engels returned to Germany in 1845, he encountered the German working-class movement and communist ideas. Later in 1845 Engels met Marx, and they embarked upon their collaboration.

Meanwhile, Marx continued to move around, leaving Paris for London and then Brussels, where he studied economics and began developing his theories. While borrowing certain techniques and language from Hegel and French socialism, he criticized Hegel, the young materialist philosopher Ludwig Feuerbach, the Young Hegelians Bruno Bauer and Max Stirner, and the liberal aspects of French socialism. In 1847, while attacking a German radical for his romanticism, Marx was asked to write with Engels a statement of principles for the Communist League. The result was *The Communist Manifesto* of 1848.

From then on Marx moved between Brussels, Paris, and Germany, but finally settled in late 1849 in London, where he spent most of his final 34 years and is buried. During those years he wrote *The Grundrisse* (1855, not published until 1939) and a major portion of *Das Capital* (between 1867 and 1880).

Marx and his family faced serious difficulties, both financially and physically. Being cut out of the family inheritance, they often lived either on the small amount he was paid for articles published in papers such as the *New York Daily Tribune* or on gifts from Engels. In 1857 a child of the Marxes died shortly after birth, and Marx's chronic liver ailment flared up, preventing him from doing much work. Engels bailed out the family with money for overdue rent and long overdue taxes (Rubel and Manale, 1975:141).

Again in 1861, the Marxes faced multiple hardships: "Marx was forced to write his friends and relatives for any aid whatever. His mother refused to help; the landlord threatened eviction; he was being sued for payment of the *Herr Vogt* printing costs; his wife was ailing; the *Presse* was printing not even half the articles he sent them" (Rubel and Manale, 1975:174).

The last 10 years of Marx's life have sometimes been described as slow deterioration and death. Without question his health problems—headaches, hepatitis, chest infections, and boils—severely restricted the creative work he was able to complete between 1873 and 1883. However, his optimism fueled in him the constant hope that good health was just ahead. The result of deterioration plus optimism was a large amount of unpublished and unfinished writing at his death, including *Das Capital*. He never wrote the major work on classes that he intended to. His unpublished material had to be unearthed and presented to the reading public by Engels or by later scholars.

Engels lived 12 more years after Marx died. He spoke at Marx's graveside in 1883, stressing both Marx's theoretical insights into capitalist society and his revolutionary mission. From then on, Engels spent his time issuing new editions of old works, such as the *Manifesto*, and publishing formerly unpublished works of Marx, such as *The Critique of the Gotha Programme* and the *Theses on Feuerbach*. In addition, Engels himself wrote several books and articles, the most important being *The Origin of the Family, Private Property, and the State*. Engels applied the dialectic to biology and other scholarly areas in which Marx was not interested (on science, see Engels, 1878). Finally, Engels's most important contribution after Marx's death was completing the last two volumes of *Das Kapital* and summarizing it in a single, brief volume.

To understand Marx's and Engels's radicalism, we must try to envision the European and world setting in which they lived and worked. Many nineteenth-century events are listed in the book's Timeline. One clear account of Marx's life (Rubel and Manale, 1975) divides it into six time periods, beginning each section with a summary of important world events. France had gone through its **bourgeois** or middle-class revolution and, in the first half of the nineteenth century, continued to struggle politically. For example, Napoleon was emperor for some time, while democrats and socialists sought to reinforce bourgeois/ capitalist control. Britain, the heartland of early industrial and capitalist expansion, was determined to avoid a revolution such as that in France, and it was Britain that Engels criticized in his book on the working classes (Engels, 1839). Germany was changing from a collection of provinces, such as Bavaria and Prussia, into a nation-state under the dynamic—even ruthless—leadership of Bismarck.

Many events during Marx's and Engels's lifetimes sound strangely familiar to us today. In 1848 Europe experienced its worst economic depression, as a poor harvest coincided with a slump in business. Southern Italians rose up against the North, and Austria joined them. During this time, representatives of Rome and Venice struggled to unite Italy, both against Austria and against an independent southern Italy. In France, radicals and socialists staged an unsuccessful coup attempt, while in Germany revolution was avoided by giving in to liberal pressure for a Reich, or nation, instead of the previous loose confederation (Rubel and Manale, 1975:33–34).

The 1850s saw the Crimean War between Russia and Turkey—one instance of Russia's ongoing quest for Balkan territory. The British continued to fight periodic wars with the Chinese, to keep open the trade in Chinese opium. A commune was established in Paris, with the aim of making France a communist country; it was soon quelled, however. At the end of the 1850s Darwin published his *Origin of Species* in Britain (Rubel and Manale, 1975:90–92), and European thinkers and writers began to lose much of their optimism about humanity.

In the 1860s a rebellion in the southern United States was put down and the slaves were freed, a development that Marx and Engels supported enthusiastically. As you can see in the Timeline, many technological advances continued to appear, including the laying of the first transatlantic cable, the opening of the Suez Canal, the steam engine, and Mendel's work on the hybridization of plants (Rubel and Manale, 1975:193).

Then in 1873 a commercial slump in the United States preceded another economic crisis in Europe (Rubel and Manale, 1975:279). Also during the 1870s, Croatia and Bosnia did battle, Germany and Austria-Hungary signed a peace accord, Queen Victoria was declared Empress of India, the Fabian (Socialist) Society was founded in England, and the telephone was invented (Rubel and Manale, 1975:279, 284–285).

We might summarize the foregoing rapidly stated nineteenth-century events as follows:

1. Major technological changes bound the world closer together, while increasing the gap between owners and workers.

2. Political struggles, for land or power, were rampant—involving Britain, France, Germany, Russia, Austria, and others.

3. Socialists and communists organized, but revolted unsuccessfully against bourgeois governments.

4. Economic crises occurred periodically, demonstrating to Marx and Engels the fragility and contradictions within capitalism.

It was the characteristics of capitalism—economic contradictions, oppression, power politics, revolution—to which Marx and Engels spoke.

Marx's and Engels's Central Theories and Methods

To introduce Marx's theories, it would be well to address two major questions: (1) his themes and intentions, and (2) whether or not they changed over his lifetime. The issue of intentions is difficult to unravel, in part because commentators have already produced so many interpretations of and viewpoints on what Marx *really* said and meant. Numerous interpretations of what Marx said are available, but the continuing question concerns what he was trying to say, or meant by what he said (Ollman, 1971:xvi). Intentions, of course, are seldom completely resolved. So we will interpret as best we can, and then allow Marx's insights to speak to our own time—even though this will go beyond what he could possibly have known or understood regarding the future.

The second question is whether or not Marx's focus changed over his lifetime. Several commentators, drawing primarily on his pre-1850 writings and on Volume 1 of *Das Capital*, concluded that the young Marx was a humanist interested in alienation, whereas the older Marx was an economist interested in labor and capital (see, for example, Zeitlin, 1967). However, for English-speakers who do not know German, fairly recent translations of the *Grundrisse* and of the *Critique* of 1859 have filled in the gap between his writings in the 1840s and after 1860.

Commentators, writing with such publications as the *Grundrisse* at their disposal, now generally conclude that Marx's work involved a slow evolution, rather than a dramatic change of focus from humanism to economics. The introduction to the *Grundrisse* states: "Marx's intellectual development is a process of 'self-clarification' (to use his own expression), which cannot either be split into periods or treated as a monolith" (McLellan in Marx, 1855:14). When the *Grundrisse* and *Critique* from the late 1850s are compared with his earlier and later writings, the gradual evolution of his concern with alienation in his writings on capitalist economics becomes evident.

Marx and Engels were social scientists and philosophers. Thus, they analyzed the contradictions and struggles between subgroups, while also prescribing and predicting change in the form of a final revolutionary upheaval. Their work began with, but disagreed with, Hegel's metaphysical and dialectical ideas of reality and truth as being in the spirit world. For Marx and Engels, the material world was reality. Their central concern was the oppression of the working classes under capitalism, and the resulting alienation of humanity from the meaning of labor. We will introduce these central issues regarding the evils of capitalism under three headings: dialectical materialism, alienation, and capitalist economics.

Dialectical and Historical Materialism   As Marx was being buried in Highgate Cemetery in London, his friend Engels summarized his theoretical contribution:

> Marx discovered the law of development of human history: the simple fact—hitherto concealed by an overgrowth of ideology—that mankind must first of all eat, drink, have shelter and clothing, before it can pursue politics, science, art, religion, etc.; that therefore the production of the immediate material means of subsistence and consequently the degree of economic development attained by a given people or during a given epoch form the foundation upon which the state institutions, the legal conceptions, art, and even the ideas on religion, of the people have been evolved, and in the light of which they must, therefore, be explained, instead of vice versa, as had hitherto been the case. (Tucker, 1978: 681)

In other words, physical survival and material production are basic to people's lives, and also to their prevailing ideas about society, human nature, what is good, even the gods.

Why was this idea revolutionary? The dominant philosophy in Germany at that time was that of G. W. F. Hegel. For Hegel, thought and mind were real, not the material world, and truth was sought, but never grasped, in that metaphysical world, the world of ideas (1807).[2] Hegel believed truth-seeking required the **dialectic** method, or the resolution of contradictions through struggle. This struggle was between being and nonbeing, but its resolution was seeking and becoming, not arriving or completing (Hegel, 1816).

Hegel's metaphysical dialectics included three important ideas: (1) People ordinarily view the world through fixed, static, commonsense categories. (2) This gives an incorrect understanding of the world. (3) Truth must be pursued through process and contradiction, meaning that A must be understood through not-A, and reconciled by means of mental struggle (Marcuse, 1941:123–124).

Truth, then, is pursued through negation, through becoming, through the reconciliation of ideas. As Engels (1875:131) stated this very complex idea: "Dialectics comprehends things and their representations . . . in their essential connection, concatenation, motion, origin, and ending." In other words, though difficult for our minds to comprehend, reality is, more than anything else, opposition, connectedness, and process.

A poster I once saw on a bus said: "You are what you eat." The young philosopher Ludwig Feuerbach developed this notion into an alternative philosophy of human life, which he called **materialism**. Instead of trying to explain the material world as an outgrowth of thought, as Hegel had done, he and his

---

[2]That is, to Hegel reality was "in God's mind," with the material world only a poor reflection of reality.

students explained thought as derived from the material world in which we live. But Feuerbach's materialist philosophy was abstract—a set of ideas to ponder, not a basis for action in the real world of labor and oppression.

Meanwhile the Young Hegelians, Max Stirner and Bruno Bauer, were also taking strong pokes at Hegel's metaphysical conception of reality. Religion, they were saying, is a fraud, and we must get rid of such notions in order to be real, free human beings. Marx not only criticized Hegel's metaphysics, but also parted company with, and strongly criticized, these Young Hegelians, whom he called "pseudo-realists." Marx offered the following analogy:

> Once upon a time an honest fellow had the idea that men were drowned in water only because they were possessed of the idea of gravity. If they were to knock this idea out of their heads, say by stating it to be a superstition, a religious idea, they would be sublimely protected against any danger from water. (Marx, 1846:2)

Thus, said Marx, do the pseudo-radicals philosophize: the "relationships of men, their chains and their limitations, are products of their consciousness" (Marx, 1846:6): get rid of these ideas—of sin, bondage, and punishment—and humanity will be free. According to Marx, the Young Hegelians who attacked both Hegel and orthodox religion were in fact arch-conservatives. They attacked phrases with other phrases, countering "believe and be saved" with "don't believe and be saved." Neither strove to change people's conditions, only their minds.

So Marx rejected both the notion of simple nonbelief and Hegel's metaphysical view of reality, while accepting the materialist view of Feuerbach and coupling it with Hegel's dynamic and dialectical process. The result was **historical materialism**: the process of change in the real world of material, physical existence. Freedom and slavery are empirical realities, not ideas, said Marx. Both a religion and an antireligion that do not change the human condition were useless, even "opiates," putting people to sleep so they do not struggle.[3] Believe what you will, but work to change your material conditions, because they are the only reality.

Alienation   Labor, as Hegel and Marx agreed, is essential to humanity. In fact, to Marx productive labor is what separates human beings from the lower members of the animal kingdom (Marx, 1846:7). In the days of the medieval guilds and before, people were absorbed in their work. They took raw materials, made them into products (whether seeds into food, or trees into houses and furnishings), and consumed/used them.

> Owner-producer-merchant-consumer were all the same person, and creative labor gave meaning to human life. Next came the separation of the

---

[3]A recent Christian hymn says: "Give thanks with a grateful heart, give thanks to the Holy One, . . . and now let the weak say I am strong, let the poor say I am rich, because of what the Lord has done for me" (Smith, 1995). Marx would say "you can give all the thanks you want, but if you are weak, you are still weak, and if you are poor, you are still poor."

merchant class. The merchant mediates between producer and consumer, and eventually goods are no longer traded for goods, but for money. Then came the separation of owner and worker in production, especially under capitalist industrialization. This is the completion of self-estrangement or alienation. (Marx, 1846:47)

Alienation, then, results from the breaking apart of the owner-worker-product-consumer syndrome. Alienation is not peculiar to industrial capitalism (Ollman, 1971:183); neither the slave nor the serf owns his or her means of production or its product. However, in capitalist industrial society, alienation has become the common condition of life.

> The *alienation* of the worker in his product means not only that his labor becomes an object, an *external* existence, but that it exists *outside him*, independently, as something alien to him, and that it becomes a power on its own confronting him. It means that the life which he has conferred on the object confronts him as something hostile and alien. (Marx, 1844:108)

Human beings under capitalism suffer from four forms of alienation: They are alienated from their work, their product, humanity or human species-being, and other people. The meaning of the first two is obvious: Because the worker does not own or control either the means of production or the product, they are externalized. As for the third form of alienation, since meaningful labor is what makes us human, we have been alienated from the essence of our humanness. Finally, the otherness or externality of labor also results in an estrangement from other people, because we do not labor with them but compete against them (Marx, 1844:114). Marx would hardly be surprised by the increasingly individualistic (egoistic) nature of the social world today. How, he would ask, could it be any other way?

According to Marx, the capitalist owners as well as the workers are alienated. In the first place, capitalists regard the goods and services produced by the workers merely as things to sell and sources of profit. Capitalists do not care who makes or buys these items, or how the workers who make them feel about the products of their labor, or how buyers use them. The capitalists' only concern is that items are produced, bought, and paid for. In addition, capitalists are alienated by knowing that they do no productive labor. And as consumers, the only difference is that the capitalists can buy and own more things than the workers can (Ollman, 1971:155). The commodity, such as a television set or video game, becomes a **fetish** for the consumer—an item that in a hollow way pretends to give meaning to life.

Today the comment is sometimes made that the laborer works and then he or she lives. That is, the money received from work makes it possible to live, or enjoy life. Marx made such a comment a century and a half ago: "The worker only feels himself outside his work, and in his work feels outside himself. He is at home when he is not working, and when he is working he is not at home" (Marx, 1844:72).

Every so often an advertisement seeks to counter the notion of the alienated or uncaring worker. A few years ago there was an ad for an automobile company that showed a worker on the assembly line demonstrating great concern for his job and the finished product. This he did by carefully checking his work on the chrome (or door hinges or cigarette lighter), talking proudly to his co-workers about the product they were producing, and then going home with a sense of satisfaction for a job well done. Such ads are intended to offset consumer doubts about workmanship—about whether workers in fact care either about their labor or the finished product.

How would Marx remedy such virtually universal alienation under capitalism? One commentator observes that, to Marx, "private property . . . is the 'summary material expression' of alienated labor, just as the division of labor is the summary expression for the real activity which occurs" (Ollman, 1971:162). To Marx, the solution would be the abolition of private property (accumulated/alienated products) and of the division of labor (specialized tasks), which also serves to alienate the worker. Communism is the solution, Marx would say, because it is "the positive abolition of private property and thus of human self-alienation and therefore the real reappropriation of the human essence by and for man" (Marx, 1844, in McLellan, 1977:89).

The replacement of private property with common ownership of the means of production under communism will restore the owner-worker-consumer syndrome. No longer will a small number of persons own both "real" property and the labor of the workers. As for the division of labor, one of its first forms was the division between town and country. This was followed by each person's having an exclusive sphere of activity. In a capitalist society, the individual becomes

> a hunter, a fisherman, a shepherd, or a critical critic, and must remain so if he does not want to lose his means of livelihood; while in communist society . . . society regulates the general production and thus makes it possible for me to do one thing today and another tomorrow, to hunt in the morning, fish in the afternoon, rear cattle in the evening, criticize after dinner, just as I have in mind, without ever becoming hunter, fisherman, shepherd, or critic. (Marx, 1846, in Tucker, 1978:160)

Later, Marx focused less on the abolition of the division of labor than on the abolition of private property, the result of his increasing attention to capitalist economics. But did Marx lose interest in alienation and become an economist? As we have noted, apparently not. The *Grundrisse*, bridging the period between *The Manuscripts* (1844) and *Das Kapital* (1860s), includes sections such as "Money as a Symbol of Alienation in Capitalist Society," "Alienation, Social Relationships, and Free Individuality," and "Alienated Labor and Capital." Thus, Marx the humanist concerned with alienation is also Marx the economist concerned with the means of production, economic exploitation, money, commodification, and labor and surplus value.

Capitalist Economics   It has been impossible to discuss materialism and alienation without introducing many of the issues that are central to Marx's theory of capitalist economics. Marx takes issue with the bourgeois assumptions of harmonious economic relations in modern society, equality of opportunity, the freedom and mobility of both laborer and capitalist, and wages as a fixed and fair basis for the economic life of the laborer. In the unalienated, noncapitalist world of the owner-worker, one's labor is the value by which one survives.

In today's world, labor still produces value. However, labor is a commodity belonging to someone other than the laborer; it is alienated labor. Products or commodities take on a "life" of their own, apart from the producer or worker. According to Marx, "the *increasing value* of the world of things proceeds in direct proportion to the *devaluation* of the world of men. Labor produces not only commodities: it produces itself and the worker as *commodity*" (Marx, 1844:107). Just as any other commodity is "made to be sold," so one's labor has to be sold in exchange for wages.

> If labor = value, so do wages = private property. Wages represent the fact that the laborer belongs to, or is a commodity owned by, the one for whom he or she labors. (Marx, 1844:117)

An additional fact of the capitalist world is that individual workers produce **surplus value**—more exchange or commodity value than they are compensated for. If in an hour a worker produces $80 worth of products (or services), and is paid $50 per hour, the surplus value produced goes to the one owning the worker's labor—the capitalist. In fact, except when money itself is used to make money, through investment and loans, the capitalist lives from the surplus value produced by the worker.

Surplus value did not originate with capitalism; it was found in slavery and feudal systems as well. However, with industrialization and the mass commodification of labor, surplus value increased manifold. The capital of the capitalists became, as Marx and Engels put it, ever more colossal. From time to time newspaper or magazine articles appear with some version of the title "And the Rich Get Richer." By 1995 Bill Gates of Microsoft was worth $14.8 billion; over the next four years his worth increased some $20 billion per year. While not every successful individual's wealth increases that rapidly, one estimate is that the wealth of the wealthiest 400 Americans increases between 25% and 30% per year—far above the growth in net worth of the average American.

Marx did not only say that the rich get richer. He argued that, as productive forces increase, the poor also get poorer, meaning that "pauperization" occurs. Some, like Durkheim, have claimed that, while the gap between top and bottom may become greater, so that the workers have a relatively smaller portion of the total value produced, they do not become poorer in absolute terms. Quite possibly, however, as workers in the developed countries rise economically, those in less developed countries may actually be worse off than before. In other words, for the world as a whole, Marx may have been right.

In his *Critique of the Gotha Programme*, Marx noted that surplus value could be increased for the benefit of the capitalists in two ways: "by extending the work day or by developing the productivity, that is, increasing the intensity of labor power (Tucker, 1978:535). Engels suggested a third way: Some small business owners or owner-workers (**petit bourgeoisie**) are driven out by competition, fail financially, and end up in the working class, or **proletariat**. This increases the ratio of workers to capitalists, thereby producing more surplus value for each capitalist. Of these three, the least likely to occur today is an increase in the length of the workweek; the most likely is a dramatic increase in productivity. This makes it possible to increase workers' wages, shorten their workweek, and still increase the profit or surplus value of the capitalists.

Although Marx and Engels knew nothing of today's "downsizing," they did recognize the danger to capitalism of laying off workers, increasing the "army of unemployed." These unemployed, they suggested, could become a powerful force against the status quo. Capitalists today offset this possibility by establishing new enterprises that produce new, more esoteric goods and services. For example, a billboard in Dallas advertises "Datashred: Mobile Document Disintegration"—that is, a company that shreds and takes away old computer printouts. Another company expanded its regular cleaning service into the suicide cleanup business. According to one of the partners, "We think we've got a growing business. . . . We even researched suicide statistics in a library. And we think the next generation will have a high suicide rate" ("Suicide Cleanup," 1979). By establishing such new and diverse enterprises, capitalism may be able to limit the number of unemployed. Otherwise, according to Marx and Engels, the petit bourgeoisie will be driven into the proletariat, and proletarians into unemployment.

In discussing Marx's theory of capitalist economics, we need to speak briefly of the **relations of production.** Such relations involve the totality of economic life—private or communal property, technology, and people in society. They encompass both the *means* of production, including both social and technological aspects, and the *mode* of production, focusing on the social aspect, including class relationships (Marx, in Bottomore, 1963:52). For Marx, the relations of production expressed or embodied not only class, but alienation and labor/value as well.

Although it would be interesting to discuss other aspects of Marx's and Engels's economic theory, such as the role of money and land,[4] we will bring this discussion to a close with a few comments on "The Fetishism of Commodities" (Marx, 1867). A commodity, as we have noted, can be either labor or its product. It has what Marx called **use value**, or utility, which includes both what owners can accomplish that they could not without the commodity, and how long the use value will last. The use value of many capitalist commodities (locks, guns, even churches) is tied strictly to the alienated nature of that society (Ollman, 1971:186). In addition, commodities may become fetishes, so that even with no actual use value, or utility, they may be desired by the consumer (Marx, 1867). **Fetishes** are commodities that become ends in themselves, without giving true meaning to life (Kamenka, 1983:567). In contemporary U.S. society, much conspicuous consumption—the fancy car, prestigious home, name-brand clothing is, Marx would say, a matter of fetishism. In Chapter 10 you will see what another economic theorist, Thorstein Veblen, had to say about accumulation and waste in capitalist societies.

Nature of Humans, Society, and Change

In an essay on a young man's choice of a profession, Marx wrote: *"Man's nature is such that he can only attain his own perfection when working towards . . . the general welfare of his world"* (Marx and Engels, 1848, 1:167). Human

---

[4]References to money include *The Grundrisse* (1855:63), *The Manuscripts* (1844:147), and many portions of *Das Capital* (1867). On land, see *The Manuscripts* (1844:42).

perfection is possible, according to Marx, but only as we seek to improve or perfect our world. A part of that perfection is human and political freedom: "Freedom is so essentially a part of human nature that even its opponents help to realise it in combatting its reality; . . . the mortal danger therefore for every human being is that of losing his freedom" (Marx, 1846, 1:51, 60). So, freedom and perfectibility are humanity's goals.

However, Marx, like Hegel, saw *society's* reality as imperfect, even negative (Marcuse, 1941:312). This imperfection arises in the historical process: "All history is nothing but a continual transformation of human nature" (Marx, in Ollman, 1971:81). The transformation involves the alienating of person from person, so that the human as social being is replaced by the individualist and egoist (see Marx, 1844:138).

To summarize, Marx saw (1) humans as capable of good, even of perfection; (2) society as imperfect, bad, full of contradictions, oppression, isolation, and alienation; and (3) human perfection to be sought in the betterment or reintegration of society. Though it is something of an oversimplification, Marx would say that *human nature is good, society is bad or alienated,* and our goal is to remake society in the image of the good in humanity.

The degradation of society, according to Marx and Engels, was the result of both alienated labor and private property. The human condition had become one in which people no longer had the drive to see, hear, love, and think, but only to *have,* to own what was seen, heard, loved, and thought about. The goal of the communist future is to get rid of such greed, to make it so people no longer satisfy their own needs by depriving others (Ollman, 1971:94, 109).

This view of human perfectibility was in large part a reaction to other prevalent theories of change, or nonchange. As you have already seen, Marx and Engels rejected standard religious ideas both about humans as made in the image of God and humans as stained by original sin. For centuries, Marx noted, Europeans were controlled by Catholic priests, but with Luther's Reformation the struggle came to be with the priestly nature of the heart (Marx and Engels, 1964:51). It was from the enchained heart, the "priest within," and the biblical myths that the Young Hegelians had tried (unsuccessfully, according to Marx and Engels) to free people's minds.

Another prevalent theory with which Marx and Engels took issue was that of Father Thomas Malthus, who argued in his 1798 *Essay on the Principle of Population* that production increases arithmetically, while population increases geometrically. His theory has certainly not proved true in the intervening 200 years, but more important is the ideological position. Malthus had written a tract in favor of the English ruling class and opposed to "Poor Laws" and other potential disruptions of privilege in British society (see Meek, 1954). Thus, Engels saw Malthus as arguing against both the French Revolution and the supposed perfectibility of humanity. Malthus himself made his status quo conservatism quite clear in his second edition:

> A man who is born into a world already possessed, if he cannot get subsistence from his parents on whom he has a just demand, and if the society do not want his labour, has no claim of *right* to the smallest portion of food,

and, in fact, has no business to be where he is. (Malthus, 2nd edition; in Meek, 1954:531–532)

Ideologically, then, Malthus was a forerunner—along with Darwin—of the American W. G. Sumner (see Chapter 3), who argued that the survival of the fittest means we should not help the needy, because only the fittest should survive. It was in response to such reasoning that Engels wrote *The Condition of the Working Class in England* (1839).

Marx and Engels, then, can be viewed as both practical and ideological radicals, stating that capitalist society ought to not just be tinkered with, but overthrown. Of course, they would argue that they were not ideologues at all, but only observers and interpreters—theorists—of the course of human history.

Marx and Engels recognized that technology was changing continuously, and that this change was centered on the means of production. They also noted that, from time to time, there were power grabs, or changes in the ruling class that controlled the state and economy. To them, however, the most important form of change is revolution, as the oppressed workers of any age rise up against their oppressors.

Class, Gender, and Race

Although Marx never wrote a major work on classes, they are an important part of his economic thought. Engels said more than Marx about women and gender, but, aside from the U.S. Civil War and colonialism, neither commented at length on race.

Classes   In the *Communist Manifesto*, Marx and Engels declared that the "history of all hitherto existing society is the history of class struggles" (1848:9). "*All past history*," wrote Engels, "with the exception of its primitive stages, was the history of class struggles; . . . these warring classes of society are always the products of the modes of production and of exchange—in a word, of the economic conditions of their time" (1884:135). Expanding on that theme in 1886, Engels wrote that modern history proves "that all political struggles are class struggles, and all class struggles for emancipation, despite their necessary political form—for every class struggle is a political struggle—turn ultimately on the question of *economic* emancipation" (in Marx and Engels, 1964:259). In other words, classes are social units, based on their relation to the means of production. The owners are a class, and so are the workers; if the owners were also workers, there would be no classes.

Marx distinguished objective, static groups in any society, such as the Europe of 1850, from the two-class system ending in revolution. Among the objective and transitory classes he identified in Germany were the feudal nobility and landowners, the bourgeoisie, the petit bourgeoisie, the peasantry, agricultural workers, industrial workers or proletariat, and the subproletariat. However, as a philosopher of history, he saw but two antagonistic classes in the long run.

The transitory nature of these objective classes can be illustrated by the feudal nobility and petit bourgeoisie. The nobility are the leftovers, or remnants, of an earlier stage of economic development, and are being replaced by bourgeois **capitalists,** or those in control of industrial production. The **petit bourgeoisie** are small owners who still work their own means of production, or owner-workers. Today, for example, a woman or man who owns and runs a small diner in a big city may cook the food and serve it to the customers. This person employs no one, owning and working his or her own business. According to Marx, the petit bourgeoisie are not able to compete with large businesses (such as the restaurant chains of today) and are eventually driven out of business and into the proletariat or working class. Thus, existing classes will eventually evolve into two antagonistic classes, the bourgeoisie and the proletariat (Marx and Engels, 1848:32). "Of all the classes that stand face to face with the bourgeoisie today, the proletariat alone is a *really revolutionary class.* The other classes decay and finally disappear in the face of modern industry; the proletariat is its special and essential product" (Marx and Engels, 1848:26).

Because previous European society also involved class struggle, Marx and Engels noted, the bourgeoisie may be viewed as revolutionary relative to the feudal lords. That, after all, was what the French Revolution was about. In modern industrial society, however, "the proletariat is revolutionary relative to the bourgeoisie because, having itself grown up on the basis of large-scale industry, it strives to strip off from production the capitalist character that the bourgeoisie seeks to perpetuate" (Marx and Engels, 1848:26). History, then, has involved more than one class struggle, but the next one—between bourgeoisie and proletariat—will be the last.

The process, according to Marx and Engels, involves four stages of polarization: common conditions, consciousness or awareness, organizing, and revolution. Let us examine each of these stages.

From the beginning of their control, members of the ruling class—in modern industrial society, capitalists—are aware of the fact that they have reason to cooperate and work together. They are a **class-for-themselves**, meaning that they are aware of their common interests. The workers, however, are a **class-in-themselves**: Though living under common conditions, they do not recognize their common interests.

The second stage toward revolution is when the proletariat develops class consciousness, thus becoming a class-for-themselves. The development of such awareness or consciousness by the workers is only a matter of time, but it develops slowly for two reasons. First, the workers are in competition with each other for jobs, goods, and so on (Marx and Engels, 1848:14). For example, in the United States in 1960, when an influx of Cubans arrived in Miami, several cab drivers were interviewed by *Time* magazine. A common theme in their responses was, "Well, I don't know any of them, but I don't like them because they are taking our jobs." The capitalists foster such working-class divisions, utilizing the principle of "divide and keep conquered." Second, good deeds by the bourgeoisie make the proletariat feel appreciated, and make the bourgeoisie feel good, so that neither class is motivated to change the status quo.

However, the development of class consciousness on the part of the proletariat is, according to Marx and Engels, inevitable. The proletariat will become a class-for-themselves for two reasons. First, by herding them together into factories, the bourgeoisie weld them together, as they discuss and recognize their common interests. In factories, wrote Marx and Engels, the bourgeoisie oversees the production of products, but "produces, above all, its own grave-diggers" (Marx and Engels, 1848:21). In the 1960s Nikita Khrushchev, then head of the Soviet Union, came to the United States to speak at the United Nations. While in the United States, he was given the opportunity to talk to some factory workers. The next day's headlines quoted Khrushchev as saying "We will bury you," which was interpreted by the U.S. media to mean he believed that Russia would bury the United States. What he had done, in fact, was quote from the *Manifesto*: "In you workers the capitalists have produced the grave-diggers of capitalism."

The other reason the proletariat will become a class-for-themselves is that a few members of the bourgeoisie who understand history will break away and join the proletariat.

> Just as, therefore, at an earlier period, a section of the nobility went over to the bourgeoisie, so now a portion of the bourgeoisie goes over to the proletariat, and in particular, a portion of the bourgeois ideologists, who have raised themselves to the level of comprehending theoretically the historical movement as a whole. (Marx and Engels, 1848:19)

These ex-bourgeois would be leaders, understanding history and helping the workers develop a sense of awareness and purpose. The revolution would occur with or without the aid of these "lapsed" bourgeoisie, but they could hasten it. Spencer and Sumner (see Chapter 3) presented a similar idea: The great leader is the person who sees the direction history is moving, and becomes a spokesperson for that movement. Marx and Engels, of course, saw themselves as two such leaders.

The third stage is organization, followed by the fourth and final stage, revolution. Despite power skirmishes that occur from time to time between groups seeking to rule, the final revolution will be when the proletariat rise up against the capitalist bourgeoisie. This revolution will be of the workers against their own national bourgeoisie, but it will eventually be worldwide. In *The German Ideology*, Marx observed: "The world became the focal point of both raw materials and commerce. Thus, while the bourgeois of each nation retained national interest, big industry created an international class in which nationality is dead (the proletariat)" (1846:57). Modern industrial society is nothing but the uneasy coercive linking of a national bourgeoisie and its workers, but this linking means nothing to the workers. The important units of analysis for Marxists are the subgroup or class and humanity, not the nation-state that was so central to Durkheim.

The outcome of the revolution will be the communist society. Hegel believed that human beings never grasp the truth, but for Marx and Engels the dialectical process will come to fruition in communism:

> Communism differs from all previous movements in that it overturns the basis for all earlier relations of production and intercourse, and for the first time consciously treats all natural premises as the creatures of men, . . . and subjugates them to the power of the individuals united. (Marx and Engels, 1848:64)

Before the revolution the ruling class has always treated its controlling interest as if it were the general interest ("What's good for General Motors is good for the country"). The difference after the revolution is that the proletariat's interest will be the general interest.

Between capitalism and communism, according to Marx, the revolution will be followed by a transitory phase: the dictatorship of the proletariat. This dictatorship will be essential to every postrevolutionary society for a while, as the rest of the world goes through the revolution. In summary, Marx stated in an 1852 letter to a friend that he had proved

> (1) that the *existence of classes* is only bound up with *particular historical phases in the development of production*, (2) that the class struggle necessarily leads to the *dictatorship of the proletariat*, (3) that this dictatorship itself only constitutes the transition to the *abolition of all classes* and to a *classless society*. (in Tucker, 1978:220; Rubel and Manale, 1975:104)

Since the state had always been the instrument of class oppression in the hands of the ruling class, Marx and Engels believed it would eventually shrivel up or wither away for lack of a purpose. By sweeping away the old conditions of capitalist production, of owner and worker, of oppressor and oppressed, the proletariat will have abolished the conditions for class antagonism, and thus the necessity for the state.[5]

Why, then, has the state not withered away in avowedly communist societies of the twentieth century? Later Marxists argue that it cannot not wither away anywhere until the worldwide revolution is complete, because the force at the disposal of capitalist nations is always a threat. The final revolution, then, is still one historical stage away, but it will end class-based history as we know it. In this communist world, machines will serve workers, not dominate them. Distribution of products will be equal and complete, with each worker also an owner (Marx, 1855:76, 152).[6]

Gender   An important theme in Marx's and Engels's work was the oppression and emancipation of women. In *The Holy Family*, Marx observed:

> The humiliation of the female sex is an essential feature of civilization as well as barbarism. The only difference is that the civilised system raises to a compound, equivocal, ambiguous, hypocritical mode of existence every vice that barbarity practises in the simple form. . . . Nobody is punished more for keeping woman a slave than man himself. (Marx, 1845, in Rubel and Manale, 1975:54)

Gender equality, then, is a central aim of communist society.

However, in Marx's and Engels's work, as well as in subsequent Marxism, the "woman question" took second place at best to what was regarded as the

---

[5]For more on the state, see Engels, 1884:317ff.

[6]Marx and Engels never presented a complete picture of what postrevolutionary communist society would look like, but Marx gave hints in the *Grundrisse* (1855), and Rubel and Manale add some useful comments (1975:298, 324).

more critical emancipation of the proletarian class. That is, the theoretically nongendered proletariat described by Marx was seen in male terms (Delphy, 1984:160). First the revolution, then the "woman question," in Marx's (and later Lenin's) view.

Part of the reason for their incomplete theorizing about gender is that both Marx and Engels saw relations between men and women as located primarily in the family. They saw the original division of labor as the natural division occurring in heterosexual relations, which developed early in history. The first form of oppression was that of women by men in the family.

Later Engels, in *The Origin of the Family, Private Property and the State*, tried to provide a materialist explanation of gender relations. He stated that the determining factor in historical materialism is the "production and *reproduction* of immediate life" (1884:25). In early barbaric society, when sexual relations were casual and unregulated, paternity was difficult to establish with certainty. Thus, the first family form was based on the original biological link between mother and child. This link gave women high status. Descent through the female line provided the "material foundation for the predominancy of women which generally obtained in primitive times" and gave rise to primitive matriarchy, or female rule (Engels, 1884:61).

Gradually, a pattern of stable relations between a heterosexual married pair developed. According to Engels, women themselves pushed for the establishment of monogamy, because unregulated sexual relations were degrading to women. They "fervently . . . longed for the right to chastity, to temporary or permanent marriage with one man only, as a deliverance" (Engels, 1884:64). The push for monogamy could not have originated with men, since they "have never—not even to the present day—dreamed of renouncing the pleasures of actual group marriage." Consequently, monogamy was, and is, strictly enforced for "women only, of course" (Engels, 1884:64).

Eventually, monogamy made **patriliny,** or tracking through the male line, possible. But patrilineal descent became important only when significant economic surpluses developed. Surplus meant that wealth could be passed on to one's descendants. Surplus was controlled by men because of the "natural" gender division of labor. In the family "there springs up naturally a division of labour, caused by differences of sex and age, . . . based on a purely physiological foundation" (Marx, *Capital*, 1867, 1:351). This division of labor, a "pure and simple outgrowth of nature," meant that "men went to war, hunted, fished, provided the raw material for food and the tools necessary for these pursuits. The women cared for the house, and prepared food and clothing; they cooked, weaved, and sewed," and cared for the children (Engels, 1884:149).

Through the domestication of animals, development of better agricultural techniques, and introduction of slavery, the man acquired "more important status in the family than the woman." The increased wealth and status of the man, combined with monogamy, enabled him to "overthrow the traditional order of inheritance in favor of his own children." The result was "the *world-historical defeat of the female sex*" and the establishment of patriarchy (Engels, 1884:67–68).

Engels did not explain why fathers decided they wanted to pass their wealth on to their children, although Marx commented that the transition to father right "appears altogether to be the most natural transition" (Engels, 1884:67). The immediate effect was the establishment of the patriarchal family, in which the sexual fidelity of women was enforced in order to ensure legitimate offspring for the patriarch.

The first form of oppression, then, was "that of the female sex by the male" (Engels, 1884:75). This oppression was cemented as the state arose to protect the property interests of owners, such as the feudal aristocracy and later the bourgeoisie. In fact, in the propertied classes the man represents the bourgeoisie and the wife the proletariat (Engels, 1884:82).

The remedy for women's oppression is the same revolution as the one that will abolish class oppression. First, women must be drawn into paid work. The "emancipation of women and their equality with men are impossible and must remain so as long as women are excluded from socially productive work and restricted to housework" (Engels, 1884:152). Women's entry into productive work is their entry into class relations; without control over production and property, women are doomed to subordination (Sydie, 1987:101).

Engels suggested that modern large-scale industry encourages the participation of women. However, he argued, their emancipation would also require abolition of the monogamous patriarchal family. So far, Engels's optimism seems to have been misplaced, as women have continued to be the primary providers of domestic labor and child care, whether or not they hold jobs. More important, gender inequities remain in socialist countries after revolutions that were expected to solve the "woman question."

Formal gender equality is not the only change the Marxist revolution is expected to bring. Engels also saw the abolition of unequal property relations as the means of producing "true sex love." He described this as a "reciprocal love" that is relatively permanent, but in the event of a "cessation of affection" and its "displacement by a new passionate love," he condoned separation as a "blessing for both parties as well as for society" (Engels, 1884:88). The idyllic conditions for women's equality with men and for the development of true sex love envisaged by Engels are complicated, however, by the fact of reproduction that, as noted earlier, is the "natural" basis for the initial inequality between the sexes.

The difficulties that orthodox Marxism has had with gender issues became a significant concern for feminists in the early 1970s, as you will see in Chapter 22. A major difficulty is that Marx and Engels, blinded by the entrenched patriarchy of their day, did not clearly identify women as members of the oppressed proletariat (Sydie, 1987:122). In other words, the revolution—as both theorized and experienced—has been inadequate to produce gender equality.

Race   Marx and Engels said little directly, but much indirectly, about race and ethnicity. Although they may have harbored some of the racial biases of their day, their concern with oppression included those in other places. Marx, for example, was very critical of British colonial policies. In 1859 he "exposed the system of oppression whereby the colonialists pretended to assume responsibility over foreign territories in order to educate them in the principles of liberty. The facts showed that 'to be free at home, John Bull [Britain] must enslave abroad'" (Rubel and Manale, 1975:153). In addition, Marx wrote to U.S. leaders, supporting the freeing of slaves, and in *Das Kapital* he stated that labor cannot be emancipated in the white skin when those with black skins are enslaved (Marx, 1867).

However, in the *Grundrisse* Marx stated that "certain races, climates, natural conditions, such as distance from the sea, fertility of the soil, etc., are more favorable to production than others" (Marx, 1855:20). With no further elaboration of this theme, we are left to wonder just how Marx viewed specific racial groups. Freedom and equality, however, were always his central themes.

Engels, in his treatment of the stages of civilization, talks at length about savagery and barbarism, borrowing from Lewis Henry Morgan's work on native Americans. However, his analysis relies on agricultural and technological changes, such as the smelting of iron, and does not connect the stages with specific racial or ethnic groups. Engels's racial attitudes are unclear. His focus—like that of Marx—was economics, oppression, class, and to a lesser extent, gender.

Other Theories and Theorists

Praxis, or Action   Marx and Engels were not just socioeconomic theorists; nor were they just utopian philosophers. They sought to understand society in order to change it—and believed that thought must not be separated from action, or praxis.

In the *Manifesto*, Marx and Engels made clear some of the things that needed changing. First was private property. As they saw it, abolishing private property would not make much difference to most people. "It is already done away with for nine-tenths of the population; its existence for the few is solely due to its non-existence in the hands of those nine-tenths" (1848:25). Their intention was to do away with bourgeois control of property, including control of the means of production.

Second, the family as we know it had to be abolished—the patriarchal family unit in which women were treated as "domestic slaves," as property.

Third, country or nationality, a concept so central to Durkheim and others, had to be abolished. Nationality has meaning only for the capitalist class. The workers, as their consciousness increases, will recognize that the worldwide proletariat is their reference group, not the nation-state where they are exploited.

Fourth, traditional religion and concepts of morality must be abolished. Such ideas have, in every age, been produced by and are supportive of the ruling class. Instead of moral notions and religious doctrines, Marx and Engels intended to introduce a moral society (1848:29).[7]

Finally, of course, the communist program and the revolution will abolish class exploitation.

---

[7]Many institutional religionists have latched onto this conception, and the earlier comment that religion puts people to sleep like opium, to label communism as an immoral, or at least an amoral, system. Large numbers of books with some version of the title *Christianity and Communism* have appeared, each arguing that the former is a system of morality, and the latter is not. Marx and Engels's response would be that these religious critics are swayed by ruling-class morality, not the morality of a moral society.

Some of the bourgeoisie have an action program of their own, Marx and Engels noted. "A part of the bourgeoisie is desirous of redressing social grievances, in order to secure the continued existence of bourgeois society. 'The bourgeois,' they say, 'are bourgeois for the benefit of the working class'" (1848:38). But Marx and Engels believed that such liberalism simply slows down the class polarization leading to the revolution. So does reformism, including unionism, which focuses the workers' attention on shorter workweeks, more pay, and better working conditions, rather than on the revolution.

As part of their action program, Marx and Engels declared, "Communists support all revolutions against the existing order" (1848:44). For example, when the Cuban revolution occurred, it was primarily a peasant revolt, with the farmworkers seeking to break up the sugar cane plantations and gain ownership of land. However, U.S. capitalists opposed it and blockaded Cuba, and when Russia stepped in to support the rebels, Cuba began to identify with Marxist thought.

Relation to Other Theorists   We turn now from Marx's and Engels's praxis to their relation to other theorists. It is not necessary to reiterate what has already been said about their relation to Hegel, Feuerbach, the Young Hegelians, or even Malthus. However, Darwin deserves further mention. A year after it appeared, Marx read Darwin's *On the Origin of Species*, reporting to Engels that "although elaborated in a crude English manner, this is the book that contains the biological basis of our conceptions" (quoted in Rubel and Manale, 1975:169).

In an interesting letter to another writer, Engels noted that both he and Marx were struck by the similarity of Darwin's treatment of plants and animals and Malthus's treatment of population. However, continued Engels,

> I came to a different conclusion from yours: namely, that nothing discredits modern bourgeois development so much as the fact that it has not yet succeeded in getting beyond the economic forms of the animal world. To us so-called "economic laws" are not eternal laws of nature but historic laws which arise and disappear. (quoted in Meek, 1954:81)

Engels was suggesting that the human world of economics should not be bound by Darwinian principles, but should be able to use the principles of cooperation found in plants and lower animals.

In another letter, Engels wrote that he accepted the theory of evolution but took the method as provisional and incomplete. Before Darwin, Engels observed, the very people

> who now see nothing but the *struggle* for existence everywhere were stressing precisely the *co-operation* in organic nature—how the vegetable kingdom supplies the animal kingdom with oxygen and foodstuffs while the animal kingdom in turn supplies the vegetable kingdom with carbonic acid and manures. . . . Both conceptions have a certain justification within certain limits, but each is as one-sided and narrow as the other. (quoted in Meek, 1954:175, 186)

According to Engels, both cooperation and competition are part of life—and bourgeois economic principles are not only not eternal, they are incomplete,

and can and must be changed. Darwin's mistake, in Engels's view, was that selection and adaptation may mean regression just as well as progress, and one-
sided evolution may very well exclude evolution in what might have been several other positive directions.

Durkheim, discussed in Chapter 4, was half a century younger than Marx,
and was finishing his thesis as Marx died. Marx, of course, did not see the division of labor, a central issue for Durkheim, as the new "glue" for society, but
rather as a problem to be solved by the communist revolution. In the *Manuscripts*,
Marx wrote that "the *division of labor* is the economic expression of the *social character of labor* within the estrangement. Or, since *labor* is only an expression of human activity within alienation, . . . *the division of labor*, too, is therefore nothing
else but the *estranged, alienated* positioning of human activity" (1844:159). Thus,
Marx saw the division of labor as one expression of society's problem, while
Durkheim saw it as the solution to the problem.

One further point of connection between Durkheim and Marx is found in
the *Manuscripts*. Raising wages, wrote Marx, causes workers to work harder,
thereby shortening their lives. This "shortening of their life span is a favorable
circumstance for the working class as a whole, for as a result of it an ever-fresh
supply of labor becomes necessary" (Marx 1844:67). This is consistent with
Durkheim's point that what is abnormal (in this case, unhealthy) for the individual may be normal (healthy) for society—especially an alienated society.

Critique and Conclusions

Critiques of Marx and Engels   The easiest way to dismiss Marx is to say that
the notion of a final revolution, with everyone living happily ever after, is absurd. Nearly all the critics have started with this point. If, as Engels said, Marx's
"real mission in life was to contribute . . . to the overthrow of capitalist society,"
it is no wonder capitalist writers, in control of the means of communication,
have ignored, dismissed, misunderstood, or vilified him.

There was no end to the lies about Marx, aimed at discrediting him. On July
30, 1871, for example, a Berlin newspaper with ties to the Prussian government
claimed that socialist agitators, including Marx, "were enriching themselves at
the expense of the unsuspecting working class" (Rubel and Manale, 1975:268).
Nothing could be more ironic than such a rumor about the poverty-stricken
Marx. As is still true today regarding public figures, the rejoinder to such misin-
formation never has the impact of the original accusation.

As for ignoring and dismissing, Marx wrote to a friend in 1869 about the latest critiques of *Capital*:

> A lecturer in political economy at a German university writes to me that I
> have fully convinced him, but that his position absolutely *forbids* him and
> other colleagues from *expressing* this conviction. The cowardliness of the
> academic mandarins, on the one hand, and the conspiracy of silence with
> the bourgeois and reactionary press, on the other, are doing me great harm.
> (Rubel and Manale, 1975:242)

Ollman (1971) suggests that distortions of Marx may be due, at least in part,
to the limitations of our minds. Engels makes this point in his book against

Dühring (1878): The human mind has trouble grasping process; we tend to see the world statically, as if in a series of snapshots. Relational and processual thinking is difficult at best, impossible at worst. Furthermore, notes Ollman, Marx was too cavalier in his use of language. Sometimes he used different words for the same idea; at other times he used the same concept for slightly different ideas.

The final point on misunderstanding has to do with what later Marxists have called "false consciousness." We have been "brainwashed" into believing that capitalism is good for all of us. Workers attempting to make sense of the world may be religious, or patriotic, or racist trade unionists, or all three. Marx would say that people who are alienated and oppressed simply cannot think straight (Ollman, 1975:238).

But we must not dismiss all questions about Marx and Engels as coming from either the unenlightened or those with a vested interest in capitalism. Some criticisms—besides the unlikelihood of a final revolution—are worth noting. First, if productive labor is what separates humans from the rest of the animal kingdom, what is the position of hunters and gatherers, who do not produce, but only gather? Marx would of course say that they are humans—but this begs the question of the role of productive labor in defining the human condition.

Second, what are the possibility and efficacy of Marx's and Engels's solutions to the problem of alienation? Is alienation to be defined by private property and the division of labor, by the exploitation resulting from nonworking owners, nonowning workers, and specialization? If so, can either or both of these be reversed? While common ownership seems at least somewhat do-able, despecialization would seem to be virtually impossible.

Third, can we either understand or solve the issue of gender inequality with an economics-centered view of change? Feminist writers don't think so. Equal economic opportunity may be part of the solution, but it omits the family-based and personality/psychology-based aspects of the issue.

Contributions and Conclusions   Despite the shortcomings of Marx's and Engels's theory, we must recognize their contributions to social thought.

More than any other thinkers, Marx and Engels have made us see the importance, if not primacy, of economics in affecting the human condition. This importance is both in its relation to political, religious, and other ideas, and in *the criticism of worldwide capitalism*. In this view, economic subgroups and the human race are crucial; nation-states are transient.

Marx and Engels questioned the conservative view that society is like a cooperating organism. Spencer and many earlier thinkers had seen society as a collection of people agreeing to the rules—people who "like it here"—and cooperating and competing in society's best interest. Engels did admit that evolutionary society includes both conflict and cooperation. But his and Marx's contribution was to show that the historical process is one of class struggle and revolution, of coercion more than consensus. Against consensus, cooperation, and equilibrium, Marx and Engels posed interest groups, exploitation, and conflict. The argument has raged ever since and is perhaps the most central ideological and theoretical debate about modern society in this book.

Equally important, their radical philosophy of change was bound to influence the real world of politico-economic activity. This influence in the nineteenth century was primarily in secret societies and cell groups, but during the twentieth century nation-states calling themselves Marxist and communist emerged.

Marx was far-sighted, if not prescient, in his view of capitalist society. In the *Grundrisse* he mentions "the influence of automation on society," and though he could not have imagined how far it would go, he seems to have seen the possibility of machines running machines. In the same volume he also noted how "agriculture comes to be more and more merely a branch of industry and is completely dominated by capital" (1855:8, 41). Today we call it agribusiness. In the *Manuscripts* he spoke of humans as "regressing to the cave dwelling," by which he meant the modern urban apartment house—though, of course, he could not have imagined today's skyscrapers (1844:155). In their work on Malthus, Marx and Engels noted the opposition to welfare, framed in terms that those who do not work should not live (Meek, 1954)—a truly modern attitude. In 1870, Marx predicted that war between Germany and Russia "will act as the midwife to the inevitable revolution in Russia" (Rubel and Manale, 1975:259). And so it did.

Final Thoughts

We have many reasons to continue studying the thought of Marx and Engels. But just before his death, Marx made the famous statement "I am no Marxist." He may have meant that, with so many misinterpretations of his thought, he could no longer identify with the label. Or, as Rubel and Manale suggest, the remark could "be taken as a protest against any kind of name worship as fetishistic and contrary to the principle of self-emancipation on which the working-class movement is based" (1975:329). The leader seeking to change society for the better is not likely to desire personal honor so much as the success of the movement with which he or she is identified.

No theory has faced more critical and ideological judgments than that of Marx and Engels. But, as we will see in Chapter 6, the next generation of Marxists expanded on Marx's and Engels's theory and sought to apply it to the modern industrial world.

References

de Aenlle, Conrad. 1997. "Eco-Friendliness Is Not the Business of Business." *International Herald Tribune*, June 7–8.

Delphy, Christine. 1984. *Close to Home* (Diana Leonard, Trans. and Ed.). London: Hutchinson, in association with The Explorations of Feminism Collective.

Engels, Friedrich. 1839/1968. *The Condition of the Working Class in England*. Stanford, CA: Stanford University Press.

———. 1875/1955. *Socialism: Utopian and Scientific*. In *Selected Works* (vol. 2, pp. 93–155). Moscow: Foreign Languages Publishing House.

———. 1878/n.d.. *Herr Eugen Duhring's Revolution in Science*. New York: International Publishers.

————. 1884/1972. *The Origin of the Family, Private Property and the State*. New York: Pathfinder Press. [Also in*Selected Works* (vol. 2, pp. 170–326). Moscow: Foreign Languages Publishing House, 1955.]

————. 1886/1964. *L. Feuerbach and the End of Classical German Philosophy*. In *Marx and Engels on Religion* (pp. 213–268). New York: Schocken Books.

Hegel, Georg W. F. 1807/1910. *The Phenomenology of Mind*. New York: Macmillan.

————. 1816/1929. *The Science of Logic*. New York: Macmillan.

Kamenka, Eugene. 1983. *The Portable Karl Marx*. New York: Penguin Books.

Marcuse, Herbert. 1941. *Reason and Revolution*. New York: Oxford Press.

Marx, Karl. 1844/1964. *Economic and Philosophic Manuscripts of 1844*. New York: International Publishers.

————. 1855/1971. *The Grundrisse* (David McLellan, Ed.). New York: Harper and Row.

————. 1867/1972. *Das Kapital: Kritik der Politischen Okonomie*. Hamburg: I.Bd., Buch I.

————. 1963. *Early Writings* (Thomas Bottomore, Ed.). London: C. A. Watts.

————. 1964. *Selected Writings in Sociology and Social Philosophy* (T. Bottomore and M. Rubel, Eds.). London: McGraw-Hill.

Marx, Karl, and Friedrich Engels. 1846/1964. *The German Ideology* (S. Ryazanskaya, Trans.). Moscow: Foreign Languages Publishing House.

————. 1848/1935. *The Communist Manifesto*. In Marx and Engels, *Selected Works* (vol. 1). London: Lawrence and Wishart.

————. 1848/1935. *Selected Works* (2 vols.). London: Lawrence and Wishart.

————. 1964. *On Religion*. New York: Schocken Books.

McLellan, David. 1977. *Karl Marx: Selected Writings*. Oxford: Oxford University Press.

Meek, Ronald L. (Ed.). 1954. *Marx and Engels on Malthus*. New York: International Publishers.

Ollman, Bertell. 1971. *Alienation: Marx's Conception of Man in Capitalist Society*. Cambridge: Cambridge University Press.

Rubel, Maximilien, and Margaret Manale. 1975. *Marx Without Myth*. Oxford: Basil Blackwell.

Smith, Henry. 1995. "Give Thanks." *Chalice Hymnal*. St. Louis: Chalice Press.

"Suicide Cleanup Their Business." 1979. *Wisconsin State Journal*, October 26.

Sydie, R. A. 1987. *Natural Women, Cultured Men: A Feminist Perspective on Sociological Theory*. Toronto: Methuen.

Tucker, Robert C. 1978. *The Marx-Engels Reader*. New York: W. W. Norton.

Zeitlin, Irving. 1967. *Marxism: A Reassessment*. Princeton, NJ: D. Van Nostrand.

Chapter 6

Marxism Extended
Lenin and Luxemburg

Those who seek to change society radically may be crushed or ignored, undermined or misunderstood, but they often effect change as well. In the previous chapter we met Marx and Engels, whose radical theory/ideology continues to influence our world. In this chapter you will meet the next generation of radical anticapitalists, V. I. Lenin and Rosa Luxemburg, who were more active than Marx and Engels in actually attempting to overthrow the capitalist and imperialist status quo.

Lenin was effectively neutralized before his death by the communist government he had been so instrumental in establishing in the Soviet Union:

> By the time he started to concentrate on the dreadful danger of Stalinist bureaucratization . . . it was too late. It is pathetic to see Lenin, a genius of realistic strategy, behaving like a desperate utopian from 1923 to the moment of his death, insistently putting forth hopeless schemes—like the proposal to create a majority in the Central Committee from working-class cadres in order to neutralize the Party bureaucrats. Lenin's great tragedy was that his incomparable, instrumentally concrete, intensely practical strategy in the end defeated him. (Meszaros, 1972:36)

As for Luxemburg, she was crushed by the German police:

> Rosa Luxemburg decided with a heavy heart to lend her energy to . . . the *coup* [attempt that] was . . . a fizzle. But neither she nor her close associates fled for safety as Lenin had done in July, 1917. They stayed in the capital, hiding carelessly, . . . trying to direct an orderly retreat. On January 16 (1919) . . . Rosa Luxemburg was seized, along with Karl Liebknecht and Wilhelm Pieck. Reactionary officers murdered Liebknecht and Luxemburg while "taking them to prison." (Waters, in Luxemburg, 1970:18)

Lenin and Luxemburg were more than radical activists. They both contributed theoretically and ideologically to the ideas of Marx and Engels, so that all four have helped to shape the Marxism of today.

V. I. Lenin (1870–1924)

Vladimir Ulyanov was born in Simbirsk on the Volga River in 1870.[1] Vladimir had three sisters, one of whom lived but a short time, and one brother. The surviving sisters, Maria and Anna, along with his mother, wife, and mistress, never ceased their concern for Vladimir, especially as he began to play a major role in Russian political life. Later on, Vladimir used several pen names and pseudonyms, but he came to be known as Lenin, the name we will use from this point on.[2]

In 1887, his older brother Alexander was drawn into a plot to assassinate the Russian tsar. The plot was discovered and Alexander was executed at age 21, when Lenin was 17. Lenin, though affected by his brother's death, continued with his schooling and passed his examinations. He began to read Marx's *Capital* in 1888, but he became a revolutionary primarily in response to Alexander's execution, not to reading Marx.

The year of his brother's death, Lenin graduated from the *gymnasium* and entered the University of Kazan to study law. While studying he also became active in revolutionary student groups, and for the next few years he was involved both in his studies and in student activism (Fischer, 1964). By 1890 he had studied *Das Kapital* and the *Manifesto*, had been arrested and released, and had been given a position as an assistant attorney in Samara. During the next four years he spent time traveling, studying, writing, practicing law, serving time in prison, and developing his version of Marx's and Engels' ideas. From at least the beginning of 1895 on, he was under surveillance by Russian authorities as a revolutionary, even when traveling abroad. In 1897 he was sentenced to three years' exile in Siberia, where he continued studying and writing. Upon his release he illegally visited Petersburg (Petrograd) and, after interrogation, went abroad. For the next few years Lenin lived primarily in Munich and Geneva. During this time he wrote and organized, and even visited Marx's grave in London.

While in law school Lenin met Krupskaya, and they were married five years later. She was his wife and collaborator for the next 25 years. For almost 20 years after his death, she continued as his biographer and interpreter.

---

[1]Much of the background material on Lenin's life is taken from an unsympathetic book by Stefan Possony (1964). However, the early portion of Possony's work is both thorough and reasonably unbiased, only becoming clearly polemical as he relates Lenin's accession to power. We will avoid reference to the latter part of his book.

[2]The name "Lenin" is difficult to trace. The best guess is that it derives from the time he spent in exile near the Lena River in Siberia. Lenin, then, would mean "man from the Lena."

Lenin has been described in many ways, especially by those seeking to glorify him as a superhuman genius. According to one biographer, at age 23 "he
was characterized by a forceful intellect, a fairly broad education, a strong capacity for work, enormous will power, and a dominant power urge. . . . From
the start, his work was polemic in nature and his arguments were dogmatic,
one-sided, and self-serving" (Possony, 1964: 388–389).

The "power urge" did not seem to include sexual activity, and his sexual attraction to Krupskaya seemed negligible. Later he told Clara Zetkin that he was
in fact strongly critical of a notion that had been attributed to him—that sexual
desire "is as simple and trivial as 'drinking a glass of water'" (Lenin, 1921a:692).

Lenin was a unique combination of theoretician and political leader. While
stressing the unity of theory and practice, he felt there were times when the
former had to be altered to serve the needs of the latter. The clearest examples
come from his writings in 1905, 1917, and 1921.

In 1905, the "Bloody Sunday" massacre, involving both peasants and workers, occurred outside the Winter Palace in Petrograd. At that time Russia was
losing a war in the east with Japan, and Lenin was in Switzerland. Lenin soon
returned to Russia but, perceiving that an open revolution was premature,
wrote that Russia was not ready for the proletarian revolt; it was still too agrarian and too backward economically.

> Only ignorant people fail to see the bourgeois nature of the democratic
> transformation going on at present. To wish to attain socialism by other
> ways, without passing through the stage of political democracy and capital-
> ism, is merely to arrive at ridiculous and reactionary conclusions, in the
> political as well as in the economic fields. (Lenin, 1905:40–41)

In other words, the revolution in Russia, when it came, would be slow and tor-
tuous, passing through the necessary phase of bourgeois capitalism before true
socialism and then communism.

Twelve years later, during World War I, the tsar's government toppled—the
result of heavy losses in the war, a rebellious army unwilling to fight, and an
economy in peril. Several months later Lenin stepped into this vacuum with his
no-compromise, utilitarian, power-centered approach. His Bolshevik party used
the support of the peasant or Narodnik party, who wanted land reform, the
Mensheviks, and the Social Democrats to gain control. However, once Lenin's
position of power was established, he cut the Narodniks and others out of the
alliance. He began immediately to nationalize the means of production and the
banks, and even made some attempt at collectivizing the farms—which the
peasants had hoped to own.

At this point, in 1917, Lenin wrote confidently of the immediate transition
of Russia to a socialist state, without the intermediate phase of bourgeois capitalism: "The dialectic of history is such that the war [in Europe] has enor-
mously accelerated the transformation of capitalist monopolies into state monopolies and thereby brought the advent of socialism considerably nearer"
(Lenin, 1917a:217). Moving rapidly without the reform liberals (or revision-
ists), without the Mensheviks (who continued to believe in slow revolution via

capitalism), without the Narodniks, and without the budding bourgeoisie, Lenin proceeded in 1917 to begin constructing his version of socialist society.

By 1921, however, events in Russia forced Lenin to change his mind again. Civil War and the inability to reap surpluses from the farmers in order to feed industrial workers had made a shambles of the Russian economy. At that time he wrote of the isolation, backwardness, and fragmentation of Russian society.

> Is it to be imagined that under such conditions Russia can pass immediately to socialism? . . . We went too far on the path of the nationalization of commerce and industry, and in the suppression of local trade. Was it a blunder? Yes, without question. . . . Capitalism will remain inevitable so long as we are unable to effect a direct transition from small industry to socialism. An attempt to completely suppress private trade—which amounts to capitalism—would be an absurdity because such a policy is economically unfeasible, and it would be suicide because a party which attempted it would be doomed to failure. It is not the growth of the petty bourgeoisie that has to be feared, but the prolongation of famine, of misery, of the shortage of food. (Lenin, 1921a:521, 530)

How, then, as a committed Marxist, did Lenin justify backing away from his 1917 position to a position similar to the one he had held in 1905? He did so by treating conditions in 1917 as deviant, and by admitting that he had misread them. The war economy, which he called "war communism," explained the massive but mistaken nationalization following the revolution. According to Lenin, writing in 1921:

> "War communism" consisted in taking from the peasants the surplus of their produce and sometimes even part of what was necessary for their subsistence. We made requisitions in order to feed the army and the workers. . . . "War communism" was necessitated by the war and by the ruin of the country. It has not been and could not be a policy answering to the needs of the proletariat. It was a temporary measure. (Lenin, 1921a:518, 533)

Thus, beginning in 1921, Russia had a mixed economy, with banks and heavy industry state-owned, but with small industry capitalistic. Peasants were subjected to a grain tax, but were allowed to sell their surplus on the open market. The new theoretical keynote was gradualness. The New Economic Policy, Lenin believed, need never be changed; it would wither away when it was no longer needed. The dramatic moves of 1917 had been deviant and wrongheaded.

Two conclusions may be drawn from this history. First, Lenin was practical enough to admit his mistakes. Second, Lenin was not just a Marxist, but a Russian Marxist, interpreting Marxist theory according to the needs and problems of Russian society.

Lenin's Central Theories and Methods

Lenin's contributions to theory included its relation to practice, as well as his views on dialectics, imperialism, revolution, and the state.

Marx's early writings made clear his belief that "to understand is to change," or that theory must not be separated from practice. As noted above, this was also a major theme for Lenin. In 1902 he wrote: "Without revolutionary theory there can be no revolutionary movement. The idea cannot be insisted upon too strongly at a time when the fashionable preaching of opportunism goes hand in hand with an infatuation for the narrowest forms of practical activity" (Lenin, 1902:19). Near the end of his life, Lenin criticized Marxists whose conception is "impossibly pedantic" (Lenin, 1922:703). He also criticized Stalin and others who were bureaucratizing the Russian government, while isolating Lenin and treating him as an irrelevant icon and figurehead.

Dialectics   In 1914 Lenin discovered (or rediscovered) Hegel. From then until his death, he spent time studying and writing about Hegel's dialectic, but, of course, within a Marxian framework (see Anderson, 1995). One of Lenin's most creative contributions was his distinction between good and bad idealism and materialism. Bad idealism is found in Hegel's assertion that the universal reality is thought or ideas. Bad materialism is a completely one-sided belief that the material is all there is. For Lenin, as in some of Marx's writings, idealism and materialism are good when they recognize each other, and dialectically interact and transform each other. Lenin did not repudiate or reject Hegel, but argued that dialectic reality involves both the material and the ideal, while emphasizing the former (Anderson, 1995:102).

The dialectic idea was useful to Lenin in another way. It allowed him to see both the Great War (World War I) and the expansion of imperialism as steps toward the revolution. These both increased awareness of the evils of capitalism, and will lead eventually to worldwide revolution, which he assumed would begin in Russia. Thus, dialectic or Hegelian thinking became a part of Lenin theoretical arsenal.

Imperialism   Few statements before Lenin wrote his 1917 treatise on *Imperialism* had been as clear and precise in explaining this nineteenth-century European phenomenon. Of course, Marx and Engels could not have foreseen what Lenin observed in the early twentieth century. In 1885 the European nations had carved up Africa into colonies and protectorates, and Lenin recognized the same occurrences in Latin America and in Asia.

Lenin discussed *imperialism* in connection with both colonialism and monopoly capitalism. In his Preface to the French and German editions, written in 1920, he described the war of 1914–1918 as "imperialist (that is, an annexationist, predatory, war of plunder) on the part of both sides; it was a war for the division of the world, for the partition and repartition of colonies and spheres of influence of finance capital, etc." (Lenin, 1917b:206). In *Left-Wing Communism*, written in 1920, he expressed this idea even more graphically: "tens of millions were killed and maimed for the sole purpose of deciding whether the British or the German robbers should plunder the largest number of countries" (Lenin, 1920a:614).

One of the more interesting expressions of the colonial mentality is found in Cecil Rhodes's[3] comments to a journalist friend as quoted by Lenin:

---

[3] Rhodes scholarships for study in the United Kingdom were named for him.

I was in the East End of London [a working-class quarter] yesterday and attended a meeting of the unemployed. I listened to the wild speeches, which were just a cry for "Bread! Bread!" and on my way home I pondered over the scene and I became more than ever convinced of the importance of imperialism. . . . My cherished idea is a solution for the social problem, i.e., in order to save the 40,000,000 inhabitants of the United Kingdom from a bloody civil war, we colonial statesmen must acquire new lands to settle the surplus population, to provide new markets for the goods produced in the factories and mines. The Empire, as I have always said, is a bread and butter question. If you want to avoid civil war, you must become imperialists. (Lenin, 1917b:236)

Such colonialism, accompanied by uneven economic development, is the essence of modern **monopoly capitalism,** the international version of the class struggle within nation-states. Capitalists in imperialist nations can readily expand their influence to less developed countries, overwhelming local producers in the process. The result is a worldwide monopoly for the capitalists of wealthy nations.

Using 1910 data from the *Bulletin of the International Statistical Institute,* Lenin found that of 600 billion francs worth of financial securities current at that time, Great Britain, the United States, France, and Germany owned 80 percent. Except for a few other countries, such as Russia, Japan, and Holland, the rest of the world of 1910 consisted of debtor nations—a fact as true today as it was then, though the distribution among nations has shifted, especially toward the United States and Japan.

An important basis for monopoly control, wrote Lenin, is control over raw materials. He noted "with what zeal the international capitalist associations exert every effort to deprive their rivals of all opportunity of competing, to buy up, for example, ironfields, oilfields, etc." (Lenin, 1917b:239). Finance capital seeks to control not only known sources of raw materials but potential sources, "because present-day technical development is extremely rapid, and land which is useless today" may not be so tomorrow (Lenin, 1917b:240). Capitalists control a combination of raw materials (including those in poor nations), manufacturing, financing, and markets. For example, observed Lenin, raw materials are transported from the dependent nations to the industrial/colonial powers, where goods are manufactured and subsequently sold back to where the raw material came from. This had occurred in the textile industry between Britain and India, as well as elsewhere. Of course, Lenin could not have foreseen the replacement of colonialism with multinational corporations operating independently and with little national allegiance.

Lenin summarized the basic features of **imperialism** as follows:

(1) the concentration of production and capital has developed to such a high stage that it has created monopolies which play a decisive role in economic life; (2) the merging of bank capital with industrial capital, and the creation, on the basis of this "finance capital," of a financial oligarchy; (3) the export of capital as distinguished from the export of commodities acquires exceptional importance; (4) the formation of international monopolist capitalist associations (such as cartels) which share the world

among themselves, and (5) the territorial division of the whole world among the biggest capitalist powers is completed. (Lenin, 1917b:244)

According to Lenin, the reason why imperialism is not seen as the world's primary problem is that bourgeois scholars and the media defend it, often in a somewhat veiled form. Reform ideas, such as government supervision of the trusts or banks or Rhodes's notion of out-migration, are presented to convince people that monopoly capitalism is being improved, while nothing important is actually changing. "Cynical and frank imperialists [like Rhodes] who are bold enough to admit the absurdity of the idea of reforming the fundamental characteristics of imperialism are a rarer phenomenon" (Lenin, 1917b:259).

Where, then, is imperialism headed? What will be the eventual outcome of the capitalist/imperialist/colonial world? Lenin predicted the following result of the European war of 1914–1918: "Out of the universal ruin caused by the war, a world-wide revolutionary crisis is arising which, however prolonged and arduous its stages may be, cannot end otherwise than in a proletarian revolution and in its victory" (Lenin, 1917b:207). In some of his more farsighted writing, he predicted independence movements in Poland, the Arab nations, India, China, and elsewhere. These uprisings, however, are not so much nationalistic as subparts of the worldwide working class revolution.

Revolution   In Marx's writings, the revolution often seemed inevitable. Lenin, however, was unwilling to wait for the proletariat to become a class-for-themselves, organize, and revolt en masse. He saw his small Bolshevik party as the **vanguard**—the advance contingent or leaders of the revolution. As early as 1902, 15 years before the Russian revolution, Lenin argued that assuming the label of vanguard was not enough: "we must act in such a way that *all* other contingents recognize and are obliged to admit that we are marching in the vanguard" (Lenin, 1902:53). After the revolution, the vanguard will establish the **dictatorship** of the **proletarian** party, or working-class leaders of the communist state.

Following the Russian revolution, monopoly capitalism will be overthrown country by country. Lenin wrote in 1915:

> Uneven economic and political development is an absolute law of capitalism. Hence, the victory of socialism is possible first in several or even in one capitalist country alone. After expropriating the capitalists and organizing their own socialist production, the victorious proletariat of that country will arise *against* the rest of the world—the capitalist world—attracting to its cause the oppressed classes of other countries, stirring uprisings in those countries against the capitalists, and in case of need using even armed force against the exploiting classes and their states. . . . [This] will more and more concentrate the forces of the proletariat of a given nation or nations, in the struggle against states that have not yet gone over to socialism. (Lenin, 1917b:203)

Thus, in any given nation the vanguard will lead the uprising against its own bourgeoisie. But the proletariat are international, not national. Therefore, as the international proletariat grows, the revolution will become worldwide. All but the role of the vanguard had been predicted by Marx as well.

Lenin clarified the relation between theory and the revolutionary practice of the proletariat in "One Step Forward, Two Steps Back," written in 1904 following the Second Congress. "In its struggle for power the proletariat . . . can, and inevitably will, become an invincible force only through its ideological unification on the principles of Marxism being reinforced by the material unity of organisation, which welds millions of toilers into an army of the working class" (Lenin, 1904:119).

Lenin waffled, however, on whether or not the bourgeois revolution had to precede that of the proletariat. As noted above, Lenin's early work indicated his belief that bourgeois capitalism must come first. "A bourgeois revolution is *absolutely* necessary in the interests of the proletariat. The more complete, determined, and consistent the bourgeois revolution, the more assured will the proletariat's struggle be against the bourgeoisie and for socialism" (Lenin, 1905:124). But Lenin's view on this changed as his political role changed, first to the possibility of skipping the capitalist stage, and then back to the concept of gradualness with the New Economic Policy of 1921.

Lenin made one further point on revolution that expanded on Marx's position that communists support all revolutions against the existing order. In his brief 1920 comment on national and colonial issues, Lenin noted the need to "strive to lend the peasant movement the most revolutionary character by establishing the closest possible alliance between the West-European communist proletariat and the revolutionary peasant movement in the East, in the colonies, and in the backward countries generally" (Lenin, 1920c:624). Thus, to Lenin, the proletariat needed the collaboration of the peasants in the poorer countries. Later Marxists carried this even further, arguing that the revolution must occur first in the most backward countries, at the fingertips of the capitalist world.

The State   In *State and Revolution* (1917c), one of his best-known works, Lenin stressed the importance of the dictatorship of the proletariat once again. In addition, he further spelled out the role of the Bolshevik party, both as the vanguard of the proletariat and as the state leaders in the name of the proletariat. [4]

However, the central thesis of *State and Revolution* is neither the vanguard nor the party. Looking at the tsarist government that he would replace and at the nation-states around Russia, Lenin argued that the bureaucratic apparatus of government is by nature bourgeois—and therefore must be smashed, not usurped or taken over. The division of labor that gives bureaucracy its character is antirevolutionary and, therefore, anticommunist. Raya Dunayevskaya, an important twentieth-century Marxist, described the bourgeois state as Lenin saw it:

> Basing himself on Marx's concept that "centralized state power, with its
> ubiquitous organs of standing army, police, bureaucracy, clergy, and
> judicature—are organs wrought after the plan of a systematic and hierar-

---

[4]An outstanding book focusing on Lenin and the Bolshevik party is Adam Ulam's *The Bolsheviks*, written in 1965 and republished with a new preface in 1998, after the breakup of the Soviet Union.

chic division of labor," Lenin now saw that the need of his time was to *destroy bureaucratism.* . . . That now became the key to his theory and his practice. It was a new organization of thought in the true Hegelian-Marxian manner. (Dunayevskaya, 1958:191)

Lenin, we have said, was in many ways a practical politician. However, his action never strayed far from his theorizing—even though the theory sometimes had to be adjusted to the needs of the time. Even during the revolution of 1917, Lenin put much effort into studying Marx and Engels, with a view to explaining the transformation of the state in a global revolution (Harding, 1978, 2:83).

In place of a bureaucracy, Lenin proposed "workers councils" or cadres that would represent the proletariat and keep the postrevolutionary government from forgetting its goals. However, Lenin was still fighting against bourgeois bureaucratization when Stalin came to power. As the Soviet state moved away from his theoretical ideals, Lenin was left isolated.

In summary, Lenin's theory (and ideology) made the following points: (1) Theory and practice must be kept together. (2) Hegel's dialectic was useful in understanding both world history and current events. (3) The world of imperial capitalism—which includes colonialism and a dramatic increase in monopoly capital—is a world of dramatically increasing inequality, both within and between societies. (4) The vanguard had to lead the way in thinking through the revolution and in organizing the proletariat. (5) The bourgeois or middle-class revolution might or might not precede the revolution of the proletariat; however, revolt by any oppressed people is a step in the right direction, leading toward a socialist world. (6) The bureaucratic bourgeois state must be smashed, and replaced by a revolutionary, worker-led government, literally "of the people."

Nature of Humans, Society, and Change

Lenin's view of human nature can only be inferred. The very fact of his belief in a revolution to correct the ills of the world indicated a conviction that humans could envisage and bring about that better world. Like Rousseau in the 1700s and Marx in the 1800s, Lenin saw in humans the "good" needed to bring into being an unalienated world, a world of equality and unselfishness. Communist morality is embodied in the struggle of the working people against all forms of exploitation.

As for society and change, they were the focal points of Lenin's life's work. The society of Lenin's experience, first aristocratic (tsarist) and then capitalist, was evil and had to be changed. For Lenin, however, change was not evolutionary but revolutionary. That is, the capitalist world is neither self-corrective if left alone, nor is it likely to be improved by liberal "tinkering." It must be overthrown and replaced by a world in which class rule is abolished and the state withers away.

Class, Race, and Gender

Class   In much of Lenin's argument regarding imperialism and the revolution, the underlying factor was class. All institutions and ideas are class-based.

"People always have been the foolish victims of deception and self-deception in politics, and they always will be until they have learnt to seek out the *interests* of some class or other behind all moral, religious, political, and social phrases, declarations, and promises" (Lenin, 1913–1922: 644).

For Lenin, unbiased theory about *capitalism* was an oxymoron: "There can be no 'impartial' social science in a society based on class struggle. In one way or another, *all* official and liberal science *defends* wage slavery, whereas Marxism has declared relentless war on that slavery" (Lenin, 1913–1922: 640). Bourgeois nationalism seeks to propagandize for an "allegedly integral national culture," meaning one believed in and supported by all classes, oppressed as well as ruling. Lenin saw things differently. In his speech to the "Youth Leagues," Lenin gave one of the better Marxist explanations of what **classes** consist of:

> Classes are that which permits one section of society to appropriate the labour of another section. If one section of society appropriates all the land, we have a land-owner class and a peasant class. If one section of society owns the factories, shares and capital, while another section works in these factories, we have a capitalist class and a proletarian class. (Lenin, 1920b:668)

Lenin did not bother to objectively describe existing classes, as Marx had done. Rather, he focused entirely on the coming class struggle and revolution, followed by the dictatorship of the proletariat. "Only he is a Marxist who *extends* the recognition of the class struggle to the recognition of the *dictatorship of the proletariat*" (Lenin, 1917c: 334). In other words, the proletariat dictatorship is a necessary stage of postrevolutionary socialist society. Because a spontaneous workers' movement might lead to its subordination to bourgeois ideology, centralized control by the vanguard is essential. This vanguard should be organized like an army, with the discipline and centralization of an army, and with power in the hands of the officers, or central committee. To Lenin, the difference between this dictatorship and that of the capitalist bourgeoisie, or of the aristocracy before it, is that, because class is obliterated, proletarian dictatorship is on behalf of all people. The bourgeoisie, noted Lenin, sneered at the classless society as sheer utopian nonsense. But to Lenin a classless society will be natural once the revolution is complete.

Gender Lenin expected the benefits of a classless society to be extended to women. Like most Marxists, Lenin considered the "woman question" to be a matter of oppression, to be corrected by revolutionizing the economics of the larger society. In telling fellow revolutionary Clara Zetkin how she should write her statement for "women Party comrades," he stated:

> The theses must emphasise strongly that true emancipation of women is not possible except through communism. You must lay stress on the unbreakable connection between woman's human and social position and the private ownership of the means of production. (Lenin, 1921b:695)

Lenin went on to declare his hatred of the privileged position of men, who sit by and watch a woman "wear herself out with trivial, monotonous, strength- and time-consuming work, such as her housework, and watching her spirit shrinking, her mind growing dull, her heartbeat growing faint, and her will growing slack" (Lenin, 1921b:697). He pointed out that postrevolutionary Russia was seeking to shift housekeeping and educational functions from the household to the society. "Woman is thus being relieved from her old domestic slavery and all dependence on her husband. She is enabled to give her capabilities and inclinations full play in society" (Lenin, 1921b: 698). In closing, however, he admitted that gender role changes had been too small to be considered real emancipation.

Lenin was not so radical in his opinions about sex as were some of his revolutionary comrades. Inessa Armand, Lenin's friend and perhaps mistress, intended to write a pamphlet on free love along the lines of Engels's *Origin of Family, Private Property, and the State*. But Lenin argued with her from his sexual conservatism, and she never published her pamphlet (see Fischer, 1964:78–81). In a brief speech in 1913 to a congress on prostitution, however, Lenin noted that the two bourgeois methods for curbing prostitution were religion and the police, pointing out that these were hypocritical solutions of a bourgeoisie for whom prostitution is but an extreme form of women's slavery.

Race   Lenin had strong views on racial oppression and expended some effort in exposing the racism of Western capitalism, especially that of the United States. In his *Notebooks on Imperialism*, which followed his earlier treatment of imperialism, he discussed the position of blacks in the United States, as well as racism and nationalist chauvinism within socialism itself (Lenin, 1921b). But he did more than discuss racism. He influenced the establishment of the American Communist party in the 1920s, a party that had a written policy of expelling any member exhibiting anti-black racism. And, as already noted, Lenin wrote about the coming uprising of the colonized, mostly nonwhite, peoples. Thus, although race was not his central focus, it was certainly a part of his view of the capitalist world as being coercive and oppressive.

Other Theories and Theorists

Lenin said more than Marx had about postrevolutionary socialism, because he was in charge of an avowedly socialist nation for the last six years of his life. One point he made about such a society concerned competition. The bourgeoisie, he observed in 1918, loved to spread the rumor that "socialists deny the importance of competition. In fact, it is only socialism which, by abolishing the enslavement of the people, for the first time opens the way for competition on a really mass scale" (Lenin, 1918:449). Another of his socialist ideas was the "subbotnik." This "unpaid working sabbath" was intended to become a tradition that would "demonstrate the conscious and voluntary initiative of the workers" in helping with needed projects (Lenin, 1919:480). But it hardly survived beyond Lenin's death.

Lenin's theory and ideology totally rejected three other forms of societal activity: anarchy, reformism or revisionism, and bureaucratization. Some have argued that Lenin's antistatism meant that he himself was an **anarchist**, or someone opposed to all structure and organization. However, Lenin remarked that anarchists are utopians who seek to dispense immediately with all administration. "These anarchist dreams, based upon incomprehension of the tasks of the proletarian dictatorship, are totally alien to Marxism, and, as a matter of fact, serve only to postpone the socialist revolution until the people are different" (Lenin, 1917c: 344).

Of even greater concern to Lenin (as to Marx) was **reformism**, also known as revisionism or economism. Bourgeois reformism includes unionization—with unions seeking shorter hours, higher wages, and better working conditions. Any such liberal tinkering with the economy has but "one aim: to allay the unrest of the people, force the revolutionary class to cease, or at least slacken, its struggle" (Lenin, 1914:287).

By the end of his life, as we have noted, Lenin's greatest fear was bureaucratization. Stating that the Communist party needed to tap into the great talent of the Russian people, Lenin noted that the party was "displaying 'a passion for bossing.'" The main enemy was the bureaucracy that was springing up (Dunayevskaya, 1958:195). The disease of bureaucratization, according to Lenin, was seen in a growing administrative mentality. Observing Stalin's increasing control and his handpicking of secondary leadership, Lenin made the following comment in a letter written in 1921: "The fight against bureaucratism in an utterly worn-out peasant country takes a long time and has to be carried on tenaciously without losing heart at the first setback" And in 1922 he described how the "vile bureaucratic bog *draws us* into the writing of papers, endless talkfests about decrees, the writing of decrees, and real live work drowns in that sea of paper" (Lenin, 1921–1922:717). Even as Marx had sought to undo the *division of labor*, so Lenin opposed (however ineffectually) the overt division of labor found in bureaucracy. In the next chapter we will see Max Weber theorizing that, whether we like it or not, bureaucracy is the wave of the future. Lenin did not like it.

Critique and Conclusions

Lenin's major contribution to Marxist theory was his work on imperialism.[5] A second contribution was to the class struggle and revolution itself, with a major emphasis on the role of the "vanguard." His third contribution was his ideas on postrevolutionary socialist society, specifically the dictatorship of the proletariat and the antibureaucratic character of such a society.

Criticisms of Lenin have come, not surprisingly, primarily from bourgeois thinkers. Lenin himself acknowledged such critics: "Throughout the civilised world the teachings of Marx evoke the utmost hatred of all bourgeois science" (Lenin, 1913–1922:640). Dunayevskaya observed: "Lenin's enemies are legion nowadays. There is always a lot of talk about his having been a 'democrat' and an exponent of 'workers management from below' only 'in theory,' but that as soon as *State and Revolution* was put away as a book, the practice of governing

---

[5]Some have argued that Lenin's work on imperialism was almost totally dependent on other writers. However, if the *Notebooks* are considered in addition to his small popularized tract on imperialism, it becomes obvious that Lenin's contributions were substantial.

made him a dictator" (Dunayevskaya, 1958:201). This same criticism, focusing on Lenin's centralist and nationalist tendencies, is found in the writings of Rosa Luxemburg.

Rosa Luxemburg (1871–1919)

Rosa Luxemburg was born in the small town of Zamosc, in Poland, near the Russian border. She was born into an enlightened Jewish family, meaning that it had broken out of the circle of ghetto culture and traditions and absorbed the general culture of the country. When Rosa was two, her family moved to Warsaw. At age five, she suffered from a hip ailment that was wrongly diagnosed and treated. The year of her recovery was spent learning to read. She never fully recovered, and throughout her life she walked with a slight limp.

The top school in Warsaw was almost exclusively reserved for Russian children, and even in the next tier of schools, such as the one Luxemburg attended, Polish was not to be spoken. By the time she finished school in 1887, she was already a member of a revolutionary socialist group and was studying Marx and Engels (Frolich, 1969:17 21). She was gifted with many talents, including drawing and painting. She read great literature in Russian, Polish, German, and French, and she wrote poetry in the first three of these languages. She was fascinated by animals and especially by plants, being able to identify large numbers of flowers and trees. In 1889 she fled from Poland and went to the University of Zurich, where she enrolled in natural science. The world of plants and animals remained a lifelong passion and refuge from politics (Frolich, 1969:24).

In 1890 Leo Jogiches came to Zurich, and their friendship became a partnership for life. Clara Zetkin, a friend of both Lenin and Luxemburg, wrote of Leo Jogiches: "He was one of those rare men who can tolerate a great personality in the woman by his side, working with him in loyal and happy comradeship, without feeling her growth and development as a limitation on his own personality" (quoted in Frolich, 1969:28). In 1899 she went through a formal marriage with Gustav Lubeck, for the purpose of obtaining German citizenship, so that the German police would not look upon her as a foreigner.

During her adult life, most of which was spent in Germany, Luxemburg wrote, gave lectures on economics from time to time, and even edited the *Leipziger Volkszeitung* for a few months in 1902. According to a major biographer, J. P. Nettl, Luxemburg was "primarily a journalist, a pamphleteer. She wrote fast and with few corrections. . . . She had no interest in expounding Marxism for its own sake—not even with a view to making it popular" (Nettl, 1966, 1:36–37). Her goal was always to serve the revolution.

Luxemburg's personality seems to have incorporated both a humanitarian concern for suffering and (like Lenin) a willingness to engage in conflict, especially intellectual. Over and above this was a boundless energy and optimism. However, from 1914 to the end of her life she was in trouble with the German authorities. While in prison she was often in poor health, and able only to write letters to friends such as Zetkin. Her good spirits only gave way during the last few months before she was murdered by the German police.

An important part of Luxemburg's intellectual attention was focused on Russia, both before and after Lenin's takeover. Thus, each made many references to the other. An even more important concern was Germany, especially as the 1914–1918 war laid bare capitalist imperialism, seeming to increase the feasibility of a proletarian uprising. But her primary goal, the arousal of the German socialists to the proletarian revolution, was never fulfilled.

Luxemburg's Central Theories and Methods

Although Luxemburg was a Marxist, she did not simply repeat Marx's formulas and theoretical ideas. She contributed to the understanding of reformism/revisionism, imperialism and militarism, nationalism and self-determination, and spontaneity/determinism.

Reformism/Revisionism   As early as 1898, Luxemburg expressed her concern with the Social Democrats in Germany over their reformism (Luxemburg, 1900:70–71). Although Marx and Lenin had both cautioned about merely tinkering with society, Luxemburg explained that the more workers' energies were wasted on immediate, bourgeois-granted goals, the more the revolution receded into the future.

Luxemburg's primary opponent in Germany was Eduard Bernstein, a politician who believed that socialism, through bourgeois reforms and unionization, would gradually take over in turn-of-the-century Germany (Frolich, 1969:71). Luxemburg countered that each reform, each minute concession by the bourgeoisie, was just another palliative confirming the wage-slavery of the proletariat. The capitalists would, as Marx had said, use any method to hold their ruling position: force, good deeds, or propaganda. It is the system that is evil and has to be radically changed. Whether the workers are momentarily satisfied is not the key issue.

Imperialism and Militarism   Luxemburg combined Marx's work in *Capital* with Lenin's observations in his seminal work on imperialism. Marx had made the mistake, according to Luxemburg, of examining capital accumulation within capitalist countries alone. He had envisioned the reinvestment of profit in new machinery, labor power, and productivity, but Luxemburg believed that this reinvestment would be a dead end, leading to unsalable commodities, unemployed workers, and the early stagnation of capitalism (Luxemburg, 1913:329ff). Instead of waiting for their own markets to be exhausted, capitalist countries must find raw materials and open new markets abroad, export capital, and even set up modern capitalist production in countries nowhere near the capitalist stage of production.

Imperialism, according to Luxemburg, allows for the continuation of capitalist accumulation and forestalls the stagnation of the capitalist system. Imperialism was not accidental, but "a historically necessary phase of capitalist development—in fact, the final stage of that development" (Frolich, 1969:191). Imperialism is, therefore, the mortal enemy of the proletariat of all countries. Yet as the pace of imperialism accelerates, so does "the concentration of capital, the pauperization of the middle classes, the numerical reinforcement of the proletariat" (Luxemburg, 1916b:330).

Luxemburg believed that capitalism would eventually choke on its own productivity, and she recognized that Marx had already dismissed the argument that population growth would keep pace with the need for new markets. However, Marx had also noted that new goods and services would help to postpone capitalism's stagnation. In other words, the various signs of capitalism's demise envisioned by Luxemburg might require a very long time to emerge. As for the pauperization of the middle class, this has seemed questionable to most who have followed after Marx and Luxemburg.

Militarism, according to Luxemburg, also releases some of the economic pressures within capitalism. It is more profitable than expenditures on schools and roads, because of "the incessant technical innovations of the military and the incessant increase in its expenditures." She continued:

> Militarism—which to society as a whole represents a completely absurd waste of enormous productive forces—and which for the working class means a lowering of its standard of living with the objective of enslaving it socially—is for the capitalist class economically the most alluring, irreplaceable kind of investment and politically and socially the best support for their class rule. (1899:83)

With imperialism and militarism, of course, comes war. Wars originate, according to Luxemburg, "in the competitive interests of groups of capitalism's need to expand" (1899:204). With war, the products of society are used up even faster than in simply preparing for it. In one of her most picturesque passages she expressed it thus:

> "Deutschland, Deutschland über alles," . . . "long live democracy," "long live the czar and slavery," "ten thousand tent cloths, guaranteed according to specifications," "hundred thousand pounds of bacon," "coffee substitute, immediate delivery" . . . . Dividends are rising—proletarians falling. (Luxemburg, 1916b:328)

Near the end of World War I, writing from experience rather than hypothetically, Luxemburg noted that "profits are springing, like weeds, from the fields of the dead. Business is flourishing upon the ruins" (1918:188). Thus, Luxemburg explained imperialism, militarism, and war as a single phenomenon of capital expansion and profit-making.

Nationalism and Self-Determination   Both Luxemburg and Lenin theorized in a specific historical setting: Lenin in pre- and postrevolutionary Russia, and Luxemburg in nationalistic and then warring Germany. Both were unwavering believers in the international proletarian struggle. But because of her location, Luxemburg argued that one mission of socialism was to liberate the proletariat from "the tutelage of the bourgeoisie, which expresses itself through the influence of nationalist ideology" (1916b:331). Writing in the middle of the war, she was only too aware of what nationalism was doing to Germany.

In addition, watching the Russian revolution closely, Luxemburg concluded that Lenin had made a serious mistake in making peace with Germany instead of calling for an immediate uprising of the German proletariat to join the Russian revolutionaries. In her work on the *Russian Revolution*, never finished and published posthumously, she declared that "the Bolsheviks, by their hollow nationalistic phraseology concerning the 'right of self-determination to the point of separation,' have . . . supplied the bourgeois in all border states with the finest, most desirable pretext, the very banner of counter-revolutionary efforts" (Luxemburg, 1922:53).

Luxemburg felt abandoned in her German struggle, not recognizing Russia's great need for a respite, for a chance to regroup and organize, without the pressure of war with Germany. Mary-Alice Waters, in her introduction to *Rosa Luxemburg Speaks*, argues that it was not because Rosa was opposed to the Bolshevik revolution that she criticized Lenin. It was that "she failed to comprehend the complex and contradictory aspects of the revolutionary dynamic of struggles by oppressed nationalities [such as Russia] in the age of imperialism" (Luxemburg, 1970:17). As an abstract theoretical statement, Luxemburg may have been correct: Nationalism in an unrevolutionized world strengthens capitalism. But at that moment in Russian history, Lenin felt he "could do no other." Luxemburg was correct in the long run, however: Peace strengthened Germany's hand and guaranteed the defeat, in less than three years, of the German workers' movement.

Spontaneity/Determinism   One aspect of what had come to be known in Luxemburg's time as "vulgar Marxism" was the notion of complete **economic determinism,** or fatalism. History is inexorable; change is inevitable; the working classes will bring about the revolution when the time is right. At the other extreme came the Russian revolution in 1917, led by the vanguard—the Bolsheviks—and followed by a "dictatorship of the proletariat" led by Lenin and the Central Committee. In the eyes of non-Russian Marxists such as Luxemburg, the outcome looked much like the dictatorship of a dictator, in the name of the proletariat—not like a workers' revolution.

Luxemburg's criticism of Lenin's centralism was harsh. Lenin responded that she was a vulgar Marxist who thought the proletariat needed neither leading nor educating. But deploring the lack of freedom in Russia, Luxemburg cautioned that freedom is above all freedom for the one who thinks differently. Much earlier Luxemburg had expressed her belief in grassroots workers' movements, and had stated the principle that error-admission and self-criticism were important parts of the revolution: "Historically, the errors committed by a truly revolutionary movement are infinitely more fruitful than the infallibility of the cleverest Central Committee" (1922:108).

Did Luxemburg believe, then, that it was a matter of either grassroots action and freedom to make errors or of central leadership and dictatorship? Clearly the answer is no. Her criticism was specific to postrevolutionary Bolshevism in Russia. In fact, she gave her life to the cause of leading, enlightening, and organizing the proletariat. She believed that leadership must only be as authoritarian and pervasive as absolutely necessary. Luxemburg's view was close to one of Marx's early statements: the revolution was something to be brought about, and it was inevitable.

Nature of Humans, Society, and Change

Despite disagreeing on the Russian revolution, Lenin and Luxemburg had similar views on human nature and change. The goodness in humans could be inferred from their ability to think of and plan for a better world. The nature of the capitalist world, however, was even worse than Marx had imagined, as imperialism/militarism/war had emerged from the greed of capitalist society. Any change in that world is a matter for mass revolution, which will usher in a society whose structures are based on equality, cooperation, and sharing. Only the socialist/communist proletarian revolution can accomplish this difficult but necessary task. But before the revolution could occur, the working classes must be awakened and organized, and they in turn will bring it about.

Class, Gender, and Race

Class   Luxemburg's view of classes was, of course, close to that of Marx. However, she added a major element in the organizing of the proletariat: the **mass strike**. In a 1906 pamphlet, she indicated that the mass strike against capitalist industries is not a single anarchic event, but an ongoing part of the proletarian revolt. It is "the indication, the rallying idea, of a whole period of the class struggle lasting for years, perhaps for decades" (1906:122). The mass strike idea distinguished her work from that of Lenin, who argued for the party's acting on behalf of the proletariat.

Luxemburg's ideas about class struggle were also connected to her conception of war, which both furthered the cause of capitalist imperialism and brought the revolution closer. Referring back to Engels, she wrote in 1918 of two possibilities: "either the triumph of imperialism and the destruction of all culture . . . or the victory of Socialism, that is, the conscious struggle of the international proletariat against imperialism, against its methods, against war." If the proletariat learned from the war and became "lord of its own destiny, the shame and misery will not have been in vain" (1918:196). Note that the outcome is conditional, rather than predestined. Repeating the official party line, Luxemburg stated the following as a basic principle of the new Communist International: "The class struggle within each bourgeois state against the ruling class, and the international solidarity of the proletariat of all countries shall be two inseparable maxims of the working class in its universal historical struggle for liberation" (1916a:225).

Gender   Despite Luxemburg's close friendship with the Marxist Clara Zetkin, there was no recorded conversation between the two regarding the role of women in the revolution. In her biography, however, Frolich notes that Luxemburg's strange reception by the German Social Democrats was due in part to politics being a "male affair. Not only that, but she had not contented herself with modestly asking the opinions of the 'practical politicians,' who were years her senior, but had put forward her own ideas." She had to contend with this male pettiness the rest of her life (Frolich, 1969:57). Franz Mehring had noted the same problem, observing in 1907 that "these irresponsible and petty attacks on the finest brain amongst the scientific successors of Marx and Engels are due in the last resort to the fact that its owner is a woman" (Frolich, 1969:165).

Just as Luxemburg refused to play the traditional woman's role in the party, she refused to write about women as facing any special problems:

> She considered herself, and she was, a revolutionary leader of men *and* women, and she dismissed the insults directed against her because she was a woman as simply part of the overhead of political battle. She understood that women can achieve their full liberation only with the triumph of the socialist revolution and the elimination of their economic bondage to the family institution, and she devoted all her energies to bringing about that revolution. She felt that was the greatest contribution she could possibly make toward the elimination of the oppression of women, as well as of the working class, national minorities, peasants, and all other exploited sectors of the population. (Waters, in Luxemburg, 1970:5)

Thus, like other Marxist revolutionaries, Luxemburg believed that "women's issues" were to be resolved by the class war.

Race   As with Lenin, most of what Luxemburg said about race was contained in her denunciation of imperialism. Describing the treatment of India by the British, of Congo by Belgium, of Algeria by the French, of Namibia by the Germans, and so on, she clearly condemned the exploitation of other races by Europeans (Luxemburg, 1913). Lenin, Luxemburg, and Du Bois (whom you will meet in Chapter 12) all seemed to see such imperialism/colonialism as a central international question.

Other Theories and Theorists

A few additional issues addressed by Luxemburg are worth noting. For instance, her view of religion is found in a 1905 essay, in which she commented on the reactionary nature of the Polish churches. Saying nothing about religion as the "opiate of the people," as Marx had, she took the position that democracy demanded complete freedom of conscience for every human being. When the churches aligned themselves with the bourgeoisie against the working classes, they were part of the enemy. Any defender of "this present regime of misery is the mortal enemy of the proletariat, whether he be in a cassock or in the uniform of the police" (Luxemburg, 1905:152).

Another issue that Luxemburg addressed was the parliamentary form of government. On this subject, her view was close to that of Lenin. She did not argue that the proletariat should boycott bourgeois government. Rather, she believed that parliamentary elections provide an opportunity for spreading socialist propaganda. Socialists, after all, might be elected and represented in the government. When that happens, socialists need to remember two things: (1) they were always an oppositional party, and (2) their goal is "seizing the reins of government and turning [it] into the organ of a victorious working class" (Frolich, 1969:80–82).

Finally, the unity of theory and practice was embodied in her life's work. In Marx, she observed, "the man of ideas and the man of action were inseparably bound up," so that "the socialist teachings of Marxism united theoretical knowledge with revolutionary energy" (Luxemburg, 1915:209).

Critique and Conclusions

Lenin explained imperialism's relation to capitalism, and Luxemburg expanded imperialism to include militarism and war. These were important contributions to understanding how the *capitalist world* functions—how capitalism and capitalists go about the daily pursuit of profit while keeping the working classes under control.

But criticisms abound. Bourgeois writers point out, as did the socialist Bernstein, that capitalism is gradually solving its own problems. However, while Bernstein assumed that reformism and gradualness would eventually lead to the parliamentary adoption of socialism, the bourgeois writers believe that the future belongs to capitalism. As for the working classes, in the developed nations they are part of the rulers, while in the rest of the world they are too weak or apathetic to rise in revolution. Bourgeois writers, then, vilified Lenin because of his success in Russia, and they ignored Luxemburg after her murder in Germany.

Luxemburg, although enthusiastic about Lenin's revolution, was critical of three of Lenin's policies: (1) his overcentralization of power, which led to a dictatorship at the expense of freedom; (2) his governmental bureaucracy, the very bureaucratization that he complained about in Stalin; and (3) his self-determination and nationalism, which led to making peace with Germany instead of uniting with Luxemburg's German proletariat in a widening revolution.

Luxemburg was criticized as well. Lenin argued that she was a vulgar Marxist, expecting a virtually automatic revolution from the grass roots. He and Stalin complained bitterly about her criticisms of the Russian Revolution. After all, Russia had been through it; Luxemburg's Germany had not. Other Marxist critics interpreted her criticisms of Lenin as opposition to the Russian Revolution itself. In 1923 she was attacked as an extreme right-wing Marxist, with her mistakes in *The Accumulation of Capital* interpreted as justifying and supporting capitalism. A few years later, as Communist parties swung to the right, she was attacked again, this time as an ultraleftist (Waters, in Luxemburg, 1970:9–10).

But Luxemburg also had her defenders. Leon Trotsky, an important exiled Russian Marxist, wrote in the 1930s on Luxemburg's behalf: "Rosa Luxemburg exerted herself to educate the revolutionary wing of the proletariat in advance and to bring it together organizationally as far as possible" (Trotsky, 1935:452). In fact, she gave her life to the cause of leading, enlightening, and organizing the proletariat.

Not being alive to defend herself, as she certainly could have done, Luxemburg was open to any interpretations that capitalist or communist writers wanted to use to their advantage. In fact, had she lived 15 more years, she might very well have echoed Marx: "I am not a Luxemburgist."

Luxemburg made it clear in her work that there is no direct link between democracy and capitalism. For her democracy is a much broader and more flexible concept than the nation-state. Democracy is not an end in itself; it will only truly emerge as a result of the worldwide revolution (see Bronner, 1987:111ff).

Whether analyzing capitalism, criticizing postrevolutionary Russia, or calling for revolution in Germany and the world, Luxemburg seldom deviated from her goal as stated in her illegal pamphlet to the Spartakus League, written from prison in 1916: "The fraternization [brotherhood] of the workers of the world is for me the highest and most sacred thing on earth; it is my guiding star, my ideal, my fatherland. I would rather forfeit my life than be unfaithful to this ideal" (1916a:219). And, indeed, her life was taken by defenders of the capitalism she explained and criticized.

Final Thoughts

Lenin and Luxemburg have helped us to think seriously about the combination of oppression and conflict, rather than unity and cooperation, that they believed characterizes imperialist monopoly capitalist nation-states. These two have been vilified or ignored by bourgeois theorists and ideologues, and today their radical ideology is on the defensive in the "new world order." However, additional critiques of capitalism will be found elsewhere in this book, including Chapters 11, 12, 16, and especially Chapter 17 on twentieth-century Marxism.

At the beginning of this book we indicated that much of the theoretical debate within sociology centers on the nature of capitalist society. We have been introduced to the evolutionary and functionalist schools of thought that overtly explain or covertly justify capitalism. And we have met the radicals, who denounce capitalism's ills and argue for its overthrow. In Section IV the discussion expands to include important theorists whose ideologies cannot be categorized as accurately as those in the previous four chapters: Max and Marianne Weber and Georg Simmel.

References

Anderson, Kevin. 1995. *Lenin, Hegel, and Western Marxism*. Chicago: University of Illinois Press.

Bronner, Stephen Eric. 1987. *Rosa Luxemburg: A Revolutionary for Our Times*. New York: Columbia University Press.

Dunayevskaya, Raya. 1958/1988. *Marxism and Freedom from 1776 until Today*. New York: Twayne Publishers.

Fischer, Louis. 1964. *The Life of Lenin*. New York: Harper & Row.

Frolich, Paul. 1969. *Rosa Luxemburg*. New York: Howard Fertig.

Harding, Neil. 1978. *Lenin's Political Thought* (2 vols.). New York: St. Martin's Press.

Lenin, V. I. 1902/1975. "What Is to Be Done?" In Robert C. Tucker (Ed.), *The Lenin Anthology* (pp. 12–114). New York: W. W. Norton.

————. 1904/1975. "One Step Forward, Two Steps Back." In Robert C. Tucker (Ed.), *The Lenin Anthology* (pp. 115–199). New York: W. W. Norton.

————. 1905/1960. "The Beginning of Revolution in Russia." In *Collected Works* (vol. 8, pp. 39–43). Moscow: Progress.

————. 1913–1922/1975. "On Marxism and Philosophy." In Robert C. Tucker (Ed.), *The Lenin Anthology* (pp. 639–654). New York: W. W. Norton.

————. 1914/1975. "Lecture on the 1905 Revolution." In Robert C. Tucker (Ed.), *The Lenin Anthology* (pp. 278–292). New York: W. W. Norton.

————. 1917a/1960. "April Theses." In *Collected Works* (vol. 14, p. 217). Moscow: Progress.

————. 1917b/1975. "Imperialism." In Robert C. Tucker (Ed.), *The Lenin Anthology* (pp. 203–274). New York: W. W. Norton.

————. 1917c/1975. "The State and Revolution." In Robert C. Tucker (Ed.), *The Lenin Anthology* (pp. 311–398). New York: W. W. Norton.

————. 1918/1975. "The Immediate Tasks of the Soviet Government. In Robert C. Tucker (Ed.), *The Lenin Anthology* (pp. 438–460). New York: W. W. Norton.

————. 1919/1975. "A Great Beginning." In Robert C. Tucker (Ed.), *The Lenin Anthology* (pp. 477–488). New York: W. W. Norton.

————. 1920a/1975. *Left-Wing Communism.* In Robert C. Tucker (Ed.), *The Lenin Anthology* (pp. 550–618). New York: W. W. Norton.

————. 1920b/1975. "The Tasks of the Youth League." In Robert C. Tucker (Ed.), *The Lenin Anthology* (pp. 661–674). New York: W. W. Norton.

————. 1920c/1975. "Communism and the East." In Robert C. Tucker (Ed.), *The Lenin Anthology* (pp. 619–625). New York: W. W. Norton.

————. 1921a/1975. "Communism and the New Economic Policy." In Robert C. Tucker (Ed.), *The Lenin Anthology* (pp. 518–533). New York: W. W. Norton.

————. 1921b/1975. "Dialogue with Clara Zetkin." In Robert C. Tucker (Ed.), *The Lenin Anthology* (pp. 685–699). New York: W. W. Norton.

————. 1921–1922/1975. "On Bureaucracy: From Lenin's Correspondence." In Robert C. Tucker (Ed.), *The Lenin Anthology* (pp. 714–718). New York: W. W. Norton.

————. 1922/1975. "Our Revolution." In Robert C. Tucker (Ed.), *The Lenin Anthology* (pp. 703–706). New York: W. W. Norton.

————. 1943. *Selected Works* (12 vols.). New York: International Publishers.

————. 1959–1962. *Werke* (37 vols.). Berlin: Dietz.

————. 1960. *Collected Works* (45 vols.). Moscow: Progress.

Luxemburg, Rosa. 1899/1974. "The Militia and Militarism, *Leipziger Volkszeitung.*" In Robert Looker (Ed.), *Selected Political Writings* (pp. 76–92). New York: Grove Press.

————. 1900/1974. "Social Reform or Revolution." In Robert Looker (Ed.), *Selected Political Writings* (pp. 57–71). New York: Grove Press.

————. 1905/1970. "Socialism and the Churches." In Mary-Alice Waters (Ed.), *Rosa Luxemburg Speaks* (pp. 131–152). New York: Pathfinder Press.

————. 1906/1924. "The Mass Strike, the Political Party, and the Trade Unions." In Robert Looker (Ed.), *Selected Political Writings* (pp. 121–140). New York: Grove Press.

————. 1913/1963. *The Accumulation of Capital.* London: Routledge and Kegan Paul.

————. 1915/1974. "Rebuilding the International." In Robert Looker (Ed.), *Selected Political Writings* (pp. 197–210). New York: Grove Press.

————. 1916a/1974. "Either-Or." In Robert Looker (Ed.), *Selected Political Writings* (pp. 211–226). New York: Grove Press.

————. 1916b/1970. "The Junius Pamphlet." In Mary-Alice Waters (Ed.), *Rosa Luxemburg Speaks* (pp. 257–331). New York: Pathfinder Press.

————. 1918/1974. "The Crisis of Social Democracy." In Robert Looker (Ed.), *Selected Political Writings* (pp. 187–196). New York: Grove Press.

————. 1922/1970. *The Russian Revolution* and *Leninism or Marxism?* Ann Arbor: University of Michigan.

————. 1970. *Rosa Luxemburg Speaks* (Mary-Alice Waters, Ed.). New York: Pathfinder Press.

————. 1974. *Selected Political Writings* (Robert Looker, Ed.). New York: Grove Press.

Meszaros, Istvan. 1972. *Lukacs' Concept of Dialectic*. London: Merlin Press.

Nettl, J. P. 1966. *Rosa Luxemburg* (2 vols.). London: Oxford University Press.

Possony, Stefan T. 1964. *Lenin: The Compulsive Revolutionary*. Chicago: Henry Regnery.

Trotsky, Leon. 1935/1970. "Luxemburg and the Fourth International." In Mary-Alice Waters (Ed.), *Rosa Luxemburg Speaks* (pp. 451–454). New York: Pathfinder Press.

Tucker, Robert C. (Ed.). 1975. *The Lenin Anthology*. New York: W. W. Norton.

Ulam, Adam B. 1965/1998. *The Bolsheviks*. Cambridge, MA: Harvard University Press.

SECTION IV

Sociological Theories of Complexity and Form

The German sociologists introduced in this section—Max Weber, Marianne Weber, and Georg Simmel—were as concerned as the French, British, and American sociologists of their era with the nature of modern, industrial society. They deplored the social disorder that seemed to accompany modernization and the French Revolution. Therefore, the work of the German radical theorists was important to them, particularly Marx's understanding of the economic changes that contributed to the problems of modern capitalism. But these sociologists rejected Marx's explanation of history in terms of class oppression and struggle.

These three German sociologists also found fault with positivist and evolutionary theories exemplified in the work of Comte, Spencer, and Durkheim. Thus, the Webers and Simmel framed their sociology in contrast to—often in opposition to—their work. For instance, although these German sociologists accepted the general idea of a science of society, their conception of that science differed from the positivists' idea. They believed that a science of society had to have two critical components: a focus on the human actor giving meaning to social events, and a recognition of the complexity and variability of cultures over time. The historical context and especially the meanings attributed to events, relations, and behaviors were central to the Webers and Simmel.

This focus led to a distinct conception of the methods needed to explore the social world. Sociology, they believed, should not slavishly imitate the methods of the natural sciences, but should develop its own methodology to fit the uniqueness of human society. Sociological data are not things or social facts, external to both the actor and the interpreter. Objectivity on the natural science model does not apply to the formulation of sociological research questions and answers, because social data require interpretation within their social context. Consequently, rather than search for causal laws, the sociologist must seek to understand and to approximate causation. This does not mean that the social scientist should pursue an ideological agenda. Rather, it means that the sociologist is concerned with values and motives within their social/historical context, but the investigation of such issues is not to be based on the observer's own evaluation or ideology.

The critical point for the late-nineteenth-century German sociology of the Webers and Simmel was that sociology must never lose sight of human agency. Historically and culturally situated humans give meaning to their social realities. As a result, relativism rather than causal explanation is the key to a scientific sociology. Sociologists should study not only human actions and behaviors, but also their social contexts.

These German sociologists were liberals who saw the sociological enterprise as a useful tool for social reform. Max Weber insisted that the sociologist should not be a politician; however, it is the sociologist's duty to provide clear, accurate depictions of society in order to give politicians the means to effect needed change. Marianne Weber was concerned about women's issues and about the need for sociological discourse in order to further theoretical understanding. Simmel was less active in the political arena, but that was understandable given his Jewish ethnicity in the German state. Simmel focused on social form and content, and on the ways in which individuals can resolve the problems that modern existence presents—in short, the means for personal efficacy rather than specific political reforms.

Chapter 7

Social Action and Social Complexity
Max Weber and Marianne Weber

The French development of sociology that you have read about in the Chapters 2 and 4 was paralleled by similar developments in Germany. However, the development in Germany differed because of the nature of the academic environment. Durkheim managed, after several years, to establish sociology as an academic discipline, but Max Weber and his fellow German sociologists had a much harder time establishing the legitimacy of the sociological enterprise. Until the 1930s, Germany "remained a country with sociologists but without sociology" (Bendix, 1971:44). Nonetheless, Germany produced several important sociologists—most notably, Max Weber, regarded by his contemporaries as their "generational spokesman" (Bendix, 1971:13). And one contemporary called him a genius (Green, 1974:277).

Max Weber was a sociologist, economist, legal scholar, historian, and politician. His eclectic interests gave him a broad perspective on society and contributed to his political activities. He was a "politically engaged scholar" who saw his work as contributing to the "strengthening of Germany's political, economic, and cultural position in the world" (Bendix, 1971:18). This concern with the ethical and political ramifications of sociology has also made him the "paradigmatic and exemplary sociologist" for many contemporary sociologists (MacRae, 1974:17).

We know quite a bit about the esteem his contemporaries accorded Weber because of the biography written by his wife, Marianne Weber. Much of the biographical and interpretive detail in this chapter comes from Marianne Weber. Marianne Weber was, however, a sociologist of note in her own right. Her work is just beginning to be more widely known in the English-speaking world, but on at least one occasion Marianne Weber's reputation eclipsed Max's. In her biography of Max Weber, she wrote that in 1908 she and Max attended a political meeting at which he spoke unexpectedly and passionately. As they were leaving, one man was overhead to ask, "Who's that Max Weber anyway?" He was told, "Oh, he's Marianne's guy" (Marianne Weber, 1926:407).

The central focus of this chapter is on Max Weber's work but, where appropriate, the work of Marianne Weber will also be introduced.

Max Weber (1864–1920) and Marianne Weber (1870–1954)

Max Weber was the eldest of eight children born to Max Weber, Sr., and his wife, Helene. Two of the children died very young, and the remaining siblings included two sisters and three brothers, among them the sociologist Alfred Weber. The family moved to Berlin in 1869 when Weber, Sr., became a city councillor and then a member of the Prussian House of Deputies. He was thus part of the political establishment. Weber, Sr., was on the left wing of the National Liberal Party but far from an idealist, and in the family context he was a typical bourgeois patriarch (Mitzman, 1969:17).

Weber's mother was very religious, and she discovered early in her marriage that her religious outlook was not shared by her husband. The religious and emotional differences between the two became apparent with the deaths of the two children and, in her estrangement from her husband, Helene Weber "wrapped herself in renunciation and inner loneliness" although outwardly appearing a "charming, graceful, loving woman . . . valiant, humorous, and joyful despite her inner seriousness" (Marianne Weber, 1926:60). According to Marianne Weber, the contrast between the self-sacrificing, religious mother who served her husband with "loving submissiveness" and the authoritarian father who desired nothing more than a "comfortable bourgeois standard of living" and who was "warmhearted and amiable as long as things went his way," had an effect on Weber's own marital relations and his view of his destiny in life (1926:38, 63).

Weber was an indifferent scholar at school and remembered being as "lazy as sin" as an adolescent, but he was an avid reader and made notes on all that he read. In 1877 he produced, as a Christmas present for his parents and siblings, two historical essays based on his reading. These two essays, "About the Course of German History, with Special Regard to the Positions of the Emperor and the Pope" and "About the Roman Imperial Period from Constantine to the Migration of Nations," foreshadowed his later sociological interests (Marianne Weber, 1926:46).

In 1882 Weber enrolled at the University of Heidelberg to study jurisprudence, as well as history, economics, and philosophy. There he was physically transformed from a bookish, lanky youth into a "jolly fellow." He became more like his father, joining his father's dueling fraternity and distinguishing himself by his "outstanding capacity for alcohol," which resulted in an "increase in his physical girth." The change was so striking that when his mother saw him, especially with the dueling scar on his cheek, she expressed her "astonishment and fright" by giving him a "resounding slap across the face" (Marianne Weber, 1926:69).

The paternal identification suggested by his physical appearance changed after Weber's move to Strasbourg to fulfill his obligatory year of military service. In Strasbourg he became close to his mother's sister's family, the Baumgartens. Unlike his father, Herman Baumgarten treated Weber as an intellectual peer and discussed political and intellectual issues with him, especially Baumgarten's liberal opposition to the German Chancellor Bismarck. Ida Baumgarten was as religious as her sister, but more forceful in her expression of her views. According to Marianne Weber, Ida Baumgarten used the Sermon on the Mount as an "uncompromising standard," and although Weber did not share her beliefs, he respected her sense of ethical responsibility. In addition, Ida Baumgarten's example allowed Weber to appreciate the difficulties of his mother's life with his father.

In 1884 Weber returned to live with his parents and complete his studies at the University of Berlin. He obtained his Ph.D. in 1889 with a dissertation titled "On the History of Commercial Societies in the Middle Ages." In 1891 he produced a second dissertation, "Roman Agrarian History," necessary for those aspiring to university faculty status. While pursuing these qualifications, he was "passionately interested in political events," most particularly in the possibility of a liberal opposition to the imperialistic conservatism of Bismarck and the "dangers of Wilhelm II's will to power" (Marianne Weber, 1926:115, 123).

In 1892 Weber began lecturing at the university on Roman, German, and commercial law, at the same time working as a barrister. He also produced three books, which established his reputation as a scholar.[1] Weber worked at a furious pace, subjecting "himself to a ruthless work schedule" (Mitzman, 1969:47–48). In 1894 he obtained an academic position at the University of Freiburg.

In 1893 Max Weber married a cousin, Marianne Schnitger. It was the marriage of two intellectuals. Some have claimed the marriage was unconsummated (Mitzman, 1969), but the partners were devoted to one another, as Marianne Weber's biography of Max makes clear.

Marianne Weber, née Schnitger, was the grandniece of Max Weber, Sr. Her mother, who came from a wealthy family, died when Marianne was very young, and shortly after her father, a physician, began to show signs of mental illness. Marianne went to live with her grandmother and an aunt on her father's side in a small town. When she was sixteen, her wealthy grandfather sent her to be educated at a "fashionable institute" in Hannover (Marianne Weber, 1926:173). In 1892 she went to Berlin, where she stayed with her relatives, the Weber family. After a year and a half, Marianne reported that "she was in love" with Max and eventually learned that her feelings were reciprocated.

As a presage of their intellectual partnership, Marianne reported that prior to the marriage she helped Max with the investigation of farmworkers he had undertaken for the Evangelical Social Congress. She observed that "it seemed advisable to . . . familiarize herself with scholarship as soon as possible if she was to be inwardly close to him and not to be overwhelmed by this insatiable competitor" (1926:189). Max Weber's mother was a little concerned by this turn of events, seeing "ink-stained hands six weeks before the wedding," and wondered if Marianne would ever "be satisfied with the every-day pursuits of a *Hausfrau*" (Marianne Weber, 1926:189). Marianne's response to her future mother-in-law's concern was, "Everything in due time."

---

[1] The books were not legal studies but studies in political economy dealing with East Elbian agricultural workers.

Marianne was a sociologist and a feminist. She was among the pioneering women who pursued an education and career like any man and was one of the leaders of the liberal feminist movement. In 1918 German women obtained the vote, and in 1919 Marianne Weber became the first woman member of the Baden parliament. She also produced considerable sociological research in her own right, including an important book on marriage and the legal position of women that was reviewed, critically, by Durkheim (see Chapter 4). The book, *Ehefrau und Mutter in der Rechtsentwicklung* (1907), was a critique of theories of mother rights found in the work of Engels and others and an endorsement of the idea that what was required was not a "substitute *for* marriage, but a re-form *of* marriage" (Marianne Weber, 1926:371).

In 1896 Max Weber was appointed to the Chair of Economics at the University of Heidelberg, and thereafter he became identified with that city. Heidelberg was the "city of light, the domain of Apollo, the home in all of Germany who resisted the excesses of patriarchalism," and "Weber was their natural leader" (Green, 1974:140). After World War I, Georg Simmel wrote to Marianne Weber that " a great responsibility now rested on the *Haus Weber*" in Heidelberg to reconstitute "that incomparable treasure of German culture" (Green, 1974:140).

Weber's active participation in university life was abruptly curtailed in 1897 by a breakdown, apparently triggered by a violent argument with his father over his treatment of Helene. Helene Weber had planned a visit to Max and Marianne by herself, when her husband suddenly decided to accompany her. According to Marianne, Weber, Sr., felt that Helene "belonged to him, that his interests and desires took precedence over hers and everyone else's, and that he had the right to determine the time and duration of her vacation" (1926:230). The son was furious with his father and, "no longer able to contain his pent-up anger" over the tyrannical treatment of his mother over the years, he told his father that his mother had the right to visit when she wished and then ordered his father out of the house. This affront to traditional patriarchal authority was compounded by his father's death some weeks later without any further contact with his eldest son. Shortly after the funeral, Max Weber suffered a breakdown that left him incapable of sustained intellectual work. Marianne Weber reported that "everything was too much for him; he could not read, write, talk, walk, or sleep without torment" (1926:242).

The opposition between the paternal and maternal influences that had been in conflict throughout Weber's childhood came to a head with this violent repudiation of his father and defense of his mother's "spiritual rights." The repudiation took its toll by disturbing the delicate psychological balance Weber had constructed for himself between his mother's religiosity and self-discipline and his father's selfish egoism and patriarchal authoritarianism (Mitzman, 1969:168–169). These personal demons never disappeared, and they formed the background to his subsequent work on the alienating nature of modern capitalist society.

From the time of his breakdown until 1917, when Weber took a professorship on a trial basis at the University of Vienna, he was a private scholar. In the turmoil of 1917, right after Germany's defeat in World War I, some Social

Democrats suggested Weber's name as a possible Chancellor. The suggestion was not followed through, but Weber did go to work as a political adviser for the newspaper *Frankfurter Zeitung* in 1917 and wrote essays on the new form of government needed for German reconstruction after the war.

Despite the periods of debilitating psychological problems, Weber produced a prodigious amount of work. With the exception of 1901, he published every year (Kasler, 1988:12). Weber's productivity was helped by the coeditorship he assumed of the *Archiv für Sozialwissenschaft* in 1904. The journal had been bought by Edgar Jaffe, who essentially "presented it to Max Weber" and in this way brought Weber's career to life again after the breakdown (Green, 1974:27). The *Archiv* became the leading German sociological journal.

A considerable amount of Max Weber's work remained unfinished and unpublished at his untimely death from pneumonia in 1920. The translation and publication of much of this work have been relatively recent. In an effort to chart a course through the wealth of this material, we concentrate on some of the central themes, recognizing that this focus does not do full justice to the totality of the Weberian opus. Marianne Weber's work will be noted throughout the chapter.

Weber's Central Theories and Methods

A central theme in Max Weber's work was his concern with the problems of Western civilization, especially the rationalization and demystification of all aspects of modern social life—"the 'disenchantment of the world'" (1946:155). He was concerned with the radical transformations in social life that distinguished modern from traditional society. He was also interested in the methodology that sociologists would use to understand those transformation.

Rationalization   Like Marx, among others, Weber noted that one of the most important historical transformations was the rationalization of economic structures to produce modern capitalism. By **rationalization** he meant the process of making life more efficient and predictable by wringing out individuality and spontaneity in life. In *The Protestant Ethic and the Spirit of Capitalism* (1904–1905:21), Weber characterized rational capitalism as the "most fateful force in our modern life." He noted that the capitalist "pursuit of wealth, stripped of its religious and ethical meaning" produced "specialists without spirit, sensualists without heart" (1904–1905:182). Weber was aware that capitalism had existed in a number of societies in various historical periods, but he claimed that the "sober bourgeois capitalism" of the West had developed "types, forms, and directions which had never existed elsewhere" (1904–1905:20).[2]

---

[2] Max Weber continued his investigation of the historical background to this peculiar form of Western rationalization in a work to be called *An Outline of Social Economics*. The work was not completed before his death, but Marianne Weber and Johannes Wincklemann compiled the notes for this work into the two-volume *Economy and Society* (1925).

Weber's studies of modern, rational capitalism were important responses to Marx's analysis of capitalism. Weber had a "great admiration for Karl Marx's brilliant constructions," but he rejected the elevation of "material factors" as "absolute and being turned into the *common denominator* of causal explanations" (Marianne Weber, 1926:335). Both Weber and Marx sought to discover the historical causal relationships that had led to the current state of modern society, but Weber did not claim, as Marx did, that "material factors," or economic interests, could explain every aspect of social reality (Sayer, 1991:109).

Ideas, in Weber's view, especially religious ideas, were important components of practical action. Weber's position on the relationship of material factors to ideas and beliefs is summed up in his "switchmen" metaphor:

> Not ideas, but material and ideal interests, directly govern men's conduct. Yet very frequently the "world images" that have been created by "ideas" have, like switchmen, determined the tracks along which action has been pushed by the dynamic of interest. (1915b:280)

Nonetheless, "No economic ethic has ever been determined solely by religion" (1915b:267–268).

Weber's interest in modern rational capitalism was reflected in many of his disparate analyses of the nature of power and authority, the characteristics of bureaucratic organizations, the nature and form of Western art, the characteristics and importance of city development, the nature and importance of world religions. The context, both personal and theoretical, for all these analyses was Weber's understanding that modern society was increasingly a place in which the transcendental world of gods was giving way to science and the rational calculation of social actions.

Weber took a particular interest in politics. He observed that, in contrast to economics, politics came into "direct competition with religious ethics at decisive points" (1915a:334). For example, the "Sermon on the Mount says 'resist no evil'. In opposition, the state asserts: 'You *shall* help right triumph by the use of *force*, otherwise you too may be responsible for injustice'" (1915a:334). Force breeds force, however, and success depends "ultimately on power relations and not on ethical 'right,' even were one to believe it possible to discover objective criteria for such 'right'" (1915a:334). Thus modern, pragmatic politics introduces an ethical dilemma: How can any state that uses force to achieve justice avoid injustice?

The progression from faith to secular pragmatism was also mirrored in, and facilitated by, the triumph of Western science. The religiously motivated search for authentic "truths" had fueled the development of science. But the development of science produced the search for efficient means-ends calculation and mastery over the natural world, which displaced the religious monopoly on "truth" in the modern world.

Weber pointed out that the belief in the "value of scientific truth is a product of certain cultures and is not a product of man's original nature" (1903–1917:17). More specifically, the rationality of Western capitalism depended on the "calculability of the most important technical factors." In other words, it depended on the sciences, "especially those based on mathematics and exact and rational experiment" (1904–1905:24).

Sociological Methodology   Weber's views on Western science are reflected in his views on the appropriate methodology for sociology. Social theorists, as you have seen in previous chapters, had been debating the characteristics of the natural sciences as opposed to the human or social sciences, and the methodology appropriate to their study. Comte believed that the methods of the natural sciences, with the addition of comparison, could be transposed to the social sciences. Other theorists, such as Simmel, disagreed, insisting that the subject matter of the social or human sciences meant that different methods were required. The natural sciences looked for the common characteristics of empirical data in order to formulate abstract, universal laws, but the human and social sciences studied unique, historical individuals and events in order to understand their specific meaning.

Weber attempted to steer a middle course between these two positions. He insisted that "interpretive understanding of social action" was the subject matter of sociology but did not preclude objective research (1925, 1:4). The sociologist went beyond the scientist's demonstration of "functional relationships and uniformities" to illustrate the "subjective understanding of the action" (1925, 1:15):

> The type of social science which we are interested in is an *empirical science* of concrete reality . . . . Our aim is the understanding of the characteristic uniqueness of the reality in which we move. We wish to understand on the one hand the relationships and cultural significance of individual events in their contemporary manifestations and on the other the causes of their being historically *so* and not *otherwise*. (1903–1917:72)

The reflexive nature of human beings meant that a different methodology was essential for sociology. Statistical uniformities could produce sociological generalizations, but only when they were "manifestations of the understandable subjective meaning of the course of social action" (1925, 1:12). This "empathetic understanding" is different from the requirements of natural science research, although "aside from pure mechanics, even the exact natural sciences do not proceed without qualitative categories" (1903–1917:74). Understanding, or **verstehen,** must be present for sociological interpretation of causes.

Weber distinguished two types of verstehen: **direct observational** understanding and **explanatory** understanding. For example, from facial expressions and gestures we can often have direct observational understanding of an angry outburst. Explanatory understanding is achieved when we understand what prompted the outburst at that precise time and place (1925, 1:18).

A sociologist cannot understand the meaning of an individual's behavior to that person. But to the extent that the behavior is typical for multiple individuals in a given situation, the sociologist can formulate generalizations that can provide the basis for causal linkages.

The sociologist, however, is usually confronted with a plurality of causes affecting social or historical events. Weber suggested that the way to cope with this problem is to ask whether the event, or chain of events, would have been different if some specific cause had been removed. If the answer is yes, then there is an objective possibility that the cause had a decisive effect. The isolation of such a cause is the isolation of a probability, however; it is not the isolation of an invariant cause-effect relationship.

Furthermore, the significance of the action must be taken into account. For a causal linkage to exist, there must be some proof that the action is normally taken to be a meaningful response. In other words, there must be some "approximation to an average or pure type"—what Weber termed an **ideal type**—that could provide the basis for estimating objective possibilities (1925, 1:12). Sociology must formulate ideal types to make significant contributions to the causal explanation of historical and cultural events.

Ideal types focus sociological inquiry by sorting out the characteristics that define the phenomenon under investigation and provide the sociologist with the tools to understand the variability of actual social and historical phenomena. For example, Weber's ideal type bureaucracy is defined as a rational form of administration that performs with maximum efficiency. As you know from any confrontation with bureaucracy, rationality often seems elusive and efficiency a risible description. The point is, however, that the ideal type allows you to understand how and why these irrational and inefficient bureaucratic behaviors occur.

Ideal types are abstractions that emphasis the core or central elements of the phenomenon. The ideal type is not a hypothesis; rather it "offers guidance to the construction of hypotheses." Neither is it a description of reality, but "it aims to give unambiguous means of expression to such a description" (1903–1917:90). Thus, no ideal type is a mirror image of empirical reality, and it cannot be judged true or false; it must be judged on its typicality and "adequacy at the level of meaning" (1925, 1:20). For example, ideal type power emphasizes the distinctive, typical characteristic of "pure" power in a variety of social and historical contexts. The type is "pure" in that it depicts the bare bones of power, uncontaminated by the compromises and adjustments encountered in the day-to-day exercise of power. "In its conceptual purity" the ideal type "cannot be found empirically anywhere in reality. It is a *utopia*" (1903–1917:90).

However, an ideal type is not ideal in the sense of a standard of perfection or an ultimate goal. Ideal types do not embody "essence" or "truth," and they do not relate in a one-to-one fashion with the ideas or understandings of the actual participants in the reality to which the type refers. Rather, ideal types are constructed by sociologists and therefore are constructed from "particular points of view" (1903–1917:81).

The evaluative basis for the construction of ideal types does not, in Weber's view, compromise the objectivity of the research. Any type of scientific inquiry is prompted by interests or values; it is only because of the investigator's evaluative ideas that the subject matter is selected and meaningful knowledge produced (1903–1917:82). The key to objectivity is conducting the research according to rational, objective methods. The research must be clearly conceptualized, the conventional rules of evidence must be followed, conclusions must be drawn only on the basis of the evidence, and no moral or political status should be attributed to the conclusions reached by the scientist *as* scientist.

Weber was particularly opposed to sociologists' using their work to advance their own personal beliefs and values: the "prophet and the demagogue do not belong on the academic platform" (1919b:146). The "elementary duty of scien-

tific self-control" demanded a "sharp distinction between the logically comparative analysis of reality by ideal-types in the logical sense and the value-judge-
ment of reality on the basis of ideals" (1903–1917:98).

Nature of Society, Humans, and Change

Weber was well aware that many sociologists of his time, such as Durkheim and
Spencer, were concerned with defining the concept of society. Weber, however,
assiduously avoided treating society, or any social grouping, as a sui generis entity (Frisby and Sayer, 1986:68). For Weber, sociology was concerned with understanding the meaning, causes, and consequences of **social action**:

> We shall speak of "action" insofar as the acting individual attaches a
> subjective meaning to his behavior—be it overt or covert, omission or
> acquiescence. Action is "social" insofar as its subjective meaning takes
> account of the behavior of others, and is thereby oriented in its course.
> (1925, 1:4)

Social action could include "failure to act" as well as "passive acquiescence" and
could involve a "past, present, or future" orientation to the behavior of others.
In addition, "others" could be specific individuals known to the actor or an "indefinite plurality . . . entirely unknown as individuals" (1925, 1:22). In all cases,
the action that was sociologically interesting was meaningful action.

Weber identified four types of meaningful social action (1925, 1:25–26):

- **Instrumental rational action** occurs when the "end, the means, and the
  secondary results are all rationally taken into account and weighed." The
  prototypical form of such action is action based on objective, scientific
  knowledge.

- **Value-rational action** is action based on a "conscious belief in the value
  for its own sake of some ethical, aesthetic, religious, or other form of
  behavior, independently of its prospects of success." The key here is that the
  action is an end in itself rather than a means.

- **Affectual action,** or emotional action, sits at the border of behavior that is
  "meaningfully" oriented and may, on occasion, go "over the line"—as, for
  example, in "an uncontrolled reaction to some exceptional stimulus."

- **Traditional action** is action determined by "ingrained habituation." Like
  affectual action, traditional action is also borderline meaningful because in
  most cases the action is an "almost automatic reaction to habitual stimuli
  which guide behavior in a course that has been repeatedly followed." It is
  action on the order of "it has always been done this way." Weber suggests
  that most everyday action is of this type.

The four types of action are pure forms or ideal types, and Weber was well
aware that in practice any social action can involve some combination of these
motivations. But for Weber, it was the first two forms—instrumental rational
action and value-rational action—that were of greatest interest and often the
most difficult to separate. Consider the relationship between capitalism and
Protestantism.

The Protestant Ethic and the Spirit of Capitalism   Both Marx and Weber investigated capitalism, focusing on the predicament of modern individuals when the economy becomes human destiny (Lowith, 1993:48). And both theorists took a pessimistic view: for Marx, it was alienation; for Weber, rationalization. Weber found most troubling the way that rationalization produced a "disenchantment of the world" involving a retreat of the "ultimate and most sublime values" from public life into private life, with the resulting loss of any sense that the world has meaning (1919b:155).

In *The Protestant Ethic and the Spirit of Capitalism*, Weber illustrated how the "specific and peculiar rationalism of Western culture," tied to the "technical and economic conditions of machine production," was originally motivated by religious values. But in time religious values fell by the wayside, and the technical and economic aspects became an irresistible force determining everyone's lives and enclosing them like an "iron cage" (1904–1905:181).

Weber demonstrated that the Protestant injunction to an ascetic existence was the key motivational factor shaping the rationalization of modern Western societies. More specifically, although capitalism had existed in a number of societies in various historical periods, Weber pointed out that the "sober bourgeois capitalism" of Western societies developed "types, forms, and directions which have never existed before" (1904–1905:20).

> It is only in the modern Western world that rational capitalistic enterprises with fixed capital, free labor, the rational specialization and combination of functions, and the allocation of productive functions on the basis of capitalistic enterprises, bound together in a market economy, are to be found. (1925, 1:165)

Most notably, Western capitalism pursued profit as an end in itself and work as a moral injunction. The **spirit of capitalism** was the rational pursuit of gain (an instrumental action); the **Protestant ethic** was "routine activity on the world" or dutiful work in a calling (a value-rational action) (1904–1905:80).

The structural supports for Western capitalism were found in cities. Capitalism was an urban phenomenon. The power of popes and kings and princes had been successfully challenged by early city-states, which were able to break away and claim legal and political autonomy. In the city the laborer could become a "free man," and the burgher class could evolve, claiming individualistic civil liberties guaranteed by a procedurally rational legal system of impersonal rules. These developments broke the hold of traditional **feudal** hierarchies in the West and provided the climate for the expansion of nonagricultural activities, most notably manufacturing and international trade.

Other structural features important to the development of capitalism included the separation of household accounts from those of the business enterprise, and, over time, the physical separation of the household from the productive sphere. For example, the "large capitalistic households of medieval cities" retained the extended household unit, but "household communism" was replaced by a calculative rational association. A male individual born into the household became a "potential business partner of the rationally managed enterprise" (Weber, 1925, 1:377). The separation of the household from the enterprise and the crucial separation of the two for "accounting and legal purposes," so critical to rational capitalist development, had clear gender implications. The household became the proper domain of women, and the productive enterprises predominantly the domain of men—at least in respect to control over production and consumption. The rationally organized capitalist productive process was therefore basically the *"battle of man with man"* (1925, 1:93).

The "battles" in the capitalist marketplace were the antithesis of the battles of a traditional or feudal warrior brotherhood. The warrior brotherhood undertook heroic deeds for a cause or a leader. Capitalist battles were detached, impersonal, calculating conflicts oriented to an object—money—rather than to a person or cause.

Weber pointed to Benjamin Franklin's advice in *Poor Richard's Almanac* as an example of rational capitalist motivations and practices. Franklin was the author of such injunctions as "Remember, that *time* is money," "Money can beget money," and the "most trifling actions . . . affect a man's credit. . . . The sound of your hammer at five in the morning, or eight at night, heard by a creditor, makes him easy six months longer" (1904–1905:48–49). For Franklin, life was "dominated by the making of money, . . . as the ultimate purpose of life." This utilitarian approach to acquisition was combined with the "strict avoidance of all spontaneous enjoyment of life" (1904–1905:53). But the idea of money-making as an end in itself was "contrary to the ethical feelings of whole epochs," including the preceding epoch in the West, in which "acquisition for its own sake was . . . a *pudendum*," or sin, in the eyes of the Catholic Church and dangerous for any individual seeking salvation (1904–1905:73).

How, Weber asked, could an activity like making money, which had previously been only tolerated at best, become a "calling" in the sense understood by Franklin? The question was particularly interesting given the economic context of Franklin's reflections: "backwoods small bourgeois circumstances of Pennsylvania in the eighteenth century, where business threatened for simple lack of money to fall back into barter, where there was hardly a sign of large enterprise, where only the earliest beginnings of banking were to be found." And yet, for Franklin, the rational pursuit of gain was the "essence of moral conduct, even commanded in the name of duty" (1904–1905:75). Referring to Marx's work, Weber declared that in Franklin's case to "speak here of a reflection of material conditions in the ideal superstructure would be patent nonsense" (1904–1905:75). The background to the idea of acquisitive activity as a calling, or an ethical duty, so "irrational from the standpoint of purely eudaemonistic self interest," and minimally supported in Franklin's case by existing economic conditions, was to be found in Protestantism (1904–1905:78).

The idea of a worldly **calling**—"a religious task set by God"—was first advanced by the Protestant reformer, Martin Luther (1904–1905:79). Luther rejected the idea that the most virtuous existence was a monastic one and suggested that God looked upon such renunciation of worldly obligations as a selfish act. To live acceptably to God was to live in the world, fulfilling one's worldly duties (1904–1905:81).

Luther's endorsement of worldly activity as righteous activity was an important change, but John Calvin's ideas about predestination were even more significant, in Weber's view, for the development of Western capitalism. For Calvin, and the Puritans, all individuals were alone with God and could not look to others, such as priests, for intervention on their behalf before God. Such intervention would be futile anyway, because each individual's fate was predetermined. Some individuals were part of the elect—the saved—and others were damned. For any individual to assume that penance or good works could change God's mind was an insult to God, whose decrees had been "settled from eternity" and could not be changed by human action. Consequently, those who were damned could never redeem themselves, just as those with God's grace could never lose that favor. More troubling, however, was that individuals could not know with any certainty whether or not they were of the elect. Weber suggested that this dour situation accounted for the Puritan opposition to hedonistic activity, most especially any idolatry of the flesh—that is, any erotic or sensual enjoyment (1904–1905:105).

Predestination was a strict and austere doctrine as well as a psychologically disturbing one. Simple piety and good works were no guarantee of election although, as God's creation, all individuals had an obligation to behave as though they were saved. Weber believed that anxiety on the part of the faithful about their fate generated a search for "proof of election." This search involved two injunctions. First, all individuals had an "absolute duty" to consider themselves chosen and to regard any doubts as "temptations of the devil" (1904–1905:158). Second, all individuals, rich or poor, had a duty to work hard in their calling for the glory of God on earth. As Franklin pointed out, time is money, and thus "every hour lost is lost to labor for the glory of God" (Weber, 1904–1905:158).

Hard work in a calling was an exercise of ascetic virtue and would normally bring material rewards to the diligent believer. These rewards could provide psychological comfort to the believer, on the assumption that surely God did not reward those who were damned. Wealth was condemned if it led to sinful idleness and indulgence. But wealth obtained from hard work in one's calling was morally "clean" because the worker was merely God's servant, duty bound to increase God's wealth on earth.

The acquisition of wealth as a result of "restless, continuous, systematic work in a worldly calling" was interpreted as the "surest and most evident proof of rebirth and genuine faith." This "proof" was the "most powerful lever for the expansion of that attitude towards life which we have here called the spirit of capitalism" (Weber, 1904–1905:172). Restless activity, combined with religious limitations on the consumption of wealth for personal ends, meant that the accumulated capital would be productively reinvested in the enterprise—capital would generate more capital. Consequently, the fundamental nature of the "spirit of capitalism, and not only that but of all modern culture: rational conduct on the basis of the idea of a calling, was born . . . from the spirit of Christian asceticism" (1904–1905:180).

Protestant asceticism "strode into the market-place of life, slammed the door of the monastery behind it, and undertook to penetrate just that daily routine of life with its methodicalness, to fashion it into a life in the world, but neither of nor for this world" (Weber, 1904–1905:154). By the twentieth century, however, as Weber pointed out, capitalism no longer needed the direct support of religious belief to continue on its profitable way.

In 1904 Max and Marianne Weber visited the United States to attend a scholarly conference held during the Universal Exposition in St. Louis. This visit gave Max Weber the opportunity to continue his research into the association between capitalism and Protestantism. He concluded that in the United States "the pursuit of wealth, stripped of its religious and ethical meaning, tends to become associated with purely mundane passions, which often actually give it the character of sport" (1904–1905:182).

Early capitalists may have had God on their side and, given the injunction to forego pleasure and constantly seek profit, they were likely to be successful. But continued success and profit required constant vigilance and accurate calculation of the risks involved in any venture. Capital accounting and double-entry bookkeeping were two techniques that served this need (Weber, 1925, 2:1156). Capitalism also required the development of rational, universally applied laws and regulations and rationalized administrative structures, notably bureaucratic structures. As Weber pointed out, the development of modern corporate organizations in any field paralleled the "development and continued spread of bureaucratic administration" (1947:337). Finally, capitalism required the collusion of political powers in the form of authority that Weber called rational-legal authority. Let us take a closer look at how Weber viewed power and bureaucracy in capitalist societies.

Power and Legitimation   Weber understood social relations as basically conflict relations. The key determinant in social relations was **power,** which he defined as the "probability that one actor within a social relationship will be in a position to carry out his will despite resistance, regardless of the basis on which this probability rests." A more refined definition, he went on, would include the basis for the "probability that a *command* will be obeyed." **Domination**, a related concept, he defined as the "probability that a command . . . will be obeyed by a given group of persons" (1925, 1:53).

Weber pointed out that every social sphere, without exception, was influenced by structures of domination. The concept could be applied to relations in a "drawing room as well as in the market, from the rostrum of a lecture hall as well as from the command post of a regiment, from an erotic or charitable relationship as well as from scholarly discussion or athletics" (1925, 2:943). Weber was primarily concerned, however, with domination relating to administration. Domination "expresses itself and functions through administration," and every administration "needs domination, because it is always necessary that some powers of command be in the hands of somebody" (1925, 2:948).

Because the term had such broad application, Weber thought it "scientifically useless," and he concentrated on two "diametrically contrasting types of domination." The **indirect form of domination** involved control over goods or marketable skills, which could be used to constrain the activities of others so that they behaved in the manner required by, and in the interests of, the monopolistic entity. For example, banks and credit institutions could impose conditions for credit to which customers, if they required credit, had to submit. But customers had no binding obligation to submit; they could try to find alternative arrangements. In contrast, the **direct form of domination** involved control over others and an "absolute duty to obey, regardless of personal motives or interests" (1925, 2:943).

Although the border between these two forms of domination was fluid, Weber maintained that there was a "clear-cut antithesis between factual power which arises completely out of possession and by way of interest compromises in the market, and . . . the authoritarian power of a patriarch or a monarch with its appeal to the duty of obedience as such" (1925, 2:943). The latter form involved the "authoritative power of command," meaning that the "manifested will (*command*) of the *ruler* or rulers is meant to influence the conduct of one or more others (*the ruled*) and actually does influence it in such a way that their conduct to a socially relevant degree occurs as if the ruled had made the content of the command the maxim of their conduct for its very own sake." The ruled are obedient and, more important, believe that they *should* be obedient. That is, the command is "accepted as a 'valid' norm"; it has **legitimacy** (1925, 2:946).

All forms of domination require self-justification, or legitimation. Weber outlined three principles of legitimation: traditional, charismatic, and rational-legal (1925, 2:954). These are all ideal types of domination/legitimation; the forms "occurring in historical reality constitute combinations, mixtures, adaptations, or modifications of these "pure" types" (1925, 2:948).

Traditional domination is based on tradition or custom that justifies, or even sanctifies, the position of the ruler. A basic form of traditional domination is patriarchy, centered in the household group or clan. The claim to legitimacy is based on descent from some founding father in the distant past or on a connection with a god or some divine event. If the claim is based on some divine connection, the divine may be male or female, but the claim is always made through the male line. The patriarch exercises personal power. The ideal-type patriarch exercises power without restraint, "unencumbered by rules," at least to the extent that he is not "limited by tradition or by competing powers," as is likely to happen in reality (1925, 2:1006).

The sanctity of tradition may provide subordinates with some protection from the arbitrary power of the patriarch, although the patriarch may interpret, revive, or even discover traditions, giving him a degree of freedom from such control. The patriarch is, however, dependent on the subordinate's willingness to obey because of reverence for tradition and custom. If the patriarch repeatedly violates traditions or customs, he jeopardizes the subordinate's compliance. Opposition to the patriarch is opposition to the *person*, not to the *form* of domination. The wicked, cruel, or incompetent patriarch may be overthrown, but he will be replaced with another patriarch in accordance with tradition and, usually, along hereditary lines of patrilineal succession.

The extension of patriarchal domination from the household is found in various forms of patrimonial domination, including feudalism. The patrimonial ruler or feudal overlord retains, in theory, absolute powers of command over his subjects. In fact, his powers are likely to be considerably muted by custom and tradition and by the administrative structure that necessitates his delegating some power to selected, favored subjects. Administratively, however, the important aspect of traditional domination—whether of the household patriarch or of the prince or lord—is that the administration of the domains is *personally held*, and thus there is no separation between public and private spheres.

Although women may, on exceptional occasions, assume power in feudal or patrimonial systems, they are usually "stand-ins" for their male kin or offspring, and their exercise of power is unusual and short-lived. Patriarchal power is pure male power and derives from the bases for household authority—superior strength and practical knowledge and experience. According to Weber, it is the power of "men as against women and children; of the able-bodied as against those of lesser capability; of the adult as against the child; of the old against the young" (1925, 2:359). In fact, for the patriarch, *all* women under his command are his subjects and their offspring are "his" children, "whether the woman is a wife or a slave, regardless of the facts of paternity" (1925, 2:1007).

The mother-child relationship was, in Weber's view, simply a natural, presocial relationship that only became a social relationship when men organized households and acquired control over women's sexuality so that the connection between (male) parent and child could be legally established. Weber claimed that the great empires of the Far and Near East, of India and the Mediterranean, as well as Northern Europe, all developed out of patriarchal household organization. He concluded that the concept of matriarchy was a mistake and "imprecise" because there was "no serious evidence" of any other form of kinship arrangements other than patrilineal relationships "ever since kinship relations . . . [have] been regulated by Law" (1925, 1:372).

Like traditional domination, charismatic domination is also personal. However, it is based on the fortuitous or timely qualities of the individual leader or ruler, "by virtue of which he is considered extraordinary and treated as endowed with supernatural, superhuman, or at least specifically exceptional powers or qualities" (1925, 1:241). The important point is that the leader is regarded as charismatic by the followers, whose recognition is freely given, usually as a result of some extraordinary deed or miracle. Thus, the followers are not subjects but disciples. As such, they will withdraw their support if the leader "appears deserted by his god or magical or heroic powers, above all, if his leadership fails to benefit his followers" (1925, 1:242).

Charismatic domination has no established administrative structures. The followers are not "officials," and "least of all are its members technically trained." In addition, there is no such thing as "appointment or dismissal, no career, no promotion." Agents of the leader are selected on the basis of their devotion to the leader. They are given "charismatic authority by their chief," or they may possess their own charisma (1925, 1:243).

The charismatic leader repudiates any involvement in "the everyday routine world," so that there is no rational economic activity in a society characterized by this form of domination. Indeed, charisma is a "typical anti-economic force." Pure charisma is a "call," a "mission," or a "spiritual duty," with the result that it can tolerate "with an attitude of complete emotional indifference, irregular, unsystematic acquisitive acts" such as bribery, extortion, begging, and other forms of economic solicitation in pursuit of its goal (1925, 1:245).

Weber regarded charisma as the greatest revolutionary force and believed that it could arise under either traditional or rational-legal forms of domination to challenge the existing order. The challenge is not arbitrary, but based on a felt need or an exceptional situation that the charismatic leader's powers are able to address. But the success of the charismatic leader depends on constant proof of such powers. Moreover, because charisma, in its pure form, is personal and opposed to any everyday, routinized structures, charisma can only extend through the life of the individual. Even in his lifetime, if he is successful, his personal charisma will gradually become routinized. The routinization of charisma generally produces a traditional form of domination, although rational-legal forms may arise, especially in modern societies.

Weber pointed out that routinization is not important to the followers, who will live "communistically in a community of faith and enthusiasm, on gifts, booty, or sporadic acquisition" while the leader is a force of revolutionary opposition (1925, 1:251). But when the movement meets with success, then the "anti-economic factor" has to be altered and a fiscal organization set up to provide for the needs of the leader and his immediate followers. Structures have to be set up to raise taxes and other contributions for the support of the regime. In addition, if charisma is not to remain a "purely transitory phenomenon," routinization will also have to involve plans for succession. This problem of succession is solved in a variety of ways: by searching for a new possessor of charisma, as in the selection of a new Dalai Lama; by seeking revelation through oracles, divination, or other magical practices; or by transforming charisma into hereditary domination.

Like traditional power, charisma is generally male power. Some female saints and mystics may be accorded a form of charismatic power, but their power is exercised on the world from *outside* that world—from the metaphorical, if not actual, cloister. Male charismatic power may also rest on otherworldly claims, but it is power exercised *in* the world.

The complete antithesis to charismatic domination—both in the characteristic exercise of power and the administration of that power—is **rational-legal domination.** It is based on a belief in the sanctity of formal rules and laws and thus on the legitimacy of the legally appointed ruler. Weber (1925, 1:217–218) listed five mutually interdependent ideas that signify the pure type of rational-legal domination:

- Any legal norm is valid on the grounds of "expediency or value rationality or both" and commands the obedience of all within the "sphere of power" or within the relevant organization.

- The legal norms are a "consistent system of abstract rules" that have "normally been intentionally established" and that are then applied to particular cases.

- All are subject to the law, even those who exercise legal authority, and all must behave according to the legal norms.

- Obedience is a consequence of membership (citizenship) in the organization, and individuals obey only the law.

- Members of the organization "obey the person in authority" because he or she is legally designated or elected; they do not "owe obedience to him as an individual."

Rational-legal domination is, in the pure type, gender neutral. Technical qualifications and merit are the basic entry stipulations, so assuming that both genders can attain those qualifications, bureaucratic office and rational-legal power are available to women as well as men. In addition, conduct in office is regulated by impersonal, formal rules and regulations, which should presumably not be subject to gender discrimination. But Weber recognized that the pure type of rational-legal domination was not to be met with in reality, meaning that it was not in practice gender neutral except in one regard—its alienating effect on both men and women.

Bureaucracy   For Weber, the purest type of rational-legal authority was **bureaucracy** (1925, 1:220), defined in its ideal type by these characteristics:

- Official business is conducted on a continuous basis.
- Business is conducted in accordance with stipulated rules.
- Every official's responsibility and authority are part of a hierarchy of authority.
- Officials do not own the resources necessary for them to perform their assigned functions, but they are accountable for the use of those resources.
- Offices cannot be appropriated by their incumbents in the sense of property that can be inherited or sold.
- Official business is conducted on the basis of written documents.

Bureaucracy, in Weber's analysis, fit the spirit of rational capitalism. A capitalist market economy demanded that "the official business of administration be discharged precisely, unambiguously, continuously, and with as much speed as possible" (1946:215). Just as bureaucracy was indispensable to capitalism, "capitalism is the most rational economic basis for bureaucratic administration" (1925, 1:224).

Weber pointed out that bureaucracy "promotes a 'rationalist' way of life," and the "bureaucratization of all domination very strongly furthers the development of 'rational matter-of-factness' and the personality type of the professional expert" (1946:240). The elimination of all personal relations and feelings is characteristic of the personality and action of ideal-type bureaucrats, who are:

- Personally free and only subject to authority in relation to their impersonal official obligations
- Appointed to their positions on the basis of contract
- Organized in a clearly defined hierarchy of offices
- Able to exercise authority delegated to them in accordance with clearly defined impersonal rules
- Separated from ownership of the means of administration
- Subject to strict discipline and control in the conduct of their office
- Appointed to and placed in jobs on the basis of technical qualifications
- Rewarded for their work with a regular salary and the prospects of regular advancement in a lifetime career

The more bureaucracy is "dehumanized, the more completely it succeeds in eliminating from official business love, hatred, and all purely personal, irrational, and emotional elements which escape calculation" (1946:216).

Rational-legal domination, enshrined in bureaucracy, was the basis for the development of the modern, capitalist Western state (Weber, 1925, 1:223). However, Weber pointed out that socialism would not eliminate the bureaucratization of life. On the contrary, it would increase the scope and power of bureaucracy, because socialism would require a "still higher degree of formal bureaucratization than capitalism" (1925, 1:225).

Capitalist or socialist, the rationalization of life increasingly restricted charisma and other individualistic conduct and produced a profoundly dehumanizing, alienating existence. Weber pointed to the "American system of 'scientific management' . . . with its rational conditioning and training of work performances" as an example. The result of scientific management was an adjustment of the "psycho-physical apparatus of man" to the demands of the task and the machine so that the individual was "functionalized" and "shorn of his natural rhythm as determined by his organism" (1925, 2:1156).

Social Change   In discussing change, Weber focused on the way in which historical changes in worldviews, most especially religious worldviews, had produced profound transformations in all aspects of social life. Unlike other theorists, such as Marx, Comte, or Durkheim, Weber did not have any linear conception of social evolution or any commitment to ideas of beneficial progress. On the contrary, Weber was profoundly pessimistic about the dehumanizing trajectory of modern, rationalized, bureaucratized life.

Furthermore, Weber did not subscribe to any utopian notions of future society. His assessment that socialism, for example, was not the answer to modern alienation was prescient, as has been apparent in the socialist experiments of recent times. He pointed out that "the lot of the mine worker is not the slightest bit different whether the mine is privately or publicly owned." The only difference is that if "strikes against the state are impossible," as they would be in a socialist state, the "essential dependence of the worker is increased" (1925, 1:254–255).

As you saw earlier, Weber insisted that both ideas and material interests must be examined together in any explanation of social change. But in his "switchmen" metaphor, he pointed out that ideas could take on a dynamic of their own and, in doing so, affect the historical process.

According to Weber, charisma was one of the ways in which the power of ideas was revealed. Through the actions and beliefs of charismatic individuals, new belief systems arose that initiated profound social changes. In a "revolutionary and sovereign manner, charismatic domination transforms all values and breaks all traditional and rational norms" (1925, 2:1115). The routinization of everyday life is challenged by the charismatic leader because charismatic beliefs transform individuals "from within" and shape "material and social conditions according to its revolutionary will" (1925, 2:1116). Although charisma is fated to succumb eventually to traditional or rational-legal forms of domination, some part of the charismatic vision will survive routinization and produce social change.

Thus Weber may have hoped for some charismatic deliverance from the "iron cage" of rationalized industrial capitalism and the bureaucratic state. But he was not optimistic.

Class, Gender, and Race

Class   For Marx, the bourgeoisie and the proletariat were the pivotal social classes in capitalism because of their contrasting positions in the productive process, but they only became class actors when they became a community, conscious of their common situation. For Weber, social classes were not communities but simply groups that shared a common economic position in the marketplace. He characterized **social classes** as

> 1. A number of people [having] in common a specific causal component of their life chances, insofar as 2. this component is represented exclusively by economic interests in the possession of goods and opportunities for income, and 3. is represented under the conditions of commodity or labor markets. This is a class situation. (1925, 2:927)

The basic determinant of all class situations was, however, property or lack of property.

In contrast to classes, Weber defined **status groups** as communities distinguished in terms of positive or negative social estimations of honor. Status honor is linked to a "specific *style of life*" that is "expected from all those who wish to belong to the circle." Status may be linked to class situation, but more often than not it stands "in sharp opposition to the pretensions of property," so that both the "propertied and the propertyless people can belong to the same status group" (1925, 2:932). Status stratification involves monopoly over "ideal and material goods or opportunities" and status honor always rests on "distance and exclusiveness" from other groups (1925, 2:935). Generally, Weber saw status groups as more important under relatively stable social conditions, and classes as more important in periods of "technical and economic transformations" (1925, 2:938).

In Weber's typology, whereas classes belong to the economic order and status groups to the social order, **parties** "reside in the sphere of power" (1925, 2:938). The action of political parties was always planned and determined by set goals. These goals might represent either class or status group interests. But parties need not be purely class or purely status parties; in fact, they are more likely to be mixed types, or to be neither. Parties vary in terms of the group(s) they serve, the means they use to seek power, and the ends they espouse, but "above all else, they vary according to the structure of domination" (1925, 2:939). Very often, their lofty goals were simply camouflage for "cravings of revenge, power, booty, and spoils" (1919a:125).

The fact that all parties struggle for domination was what made politics, especially revolutionary politics, so disturbing in Weber's view. For example, in 1919 Weber was in Munich during the revolutionary turmoil, when a soviet-style republic was proclaimed twice and put down on both occasions. He was not sympathetic to either the revolutionaries or the government forces that suppressed the uprisings and declared, "To restore Germany to her old glory, I would surely ally myself with any power on earth, even with the devil incarnate, but not with the force of stupidity. So long as madmen carry on in politics from right or to the left, I shall stay away from it" (Marianne Weber, 1926:673).

Weber was involved in politics as a detached adviser at various points in his career. In 1918, in the aftermath of the war, he was a founding member of the German Democratic Party and an adviser to the German delegation at the Versailles peace conference. There was also an unsuccessful move to make him a candidate for the Presidency. Nevertheless, Weber, who was "never a party man," maintained a "measure of political and intellectual distance" from political battles (Coser, 1977:256). He concluded that politics was only work for the truly "heroic" man under the political conditions of the early twentieth century.

Race   Weber's ideas about social classes, status groups, and parties affected his conceptualization of race and ethnicity. Although race and ethnicity might be anchored in ideas about biological as well as social differences, they were not, in Weber's view, "natural" but were socially determined in relation to the dynamics of power. For example, ethnicity was a "presumed identity" that became a group identity when it was made the basis for a political party. And "race identity," defined as "common inherited and inheritable traits that actually derive from common descent," depended on the subjective perception of such common identity. When a racial group was so identified, the resulting social action was usually negative: "Those who are obviously different are avoided and despised or, conversely, viewed with superstitious awe" (1925, 1:358). But these reactions were not "natural"; they depended on one group's attempt to monopolize social power and honor (1925, 1:386).

Weber pointed out that racial and ethnic differences had less to do with "aesthetically conspicuous differences of the physical appearance" than with the "perceptible differences in the *conduct of everyday life*"—that is, in the differences in "clothes, in the style of housing, food and eating habits, the division of labor between the sexes and between the free and the unfree" (1925, 1:390–391).

As with status honor generally, it was the sense of honor that was important in race relations. In the case of southern U.S. race relations, Weber suggested:

> The "poor white trash," i.e., the propertyless and, in the absence of job
> opportunities, very often destitute white inhabitants of the southern
> states . . . in the period of slavery, were actual bearers of racial antipathy,
> which was quite foreign to the planters. This was so because the social
> honor of the "poor whites" was dependent upon the social *declassement* of
> the Negroes. (1925, 1:391)

Weber's discussion of race and ethnicity emphasized the social and historical nature of discrimination and prejudice. For example, he pointed out that the "existence of several million mulattoes in the United States speaks clearly against the assumption of a 'natural' racial antipathy." The fact that sexual relations between races might be regarded with horror by both sides was "socially determined by the previously sketched tendency towards the monopolization of social power and honor, a tendency which in this case happens to be linked to race" (1925, 1:386). Historically, Weber noted, racial antipathy was more likely to be consolidated when it was accompanied by a "memory of an actual migration, be it colonization or individual migration" (1925, 1:388).

Like all status groups, racial and ethnic groups can be negatively as well as positively privileged, which translates into differences in orientation to the world. Positively privileged groups have a sense of their human dignity that is related to their "being"—that is, their "beauty and excellence"—so that their "kingdom is 'of this world'" and they "live for the present . . . by exploiting their great past." Negatively privileged groups cultivate a sense of human dignity that is related to the future. These groups are "nurtured by the belief in a providential mission," or by a belief that "the last will be first" in another life, or that in this life a Messiah will appear who will "bring forth into the light of the world which has cast them out the hidden honor of the pariah people" (1925, 2:934). The continued relevance of these observations to current ethnic and racial conflicts is readily apparent. Martin Luther King's "I Have a Dream" speech was a future-oriented dream, just as white supremacist references to glorious Confederate tradition are present- and past-oriented.

Gender   Weber's views on gender were related to his views on power. They were also influenced by his wife's work.

Marianne Weber was a feminist activist and scholar throughout her life, and Max Weber was thus involved in feminist circles in Heidelberg. Marianne claimed that her involvement with the women's rights movement "delighted" her husband and that he was "soon more of a feminist than she was." She reported that, in a debate about women's rights, Max responded to one of the "leading lights" of the university with a short comment illustrating the misunderstanding of the speaker and in doing so "sketched the whole question of women's rights, and expressed the innermost thoughts of women which, for the time being, they can only stammer indistinctly" (1926:229).

According to Marianne, Max viewed women "primarily as human beings and only secondarily as members of the opposite sex," although he did expect them to "display an animated grace and reserve designed to serve as a guide for man's behavior." He took seriously "any sign of scholarly interest on the part of a woman and was pleased when it was expressed graciously," but he was "irritated by the . . . [Berlin style], meaning a certain kind of forced self-assurance . . . that manifested itself in pseudo clever or witty altercations and robbed a rosebud of a girl of her fragrance even before she had fully opened up" (Marianne Weber, 1926:110).

Despite such endorsements, feminism was not for the Webers a way to overthrow marriage, but only a way to make it less authoritarian (Mitzman, 1969: 279). Max Weber denounced the argument for free love and children out of wedlock as "crude hedonism and an ethic which would only benefit the man as goal of the woman!" Marianne's view of marriage was that "claims to mutual possession are not justified," but "fidelity and exclusiveness in the sexual sphere are a matter of course." Marriage for the Webers was not only an ideal from which individuals could not exempt themselves at will, it was also "an *ethical norm* of sexual union" (1926:371).

There is, however, a certain irony in these positions. It would seem that Max Weber was not immune to the pleasures of erotic and extramarital love. In 1910 the Webers were in Venice with the Jaffes, friends from Heidelberg. Edgar Jaffe was Max Weber's publisher and coeditor on the *Archiv*; Else Jaffe, one of Marianne's friends, had briefly been one of Max's students. When Marianne had to leave early to attend a feminist conference, Max Weber and Else Jaffe may have become lovers (Green, 1974:166). Their relationship continued until Max Weber's death, and Else Jaffe was at his bedside, along with Marianne, during his final illness.[3]

Max Weber's public position on issues of free love, marriage, and ethical standards was tied to his views on the asceticism demanded by modern capitalism. Salvation religions, such as Protestantism, were profoundly antagonistic to anything that took individuals "out of themselves," including sexuality. As Weber stated, salvation religions existed in "profound tension with the greatest irrational force of life: sexual love" (1915a:342). Modern monogamous marriage represented the necessary routinization of sexuality in a capitalist society: "Inner-worldly and rational asceticism . . . can accept only the rationally regulated marriage" as the means to control man, who is "hopelessly wretched by virtue of his 'concupiscence'" (1915a:349). The only way to produce the rational, self-disciplined, moral individual who would labor diligently in his "calling" was to channel his sexuality into marriage.

The asceticism of modern life "gathers the primal, naturalist and unsublimated sexuality of the peasant into a rational order of man as creature" and thus controls the "diabolical power" of sexuality, which could endanger salvation and civilization (1915a:349). The contrast between rationally regulated life and "magical orgiasticism and all sorts of irrational frenzies" was accomplished by controlling sexuality in marriage (1915a:344).

Weber's sentiments regarding marriage were a reflection of his own situation. For Weber, marriage should be a relationship in which each assumes an "ethical responsibility for another" (1915a:347). As he saw it, marriage should embody something unique: the "transformation of the feeling of love which is conscious of responsibility throughout all the nuances of the organic life process, 'up to the pianissimo of old age,' and the mutual granting of oneself to another and becoming indebted to each other (in Goethe's sense). Rarely does life grant such value in pure form. He to whom it is given may speak of fate's fortune and grace—not of his own 'merit'" (1915a:345).

The routinization of sex in marriage stood in contrast to, but at the same time encouraged, eroticism. In Weber's view, eroticism, the "joyous triumph over rationality," could occur in modern, rationalized society only in extramarital relations (1915a:343). Eroticism, precisely because it was removed from the everyday routines, was the "only tie which linked man with the natural fountain of life"—that is, to woman. For Weber, women were the representatives of the more primitive, natural state and represented for modern man the "gate into the most irrational and thereby the real kernel of life" (1915a:345).

Erotic love might offer the "unsurpassable peak of fulfillment" in the fusion of "souls to one another," but erotic love was dangerous, especially for women. Weber noted that for the warrior brotherhood the "possession and fight for women has ranked about equally with the fight for treasure and the conquest of power" and, in what he called the "period of knighthood romance," capturing a

---

[3]Mitzman (1969:387) also reported that Weber began an affair in 1911 with the musician Mina Tobler that "lasted in full intensity until 1914, and on a less passionate level until his death in 1920."

woman was the high point of any heroic war (1915a:345). Although erotic relations had progressed in Western society from the outright brutality of the warrior to the more civilized relations of "salon culture," nevertheless Weber maintained that the "erotic relation must remain attached in a certain sophisticated manner, to brutality" (1915a:348). Brutality need not be physical, it can also be spiritual, involving the psychological oppression of one partner in order for the controlling partner to derive pleasure "in the other." The "other" is the means for the pleasure of the more powerful partner, although this coercion, Weber maintained, was "never noticed by the partners themselves"—a point that abused spouses would question (1915a:348).

Although this brutality was seemingly gender neutral, it must have been masculine in its origins. "Heroic ecstasy and heroic regeneration" were the erotic experience of the warrior and, in Weber's account, the first indication of the sublimation of sexuality. In Weber's discussion, men of action match the image of the heroic warrior, whereas loving women suggest vulnerable dependency (Bologh, 1990:165). Love is distinguished from eros in salvation religions, which promote brotherly love. The irrational force of life—sexual love—could have no place in the public world of men that grew out of such religions (1915a:343).[4]

Conflict and the search for power were, for Weber, endemic in all social relationships, certainly including the love relationship. The capitalist world of rational calculation and profit demanded the sublimation of erotic desire in sober marriage. Sex itself thus became a form of calculation, permitted only as a "means willed by god for the increase of His glory according to the commandment, 'Be fruitful and multiply'" (Weber, 1904–1905:158).

Marianne Weber also wrote a series of essays on gender relations in marriage and erotic relations. She defended women's capability of and need for sexual pleasure in the face of late Victorian sentiments that idealized the asexual woman. Marianne Weber also presented a clear analysis of the gender conflict that patriarchal marital relationships, favored by bourgeois capitalists, could produce.

> The richer and the more autonomous her personality, the more difficult must be her principled subjection. If she strongly strives for independent activities and intellectual growth, her husband, concerned about his authority, must necessarily feel ill at ease. His anxiety is not calmed as long as he is not continuously certain of mastery over her inner life. (quoted in Bendix, 1971:11)

---

[4]Mitzman (1969:291) suggests that Max Weber tried to separate his own erotic experiences from his public life and companionable marriage. Mitzman also claims that Max never told Marianne about his affairs (although there are hints in her biography of Weber that she was aware of them, at least of the affair with Else Jaffe). Max Weber's "unconsummated love for Marianne at times appears similar to the acosmic mystical love he . . . analyzed at length in his sociology of religion." Although this Calvinist perspective did not desert him, after 1910 he seemed more receptive to "anti-modernist, erotic, mystical, and aristocratic views that were incompatible . . . with this inherited asceticism."

Marriage to Max did not curb Marianne's intellectual growth, although she felt that her mother-in-law's marriage was an example of just such stifling of a woman's talents and needs.

Marianne Weber recognized the need for women's contributions to the "suprapersonal" world. In addition, she advocated women's need for financial independence, including the possibility of her being paid for housework—an idea still being proposed today.

During her professional life, Marianne Weber surrounded herself with important social scientists, including Georg Simmel (Chapter 8), Gertrude Simmel, and Robert Michels (Chapter 9), and she was politically active in feminist circles in Berlin. Marianne lived for more than 30 years after her husband's death, and her salon continued until disrupted by the rise of Nazism. But although she was a sociological theorist of some note in her own place and time, her work is only now beginning to be known in the English-speaking world (Lengermann and Niebrugge-Brantley, 1998).

Other Theories and Theorists

Max Weber was convinced that sociological knowledge had, and must have, practical value. But he was aware that such knowledge, like any scientific knowledge, could be used unethically, particularly when the scientific specialist ventured into the world of practical politics. He cautioned that scientists and academics should not become politicians in the classroom or the laboratory.

The issue of ethics was one of Weber's constant concerns. In his essay "Politics as a Vocation" (1919a), Weber contrasted the "ethic of ultimate ends" with the "ethic of responsibility" and suggested that a pure ethic of ultimate ends usually meant abandoning responsibility for the consequences. For example, if the implementation of some desirable end led to problems, then the blame was typically placed not on the instigator but on "the world, or the stupidity of other men, or God's will who made them thus" (1919a:121). But someone with an ethic of responsibility would take the "average deficiencies" of people into account and would not blame them for the outcome of his or her actions (1919a:121).

For practicing politicians, the ethic of responsibility was the more desirable. But Weber pointed out that although "politics is made with the head, . . . it is certainly not made with the head alone" and, ideally, the ethic of ultimate ends and the ethic of responsibility would be found together. The "genuine man—a man who *can* have the 'calling for politics'" was one in whom the ethics were in unison (1919a:127). Such ethics were particularly important in the modern world. The "increasing concern with the satisfaction of immediate, everyday needs," the decline in religion and faith, and the "leveling of far-reaching ideals" made the need for an ethical ideal imperative (Schroeder, 1992:16).

Weber thought of himself as a politician, and, as indicated earlier, he did intervene in practical politics at various points in his career. Earlier in his life he had remarked that he was not a "real scholar," and Marianne Weber believed that he gave the appearance of a "born fighter and ruler even more than a born thinker" (1926:166). She stated that in much of Weber's work the "researcher and the politician" complemented each other. The principles guiding Weber's selection of material were "first and foremost, political passion, then a sense of justice . . . and . . . the conviction that human *happiness* was not the most important thing, but that *freedom* and human *dignity* were the ultimate and highest values whose realization should be made possible for everyone" (1926:306).

The essay "Politics as a Vocation" was developed from a lecture Weber gave to Munich students in the "revolutionary winter of 1918–19" when many German students were seeking ways to restructure their society in the aftermath of defeat. Weber cautioned against too idealistic a belief in the construction of a "pure" social order animated only by ideals of "justice and brotherhood," which Russian Bolshevism had initially advanced (Marianne Weber, 1926:682). Weber indicated that the road to such ideals "ran through the utmost inhumanity, without any guarantee that the goal would be reached" (1926:682).

Weber was intrigued by Sigmund Freud's ideas, but he rejected the interpretation of those ideas in the work and practice of Otto Gross, a psychiatrist and disciple of Freud. Gross advocated the elimination of monogamy, which represented, he said, the worst repression of emotional and sexual health. Gross instead recommended eroticism and singled out the female or maternal principle as the primary source for a healthy and happy life. Eroticism and the superiority of instinct and intuition over the patriarchal values of science and reason gave rise to a movement of "aesthetic and libidinal liberation" that was influential among many young intellectuals in Heidelberg (Roth, 1991:273).[5]

Else Jaffe was one of those intellectuals; she became one of Gross's lovers and bore his child in 1907. Weber was aware of the affair and disapproved, perhaps because he already had "more than friendly feelings" toward Else at the time (Green, 1974:55–56). When Gross submitted an article to the *Archiv* opposing patriarchy and advocating free love, Weber rejected it on the grounds that, although he found Freud's ideas "scientific," he could not accept the "prophetic" interpretation of those ideas in Gross's article. He stated that Gross's ideas were "not value-free" and did not "satisfy the demands of reasonableness and objectivity" (Green, 1974:56). Gross's ideas and practices were anathema to Weber, but they were important to Weber's reflections on the nature of love and eroticism in the disciplined world of modernity.

Critique and Conclusions

Max Weber's large corpus of work, only a portion of which is discussed in this chapter,[6] has been and remains the basis for a number of contemporary theoretical formulations. At the same time, his work has aroused its share of controversy. Even in his own lifetime, the thesis of *The Protestant Ethic and the Spirit of Capitalism* was disputed.

Still, the classical sociological canon has tended to be the theoretical troika of Durkheim, Marx, and Weber. Weber's work was, in many ways, a critique and

---

[5]Roth (1991:273) suggests that the views and practices of Gross and his disciples were very similar to the counterculture of the 1960s.

[6]Significant omissions are Weber's work on the sociology of music and art, as well as his magisterial analysis of world religions.

correction of Marx's work, as we have noted in this chapter. It was also largely a repudiation of Durkheim's reification of collective concepts, such as the *sui generis* understanding of society, as well as his methodological position. For Weber, sociology was an interpretive exercise that took the individual and individual action as the basic unit of analysis. When examining concepts such as the state, association, or feudalism, the "task of sociology is to reduce these concepts to 'understandable' action, that is without exception, to the actions of participating individual men" (1947:55).

Unlike Marx, Weber had no utopian expectations about the future of society, and he was equally skeptical of Durkheimian sociology's ambition to produce solutions to the problems of the day. For Weber, sociology was an empirical science that could clarify the nature of a problem or situation, but it could not dogmatically assert a solution. The sociologist might select a topic on the basis of interest or ethical values but had to hold personal values in abeyance during the inquiry.

This aspect of Weber's methodology came under attack at a conference held in Heidelberg in 1964 to celebrate the hundredth anniversary of his birth. The attack came from Herbert Marcuse, who claimed that Weber's separation of values from science resulted in the subjection of science to nonscientific, even irrational, values. However, Weber's value-free sociology was defended on this occasion by Talcott Parsons.[7] The event marked, as one sociologist has noted, the "beginning of the great onslaught on Weber as arch representative of liberal or bourgeois social science, an onslaught carried forth by a new political generation without any memories of the Second World War and hence without any personal yardsticks for comparing the present with the past" (Roth, 1991:265). More recent "recoveries" of Weber have been more positive in their evaluation of his methodological and political stance. Sayer concludes that Weber's pessimism about the modern age "should be taken seriously" in light of the wars and atrocities of the late twentieth century (1991:55).

Final Thoughts

Max Weber was preoccupied with the issue of power and conflict. The search for power was, he believed, endemic in all social relationships. On that basis, you might be tempted to classify him, like others who were critical of the distortions of modern capitalism, as ideologically radical. However, Weber's sociology was a detached analysis of power in social life, and he was in most respects a man of his class and era (Bendix, 1962:6). At the same time, he was quite puritanical (Bendix, 1962:6). For example, as you have seen, Weber suggested that the capitalist world of rational calculation and profit necessarily involved the sublimation of erotic desire. Modern capitalism required sober marriage in

---

[7]Marianne Weber stated that for Max Weber, "Intellectual freedom was . . . the greatest good, and under no circumstances was he prepared to consider even the interests of political power as more important and attainable for the individual" (1926:120). Weber's "ethic of tolerance" transcended racial, ethnic, and political divisions.

which sex was a form of calculation (1904–1905:158). This detached analysis of the effects of capitalism and Protestantism was accompanied by a rejection of any notion of matriarchy and "socialistic theories of marriage."

Weber's analysis of the alienating nature of modern existence remains significant. He pointed out that rationalized relationships invariably produce irrational outcomes as individuals seek an escape or a return to an "enchanted" world. In a "world robbed of gods," there is a dangerous split between rational understanding and mastery over the natural world, on the one hand, and the human need for "mystic" experience, on the other (1915b:282). This split continues to describe the contradictory nature of modern societies. For example, in our secular, rational society we have seen the proliferation of fundamentalist religious movements as well as mystical, even magical, beliefs. The very successes of science and technology have also generated disturbing environmental and social problems. The search for nonrational ways to escape the rationalization of modern life in order to protect human dignity and self-worth will undoubtedly continue.

Weber was profoundly pessimistic about the possibilities of reenchanting the world. He saw little chance of escaping this alienating existence and saw not summer's bloom ahead but the polar night of icy darkness and hardness (1919a:128). But it was precisely because of this bleak future, he believed, that sociologists had a critical task to perform. Their constant scrutiny of the meanings and consequences of social action, their attempt to provide clarity in a confusing world, was essential to our ability to make informed choices and maintain our human dignity and freedom.

References

Abraham, Gary A. 1992. *Max Weber and the Jewish Question*. Urbana and Chicago: University of Illinois Press.

Aron, Raymond. 1970. *Main Currents in Sociological Thought* (2 vols.). New York: Anchor Books.

Bendix, Reinhard. 1962. *Max Weber: An Intellectual Portrait*. New York: Anchor Books.

———. 1971. *Scholarship and Partisanship*. Berkeley: University of California Press.

———. 1984. *Force, Fate, and Freedom*. Berkeley: University of California Press.

Bologh, Roslyn. 1990. *Love or Greatness: Max Weber and Masculine Thinking—A Feminist Inquiry*. London: Unwin Hyman.

Coser. Lewis A. 1977. *Masters of Sociological Thought*. New York: Harcourt Brace Jovanovich.

Drysdale, John. 1996. "How Are Social-Scientific Concepts Formed? A Reconstruction of Max Weber's Theory of Concept Formation." *Sociological Theory, 14,* 71–88.

Eisenstadt, S. N. 1968. *Max Weber on Charisma and Institution Building*. Chicago: University of Chicago Press.

Frisby, David, and Derek Sayer. 1986. *Society*. London: Tavistock Publications.

Green, Martin. 1974. *The von Richthofen Sisters: The Triumphant and Tragic Modes of Love*. London: Weidenfield and Nicolson.

Kalberg, Stephen. 1996. "On the Neglect of Weber's *Protestant Ethic* as a Theoretical Treatise: Demarcating the Parameters of Postwar American Sociological Theory." *Sociological Theory, 14,* 49–70.

Kasler, Dirk. 1988. *Max Weber: An Introduction to His Life and Work*. Chicago: University of Chicago Press.

Lengermann, Patricia Madoo, and Jill Niebrugge-Brantley. 1998. *The Women Founders: Sociology and Social Theory 1830–1930*. New York: McGraw-Hill.

Lowith, Karl. 1993. *Max Weber and Karl Marx*. London: Routledge.

MacCrae, Donald. 1974. *Max Weber*. Harmondsworth, England: Penguin.

Mitzman, Arthur. 1969. *The Iron Cage: An Historical Interpretation of Max Weber*. New York: Alfred A. Knopf.

Roth, Guenther. 1991. "Max Weber: A Bibliographical Essay." In Peter Hamilton (Ed.), *Max Weber: Critical Assessments* (vol. 1, pp. 264–279**).** London: Routledge.

Runciman, W. G. (Ed.). 1978. *Weber: Selections in Translation* (Eric Matthews, Trans.). London: Cambridge University Press.

Sayer, Derek. 1991. *Capitalism and Modernity: An Excursus on Marx and Weber.* London: Routledge.

Schroeder, Ralph. 1992. *Max Weber and the Sociology of Culture*. London: Sage.

Turner, Stephen P., and Regis A. Factor. 1994. *Max Weber: The Lawyer as Social Thinker*. London: Routledge.

Weber, Marianne. 1907. *Ehefrau und Mutter in der Rechtsentwicklung*. Tübingen: J. C. Mohr.

———. 1919/1997. *Frauenfragen und Frauengedanken*. Tübingen: J. C. Mohr.

———. 1926/1975. *Max Weber: A Biography* (Harry Zohn, Trans. and Ed.). New York: John Wiley & Sons.

Weber, Max. 1903–1917/1949. *The Methodology of the Social Sciences*. Toronto: Collier-Macmillan.

———. 1904–1905/1958. *The Protestant Ethic and the Spirit of Capitalism* (Talcott Parsons, Trans.). New York: Charles Scribner's Sons.

———. 1915a/1946. "Religious Rejections of the World and Their Directions." In H. H. Gerth and C. Wright Mills, *From Max Weber: Essays in Sociology* (pp. 323–359). New York: Oxford University Press.

———. 1915b/1946. "The Social Pathology of the World Religions." In H. H. Gerth and C. Wright Mills (Eds.), From Max Weber: *Essays in Sociology* (pp. 267–301). New York: Oxford University Press.

———. 1919a/1946. "Politics as a Vocation." In H. H. Gerth and C. Wright Mills, *From Max Weber: Essays in Sociology* (pp. 77–128). New York: Oxford University Press.

———. 1919b/1946. "Science as a Vocation." In H. H. Gerth and C. Wright Mills, *From Max Weber: Essays in Sociology* (pp. 129–156). New York: Oxford University Press.

———. 1921/1962. *The City* (Don Martingdale and Gertude Neuwirth, Trans. and Eds.). New York: Collier Books.

———. 1922/1964. *The Sociology of Religion* (Ephraim Fischoff, Trans.). Boston: Beacon Press.

———. 1925/1978. *Economy and Society* (2 vols.) (Guenther Roth and Claus Wittich, Eds.). Berkeley: University of California Press.

———. 1946. *From Max Weber: Essays in Sociology* (H. H. Gerth and C. Wright Mills, Trans. and Eds.). New York: Oxford University Press.

———. 1947. *The Theory of Social and Economic Organization* (Talcott Parsons, Ed.). New York: Free Press.

Chapter 8

The Sociology of Form and Content
Simmel

The modern age defined itself as, above all, the kingdom of Reason and rationality. (Bauman, 1987:111)

As you saw in Chapter 7, Max Weber defined modernity as rationalization. Georg Simmel, a contemporary, compatriot, and friend of Weber's, had a similar opinion. Both theorists pointed out that the benefits of *rationalization* and *industrialization*, embodied in science and technology, were offset by the environmental and military excesses that scientific and technological "progress" allows. Furthermore, modern life produces a great deal of alienation and anomie among individuals. Thus, these two German sociologists questioned the idea that rationality has triumphed in all areas of social life. Despite Nietzsche's claim, God has not died for most people in the modern world. "Irrational" religious and magical beliefs are still significant motivators for many individuals. Simmel has been called the sociologist of *modernity* because of his intense focus on this issue (Frisby, 1986). His insights into the stresses, discontents, contradictions, and excitement of modern life are documented in his numerous essays and in his major works.

Simmel's analysis of modern society was focused primarily on the individual experience of modernity, especially the experiences of the modern city dweller. He observed that the "tumult of the metropolis" gave rise to a "mania for travelling, . . . the wild pursuit of competition and . . . the typically modern disloyalty with regard to taste, style, opinions and personal relationships" (1900:484). In Simmel's analysis, the excitement of metropolitan existence was tied inextricably to the anomie and alienation that he perceived in modern life. Simmel's ambivalence about modernity did not lead him to conservative nostalgia for some past social existence or to radical suggestions for change. In fact, Simmel's position on the question of social change was more objective than the position taken by some of the positivist sociologists, such as Durkheim.

Simmel's sociology has been called formal sociology because he observed that social interactions always occur in **forms**, whether institutional forms such as the state, church, and family or more general forms such as competition, co-operation, conflict, and hierarchy. Simmel's analysis of sociological forms was balanced, however, by his numerous investigations of the **content** of those forms, including social types such as the stranger, the coquette, the miser, and the spendthrift. In this chapter you will learn how Simmel came to these ideas.

Georg Simmel (1858–1918)

Georg Simmel was the youngest child of a successful Jewish businessman living in Berlin. His father died when he was young, and a family friend, the owner of a music publishing business, became Simmel's guardian. When his guardian died, he left Simmel a substantial legacy, providing a welcome supplement in Simmel's early years to his precarious income from teaching.

Simmel attended the University of Berlin, studying history, philosophy, and psychology. He was awarded his doctorate in 1881 with a dissertation on Kant's philosophy of nature. In 1885 he became a Privatdozent, or lecturer, at the University of Berlin. The Privatdozent position was unpaid, and Simmel had to rely on student fees for remuneration. Fortunately, he was a popular lecturer and attracted large numbers of students. Despite Simmel's popularity as a lecturer and his prolific output of books and articles, it was not until 1901 that he was given the title Ausserordentlicher Professor (Extraordinary Professor). This was a purely honorary title, however, and Simmel's marginal status in the academy continued.

Simmel tried to obtain a full-time, remunerated position at a German university, but despite the support of many influential contemporaries, including Max Weber, he was unsuccessful. In 1914 he was finally given an appointment at the University of Strasbourg. When he arrived, however, the lecture halls were being converted into military hospital wards and the dormitories into barracks, so that the long-awaited appointment was a great disappointment.

A major problem for Simmel in his search for a full-time academic appointment was the anti-Semitism that pervaded the German academic community at the time. When Simmel was being considered for the Chair of Philosophy at the University of Heidelberg in 1908, the faculty supported his candidacy. But the minister of education for Baden asked a Professor Schaefer at the University of Berlin for an evaluation of Simmel. Schaefer's report suggested that Simmel was quite unsuitable, that he was a "dyed-in-the-wool Israelite, in his outward appearance, in his bearing, and in his manner of thinking." Schaefer conceded that Simmel was a popular lecturer, but added that he attracted mainly women and an "extraordinarily numerous contingent of the oriental world" and that generally "one does not come away from his lectures with too much of positive value; but it is pleasant to be offered up this and that titillating stimulation or volatile intellectual pleasure." Schaefer concluded that he did not believe the "level of Heidelberg would be raised by allowing even broader scope . . . to the world view and philosophy of life which Simmel represents, and which, after

all, are only too obviously different from our German Christian-classical education." Simmel's specialty, sociology, had yet to "earn its position as a scholarly
discipline," and it would not be "right to give official standing to this orientation," especially to one who "operates more by wit and pseudo-wit than by solid
and systematic thinking" (Schaefer, in Coser, 1965:38–39). Marianne Weber reported that Weber "never forgave those involved for their failure to bring this
philosopher to Heidelberg" (1926:358).

Simmel's academic problems were complicated by the association of sociology
with socialism in the minds of many contemporaries, as well as the association of
socialism with Jewish intellectuals. In his early years, Simmel was associated with
socialist circles in Berlin, but he became critical of historical materialism as a philosophy and of the orthodoxy of many socialist political parties (see Frisby,
1984:25).

Simmel's difficulties with the academic community stood in contrast to his
social life in Berlin. Simmel's wife, Gertrude, was a philosopher who published
work on religion and sexuality under the pseudonym Marie-Luise Enckendorf.
She was also responsible for making their home a "stage for cultivated gather-
ings where the sociability about which Simmel wrote so perceptively found a
perfect setting" (Coser, 1977:196). The Simmels held weekly salons attended by
a small, exclusive group of talented intellectuals and artists (Frisby, 1984:36).
Among them were the poets Stefan George and Rainer Marie Rilke, the philosophers Henri Bergson and Ernst Troeltsch, as well as Max and Marianne Weber
and other members of the Heidelberg circle that collected around the Webers'
salons. Marianne Weber recorded that Simmel often visited them in Heidelberg
and that he "won everyone's heart not only with his exceptional conversational
skills but also with his kindness, warmth, and genuine humanity" (1926:370).

Simmel also held private seminars in his home, and among the students who
attended were the sociologists Georg Lukacs and Karl Mannheim. It has been
noted that nearly every intellectual of Simmel's era was at one point or another
influenced by him (Coser, 1977:199). Simmel certainly had an influence on the
first American sociologists; for example, George Herbert Mead took courses from
Simmel when he was in Europe. Simmel's work was especially influential among
the sociologists of the Chicago School. Many of his essays were translated and
published in the early issues of the *American Journal of Sociology*, and his reflections
on the modern metropolis were important to the urban sociology of the time.
Simmel's influence over American sociology declined from the 1930s until the
mid-1950s, although later he was recognized as "in many ways the most imaginative and intuitive of all the great sociologists" (Nisbet, 1966:19).

Despite Simmel's marginality in the German academy, he was, along with
Max Weber and Ferdinand Tonnies, responsible for the establishment of sociology in the German university system. There were no chairs of sociology prior to
1918 in German universities, and the discipline was regarded as intellectually suspect by many. In fact, Simmel himself wrote, in a letter to a colleague, "it is . . .
somewhat painful to me to find that I am only recognized abroad as a sociologist—whereas I am indeed a philosopher. I see philosophy as my life-task and
engage in sociology really only as a subsidiary discipline" (quoted in Frisby,
1984:25).

From the wealth of sociological as well as philosophical material that Simmel produced, we have selected only a few of his important sociological works to illuminate his sociological outlook—among them, his *Philosophy of Money*, his critical essays "How Is Society Possible?" and "The Problem of Sociology," and some essays dealing with specific social types and forms. Simmel produced a great deal of innovative sociological material, however, that you might find rewarding to read.[1]

Simmel's Central Theories and Methods

Simmel regarded sociology as the study of social interaction. To carry out this study, he proposed to abstract the forms of social interactions from the content. For example, he was interested in how conflict is structured (its form) irrespective of whether it is marital conflict, global conflict, or ethnic conflict (its content). In a manner of speaking, the difference between form and content is a matter of perspective: The "same thing . . . looked at from above, appears as form" but must be labeled "content . . . [when] looked at from below" (1908b:172).

Because of Simmel's emphasis on forms of social interaction, his sociology has often been labeled **formal sociology**. This label is misleading, however, because Simmel's sociology was not the "abstract classification of social forms or an endless typification and taxonomy of social interactions" that the formal or "pure" sociology characterization implies (Frisby, 1984:62).

Simmel's point is that basic forms of social interaction—such as conflict, cooperation, and competition—are to be found in a variety of contexts. The content of each interaction might vary, but the form would be consistent with other interactions of that type.

> Superiority, subordination, competition, division of labor, formation of parties, representation, inner solidarity coupled with exclusiveness toward the outside, and innumerable similar features are found in the state as well as in a religious community, in a band of conspirators as in an economic association, in an art school as in a family. However diverse the interests that give rise to these sociations, the forms in which the interests are realized are identical. (Simmel, 1908e:26)

Social phenomena are thus "composed of two elements which in reality are inseparable: on the one hand, an interest, a purpose, or a motive; on the other, a form or mode of interaction among individuals through which, or in the shape of which, that contents attains social reality" (1908e:24).

The uniformity of modes of interaction occurs because they all involve **exchange**—the "purest and most developed kind of interaction." All activities, "every conversation, every affection (even if it is rejected), every game, every glance at another person" are exchanges of "personal energy" (1900:82). Exchange "creates an inner bond between men—a society in place of a mere collection of individuals" (1900:175).

---

[1] For some comments on Simmel's work and new translations of some of his essays, see *Theory, Culture and Society, 8*(3), 1991. For discussions of Simmel's contemporary theoretical significance, see Kaern, Phillips, and Cohen (1990).

For Simmel, the distinctive nature of sociology is its concern with the separation of form and content in exchange relationships:

> To separate, by scientific abstraction, these two factors of form and content which in reality are inseparably united; to detach by analysis the forms of interaction or sociation from their content (through which these forms become social forms); and to bring them together systematically under a consistent scientific viewpoint—this seems to me the basis for the only, as well as the entire, possibility of a special science of society as such. Only such a science can actually treat the facts that go under the name of sociohistorical reality upon the plane of the purely social. (1908e:25)

The abstraction of form from content is what differentiated sociology from psychology or history, although it draws on both these other disciplines. Psychological processes underlie the forms that sociology abstracts, and these sociological forms become the "material for the induction of timeless uniformities." Or the forms may be examined in terms of specific times and places, providing data "in the service of history" (1908e:29).

In comprehending the nature of forms, wrote Simmel, the sociologist may learn from "a great many fields—political science, economics, history of religion, history of art, and so on," but the central focus for sociology is to ascertain from all the facts what is the "pure form of human behaviour" in any particular situation or context. For example, in examining competition, the task of the sociologist is to "ascertain from all the facts what competition is as a pure form of behaviour; under what circumstances it emerges and develops; how it is modified by the particular character of its object; by what contemporaneous formal and material features of society it is increased or reduced; and how competition between individuals differs from that between groups" (1908e:29).

In advancing this idea of pure forms as the basic subject matter of sociology, Simmel used an analogy with geometry: "Geometry studies the forms through which any material becomes an empirical body, and these forms as such exist, of course, in abstraction only, precisely like the forms of sociation. Both geometry and sociology leave to other sciences the investigation of the contents realized in the forms" (1908e:28). However, having made the analogy, Simmel recognized its limitations. Unlike geometry, which can "construct the whole range of possible formations from a relatively few fundamental definitions," sociological forms can only apply to a "limited range of phenomena." For example, very little is gained from knowing that superordination and subordination are common to almost any human interaction. What the sociologist needs to know is how these forms are manifested in reality. Discovering the specifics is a mixed blessing for sociologists, because the forms "lose in applicability what they would gain in definiteness" (1908e:28). Although no pure forms exist in reality, they have methodological significance as **ideal types**—"categories of knowledge to master the phenomena, and to organize them intellectually" (1908b:172).

This idea of form and content can be applied to Simmel's conception of sociology itself. He considered it a new scientific discipline and a method of research with its own content, but with a form similar to the other human or social sciences (Litchblau, 1991:37).

The goal is to understand both society and individuals, although Simmel tried to avoid focusing on individuals as well as treating organizations and institutions such as the state or the church as autonomous social actors (Turner, 1992:165–166). Simmel insisted that there was "no such thing as interaction" as such—"only specific kinds of interaction" (1908e:27). His method, he claimed, was "finding in each of life's details the totality of meaning" (1900:55). This method is central to Simmel's views on the nature of society, humans, and social change.

Nature of Society, Humans, and Change

In two of his more important essays, Simmel laid out his basic theories of society and human nature. In "The Problem of Sociology," he stated that if "there is to be a science whose subject matter is society and nothing else," it must be one that examines the multitude of social interactions that constitute what is called "society" (1908e:25). Simmel was quite clear that an entity, "society," did exist and that it had its "own vehicles and organs by whose claims and commands the individual is confronted as by an alien party" (Wolff, 1950:58). But it was an entity whose "reality" lay in the minds and actions of individual human beings.

In "How Is Society Possible?" Simmel posed and answered a fundamental question. He argued that society was possible because it was an **object of knowledge** for individuals, expressed in their patterns of interaction.

Simmel's question about the possibility of society was a takeoff on Kant's inquiry "How Is Nature Possible?" Kant had argued that nature was a real entity *only* as a result of human understanding. That is, perceptions of color, taste, tone, temperature, resistance, and smell "only become nature through the activity of the mind which combines them into objects and series of objects, into substances and attributes, and into causal connections" (1908d:6). Nature is not present in its elements but is produced by the "observing subject"; individuals "name" nature.

The direct identification analogous to naming nature, argued Simmel, is not possible with society because society is inseparable from its elements, which are individuals. Individuals know that they are social individuals and have the "feeling and the knowledge of determining others and being determined by them" (1908d:7). The abstract idea of society may not be conscious in all individuals, but all individuals know the "other is tied to him—however much this knowledge of the other as fellow sociate . . . is usually realized only on the basis of particular, concrete contents" (1908d:8). Therefore the **meaning** of social actions and interactions is the significant subject matter of sociology.

According to Simmel, **sociation** between individuals, or social interaction, is always socially incomplete. Each individual has a "core of individuality" that is absent in some degree or other from any interaction. As a result, interaction occurs on the basis of generalizations and typifications. That is, we know someone "not in terms of his pure individuality" but by the "general type under which we classify him" (1908d:10). Thus the claim that no one can know the "real you" is, for Simmel, exactly the case. He suggested that people typify others in terms of qualities—good, bad, moral, immoral—as well as in terms of activities—teacher, student, athlete, couch potato. In addition, group members see each other not simply in terms of their particular roles within the group but also as members of "my group," so that "people look at one another as if through a veil" (1908d:11).

> We see the other not simply as an individual but as a colleague or comrade or fellow party member . . . and this inevitable, quite automatic assumption is one of the means by which one's personality and reality assume, in the imagination of another, the quality and form required by sociability. (1908d:11)

All social interaction rests, however, on the idea of a "real, unconditionally individual nature" that is only veiled by the typifications necessary for interaction.

In Simmel's analysis, the relationship between society and the individual is **dialectical**. The individual "exists both for society and for himself" so that the individual is "contained in sociation and, at the same time, . . . confronted by it" (1908d:17). Individuals are born into and influenced by their social and cultural milieu, but as self-conscious individuals they stand opposed to that milieu, and out of that opposition they transform the milieu. For example, a moral command "confronts us as an impersonal order to which we simply have to submit"; however, "no external power, but only our most private and internal impulses" produce obedience to the command (1908c:118).

According to Simmel, the forms of social life as well as the individual personality are characterized by this ambivalence. Conflict, for example, is an integral and inevitable part of social interaction, as is cooperation; a relationship or interaction totally devoid of conflict is logically, and empirically, impossible. He suggested that "happiness, though it is the object of all our endeavours, would be mere boredom if it were ever achieved as an eternal state" (1900:166).

Conflict and cooperation involve both a psychological and a sociological dimension. For example, Simmel noted that "hostilities are the bitterest that arise on the basis of previous and somehow still felt communion or solidarity (hatred between blood relatives has been called the most burning hatred)" and the "deepest hatred grows out of broken love" (1908e:34). These feelings and situations can be understood both psychologically and sociologically. But from the sociological point of view, "we are not interested in the psychological processes that occur in each of the two individuals but in their subsumption under the categories of union and discord." Sociologically, we are interested in the question, "Up to what point can the relation between two individuals or parties contain hostility and solidarity before depriving the relation of the character of solidarity or giving it that of hostility?" (1908e:34). The sociological interest is in the form taken by the relationship, rather than its content. In fact, individuals are themselves forms, sociologically speaking:

> Society claims the individual for itself. It wants to make of him a form that it can incorporate into its own structure. And this societal claim is often so incompatible with the claim imposed on the individual by his striving after an objective value, as only a purely egoistic claim can be incompatible with a purely social one. (Wolff, 1950:61)

According to Simmel, however, society is only one of the forms affecting an individual life: It is "neither essential to all forms nor is it the only one in which human development is realized." The pure "objective realms" of "logical cognition or metaphysical imagination, the beauty of life or its image in the sovereignty of art, the realms of religion or of nature—none of these, to the extent to which they become our intimate possessions, has intrinsically and essentially anything to do with 'society'" (Wolff, 1950:62). "Mankind" and society represent "two different vantage points" that "measure the individual by different standards." These standards may be in conflict:

> What ties us to mankind and what may contribute to the development of mankind—religious and scientific contributions, inter-family and international interests, the aesthetic perfection or personality, and purely objective production that aims at no "utility"—all this, of course, may on occasion help develop the historical society of which we are members, but, essentially, it is rooted in claims that go far beyond any given society, and that serve the elevation and objective enrichment of the type of "man" itself. They may even be in pointed conflict with the more specific claims of the group that for any given man represents "his society." (Wolff, 1950:63)

All human beings, Simmel maintained, have a part of the self that is "outside" society, although the extent of the "non-social element," or personal self, as opposed to the social self will vary among individuals. For example, with friends and loved ones, what the individual "preserves for himself after all the developments and activities devoted to the friend or beloved are taken care of is almost nothing" (1908d:13). The opposite situation occurs when the individual participates in the modern economy. In the interactions of producing, buying, and selling, the exchange relations with others are (ideally) purely objective, and the "individual life and tone of the total personality is removed from the social action" (1908d:14). It was this objective, material culture that produced the "tragedy" of modernity because it stifled and perverted the humanity of human beings. In actual day-to-day interactions, individuals move between these two extremes, but the nature of social life "consists of the fact that life is not entirely social" and society is a "structure which consists of beings who stand inside and outside of it at the same time" (1908d:14–15).

Simmel's views on the relationship between social change and conflict, the influence of money on human interaction, and the "objective culture" (things) that money buys are discussed in the following sections. Underlying his ideas on all these matters, however, is his basic understanding that individuals have a life apart from the part they play in society.

Social Change and Conflict   To Simmel, social change is primarily change in the nature of human beings. Although "society" is a force over individuals, sociologically it is the plurality of individual interactions that create society. More specifically, in Western society, according to Simmel, **social change** means progress toward equality, freedom, and individuality (Phillips, 1990:26).

Change is marked by **social conflict,** Simmel pointed out, and conflict has usually been regarded as a destructive force that should be prevented. But conflict, he maintained, is often a source of group integration and solidarity. Thus, social conflict involves cooperation as well as conflict and competition: "Whilst antagonism by itself does not produce sociation, it is a sociological element almost never absent from it" (1908e:25). In addition, conflict never takes a singular form. It varies in intensity, duration, context, and so on.

For example, Simmel suggested that similarity would "sharpen the antagonism" for people who regarded their relationship as close. In fact family members "often do one another worse or 'wronger' wrong than complete strangers do" (1908b:44). A family conflict may arise when the "harmonizing forces" weaken, but the similarity of "characteristics, leanings, and convictions" means that "divergence over a very insignificant point makes itself felt in its sharp contrast as something utterly unbearable" 1908b:44). The intensity, even the violence, of conflict when it occurs in intimate relationships is connected to the assumption that the parties should share common or complementary characteristics.

The love relationship is most especially subject to bitter reactions, and when the relationship fails, there is often a desire for vengeance.

> To have to recognize that a deep love—and not only a sexual love—was an error, a failure of intuition, so compromises us before ourselves, so splits the security and unity of our self-conception, that we unavoidably make the object of this intolerable feeling pay for it. We cover our secret awareness of our responsibility for it by hatred which makes it easy for us to pass all responsibility to the other. (1908e:93)

Simmel's observations seem to reflect what frequently happens in cases of marital separation and divorce. Rejection of the other is usually most violent when the parties have been formally joined together, so that "separation does not follow from conflict but . . . conflict from separation." "Amicable" divorces often break down in the face of separation, and the "renegade hates and is hated" often with more intensity than would be the case of conflict between comparative strangers. As Simmel pointed out, "the (sociologically very significant) 'respect for the enemy' is usually absent where the hostility has arisen on the basis of previous solidarity" (1908e:95).

Conflict is different, Simmel suggested, when the parties recognize that they are different and opposed to each other. The pure form of such conflict is legal conflict, in which "nothing enters its whole action which does not belong to the conflict *as such* and serve its purpose." Any third-party interference, or any subjective interests, are excluded by the "objectivity with which only the fight and absolutely nothing else proceeds" (1908b:36). The delegation of such conflicts to professionals—lawyers—illustrates the nature of this form of conflict, the content of which is objectively obtained by the "clear separation of the controversy from all personal associations which have nothing to do with it" (1908b:37).

Another pure form of conflict, in Simmel's analysis, is competition for the "favor of one or more third persons." In this case, the two opposing parties interact in the pursuit of a common goal but "fight *against* a fellowman *for* a third one." The conflict can be pursued in a "thousand ways," through the "socio-logical means of persuasion or conviction, surpassing or underselling, sugges-tion or threat" (1908b:88). But the result, ironically, can be the founding of a relationship with the original opponent, as when rival companies form a cartel or hostile nations band together to fight a common enemy. Conflict can thus increase the integration and solidarity of a group, as well as promote peaceful coexistence for former opponents.

Conflict and cooperation, noted Simmel, involve different forms of adminis-tration. For example, war needs a "centralistic intensification of the group form" that is best guaranteed by despotism (1908b:88). A group at war does not toler-ate members' deviation from the group's aims. Draft dodgers, and even consci-entious objectors, may be seen as threats to the necessary solidarity of the total group and will therefore be dealt with severely. In peacetime, group control can be more relaxed and "antagonistic members" tolerated because "each of them can go his own way and can avoid collisions" with the majority. War, however, "pulls the members so tightly together and subjects them to such a uniform im-pulse that they either must completely get along with, or completely repel, one another" (1908b:92–93). This is why, Simmel pointed out, "war with the out-side is sometimes the last chance for a state ridden with inner antagonisms to overcome these antagonisms, or else break up indefinitely" (1908b:93). Indeed, this was the theme of the 1997 film *Wag the Dog*, in which a U.S. president simu-lates a war to cover up an indiscretion.

In Simmel's discussion of conflict, he noted a peculiar characteristic of con-flict in modern Western societies: Competition is its defining characteristic. The impersonality of modern life makes competition easier. Individuals can treat others as "objects" and therefore "fair game" in the competitive race for material gain. The objectification of others and the pursuit of material, or objective, ends enable competition to attain the "cruelty of all objectivity, a cruelty which does not consist in the enjoyment of the other's suffering but, on the contrary, the elimination of all such subjective factors from the whole action." This indiffer-ence to personal feelings or "subjective" elements is characteristic of "logic, law, and money economy," and it makes people "who are not at all cruel," or at least do not think that they are, "practice the harshness of competition—and with a certain consciousness of not wishing to do anything bad" (1908b:84). Nonethe-less, competition, along with conflict, is what fuels social change in modern so-ciety. Such questionable moral interactions found in modern, metropolitan life are what fascinated Simmel.

Money and Exchange Relations   In one of his major works, *The Philosophy of Money* (1900), Simmel explored the way in which social relations are trans-formed by a modern money economy (Frisby, 1984:96). As you have seen, for Simmel, the overarching form of social interaction is **exchange**. Exchange is the "sociological phenomenon *sui generis*, an original form and function of social life" (1900:100). And a prime mechanism of exchange is money. Money represented, for Simmel, a "means, a material or an example for the presentation of relations" in the "most profound currents of individual life and history" (1900:55).

The Philosophy of Money was ostensibly a critique and extension of Marx's discussion in *Capital*.[2] Simmel himself remarked that "Not a single line of these investigations is meant to be a statement about economics" but rather an inquiry into the "pre-conditions" of monetary exchanges and the "non-economic values and relationships" that emerge (1900:54–55). The work attempted "to construct a new storey beneath historical materialism." This new "storey" comprised an analysis of how a money economy transformed social and cultural life in modern society. He summed up his approach as follows: "Every interpretation of an ideal structure by means of an economic structure must lead to the demand that the latter in turn be understood from more ideal depths, while for these depths themselves the general economic base has to be sought, and so on indefinitely" (1900:56).

In the first part of the book, Simmel examined the nature of the social interactions that contributed to the development of a money economy. In the second part, he examined the consequences for social interaction of the progressive development and extension of a money economy.

Exchange, for Simmel, is the basic form of social interaction. Individuals seek to satisfy certain needs and desires by exchanging valued items or actions with others, or by expending labor power on nature. Objects are valued when they are needed or desired; thus, exchange always has a subjective character. The specific character of exchange is "to deal with the equality of values." In a barter economy, goods are exchanged for goods, but the exchange of equivalent values in those goods is difficult to achieve. Money simplifies the transaction. Money is able to "express the value relation between . . . objects" that may not be identical or even similar (1900:147).

Over time, according to Simmel, money becomes a **pure form,** in the same way that "objective laws of custom, law and morality" eventually become the "ideal products of human conceptions and valuation, which in our mind now stand beyond the will and action of the individual" (1900:174). Money becomes a **reified** social function, standing "beyond the individual objects related to it, in a realm organized according to its own norms" (1900:176). This occurs when exchange becomes more than a "private process between two individuals" and becomes an activity backed by the whole community (1900:176–177). As a representative of the community, the government establishes currency, stock markets, and other means of formally regulating monetary exchanges. Money gains a "sociological character" as a reflection of the stability and reliability of social relations. Only in a "stable and closely organized society that assures mutual protection and provides safeguards against a variety of elemental dangers . . . [is

---

[2]It was "ostensibly" a reaction to Marx's work because most commentators agree that Simmel does not come to grips with Marx's views on the labor theory of value. The general conclusion is that Simmel looks at the economy "from the side of demand and thus from the side of consumption and distribution, thereby allowing supply to be more or less a function of demand. Marx starts from supply, from production" (Brinkman, quoted in Simmel, 1900:26). Where Simmel does come close to Marx is in his theory of alienation.

it] possible for such a delicate and easily destroyed material as paper to become the representative of the highest money value" (1900:172).

The essential function of money is to provide a concrete "expression and . . . representation of the economic value of things" (1900:198). Money is therefore only valuable because it is the "means for the acquisition of values" (1900:228). Money is a tool and, like any social institution, allows the individual to attain "ends for which his personal abilities would never suffice" (1900:209). For example, the legal forms of "contract, testament, adoption etc." give the individual a "collectively established tool that multiplies his own powers, extends their effectiveness and secures their ends" (1900:209).

Exchange based on money has a couple of benefits to society:

- It contributes to self-sufficiency and individual freedom. By making exchanges and interactions more impersonal, money decreases individual dependency on others. For example, Simmel suggested that the wage laborer has more freedom than the peasant: "Certainly the worker is tied to his job almost as much as the peasant to his lot but the frequency with which employers change in a money economy and the frequent possibility of choosing and changing them that is made possible by the form of money wages provide an altogether new freedom within the framework of his dependency" (1900:300).

- It allows exchanges between individuals located at great distances from one another and thus extends the number of possible social interactions. As Simmel noted, "one of the few rules that may be established with some degree of generality concerning the form of social development is this: that the enlargement of the group goes hand in hand with the individualization and independence of its individual members. . . . The importance of money for the development of individuality is thus very closely related to the importance it possesses for the enlargement of social groups" (1900:346–347).

This somewhat rosy picture is countered by the fact that individuality and freedom of choice also isolate the individual from others and from valued objects, and thus contribute to the anomie of modern life. The abstraction and impersonality of social relations also contribute to the intellectualization of life. Money becomes a symbol that increasingly loses any specific connection to objects, which "presupposes a remarkable expansion of mental processes" and a "fundamental re-orientation of culture toward intellectuality." The idea that "life is essentially based on intellect, and that intellect is accepted in practical life as the most valuable of our mental energies, goes hand in hand with the growth of a money economy" (1900:152).

Money and intellect share a "matter-of-fact attitude in dealing with men and things" (Wolff, 1950:411).

> Money places the actions and relations of men quite outside of men as human subjects, just as intellectual life . . . moves from personal subjectivity into the sphere of objectivity which it only reflects. This obviously implies a relationship of superiority. Just as he who has money is superior

to he who has the commodity, so the intellectual person as such has a certain power over the more emotional, impulsive person. (1900:436)

The superiority of money and intellect means that the emotional, impulsive person is thought of as more "one-sided, more committed and prejudiced than the intellectual person," who is deemed to have the "superior view and the unlimited possibilities of use of all practical means" (1900:436–437).

Money is thus the "breeding ground for economic individualism and egoism" and produces self-sufficient manipulators who feel justified in using any means necessary to get what they want in exchanges with others (1900:437).[3] Oddly, such manipulators often consider their motives and behavior to be entirely benign:

> Certainly there is something callous about the purely rationalistic treatment of people and things. Yet this is not a positive impulse but simply results from pure logic being unaffected by respect, kindness and delicacies of feeling. For this reason, the person who is interested solely in money is unable to comprehend why he is reproached with callousness and brutality, since he is aware of the logical consistency and pure impartiality of his behavior but not of any bad intentions. (1900:434)

The real danger of basing exchange on money, in Simmel's view, is that, in the end, money will become the determinant of all values. A "crisis of culture" occurs when "the desire for money far exceeds the desire for the things it can buy." Money thus changes from a means to an end in itself, with damaging consequences for the individual and for culture as a whole (1900:431).

Objective Culture   Simmel defined **culture** as the "enhancement and refinement of certain human energies whose original manifestations we term 'natural'" (1900:446). Thus, a fruit tree is "cultivated," but the "bare marble block is not 'cultivated' to produce a statue." In the latter case, "will and intelligence" beyond the natural or raw material are required. By "cultivating objects" with will and intelligence, their value is increased "beyond the performance of their natural constitution," and in this process "we cultivate ourselves" (1900:447).

The material products of this mental and practical labor Simmel termed **objective culture**—that is, "works of art, machinery, tools and books" produced by human beings (1900:446). Objective culture is produced by what he called **subjective culture**—that is to say, by human intentions, purposes, and desires—so that "in refining objects, man creates them in his own image." As the objects and things of objective culture increase, there is a corresponding "growth of *our* energies" (1900:447). The "independent values of aesthetic, scientific, ethical, eudaemonistic and even religious achievements are transcended in order to integrate them all as elements in the development of human nature beyond its natural state" (1900:447).

---

[3]Self-help books that advise individuals how to be successful in business have exactly this goal in mind.

The problem for modern society, according to Simmel, is that the sheer pro-liferation of objective culture overwhelms the individual mind. Individuals pro-duce objective culture for their own personal development as autonomous be-ings, but the tragedy of modern culture is that this autonomy is threatened by the very objects that individual creativity produces. For example, consumers in modern Western society can become fixated on the acquisition of "things" well beyond what they require for the reasonable satisfaction of life. The "ubiqui-tous tragedy of culture" is that human beings can only live in relation to forms that have come to have "their own independent existence and significance" (1900:257).

Furthermore, the sophistication of the tools and technologies of culture may outpace the sophistication of those who use them; the "cultural growth of the individual can lag considerably behind the cultural growth of tangible as well as functional and intellectual objects" (1900:463). Simmel pointed, for example, to the transformation of the military:

> The work of the individual soldier has essentially remained the same for a long time, and in some respects has been reduced through modern meth-ods of warfare. In contrast, not only the material instruments but, above all, the completely impersonal organization of the army have become extremely sophisticated and a real triumph of objective culture. (1900:449)

Simmel would have regarded present-day computer-dependent warfare as fur-ther confirmation of this point. Our tools of war have made us far more efficient warriors than ever before, but they have not made us any better at resolving conflict peaceably.

The money economy fuels the domination of objective culture because it encourages the exclusion of "irrational, instinctive, sovereign traits and im-pulses which aim at determining the mode of life from within, instead of receiv-ing the general and precisely schematized form of life from without" (Wolff, 1950:413). Simmel pointed to the passionate hatred of the money economy by the art critic John Ruskin and the philosopher Nietzsche, who saw it as destroy-ing the soul of humanity through the quantification of the aesthetic.

The manifestation of objective culture and the triumph of a money economy, according to Simmel, are found in the modern metropolis. The metropolitan sub-ject manifests a "blasé attitude," an indifference, that "expresses all qualitative differences of things in terms of "how much?" and erases the "individuality" of any object or person (Wolff, 1950:414).

Simmel saw money as both alienating and necessary in modern metropoli-tan life. Social relations become objectified with the elimination of all "personal nuances and tendencies," so that there is an "inner barrier" between people. That barrier, however, is "indispensable for the modern form of life" in a me-tropolis. The "jostling crowdedness and the motley disorder of metropolitan communication would simply be unbearable without such psychological dis-tance" (1900:447). The anonymity and frantic pace that mark metropolitan life are thus produced by and, at the same time, reinforce the fact that money has become an end rather than a means.

Psychologically, the focus on money and things results in the "lack of something definite at the centre of the soul." Human beings are impelled to seek "momentary satisfaction in ever-new stimulations, sensations and external activities. Thus it is that we become entangled in the instability and helplessness that manifests itself as the tumult of the metropolis, as the mania for travelling, as the wild pursuit of competition and as the typically modern disloyalty with regard to taste, style, opinions and personal relationships" (1900:484). Did Simmel manage to describe anyone you know?

The paradox—the "real, ubiquitous tragedy of culture"—is that human beings can only live in relation to forms that come to have "their own independent existence and significance" (1900:257). This contradiction between objective and subjective culture has particular significance with regard to gender relations.

Class, Gender, and Race

Simmel did not comment on class or race directly, but his comments on gender were extensive. In addition, in his formal sociology he looked at superordination and subordination, competition and cooperation, conflict, and group affiliations—all illustrating the contours of social relationships and thus applicable to class, gender, and race. In all of the social forms affecting social relationships, the key was **dualism,** as proposed by Durkheim. Simmel explained forms of social life in terms of dualisms such as conformity and individuation, antagonism and solidarity, compliance and rebelliousness, and freedom and constraint (Levine, 1971:xxxvi–xxxvii).

Class   Simmel's discussion of superordination and subordination was related to his belief that socialism and anarchism represented a "sociological error." He began by pointing out that the "quest for freedom and the attainment of freedom" had as its "correlate or consequence, the quest for domination and the attainment of domination." In Simmel's view, both "socialism and anarchism deny the necessary character of this connection" (Wolff, 1950:282).

Furthermore, Simmel argued, concentrating on the elimination of inequality ignores the subjective feelings that produce and preserves inequalities. Sociologists need to address the "consciousness of degradation and oppression, in the descent of the whole ego to the lowness of the social stratum, and, on the other hand, in the personal haughtiness into which self-feelings are transformed by externally leading positions" as much as they needed to address the technical means for the "elimination of command and subjection." He concluded that if the "association between super-subordination and the feeling of personal devaluation and oppression" could be dissolved, then there is no logical reason why the "feeling of dignity and of a life which is its own master, should stand and fall only with socialism" (Wolff, 1950:283).

Simmel did recognize, however, that industrial production presented a problem. A complex division of labor is only possible if workers are paid in money rather than goods. The highly specialized labor characteristic of modern

capitalism, however, is of "little value for the total personality which often becomes stunted because of the division of energies that are indispensable for the
harmonious growth of the self" (1900:454). Like Marx, Simmel recognized the
alienating character of industrial production:

> The fact that labor now shares the same character, mode of valuation and
> fate with all other commodities signifies that work has become something
> obviously separate from the worker, something that he not only no longer
> *is,* but also no longer *has.* For as soon as his potential labor power is
> transposed into actual work, only its money equivalent belongs to him
> whereas the work itself belongs to someone else or, more accurately, to an
> objective organization of labor. (1900:456)

As regards consumption, Simmel observed that capitalist industrial organization allows for the efficient production of more goods, but that they are stan-
dardized, impersonal goods that can appeal to the mass of individuals. Consumer goods cannot be designed for the "subjective differentiation of taste" if
the goods are to be produced "cheaply and abundantly enough in order to satisfy the demand for them" (1900:455). Furthermore, the products of consumer
culture have an "autonomous character," in that the "worker is compelled to
buy his own product if he wishes to have it" (1900:456). For all individuals in
modern society, "cultural objects increasingly evolve into an interconnected enclosed world that has increasingly fewer points at which the subjective soul can
impose its will and feelings" (1900:46). In this connection, think of all the
people today who spend hours and hours shopping without increasing their
feelings of personal well-being.

Despite Simmel's position that modern, capitalist, industrial society is profoundly alienating, unlike Marx he did not believe that socialism or communism is the answer. In fact, Simmel suggested that in modern society, with its
separation of position and objective content from personality and subjective
content, and the stress on technical qualifications, "special talent . . . has a much
greater chance of rising to a higher position." This possibility of upward mobility, Simmel maintained, undermines socialist assumptions. He concluded that:

> However much socialism abhors this blindly contingent relationship
> between the objective scale of positions and the qualification of persons, its
> organizational proposals nevertheless amount to the same sociological
> form. For, socialism desires a constitution and administration which are
> absolutely centralized and hence, by necessity, rigorously articulated and
> hierarchical; but, at the same time, it presupposes that all individuals are, a
> priori, equally capable of occupying any position whatever in this hierar-
> chy. (Wolff, 1950:294)

Simmel suggested that if hierarchy could simply be retained as a "technical-
organizational" value, and subordination and superordination were reciprocal,
then the "organizational value of super-ordination" would be preserved without
its "oppressiveness, one-sidedness, and injustice" (Wolff, 1950:285). He pointed
to marriage as the approximation of this ideal: "The relationship of marriage . . .
owes its inner and outer firmness and unity, at least in part, to the fact that it

comprises a large number of interest spheres in some of which the one part and in others the other part, is superordinate" (Wolff, 1950:288). Simmel concluded that what was called equality of men and women in marriage, "as a fact or as a pious wish—is actually . . . such an alternating superordination and subordination" (Wolff, 1950:288). However, the notion that husband and wife alternate superior/subordinate positions, leading to a balanced, more or less equal relationship, is somewhat questionable when Simmel's ideas on the nature of men versus women are taken into account.

Gender   Simmel paid a great deal of attention to the dynamics of gender relations. Apart from Spencer, Simmel was one of the few classical sociologists who developed a theory about transformations in gender relations as integral to the progress of modernization (Van Vucht Tijssen, 1991:203). The contradiction he noted between objective and subjective culture was of particular significance.

Simmel's discussion of changing gender relations was, like that of Weber, colored by his aversion to the rigid patriarchalism that characterized much of German society at the time. He also sympathized with the aspirations of the liberal women's movement in which his wife, as well as Marianne Weber, was involved. However, like Max Weber, Simmel's conclusions with respect to gender relations were framed by the assumption of a fundamental, unchangeable biological difference between men and women that had invariable social consequences.

Most notably, Simmel believed that women were estranged from specialized, objective culture because of their closer connection to nature and thus their inability to differentiate themselves to create an autonomous life. Objective culture is "thoroughly male";

> it is men who have created art and industry, science and commerce, the state and religion. The belief that there is a purely "human" culture for which the difference between men and women is irrelevant has its origin in the same premise from which it follows that such a culture does not exist— the naïve identification of the "human" with "man." (1984:67)

Where women did participate in the production of culture, according to Simmel, they were successful only to the extent that they incorporated the "male spirit" into their work. When an "act of original production is demanded," he declared, women fail (1984:74). Thus, if women wanted to participate in objective culture, they had to accomplish something that "*men cannot do*. This is the core of the entire problem, the pivotal point of the relationship between the women's movement and objective culture" (1984:75).

The difficulty with women's entry into objective culture resided in what Simmel saw as the fundamental, "natural" differences between men and women. Women do not experience the subjective/objective dichotomy as men do. Rather, women's lives are subjective, characterized by immediate, not detached, experience (1984:42–43). An objectification of women's experience, or the production of feminine culture, is therefore impossible. Only men can separate objective actions from subjective personality, fragment their lives and defer goals and desires, and use energy in performances that "signify" something rather than existing in a "state of harmonious and self-contained repose" (1984:112).

> Knowledge and creation are dynamic relationships in which our existence is . . . drawn out of itself. They represent a displacement of the centre, an annulment of that self-contained completeness of being which constitutes the meaning of life for the female type, even with all its external activity and its devotion to practical tasks. (1984:112)

The "tragedy" of modern culture is therefore a tragedy for men alone.

The difficulties that women have with objective culture are compounded by the specific consequences of the equation "the objective = the male." The fact that men claimed the status of the *"generally human"* is "grounded in the *power position* of men." If the relationship between men and women is seen as akin to the relationship between master and slave, suggested Simmel, then it is clear that one of the master's privileges is that "he does not think about the fact that he is master"; in contrast, the slave can never forget her (his) status. As a result, "the man as master does not take as vital an interest in his relationship to the female as the woman must take in her relationship to the male" (1984:103).

In addition, the master makes all the rules. Therefore, women always encountered in their "accomplishments, convictions, and the practical and theoretical content of their lives" the absolute standards that are "formed by the criteria that are valid for men" (1984:105).

> Because the male prerogative imposes this duality of standards on women—the masculine as trans-sexually objective, and the specifically female standard that is directly correlated with and often diametrically opposed to this—there is actually no standpoint from which women can be unconditionally valued. (1984:105)

The dominance of masculine objectivity is a problem for any transformation of gender relations. The women's movement itself, Simmel argued, was simply the result of transformations in the division of labor in the modern, masculine world. Simmel recognized, however, that changes in the division of labor had different consequences for proletariat women as opposed to the bourgeois women. For the proletarian woman, the changes provided "economic and social freedom" from the "all-embracing ties of domesticity that subordinated her to her man" (1984:182). For bourgeois women, it removed many of the service and production activities from the home, leaving them "deprived of an adequate outlet for their energy." Bourgeois women, therefore, long to have the "freedom to engage in economic or other activities," in contrast to proletarian women who want to "return to the home" (1984:183).

These different class interests, however, do not affect women's rights within society, so that "marital laws, property laws, custody of children, etc., are of equal concern to both classes" (1984:183). Consequently, the division of labor that gives rise to the women's movement and the class divisions within that movement also produce a source of female solidarity that may transcend class divisions. The same issues have perplexed more recent women's movements, as you will see in Chapter 22 .

Despite Simmel's perceptive analysis of gender power relations (an analysis that remains important to current feminist debates), his ideas about women's "nature" in contrast to men's colored his conclusions about any future transformations in those relations. In Simmel's view, the differences between men and women were based on unchanging, biological differences. For example, Simmel suggested that men's sexuality was focused on the desire for, and consummation of, a relationship, whereas women's sexuality "unconditionally and directly constitutes her ultimate being" (1984:107). Women are more "closely and deeply rooted in the dark, primitive forces of nature than are men" (1900:378). For the man, "sexuality is something he does; for the women it is a mode of being" (1984:109).

Consequently, Simmel saw prostitution as the ultimate degradation for a woman. Because the sexual act involves a woman's "total self," the surrender of "her most intimate and personal quality, which should be offered only on the basis of a genuine personal impulse and also only with equal personal devotion on the part of the male" for a "totally impersonal, purely extraneous and objective compensation" is "unsuitable and inadequate" (1900:377–378). Of all human relationships, Simmel suggested, prostitution was the one that fundamentally contradicts Kant's moral imperative—"never to use human beings as means"—because for both parties prostitution is a relationship of "mutual degradation to mere means" (1900:377).

According to Simmel, a woman's authentic being is of a "constant nature," having as a prime psychological trait "fidelity"; in contrast, men's detachment and objectivity creates a "disposition in favor of infidelity" (1984:71). A "girl who has gone astray only once loses her reputation entirely" because women's infidelity is "more harshly judged than a man's (of whom it seems to be believed that an occasional purely sensual indulgence is compatible with loyalty to his wife in every spiritual and essential respect)." In fact, the "worst rake can still rise from the mire by virtue of other facets of his personality and no social status is closed to him" (1984:71). The double standard is thus a natural standard in Simmel's view.

Simmel's comments in this regard were somewhat self-serving: He had a son from his marriage and a daughter from his lifelong affair with the writer and poet Gertrude Kantorowicz. But in a "highly original ethical interpretation of marital fidelity he determined never to see this daughter" (Vromen, 1990: 320).

Simmel, like Durkheim, suggested that women might be more active in cultural pursuits. But he went further, suggesting that given women's empathetic abilities they might also be more active in medicine. His main conclusion was, however, that the "home remains the supreme cultural achievement of women" (1984:97). He speculated on the possibility of an "autonomous *femininity*" that might be promoted by an initial "mechanical leveling of education, rights, occupations, and conduct" but insisted that the basic difference remained: cultural objectivity contradicted the "innermost essence of the distinctly female existence" (1984:99).

The major problem with Simmel's analysis of gender relations is that for him women remained culturally subordinate to men, trapped by their biological nature. Simmel recognized the "male bias of culture" but failed to escape that bias himself, remaining "imprisoned in a romantic conception of the eternal and universal female principle" of *schöne Seele* (beautiful soul).[4] Nonetheless, Simmel's idea that the feminization of culture might mitigate the tragic alienation men experience in modern society remains an important issue in current feminist discussions.

Race   Simmel did not discuss race explicitly, but his essay "The Stranger" helps to illuminate the ambiguous social interactions that racial difference often generates within a society. The underlying idea is that societies tend to assign the status of stranger to individuals who are in some way different from the majority of group members. The stranger is "an element of the group itself . . . whose membership within the group involves both being outside it and confronting it" (1908f:144).

Designating a stranger involves specific forms of social interaction. First, interaction with the stranger is a combination of attraction and repulsion. Simmel suggested that the stranger historically made his appearance as a trader. The trader is "required for goods produced outside the group," but the trader "intrudes as a supernumerary . . . into a group in which all the economic positions are already occupied." He noted that the "classic example of this is the history of European Jews" (1908f:144). Although the Jews supplied necessary goods and services, they were treated differently from others who fulfilled similar roles within the society. For example, in medieval Frankfurt Jews were assigned a fixed tax, unlike Christians whose taxes varied according to their incomes. This tax was fixed because the "Jew had his social position as a *Jew*, not as the bearer of certain objective contents" (1908f:149). The stranger is thus seen not as an individual but as a stranger of a "certain type."

The stranger is also "near and far *at the same time*." Having general attributes in common (nearness) simply highlights those that are different (distance). For strangers to a "country, the city, the race, and so on, what is stressed is again nothing individual, but alien origin" (1908f:148). The near and far character of the stranger also accounts for the stranger's objectivity.

> Because he is not bound by roots to particular constituents and partisan dispositions of the group, he confronts all of these with a distinctly "objective" attitude, an attitude that does not signify mere detachment and nonparticipation, but is a distinct structure composed of remoteness and nearness, indifference and involvement. (1908f:145)

Simmel's discussion of the stranger can be applied to the position of different races that have been incorporated into a society. For example, African Americans are citizens of the United States but are often regarded, and often feel themselves, as detached from and not fully incorporated into U.S. society. Their nearness to other members of the group is balanced by their invariable difference.

---

[4]Marianne Weber criticized Simmel's essay on "Female Culture." She objected to his "radical polarity of the genders" and claimed that Simmel "failed to appreciate women's need to determine their own choices." She also pointed out that women need to, and have the ability to, contribute to objective culture. In sum, she thought Simmel's analysis elitist (quoted in Vromen, 1990:334–336).

Other Theories and Theorists

Simmel claimed he was both sociologist and philosopher, and his work reveals precisely such a combination. Although his central focus was the forms of social and cultural life and how these unfold through creative human efforts, he was also concerned with the Kantian issue of the source of moral values and how an ethical life can be lived. His comparative analysis of the philosophers Schopenhauer and Nietzsche explored these themes.

Both Schopenhauer and Nietzsche were concerned with the profound anomie and alienation of modern life and the degradation of traditional values and standards. They decried the absence of a solid ethical basis for the conduct of individual and social life, and they did not believe that reason could fully replace the old, presumed certainties of traditional values.

Schopenhauer agreed with Kant that ultimately the external world could not be known by human beings, nor was rationality the answer to knowledge of reality or ethical actions. Schopenhauer asked, "What is life, what is its meaning, purely *as* life?" (Simmel, 1907:379). His answer was that life is the will to life. Life is not defined by its contents, ideas, or state of being; it is a state of self consciousness. Thus Simmel remarked, "Schopenhauer . . . shifted the axis of our perspective on man. Rationality no longer constitutes the veiled but basic reality" (1907:29). Schopenhauer's "philosophical expression for the inner condition of modern man" is that the "essence of the world and ourselves has its total and only decisive expression in our will" (1907:5). All that human beings can know is their own needs and desires—their own will.

According to Simmel, Schopenhauer did not see knowledge as a form of enlightened rational will, but as a realization of the arbitrary play of instincts and the "unremitting monotony" of human life (1907:8). The human tendency to seek a final goal in life was thus thwarted, because there was nothing "outside of the will" and will was "identical with life" (1907:5). As a result, Schopenhauer's formulation was ethically problematic. If existence was simply a "phenomenon of will," then any injustice, any of the "pains and absurdities of the world," could be justified as the responsibility of will: "The world is as it is because it wants things to be that way" (1907:67). The only escape was through individual transcendence of the demands of the will, which was only possible in the "renunciation of life" of the "ascetic saint." Such renunciation, however, was not a collective, social solution to the conflicts and problems of modern life.

Nietzsche took up Schopenhauer's concern with the meaning of life but came to an opposite, less pessimistic conclusion, in Simmel's view. According to Simmel, Nietzsche's reformulation of Schopenhauer was a consequence of his study of evolutionary Darwinism, which allowed him to "find in the fact of mankind's evolution the possibility of saying 'yes' to life" (1907:5).

> Nietzsche takes a totally new concept of life, which is very much opposed to that of Schopenhauer, from the idea of evolution: life is in itself, in its intimate and innermost essence, an increase, maximization, and growing concentration of the surrounding power of the universe in the subject. Through this innate urge . . . life can become the goal of life. Thus, the question of a final goal beyond life's own natural process becomes moot. (1907:6)

The evolution of humanity was not without pain and difficulty, according to Nietzsche. Just as Kant understood morality as the individual's painful rejection of sensual nature through reason, Nietzsche "transfers this connection beyond the individual to mankind: only discipline attended by great pain has brought forth 'all elevation of humanity' " (1907:166).

The difficulty was that the majority of individuals, in Nietzsche's view, were incapable of understanding and attaining the strength of will necessary to move humanity to objectively higher levels. Only those individuals willing to endure severe personal discipline in the conduct of their lives could become Übermenschen ("overmen"). Historically, especially in Christian doctrine, the "weak, the mediocre, and the insignificant" had attained power over the "strong, noble, and exceptional" (1907:138). This doctrine, according to Nietzsche, was a reversal of an earlier estimation that it was "good" to be strong, dominant, a winner. The Christian doctrine celebrated the individuals who renounced their will and abased the self for others. The consequence of what Nietzsche called "slave morality" was, in Simmel's words, a "lowering and levelling of the general human type" (1907:139).

> The herd animal has achieved victory over the highest and superior specimens of its species through the demand that . . . the mentality of the suppressed and retarded majority, become the general norm and goal. . . . the Christian, democratic, and altruistic notions of value are intended to make the powerful serve the weak, the healthy administer to the ill, and the mighty to submit to the lowly. (1907:139)

The elevation and transformation of modern existence required the perfection of the highest human beings, which was the sole purpose of life in Nietzsche's view. Simmel suggests that in this way Nietzsche's philosophy "exalts and glorifies life" (1971:387).

Simmel's endorsement of Nietzsche as opposed to Schopenhauer does not provide any final philosophical comfort. According to Simmel, "life is the antithesis of form" because "Life is always more life than there is room for in the form allotted by and grown out of it" (1971:370). Consequently, the "essence of life would be denied if one tried to form an exhaustive conceptual definition" (1971:392, fn.1). Life tries to transcend form, but the human processes of "thinking, wishing, and forming can only substitute one form for another." This conflict between life and form has appeared in other historical periods but has, in Simmel's view, become most clearly revealed in modern life.

Simmel concluded that in modern society, "Life is a struggle in the absolute sense of the term which encompasses the relative contrast between war and peace: that absolute peace which might encompass this contrast remains an eternal . . . secret to us" (1971:393). Human transcendence can be achieved only through the recognition that life is a "boundless continuity," as Schopenhauer believed, as well as being "individuality encased in form" as suggested by Nietzsche (1971:368). Modernity forces the clear recognition of a central human dilemma: the "true self" is encased in cultural forms that the self must transcend.

Critique and Conclusions

A major theme that runs through Simmel's sociological and philosophical work is a critical analysis of the forms, nature, and processes of *modernity*. Like his friend Max Weber, Simmel recognized the profound contradictions that modern *capitalist society* represented. Rationalization and objectivity offered greater freedom to individuals while at the same time constraining and regimenting life. Money was a prime symbol of these contradictions. Money provides individuals with greatly expanded opportunities for social interaction at the same time that it depersonalizes the relationships that emerged from those interactions. The abstract measure of value that money represents stands in contrast to the human value of the individual. Individuals are alienated from one another not because they are isolated from others, but because others are anonymous. This anonymity engenders an "indifference to their individuality, a relationship to them without regard to who it is in any particular instance" (Simmel, 1991:21).

To some extent, Simmel shared Weber's pessimism about the future of humanity in a depersonalized, bureaucratized world. In fact, Simmel and Weber may have discussed the idea of an aesthetic escape from the rationalized world of modernity (Abraham, 1992:135). Weber came to see eroticism as one means of escape but was less sympathetic to Simmel's preoccupation with subjective culture, the human soul, and the natural, organic source as the critical problem of modernity. However, Simmel's idea of the tragic but inescapable search for the "true self," immune to the problems and pressures of social life, remains an important contemporary issue, exemplified in the many best-selling self-help and pop psychology books.

Because of the sheer brilliance, range, and diversity of his interests, Simmel did not fit easily into the rigid hierarchies of the German academic world at the turn of the century (Coser, 1977:210). His Jewish heritage was, as you have seen, also a handicap in the German academy. Simmel's status as an academic and intellectual outsider has been one of the themes that appear in evaluations of his work. One contemporary thought Simmel's work "fragmentary and incomplete," although he did suggest that this may have been what Simmel intended and, in that respect, it was an "important advance over the older sociologists who foundered on their mania for systems" (Leopold von Wiese, quoted in Coser, 1971:53). In the mid-twentieth century, Simmel was characterized as the "marginal man, the stranger," who presented his "academic peers not with a methodical, painstakingly elaborated system but with a series of often disorderly insights, testifying to amazing powers of perception" (Coser, 1965:36).

However, another contemporary, Georg Lukacs, called Simmel the "most significant and interesting transitional figure in the whole of modern philosophy" because of his ability to see "the smallest and most inessential phenomenon of daily life so sharply *sub specie philosophiae* that it becomes transparent and behind its transparence an eternal formal coherence of philosophical meaning becomes perceptible" (1991:145). Lukacs characterized Simmel as the philosopher of "Impressionism" who was able to proceed from an appreciation of the particular to "embrace the totality of life" (1991:148).

Lukacs also maintained that it was Simmel's sociology that laid the groundwork for the sociological work of Max Weber and other German sociologists, despite their methodological differences from Simmel. However, Simmel did not create a "School." He himself declared that he would die "without intellectual heirs, and that is as it should be. My legacy will be, as it were in cash distributed to many heirs, each transforming his part into use conformed to *his* nature" (quoted in Coser, 1977:198–199). It is the richness of this scattered legacy that makes Simmel's work fresh and sociologically relevant.

Final Thoughts

It is just as impossible to cover in a short chapter the wealth of material that Simmel produced as it was to cover Max Weber's work. We have examined only a few of Simmel's fascinating essays on various manifestations of sociability, and we have paid no attention to his interesting work on various artists, such as Goethe and Rembrandt.

Simmel was influenced by the German philosophers Kant, Hegel, Schopenhauer, and Nietzsche, as well as by Spencer's evolutionism. He was also indebted to Marx, and his *Philosophy of Money* is an important complement to Marx's analysis of capitalist society. More than anything else, however, Simmel was a philosophical sociologist concerned with how human beings can define their humanity in the context of an overwhelmingly objective culture.

References

Abraham, Gary A. 1992. "Within the Weber Circle": A Review of Lawrence A. Scaff, *Fleeing the Iron Cage.*" *Theory, Culture and Society, 9*(2), 129–139.

Bauman, Zygmut. 1987. *Legislators and Interpreters: On Modernity, Post-Modernity, and Intellectuals.* Cambridge: Cambridge University Press.

Coser, Lewis A. (Ed.). 1965. *Georg Simmel.* Englewood Cliffs, NJ: Prentice-Hall.

———. 1977. *Masters of Sociological Thought.* New York: Harcourt Brace Jovanovich.

Frisby, David. 1984. *Georg Simmel.* London: Tavistock.

———. 1986. *Fragments of Modernity: Theories of Modernity in the Work of Simmel, Kracauer, and Benjamin.* Cambridge, MA: MIT Press.

———. 1992. *Sociological Impressionism: A Reassessment of Georg Simmel's Social Theory.* London: Routledge.

Kaern, Michael, Bernard S. Phillips, and Robert S. Cohen (Eds.). 1990. *Georg Simmel and Contemporary Sociology.* Dordrecht: Kluwer Academic Publishers.

Levine, Donald N. 1971. "Introduction." In Georg Simmel, *On Individuality and Social Forms* (pp. ix–lxv). Chicago: University of Chicago Press.

Levine, Donald N., Elwood B. Carter, and Eleanor Miller Gorman. 1976. "Simmel's Influence on American Sociology." *American Journal of Sociology, 81,* 813–845.

Litchblau, Klaus. 1991. "Causality or Interaction? Simmel, Weber and Interpretive Sociology." *Theory, Culture and Society, 8*(3), 33–62.

Lukacs, Georg. 1991. "Georg Simmel." *Theory, Culture and Society, 8*(3), 145–150.

Nisbet, Robert. 1966. *The Sociological Tradition.* New York: Basic Books.

Phillips, Bernard S. 1990. "Simmel, Individuality, and Fundamental Change." In Michael Kaern, Bernard S. Phillips, and Robert S. Cohen (Eds.), *Georg Simmel and Contemporary Sociology* (pp. 9–12). Dordrecht: Kluwer Academic Publishers.

Simmel, Georg. 1900/1978. *The Philosophy of Money* (Tom Bottomore and David Frisby, Trans.). London: Routledge & Kegan Paul.

———. 1904/1980. *Essays on Interpretation in Social Science* (Guy Oakes, Trans. and Ed.). Totowa, NJ: Rowman and Littlefield.

———. 1907/1991. *Schopenhauer and Nietzsche* (Deena Weinstein and Michael Weinstein, Trans. and Eds.). Amherst: University of Massachusetts Press.

———. 1908a/1971. "Conflict." In Donald N. Levine (Ed.), *On Individuality and Social Forms* (pp. 70–95). Chicago: University of Chicago Press.

———. 1908b/1955. *Conflict and the Web of Group Affiliations* (Kurt H. Wolff and Reinhard Bendix, Trans.). New York: Free Press.

———. 1908c/1971. "Domination." In Donald N. Levine (Ed.), *On Individuality and Social Forms* (pp. 96–126). Chicago: University of Chicago Press.

———. 1908d/1971. "How Is Society Possible?" In Donald N. Levine (Ed.), *On Individuality and Social Forms* (pp. 6–22). Chicago: University of Chicago Press.

———. 1908e/1971. "The Problem of Sociology." In Donald N. Levine (Ed.), *On Individuality and Social Forms* (pp. 23–35). Chicago: University of Chicago Press.

———. 1908f/1971. "The Stranger." In Donald N. Levine (Ed.), *On Individuality and Social Forms* (pp. 143–149). Chicago: University of Chicago Press.

———. 1971. *On Individuality and Social Forms* (Donald N. Levine, Ed.). Chicago: University of Chicago Press.

———. 1984. *Georg Simmel: On Women, Sexuality, and Love* (Guy Oakes, Trans. and Ed.). New Haven, CT: Yale University Press.

———. 1991. "Money in Modern Culture." *Theory, Culture and Society, 8*(3), 17–31.

Turner, Bryan S. 1992. *Max Weber: From History to Modernity.* London: Routledge.

Van Vucht Tijssen, Lietke. 1991, "Women and Objective Culture: Georg Simmel and Marianne Weber." *Theory, Culture and Society, 8*(3), 203–218.

Vromen, Suzanne. 1990. "Georg Simmel and the Cultural Dilemma of Women." In Michael Kaern, Bernard S. Phillips, and Robert S. Cohen (Eds.), *Georg Simmel and Contemporary Sociology* (pp. 319–340). Dordrecht: Kluwer Academic Publishers.

Weber, Marianne. 1926/1975. *Max Weber: A Biography* (Harry Zohn, Trans. and Ed.). New York: John Wiley & Sons.

Weinstein, Deena, and Michael A. Weinstein. 1993. *Postmodern(ized) Simmel* London: Routledge.

Wolff, Kurt H. 1950. *The Sociology of Georg Simmel.* New York: Free Press.

SECTION V

Sociological Theories of Politics and Economics

To this point you have been reading about the theories of the founders of sociology and their forebears. These early sociological theorists were struggling to outline a new discipline in a world undergoing significant change. In the process they established several basic schools of thought that are still influential in sociology. Chapters 3 and 4 introduced evolutionary and functional theories, which support the status quo. They assume or claim that society is good, that it is self-corrective, and that it is consensual and like an organism. Because these theories were produced within Western capitalist societies, they justify capitalism. (Remember that in a Buddhist or socialist society, an ideology that supports Buddhism or socialism, respectively, would be considered status quo conservative.)

In Chapters 5 and 6 you became acquainted with radical theories, which argue that capitalist society is bad and coercive, human nature is good, and society needs a complete overhaul through conflict to bring it more in line with the goodness in humans. In Chapters 7 and 8 you met three German theorists with an eclectic set of concerns and perspectives. They analyzed the complexity of Western capitalist society in terms of stratification, authority relations, religion, gender issues, the form and content of social groups, and many other issues confronting humanity.

Section V focuses on theoretical responses to Marxism's radical criticism of capitalism, which has both political and economic components. Here we address three bases for societal leadership: force, ingenuity, and splendor.

> [We] strive to rule over men to demonstrate the ability and force of the body, or spiritual force, or for the splendor of civil life. One recognizes that men may become in some part masters of others in all three ways. And firstly, in respect to physical *force*, this is what binds the conquerors to the conquered. Secondly is the force of *ingenuity*, that which the wise use with respect to the ignorant and the shrewd with respect to the foolish. The third, finally, is the *splendor* and luxury of civil life by which the great and

223

the rich through the pomp of living dominate those who cannot afford to behave similarly. (Genovesi, 1820:292, italics added)

The first two bases for leadership—force and ingenuity—are primarily political, while the third—splendor—is mainly economic.

Section V (Chapters 9 and 10) introduces the political sociology and economic sociology theories that responded to the two major aspects of the radical anticapitalism of Marx and has followers. Almost uniformly, criticism of Marxism begins with the concept of a final revolutionary overthrow of capitalism. The critics consider the notion of a classless society without a state or a ruling elite, and with everyone living "happily ever after," as utopian, and therefore untenable. The theoretical response is that there will always be a ruling elite, and any major change simply involves who is in charge.

In Chapter 9, Robert Michels argues that there is an "iron law" of oligarchy, or rule by a few—meaning that a small number of people run any institution, including the government. Neither monarchy nor democracy is possible. Furthermore, Vilfredo Pareto claims not only that there is a circulation of elites, but that success in politics is enhanced by cynicism and hypocrisy—that is, by manipulating one's message to fit the audience—and that success is its own justification. Ideologically, such critics of radicalism are conservative, in the sense that they believe nothing important ever changes, only the personnel in positions of leadership. However, Pareto would argue (as do the positivists) that this is not ideological at all, but is simply reality—that his theory is not just political, but deals with the character of both human nature and society.

Chapter 10 introduces economic sociology, with its criticisms focusing on the functioning of the capitalist system. In that chapter, Thorstein Veblen argues that the leisure class is an extension of the capitalist owners of the means of production, and that in the early twentieth century the "captains of industry" ran everything, even education. Joseph Schumpeter offers a theory of stratification that relates rewards to aptitude, and he is fascinated by entrepreneurship in the capitalist world.

Ideologically, Veblen is a serious and insightful critic of capitalism—a would-be radical—but unlike the radicals (or even the liberal reformers), he believes that little if anything can be done to cure capitalism's ills. Schumpeter, on the other hand, does not just see the prediction of a final revolution as mistaken; he is ideologically positive toward many aspects of modern capitalist society, though he finds capitalist imperialism as somewhat irrational. However, despite his conservative ideology, he perceives in the future a move toward at least partial socialism, or government takeover of certain portions of the economy.

We turn now to these political and economic theoretical reactions to Western radical theory. You will see that each new set of ideas adds to the complexity of the theoretical landscape.

Reference

Genovesi, Antonio. 1820. *Lezioni di Commercio ossia de Economia Civile*. Milan: Silvestri.

Chapter 9

Political Sociological Theories
Pareto and Michels

Richard Nixon was an important political figure in late-twentieth-century U.S. politics. Early in his career he was involved in the anticommunist witch-hunts, and he made his reputation as a fighter for American capitalist democracy. Losing the campaign for the presidency in 1960, he ran again in 1968, during the Vietnam War, and was elected. Instead of reducing U.S. involvement in the war, he broadened it to include Laos and Cambodia. Reelected in 1972, he did an apparent about-face by initiating serious dialogue with Communist China. However, in 1974 his role in the Watergate break-in finally came to light, and he was forced to resign.

In the past 25 years much new material on Nixon has been made public, especially a massive number of tapes of Oval Office conversations. This information has reinforced the view of Nixon as an expedient politician, able to manipulate images and behaviors to suit the needs of the moment, and to increase the likelihood of success. In a television interview several years after his resignation, Nixon said, "There's a lot of hypocrisy . . . in political life. It's necessary in order to get into office and in order to retain office." A president is "not lying in an immoral sense" when "he says what he doesn't believe" (Richard Nixon, on "Good Morning America," quoted in the *Capital Times*, October 28, 1982, p. 14).

This chapter is on society and politics. It is about political behavior, and about ruling elites. Though it covers a variety of issues concerning human relations, the primary focus is **power,** or the ability to gains one's ends, with or without the opposition of others.

One hundred years before Nixon's time, Karl Marx analyzed politics in terms of the capitalist ruling class, oppression, the state, and revolution. By the latter part of the nineteenth century, Marx's views had evoked responses from several important thinkers. Vilfredo Pareto in Italy produced a theory of politics as a subfocus within his general theory of society—a theory that distinguished between actual human motives and rationalizations for behavior. Soon

225

thereafter, the cosmopolitan Robert Michels wrote about politics, both in his 1911 book *Political Parties* and in his *Lectures*, published in 1927. We begin with Pareto.

Vilfredo Pareto (1848–1923)

Few writers have elicited more intense reactions than Vilfredo Pareto. One writer called Pareto "the adversary of humanitarian democracy" (Zeitlin, 1994:192); another described him as "a humanist who fought ceaselessly for democracy [and] for freedom of any sort" (Lopreato, in Pareto, 1916b:xx). Why such differing interpretations of this man? The answer lies in Pareto's response to the times in which he lived, and others' fragmentary knowledge of his work. The most sensitive treatment of Pareto's life and work is Placido Bucolo's 1980 book *The Other Pareto*, in which he drew upon newspaper articles and letters written by Pareto over a 50-year period.

Vilfredo Pareto was born in Paris to an Italian political-exile father and a French mother. When Vilfredo was a small boy, the family moved back to Italy, where he gradually became inbued with humanitarian/democratic ideals. "In reality," wrote Bucolo (1980:3) "Pareto's drama is the drama of Europe, which—an impotent witness—watches its own destruction, ready to resign the mastery of the world and become the slave of its passions. It [Europe] decays from the condition of a freeman to that of an instrument, more and more powerless in the face of an arrogant bureaucracy."

The power-hunger of Europe's leaders, culminating in World War I, was paralleled by Pareto's increasing cynicism about political life. The cynical portions of his work became known in the West before his earlier works, and his writings about fascism, especially that of Mussolini in Italy, were misunderstood as sympathetic with the brutal totalitarianism of Italy—which began before, but developed after, Pareto's death. According to Bucolo (1980:285), "A worse fate could not have befallen Pareto—scientist, anti-metaphysician, anti-totalitarian, anti-colonialist, anti-militarist, than that of being quoted as the ideologue of a regime which was gradually losing all those characteristics to which Pareto had given his initial, incontestable support."

Not only did events in Europe affect Pareto's view of society and politics, but so did his private life. He suffered two political defeats, in 1880 and 1882, which he saw as resulting from corrupt practices by his opposition. Soon thereafter, his friend Maffeo Pantaleoni was forced to resign his teaching post because he had criticized a customs duty policy on wine. Pareto considered himself partly to blame because he had quoted the incriminating article in print (de Rosa, 1962:143).

In 1893 Pareto was appointed to the Chair of Political Economy at Lausanne, where he taught for the next 20 years. In the same year, Crispi became Prime Minister of Italy and began to imitate Bismarck of Germany in making Italy into a military and colonial power.

In 1901 Pareto inherited a substantial fortune, and moved to a villa at Celigny. He knew how to enjoy "the good life," and criticized those who did not:

> As regards the bitter hatred which some elated moralists display against less ascetic men, it has its origin not only in that religious and sectarian sentiment for which the heretic will die and destroy himself, but it springs also from that envy which unknowingly and unintentionally the non-enjoyer resents in the enjoyer, or the eunuch in the virile man. (Pareto, 1901:45)

Later that year his wife ran off with a servant—a deeply disturbing experience for Pareto. After that, according to Zeitlin (1994:228), he came to be known to the intellectual world as "the hermit of Celigny," although he continued to entertain his friends, including both Pantaleoni and Michels.

An extremely sensitive man, all these events affected Pareto deeply, and gradually altered his liberal humanitarian view of history and the world.

Pareto's Central Theories and Methods

Pareto was greatly influenced by the work of another Italian, Niccolo Machiavelli. In *The Prince* (1532), Machiavelli had set for himself the problem of discovering "the best means available to princes for holding their power" (Pareto, 1916b:254). Although Machiavelli had not argued that princes *should* stay in power, the methods he described included deceit and force as well as the use of argument. Pareto thought that Machiavelli's arguments were very insightful in explaining history and society.

Pareto's theory included not only general sociology and politics, but economics and other issues as well. In this section we will deal with his general social theory and his theory of political elites; economics and other theoretical issues will be considered under Other Theories and Theorists.

Residues and Derivations   The core of Pareto's work, and also the most controversial, was his general theory of residues and derivations. Put simply, **residues** are the reasons or motives for behavior, while **derivations** are the excuses (justifications, rationalizations) we give for our behavior.

By residues Pareto meant the bases of human action, the sentiments that determine behavior. He used the term synonymously and interchangeably with instinct, need, and motive, but especially with sentiment (Pareto, 1916b:xxxi). Of these "springs of human action," six were most important:

1. The instinct for combinations (change)

2. Persistence of aggregates (non-change)

3. Self-expression or activity—the need to do something, to express feelings through actions

4. Sociality, or sociability

5. Integrity or integration with others and with one's social setting

6. Sex residues (Pareto, 1916b:120–122; Bucolo, 1980:204–212)

Although all these had a place in Pareto's theory, the first two—change and non-change—were central.

To illustrate the residue involving combinations, or change, Pareto offered two very different examples: the scientist working in a laboratory, and the person

playing a game of chance. In both instances the individual is seeking new combinations—whether through rational norms in the lab or through "luck" in the
game of chance. Combinations, then, may be rational or irrational, based on
sound factual reasoning or on various kinds of faith. Regardless, the impetus to
combine, Pareto argued, is a basic part of human nature (1916b:122–127).

By contrast, the residue for group persistence, or non-change, is the need to
conserve. Humans perpetuate certain beliefs and ways of behaving, often solving the same problem in the same way again and again. This residue may be
called habit on the individual level, or culture on the societal level. Persistence
is often so strong that it may outlast the conditions for its existence. Pareto gave
as an example the old tradition of burying objects with a deceased person. The
idea was for these objects to be available in a life after death, so that patterns
could be continued even then (1916b:132). Motives for persistence, according
to Pareto, include relations with loved ones, with social class, and with one's native land (Bucolo, 1980:207).

Paralleling these important needs of individuals—to change and to conserve—are equivalent characteristics of societies as a whole. Pareto described
the two extreme types of societies: at one extreme, "a human society in which
each individual each day behaved independently of the past" and of other individuals, so that new combinations were ubiquitous; at the other, "a society in
which each person is assigned his role, from birth to death, and from which
there is no escape. Stability here would be very great, society would be crystallized" (1906:314). Actual societies, he suggested, fall between these two extremes. Just as human beings exhibit an intermingling of the residues for new
combinations and persistence, so societies are characterized by both change and
non-change, but with some dominated more by one or the other.

Although the mix of residues differs, the residues themselves never change;
they are the essential underlying motives and sentiments. What does change,
according to Pareto, are the derivations—the intellectual systems of justification
with which individuals camouflage their motives in order to give themselves a
look of rationality. Derivations are the reasons we give for behaving as we do, or
for wanting someone else to behave a certain way. At opposite ends of the spectrum, purely instinctual behaviors, such as eating, do not involve derivations,
nor do what Pareto called "logico-scientific" outcomes, such as experiments
with chemical reactions. However, derivations figure in all the intermediate
cases, arising whenever people try to explain their behavior (including *what*
they eat) or justify what they want someone else to do. Explanation is almost
always rationalization, argued Pareto, seldom expressing the real reason or basis
for behavior. "Man, although impelled to act by nonlogical motives, likes to tie
his actions logically to certain principles; he therefore invents these *a posteriori* in
order to justify his actions" (1901:27).

Examples of derivations can be seen in the persuasive mechanisms people
use to get others to behave in certain ways. One is an appeal to human authority: "because I said so" or "because I am your mother." Another is metaphysical,
appealing to external authority: "because God will punish you." Pareto noted
that people often state their aims in theological or metaphysical derivations,
"while the practical purpose of human beings is the welfare and prosperity of

themselves and their societies" (1916b:234). Finally, people offer verbal proofs: "Vote for me because I favor democracy and will work for the people." Here a political candidate is relying on catch-phrases such as "democracy" and "working for the people," hoping no one will ask what they actually mean.

Some derivations rely on "incidental sentiments determining choice of terms" (Pareto, 1916b:193), as in the everyday "propaganda-speak" of today. One country's "leader" is another country's "warlord"—the choice of term depending on the positive or negative sentiment it evokes. For example, in the Persian Gulf War, U.S. missiles were "Patriots," while Iraq's were "Scuds." A Patriot shooting down a Scud gave a sense of pride to those in the United States keeping track of the war.

The relationship between residues and derivations involves the problem of logic and illogic. Logic, according to Pareto, is derived from success. If we act in a way that brings about the outcome we desire, we are acting logically. Logic is not based on confessing or recognizing our real motives; it is based on doing/ saying whatever gets us what we want. A by-product of this view, drawing upon Machiavelli, is Pareto's **political cynicism**. An effective derivation is logical; believing one's own message while failing in one's aim is illogical. Politically, then, cynical or hypocritical political leaders who do not believe their own message are acting logically. Thanks to their ability to change their viewpoint to suit their audience, they will be successful. True believers act illogically, because they are incapable of altering what they say to fit their audience. Thus, as Nixon said, hypocrisy may be necessary to be successful in politics—and for Pareto, success is logical.

Pareto believed that the majority of politicians are non-logical, because they tend to believe what they say (especially if they repeat it enough times). "Often the person who would persuade others begins by persuading himself; and even if he is moved in the beginning by thoughts of personal advantage, he comes eventually to believe that his real interest is the welfare of others" (Pareto, 1916b:114). Somewhat sarcastically, Pareto observed, "to be moved with compassion for the poor and destitute in the midst of luxuries agreeably stimulates the senses. . . . It is sweet to enjoy one's wealth and to discuss equality . . . to play with words and future promises" (1901:68).

All this comes very close to saying "The end justifies the means." Cartoonist Bill Watterson (*Calvin and Hobbes*) expressed it this way:

> *Calvin*: I don't believe in ethics anymore. As far as I'm concerned, the ends justify the means. Get what you can while the getting's good—that's what I say! Might makes right! (Pounding his fist) The winners write the history books! It's a dog-eat-dog world, so I'll do whatever I have to, and let others argue about whether it's right or not.
>
> (Hobbes pushes Calvin into the mud.)
>
> *Calvin*: Hey-y! Why'd you do that?!?
>
> *Hobbes*: You were in my way. Now you're not. The ends justify the means.
>
> *Calvin*: I didn't mean for *everyone*, you dolt! Just *me!*
>
> *Hobbes*: Ah-h . . .

In the course of human history the residues never change, because they are the motives or bases for all human action. What changes are the derivations, which are complete and complex enough to include the various ideologies that appear throughout this volume. Later we will see how Pareto's ideas relate to those of other theorists of his day. For now, Pareto's views on political cynicism and hypocrisy lead us to his treatment of ruling elites.

The Circulation of Elites   Those who run for office never say "Vote for me because I want power, I want to run things." If they revealed their true motivations, what would happen? Pareto argued that if "the new elite were clearly and simply to proclaim its intentions which are to supplant the old elite; no one would come to its assistance, it would be defeated before having fought a battle" (1906:92). So, utilizing whatever derivations they can devise, an elite and a would-be elite struggle for political power.

According to Pareto, "society is always governed by a small number of men, by an *elite*, even when it seems to have a completely democratic organization" (1906:312). Not only was democracy inconceivable to Pareto, so was mass revolution; "almost all revolutions have been the work, not of the common people, but of the aristocracy" (1906:92). However, sometimes the poorer classes "derive some advantage, as a by-product, from the struggle between the *elites*" (1906:301).

Pareto suggested that elites may use cunning or force to achieve their aims, but that a new elite ordinarily takes control by the use of force. Then, as the new elite's authority is legitimated or legalized, they are followed by perpetuators or administrators, "shrewd but cowardly individuals who are easily overthrown by violence, whether from abroad or from within." These administrators are "timid but often honest souls who believe in the efficacy of the law against force of arms. They are constantly declining in vigor, and are busy digging their own graves" (Pareto, 1916b:342, 384). Despite a loss of vigor, however, administrators are not necessarily less violent; often "the weak are precisely those who are also violent" (Pareto, 1901:71).

These mechanisms result in the circulation of elites, as "lions" are followed by "foxes"—that is, as leadership by force is followed by leadership by cunning. Note that "circulation" does not imply historical change or progress, but simply going around and around.

Why do elites continue to circulate? The weakening of those in power is not so much a result of their becoming fat, lazy, and unconcerned as it is a result of their inherent conservatism. Their support for or conservation of a system that is becoming increasingly anachronistic leaves them open to overthrow by a forceful new elite with a (supposedly) new idea.

Most of the time the lions and foxes simply take turns feeding on the sheep, the masses. As Pareto put it, "The world has always belonged to the strong. . . . Men only respect those who make themselves respected. Whoever becomes a lamb will find a wolf to eat them" (Bucolo, 1980:125). If the masses do threaten to cause trouble for the elite in power, Machiavelli had said, they will be either cajoled or exterminated (Machiavelli, 1532). Pareto's version was that the masses would be absorbed or eliminated, either bought off or wiped out.

The more humanitarian approach—absorbing the agitators—can be illustrated by the experience of José Gonzalez (pseudonym) of Colombia, South America. As an undergraduate, Gonzalez was a committed Marxist who continually organized students for study groups and protests against the Colombian government and its links with the United States. After being jailed several times, Gonzalez was finally called into the office of the Colombian President. Aware of the extermination of rebel leaders in the Colombian mountains, Gonzalez was convinced that he was to face the same fate. Instead he was asked, "How would you like to go to the United States for graduate study?" Recovering from his surprise, he indicated that he would think about it and would decide before graduation.

According to Gonzalez, the hope of his government was that study in the United States would retool his ideology—that he would return to Colombia a confirmed capitalist. At graduation, he accepted the proposal, and was sent to Brattleboro, Vermont, to the Peace Corps volunteers' preparation center for his prestudy "briefing." (The choice of location may have been less than optimal for José's ideological conversion, since many Peace Corps volunteers at that time were joining up precisely because they were disenchanted with U.S. society.)

Gonzalez decided to study social psychology at the University of North Carolina, hoping that this course of study would leave his ideology intact. He later returned to Colombia to teach and continue his radical organizing. Whether in José's case the government subsequently turned from attempted absorption to elimination—the more violent means of dealing with troublemakers—is unknown.

In summary, Pareto's theory of political elites was that elites use derivations to seek and hold power, circulate, and try to keep the masses under control by absorption or elimination.

Methods   Pareto's writings stressed measurement, or operationalization, and the scientific method. Though he used such methods infrequently in his own writings, it is clear that he favored careful statistical analysis in the study of economics, and sought to make sociology and economics resemble as closely as possible the natural sciences.

Near the end of his life, he wrote, "I determined to begin my *Treatise*, the sole purpose of which . . . is to seek experimental reality, by the application to the social sciences of the methods which have proved themselves in physics, in chemistry, in astronomy, in biology, and in other such sciences" (quoted in Coser, 1977:387).

Nature of Society, Humans, and Change

Pareto's *ideology* changed gradually during his life. He began as a cautious liberal. Wanting to believe in progress, Pareto wrote in 1892:

> For their ideas to be victorious, the Liberals must always abstain from the
> chicanery and tricks of petty politicians, who will always win that sort of
> game. They must hold fast to a doctrine which is organic, sincere, right and

honest, paving a way where they cannot be followed by those who have acquired their power by lies and deceit. (Bucolo, 1980:60)

Note that "sincere, right and honest" is hardly consistent with the political cynicism discussed earlier.

By 1900 Pareto's disillusionment with liberalism had begun, and he compared socialism favorably with liberalism in Europe: "The Socialists . . . in the fight for freedom . . . take the place vacated by the Liberals . . . . the Socialists, more or less alone, resist the oppression of governments and fight against militarism" (Bucolo, 1980:117). Gradually his position altered from the liberal notion of making the world a better place to an apparent belief that nothing could be done to change the world. According to Bucolo, however, Pareto continually made the distinction "between men as they are and as some would like them to be." He "never excluded the possibility that foresight and wisdom of the few could become that of the many" (Bucolo, 1980:146). Despite this qualification, it is clear that during the final 25 years of his life, Pareto became increasingly conservative—though he would call himself a nonideological realist—about society and power.

Over time, then, Pareto became increasingly cynical about *human nature*. He did not say that humans are evil, but rather that in seeking power they camouflage their motives to make them seem higher (more altruistic) than they really are. While one commentator concluded that Pareto despised humanity. Bucolo disagreed: Pareto had "never despised humanity as such, then or before. He had despised petty politicians: those who, while claiming to act rationally had done no more than obey their instincts" (Bucolo, 1980:145).

Pareto did not see society as good or evil, but as a mixture of primarily self-seeking characters. He denied that more education would result in fewer criminals, and he saw no solution for society's problems and inadequacies.

Some affirm that alcoholism is the cause of all evil. Others think it is immoral literature. Still others—the majority—blame the unequal distribution of wealth. They inflict any absurdity on us in order to avoid admitting that in the human species, as in all living species, individuals are not born alike; they have different characters, and that certain individuals are fitted for the environment in which they live, whilst others are not. (Bucolo, 1980:161)

Thus, he believed that some people are better adapted than others to the social world in which they are born and raised. Later theorists of culture echoed this point, arguing that those who, because of their hereditary makeup, are maladjusted in one society might have been fitted for or normal in another.

Pareto saw history and change as resulting from the combination of unchanging residues and the circulation of elites. Change occurs only in the derivations, or justifications (including ideologies), that individuals give for their behavior. Early in his life, Pareto had attempted to work for justice and a better world, but gradually he gave up the notion of change in favor of what Bucolo called an eternal history. Does this make him an ideological *status quo conservative*? Sidney Hook's answer was that although Pareto was probably not a fascist in Mussolini's terms, he was definitely a conservative. Hook based this conclusion on one sentence from Pareto: "The centuries roll by, human nature remains the same" (Hook, in Pareto, 1916a:748). Pareto would doubtless argue that the combination of cynicism, hypocrisy, and non-change made him not a conservative, but a realist.

Class, Gender, and Race

Pareto's comments on *class* are found in his discussion of the circulation of elites. As for *gender,* Pareto believed that patriarchy was the natural and universal social form among civilized peoples. The patriarchal family was the "only one concretely existing, and . . . deviations from it, which had been noted even in ancient times, were of little or no account" (1916a, 2:613). Pareto observed that Engels's reconstruction of the evolution of the family, starting with "sex promiscuity or community in women," testified to his "mental ingenuity and lively imagination," but was "scientifically erroneous." Engels's theory was useful, however, in illustrating "the immense amount of fatuity, stupidity, and hypocrisy that lurked in certain forms of bourgeois idealism" (Pareto, 1916a, 2:613, 614).

Pareto had little time for the equality claims of feminists. Like some present-day commentators, Pareto believed that feminists were hysterical women "in want of a mate" who persecuted "women who have lovers simply because they have been unable to find men of their own" (1916a, 2:696). He also contended that feminism could only arise when a society was wealthy. Linking feminism to wealth, Pareto noted the "licentiousness of certain emancipated women in the United States" and the "hypocrisies of German sex-reformers," such as Marianne Weber (1916a, 1:39, 75).

Although Pareto did not endorse feminism or women's right to vote, he did point out that women's demands for equality revealed the hypocrisy of many so-called democracies:

> Both European and American democracies profess to be founded on principles of thorough-going equality between human beings. . . . But that fine principle is forgotten when it is a question of women. By a neat trick of sleight-of-hand, equality of human beings becomes equality of males, nay of certain males. (1916a, 2:735)

Pareto viewed women as naturally fickle and promiscuous. He was scathing about the reformist assumption that capitalism was the primary cause of prostitution. Whatever the economic context, Pareto insisted that there would be women willing to sell themselves: "The woman of the petty bourgeoisie sells herself to get a stylish hat, the society woman sells herself to get a string of pearls—but they both sell themselves" (1916a, 3:1318).

For most women, Pareto claimed, prostitution is "a case of vanity and love of extravagance" or a case of "indolence," for there are those "those in higher social circles . . . who like this profession the way a hunter likes hunting and the fisherman fishing." Consequently, those reformers who "organize leagues against obscenity and the 'white-slave trade'" are misguided. Pareto believed it foolish to "worry so much about the seduction of women and so little about the seduction of men" (1916a, 3:1319). In fact, it is usually the woman who leads the man astray. In the case of "the unfaithful clerk, the dishonest cashier, the absconding banker, the army officer turned spy," Pareto advised, look for the woman behind it. Finally, "from the experimental standpoint," Pareto believed it was an open question "whether prostitution may or may not be the occupation best suited to the temperaments of certain women, . . . and whether prostitution is, or is not, within certain limits beneficial to society as a whole" (1916a, 2:862–863).

Pareto used many references to historical and mythological women in his works. His ideal woman was Fortunata, depicted in Petronius's *Satyricon*. Fortunata devoted herself to "domestic economy, and once when her husband had been ruined she gave him her jewels—in that too differing . . . from many women in our plutocracy who make haste to divorce men who cease to be able to keep them in luxury" (1916a, 4:1894).

Pareto's misogynist views very likely had some basis in his personal experience. As noted in the introduction, when Pareto was 41, he married a younger woman who, shortly after the marriage, absconded with the cook and some of Pareto's possessions. Pareto was understandably bitter about this event, and it probably reinforced his view that women were untrustworthy whores at heart. Certainly women, along with less well-educated men were, in his view, incapable of scientific thinking. Women exhibited the "sentiments of inferiors"—that is, the sentiments of "subordination, affection, reverence, fear,— which was appropriate because beneficial to the maintenance of order in society" (1916a, 2:687).

Pareto's views on *race* appear to have been more liberal. He observed that in the United States there were hotels where "a person cannot have his boots polished because it an offence against Holy Equality for one person to polish another's boots." But these same people would not "allow a Negro to be accommodated at a hotel that they frequent, or ride in a railway coach which has the honor of transporting them" (1916a, 2:734). Thus, it is not only the status of women that exposes the practical hypocrisies of capitalist democracies.

Other Theories and Theorists

Pareto's Economic Theories   Though Pareto's views of society and elites were his primary focus, he also sought to understand economics. Although other economists have not adopted it, Pareto used the term **ophelimity** to mean the pleasure that a certain quantity of a thing affords the individual (1906:112). According to Pareto, differences in ophelimity are due to differences in taste, coupled with the obstacles encountered in gratifying one's tastes. Markets and prices do not by themselves determine economic behavior, but depend on "the opposition of tastes and obstacles" (1906:152). The more intense and widespread the taste for an item, and the more obstacles there are to obtaining it, the higher its value and its price.

Another important part of Pareto's economic theory is capital, of which he listed three kinds: (1) Land capital is immovable property that can be mined or developed. (2) Mobile capital includes machines, transport means, household goods, and money. (3) Human capital is "the cost of production of a human being . . . what is strictly necessary to keep him alive and train him" (Pareto, 1906:300). The concept of human capital has been expanded recently in economics, but Pareto was one of the earliest writers to recognize its importance. These three forms of capital are used in the "free market" system to increase one's bargaining position relative to others.

Although individual economic behavior was of some interest to Pareto, he was much more concerned with economic systems, their upswings and downswings (Pareto, 1906:383). According to his analysis, upswings result when entrepreneurs expand production by transforming savings into development, often using credit. Investors likewise extend themselves to have a part in a productive boom. Downswings occur when markets become glutted and/or stagnate (because tastes are satisfied with few obstacles for the individual), and the producers and investors reduce and retrench (1906:321–380). Schumpeter, whose theories are discussed in Chapter 10, had similar views.

One further issue in economics raised by Pareto was the dichotomy between altruism and egotism. Some social theories are based on altruism (recall Durkheim's altruistic suicide), but most theories of human behavior assume the primacy of egotism. According to Pareto, "it is customary to assume that man will be guided in his choice exclusively by consideration of his own advantage, of his self-interest" (1906:105). This premise for human behavior was later expanded into exchange theories, which argue that humans seek the most profit or benefit at the least cost. We will return to exchange theories in Chapter 21.

Pareto felt very strongly that the ruling class, especially in Italy, did not understand the laws of economics. In his *Lettres d'Italie* he wrote: "Unwilling to take the trouble to study political economy—as they believe they will find it condemns their actions—the governing class deny that the natural laws of production and the distribution of wealth exist" (quoted in de Rosa, 1962:31).

Pareto in the Community of Scholars   The relation of Pareto to other theorists begins with Gaetano Mosca, who published *The Ruling Class* (1884) twenty years before Pareto's *Manual of Political Economy* appeared. When Pareto's book was published, it was apparent to many, but especially to Mosca, that Pareto's discussion of elites paralleled Mosca's. In fact, Mosca accused Pareto of having "copied shamelessly," to which Pareto responded by eliminating the few references to Mosca in a subsequent printing of his book (Mongardini, in Albertoni, 1982:80). Later, Pareto claimed that it was after his publication of *I Sistemi Socialisti* in 1902 that he began to see Mosca's writings quoted (Jensen, in Albertoni, 1982:134). In any case, the relation of the two scholars was anything but friendly. As one observer put it, "Pareto himself made a major effort to persuade his readers that he was the intellectual fountainhead and Mosca simply a parroter of commonplace ideas" (LaPalombara, in Albertoni, 1982:137).[1]

---

[1]Although some of Pareto's ideas, especially on political power, may have originated with Mosca, Pareto's general theory goes beyond Mosca's political theories. For those wanting to know more about Mosca, we suggest his major book, *Elementi di Scienza Politica*, translated under the title *The Ruling Class* (Mosca, 1884). An outstanding treatment of Mosca's influence outside Italy is *Studies on the Political Thought of Gaetano Mosca*, edited by Ettore Albertoni (1982).

Pareto was also dismissive of Rousseau's image of the ideal "native" or "savage" as a baseline for judging what society's rules have done to human nature (see Chapter 1). Rousseau was not describing a "primitive" human who actually existed, but Pareto nonetheless took exception to his description of the so-called happy savage. "Facts show that nothing is more wretched than the life of a savage, that the average life span is very brief and that they are subject to every type of illness" (quoted in Bucolo, 1980:158).

Pareto's criticism of Marx began, as did that of most non-Marxists, with a rejection of the inevitable final revolution. Whereas Marx had seen the "history of all hitherto existing societies" as class conflict, Pareto wrote that "the history of man is the history of the continuous replacement of certain elites: as one ascends, another declines" (1901:36). Nevertheless, Pareto's definition of **socialism**, which included communism, was very close to Marx's: "schools or sects which have a common quality: that of wanting a total renovation of society: changing, especially, the basis of property and also that of the family; increasing the power of the state and diminishing the freedom of the individual, with the aim of favoring the less well-off" (quoted in Bucolo, 1980:44).

In one of Pareto's major passages on Marx, he seemed to agree with the view, espoused by Marx and Sumner, that a great leader is one who sees the direction history is moving and enunciates that position. Pareto also pointed out that society may hold allegiance to a "leader" even after that person's ideas have been proved false.

The Marxian theory of value is not valid; after they had tried out various and subtle interpretations, we now witness some of the most educated Marxists going so far as to say that Marx never intended to set up a theory of value. All this has hurt the socialist faith little or not at all. It was not the book by Marx which has created the socialists; it is the socialists who have made Marx's book famous. (1901:100)

Pareto added that, similarly, Voltaire did not produce skepticism; rather, skepticism made Voltaire's books famous.

Pareto's criticisms often had a sarcastic, cutting edge to them. He was critical of those like Durkheim who thought a new morality could be built on scientific principles and understanding. People do not and never will operate on such principles, Pareto wrote, but will excuse and rationalize their behaviors. He criticized not just the revolutionaries or radicals, such as Marxists, but later in life he also criticized liberal humanitarians who thought society could be made better (or good) by tinkering with it, by bringing in new derivations. Pareto was critical of evolutionary thinking that assumed progress and betterment. Society, he said, never changes much, and when it does make progress, as toward freedom, it is as an indirect result of elites' striving for other, more personal goals. Functionalism's notion of society as integrated or interdependent made sense to him, but not predicated on the parts' working together for the good of the whole. Perception of that sort of integration is based on illogic and hidden sentiments or residues.

Pareto was not always critical. For example, he echoed, at about the same time (1900), Herbert Spencer's idea that industrialization will result in a less violent or warlike form of evolution. Though World War I changed such ideal-ized and progressive perceptions, Pareto wrote in 1901 that our "societies are certainly much more industrialized and less warlike than the societies of the past century" (1901:74). Again, sounding very much like Max Weber, Pareto wrote that scientific objectivity may be desirable, but it is impossible.

All in all, Pareto appeared to gain satisfaction from criticizing the work of his colleagues as based upon their derivations. He wrote to his friend Pantaleoni: "Not because of any merit of my own, but because of the circumstances in which I found myself, I have no prejudices of any kind . . . which hinder others to do scholarly work in this field. I am not tied to any party, any religion, or any sect; therefore, I entertain no preconceived ideas about phenomena" (Pareto, in de Rosa, 1962). He was understandably unpopular among those committed to an ideology, and among scholars in general.

Critique and Conclusions

Those who believe that human nature is good and society bad find Pareto dis-turbing. Pareto was a "debunker." One commentator stated:

> He was utterly unable to tolerate sham, deception, and corruption. This intolerance manifested itself in various ways, including a debunking attitude that has irritated many a believer in one political doctrine or another. Democracy, which Pareto usually put in quotation marks, was one of his favorite targets. (Farina, in Pareto, 1916b:xvi)

Both Marxists and defenders of capitalist democracy labeled Pareto a fascist. Mussolini's offer in 1922 of an appointment to the Italian Senate helped to con-firm that label. Pareto turned down the position at first, later accepted it, but never filled it because of ill health.

The issue of fascism deserves further mention. His support for Mussolini's re-gime was based on its early emphasis on law and order, which was what Pareto believed postwar Europe needed more than anything else. J. J. Schumpeter, the economic sociologist whose work is introduced in Chapter 10, had this to say about Pareto:

> Mussolini honored himself by conferring senatorial rank on the man who kept preaching moderation and who stood throughout for the freedom of the press and academic teaching. . . . To his last day Pareto refused to embrace this *ism* as he had refused to embrace any other. (quoted in Meisel, 1965:35)

In a few years Pareto might no longer have supported the totalitarian govern-ment that Mussolini's had become—though this, of course, is speculation.

In summary, then, Pareto's insights included, first, his "contribution" to the fascist concept of order and control. Following Machiavelli, he argued that power is inevitable, is its own justification, is based on the best use of deriva-tions, and is usually cynical when employed correctly and successfully. Second, though we have dealt with it only briefly, Pareto stressed measurement, or operationalization, and the scientific method. Third, he pointed out the illogic in human behavior, distinguishing motives, or residues, from the reasons that people give and often believe. The central issue raised by Pareto's theory is whether or not society is primarily the result of an ideological overlay of rationalizations. Finally, Pareto argued that elites merely circulate between lions and foxes, while feeding on the sheep, or the masses.

Robert Michels (1876–1936)

Robert Michels made all of Europe his home. He was a man of Western culture, having a French mother, a German father, and an Italian ancestry. He studied in various countries, but his early radicalism kept him from an academic appointment in Germany. He was connected with the German socialists, whom Luxemburg later criticized for their conservatism and nationalism, during World War I. In fact, it was the abrupt about-face of the German socialists that led to Michels's pessimistic and critical work, in which he denied that genuine democracy, socialist or otherwise, is possible (see Lipset, 1968). Michels argued, however, that although democracy is impossible, it is the goal to strive for.

Michels argued that only a charismatic leader, of the type Weber described, could neutralize, or even retard, tendencies toward **oligarchy**, or rule by a few. In the 1910s and 1920s, Michels's example of charisma was Mussolini in Italy. In 1928, he left his position at the University of Basle to accept a chair at the University of Perugia offered to him personally by Mussolini, and he subsequently became a naturalized Italian citizen.

Despite his tenuous relation with the German academic scene, his affection for German culture never ceased, and in 1910, along with Max Weber, he helped organize the German Sociological Society. Theorists such as Weber and Joseph Schumpeter were strongly influenced by Michels's ideas.

His book *Political Parties*—in which he enunciated the "iron law of oligarchy"—first gave the English-speaking world access to Michels, but in 1927 he gave an important set of lectures, subsequently printed, on political sociology. His *First Lectures*, published in 1949, included portions of these 1927 lectures plus other previously published papers. These two volumes make clear both his debt to, and his criticisms of, Karl Marx, as well as his relation to numerous other theorists.

Michels's Central Theory and Methods

Michels was a theorist of political sociology. As such, he did not deal with several of the topics that concern us in this volume. Unlike Pareto, he did not present a complete theory of society or human nature; nor did he focus at length on economics. We begin with his theory of oligarchy.

Political Organization and Oligarchy   Sociology does not have many laws, or principles that always hold true. Michels argued in support of one: the **iron law of oligarchy**, or rule by a few. He pointed to "the existence of immanent oligarchic tendencies in every kind of human organization." He argued that "oligarchy is, as it were, a preordained form of the common life of great social aggregates," and summarized, "Who says organization, says oligarchy" (1911: 290, 401).

For Michels, the iron law of oligarchy essentially meant that democracy, mass movements, and organization of the masses for revolution are impossible. "History seems to teach us that no popular movement, however energetic and vigorous, is capable of producing profound and permanent changes in the social organism of the civilized world" (1911:392).

Michels refined Pareto's idea of the alternation between lions and foxes and the circulation of elites. The nobility, he pointed out, were often reduced to selling their residence or goods in order to assure financial survival. In fact, he noted, many modern cities developed when the old nobility gave up "the occupancy of its palaces which were located mostly in the center of the city" (1927:73). Nor did the ruling class simply degenerate; they were "rejuvenated by the entry of heterogeneous elements of the middle class." In Germany "we have witnessed the process of absorption of the young industrial middle class by the old hereditary aristocracy" (1927:78). Likewise, many "families of the old aristocracy disappear into the masses," rather than becoming extinct (1927:104). Thus, Pareto's "circulation" was not simply a process of rises and falls, but involved absorption and decline of units as well.

Marx and the Revolution   Michels, like Pareto, saw great merit in Marx's views on economics and inequality. However, Michels went further than most in spelling out the problems with Marx's political views. Michels did not believe the proletariat would abolish the state. Instead, the aim of opposition leaders is to permeate the state, to compete for positions within it, and eventually to control it. Referring to Mosca's work, Michels argued that so-called "class struggles consist merely of struggles between successively dominant minorities" (1911:377). Marx, and especially Lenin, had noted that the immediate consequence of the proletarian revolution would be a dictatorship of the proletariat, followed by a gradual evolution to communism. Michels, however, noted that administration of social wealth always requires an extensive bureaucratic hierarchy, which leads "by an inevitable logic to the flat denial of the possibility of a state without classes," or of a classless, stateless society (1911: 383). Thus, oligarchic tendencies in all organizations preclude a final revolution leading eventually to communism.

According to Michels, there were three further reasons against a final revolution. First, leadership in any sphere is not only oligarchic but inherently conservative. Though revolutionary sentiments might help union leaders gain their positions, the notion of revolution gives way to "the hope that there shall long continue to exist a proletariat to choose them as its delegates and to provide them with a livelihood." Identifying with the system that spawned them, "the officials of the trade unions, wearing evening dress, meet the employers in sumptuous banquets" (1911:305, 311). In other words, they identify upwards with capitalist society instead of with the working classes, much less with any sort of radical ideology.

Second, the revolutionary bonding of the masses is negated by the general increase in wealth in capitalist societies, resulting in several strata of workers

(1911:295). The workers are no longer—if they ever were—simply "the poor." They include the well-off, the less well-off, and the poor, and their "common interest" in revolution is hardly clear. When wealth disparity is coupled with Durkheim's division of labor into institutional spheres, working-class patterns come to resemble a checkerboard. Such differentiation made the revolutionary unification of the proletariat impossible for Michels to imagine.

Third, the possibility (or at least ideology) of social mobility, for oneself or one's children, causes the "system" to be seen not as oppressive, but as a source of opportunity (1911:305). Michels observed that "wherever there remains in the workers any hope whatever, founded or unfounded, of approaching emancipation or elevation to the dignity of proprietors, anti-capitalistic movements do not take root or at least do not thrive" (1927:82). In other words, as long as I see it possible to make the system "work for me" or for my children, I have no desire to overthrow it. Even when it is obvious that my racial or ethnic group has been discriminated against, belief in a bourgeois education as the door to success will reduce my revolutionary fervor. Regarding mobility, Pareto had pointed out, "the governing class is required to absorb only a small number of new individuals in order to keep the subject class deprived of leadership" (1916a:311).

Thus, the oligarchic and conservative tendencies of the labor leaders, the differentiation of the workers both horizontally and vertically, and the ideology of mobility all obscure the likelihood of mass revolution.

Nature of Humans, Society, and Change

Did Michels's view of the factors that curb mass revolution make him a pessimist about humans and change? Though he nowhere indicated a preference for revolution, he did express his views on the socialist/communist thinkers. Their great error, he wrote,

> an error committed in consequence of their lack of adequate psychological knowledge, is to be found in their combination of pessimism regarding the present, with rosy optimism and immeasurable confidence regarding the future. . . . Within the limits of time for which human provision is possible, optimism will remain the exclusive privilege of utopian thinkers. (Michels, 1927:403)

Perhaps the most insightful treatment of Michels's outlook is found in de Grazia's introduction to his *First Lectures*:

> If one searched his life and writings for his hierarchy of values, I believe one would have to place . . . individualism, even anarchy, first and derive from that his succeeding values. . . . One finds in his later writings pensive, regretful references to the unattainable ideal of the Jeffersonian . . . democrat. Alongside this value . . . one would place his romanticism, born of his cosmopolitan family background, the wonderful milieu of prewar intellectualism in Europe, and his education, which was steeped in tradition and history. (de Grazia, 1927:7)

This assessment seems quite accurate, except perhaps the notion that Michels had anarchic tendencies. Michels did see the individual as social actor, and believed that democracy was desirable, if unattainable. His main theoretical contributions concerned oligarchy and the Marxist revolution.

Class, Gender, and Race

Michels's views on classes and social mobility are related to those of Marx. Michels stated that machine work deserved the criticism of Marx, de Tocqueville, and others. The irresponsibility and unintelligibility of such work constitute "a fearful incubus for the worker, rendering him liable to apathy and indifference, or to rebellion" (1927:13). Other scholars, such as Veblen, agreed with Michels that apathy was in fact more likely than either rebellion or revolution.

Another important point that Michels raised about class concerned the way in which members of a given class may identify either up or down. He noted that owners of great estates in Russia, Italy, and France had renounced their wealth, lived a modest life, and given themselves to the betterment of those less well off. Likewise, peasants and the very poor, "because of inherent conservatism or because of intense gratitude and faithful devotion to their master, would consider an injustice every law, even if enacted for their welfare, that would obstruct the full freedom of private property" (1927:26). Later Marxist writers would interpret this as "false consciousness," a result of the ruling class's control over the means of propaganda and hence over people's thinking.

Finally, Michels added to Marx's discussion of the petit bourgeoisie. Marx had defined them as owner-workers—those who owned and worked their own means of production. Though he did not use the term "petit bourgeoisie," Michels added the following description:

> How many workers are there who live not only by the earnings of their own labor, but enjoy also a small revenue, obtained by them from a small rural property or joint-property, or from small savings invested in a savings bank. . . . In such a case they are both the "exploited," inasmuch as the system subtracts day by day a part of the work done by them, the so-called plus-value . . . and the "exploiters," inasmuch as they themselves also live by the fruit of somebody else's labor. (1927:32)

To Michels, then, the petit bourgeoisie included not only owner-workers, but also laborer-investors.

Michels made no reference to race and very little to gender. He wrote in passing of the coquette who flirts but resists, eventually causing a man "to give her the greatest satisfaction that man can give to woman, that of marrying her" (1927:127), using this example as an analogy for the party leader who keeps his constituents at a distance so that their desire for his leadership becomes greater. He also described the wealthy married man whose love affair with money is such as to drive his wife into the arms of another man, seeking the attention that is unavailable from her wealth-seeking husband (1927:28).

Michels's third comment on gender is one that Charlotte Gilman was to make much of (see Chapter 11). According to Michels, the woman, in "her mania for luxury," serves "as a powerful stimulus for the creation . . . of the means of satisfying her longings" (1927:54). Female consumption, that is, increases the competitiveness and striving for things characteristic of *modern industrial society.*

From these small allusions to women it is apparent that Michels did not treat gender as a separate issue, but referred to women only in relation to men—not unusual for that time. By the same token, he did not provide enough information on which to construct his overall view of gender.

Other Theories and Theorists

You have already seen Michels's intellectual relation to Marx's theories and to Pareto's circulation of elites. His connection with Max Weber, whom he knew, also deserves mention. As noted in Chapter 7, Weber saw the social world as too complex to ever be completely understood. Michels, in turn, sounded quite Weberian on the subject of disentangling the determining causes of historical events. One must, he suggested,

> establish their multiple character and the relations existing among them; he must define, limit, and verify the different measures of participation by certain qualitative elements known *a priori*, such as the economic factor, race, tradition, and others. Put another way, he must eviscerate the problem with the object of tracing, with care and precision, the quantitative proportions of qualitatively pre-established co-efficients. (1927:59)

Michels supplemented Weber's treatment of religion, pointing to the differences between Protestant, especially Puritan, Christianity and Catholicism. Protestant virtue consists of the accomplishment of one's duties, he observed, whereas Catholicism creates a more carefree and artistic temperament. Protestantism, Michels suggested, gives an impetus to individual initiative because the individual is directly responsible to God, without any intercession by priests, saints, or altruistic prayers (1927:34).

Michels also expanded on Weber's view of charisma. Charismatic leadership, observed Michels, tends to be noneconomic in character. The leader is often seen as having a transcendental mission and is given charity, rather than a salary, by his or her followers. Later Michels added that the fascist leader, such as Mussolini, is able to establish control precisely because of charismatic qualities (1927:111, 113, 131).

Finally, Michels expanded on Weber's view of parties. Weber had described the party as an organization that directly seeks power in society. Michels agreed, but distinguished the following types of parties: (1) The charismatic party is based on emotion and enthusiasm. (2) The economic or class-based party is often found among the working class. (3) A political party might be based on the moral ideas of a particular culture, such as "family values," defined in a very specific way. (4) The confessional party is based on religion, seeking to establish some sort of heavenly kingdom on earth, or seeking to prepare its members for a better life afterward. (5) The nationalist party is based on patriotism and is usually grounded in allegiance to a "fatherland" (1927:138–139, 156–157).

Thus, just as he did for Marx's and Pareto's theories, Michels added to the complexities introduced by Weber, showing that the world of political life and history is indeed multifaceted.

Critique and Conclusions

A central contribution of Michels, as well as Pareto and Mosca, was the concept of elites and oligarchy. The proletarian revolution, they each believed, is untenable—though certain elites might pretend to "speak in the name of the proletariat." Society is always run by a small party or small number of individuals, and this will never change. Michels explained the complexity of the world of elites and power in a readable manner.

Final Thoughts

When we introduced Pareto at the beginning of the chapter, we indicated that there have been strong differences of opinion about him and his work. In fact, it is extremely difficult for scholars (and for us) to be neutral about Pareto. To agree with his assessment of human behavior and society, one must give up optimistic liberal or radical thinking, a rational functionally integrated view of society, and the notion of evolutionary progress. If we reject his ideas because of our political or religious beliefs and ideologies, he laughs at our illogic, about how we have been "hoodwinked" by our own derivations.

Pareto saw himself as the only real social theorist—the rest of us are ideologues. His critics would say he was not really a theorist at all, because he explained nothing regarding the course of human history. Given that the residues never change, he was dealing with constants, with only the superficial derivations undergoing change as people think up new ones.

References

Albertoni, Ettore A. (Ed.). 1982. *Studies on the Political Thought of Gaetano Mosca*. Milano/Montreal: Comitato Internazionale Gaetano Mosca per lo Studio della Classe Politica. (papers by Jensen, LaPalombara, Mongardini)

Bucolo, Placido. 1980. *The Other Pareto*. New York: St. Martin's Press.

Coser, Lewis A. 1977. *Masters of Sociological Thought*. New York: Harcourt Brace Jovanovich.

de Grazia, Alfred. 1927/1949. "Introduction." In Roberto Michels, *First Lectures in Political Sociology*. Minneapolis: University of Minnesota Press.

de Rosa, Gabriele. 1962. *Carteggi Paretiani, 1892–1923*. Rome: Roma Publishing.

Lipset, Seymour Martin. 1968. "Introduction." In Robert Michels, *Political Parties*. New York: Free Press.

Machiavelli, Niccolo. 1532/1979. *The Prince*. Middlesex, England: Penguin.

Meisel, James H. 1965. *Pareto and Mosca*. Englewood Cliffs, NJ: Prentice-Hall.

Michels, Robert. 1911/1959/1968. *Political Parties*. New York: Dover.

———. 1927/1949. *First Lectures in Political Sociology*. Minneapolis: University of Minnesota Press.

Mosca, Gaetano. 1884/1939. *The Ruling Class*. New York: McGraw-Hill.

Pareto, Vilfredo. 1901/1968. *The Rise and Fall of the Elites*. Totowa, NJ: Bedminster Press.

———. 1902/1951. *I Sistemi Socialisti* (Celertino Arena, Ed.). Turin, Italy: C. Arena.

———. 1906/1971. *Manual of Political Economy*. New York: Augustus Kelley.

———. 1916a/1935. *The Mind and Society* (Arthur Livingstone, Ed.) (4 vols.). London: Jonathan Cape.

———. 1916b/1980. *Trattato di Sociologia Generale* (*The Mind and Society*, edited and abridged by Giulio Farina). Minneapolis: University of Minnesota Press.

Zeitlin, Irving M. 1994. *Ideology and the Development of Sociological Theory* (5th ed.). Englewood Cliffs, NJ: Prentice-Hall.

Chapter 10

Economic Sociological Theories
Veblen and Schumpeter

If I were a rich man. . . .
I'd build a big tall house with rooms by the dozen. . . .
There could be one long staircase just going up
and one even longer coming down;
And one more leading nowhere *just for show.* . . .
The most important men in town will come to fawn on me;
They will ask me to advise them. . . .
And it won't make one bit of difference
If I answer right or wrong.
When you're rich they think you really know.
If I were rich, I'd have the time that I lack
To sit in the synagogue and pray, . . .
And I'd *discuss the holy books with the learned men
seven hours every day;*
This would be the sweetest thing of all. . . .
    (Harnick/Bock, 1964; emphasis added)

Tevye's song from *Fiddler on the Roof* introduces us to two social scientists who approach theory primarily from an economic perspective. They are Thorstein Veblen and Joseph Schumpeter, each of whom was primarily an economist and secondarily a sociologist. In addition, each constructed a theory of classes, as well as writing about economic development and change.

In an essay on Vilfredo Pareto, Schumpeter (1949:147) wrote:

Could we confine ourselves to Pareto's contributions to pure theory, there would be little need for glancing at the man and his social background and location. But into everything that was not a theorem in the pure logic of economics the whole man and all the forces that conditioned him entered so unmistakably that it is more necessary than it usually is in an appraisal of scientific performance to convey an idea of that man and of those forces.

245

One commentator has noted that this is every bit as true of Schumpeter as it is of Pareto (Smithies, in Harris, 1951:15). For that matter, it is true of most of the thinkers you meet in this volume, but especially so of these two economic sociologists.

Thorstein Veblen, 1857–1929

Thorstein Veblen was an American thinker and academic who was foremost a critic, then a theorist, and to some extent a reformer. He would like to have been a radical, but believed little could be done to change the course of capitalist history.

Veblen was a Norwegian-American farm boy who grew up in the Midwestern United States. He was born in Wisconsin, but the family was driven off their first farm and migrated to Minnesota. There the family became relatively successful at farming through hard work and frugality, although a portion of their second farm had to be sold to pay interest and taxes. Such experiences resulted in his family's hatred of "tricksters, speculators, and shyster lawyers" (Coser, 1977:276).

Thorstein was personally out of step with the political and Lutheran religious orthodoxy around him, and his keen mind handled this maladjustment through wit, sarcasm, and criticism. He was described, in the introduction to the 1957 edition of *The Higher Learning in America*, as an unhappy man. "When he received his Ph.D. from Yale in 1884 there was no academic position available, and the next seven years . . . he lived on his family's farm, isolated, unhappy, seemingly rejected and as a result rejecting the America of which he was not a part" (Hacker, in Veblen, 1918:ix).

At the age of 34 he began moving from university to university, never staying long or finding security in any one. But despite his academic wanderings and marginality, Veblen, thanks to his writings and intellect, made a reputation for himself as a critical social scientist.

Veblen's Central Theories and Methods

Veblen was, to some extent, an evolutionist in the line of Spencer and Darwin. However, although he believed in technological change and advance, he was critical of capitalism, and he did not believe in human progress, whether through evolution or a Marxist revolution.

Veblen and Marx   Had Veblen been more optimistic about the ability to change society, he might have been a Marxist. But in various writings Veblen raised the same criticisms of Marx as others were making: History is goalless, not goal-oriented; the poor do not become increasingly miserable; and there is not likely to be a growing reserve army of unemployed workers.

In addition, Veblen questioned the whole idea of economic laws, especially those propounded by Marx. Why does a human being have the right to the total value of her or his labor? Although this may seem justifiable, such laws were to

Veblen always apologies for some system of ideas. Furthermore, deprivation, even when it occurs, does not lead to revolution, but to deterioration, subjection, and apathy. Human beings, Veblen observed, simply do not act rationally to increase pleasure (as Rousseau and Marx believed); rather, they act to perpetuate institutions. In other words, people are more comfortable avoiding change.

Marx missed some other important points, according to Veblen. First, Marx saw industrial productivity as closely related to economic crises. Veblen noted that money supply and price-setting complicate this relationship; that is, productivity is but one element in economic life. Today it is argued that business is a bundle of assets more than it is a matter of production. Second, Marx treated production costs as fixed, whereas Veblen saw such costs as decreasing as machines produce ever more efficiently (Veblen, 1904:185, 229).

The small capitalism of Marx's time had evolved into large-scale industry by Veblen's time. Noting this transformation, Veblen viewed enterprises as so far removed from their customers that there is no longer any personal contact that might mitigate the industrial owners' and managers' otherwise ruthless behavior. Those concerned about multinational corporations today make this same point. The use of child labor in Indonesia is acceptable to management and unknown by customers unless some group raises public awareness.

Despite his *criticisms of capitalism*, Veblen did not conclude with Marx that the system was due to be overthrown. Habits and institutions are too tenacious, and big business and industry become ever bigger. The capitalist pricing and commodity system, with its single-minded focus on profit, is at the heart of the society's economic problems. We think we are free under capitalism, observed Veblen, but we are free only to spend, to be consumers, to support capitalism. The notion of capitalism's being overthrown by an exploited and unhappy proletariat simply made no sense to him.

Ownership and Capitalist Waste   Veblen referred to the managers of large-scale enterprises as "captains of industry." They are the new aristocracy, uncontrolled by government but controlling more and more of the world's resources (as Lenin also noted). They speak on all subjects, and people see business wisdom as a sign of general wisdom (as in Tevye's song).

The captains of industry act benevolently, as befits their wealth and position. Businessmen are not primarily humanitarians, though they show constraint and do "good things" from time to time (Veblen, 1904:42). Examples of such deeds include Andrew Carnegie's building libraries, just as computer companies today give hardware to schools, locking them into computer technology. Pareto, likewise, had noted some acts that benefit society while the individual is pursuing personal ends. Marx too had noted that the good capitalist, while doing nice things to keep the "have-nots" quiet, does not allow humanitarian motives to get in the way of profit.

Important to capitalist business enterprise is what Veblen called **sabotage**, or the destruction (waste) of goods and resources. This destruction is both direct, in the case of war, and indirect in the sense of what we now call "built-in obsolescence." War brings prosperity not just because it maximizes productivity, but also because it results in the direct destruction of goods. The "advanced" nations profit considerably from proselytizing or punishing the more "backward," often backing such dealings with force. Writing before World War I, Veblen noted that "when a modern government goes to war for trade purposes, it does so with a view to reestablishing peace on terms more lucrative to its business men" (Veblen, 1904:296).

An example will illustrate Veblen's point. While the Persian Gulf War of 1991 was still in progress, U.S. Secretary of State James Baker announced the setting up of the Middle East Bank for Reconstruction and Development, to help rebuild the region. "The entire region, including Iraq [which the United States was bombing at the time], 'warrants the same spirit of multilateral commitment to reconstruction and development' as the world's developed nations have shown in other areas, including Europe and Latin America, Baker said" ("Middle East Bank for Reconstruction," 1991). Though such destruction/reconstruction is not always so blatantly admitted, it became even more apparent in this instance. A few days after Baker's announcement, the *Baltimore Sun* reported:

> San Francisco–based Bechtel Group Inc. appears to be the biggest winner so far among U.S. companies scrambling for a chunk of the multibillion-dollar reconstruction effort in Kuwait. . . . A bulk liquefied petroleum gas facility that Bechtel constructed . . . from 1960–1962 cost $1 billion, and now is worth $3 billion, said the executive, who asked not to be identified. "For everything they're talking about repairing now, it could cost $20 or $30 billion by the time the project's finished," he said. ("Bechtel Group Gets Big Chunk of Kuwait Reconstruction Bucks," 1991)

So whether it be the enemy (Iraq) or the friend (Kuwait), one form of sabotage is direct destruction and reconstruction in war.

Veblen also saw a portion of resource waste as stemming from **obsolescence**. Were he alive today, he would have understood the "throwaway" society, and the making of goods in such a way as to guarantee their early demise. Newspaper articles—for example, "Self-Destructing Videos" (1989) and "Clothes Grow More Costly, Less Durable" (1989)—often refer to this aspect of consumer society.

Veblen simply recognized, as did Marx, that capitalism needs to be creative to keep capital flowing to the capitalists. Marx, you recall, saw part of the solution in esoteric goods and services; Veblen added that waste, destruction, and sabotage are also essential. This description of capitalism suggests Veblen's cynical view of the nature of modern society.

Nature of Society, Humans, and Change

Much of Veblen's theory and ideology regarding capitalism centered on the wealth of industrial managers and owners. Although he linked this wealth to the distress of the masses, this distress was not central to Veblen's thinking. His focus was the wealth of the great owners, the "captains of industry."

Much of what Veblen had to say about society has already been introduced, but it might be well to summarize at this point. Veblen for the most part considered societies and their institutions to be imperfect, if not bad, but it is not clear that he believed human nature to be good—as many radicals, from Rousseau to

Marx, did. He was not a radical because he was pessimistic about changing institutions (such as economies) and societies for the better. Rather, he believed that habits are too ingrained and that support for institutions dominates the desire for improvement. Technological change is evolutionary and cumulative, but most societal change, as Pareto would agree, is neither progressive nor goal-oriented.

Class, Gender, and Race

Class   The book that established Veblen's reputation as an acerbic and astute writer was his first, *The Theory of the Leisure Class*, published in 1899. Class was a primary focus of Veblen's attention, with gender less so, and with references to race almost incidental.

Veblen's theory of class began with the claim that there is in humans an instinct of workmanship—a need to create, to do something (Veblen, 1914). At the earliest stages of human development, when there was no economic surplus, people worked and struggled simply for subsistence or survival. There was, however, also a universal desire for status, and gradually the ability to produce a surplus made accumulation possible.

Veblen's central thesis was that humans did not use the growing surplus for useful purposes; rather, they used the surplus to impress other people (Chase, in Veblen 1899:xiv). Some theorists, according to Veblen, had interpreted continued accumulation as due to the desire for greater creature comforts (such as a more comfortable chair or bed). But he saw accumulation as an end in itself, for the sake of repute and esteem. This desire manifested itself increasingly as surpluses grow.

The lower "barbarian" culture strove to increase surplus by means of predation, including capture and conquest. In the past, then, aggression had been the accredited form of action, with booty as the resulting trophy (Veblen, 1899:17). Later, manual labor came to be seen as particularly repugnant: "Whatever has to do directly with the everyday work of getting a livelihood, is the exclusive occupation of the inferior class" (Veblen, 1899:2).

As industrial society displaced the earlier predatory society, accumulated property replaced trophies of predatory activity as the symbol of success. For the lower classes, the effort to stay above the subsistence level might make them industrious and frugal, because for them productive labor was necessary (Veblen, 1899:35). But for those better provided for, not just manual labor but any form of labor became distasteful. No longer the predatory warrior, the high-status person now sought to avoid all work, to engage in conspicuous leisure. Conspicuous leisure now involves waste, of time and things. According to the song, if Tevye were rich, he would put up an extra staircase "just for show," and would spend seven hours every day discussing the holy books with the learned men; these ambitions, Veblen would say, are characteristic of the leisure class.

An important aspect of conspicuous leisure involves manners and decorum, because, as Veblen put it, "good breeding requires time, application, and expense, and can therefore not be compassed by those whose time and energy are taken up with work" (1899:49). The 14-piece place setting, the multicourse meal, and other minute aspects of good manners are obvious examples of both good breeding and conspicuous leisure. The leisure class learn these subtleties, in part, at the appropriate schools, which teach lessons about taste and discrimination regarding the appropriate articles and styles of consumption. The time of the leisure class is spent in drives, clubs, sewing circles, charity events, and other social functions, which they describe as irksome but unavoidable, but to the outside observer seem merely to waste time (Veblen, 1899:65). An article in the *International Herald Tribune* observed:

> It is not money but a whole way of life that is specific to that class—the rules of etiquette, special institutions such as the *rallyes* and private clubs that do not exist in other classes. . . . If the upper crust have succeeded in maintaining a world apart, they have also assured the impenetrability of that world by rituals of etiquette inaccessible to the uninitiated, by private clubs such as the Jockey, the Travellers, the Interallie and the Automobile club, and by the *rallyes,* weekly dances for their children which serve as a marriage market and as a means of excluding unwelcome social elements. ("Room at the Top: Life in Paris's Posh Quartiers," 1990)

Another way the "upper crust" produce and demonstrate leisure is by having servants. The servants who answer the door, do the gardening, or drive the car are demonstrating that the master need not do such tasks but can pay to have them done (Veblen, 1899:63, 66). The key, then, is to demonstrate both accumulated resources and time on one's hands.

Not only is time to be wasted unproductively, but so are goods. Conspicuous consumption is an essential characteristic of the leisure class. It is particularly important in a populous and anonymous society in which others do not know you, or your parents, or your character, but they see what kind of car you drive and how you dress (Veblen, 1899:86). Conspicuous consumption as a precept filters down to the lower classes, who are capable of consuming but not of accruing leisure (Veblen, 1899:105). Veblen went on to note that even religion and sports (participatory and spectator) could be viewed as examples of conspicuous consumption and leisure (1899:119, 255, 397).

In the larger society the leisure class is for the most part conservative, even reactionary in some ways, seeking "to retard change and to conserve what is obsolescent." They are parasitic, diverting what they can to their own use and retaining or accumulating what they can (Veblen, 1899:198, 209). Veblen intimated that, in their conservatism, the leisure class goes so far as to lose the instinct for self-preservation. Leisure and accumulation, then, eventually lead to the weakness and stagnation of this class, especially as they are supplanted by the new rich, or "nouveau riche."

Gender   What was called in Veblen's time the "woman question" is treated at some length in *The Theory of the Leisure Class* (1899:354–362). However, Veblen was not completely clear in his presentation. He noted, first of all, a body of common sense that placed women in a position ancillary to that of men. Men and women may have begun history sharing the drudgery of life, but as time went by poor women carried out more and more of the hard tasks (1899:13).

Women's subordination to men did not change greatly with industrialization, but the role of high-status women did. The wife, who in predatory society was "the drudge and chattel of the man . . . [and] the producer of goods for him to consume, has become the ceremonial consumer of goods which he produces" in the middle class, and the consumer of goods produced by others in the leisure class (Veblen, 1899:83). The leisure-class woman is petted, debarred from vulgarly useful employment, and required to consume conspicuously, often vicariously for her husband (1899:354–358). All these, noted Veblen, are characteristics of the unfree. (The woman's role as consumer had been discussed a year earlier by Charlotte Perkins Gilman, as you will see in Chapter 11.)

Veblen did not assert, however, that drudgery and leisure are the way women's lives ought to be. Sentiment was growing, he observed, that this whole arrangement of vicarious life, or life lived through the male, was somehow a mistake. Although it may have been good for its time and place, "it does not adequately serve . . . life in a modern industrial community" (Veblen, 1899:358).

At the same time, however, Veblen referred to modern women as "less manageable," suggesting that by youth, education, and temperament, they were "out of touch with the traditions of status received from the barbarian culture" and that they had reverted to self-expression and workmanship (1899:356). The term "reverted" is confusing unless we recall Veblen's earlier point that in subsistence societies women and men had both worked hard—that only later did women become first drudges and then leisure-time consumers. Thus, some women of his day were seeking to recapture a working lifestyle—a "more generic type of human character, . . . a less differentiated expression of human nature" (1899:361).

These closing words suggest that Veblen considered women's liberation (to use today's term) to be not at all inconsistent with human nature. Yet he described the "barbarian" and modern conservative gender traditions positively enough to make us wonder if he was consistently critical of women's past or supportive of their liberation.

Race   The racial and ethnic biases of Veblen's day show up several times in his treatment of business and industry. The clearest example is his observation, in a footnote, that northern Europeans, especially Germans and Scandinavians, are efficient at war-making and are "apparently, on the whole, also the ones most generally endowed with industrial initiative and a large aptitude for the machine technology and scientific research" (1904:396). Though he nowhere stated that racial/ethnic differences are innate, a bias in favor of those of European ancestry is apparent.

Other Theories and Theorists

In this section we will examine two of Veblen's less central issues: higher education and exchange theory. Then we will briefly look further at his relation to Marx and Pareto.

Business and Higher Education   Veblen's book *The Higher Learning in America* (1918) combined his understanding of capitalism and big business with his alienation from the academic community. It included both theoretical insights and exaggerations.

"What is the 'work' of higher education?" Veblen asked. His answer was that it involves "two lines of work, distinct but closely bound together: (a) scholarly and scientific inquiry, and (b) the instruction of students" (1918:12). What he observed, however, was that higher learning tends to concentrate on "decorative real-estate, spectacular pageantry, bureaucratic magnificence, elusive statistics, vocational training, genteel solemnities and sweat-shop instruction"—none of which is closely related to the university's primary concerns (1918:128). Above all, Veblen stressed, "work that has a commercial value does not belong in the university" (1918:110). To Veblen, the classic concept of higher education—that is, learning for its own sake—is still the only appropriate one.

The governing boards of universities used to be drawn largely from the clergy, Veblen noted, because early American colleges were primarily for professional training, mostly of clergy but also of schoolmasters (1918:16). At the turn of the twentieth century, however, businessmen and politicians had come to substitute for clergy, and since businessmen controlled politics, "discretionary control in matters of university policy now rests finally in the hands of businessmen" (1918:45, 46).

This takeover reflected the increasing importance of corporations and the secularization of society. "Business success is by common consent . . . taken to be conclusive evidence of wisdom even in matters that have no relation to business affairs" (Veblen, 1918:50). As Tevye's song points out, "if I were a rich man," it wouldn't "make one bit of difference if I answer right or wrong; when you're rich they think you really know."

Veblen cynically described the work of university governing boards and administrations as prestige, publicity, plant, and perpetuation—keeping the wheels turning (1918:99, 163). Competition for students and for funds required these functions, though they have little or nothing to do with a university's real work.

Even today, faculty might organize or unionize, but they do not because they see themselves as free professionals, not as employees of a given institution of higher learning, receiving wages for their work (Veblen, 1918:86). This is not altogether wrongheaded on the part of faculty, whose goal is supposed to be the pursuit of knowledge and learning. However, administrators expect faculty to help in luring both students and funds. Reflecting his own isolation and alienation from the academic scene, Veblen observed that the academic "may make his chance of preferment less assured, and may even jeopardize his tenure, by a conspicuously parsimonious manner of life, or by too pronounced an addiction to scientific or scholarly pursuits, to the neglect of those polite exhibitions of decorum that conduce to the maintenance of the university's prestige in the eyes of the (pecuniarily) cultured laity" (1918:119). In other words, an appropriate and "acceptable" lifestyle is as important as the pursuit of learning for university faculty.

Veblen took a very negative view of the money paid to athletes and their coaches, justified by "threadbare subterfuges" as a part of higher education

(1918:90, 92). Like so many of his insights, this one is even truer today than when he wrote, and is entirely consistent with his description of university administrations and governing boards as focused on publicity and prestige.

Thus, to Veblen, seats of higher learning had strayed far from their goals. Even when they took "playful excursions" into creativity and originality, they soon returned to the orthodox commonplaces. Universities, in other words, are conservative, serving the needs of the business community while forgetting their mission (1918:133). In many ways, the modern university is just another of Max Weber's large capitalist bureaucratic organizations.

Exchange Theory   Veblen did not develop an exchange theory (the focus of Chapter 21), but he did speak to one of its issues. Exchange theory has as a central tenet that people make exchanges in which they try to maximize gain or profit and to minimize cost. Another tenet is that even altruistic behavior can be explained in terms of profit, because it makes you feel good and may cause others to see you as a good person. Veblen observed that "many ostensible works of disinterested public spirit are no doubt initiated and carried on with a view primarily to the enhanced repute, or even to the pecuniary gain, of the promoters" (1899:340). Marx and Pareto saw much philanthropic behavior as intended to entrench the elite's ruling position; Veblen saw it in almost the same way, as a matter of exchange—reputation and gain for good deeds.

Veblen and Pareto   The relation of Veblen's economic theory to that of Marx has already been discussed. In addition, Veblen's ideas can be compared to Pareto's. Besides their similar views of exchange, Veblen's ideas remind us of Pareto's circulating elites, the lions and the foxes. Veblen spoke of two "barbarian" traits, "ferocity and astuteness," both "expressions of a narrowly self-regarding habit of mind" and both "of no use for the purposes of collective life" (1899:275). Likewise, Veblen's view of society as technologically evolutionary but goalless is reminiscent of Pareto's more extreme view that nothing important ever changes, only the derivations used to justify the unchanging residues.

Critique and Conclusions

One criticism of Veblen concerns the idea that the leisure class loses the instinct for self-preservation. As an example, as the barbarians poured into Rome, it is hard to imagine that the Romans simply did not care what happened to them, which is what Veblen seems to imply. However, the Romans may have forgotten how to protect themselves. In other words, it is more likely that the leisure class loses the know-how, not the instinct, of self-preservation.

Another criticism is that Veblen's view of gender is based on a misreading of so-called predatory or barbarian societies. His notion that in very early societies women were ancillary or subordinate to men is questionable. Rousseau had argued that an early characteristic of gender was role similarity and virtual equality. A hundred years after Rousseau, anthropological studies indicated that women enjoyed greater power and economic centrality in quite a few hunter-gatherer and agricultural societies, such as the Iroquois, than Veblen recognized.

As for Veblen's contributions, many have stood the test of time. Veblen recognized that innovations accelerating the pace of production would eventually make their way into use, and that those who do not adopt them will be "left out of the running" (1914:314). Although he could not have foreseen either automation or computerization, their development and adoption would have made sense to him. They simply provide further bases for obsolescence, and for the displacement of people by machines.

A basic instinct of human beings, according to Veblen, is "to do something"—to work, create, construct. In the industrial world, the creators are the scientists, inventors, and engineers, while the businessmen are the exploiters and leisure class, and the workers are only the workers. Though he did not try to blueprint a utopia, it is clear that Veblen thought the engineers should take over industrial processes and make them work for humankind, rather than being under the control of the industrial "captains," whose only goals are exploitation and profit (Hacker, in Veblen 1918: vii). Later, John Kenneth Galbraith (1971) would argue that the engineers and scientists have in fact taken over, and that managers and boards of directors simply rubber-stamp the engineers' decisions. But the problem is one of definition: "Taking over" to Veblen meant controlling, possibly owning, the resources and operations, while to Galbraith it meant making the important techno-productive decisions.

To Veblen, the villain was capitalism itself—business exploitation and profit. In his view, the entrepreneurial adventure capitalism of Marx's time is declining. However, it is not and will not be replaced by socialism, Marxist or otherwise. In fact, he considered socialist proposals to be "ill-defined and inconsistent and almost completely negative." Veblen found Marxism's "withering away of the state" or political institutions particularly untenable (Veblen, 1904:337, 356).

According to Veblen, the future of capitalism will be more and more powerful managers and ever-larger businesses. The multinational corporation of today is but an extension of Veblen's view of the future. Though he may have disliked his prediction, it was that capitalism will become more centralized, more finance-based instead of product-based, with the profits—as Marx had said—becoming ever more colossal.

Joseph Schumpeter, 1883–1950

Schumpeter is seldom discussed in a book on social theory. However, he was more than an institutional economist; he was an historical social scientist whose work paralleled that of Veblen, in that he wrote about capitalism's characteristics and future.

Joseph Schumpeter was born in Austria to an affluent Moravian Christian family. His work and personality are best understood if we keep in mind his quasi-aristocratic beginnings and his childhood as the only son of a young widowed mother. His devotion to his mother and to the centrality of intergenerational relations were manifested in his two marriages—one to an older woman and one to a much younger one—and in his commitment to his students, whom he often treated as sons (Smithies, in Harris, 1951:16). With his contemporaries and colleagues, he was much less successful.

Schumpeter was a social scientist, a historian, and at certain times a politician and a finance minister. He wrote his first major book in 1911 (though a lesser book had preceded it), two important essays in the 1930s, and a second major book in 1942. His most daunting book, *The History of Economic Analysis*, appeared posthumously in 1954, edited by his wife, Elizabeth Boody. Thus, his work covers the first half of the twentieth century, and is presented here in order to relate his ideas to those of Veblen and Marx.

Schumpeter's early career has been described as follows:

> Schumpeter's scientific output during the years between his graduation from the University in 1906 and the end of the First World War was stupendous, especially if one considers that during that period he lived in five different places with as many different cultures, located in four countries on three continents, and that according to reports he made full use of the many opportunities to enjoy life which prewar Vienna and London, not to speak of Cairo and Czernowitz, offered in abundance. (Haberler, in Harris, 1951:27)

Schumpeter held various nonacademic positions in Austria and Germany during World War I. During the 1920s, he was an academic while also writing on various economics topics for magazines. A major change in his career occurred when he went to Harvard in 1932 and began devoting his full time to teaching and research (Hoselitz, in Schumpeter, 1934:vi). His work, then, spanned two continents and four decades, but he always believed that a scholar's first 30 years of life were crucial.

Schumpeter's interpersonal inadequacies manifested themselves in an unusual way. Despite his impressive intelligence and encyclopedic knowledge, he had trouble winning over his contemporaries to his views (Smithies, in Harris, 1951:16). Time and again he seemed to stack the cards against himself so as to lose an argument with honor. This may explain his refusal to dogmatize in order to attract not just students, but disciples, to a potential Schumpterian school of thought; it may also explain the paradoxes in his arguments that give capitalists, socialists, and intellectuals alike reasons for rejecting them (Smithies, in Harris, 1951:16).

Schumpeter's Central Theories and Methods

A key contribution of Schumpeter's sociological theory was a view of capitalism in motion, developing a "'moving picture' ('film') of industrial capitalism in action, growth and decline, the role of its controlling class . . . [and] the capitalist entrepreneur, as he grows and changes from the ingenious craftsman and venturesome merchant to the head of an industrial family and finally the executive of a big corporation" (von Beckerath, in Harris, 1951:113). Besides capitalism in motion, Schumpeter dealt at length with Marxism and with imperialism as an aspect of twentieth-century capitalism.

Schumpeter sought to discover the ideological biases of other social scientists, though not in the "debunking" style of Pareto. While admitting that some sort of vision was essential to prescientific philosophy, he maintained a positivist faith in scientific inquiry and objective truth (Smithies, in Harris, 1951:17).

He, perhaps more than Max Weber, felt that objectivity was not only desirable but possible. Yet his aristocratic bias toward capitalism must have been apparent to him, and very likely helped him to realize, as Weber did, that freedom from ideology is never completely possible (Smithies, in Harris, 1951:21).

Schumpeter and Marx   Schumpeter's treatment of Marx is much more thorough than Veblen's. In fact, the first 58 pages of *Capitalism, Socialism, and Democracy* (1942) provide an excellent summary of Marxism—perhaps the best and most balanced treatment by anyone, Marxist or otherwise. Schumpeter observed that various social thinkers have treated history as the struggle between races, or as the relation between vocational groups, or as a matter of material production. On this Schumpeter agreed with Marx: History is primarily about economics.

However, according to Schumpeter, Marx "never, as far as we know, worked out systematically what it is plain was one of the pivots of his thought"—namely, that history is about classes and class struggle (1942:14). What Marx did was discuss in various places the issues of class consciousness and revolution. Even more important to Schumpeter was the way Marx tied class theory to the inevitability of socialism/communism. Calling it a "bold stroke of analytic strategy," Schumpeter noted that Marx had linked "the fate of the class phenomenon with the fate of capitalism in such a way that socialism, which in reality has nothing to do with the presence or absence of social classes, became, by definition, the only possible kind of classless society, excepting primitive groups" (1942:19). While this "bold stroke" made it possible for Marx to build an edifice leading from classes to consciousness to revolution to communism/socialism, it also, according to his critics, "painted Marx into the corner" of a narrow prediction for the future.

Another of Schumpeter's criticisms of Marx's view of classes was that by "attributing—quite unrealistically—to the masses his own shibboleth of 'class consciousness,' he undoubtedly falsified the true psychology of the workman (which centers in the wish to become a small bourgeois)" (1942:7). This, you will recall, was also one of Robert Michels's criticisms of Marx: As long as workers see the opportunity for mobility, for themselves or their children, they identify with capitalism instead of seeking to overthrow it.

Schumpeter found in Marx, especially in the *Manifesto*, a glowing account of the achievements of *industrial capitalism*, with its colossal productive forces. This original and authentic Marxian view, commented Schumpeter, is strikingly more positive than and different from "the views of the vulgarized Marxism of today or from the Veblenite stuff of the modern non-Marxist radical" (1942:7)—an interesting label. However, Marx's insistence that not just productive forces, but technology itself, creates a given class system "stresses the technological element to a dangerous extent" (1942:12).

Schumpeter criticized Marx's labor theory of value at length. While labor produces value and capital, capital also produces capital, and is also used in creating the means of production themselves (1942:32). Likewise, overproduction might reduce prices, thereby affecting the value of labor. Schumpeter, like other critics, saw Marx's view of the production of value as oversimplified.

In summary, Schumpeter criticized Marx for presenting "a long list of con-clusions that do not follow or are downright wrong; mistakes which if corrected change essential inferences, sometimes into their opposites." Yet he qualified his verdict on two grounds: Marx's critics were far from always right, and Marx's contributions to the analysis of capitalist society outweighed his narrowness and his mistaken predictions of the future (1942:43). After all, Schumpeter noted, Marx's goal was to "found a homogeneous party based upon the organized pro-letariat of all countries that would march toward the goal without losing its revolutionary faith and getting its powder wet on the road." Compared to such a goal, the mistaken details of Marxism were of little consequence (1942:319).

Economic Development   Schumpeter's other major theoretical concern was economic development, and many of these ideas were produced before he turned 30 years of age. Manifesting a status quo conservative capitalist view of economics, he noted that economic activity might stem from a variety of mo-tives, but "its *meaning* is always the satisfaction of wants." The leading character-istics of a commercially organized state are "private property, division of labor, and free competition" (Schumpeter, 1911:10, 5). Schumpeter assumed an eco-nomic system's tendency toward equilibrium—a basic functionalist assumption (1911:62).

An economic system, according to Schumpeter, is actually run by the de-mands of the consumer. The assumption is that "the means of production and the productive process have in general no real leader, or rather the real leader is the consumer. The people who direct business firms only execute what is pre-scribed for them by wants or demand and by the given means and methods of production" (1911:21). As today's producers of magazines, movies, and toys put it: "We only give them what they want." Yet Schumpeter admitted there was a circular flow, in which producers innovate or initiate economic change and then educate (brainwash) the consumer, who must be "taught to want new things" (1911:65).

Schumpeter defined **economic development** as "the carrying out of new combinations." He presented an insightful list of possible factors in such innova-tion: (1) a new good, or new quality of a good; (2) a new productive method; (3) the opening of a new market; (4) a new source of raw material; or (5) a new organization, such as monopolization or decentralization (1911:66).

Schumpeter noted that the entrepreneur or innovator has to resort to credit, because he or she could not, by definition, rely on returns from previous production. This assumed that the innovator is, in fact, starting from scratch, and is not involved in the previous production of something else—a question-able assumption.

The **entrepreneur** was central to Schumpeter's view of development, and he spent much time and effort describing the entrepreneur's character and motives. The primary characteristic of the entrepreneur is leadership, manifested in several ways: ability to escape conventional thinking, ability to live with uncertainty, and willingness to tolerate the disapproval of those who are bound by conventional-ity (1911:86–89 *et passim*). The motives of the entrepreneur are not primarily of a hedonistic or egoistic nature. They are, rather, (1) kingdom building, giving a sense of power and independence; (2) success, for its own sake and to prove one-self superior to others; and (3) the joy of creating, of exercising one's imagination, ingenuity, and energy (1911:92–93).

Schumpeter observed that entrepreneurial activity is cyclical: Periods of in-novative boom, which he called swarm-like, are followed by assimilation (eco-nomic lions and foxes). Innovation is swarm-like in that "the appearance of one or a few entrepreneurs facilitates the appearance of others" (1911:228). Over time, however, innovation declines under capitalism. Entrepreneurs reinvest their profits and retire, thus liquidating their enterprise or consolidating it with others (1911:99).

Will the result be the eventual stagnation of capitalism? Schumpeter's an-swer to that question came 30 years later; his view of the future of capitalism will be discussed later under Other Theories and Theorists. However, he did sug-gest that the outbreak of war "may cause [economic] disturbances big enough for a crisis to be spoken of" (1911:220)—a position directly opposite to Veblen's and Luxemburg's that war gives rise to economic prosperity.

Nature of Society, Humans, and Change

Schumpeter's views on society were scattered through his work on economics. He nowhere indicated that he believed in the goodness of either society or hu-man nature. In fact, his descriptions of *capitalist society* lead one to conclude that, although he was sympathetic with the capitalist entrepreneur and enterprise, he saw economic and other institutions as a decidedly mixed bag.

His treatment of social change was hardly one of evolutionary progress. He believed that change in institutions is real and important (unlike Pareto), but that it involves rise, stagnation, and fall. Change results from the activities of a society's leaders (its "aristocrats"), but also from changes in monetary, political, and productive policies. Like Weber, Schumpeter saw society and its change as too complex to analyze monocausally or unidirectionally, as Marxists seemed to do. Schumpeter tried hard to avoid ideology and to analyze society with positiv-istic objectivity. So, despite his capitalist sympathies, he did not predict an even-tual victory for capitalism over its radical foes.

Class, Gender, and Race

Schumpeter stated at the outset of his 1934 essay that he was treating classes "in an ethnically homogeneous environment"—not because race/ethnicity is unimportant, but because the "essential nature" of social stratification based on class requires ignoring certain external factors, such as race (Schumpeter, 1934:102). He then indicated that his concern with class was fourfold: the for-mation, nature, cohesion, and concrete causes and conditions of an historically given class structure (1934:107).

A key characteristic of a **class**, according to Schumpeter, is that it is aware of its identity, and has a characteristic "spirit" or ethos (1934:107). For Schumpeter, class awareness or identity is somewhat like Marx's "class-for-itself," with non-members of a class sometimes working on behalf of that class, and against their own class (1934:110)—reminiscent of Marx's members of the bourgeoisie who break away and work on behalf of the proletariat.

Schumpeter's view of classes resembles that of the functionalists (see Chapter 14), who argued that class hierarchy is determined by the significance to society of the function performed. According to Schumpeter, the "position of each class in the national structure, depends, on the one hand, on the significance that is attributed to that function, and, on the other hand, on the degree to which the class successfully performs the function" (1934:137, 157). Another key aspect of class ranking is replaceability. Thus, a banker or businessman is of a higher class than a janitor or factory worker because the duties performed by the former require more training, because those duties are more highly valued by society, and because such individuals would be harder to replace.

According to Schumpeter, individuals are born into a class because they are born into a family—which he saw as the true unit of class theory. They are not, however, "stuck." Mobility might occur because of an historical accident that thrusts one function forward and diminishes the status of another (such as the decline of the blacksmith with the introduction of the automobile). Like Veblen, Schumpeter wrote of "being crowded out of business" as a function declines in importance or a new product supersedes an old one.

More important in changing one's class position and status, however, is **aptitude,** as "the class member performs with more or less success than his fellows those activities that he must perform in any event" (1934:132). By itself, the demonstration of aptitude is not enough to change a person's class position: The least competent banker is still of a higher class than the most skilled janitor. Rather, aptitude, or its lack, must result in raising or lowering one's position: The banker might be demoted or fired, while the janitor might be promoted.

Prestige could take on a life of its own, outlasting the aptitude that gave rise to it. Such prestige might also spread to other areas of life, in which the individual is less "apt" (Schumpeter, 1934:166). On this point Schumpeter differed from Veblen, however, arguing that the "warlord was automatically the leader of his people in virtually every respect. The modern industrialist is anything but such a leader" (1934:167). Schumpeter thus rejected Veblen's view that success in business is seen as a sign of general wisdom.

According to Schumpeter, aptitude is very likely distributed in society along a normal curve. At the upper end of the curve are a few with great ability—an idea that reflected Schumpeter's elitist or aristocratic view of society (Harris, 1951:1). Class differences are minute, to be distinguished in small increments. But this distribution is not random or chance. At least a portion of it is inherited within families, making classes stable from generation to generation.

Schumpeter's theory of classes was thus based primarily on functional importance and individual aptitude, on societal need and individual ability. The notions of a leisure class wasting time and goods (Veblen) and/or exploiting the rest of society (Marx) were not central to Schumpeter's theory of classes.

Schumpeter's social theory did not include gender and race. He did recognize that race is an independent factor that helps to explain society's inequalities, altering the effects of aptitude and function on societal rankings or classes. However, he did not attempt to explain the workings of that factor, and he did not confront the issue of gender.

Other Theories and Theorists

Two other issues with which Schumpeter dealt were imperialism and the future of capitalism.

Economic Imperialism   Schumpeter's view of **imperialism** had both similarities with and differences from that of Lenin. Schumpeter defined imperialism as "the objectless disposition on the part of a state to unlimited forcible expansion." Although it sought hegemony or world domination, it could not be reduced to the economic class interests of that age—a mistake made by Lenin and the neo-Marxists, according to Schumpeter (1934:7).

Writing some 20 years after Lenin, Schumpeter argued that not all imperialism is political; it also takes the form of **economic imperialism**. Certain countries and their corporations employ cheap labor in less developed countries, and are able to open markets there at monopoly prices as well. Had Schumpeter been writing today, he would have noted the economic imperialism of U.S. corporations with factories in Mexico and Indonesia, and their worldwide markets. Likewise, he would have understood the "new world order" of today, with corporations, the World Bank, and the International Monetary Fund controlling access to funds.

All this ensures control by the "captains of industry" (Veblen's term) in the developed nations, and results in huge profits for organized capital and capitalists. According to Schumpeter, however, unlike Lenin, imperialism is not a necessary phase of capitalism, nor does the former develop directly as a result of the latter (1934:82–84, 89).

The Future of Capitalism   Schumpeter began *Capitalism, Socialism, and Democracy* with the lengthy discussion of Marx referred to earlier. The next two parts of that book are "Can Capitalism Survive?" and "Can Socialism Work?" His short answers to these two questions were "no" and "probably." The longer answers, however, speak to the question "Why?"

Much of Schumpeter's discussion of capitalism was quite favorable—hardly surprising, given his evident aristocratic and capitalist ideology. He argued that capitalism is doing away with poverty; in fact, the poor are gaining in relative shares of wealth, compared to the rich (1942:67). Although this may be doubtful, it was one of Schumpeter's beliefs. Furthermore, larger firms are able to drive out smaller ones—as both Marx and Veblen had predicted—so that the eventual winners in local capitalist markets are "the department store, the chain store, the mail-order house, and the supermarket" (1942:79, 85). Moreover, he did not see output slackening because of a reduction in technological changes (1942:118).

So what is capitalism's problem? According to Schumpeter, it is twofold. First, in places such as Great Britain, many people are already hostile to capitalism. Somewhat overdramatically, Schumpeter predicted: "Faced with the increasing hostility of the environment and by the legislative, administrative, and judicial practice born of that hostility, entrepreneurs and capitalists—in fact the whole stratum that accepts the bourgeois scheme of life—will eventually cease to function" (1942:156). Why the hostility to capitalism? Schumpeter believed it is because markets have become glutted, resources are giving out, inflation and recession give rise to continuous economic crises, and innovation is becoming less frequent. The result is *the stagnation of capitalism.*

The second problem is that industrial life has become depersonalized, with ownership degenerating into stock and bond holding and executives acting like civil servants. According to Schumpeter, capitalist (entrepreneurial) "motivation and standards have all but wilted away" (1942:219).

Schumpeter's predictions of large businesses driving out smaller ones and ownership becoming a matter of stocks and bonds seem to have been correct. However, his conclusion seems faulty because of his dependence on entrepreneurial innovation as the predominant factor in capitalist economic development, and because of changes that have occurred in the more than half century since he wrote. In those years, many more checks and balances have been put on "the market," in an attempt to avoid both crises and stagnation. Also, accumulation of stocks and other forms of wealth has apparently been sufficient as a basis for capitalism's success.

The outcome of Schumpeter's argument is stated very clearly in his Preface: "Can Capitalism Survive?—I have tried to show that a socialist form of society will inevitably emerge from an equally inevitable decomposition of capitalist society" (1942:xiii). And again later: "Can capitalism survive? No, I do not think it can" (1942:61). Under socialism, predicted Schumpeter, unemployment would be less, because of the elimination of crises. The government would be able to redirect people into needed employment, as planning from the top maximizes economic possibilities and the meeting of needs (1942:196).

In short, for Schumpeter, the taking over of the economy by the public sector—that is, **socialism**—would ultimately be a small price to pay for some semblance of economic stability. This outcome would certainly not be brought about by mass revolution, nor would it be complete, but it would be necessary at least in the monetary and industrial sectors (which is exactly what Lenin had tried to accomplish). Thus, whereas individual entrepreneurship is important to a country's early development, at a later stage state control will be required.

If Schumpeter's analysis is correct, his critics have said, he was either advocating socialism or was a "defeated capitalist." However, he himself argued against those who called him either a socialist or a defeatist. He claimed that his analysis was by definition neither—it was simply realism (reminding one of Pareto). "Facts in themselves and inferences from them can never be defeatist or the opposite whatever that might be. The report that a given ship is sinking is not defeatist" (Schumpeter, 1942:xi). In other words, he claimed to be seeking an objective analysis, not expressing an ideology.

Critique and Conclusions

Schumpeter was so self-critical as to believe that he never worked hard enough. He kept a diary in which he graded himself by the week on his accomplishments. These grades were seldom complimentary. If he put in a 60-hour week, he should have put in 80; if he began a major paper, he thought he should have finished it.

His dire prediction for capitalism's future was at least partially a result of post–World War II unrest in the major capitalist countries, such as Britain and the United States (Schumpeter, 1942). Strikes were rampant, as those who had sacrificed for the war effort began to seek more "goodies" for themselves. This unrest, coupled with his analysis of crisis and stagnation, led to his expectation of capitalism's decline. Although he considered this a realistic prediction, few have agreed that his analysis leads to such a conclusion.

Schumpeter's encyclopedic grasp of economic principles and methods was only peripherally related to his sociological insights. Writing sympathetically and critically on Marx, classes, entrepreneurship, imperialism, and the future, he was too eclectic and complex to establish a school of thought. His theories have been criticized by capitalist and Marxist thinkers alike, and, as in the case of Max Weber, by those who simplify in order to draw clear-cut conclusions.

Final Thoughts

When we began this chapter, we noted the importance of Veblen's and Schumpeter's backgrounds to their sociological insights. Veblen's farm background and marginal academic career were clearly related to his critical, left-leaning theory. Likewise, Schumpeter's industrial and quasi-aristocratic background led him to be interested in and sympathetic to capitalist society. In addition, his self-criticism may very well have contributed to his "realistic" prediction of capitalism's decline.

Veblen, Schumpeter, and Marx all agreed that nineteenth-century adventure/entrepreneurial capitalism was declining. Marx predicted the revolutionary overthrow of capitalism by the proletariat—and, as an optimist, he looked forward to it. Veblen, a theorist "on the left," meaning a critic of capitalism, saw the change as increasing monopoly or managerial oligopoly—a move to the right. Since he did not prefer that outcome, he could be labeled a pessimist. Schumpeter, on the other hand, argued for an equilibrium-based, entrepreneurial capitalism and for a functional theory of classes—both of which indicated a not-well-hidden capitalist ideology. Thus, when he predicted a socialist future, he might deny defeatism (or pessimism), but to the reader the label seems to fit. In other words, Schumpeter, a theorist "on the right" ideologically, saw in the future a move to the left, toward socialism.

So far, it seems that history has upheld the conclusions of Veblen more than the other two theorists. But the twenty-first century will pronounce its own judgment.

References

"Bechtel Group Gets Big Chunk of Kuwait Reconstruction Bucks." 1991, February 28. *Baltimore Sun*.

"Clothes Grow More Costly, Less Durable." 1989, April 12. *Capital Times*.

Coser, Lewis A. 1977. *Masters of Sociological Thought*. San Diego: Harcourt Brace Jovanovich.

Galbraith, John Kenneth. 1971. *The New Industrial State* (2nd ed.). Boston: Houghton.

Hacker, Louis M. (Ed.). 1918/1957. "Introduction." In Thorstein Veblen, *The Higher Learning in America* (pp. v–ix). New York: Hill and Wang.

Harnick, Sheldon, and Jerry Bock. 1964. *Fiddler on the Roof*. New York: Sunbeam Music.

Harris, Seymour E. (Ed.). 1951. *Schumpeter, Social Scientist*. Cambridge, MA: Harvard University Press. (Papers by Haberler, Smithies, and von Beckerath.)

"Middle East Bank for Reconstruction." 1991, February 1. *Capital Times*.

Morgan, Lewis Henry. 1868. *Consanguinity and Affinity of the Human Family*. Washington, DC: Smithsonian Institution.

"Room at the Top: Life in Paris's Posh Quartiers." 1990, February 12. *International Herald Tribune*.

Schumpeter, Joseph A. 1911/1934. *The Theory of Economic Development*. Cambridge, MA: Harvard University Press.

———. 1934/1964. *Imperialism; Social Classes* (Bert Hoselitz, Ed.). New York: World Publishing–Meridian Books.

———. 1942/1962. *Capitalism, Socialism, and Democracy*. New York: Harper and Row.

———. 1949. "Vilfredo Pareto (1848–1920)." *Quarterly Journal of Economics*, 63, 147–173.

———. 1954. *History of Economic Analysis*. New York: Oxford University Press.

"Self-Destructing Videos." 1989, March 30. *Wisconsin State Journal*.

Veblen, Thorstein. 1899/1934. *The Theory of the Leisure Class* (Stuart Chase, Ed.). New York: Macmillan.

———. 1904/1965. *Theory of Business Enterprise*. New York: A. M. Kelley.

———. 1914. *The Instinct of Workmanship and the State of the Industrial Arts*. New York: Macmillan.

———. 1918/1957. *The Higher Learning in America*. (Louis M. Hacker, Ed.). New York: Hill and Wang.

———. 1919. *The Place of Science in Modern Civilization*. New York: W. B. Huebsch.

SECTION VI

Other Voices in Sociological Theorizing

Section I introduced theory and theorizing, as well as three important early nineteenth-century "parents" of sociology. In Section II you encountered capitalist conservative theory and ideology: evolution and functionalism. Section III presented the radical anticapitalist response, and Section V the sociopolitical and socioeconomic reactions to Marxism. While there are many internal variations within each section, these four sections are structured and coherent.

Section IV, however, consisted of three German theorists, the Webers and Simmel. The Webers' encyclopedic concerns included complexity and objectivity, while Simmel's involved form and content. Aside from the fact that they wrote at the same time, in the same country, and were all three concerned with human action and meaning, they can hardly be considered to represent a single school of thought.

In Section VI we again include chapters which, at first glance, appear only slightly connected. Throughout the first ten chapters, however, two foci of attention have been gender and race—the former in the work of Marianne Weber and Rosa Luxemburg, among others, and the latter especially in the Marxists. C. P. Gilman and Beatrice Webb (Chapter 11) wrote a generation after Martineau, and were contemporaries of Luxemburg. But, unlike Luxemburg, they were not radical anticapitalists. While giving a feminist perspective to their theorizing, they were theoretical and methodological generalists, writing about society, not just gender. And W. E. B. Du Bois (Chapter 12), the first African American theorist to be included in this volume (not the last), did not restrict his writings to race. He lived 95 years, and wrote insightfully on many aspects of the capitalist and colonial worlds.

Chapter 13 could very well be a section in itself. However, there are two main reasons why C. H. Cooley, G. H. Mead, and Sigmund Freud are included in a single chapter of Section VI. First, the careers of all three straddled the turn of the twentieth century, completing the transition from the "classic" theorists of society to the strictly twentieth-century theorists. Second, and more important, all three focused on micro-theory, or the development of the self and personality in society, which has not been a major orientation of this volume so far. But none of the three ignored the larger sociocultural context. In fact, Mead was decidedly evolutionary in much of his theorizing, and Freud spent the last 15 years of his life writing about culture and social structure.

In this section, then, we examine society from the perspective of two early-twentieth-century women, a towering African American scholar and activist, and three men who related the self to society.

Chapter 11

Society and Gender
Gilman and Webb

In the early 1800s, Harriet Martineau wrote about society from both a theoretical and methodological perspective. A generation later, three things were happening in Europe and the United States with regard to women and gender. First, Western women were actively seeking rights that had been denied them, such as property ownership and especially the vote. Second, increasing numbers of women, such as Marianne Weber and Rosa Luxemburg, were theorizing about society. Third, women and some men were writing about gender itself.

We come now to two women, contemporaries of Weber and Luxemburg, who contributed greatly to theories of both society and gender. They both lived in the English-speaking world and knew each other, but they differed in their emphasis on theory versus methods, and in their views of gender. Many of today's gender issues were foreshadowed by Gilman and Webb, but by the mid-twentieth century they had disappeared from the scholarly accounts controlled by male scholars. Only in the last quarter of the twentieth century have they been rediscovered and appreciated.

Charlotte Perkins Gilman (1860–1935)

Charlotte Gilman was born into one of the most famous nineteenth-century U.S. families, the Beechers. Her aunt, Harriet Beecher Stowe, wrote *Uncle Tom's Cabin*, a work that fueled the antislavery movement. The family also included two famous preachers, Henry Ward Beecher and Lyman Beecher, and another woman intellectual, Catherine Beecher. Undoubtedly, this intellectual background fueled her career, but her perspective was also shaped by her own early experiences.

When Charlotte was two years old her father abandoned her mother, "resulting in financial strain for her mother and a lasting sense of rejection in Charlotte" (Deegan and Hill, 1997:1). Gilman described her mother's life as "one of the most painfully thwarted I have ever known." After having a "flood" of admirers, her mother became "a deserted wife," and as the "most passionately domestic of home-worshipping housewives, she was forced to move nineteen times in eighteen years, fourteen of them from one city to another" (Gilman, 1935:8). Charlotte, her mother, and her brother, Thomas, were the Beechers' "poor relations," often "fleeing . . . on account of debt" (1935:9). In a typical nineteenth-century pattern, her brother was sent to Massachusetts Institute of Technology, while Charlotte educated herself for the most part. She initially made a living painting and writing short stories and poetry.

In 1882 Gilman met the painter Charles Walter Stetson, and in 1884 they were married. A year later Katherine was born, and Charlotte hoped that the weakness and depression she attributed to pregnancy would pass, but although the pregnancy was normal enough, Charlotte was "plunged into an extreme of nervous exhaustion which no one observed or understood in the least" (Gilman, 1935:89). What appears to have been a severe case of postpartum depression was inaccurately diagnosed as hysteria, and a specialist recommended a totally domestic life as a cure, warning that she should "never touch pen, brush or pencil" again as long as she lived (1935:96). This was clearly the wrong remedy for Gilman, although the experience did produce a powerful, semiautobiographical story, "The Yellow Wallpaper," in 1890. Several medical men praised this story as the most illuminating description of "nervous prostration," and it changed their treatment of the condition. Gilman noted:

> Identical patterns of depression and anxiety have been observed in fathers and adoptive mothers, negating the idea that it is a maternal hormonal condition. Today there is some acceptance that social pressure on women to drop all outside interests for motherhood is a major factor in emotional breakdowns following childbirth. (quoted in Nies, 1977:134)

Gilman's recovery came when she left her husband and moved to California with her child. She and her husband divorced amicably in 1894, and he married one of her close friends, Grace Channing. Gilman, with no money and in debt, sent her daughter to stay with her father and his new wife, whom Katherine had "known and loved since babyhood" and "loved as another mother" (Gilman, 1935:162). Gilman's willingness to "give up" her child aroused outrage, and she was accused of insanity, for "no normal woman would give up her child." The mythology of fulfillment through motherhood made an accurate diagnosis of Gilman's problem impossible in her own day. It also made her decision incomprehensible to "pure-minded San Franciscans" (1935:167), though her rationale seems eminently logical now. She pointed out that "since the father longed for his child and had a right to some of her society; and since the child had a right to know and love her father," it seemed the right thing to do (1935:163). In her autobiography, she asserted that it had also been the best thing for the child.

After the breakdown Gilman (like Max Weber) suffered from periods of depression and anxiety, or bipolar mood swings. And, like Weber, when she worked, she worked furiously, completing her first major work, *Women and Economics* (1898), in a very short period of time. This book gave her international fame, and she continued to write prolifically, producing sociological texts as well as feminist novels and stories. Gilman used both her novels and her sociology to stress the idea that "a common humanity was the cardinal fact about both sexes," and women are not "undeveloped *men*, but the feminine half of humanity in undeveloped form" (Degler, in Gilman, 1898:xxi, xxiii).

In 1900, Charlotte married G. Houghton Gilman, who gave her freedom, acceptance, and admiration—a combination that freed her to do her work (Lengermann and Niebrugge-Brantley, 1998:111). Throughout her adult life she also experienced an often-thwarted attraction to other women, beginning with Martha Luther in 1881.

In 1890 she wrote to Grace Channing:

> It is awful to be a man inside and not able to marry the woman you love! When Martha married it cracked my heart a good deal—your loss will finish it. . . . I think of you with a great howlin' selfish heartache. I want you—I love you—*I* need you for *myself!* (quoted in Lane, 1990:150)

In a letter to Houghton Gilman, Charlotte referred to her passionate love for Adeline Knapp, and expressed her concern for the scandal such information would cause in the San Francisco papers. At the time Gilman lived, women were not supposed to be "agents," or active on their own behalf; thus, her actions and emotions were anything but conventional (Lengermann and Niebrugge-Brantley, 1998:107).

Gilman was not only unconventional in her loves. She had strong opinions and was able to convey them. "I had plenty to say and the Beecher faculty for saying it." As was true for many feminists at the turn of the century, the more popular she became as a speaker and the more visible her work became, the angrier this made the gender conservatives of her day. Her work lost in popular appeal, she wrote, because the "principal topics were in direct contravention of established views, beliefs and emotions" (Gilman, 1935:304).

Her response was to start her own journal, the *Forerunner*, which she wrote and published from 1909 until 1916, the final issue including the last chapter of her novel *With Her in Ourland* (1916). This novel was a sequel to *Herland* (1915), and is the story of three men who discover an all-female country in which all attributes and roles of women, especially the motherhood role, are held in the highest regard, in which women reproduce without males, and where extreme gender traits are nonexistent. *With Her in Ourland* recounts the visit of one of the male visitors and his Herlander wife, Ellador, to the United States, China, and Japan to observe the devastation produced by World War I. The contrast between Herland and Ourland astonishes Ellador, who proceeds to contrast and comment on the differences that primarily affect women.

Gilman met with public and private censure despite the success of her lectures and books. Her insights were frequently explained away by attributing them to aspects of her personal life. According to Judith Nies (1977:144), Gilman understood that

> in olden times, as a messenger of bad tidings [in this case as a threat to male privilege] she would have been killed. But modern societies have developed

more subtle ways of eliminating their messengers. Fame, then plagiarism and dilution of her ideas, then obscurity was the fate of Charlotte Perkins Gilman.

Gilman's Central Theories and Methods

Important sociological contacts who influenced Gilman's thought included Jane Addams at Hull House in Chicago and the British Fabian socialists George Bernard Shaw and Sidney and Beatrice Webb. Addams and Gilman joined the American Sociological Society (A.S.S.) in 1905, the year it was founded. For a while Gilman worked at Hull House, but she broke with Addams because "my interest," unlike Addams's, "was all humanity, not merely the underside of it; in sociology, not social pathology" (Gilman, 1935:184). Because of her interest in society as a whole, she emphasized the study of normal rather than deviant children (1900), the home more than the orphanage (1903), and marital relations (1898) (Deegan and Hill, 1997:29).

Gilman did not work within the confines of the academic ivory tower, but was recognized as an important thinker by male scholars such as E. A. Ross, an important sociologist at the University of Wisconsin, and Lester Frank Ward, a radical founder of the A.S.S. Ross called her the "most brilliant woman I have ever known." She first met Ward at an 1896 Suffrage Convention in Washington, D.C., although he had written to her previously to praise "the scientific background" in her poem "Similar Cases."

Although Gilman was in touch with British and U.S. socialists, she defined her socialism as of an early humanitarian kind, based on its first, pre-Marxian, exponents. In *With Her in Ourland* her heroine says to her husband that Americans believe in socialism too much, thinking "that every step toward economic health and development has been appropriated by Socialism, and that you cannot do one thing toward economic freedom and progress unless you become a Socialist" (1916:134). Gilman and Addams were both sympathetic to the socialist agenda because it focused on economic conditions and economic solutions. But Gilman never accepted what she called the "narrow and rigid 'economic determinism' of Marx, with its class consciousness and class struggle . . . nor the political methods pursued by Marxians" (Gilman, 1935:131).

Both Addams and Gilman rejected conflict-based methods, emphasizing democracy and education as the mechanisms for liberal social reform. However, as Deegan and Hill put it, "Her 'liberal' agenda frequently involved a radical application of these [socialist] ideals, especially for women" (1997:35). She "envisaged a new society emerging from pragmatism, populism, and nationalism. She proposed institutional modifications in economics, child care, the home, and the marketplace. Democracy and education" are the cornerstones of these changes (1997:44). Thus, she was ideologically a liberal reformer with radical ideas regarding gender. And, like Veblen, she admitted that in some ways she was more of a critic than either a reformer or a radical. Like her novelistic heroine Elladar, Gilman was able to "see the diseases easier than the cures" (Gilman, 1916:151).

In their introduction to *With Her in Ourland*, Deegan and Hill (1997:28) suggest that three major sociological themes animate this work and the earlier work, *Herland*:

1. Assertion of the excellence of women's values and abilities

2. Belief in the biological and evolutionary origin of women's superior attributes

3. A socialist vision of political and social equality between the sexes

As a basis for these themes, they suggest that Gilman was influenced by three theories (Deegan and Hill, 1997:27):

1. The cultural feminism shared by Addams, Ward, and Gilman

2. The reform Darwinism shared by Ward, Geddes, and Gilman

3. The Fabian socialism of Geddes, Addams, Gilman, and the Webbs

To these we would add a fourth:

4. Her functionalist, or cooperative, view of society

From these influences she wove a distinctive theory of feminist reform Darwinism. Her major concerns were society, in particular economics and cooperation, and gender.

Reform Darwinism   In the work of Herbert Spencer and William Graham Sumner (see Chapter 3), **social Darwinism** combined the idea of the survival of the fittest with support for the status quo, individualism, and capitalism. Lester Frank Ward, like Sumner a founder of U.S. sociology, introduced a version of social Darwinism that challenged the Spencer/Sumner view. Ward believed that their interpretation of social evolution was a simple, straightforward apology for the brutality of capitalist competition and selfishness. In his view, if Darwin's ideas are correctly applied they show that cooperation, not competition, is the means for the survival of the higher species (Nies, 1977:139).

Gilman accepted this version, known as **reform Darwinism**, stating that "We, with all life, are under the great law, Evolution." However, she agreed with Ward that care and cooperation are the social characteristics that grow directly from social evolution (Gilman, 1898:42). The organic nature of society produces the "gradual subordination of individual effort for individual good to the collective effort for the collective good" (1898:102). As the functionalists were saying, cooperation for the good of the whole gives rise to social progress. Such progress is achieved not by leaving society alone, but by tackling its ills through social reforms.

In the area of gender relations, however, reform would require a radical overhaul. The heroine in *Ourland* explains to her husband that in Herland she was used to seeing everything cared for. But "your economic philosophy" ignores such care with "that foolish *laissez faire* idea, and your politics," based on self-interest (Gilman, 1916:117). Furthermore, women's economic dependence acts as a drag on social progress because women "obtain their economic goods by securing a male through their individual exertions, all competing freely to this end" (Gilman, 1898:109). The failure of the "sex-relation" to evolve left women leading lives that resembled those "of the savage in the forest." But it need not be so, because women were initially the superior sex (1898:129). Thus, reform Darwinism argued that gender cooperation was required for progress—and progress included what we now call "feminism."

Cultural Feminism   Gilman's **cultural feminism,** arguing that historically women were equal to, if not superior to, men, was also influenced by Ward's thought. Most social evolutionists argued that women are inferior to men in terms of intelligence and physical strength and therefore the great leader and the genius, as well as the great criminal, will all be male. Ward argued instead for historical "gynaecocracy" (rule by women) and "parthenogenesis" (fertilization and reproduction by the female alone).

Ward, like Engels, believed that early society was woman-dominated, and that restricting women had impeded social evolution. His five-stage theory of societal evolution asserted that women were the unchanging trunk of the genealogical tree, whereas men had been grafted on. Ward listed five historical revolutions: (1) from asexuality to sexuality with the appearance of the male sex; (2) the passage of the male from a small fertilizing adjunct to superior size and strength; (3) the consequent societal change from matriarchy to patriarchy; (4) the progression to monogamous mating; and (5) eventually, true gender equality.

Following Ward, Gilman suggested in *Women and Economics* (1898:130) that the evolution of the male was a "long series of practical experiments" to bring him into "equality with the female." Gradually, the male as a mere "reproductive agent" became more equal to the female as he adopted feminine qualities. The female had been temporarily subjected because if the female had retained her "full personal freedom and activity, she would have remained superior to him, and both would have remained stationary" (1898:131–132). But women suffered their period of subjection for the sake of producing "a civilized man," and now "the time has come when neither he nor the world is any longer benefited by her subordination." Women could "become free, economic, social factors," and the "full social combination of individuals in collective industry" would become possible. With this freedom "a union between man and woman such as the world has long dreamed of in vain" would also occur (1898:135, 145).

Socialism   Gilman's cultural feminism and her socialism overlapped. She stated as her main interests the "basic need of economic independence" for women and the "need for more scientific care for young children," both of which "seemed . . . of far more importance than the ballot" (1898:131).[1] Gilman, like Marx, saw work as central to human existence. A woman's confinement to "motherhood" is both a denial of her independence and unfulfilling as a life task. Motherhood, as practiced and promoted, is inefficient, exploitative, and because practiced by amateurs, harmful to children.

Gilman's focus was always on collective activity. She suggested that households and the economy would be more efficient and productive if the majority of women were employed in occupations and houses were redesigned with cooperative kitchens to mass-produce food for individual families. She described

---

[1]Despite this comment, Gilman was active in support of women's suffrage and was the California delegate to the 1896 Suffrage Convention in Washington, D.C. In 1899 she went to England to attend the Quinquennial Congress of the International Council of Women, where she was lionized as the author of *Women and Economics*.

eating as "an individual function" and cooking as "a social function"—and neither "in the faintest degree a family function" (1898:240). In the "early stages of
civilization cooking was done at home, but as society develops its functions spe-
cialize, and the reason why this great race-function of cooking has been so re-
tarded in its natural growth is that the economic dependence of women has
kept them back from their share in human progress" (1898:241).

Gilman did not so much espouse socialism as offer scathing criticisms of
capitalism. In *Ourland*, for example, she observed: "Talk of blood-suckers! You
have oil-suckers and coal-suckers, water-suckers and wood-suckers, railroad-
suckers and farm-suckers—this splendid country is crawling with them—and
has not the intelligence, the energy, to shake them off" (1916:133). "You
people," the heroine Ellador says, "keep quiet and pay three times what is necessary for the right to live." The suckers are "vermin," and the endless labor of
the majority of people represents "long hours of grinding toil for other people's
profit" (1916:103). Ellador tells her husband: "You have got to see that for one
man to rob another man is bad enough; for a man to rob the public is worse;
but to rob the public *through the government* is a kind of high treason which—if
you still punished by torture—would be deserving of the most excruciating
kind" (1916:148).

Functionalism Gilman's book *Human Work* (1904) states her functionalism
most clearly. Society is the whole, and we are the parts. Human existence results only from complex interdependent activities. Reflecting Durkheim's division of labor, Gilman wrote: "Society consists of numbers of interrelated and
highly specialized functions, the functionaries being individual human animals"
(Gilman, 1904, in Lengermann and Niebrugge-Brantley, 1998:143). This statement is consistent with her cooperative evolutionary view.

Another functional element of Gilman's theory is the idea that what sets humans aside from and above the rest of the animal kingdom is mastery of the
food supply. Food, she argued, is central to evolution and to cooperative life,
meaning that for Gilman as for Marx, material needs are primary (Gilman,
1904, in Lengermann and Niebrugge-Brantley, 1998:143).

In summary, then, Gilman's theoretical focus included a cooperative and reform or liberal social Darwinism, a cultural feminism that argued that the genders are equal and in some ways women are superior to men, and the incorporation of certain aspects of functionalist socialist economics.

Nature of Society, Humans, and Change

Gilman did not believe society as it exists is good, but she did believe it possible
to make it so. Her liberal ideology was based on a view of society as cooperative,
evolutionary, and reformable. According to Deegan and Hill (1997:3), "the
chaos and hatred of *Ourland* did not defeat her belief in human nature and social improvement." Her central point was that the "business of mankind was to
carry out the evolution of the human race, according to the laws of nature" but
human beings also added "the conscious direction, the telic force, proper to our
kind—we are the only creatures that can assist evolution" (Gilman, 1898:42).

Gilman's view of human nature cannot be separated from her views on gender. In *Women and Economics* she argued that the public-private distinction made between men and women is neither natural nor healthy. The biological ability to give birth does not define a human being's place in society and, although motherhood is touted as the most fulfilling and natural task for women, it is "not motherhood that keeps the housewife on her feet from dawn till dark; it is house service, not child service" (Gilman, 1898:20).

One of her most interesting discussions of human nature occurred near the beginning of *Ourland* (1916:70), in a conversation between Terry (a macho male) and Ellador:

> Terry was almost delighted by the war. "To make war is human activity." "Are some of the soldiers women?" she inquired. "Women! Of course not! They are men; strong, brave men. Once in a while some abnormal woman becomes a soldier, I believe." "Then why do you call it 'human nature'?" she persisted. "If it was human wouldn't they both do it?" So he tried to explain . . . that it was done by men because they could do it—and women couldn't. "The women are just as indispensable in their way. They give us the children—you know—men cannot do that." . . . Ellador listened. . . . She always seemed to understand not only what one said, but all the background of sentiment and habit behind. "Do you call bearing children 'human nature'?" she asked him. "It's woman's nature," he answered back, "it's her work." "Then why do you not call fighting 'man nature'—instead of human?"

Gilman did not see *society* as good and *human nature* as bad, or vice versa. She saw society as changing and changeable, and human nature as distorted but also changeable. That is, social change is evolutionary, but also requires social reform—sometimes very difficult reform, especially in regard to gender relations. Women, she said, must "make a long jump, from the patriarchal status to the democratic, from the narrowest personal ties to the widest social involvement" (1916:179). Any changes would be products of cooperative human nature, and individualized motherhood must therefore be made into a collectively organized, specialized task. "No one thing could do more to advance the interests of humanity than the wiser care and wider love of organized motherhood around our babies" (Gilman, 1898:194).

Class, Gender, and Race

Gilman's struggle to transcend her own outsider status gave her insights that escaped many other social analysts of her day. Like Max Weber, however, she had both new ideas and blind spots. Her attitudes toward race and class were ambivalent, but her principal focus was gender.

Race and Class   Ellador's husband in *Ourland* tells her that she must be prepared for a shock: "Race and color make all the difference in the world. People dislike and despise one another on exactly that ground—difference in race and color" (1916:97). Ellador then goes on the point out the irrationality of Jim Crow race laws in the United States and the irrationality of ideas of inherent race superiority and inferiority.

However, Deegan and Hill (1997) claim that Gilman was simultaneously racist and antiracist. For example, in "A Suggestion on the Negro Problem" (1908) she maintained that it was the Negroes' inferiority that made exploitation possible. In *With Her in Ourland* Gilman's "racism, anti-Semitism, and ethnocentrism unfortunately surface," and Ellador's solution to the "Jewish problem" was for Jews "to leave off being Jews" (Kessler, 1995:76–77). Lengermann and Niebrugge-Brantley add that the older Gilman got, the more racist she became (1998:112).

As for class, Gilman criticized what she called the "narrow and rigid 'economic determinism' of Marx" and Marxist class analysis (1935:131). She was sympathetic to working-class problems, however, believing in democracy and education as the mechanisms for social reform. Yet when it came to a discussion of poor immigrants, she seemed bigoted (Deegan and Hill, 1997:45).

Gender   Gilman maintained that men and women were born equal and it was "cultural conditions that divide them" (1916:185). She listed the evolutionary, cultural pressures that have produced the excessively sexual and maternal modern woman:

> first, the action of large natural laws, acting on her as they would on any other animal; then the evolution of social customs and laws . . . burned into each generation by the force of education, made lovely by art, holy by religion, desirable by habit; and steadily acting from beneath, the unswerving pressure of economic necessity upon which the whole structure rested. (1898:69)

These cultural conditions are modified somewhat by the fact that every woman "inherits from her father a certain increasing percentage of human development, human power, human tendency; and each boy as well inherits from his mother the increasing percentage of sex-development, sex-power, sex-tendency," thus setting "iron bounds to our absurd effort to make a race with one sex a million years behind the other" (1898:69–70). In other words, a child's upbringing might reduce the gender distinction produced by culture. The persistence of gender differences is explained sociologically, however, by the fact that they are internalized and no longer recognized as either culturally determined or unnecessary.

Gilman's main point was that gender is a social construction, and economic dependence in particular is the critical factor maintaining modern gender inequality. Why, she asked, do mothers refuse help from professional child-rearers when professional specialization has been accepted in virtually every other sphere of modern life? Her answer was that women refuse because a male-centered culture has persuaded her this task is natural. As Ellador's husband put it:

> We men, having all human power in our hands, have used it to warp and check the growth of women. We, by choice and selection, by law and

religion, by enforced ignorance, by heavy overcultivation of sex, have made the kind of woman we so made by nature, that that is what it was to be a woman. (Gilman, 1916:173)

The result of these cultural constructions of gender is an overdevelopment of certain aspects of the female personality and abilities. Her sexual and maternal propensities have been exaggerated while her ability to contribute to the larger community in other ways has atrophied. "Wealth, power, social distinction, fame,—not only these but home and happiness, reputation, ease and pleasure, her bread and butter,—all, must come to her through a small gold ring" (Gilman, 1898:71). The excessive distinctions between the sexes are "disadvantageous to our progress as individuals and as a race" (1898:33).

According to Gilman, women and men are the same in intelligence and in ability to contribute to society, but, even if raised identically, the woman's childbearing function gives her a more positive or life-centered orientation to politics, religion, and other aspects of culture (Kessler, 1995:32). In *The Man-Made World* (1911) Gilman suggested that domestication of women has deprived society of women's qualities of cooperation, peacefulness, and life orientation. Male domination has led to competition and destruction.

The consequences of male domination are also reflected in religion. The morbid elements that Durkheim, for example, noted in Western religion came, according to Gilman, from the domination of men's worldview. Western religions are preoccupied with death largely because they have been almost totally developed by men. Women, who are more in touch with birth and life, would have a more life-oriented approach to religion if they were allowed to participate in what Weber called its "annunciation" or prophecy, and later in its ministry (Gilman, 1923).

Maternal love is the key to the cooperative, harmonious society because the "love of the mother for the child is at the base of all our higher love for one another" (Gilman, 1898:260). The distortion of femininity and motherhood is the fault of a male-dominated society that narrows and restricts women, at the same time blaming them for the ills of the society. As Ellador's husband states, men

have heaped . . . scornful abuse on her, ages and ages of it. . . . And then, as if that was not enough . . . we, in our superior freedom, in our monopoly of education, with the law in our hands, both to make and execute, with every conceivable advantage—we have blamed women for the sins of the world. (Gilman, 1916:173)

In her autobiography, Gilman (1935) stated that by the age of 35 she had learned that only woman as helpless victim could claim respectability; the woman who asserts herself—as in divorcing a husband—loses legitimacy.

Recent feminist literature speaks of "**alpha bias**," meaning that the genders are very different in nature, and "**beta bias**," meaning that virtually all gender differences are produced by culture and society. Gilman's views on gender are clear but mixed. Women and men are the same in intelligence and ability to contribute to society, but, even if raised identically, the woman's childbearing function gives her a more positive or life centered orientation to politics, religion and other aspects of culture.

Other Theories and Theorists

Gilman's relation to Ward's cultural feminism has already been discussed. She was sympathetic with Marx's materialism, but argued for cooperative socialism, rejecting conflict as the primary basis for change, preferring peaceful means that included education and liberal reforms. She rejected the Spencer/Sumner view of evolutionary theory, preferring the reform-based evolution of an organismic or cooperative society. Her view of religion separated her from both Marx and Durkheim, in that she saw its fundamental character as resulting from its having been produced by males.

In another response to Durkheim, Gilman wrote of specialization (Durkheim's division of labor) not just in society as a whole, but between men and women. She found gender specialization extremely unhealthy and unnatural, in that it keeps half the population from contributing to the larger society. She argued that the same functional differentiation that produces specialists in medicine, law, and other institutions is not only positive, but should be extended to many of the tasks that fall to women in the home, such as child rearing and meal preparation. These, too, she believed should be professionalized.

One further theoretical insight links her to Thorstein Veblen. Before he coined the phrase "conspicuous consumption" in his *Theory of the Leisure Class*, Gilman wrote of "the consuming female—priestess of the temple of consumption, who creates a market for all that is luxurious and enervating" or debilitating (1898:120). The resulting ruthless competition among men on women's behalf is not only damaging to those involved but fosters the U.S. male's savage individualism. Thus, both males and females are distorted by a male-dominated capitalist culture.

Critique and Conclusions

Gilman's fictional writings introduced a utopian world in which both men and women were able to experience full personal fulfillment and society became truly "humane." According to Deegan and Hill (1997:44), Gilman "envisioned a new society emerging from pragmatism, populism, and nationalism. She proposed institutional modifications in economics, child care, the home and the marketplace." The primary tools of change for Gilman were "democracy and education." Gilman supported the fight for the vote, but her feminism was less explicitly political and more fully expressed in her social writings, both fiction and nonfiction. She wrote to prompt people to change their behavior (Kessler, 1995:80).

Many of the issues Gilman wrote about remain problems for contemporary society—such as child care, the burden of a double day (or second shift) for employed women, and the enduring violence in society that is often perpetrated on the bodies of women. As a result, Gilman's work still resonates, due in part to her vision of what was possible (Kessler, 1995:81).

Gilman was resolute to the end in her commitment to "humanity." In 1932 she learned that she had cancer and when, in 1935, she could no longer work, she took her own life with chloroform (which she had obtained when first diagnosed with the condition). In her suicide note humanity, rather than her own suffering, was foremost in her mind:

Human life consists in mutual service. No grief, pain, misfortune or "broken heart" is excuse for cutting off one's life while any power of service remains. But when all usefulness is over, when one is assured of unavoidable and imminent death, it is the simplest of human rights to choose a quick and easy death in place of a slow and horrible one. Public opinion is changing on this subject. The time is approaching when we shall consider it abhorrent to our civilization to allow a human being to die in prolonged agony which we should mercifully end in any other creature. (Nies, 1977:145)

We still debate the right to choose to end one's life, just as we still debate many of the societal, economic, and gender issues Gilman raised.

Beatrice Potter Webb (1858–1943)

Beatrice Potter Webb lived through and beyond the conservative, moralistic Victorian era in Britain. She was born the eighth of nine daughters in an upper-middle-class British family, which she described thus: "I belonged to the class of persons who habitually gave orders, but seldom, if ever, executed the orders of other people" (Webb, 1926:37). She saw her father, a railway owner and financier, as a typical Victorian capitalist in his economic and political views, but nonetheless the only man Webb knew "who genuinely believed that women were superior to men, and acted as if he did" (1926:9).

Webb described her mother, Laurencina, as a scholar and a gentlewoman, an ardent student of, among other social theorists, Adam Smith and Thomas Malthus (Webb, 1926:12–13). A French political economist who visited the Potter household described Laurencina as a "female Hellenist" who was also a stylish woman of the world with "nine daughters, two nurses, two governesses, servants in proportion, a large well-appointed house, frequent and numerous visitors; throughout all this, perfect order, never noise or fuss; the machine seemed to move of its own accord. . . . In France we believe too readily that if a woman ceases to be a doll she ceases to be a woman" (Webb, 1926:13, fn.1).

Laurencina Potter was an impressive woman in many ways, but in her daughter's view she was a distant, controlling mother. Beatrice Webb thought her mother seemed to dislike women and felt that her daughters were a disappointment to her. In retrospect she found the absence of affection between herself and her mother "pitiful" because they had the "same tastes . . . and were puzzling over the same problems," and her mother had the same ambitions as her daughter—to be a published author (Webb, 1926:10).

Webb confessed that "conservative by temperament and anti-democratic through social environment," she also reacted against her father's overvaluation of women relative to men" (1926:9). A liberal father, an accomplished mother, and a more than comfortable life while growing up had the paradoxical result that Webb started life as an antifeminist. In 1889, she signed an anti-suffrage manifesto. Webb later described the signature as a "false step," but did not repudiate her stand for 17 years. Even then her change of mind was not on the basis of "abstract rights," but had to do with the situation women found themselves in because of their "special obligations" as women (1873–1924, 3:58). These special obligations were maternity and child care, and it was because the government had begun to intervene in women's special sphere that she decided women had a "positive obligation" to "claim a share in the conduct of political affairs." Consequently, for Webb, suffrage became not an issue of "rights" or an abandonment of women's special maternal roles, but simply a necessity to enable women to fulfill their special obligations more effectively (1873–1924, 3:59). Webb made her waffling on women's suffrage sound more rational than it actually was by claiming that "at the root of my anti-feminism lay the fact that I had never myself suffered the disabilities assumed to arise from my sex" (1926:303).

Webb was educated at home, except for one year spent at a girls' academy. She was a prolific reader and "self-improver" who read philosophical, economic, and theological texts, including the works of Comte and Martineau. Webb had the advantage, by virtue of her class position, of knowing many of the significant British intellectuals of her day—most particularly Herbert Spencer, the "oldest and most intimate friend of the family" (Webb, 1926:19). She learned from Spencer, but later departed from his view of society.

Another important intellectual, as well as working, relationship was with Charles Booth, who was married to her cousin Mary. In 1886 Webb began to help Booth with his inquiry into the life and labor of the London poor. Her theoretical thinking and reading gained focus, however, when she met and married Sidney Webb, a Fabian socialist. She and Sidney were once described by their friend George Bernard Shaw as "two typewriters beating as one." As a team they were both sociologists and political activists, with sociology always intended to inform politics. They often alternated the roles of primary sociological investigator and politically active citizen. They saw the advantage of this division of labor, depending on the issue at hand, in the following way:

> If one partner is predominantly and continuously the scientific investigator, with only a slight and occasional participation in active life, whilst the other partner is more continuously entangled in administration or legislation, with only secondary or intermittent personal work in investigation or research, their incessant intimate discussions may well increase the efficiency and augment the yield of both sides of each other's intellectual activities. (Webb, 1948:17)

Webb's Central Theories and Methods

Beatrice Webb saw herself as a nonideological scientific investigator. Her attention to methods of data collection made it possible for her to believe that a researcher could put "bias out of gear." For example, in her early years, Webb worked for the Charity Organization Society. She eventually found their strict utilitarian approach, combined with a moral condemnation of any "undeserving poor," uncongenial and insufficient in discovering the causes of poverty, or in providing any cure for the multitude of problems that beset the poor. What was required was a scientific examination of the causes and conditions of poverty before any social program could be developed for the alleviation of the condition. Webb's notion of "letting the research speak" is indicative of the early influence on her of Comte's positivism and Spencer's endorsement of science.

It was Spencer who taught her to "look on all social institutions exactly as if they were plants or animals, things that could be observed, classified and explained and the action of which could to some extent be foretold if one knew enough about them" (Webb, 1873–1924, 2:307). After her mother's death Webb read Spencer's *First Principles*, and although she later rejected Spencer's functional individualism, she stated that "the importance of functional adaptation was at the basis of a good deal of the faith in collective regulation I afterwards developed" (1873–1924, 2:307). In a sense Webb "inherited" Spencer after her mother's death, and they remained friends throughout his life, despite her subsequent rejection of much of his sociological perspective, and his rejection of her as his "literary executor."

Socialism, Not Spencerianism   The "anti-democratic and anti-collectivist bias" that had accompanied Webb's early Spencerian convictions underwent a significant change under the influence first of Charles Booth and later of Sidney Webb (Webb, 1926:215–216). Booth's findings from his survey of the London poor suggested that collective solutions, administered by the state, seemed the only logical answer to the alleviation of poverty and other social ills. This socialist conclusion was, of course, in direct opposition to Spencer's laissez-faire capitalism and individualism.

In 1887 Webb was working on an essay, "The Nature of Economic Science," as a result of reading Marx, but abandoned it because she began to doubt the feasibility and "desirability of a water-tight science of political economy"—although the effort did provide illuminating hypotheses for future investigation. The study of Marx and political economy in combination with her study of social pathology in the Booth research, however, did serve to call into question the dogmatic conclusions of her "revered teacher, Herbert Spencer" (Webb, 1926:250).

It is quite possible that the orderliness and comfort of the home in which she was raised, coupled with the appeal of an orderly, centralized state, resulted in her rejection of the conflict-filled, helter-skelter individualism of the capitalist evolutionists around her—including Spencer. In addition, her somewhat typical—for her time—upper-class concern for the "unfortunate" coupled with her view of the importance of an objective, scientific investigation of society, led easily into an endorsement of **Fabian socialism**, a British variant espousing gradual reform of society through government control and mainstream politics.

Methods of Sociological Inquiry   It is often difficult to separate a thinker's theory from ideology. With Webb it is more difficult than in the case of, for example, Marx or Durkheim, because she was primarily a methodologist and secondarily a theorist, who claimed to consciously avoid ideology. As she wrote in 1883, "Certainly the scientific mind seems to me the fairest, the most *purely rational*. The only test it acknowledges is *truth* (in its most literal and perhaps narrowest sense), a demonstrable accordance of idea with fact" (Webb, 1883–1924, 1:91).

In 1886 Webb began working with Booth on his survey of the London poor. It was as a sociological "brain worker," an objective observer of the social scene, that Webb distanced herself from Spencer's individualism and evolutionism and also from the feminist interests and movements of her time. After working with Booth, she undertook an investigation of the factory, in the course of which she did participant observation, taking a job as a trouser hand in one of the workshops. This research demonstrated that Webb's endorsement of science went beyond the lip service that Comte, Spencer, and other nineteenth-century sociologists paid to it.

Her own view of the nature of sociological inquiry and the role of the sociologist is spelled out in the essays appended to *My Apprenticeship* (1926) and in her book with Sydney Webb, *Methods of Social Study* (1932). The three essays in *My Apprenticeship*—"Personal Observation and Statistical Inquiry," "The Method of Interview," and "The Art of Note-Taking"—chart her progress as a methodologist and sociologist. In "Personal Observation and Statistical Inquiry," written in 1887, she noted, like Martineau before her, that observation is "vitiated *if the persons know they are being observed*" (1926:791). She commented that she had learned more about dock laborers as a rent collector than when she toured the docks with officials or visited the dockers' homes as a social investigator.

The "Observation" essay stressed the need to combine observation with statistics: "Statistical enquiry without personal observation lacks all sure foundation; while personal observation unless followed by statistical enquiry leads to no verified conclusion. The two methods are . . . equally essential acts in all scientific investigation of the structure and growth of existing societies" (1926:358). Webb noted later, however, that the essay fell short because of her ignorance at the time of other research methods, especially the need for historical method (1926:248).

In "The Method of Interview," Webb claimed that the interview is the means of scientific investigation "peculiar to the sociologist" and is "compensation for inability to use the chemist's test-tube or the bacteriologist's microscope" (1926:361). Like Martineau, she advised against taking notes during interviews, though as soon as the interview is concluded notes should be made so as not to trust memory "a moment longer than necessary." Above all, Webb stressed the "right manner of behaviour" in conducting an interview. The interview is, she thought, a "particular form of psychoanalysis," and it is easy to inhibit "free communication, or prevent the rise to consciousness of significant facts, by arousing suspicion." Consequently, the interviewer must avoid taking notes, arguing with the subject, or appearing bored, indifferent, or weary (1926:361–362).

The third essay, "The Art of Note-Taking," discussed the inductive method used by the Webbs in their investigations. Beatrice Webb saw note-taking as the sociological equivalent to the use of the blowpipe and balance in chemistry, or the prism and electroscope in physics. Every "fact" ascertained, along with its date and source and the method by which it was obtained, is recorded on a separate card or sheet of paper. The data are always written up in the same manner, allowing for a shuffling and reshuffling of the notes until they generate a "clear, comprehensive and verifiable theory." The process, Webb believed, facilitates building up "one hypothesis and knocking it down in favour of others that had been revealed or verified by a new shuffle of the notes." This "stimulating recreation" means they could "make our order of thought correspond, not with our own presuppositions, but with the order of things discovered by our investigations" (1926:369). Thus, Max Weber's concern with value-free research was reinforced by the Webbs, who stated that the collecting and organizing of facts makes such objectivity possible, if not probable.

In their methodology as well as their commitment to scientific sociological inquiry, the Webbs followed Spencer. Even in their indexing of cards they mirrored the "slips of paper" method that Spencer used to organize the massive notes from his reading. For them, society was a "vast laboratory." Sociologists must not focus on the particular questions that might interest them, but must select a specific social institution "and sit down patiently in front of it, exactly as if it were a form of energy or a kind of matter, the type-specimen of a plant or some species of animal, and go on working steadfastly to acquire all possible information about it" (Webb and Webb, 1932:40). This method of scientific inquiry, they noted, only provides knowledge of how things happen; it cannot "settle what *ought* to happen."

The "ought" depends on human values, which Beatrice Webb suggested varied by race, generation, and individual (1926:294–295). Scientific investigation of social conditions could provide the facts that, in turn, could be the means for social change, but the sociologist as scientific observer could not set out the social goals the scientific findings suggest. Science does not and could not yield the purpose of life (1926:123).

Webb's primary commitment was to social research—the "endless questioning of the nature of things, and more especially of the nature of the queer animal, man, and of the laws which force him outside, heaven knows where to" (1873–1924, 1:121–122). She characterized her partnership with Sidney as an "indissoluble combination of two strong and persistent aims." They were both scientists and socialists with a "perpetual curiosity to know all that could be known about the nature and working of the universe, animate as well as inanimate, psychical as well as material, in the belief that only by means of such knowledge could mankind achieve an ever-increasing control of the forces amid which it lived" (1948:16). It was their nonmilitant socialism, stressing societal order, that governed their view of the nature of society, human beings, and social change.

Nature of Society, Humans, and Change

For Beatrice Webb, human society and individuals were changeable—they could be reformed. She was optimistic that things could be improved, and neither society nor human beings were hopelessly corrupt. She perceived society as a "vast laboratory" in which "experiments in human relationships, conscious or unconscious, . . . are continuously being carried on" and believed that those "races" will survive and prosper who, through scientific social investigations, inquire into "how things happen." In fact, the Webbs' liberal optimism allowed them to speak of the idealist as crucial to any planning for social change.

We learn most about Beatrice Webb's view of society from her orientation toward change. In her view, change is possible and desirable, but any active intervention in promoting change needs to be based on a scientific assessment of conditions and institutions, and a commitment to promoting the "progress of mankind to even higher levels of individual distinction and communal welfare" (1948:17). Although scientific assessment could provide the facts necessary to plan for social change, the sociologist could not set out the goals that such findings suggest.

According to Webb, a three-part division of labor must be applied to the pursuit of social change:

1. *Scientist*: The sociologist provides the "facts," employing "patient methods of observation, generalisation and verification" to discover the way in which a "given end can be obtained" (1948:263).

2. *Politician*: The "man of affairs" brings a "knowledge of and capacity to control men" to the situation and chooses the process to bring about the desired ends.

3. *Idealist*: Both the sociologist and the politician are relatively useless without someone who formulates the desired ends or goals to be attained. These desired ends may emerge from metaphysics, religion, inner consciousness, or communion with a "higher and nobler life than that of common humanity" (1948:263–264).

Like many of their sociological precursors, the Webbs genuinely believed that progress is possible, but that it must be planned in accordance with reality— with the "facts"—and governed by ideals.

The separation of the roles of sociologist, political activist, and idealist was often modified in practice in the Webbs' own research and political activities. Beatrice Webb described their sociological work as separate from their "practical citizenship," although she conceded that their sociological work tended to confirm the positions they took as socialists. However, she also maintained that although their sociological work and active participation in the very institutions they investigated might call into question their objectivity, this was controlled by the nature of the partnership, with one partner as activist and the other as researcher.

Class, Gender, and Race

Class   Beatrice Webb's position on social class was complex. With her marriage to Sidney she crossed class lines. Sidney Webb's father was an accountant and his mother a shopkeeper, and his own formal schooling ended at age 15, though he continued with evening classes until he passed the Civil Service Examination. The marriage was a minor scandal in Beatrice's family and among some of her friends, because of the class difference and, more important, because Sidney Webb was a well-known socialist and one of the leaders of the Fabian Society.

Despite the marriage, Beatrice Webb never shed her sense of class superiority. When asked whether she ever felt shy about her public appearances, she was reported to have responded, "If I ever felt inclined to be scared going into a room full of people I would say to myself, 'You're the cleverest member of one of the cleverest families in the cleverest class of the cleverest nation of the world, so what have you got to be frightened of?'" (Shannon, in Webb, 1898:xiii–xiv).

Although Webb retained a sense of personal superiority that was the result of her privileged socialization, she was also conscious of the problems class privilege produced. Not the least of such problems were the "benevolent" philanthropic activities of the privileged that produced little benefit for the under-privileged but did give the privileged—as Marx had noted—feelings of "pharisaical self-congratulation" (Webb, 1948:85). It was this clear perception of the nature of class privilege that made Fabian socialism attractive to Beatrice Webb. The Fabian program of social investigation involved the gradual, controlled implementation of reforms through the socialist's involvement in government institutions and political parties. The transformations of society on behalf of the underprivileged could therefore be accomplished without any radical or revolutionary upsets, and with such changes the need for philanthropy would disappear. The key to the Fabian socialist program, according to Webb, was the inevitability of gradualness.

Webb worked consistently to improve working-class social conditions, but assumed that the cooperation of workers in such improvement was imperative. "The more of the national wealth we can divert from the rich to the regular out-goings of the poorest class—*so long as it is accompanied by the increase in personal responsibility on the part of these benefited classes*—the wholesomer for the state" (Webb, 1948:141). The Webbs staked their "hopes on the organised working-class, served and guided, it is true, by an *elite* of unassuming experts who would make no claim to superior social status, but would content themselves with exercising the power inherent in superior knowledge and longer administrative experience" (Webb, 1948:97).

Webb's confidence in the transformation of society, especially the transformation of the working class, was largely a confidence in working-class men. When Webb was investigating the Co-operative Movement, she met a number of its male working-class leaders and recorded this comment in her diary:

> The working man has still the 18th century idea of a wife for the relief of physical nature, for the bearing of children, and the ministering to his personal comforts. Suddenly he is introduced to the 19th century woman with her masculine interests and her womanly charm—womanly charm cultivated by her as an instrument of power in public life—in the movement of the masses—not as a means of satisfying personal vanity, and love of admiration. (Webb, 1873–1924, 1:281)

Despite this condescending view, Beatrice Webb was aware of the particular problems working-class women faced by being forced to balance wage work and domestic labor. Webb maintained that middle-class women require an end to restrictions on their entry into the professions, but working-class women need protective legislation to prevent their exploitation.

During World War I Webb was appointed to a War Cabinet Committee on Women in Industry that was set up to investigate the question of equal pay. Webb produced a Minority Report that advocated uniform rates regardless of which sex undertook the work. In summary, Webb pointed out that

> for the production of commodities and services, women no more constitute a class than do persons of a particular creed or race; and the time has come for the removal of all sex exclusions; for the opening of all posts and vocations to any individuals who are qualified for the work, irrespective of sex, creed or race. (1919:71)

Gender   In relating work to gender, Webb argued that nondiscrimination in the workplace is essential. In addition, she recommended that because of women's maternal responsibilities there should be a separate investigation into the public provision for maternity and childhood (Webb, 1919).

The Webbs, along with Fabian colleagues such as G. B. Shaw, endorsed motherhood as the primary role for women. For Webb, the solution to the "woman question" was not complete equality and freedom. For women to compete with men meant that many would forego motherhood or would be severely incapacitated for childbearing, and this would not benefit society. To Webb it was enough that half the population strained to compete for wealth and power; what was also needed was someone to "watch and pray, who will observe and inspire, and . . . guard and love all who are weak, unfit or distressed" (1873–1924, 1:53). Men have a special service as producers; women have a special service as "servants of the community, creators of something more precious than commodities, creators of the nation's children." The answer to the woman question was the "endowment of motherhood," making the bearing and rearing of children into an "art through the elaboration of science" (1873–1924, 1:53).

Webb recognized that she herself did not fit the natural maternal image that she promoted as the best role for women. She believed in the holiness of motherhood and in its superiority over any other occupation, and stated that if she had been younger when she married she would have chosen motherhood over a "brainworking profession."[2] She believed that women's intellectual contributions were usually "small and the ideas thin and wire-drawn from lack of matter and wide experience," and that educating women was unlikely to provide that "fullness of intellectual life which distinguishes the really able man" (1873–1924, 1:52). Webb justified her own role as a "brain worker" by arguing that the objectivity she was able to bring to bear in her sociological work depended on her denial of her female nature. As she claimed, the only way in which women could convince the world of their power was to show it. To do that, she suggested, "it will be needful for women with strong natures to remain celibate, so that the special force of womanhood, motherly feeling, may be forced into public work" (1873–1924, 1:214). Webb concluded, at the time of her marriage, that having been transformed into a thinker, it would be a mistake to throw

---

[2]This idyllic view of the maternal role was clearly class-based, having little relevance, as she recognized later, to working-class women.

away the result and, furthermore, the books and reports that she and Sidney produced were like the children she never had (1873–1924, 1:359).

In 1906 Webb wrote to Millicent Fawcett, the leader of the constitutional movement for women's suffrage, that she no longer objected to the idea of granting the electoral franchise to "women as women, whether married or single, propertied or wage-earning" (1948:363). She indicated that her endorsement of women's suffrage was occasioned by the fact that "women suffragists were being battered about rather badly, and coarse-grained men were saying coarse-grained things." So she felt she should "give a friendly pull to get things out of the mud, even at the risk of getting a little spattered myself" (1873–1924, 3:57).

Even when she endorsed the vote for women, she did not alter her view that women were constitutionally different from men and had different roles to perform in society. When women were enfranchised in June 1918, she noted in her diary that it was an "outstanding event," but that it held "no glamour" for her, as she was "wholly indifferent to" her own political enfranchisement. However, she did suggest that the "coming of the Labour Party as a political force" was largely the consequence of extending the franchise to women (1873–1924, 3:308–309).

Race   Like Gilman, Webb's comments on race are not systematically presented, and she could also be said to have been both antiracist and racist, depending on the cultural context. Webb regarded Europeans as a whole as a progressive "race" and commented that when she thought of the "future man" she forecast an "impersonality . . . perpetually disentangling the material circumstances of the universe by intellectual processes, and, by his emotional will, casting out all other feelings, all other sensations other than that of all-embracing beneficence" (1948, 2:242). Her comments about American blacks, native Hawaiians, and others in her *American Diary* (1898) reinforce the idea, however, that the "future man" she referred to was European.

On the Webbs' visit to Howard University in 1898, she recorded her impressions of the student body: "They were all so anxious to learn their lessons, so docile and modest, so naively anxious not to be physically repulsive,—in a word so painfully conscious of their inferiority of race" (Webb, 1898:39). The Webbs were not impressed by Howard University and described it as a "seedy survival; old-fashioned in its educational methods . . . and very inferior in staff and equipment" (1898:38–39).

In Honolulu she remarked that it would be interesting to study the characteristics of the three races—Hawaiians, Chinese, and Japanese—and she recorded the following impressions:

> The Hawaiians and the Chinese are amazingly complementary in characteristics: the Hawaiians sympathetic, musical, intensely amorous and incurably idle; the Chinese deliberate, silent, uncannily industrious, cautious in self-indulgence, careful of their families, and intensely acquisitive, but apparently without imagination and completely absorbed in routine and mechanical work for profit. (1898:160)

The Chinese were compared to Jews as "resembling each other in combining a low standard of life with ambition and persistent industry," and the Japanese, although "more intelligent and versatile," still had "objectionable notions as to leisure and a quite intolerable personal independence" (1898:160).

Beatrice Webb's comments on various peoples were not unusual for that time period, and certainly not for individuals of her class background. Nonetheless, one is surprised that such comments emerged from a professed socialist and self-professed objective social scientist.

Other Theories and Theorists

You will recall that Beatrice Webb was indebted to Spencer's evolutionism, but rejected his competitive view. For both Beatrice Webb and W. G. Sumner, the vision of evolution toward a more orderly and civilized society, charted by scientific sociology, was key, though they took very different directions in pursuit of this goal. Sumner (in Webb, 1898:60) remarked that "it is the greatest folly of which a man can be capable, to sit down with a slate and pencil to plan out a new social world." But that is precisely what the Webbs attempted to do.

Beatrice Webb accepted Marx's emphasis on change toward socialism, but believed—as did Gilman—that it could be brought about by legislative means. Her socialism was of the cooperative kind, and involved trade unions, not Marx's conflict-based revolution or Lenin's power-based centralization. Finally, like Weber, she believed that objective science and committed citizenship could be separated, and that science could help in avoiding bias.

Critique and Conclusions

The Webbs have been criticized for proposing a rather mechanical, unfeeling, ordered world (Bell, 1962:26). One of the Webb's contemporaries, H. G. Wells, who at one time was a friend as well as a Fabian, drew an unflattering portrait in his novel *The New Machiavelli* (1911). One of his characters, Altiora Bailey, was modeled on Beatrice Webb, and Altiora's husband on Sidney Webb. Wells wrote that Altiora's "soul was bony," and that if Altiora and her husband

> had the universe in hand, I know they would take down all the trees and put up stamped green shades and sunlight accumulators. . . . [Their world was] an organized state as confident and powerful as modern science, as balanced and beautiful as a body, as beneficent as sunshine. . . . Individualism . . . meant muddle, meant a crowd of separate undisciplined little people all obstinately and ignorantly doing things jarringly each one in his own way. (Wells, 1911:56–57)

The state envisaged by the Baileys (Webbs) was an "organized state" that would "end muddle forever." Wells's portrait of the Webbs' personalities was somewhat malicious, but he characterized them in a fashion they might have found acceptable—that is, as believing that society could run as smoothly as the household in which Beatrice had been raised.

The Webbs' commitment to a Fabian collectivist orientation made only a minor contribution to socialist thinking. They focused on the cooperative movement and on the kind of government control and planning needed to guarantee a decent life for the underprivileged. However, Beatrice's insights into methodology, especially those involving data collection, were considerable, and have lasted.

Finally, Webb's position on gender was complex, but reflected the "faces of feminism" at the turn of the century (Banks, 1981). It straddled two eras—nineteenth-century Victorian England, with its emphasis on women's unique contribution, and the more complex and diverse ideas about women that were emerging at the turn of the twentieth century. Webb condemned the existing situation of women, especially working-class women, but at the same time endorsed an idealized maternal role as women's natural contribution to the collective welfare of the society. Webb could not reconcile women's personal needs and abilities with society's preference for "self-sacrificing wives and mothers" (Caine, 1982:37). To a large extent it was Webb's construction of herself as an independent "brain worker" that impeded her feminist identification. In that role, she was obviously not a maternal woman as she had defined the ideal.

Final Thoughts

Charlotte Gilman and Beatrice Webb had several things in common. Both had a commitment to sociological research as a necessary part of social progress, both were interested in socialism, and also in gender issues. There the similarities end.

Webb was a committed socialist reformer; Gilman moved between radical and liberal reform ideas. For example, Gilman did not favor trade unions, believing that they more often sided with the elite to the disadvantage of the poor and unskilled. Webb, however, saw trade unions as an essential part of a remade socialist society.

Their backgrounds were radically different. Gilman, as a poor relation and then a single mother with few occupational skills or resources, saw firsthand the disadvantages experienced by the majority of women in a male-dominated society. Webb's privileged background meant that although she came to understand the problems faced by women, especially working-class women, her understanding came from the outside, mostly from her sociological research.

They were both good, readable writers, but because Gilman's feminist views made publication a problem at times, she started her own journal. Webb, however, found that in her experience women often had an advantage in conducting social research, as they aroused less suspicion than men, and thus gained better information. In addition, she observed that the female writer on economic questions had a "scarcity value" and was often paid more and published more readily than her male counterparts (Webb, 1948:303–304).

Gilman met the Webbs in 1896 at the International Socialist and Labour Congress and was later invited to visit them at their country retreat. She was there at the same time as George Bernard Shaw, with whom she recorded she had "some talk . . . on literary work. Very good and useful criticism" (Gilman, 1935:203). It seemed from Gilman's account of the visit that the Webbs' interest in her was on account of her first book of poems, and Gilman read some of the poems to the various visitors gathered at the Webbs' that weekend. Gilman recorded that after hearing the poems, Beatrice Webb remarked, "You will do critical work but you will never be able to do original work." Gilman interpreted this to mean that "original" meant "research work, and critical was pointing out what was the matter with society, no matter how original the analysis," which—in keeping with Webb's estimation—was indeed Gilman's primary strength (Gilman, 1935:204).

The most important difference between the two was in their views on gender. Gilman emphasized the similarities between men and women and predicted that in a future society the similarities would be seen as much greater than the differences. Society, she believed, was greatly damaged by the loss of the homebound woman's political and economic abilities. With a restructuring of society—especially a restructuring of daily physical household needs, a redesign of homes, and a change in educational practices—women could be both mothers and economically productive citizens.

Webb, on the other hand, saw motherhood as women's innate and primary role. For Webb, society would be damaged if too many women chose to be "brain workers" instead of mothers. Although she advocated changes in working conditions and benefits for women and was one of the architects of the British social welfare system, the greatest contribution women could make to the collective welfare was, in her view, their maternal devotion to children and their inspiration and support of their husbands. By today's standards, Gilman would be considered a feminist, while Webb, who lived a feminist public role, would not.

References

Banks, Olive. 1981. *Faces of Feminism*. Oxford: Martin Robertson.

Bell, Daniel. 1962. *The End of Ideology: On the Exhaustion of Political Ideas in the Fifties*. New York: Free Press.

Broschart, K. R. 1991. "Beatrice Webb (1858–1943)." In Mary Jo Deegan (Ed.), *Women in Sociology* (pp. 425–431). New York: Greenwood.

Caine, Barbara. 1982. "Beatrice Webb and the 'Woman Question.'" *History Workshop Journal, 14*, 295–319.

Deegan, Mary Jo, and Michael R. Hill (Eds.). 1997. "Introduction." In Charlotte Perkins Gilman, *With Her in Ourland: Sequel to Herland* Westport, CT: Praeger.

Degler, Carl (Ed.). 1966. "Introduction." In Charlotte Perkins Gilman, *Women and Economics*. New York: Harper & Row.

Gilman, Charlotte Perkins. 1890/1980. *The Yellow Wallpaper and Other Fiction*. (Ann J. Lane, Ed.). New York: Pantheon Books.

———.1898/1966. *Women and Economics* (Carl Degler, Ed.). New York: Harper & Row.

———. 1900. *Concerning Children*. Boston: Small, Maynard & Co.

———. 1903/1972. *The Home*. Urbana: University of Illinois Press.

———. 1904. *Human Work*. New York: McClure and Phillips.

———. 1908. "A Suggestion on the Negro Problem." *American Journal of Sociology, 14*, 78–85.

———. 1909–1916. *The Forerunner: A Journal.*

———. 1911. *The Man-Made World, or Our Androcentric Culture.* London: T. Fisher Unwin.

———. 1915/1979. *Herland.* New York: Pantheon.

———. 1916/1997. *With Her in Ourland: Sequel to Herland* (Mary Jo Deegan and Michael R. Hill, Eds.). Westport, CT: Praeger.

———. 1923. *His Religion and Hers: A Study of the Faith of Our Fathers and the Work of Our Mothers.* New York: Century.

———. 1935. *The Living of Charlotte Perkins Gilman: An Autobiography.* New York: D. Appleton-Century.

Kessler, Carol Farley. 1995. *Charlotte Perkins Gilman: Her Progress Towards Utopia With Selected Writings.* New York: Syracuse University Press.

Lane, Ann J. 1990. *To Herland and Beyond: The Life and Work of Charlotte Perkins Gilman.* New York: Pantheon.

Lengermann, Patricia Madoo, and Jill Niebrugge-Brantley. 1998. *The Women Founders: Sociology and Social Theory, 1830–1930.* New York: McGraw-Hill.

Nies, Judith. 1977. *Seven Women: Portraits from the American Radical Tradition.* New York: The Viking Press.

Sumner, William Graham. 1963. *Social Darwinism: Selected Essays* (Stow Persons, Ed.). Englewood Cliffs, NJ: Prentice-Hall.

Sydie, Rosalind A. 1996. "Beatrice Webb: Feminism and Sociology." Paper presented at the Conference of the Research Committee on the History of Sociology, International Sociological Association, Amsterdam.

Webb, Beatrice. 1873–1924/1982–1985. *The Diary of Beatrice Webb* (4 vols.) (Norman and Jeanne MacKenzie, Eds.). Cambridge, MA: Belknap Press.

———. 1898/1962. *An American Diary.* (David A. Shannon, Ed.). Madison: University of Wisconsin Press.

———. 1919/1978. *The Wages of Men and Women: Should They Be Equal?* Ann Arbor, MI: University Microfilms International.

———. 1926/1950. *My Apprenticeship.* London: Longmans, Green and Company.

———. 1948. *Our Partnership* (Barbara Drake and Margaret Cole, Eds.). London: Longmans, Green, and Company.

Webb, Beatrice, and Sidney Webb. 1932. *Methods of Social Study.* London: Longmans, Green and Company.

Webb, Sidney. 1889/1967. "Historic." In G. Bernard Shaw (Ed.), *Fabian Essays on Socialism* (pp. 46–88). Garden City, NY: Doubleday.

Wells, H. G. 1911. *The New Machiavelli.* London: Longmans.

Chapter 12

Sociological Theory and Race
W. E. B. Du Bois

W. E. Burghardt Du Bois was a social theorist, a researcher, a journalist, a college professor, a novelist, an activist—and a poet:

> Wild is the world and witless, terrible in its beauty and crime. Can one forget sunrise on Lake Baikal, the gray oaks of Nara, the hills of light of Manhattan? Who may not remember the lynching of Mary Brown, the suicides of bankers in 1929, and the cripples crawling out of Guadalcanal, Aachen, and Leyte? Behold the starving children of Europe, Asia, and Africa. Such a world, with all its contradictions, can be saved, can yet be born again; but not out of capital, interest, property, and gold, rather out of dreams and loiterings, out of simple goodness and friendship and love, out of science and missions. (Du Bois, 1945:142)

Du Bois lived 95 years (1868–1963), beginning to write while Karl Marx was alive, and still writing on the eve of Martin Luther King's march on Washington. Hardly a typical African American, Du Bois nonetheless embodied and expressed the struggle of black Americans from post–Civil War Reconstruction to the Civil Rights Act.

The currents that played upon Du Bois's life were those affecting other African Americans. He often swam upstream against both political and scholarly opinion. There was the blame laid upon African Americans for the supposed failure of Reconstruction. This he confronted in a major revisionist history book, written in 1935. There were the mistreatment and lynchings of blacks, in order to "keep them in their place." There was their movement from South to North seeking work in cities such as Philadelphia, which Du Bois studied in 1899. There was his continual disagreement with Booker T. Washington, who was popular in white society, regarding whether, as Du Bois believed, African Americans should be encouraged to seek higher education or, as Washington argued, should be "taught a trade."

Other currents were affecting most of humanity during Du Bois's lifetime. Challenges to industrial capitalism from Marxism, communist Russia, and other manifestations of socialism increasingly appealed to Du Bois. There were the sufferings of the colonial world, a world with which he identified strongly, and in which he settled at the end of his life. Finally, there were two major wars, led by the supposedly civilized nations of Europe, but engulfing much of the colonial world as well. Du Bois made trenchant observations on these issues, in the process of bringing a new perspective to social theory.

W. E. B. Du Bois (1868–1963)

W. E. Burghardt Du Bois was born in Great Barrington, Massachusetts, in 1868. On his mother's side his ancestors were Dutch and African, and on his father's side French Huguenot and African; he was two generations removed from the African ancestor on each side. In *Darkwater* (1920), he described himself as having "a flood of Negro blood, a strain of French, a bit of Dutch, but, thank God! no 'Anglo-Saxon'" (Du Bois, 1920:488).

Du Bois received a B.A. from Fisk University in Nashville, Tennessee, in 1888, having been turned down by Harvard. Coming from Massachusetts, it was the years at Fisk and summers teaching in rural Tennessee that introduced him to the black South and made it possible for him to write *The Souls of Black Folk* in 1903 (Sundquist, 1996:9). Between 1888 and 1895 he completed another B.A. and a Ph.D. at Harvard, during which time he spent two years at the University of Berlin, attending lectures by Max Weber and becoming friends with both Max and Marianne (Farganis, 1996:181).

Between 1894 and 1910 he taught at Wilberforce College, the University of Pennsylvania, and Atlanta University, where he was Professor of Economics and History for 14 years. His first switch from academia to journalism came in 1910, when Du Bois helped to found the National Association for the Advancement of Colored People (NAACP) and became editor of its journal, *Crisis*. In 1934 a disagreement with the NAACP over assimilation/separation (discussed below) caused him to leave and return to Atlanta University, where from the age of 66 to 76 he was chair of the Sociology Department. For the last four years of those years (1940–1944) he was also editor of the social science journal *Phylon*. Near the end of his life, discouraged with continuing discrimination against African Americans in the United States, Du Bois moved to Ghana—a recently independent West African nation then under the leadership of his friend Kwame Nkrumah.

Du Bois has been called one of America's greatest intellectuals. Moreover, his intellectualism was rare in that he "was truly a world figure, at home in Western antiquity, in the Germany of Goethe, and in the African village"—and, we might add, in Soviet Russia (Weinberg, 1970:xvi). Du Bois was proud of his Western education, and he wrote of his comfort with Aristotle, Shakespeare, and Alexander Dumas. He also felt that he understood African Americans, and believed that in *The Souls of Black Folk* (1903) he had written the biography of an entire people.

However, Du Bois also recognized in his personal history the possibility of the factor we would call luck or circumstance:

> *Suppose* my good mother had preferred a steady income from my child labor rather than bank on the precarious dividend of my higher training? *Suppose* that pompous old village judge, whose dignity we often ruffled and whose apples we stole, had had his way and sent me while a child to a "reform" school to learn a "trade"? *Suppose* Principal Hosmer had been born with no faith in "darkies," and instead of giving me Greek and Latin had taught me carpentry and the making of tin pans? *Suppose* I had missed a Harvard scholarship? *Suppose* the Slater Board had then, as now, distinct ideas as to where the education of Negroes should stop? Suppose *and* suppose! As I sat down calmly on flat earth and looked at my life a certain great fear seized me. Was I the masterful captain or the pawn of laughing sprites? . . . Even with these thoughts, I did not hesitate or waver; but just went doggedly to work, and therein lay whatever salvation I have achieved. (Du Bois, 1920:491–492)

Thus, while admitting his determination and hard work, Du Bois also recognized the favorable choices that had been made for him, from those by his mother to the admissions committee at Harvard.

Du Bois was clearly a man of many talents; yet always he was outside the white establishment, looking in. How did he cope? As a boy, he coped by winning—at exam time or in a footrace. As he matured, he wrote, "all I knew is that 'they' shall not keep their prizes. But how should I wrest them away? I could never decide: by reading law, by healing the sick, by telling the wonderful tales that swam in my head. . . . Why did God make me an outcast in mine own house?" (Du Bois, 1903:102). And so Du Bois worked and struggled at bridging the gap between white culture and black society.

Throughout his long life, Du Bois wrote historically, analytically, and critically, and he theorized about many aspects of society, not only about race. It is to his theoretical insights that we now turn.

Du Bois's Central Theories and Methods

Two major themes of Du Bois's work were race and class, to be discussed in a later section of this chapter. Here we will focus on four other themes: (1) political economy, including capitalism, socialism, and communism; (2) imperialism, colonialism, and war; (3) social organization and culture; and (4) leadership and power.

Capitalism, Socialism, and Communism   Du Bois's analysis of capitalism began with the period known as Reconstruction after the U.S. Civil War. The war left the North with many important elements of capitalism already in place:

> After the war, industry in the North found itself with a vast organization for production, new supplies of raw material, a growing transportation system

on land and water, and a new technical knowledge of processes. All this, with the exclusion of foreign competition through a system of import taxes, and a vast immigration of laborers, tremendously stimulated the production of goods and available services. (Du Bois, 1935a:581)

The key question after the war became, "In whose hands would lie the power which capitalist ownership gave?" Certainly not in the hands of labor or its trustees; rather "the new plan was to concentrate into a trusteeship of capital a new and far-reaching power which would dominate the government of the United States." **Super-capital**, or economic and political control by big business, developed during the 1870s in the United States. This resulted, according to Du Bois, in the failure of real democracy in the South and its perversion in the North (1935a:581, 583, 584). Du Bois's insights about post–Civil War capitalism could be applied to the capitalist world as a whole.

But had super-capitalism not done good in the world? Du Bois's answer was "There are more merchants today, surer deliveries, and wider well-being, but are there not, also, bigger thieves, deeper injustice, and more calloused selfishness instead of [concern for general] well-being?" (Du Bois, 1917:311).

Despite these anticapitalist sentiments, Du Bois sought in his first 50 years of life to try to foster the possibilities for social justice within the capitalist world— a liberal approach. However, by the end of World War I his interest in Marxism and in Lenin's Russia had begun to grow. Du Bois defined **socialism** as "a disciplined economy and political organization to which the first duty of the citizen is to serve the state; and the state is not a selected aristocracy, or a group of self-seeking oligarchs who have seized wealth and power" (Du Bois, 1958:665). The state, Du Bois continued, was "workers with hand and brain."

However, his early interest in socialism and communism did not translate into wholehearted support. Du Bois pointed out in 1931 that American communists, largely immigrants, employed an inapplicable imported Marxism that blamed American Negroes for their own situation (Du Bois, 1931b:407). And in his 1940 autobiography he stated unequivocally: "I was not and am not a Communist. I do not believe in the dogma of inevitable revolution in order to right economic wrong" (Du Bois, 1940:302). A year later, as his Marxist sympathies increased, he made the following comment, pointing out that neither communism nor capitalism should take for granted the support of the world's "colored" peoples:

> For the time being, we shall judge every nation strictly on the merits of the attitude of that nation towards our national aspirations. We have every cause to be grateful to the Communists for their active interest in the fate of colonial peoples and for their constant denunciation of the evils of imperialism. It is then left to the so-called "free" nations to convince us that they are more concerned about our welfare than the Communists, and in this regard we believe more in action than in mere words. (Du Bois, 1946:280)

By the time Du Bois reached 90 years of age he was predicting (as Schumpeter had done) that capitalism was doomed. Speaking to the emerging African nations, he said: "You can choose between groups of political union; you cannot choose between socialism and private capitalism because private capitalism is doomed!" (Du Bois, 1958:665). Nearing the end of his life, at age 93, despite his personal move toward communism, he addressed himself once more to African Americans: "It is not that I would persuade Negroes to become communists, capitalists, or holy rollers, but whatever belief they reach, let it for God's sake be a matter of reason and not of ignorance, fear, and selling their souls to the Devil" (Du Bois, 1961, in 1946/1965:338)

Imperialism, Colonialism, and War   Du Bois's contributions to the theory of capitalism were linked to his discussions of imperialism, colonialism, and war. In part, Du Bois's view of **imperialism** was similar to that of Lenin, especially with respect to the making of enormous profits by exporting surplus capital to the undeveloped countries (Lenin, 1916; Du Bois, 1945:46). But what Europe— or rather a small portion of Europe—wants from Africa, according to Du Bois, is not the exporting of capital; it is "the raw materials—ivory, diamonds, copper and rubber in which the land abounds, and even more do they covet cheap labor to mine and produce these things" (Du Bois, 1943:654). In addition, Du Bois recognized the advantages of imperialism in opening markets for the products produced by the imperial power. So, to Du Bois, imperialism provides opportunities for investment, raw materials, cheap labor, and markets.

It is impossible to discuss Du Bois's concept of imperialism without also talking about colonialism. Du Bois noted that political domination by Britain, France, Portugal, and Germany yields only small returns through colonial taxation, and is often costly to the citizens of the imperial power. However, "this governmental investment and its concomitant political control have been the basis upon which private investors have built their private empires" (Du Bois, 1943:656). So, capitalists dominate both the imperial power and its colonies. The colonies themselves, Du Bois wrote in 1945, are "the slums of the world. They are . . . centers of helplessness, of discouragement of initiative, of forced labor, and of legal suppression of all activities or thoughts which the master country fears or dislikes" (1945:17).

The imperial powers at first justified or rationalized colonialism, Du Bois noted, by sending missionaries to save souls. However, missionary work interfered "with profit and investment and soon was changed by the new science to a doctrine of natural human inferiority on the part of the majority of mankind, making them forever inferior and subservient to the ruling nations of the world" (1945:45). In a 1923 statement, white settlers in Kenya had claimed: "The controlling powers may . . . aim at advancing the black race as far along the road of progress as its capacity allows, without misgivings that the success of their endeavors will lead to a demand for their withdrawal, entailing loss of prestige and trade" (Du Bois, 1943:662).[1] Thus, the colonial argument was that Africans are inferior, hence justifiably treated as such.

---

[1] The notion of limited capacity did not die out with political colonialism. Several years after Uganda gained independence in the early 1960s, I heard ex-colonials speak of the inability of a black dental surgeon to understand what he was doing. His work was, according to these whites, a matter of rote or "cookbook" learning.

Another aspect of colonialism that Du Bois wrote about was the principle of "divide and conquer." Marx had spoken of the way in which capitalists try to keep the working classes at each other's throats. Du Bois noted that the same is true in the colonies: Moslems and Hindus are encouraged in their animosities, as are Arabs and Jews, and even Protestants and Catholics (Du Bois, 1945:109). He did not suggest that colonialism produces such antagonisms, only that the imperial powers take advantage of the existing divisions.

Central to imperialist capitalism, according to Du Bois, is war. Recalling Veblen's views on sabotage and the destruction of resources, Du Bois during World War I commented on the horror of a situation where "under equal conditions, equal armament, and equal waste of wealth, white men are fighting white men with surgeons and nurses hovering near" (Du Bois, 1917:311). During World War II he noted that not just waste but production itself brings profits to corporations:

> The result of concentration of war orders in a few great corporations has been to give 16 non-financial enterprises 50 per cent more assets than all the corporations the government owns. The assets of these 16 concerns increased in the four war years from 1939 to 1943 by $5,239,000,000—that is 20.2% or one-fifth. (Du Bois, 1945:94)

But the cause of war, Du Bois observed more than once, is not just profit; it is preparation for war. Imperial nations make war for the sake of conquest, "and conquest, not in Europe, but primarily among the darker peoples of Asia and Africa; conquest, not for assimilation and uplift, but for commerce and degradation" (Du Bois, 1917:316, 318). Thus, whites were killing whites in Europe in order to control the lands where the darker peoples lived.

Writing in his 80s on the struggle between capitalism and communism, Du Bois noted that "public officials and military men began openly to declare that if the Russians would not attack us, we would attack them to keep them from attacking us" (Du Bois, 1951:464). Again, however, he interpreted the struggle with communism as involving colonial aggression. "As big business gained in power and promoted war, what was ostensibly against Communism was really for colonial aggression in Asia and Africa (Du Bois, 1954–1955: 402). Capitalism could be understood only through wealth and power, with power supporting the accumulation of wealth. Wealth, or super-capitalism, resulted from imperialism and war, and imperialism is bolstered by the ideology of inferior races.

Du Bois made it very clear that he did not believe colonialism was "here to stay." Writing in 1945, some 15 years before the African countries rushed to independence, he wrote: "Have the present masters of the world such an eternal lien on civilization as to ensure unending control? By no means; their very absorption in war and wealth has so weakened their moral fiber that the end of their rule is in sight" (Du Bois, 1945:19, also 97).

In his 1945 work on colonialism Du Bois commented on communist Russia, suggesting that it had two possible futures: either it would become part of the imperialist world, or it would stand up against world capitalism on the side of workers and the oppressed. At the close of the chapter on Russia, he stated prophetically: "Even should the Russian experiment fail and Communism be proved unable to cope with the problems of land, property, and income, Russia deserves all credit for having at least faced the problem and for having tried to solve it" (Du Bois, 1945:122).

Social Organization and Culture   Du Bois argued that the basic element in social organization is oppression—which he himself had experienced. Response to oppression could take "three main forms: a feeling of revolt and revenge; an attempt to adjust all thought and action to the will of the greater group; or, finally, a determined attempt at self-development, self-realization, in spite of" prejudice and discrimination (Du Bois, 1901b:4). Black leaders, Du Bois noted in 1901 (1901b:4), had tried all three approaches.

Much of Du Bois's theory of social organization has already been covered in the discussion of capitalism, socialism, and communism. However, in *Darkwater* (1920) he referred to the "manure" theory of social organization. By this he meant that the dregs of humanity are considered fit only to do tasks that no human being ought to have to do. This is the foundation for "a Theory of Exclusiveness, a feeling that the world progresses by a process of excluding from the benefits of culture the majority of men, so that a gifted minority may blossom" (Du Bois, 1920:543). How, he wondered, could a democracy be built on the backs of the despised?

Du Bois reformulated his oppression or "zero-sum game" theory of culture eight years later as the theory of the Chosen People. Veblen, being one of the Chosen despite his criticism of capitalism, had spoken of the special talents of the German and Nordic peoples. Du Bois spoke of the same belief, "that everything that has been done in modern times has been done by the Nordic people; that they are . . . the salt of the earth; that if anything is done to change their type of civilization, then civilization fails and falls (Du Bois, 1926:396). In the "Manifesto of the Second Pan-African Congress" (1921b), Du Bois wondered why "in the 20th century of the Prince of Peace, in the millennium of Buddha and Mahmoud, and in the . . . Age of Reason, there cannot be found in the civilized world enough of altruism, learning and benevolence to develop native institutions for the native's good." The crux of the matter, as he saw it, is why mutual attitudes toward peoples are determined by the degree to which one could subject the other (Du Bois, 1921b:641).

Du Bois, then, presented a theory of oppression and cultural exclusiveness, which he believed to be correct for the present, but changeable. White writers have often treated blacks, especially African Americans, as having contributed to music and perhaps art, but nothing else. However, in no book has the case for multiracial cultural contributions been stated better than in Du Bois's *The World and Africa*, published in 1946. Here he wrote of the Negro African civilizations that flourished prior to the arrival of European conquistadors. He asserted that evidence favored the theory that ancient Egyptians were neither Arab nor white, but black (Du Bois, 1946:79, 106). Du Bois's scholarly work was so ignored by white academics (paralleling the fate of Charlotte Gilman) that the theory of "black Egypt" had to be rediscovered in the 1970s and 1980s. Du Bois reminded us that the contributions of the darker peoples to the growth of civilization and culture had to be obliterated in order to develop and then perpetuate the ideology of white superiority.

Although Du Bois's view of ancient Egyptian civilization as black African was central to his argument for cultural equality, his book on *The Gift of Black Folk* (1924) painted the picture with even broader strokes. In this book he reported the cultural and social contributions of African Americans as explorers, soldiers, and laborers, as well as their contributions to women's emancipation (discussed below).

On society and culture, Du Bois wrote about further specialization in a way that was very similar to Gilman. Is menial service really necessary, he asked? "Can we not transfer cooking, along with the laundry, from the home to the scientific laboratory. Cannot the training of children become an even greater profession than the tending of the sick?" (Du Bois, 1920:543). Although the point is the same, Gilman's concern was the domestic enslavement of women, whereas Du Bois was talking about the menial work assigned to African Americans—both men and women.

Leadership and Power   Oneness, singleness of vision, narrowness—these are some of the terms Du Bois used at the turn of the twentieth century to describe the **leader**, be he Jefferson Davis or Booker T. Washington. "It is," wrote Du Bois, "as though Nature must needs make men a little narrow to give them force" (Du Bois, 1903:123). In other words, the role of leader in a differentiated society (described by Durkheim) requires specialization and focus.

But when Du Bois moved from the general character of leadership to the nature of **power** or leadership in modern industrial civilization, he observed that "its foundation is the idea of the strong man—individualism coupled with the rule of might." Ideally, Americans may glorify the leader of humble origin— an Abraham Lincoln or Benjamin Franklin or Alexander Hamilton—but when they pick up their newspapers to look for the best of their society, they find few such people. Rather, "today we find the names of those who by accident and extravagance, by their show and influence, by their wealth and impudence have come by general consent to be regarded as forming the best" (Du Bois, 1907:251). Today's leaders, Du Bois would say, embody what is valued most by our culture; they "represent in their lives that which we really worship" (Du Bois, 1907:252). This comment broadens Veblen's view of the "captains of industry," who, because they have money, are seen as having general wisdom. These, according to Du Bois are "the favored Few who luxuriate in the toil of the tortured many" (Du Bois, 1921b:642).

Thus, Du Bois's two main theoretical points about leadership and power were, first, that leaders today ordinarily must be specialists and second, that leaders mirror the values and attributes most prized by their society—in modern American society, according to Du Bois, wealth, show, and impudence.

Double-Consciousness   Du Bois often felt himself to be an outcast or stranger in his own land. From this experience he developed the concept of **double-consciousness**. Writing early in his career, he spoke of his "twoness,—an

American, a Negro; two souls, two thoughts, two unreconciled strivings; two warring ideals in one dark body" (Du Bois, 1903:102). Culturally Du Bois was an American, but he also represented African American society.

Du Bois described this double-consciousness, common to African Americans, as debilitating. Having no true (or integrated) consciousness, the African American sees him (or her) self through the eyes of others, measured by others' contempt or pity (Du Bois, 1903:102). The individual feels torn asunder, and this "waste of double aims, this seeking to satisfy two unreconciled ideals, has wrought sad havoc with the courage and faith and deeds of ten thousand thousand people" (Du Bois, 1903:103).

Double-consciousness has been noted by African Americans traveling to Africa to seek their roots. In the United States they are seen as black, but in Africa they may be viewed as Americans—thus being an outsider in both places. A related concept in sociology today is that of the "marginal man"—the individual not fully integrated into either society or culture.

Nature of Society, Humans, and Change

Given Du Bois's consciousness as both American and African American, it is not surprising that more than one ideology can be found in his work. There was in Du Bois the struggle between liberal rationalism and the promise of radical socialism for a just world. Also within Du Bois were both the scientist and the critic.

Perhaps the central ideological issue that Du Bois confronted and exposed was history as ideology. His clearest statement of the problem was in his book *Black Reconstruction in America* (1935a)—specifically, its closing chapter, "The Propaganda of History":

> In a day when the human mind aspired to a science of human action, a history and psychology of the mighty effort of the mightiest century, we fell under the leadership of those who would compromise with truth in the past in order to make peace in the present and guide policy in the future. (Du Bois, 1935a:727)

In this massive work, probably his best historical research, he effectively laid to rest the argument that it was black Americans who caused the failure of Reconstruction after the Civil War, resulting in their quasi-slavery. After reviewing what other early-twentieth-century historians had said about the post–Civil War period, Du Bois wrote: "I cannot believe that any unbiased mind, with an ideal of truth and of scientific judgment, can read the plain, authentic facts of our history, during 1860–1880, and come to conclusions essentially different from mine; and yet I stand virtually alone in this interpretation" (1935a:726). Du Bois ended his historical critique by repeating a comment from an earlier time, characterizing history as "lies agreed upon"—hardly a ringing endorsement of the accuracy of the historical accounts on which many of us were raised!

Human nature, to Du Bois, is changeable. It is not immutably sinful, good, selfish, beastly, or altruistic. In 1948, at the age of 80, he observed: "Many of the old cliches have fallen into disuse; human nature can be changed and most prejudices are neither inborn nor ineradicable" (Du Bois, 1948:91). There are times, wrote Du Bois, when "human nature is horrible and human beings beastly, but the world progresses; men reel and stagger forward" (Du Bois, quoted in Sundquist, 1996:34).

Du Bois was particularly concerned with the nature of black human beings, who he felt had been slandered by whites because of the latter's vested interest in treating blacks as inferior. Du Bois described the humanity of the slaves leaving their homes and plantations following the Civil War:

> They did not wreak vengeance on unprotected women. They found an easier, more effective and more decent way to freedom. Men go wild and fight for freedom with bestial ferocity when they must—where there is no other way; but human nature does not deliberately choose blood—at least not black human nature. (Du Bois, 1935a:66)

Human nature, then, is not only diverse in its manifestations but alterable. Thus, to Du Bois, change was possible. But would change be revolutionary, evolutionary, or by liberal reform? Du Bois responded in 1921 to a criticism of the NAACP, which had been accused

> of not being a "revolutionary" body. This is quite true. We do not believe in revolution. We expect revolutionary changes in many parts of this life and this world, but we expect these changes to come mainly through reason, human sympathy, and the education of children, and not by murder. (Du Bois, 1921a:341)

Du Bois made clear at that stage of his life how he viewed change: "We who suffer and believe in *reform* must not think that we can answer . . . simply by saying that present industrial society is *not* in accordance with human nature. It *is* in accordance with human nature today, but human nature can and must and will be changed" (Du Bois, 1921a:346). Does this mean that progress is inevitable? In 1933 Du Bois said no: U.S. blacks "have imbibed from the surrounding white world a childish idea of progress. Progress means bigger and better results always and forever. But there is no such rule of life. In six thousand years of human culture, the losses and retrogressions have been enormous" (Du Bois, 1936:419).

Change is possible, but progress is not inevitable. Du Bois, then, was not an optimist, and he made this plain in *Darkwater*: "So strong is the spell of beauty that there are those who, contradicting their own knowledge and experience, try to say that all is beauty. They are called optimists, and they lie. All is not beauty. Ugliness and hate and ill are here with all their contradiction and illogic" (Du Bois, 1920:607).

Whatever optimism Du Bois had felt 50 years earlier about changing the United States through logic and liberal reform was greatly reduced after World War II, as he moved toward Marxist radicalism. One biographer described this disillusionment: America, "the promised land, was a cruel, receding mirage for people of color" (Lewis, 1993, quoted in Farganis, 1996:182). As noted previously, Du Bois eventually moved to Ghana and died there. The sole note of optimism in his last years was his firm belief in the coming freedom of the African colonies.

Class, Gender, and Race

We come now to some of the central issues in the work of W. E. B. Du Bois. He often spoke of a class structure that is also racial in nature. He stated late in life that the "workers of the world were indeed arising," and that this was not strictly a matter of race (Du Bois, 1951:468). Most of his work, however, dealt with the intertwined nature of class and race. For example, in *The Souls of Black Folk* (1903) he commented that "to be a poor man is hard, but to be a poor race in a land of dollars is the very bottom of hardships" (Du Bois, 1903:190).

The Intersection of Class and Race   In relating class and race, Du Bois made an important point regarding ecology, or spatial location. The black and white poor are often in close proximity both residentially and in the saloon, gambling house, and brothel. However, at the higher social levels, residence and activity may separate coworkers and natural friends (Du Bois, 1903:186, 196). One result of proximity at the lower socioeconomic levels is that there is more race prejudice among the middle and lower classes than among those of high status (Du Bois, 1935a:573).

Du Bois also presented characterizations of African American social classes. In 1903 he stated that 96 percent of blacks are toiling in monotony, with little time for leisure. Later in the same book he described those still on the land as 10 percent who are paupers and wanderers, 40 percent who are tenants or indentured to the land, another 40 percent who are wage earners, and the upper 10 percent who control land themselves, in most cases having "croppers" working for them (Du Bois, 1903:175, 181).

In discussing capitalist inequality, Marx and Pareto had introduced the concept of the ruling class. In his early study of Philadelphia, Du Bois described the black ruling class, or bourgeoisie, as the "caterers, clerks, teachers, professional men, small merchants, etc., who constitute the aristocracy of the Negroes. Many are well-to-do, some are wealthy, all are fairly educated, and some liberally trained" (Du Bois, 1899, in Farganis, 1996:186). He took special note of how they related to other African Americans.

Du Bois wrote of the African American middle class in 1899 that "they shrink from all such display and publicity as will expose them to the veiled insult and depreciation which the masses suffer. Consequently this class, which ought to lead, refuses to head any race movement on the plea that thus they draw the very color line against which they protest" (Du Bois, 1899, in Myrdal, 1944: 1388). Again, he noted that "so hard has been the rise of the better class of Negroes that they fear to fall if they now stoop to lend a hand to their fellows" (Du Bois, 1899:351).

In the 1930s Du Bois raised the same issue as part of his proposal for separate black businesses: If the leading Negroes, he argued, "cannot assume and bear the uplift of their own proletariat, they are doomed for all time. It is not a case of ethics; it is a plain case of necessity. The method by which this may be done is, first, for the American Negro to achieve a new economic solidarity" (Du Bois, 1935b:436). At about the same time Du Bois declared that this was a fait accompli: "There is no group of leaders on earth who have so largely made common cause with the lowest of their race as educated American Negroes, and it is their foresight and sacrifice and theirs alone that have saved the American freedman from annihilation and degradation" (Du Bois, 1931a:56).

So, had successful African Americans isolated themselves from, or "stooped to help," their poorer brothers and sisters? It is, of course, possible that between 1900 and 1930 the black bourgeoisie had become comfortable enough with their success that they no longer feared the white community's looking upon them as an inferior race. However, it is also possible that Du Bois's emphasis in the 1930s on the need for black separateness in business was such that his perception of need outran the helping behavior of successful blacks. It is also worth noting that his later Marxism sought not so much economic separateness as working-class—black and white—unity.

The Race Construct   Let us now move beyond Du Bois's treatment of class and race to the issue of the race construct, or the use of race to classify categories of people. Du Bois argued that no scientific definition of race is possible. Physical differences fade into each other almost imperceptibly.

Using only skin color and hair, there may be three major "stocks": whites, with light skin and straight or wavy hair; Negroids, with dark skin and close-curled hair; and Mongoloids, with sallow or yellow skin and straight hair (Du Bois, 1946:2). However, certain facial features are also used to distinguish between racial types: large or thin lips, flat or thin nose, eyes with folds or without—and therein lie confusions. Furthermore, according to Du Bois, nine-tenths of black Africans do not conform to the Negroid stereotype (1915a:629). For example, certain of the Bantu peoples of East Africa have facial features much more similar to those of Europeans than to those ordinarily considered in books on race to be "Negroid."

Franz Boas, a respected U.S. anthropologist, stated early in the twentieth century that "an unbiased estimate of the anthropological evidence . . . does not permit us to countenance the belief in a racial inferiority, which would unfit an individual of the Negro race to take his part in modern civilization" (Du Bois, 1908:293). Du Bois, of course, agreed, pointing out that the race construct is primarily for ideological purposes. But despite statements such as that of Boas, whites continue to use historical ideology, evolutionary arguments, and intelligence tests to try to prove the inherent inferiority of colored peoples—not only Negro slaves, but Asiatic coolies as well (Du Bois, 1946:37).

The race construct as ideology puts black people in an untenable position. Everything black is hideous, or at least wrong. "If they fought for freedom, they were beasts; if they did not fight, they were born slaves. If they cowered on the plantations, they loved slavery; if they ran away, they were lazy loafers. If they sang, they were silly; if they scowled, they were impudent" (Du Bois, 1935a:125). And so race becomes an epithet, rather than a description—an epithet predicated on overgeneralization, incorrect or fabricated evidence, and historical treatment.

An important conclusion drawn by Du Bois in the 1920s was that "the income-bearing value of race prejudice was the cause and not the result of theories of race inferiority" (Sundquist, 1996:31). In other words, racial discrimination preceded prejudice. But does race exist? Does it mean anything at all? At the Pan-African Congress of 1921, in which Du Bois was a central figure, the following resolution was adopted:

> The absolute equality of races, physical, political and social is the founding stone of world and human advancement. No one denies great differences of gift, capacity and attainment among individuals of all races, but the voice of Science, Religion, and practical Politics is one in denying the God-appointed existence of super-races or of races naturally and inevitably and eternally inferior. (Du Bois, 1946:238)

Du Bois spoke not only about the faulty racial construct and the races' actual equality, but also about the colored peoples of the world. Racial differences, according to Du Bois, are real but fuzzy, have no general connotations in terms of physical or mental differences, but have been and are being used ideologically as the basis for racial inequities (on this issue, see Sundquist, 1996:17).

Gender   Although gender was not as central to Du Bois's theorizing as race and class, he stated that the "uplift of women is, next to the problem of the color line and the peace movement, our greatest modern cause. When, now, two of these movements—women and color—combine in one, the combination has deep meaning" (Du Bois, 1920:574). In his 1924 book *The Gift of Black Folk*, he devoted an entire chapter to the contributions that black women had made to Western culture (1924:259–273).

Du Bois spoke forcefully on the issues of suffrage and education for women. In a 1915 article, Dean Kelly Miller had argued against suffrage, claiming that women are too busy with home and children to take a hand in public life, that women are weaker than men, that women are protected by men's votes, and that voting and officeholding by women are risky for society. Du Bois responded to several points in Miller's argument:

1. The "actual work of the world today depends more largely upon women than upon men." So the dilemma of the man-ruled world is whether woman is doing the world's work well or not. "If she is not doing it well why do we not take from her the necessity of working? If she is doing it well why not treat her as a worker with a voice in the direction of work?"

2. The statement that women are weaker is the same kind of "rot" that characterizes the notion that the darker races or lower classes are weaker. The accomplishments of women, despite humiliating prejudices, make it "inconceivable that any fair-minded person could for a moment talk about a 'weaker' sex."

3. The notion of men protecting or representing women with their votes overlooks the large numbers of women connected to no man. "To put this whole army . . . out of court and leave them unprotected and without voice in political life is more than unjust, it is a crime." Of course, a family might be given the vote, but by what process of rationality could it be determined that the representative should always be a man—be he genius or drunkard? Du Bois concluded this argument: "The meaning of the twentieth century is the freeing of the individual soul; the soul longest in slavery and

still in the most disgusting and indefensible slavery is the soul of womanhood" (Du Bois, 1915b:378–379).

Du Bois also questioned the way women are looked upon and treated. In
Darkwater (1920) he made the fairly up-to-date comment that women are ham-
pered because men pretend to worship virgins and mothers while actually de-
spising motherhood and despoiling virgins (Du Bois, 1920:565). Regarding education, Du Bois argued that if either gender must remain uneducated, better it
should be the father than the mother, because she is the primary rearer of the
next generation. However, noted Du Bois, males need education also if they are
to succeed in the modern world (Du Bois, 1927:146).

Other Theories and Theorists

We have already observed some of the relationships between Du Bois and Marx,
Lenin, Veblen, Schumpeter, and Gilman. We begin this section with a brief comment on Sumner and the survival of the fittest. According to Du Bois, writing in
1904, the hope of white Americans was that blacks would die out or emigrate,
thus demonstrating their "unfitness" for U.S. society. At the same time, he bemoaned the triumph of brute force and cunning over weakness and innocence—
interpreted by Sumner as survival of the fittest. Du Bois's hope was that in the
"competition of races the survival of the fittest shall mean the triumph of the
good, the beautiful, and the true; that we may be able to preserve for future civilization all that is really fine and noble and strong, and not continue to put a pre-
mium on greed and impudence and cruelty" (Du Bois, 1903:185). Thus, Du Bois's
vision of the "fittest" reminds us of Gilman's and Webb's view of evolution as the
story of cooperation, or of "goodness," more than of competition.

During the last half of his life Du Bois moved toward a more Marxist position. In *Darkwater* and in the Soviet press, he used Marxist language to describe
the connections among racism, economic inequality, and the distortion of
knowledge (Lewis, 1997:44). And at the close of an address at the age of 90,
presented by his wife to the All-Africa People's Congress, he used slightly altered Marxist language: "You have nothing to lose but your chains! You have a
continent to regain! You have freedom and human dignity to attain!" (Du Bois,
1958, in 1946:310).

He rejected much imported Marxism as not fitting the U.S. situation; yet he
clearly moved closer to communism and the Soviet experiment as he grew
older and more disillusioned with capitalist oppression and racism. His most direct homage to Marx was in *Black Reconstruction in America* (1935a), where he
quoted Marx's correspondence with Abraham Lincoln in 1865:

> Injustice against a fraction of your people having been followed by such
> dire consequences, put an end to it. Declare your fellow citizens from this
> day forth free and equal, without any reserve. If you refuse them citizens'
> rights while you exact from them citizens' duties, you will sooner or later
> face a new struggle which will once more drench your country in blood.
> (Du Bois, 1935a:354)

Even though at the very end Du Bois was hardly a true believing Marxist, his understanding of what Marx and Marxism stood for appealed to one whose life's work was for justice and equality.[2]

Several of the theoretical issues raised by Robert Michels are also found in Du Bois's work. At several points he discussed oligarchy and oligopoly, although he never referred to an "iron law" of social organization. In describing Reconstruction after the Civil War, Du Bois noted that "skilled labor proceeded to share in the exploitation of the reservoir of low-paid common labor." And while he noted that skilled labor and capital were often in competition, "they fought to share profit from labor and not to eliminate profit" (Du Bois, 1935a:597). This is close to Michels's point about the conservatism of labor leaders and their identification with the capitalist system.

Many years earlier, Du Bois had spoken about a second factor that Michels said would reduce the likelihood of revolution: the hope of mobility. Talent, wrote Du Bois, "should be rewarded." The "incentive to good, honest, effective work . . . would inspire the young to try harder, [and] it would stimulate the idle and discouraged" (Du Bois, 1899, quoted in Sundquist, 1996:353). During the Philadelphia race riots at the turn of the twentieth century, Du Bois was asked by a newspaper editor why Negroes did not fight back. Because they are still hopeful, he said. The Negro, said Du Bois, "still believes that he can in other ways gain success at some time. So long as that hope remains general, there is little chance of widespread degeneration or extinction"—or, we might add, revolution (Du Bois, 1904:369). Du Bois had earlier said that the surest way to encourage criminal behavior is to refuse Negroes remunerative work. Thus, the outcome must at least be jobs, if not actual mobility. But social mobility must be possible enough that the downtrodden masses can see examples of success and can hope—for themselves or their children.

At the age of 93, Du Bois wrote about Toussaint L'Ouverture. This black man had led the revolt in Haiti that brought freedom to the black population, which in turn had caused Napoleon to give up his dreams of an empire in the Western Hemisphere and to sell the Louisiana Purchase "for a song." Du Bois noted that Toussaint would not appear in the history books that distorted Reconstruction and treated Western history selectively. However, he noted that both Comte and Martineau hailed Toussaint as a great man. Comte "included him with Washington, Plato, Buddha, and Charlemagne as worthy to replace all the calendar saints. . . . Harriet Martineau wrote a novel on his life" (Du Bois, 1961:301).

Because of his multifaceted concerns, Du Bois's thought had connections to most of the other theorists in this volume who wrote between 1830 and 1930. As one biographer put it, Du Bois "cast light on nearly every major issue of modern social life—race and racism, democracy, equality, socialism and capitalism, imperialism, revolution, war and peace, cultural nationalism—and more" (Weinberg, 1970: xvii).

---

[2]Du Bois also appreciated the writings of Marianne and Max Weber, whom he knew well.

Critique and Conclusions

Throughout his life, the white community compared Du Bois with another black leader, Booker T. Washington. Washington fostered the keeping of talented blacks "in their place," by teaching them skilled trades instead of the liberal arts. Du Bois sought racial equality at all levels of the educational and occupational spectrum. Washington was glorified by the white community; Du Bois was vilified, or ignored. In the 1940s, Gunnar Myrdal wrote:

> We can honestly say that some of the most capable statesmen in the United States are Negroes, whatever we may think of their policies. If these men, with their training in practical politics, were white, they would no doubt be national leaders just as they are now race leaders. This was almost recognized of Frederick Douglass and Booker T. Washington, but the two other Negro statesmen of equal stature—W. E. B. Du Bois and James Weldon Johnson—have been virtually ignored by whites. (Myrdal, 1944:987)

As a result, Du Bois's thoughts on African history had to be rediscovered by a new generation of black scholars.

As Du Bois increasingly verbalized his support for the Soviet Union, he was treated as a traitor by the U.S. government. His more incendiary writings did not help. He closed his 1946 book on Africa: "Let the white world keep its missionaries at home to teach the Golden Rule to its corporate thieves. Damn the God of Slavery, Exploitation, and War" (Du Bois, 1954–1955, in 1946:291). His neutrality during the Cold War, like that of Paul Robeson and other African Americans, was seen as disloyalty by those who demanded that they take sides.

Du Bois often did not receive support from the African American community either. He did not just criticize capitalism, he was critical of many African American leaders of his time. Like Rosa Luxemburg in Germany, who criticized Russian communism and German socialism as well as capitalism, Du Bois criticized both white racism and the black press.

Though vilified and ignored, it is apparent that Du Bois contributed greatly to our understanding of the many years during which he lived. His revisionist history of Reconstruction, his meticulous treatment of the contributions of blacks to civilization, and his increasing interest in and concern for Africa all make Du Bois stand alone.

Final Thoughts

We have already noted Du Bois's prediction that the future would belong to socialism. By 1935 he had shown how the United States had became increasingly reactionary after the Civil War, and how the world order of capitalism "has brought nearer the revolution by which the power of capitalism is to be challenged" (Du Bois, 1935a:631). His analysis of this world order was correct; whether his prediction will be remains to be seen.

Du Bois began the twentieth century by stating that the issue of the century would be race (Du Bois, 1903:100). On this point he was clearly correct, as long as race is broadened to include ethnicity, and as long as mega-capitalism is added as a second issue.

In what may very well have been his last writing, Du Bois at the age of 94 addressed the role of whites in an independent Africa. He stated that good relations between races will certainly

> not be automatic; it will be in great part because men like Dr. [Albert] Schweitzer . . . would not only treat disease but train Negroes as assistants and helpers, surround himself with a growing African staff of scientifically educated natives who can in time carry on and spread his work and see that it is supported by the new African states and does not continue to be dependent on European charity. (Du Bois, 1962:675)

One of the great complaints regarding European philanthropic efforts in Africa and elsewhere has always been that Du Bois's plea is ignored—that little effort has been made to avoid neocolonialism, whether economic or medical. Likewise, too few ex-colonial whites have consciously "worked themselves out of a job," or trained their own replacements.

Du Bois would have been dismayed. Looking at an unjust and unequal world, he sought equality and peace. He seldom separated his theory from his desires or ideology. Weinberg called him "the most *un*detached person alive" (Weinberg, 1970: xiii). We have concentrated on his important theoretical insights into capitalism, imperialism, class, race, and gender—while not ignoring his hopes for a better world.

References

Du Bois, W. E. B. 1899. *The Philadelphia Negro*. Philadelphia: Publishers for the University.

———. 1901a. *The Black North in 1901*. New York: Arno Press.

———. 1901b/1996. "Booker T. Washington." *The Dial*, July 16. Reprinted in Eric J. Sundquist (Ed.), *The Oxford W. E. B. Du Bois Reader* (pp. 245–247). New York: Oxford University Press.

———. 1903/1996. *The Souls of Black Folk*. Chicago: A. C. McClurg and Company. Reprinted in Eric J. Sundquist (Ed.), *The Oxford W. E. B. Du Bois Reader* (pp. 97–240). New York: Oxford University Press.

———. 1904/1996. "The Future of the Negro Race in America," *The East and the West* 2 (January). Reprinted in Eric J. Sundquist (Ed.), *The Oxford W. E. B. Du Bois Reader* (pp. 362–373). New York: Oxford University Press.

———. 1907/1996. "Abraham Lincoln." *Voice of the Negro*, 4 (June). Reprinted in Eric J. Sundquist (Ed.), *The Oxford W. E. B. Du Bois Reader* (pp. 248–256). New York: Oxford University Press.

———. 1908/1970. "Race Friction Between Black and White." *American Journal of Sociology* (May). Reprinted in Meyer Weinberg (Ed.), *W. E. B. Du Bois: A Reader*. New York: Harper and Row.

———. 1915a/1996: "Africa and the Slave Trade." In Eric J. Sundquist (Ed.), *The Oxford W. E. B. Du Bois Reader* (pp. 628–637). New York: Oxford University Press.

———. 1915b/1996: "Woman Suffrage," *The Crisis*, 11 (November). Reprinted in Eric

J. Sundquist, (Ed.), *The Oxford W. E. B. Du Bois Reader* (pp. 377–379). New York: Oxford University Press.

———. 1917/1970. "Of the Culture of White Folk," *Journal of Race Development* (April). Reprinted in Meyer Weinberg (Ed.), *W. E. B. Du Bois: A Reader* (pp. 309–320). New York: Harper and Row.

———. 1920/1996. *Darkwater*. New York: Harcourt, Brace, and Howe. Reprinted in Eric J. Sundquist (Ed.), *The Oxford W. E. B. Du Bois Reader* (pp. 481–622). New York: Oxford University Press.

———. 1921a/1970. "The Class Struggle" and "Socialism and the Negro." *Crisis* (August, October). Reprinted in Meyer Weinberg (Ed.), *W. E. B. Du Bois: A Reader* (pp. 341–343, 344–347). New York: Harper and Row.

———. 1921b/1996. "Manifesto of the Second Pan-African Congress." In Eric J. Sundquist (Ed.), *The Oxford W. E. B. Du Bois Reader* (pp. 640–643). New York: Oxford University Press.

———. 1924. *The Gift of Black Folk*. Boston: Stratford Company.

———. 1926/1996. "Cultural Equality." *Report of the Debate Conducted by the Chicago Forum*, March 17. Reprinted in Eric J. Sundquist (Ed.), *The Oxford W. E. B. Du Bois Reader* (pp. 394–400). New York: Oxford University Press.

———1927/1970. "Boys and Girls," *Crisis* (April). Reprinted in Meyer Weinberg (Ed.), *W. E. B. Du Bois: A Reader* (p. 146). New York: Harper and Row.

———. 1931a/1970. "The Negro Bourgeoisie," *Crisis* (September). Reprinted in Meyer Weinberg (Ed.), *W. E. B. Du Bois: A Reader* (pp. 55–56). New York: Harper and Row.

———. 1931b/1996. "The Negro and Communism." *Crisis, 38* (September). Reprinted in Eric J. Sundquist (Ed.), *The Oxford W. E. B. Du Bois Reader* (pp. 400–409). New York: Oxford University Press.

———. 1935a/1962. *Black Reconstruction in America*. New York: Meridian Books, World Publishing.

———. 1935b/1996. "A Negro Nation Within the Nation." *Current History, 42* (June). Reprinted in Eric J. Sundquist (Ed.), *The Oxford W. E. B. Du Bois Reader* (pp. 431–438). New York: Oxford University Press.

———. 1936/1996. "The Field and Function of the American Negro College." *Fisk News, 6* (June). Reprinted in Eric J. Sundquist (Ed.), *The Oxford W. E. B. Du Bois Reader* (pp. 409–423). New York: Oxford University Press.

———. 1939. *Black Folk: Then and Now*. New York: Octagon Books.

———. 1940. *Dusk of Dawn*. New York: Harcourt, Brace and Company.

———. 1943/1996. "The Realities of Africa." *Foreign Affairs, 21* (July). Reprinted in Eric J. Sundquist (Ed.), *The Oxford W. E. B. Du Bois Reader* (pp. 653–664). New York: Oxford University Press.

———. 1945. *Color and Democracy: Colonies and Peace*. New York: Harcourt, Brace and Company.

———. 1946/1965. *The World and Africa*. New York: International Publishers.

———. 1948/1970. "The Negro Since 1900: A Progress Report," *New York Times Magazine* (November 21). Reprinted in Meyer Weinberg (Ed.), *W. E. B. Du Bois: A Reader* (pp. 89–98). New York Harper and Row.

———. 1951/1996. "I Take My Stand for Peace," *Masses and Mainstream, 4* (April). Reprinted in Eric J. Sundquist (Ed.), *The Oxford W. E. B. Du Bois Reader* (pp. 464–469). New York: Oxford University Press.

———. 1954–1955. "Africa and the American Negro Intelligentsia." *Presence Africaine* (December–January). Reprinted in Meyer Weinberg (Ed.), *W. E. B. Du Bois: A Reader* (pp. 384–403). New York: Harper and Row.

———. 1958/1996. "The Future of Africa." *National Guardian* (December 22). Reprinted in Eric J. Sundquist (Ed.), *The Oxford W. E. B. Du Bois Reader* (pp. 664–667). New York: Oxford University Press.

———. 1961/1996. "Toussaint l'Ouverture," *Freedomways, 1* (Summer). Reprinted in Eric J. Sundquist (Ed.), *The Oxford W. E. B. Du Bois Reader* (pp. 296–302). New York: Oxford University Press.

———. 1962/1996. "Whites in Africa After Negro Autonomy." *Albert Schweitzer's Realm: A Symposium.* Reprinted in Eric J. Sundquist (Ed.), *The Oxford W. E. B. Du Bois Reader* (pp. 667–675). New York: Oxford University Press.

Farganis, James. 1996. "Introduction." In James Farganis (Ed.), *Readings in Social Theory: The Classic Tradition to Post-Modernism* (pp. 180–182). New York: McGraw-Hill.

Lenin, V. I. 1916/1939. *Imperialism: The Highest Form of Capitalism* (vol. XIX). New York: International Publishers.

Lewis, David Levering. 1993. *W. E. B. Du Bois: Biography of a Race, 1868–1919.* New York: Henry Holt.

Lewis, David Levering. 1997. "Du Bois and the Challenge of the Black Press." *Crisis,* (July), 43–44.

Myrdal, Gunnar. 1944. *An American Dilemma: The Negro Problem and Modern Democracy.* New York: Harper and Brothers.

Sundquist, Eric J. (Ed.). 1996. "Introduction." *The Oxford W. E. B. Du Bois Reader* (pp. 3–36). New York: Oxford University Press.

Weinberg, Meyer (Ed.). 1970. "Introduction." *W. E. B. Du Bois: A Reader* (pp. xi–xvii). New York: Harper and Row.

Chapter 13

Society, Self, and Mind
Cooley, Mead, and Freud

When sociology teachers complain that they are having trouble getting their students to think sociologically, they usually mean getting them to think about society as a whole. In the United States we are more attuned to individual-level explanations. For example, we might say, he is homeless because he is an alcoholic or is too incompetent to hold a job rather than looking at the social context in which he lives, or she is divorced because she is flighty and insecure, not because a mobile society has left her without a support system for the normal stresses and strains of marriage. For the most part, the theories you have encountered so far in this book have focused on the societal level. This chapter is different. These three theorists—Charles Horton Cooley, George Herbert Mead, and Sigmund Freud—all focused on the influences affecting the development of the person or self.

Both Cooley and Mead sought to explain the self and activity of individuals. They saw the individual as an active agent influenced by the environment, including family. Freud was also concerned with the individual, but much of his theory dealt with the unconscious, the biological drives, and their control by society.

Cooley and Mead were part of an exceptional flowering of American sociology at the turn of the twentieth century. They were colleagues at the University of Michigan between 1891 and 1893. Both men were influenced by the pragmatic philosophy of William James and John Dewey, as well as by Darwin and developments in German psychology. They were concerned with the self, but also with solutions to the many social problems that had resulted from *industrialization, urbanization,* and *mass immigration* to the United States. For both Cooley and Mead, scientific sociology is the answer to the problems that challenge a democratic society.

Freud was primarily concerned with discovering the causes of psychological dysfunction. His training in medicine and his research background meant that he sought biologically determined explanations for phenomena, but he came to recognize that the life of the mind require taking account of human meaning and hidden intentions. Unlike Cooley and Mead, Freud was less hopeful about significant transformations of society, because he believed that socially danger- ous instinctual urges cannot be eliminated but only repressed, sublimated, or controlled.

Charles Horton Cooley (1864–1929)

Charles H. Cooley was born in Ann Arbor, Michigan. His father was a professor of law at the University of Michigan, as well as a Justice of the Michigan Su- preme Court. Cooley attended the University of Michigan, graduating with an engineering degree. He worked for a short time as a draftsman in Bay City, Michigan, and later as a statistician in Washington, D.C. According to his nephew, Albert Reiss, Cooley was unenthusiastic about engineering, and after reading extensively in economics and sociology, he did a graduate degree in po- litical economy and sociology at Michigan. During his college years, Cooley suf- fered from ill health, and as a semi-invalid, he read extensively and indulged in "much day-dreaming" (Reiss, 1968:3).

At that time sociology was generally regarded as a potentially subversive dis- cipline because of its focus on social issues and problems. Cooley remarked that he did not know that "sociology was . . . objected to as a '*radical* subject,'" but that he had an advantage because of his "conservative antecedents," his father being the "first Dean of the Michigan Law School" (1930:10).

While pursuing his PhD, which he obtained in 1894, Cooley began teaching at the University of Michigan, where he remained for the rest of his life— though he was sought by other universities. Cooley admitted he was fortunate to have a department chairman who "had confidence in me and allowed me to do absolutely as I pleased" (Cooley, 1930:10). In this academically idyllic situa- tion, Cooley devoted himself to a "life of unhurried contemplation and leisurely study" (Coser, 1977:316).

Cooley was involved in the early institutionalization of American sociology. He helped form the American Sociological Society in 1905 and became its presi- dent in 1918. His work laid the foundation for the subsequent development of social psychology and symbolic interactionism (see Chapter 20) in U.S. sociology.

Cooley's Central Theories and Methods

Like most of his sociological generation, Cooley was influenced by Herbert Spen- cer. He claimed that "nearly all of us who took up sociology between 1870 . . . and 1890 did so at the instigation of Spencer" but most "fell away from him sooner or later, . . . more or less completely." In fact, Cooley suggested that Spencer was not "by nature especially suited to be an observer of mankind and society" be- cause he was, by his own admission, "deficient in those sympathetic qualities which are after all the only direct source of our knowledge of other people"

(Cooley, 1930:263, 265). Spencer's "lack of insight into other minds" was, according to Cooley, a fatal handicap for "direct study of social phenomena" (1930:267). He thought that Spencer's organic analogy was not very useful to sociology and that the "conceptions drawn from physics and biology" were unhelpful in dealing with social facts (1930:283).

Like Spencer, Cooley saw society as an organism, but unlike Spencer he did not make the organismic analogy. For Cooley, as for Georg Simmel, society was a "complex of forms and processes each of which is living and growing by interaction with the others, the whole being so unified that what takes place in one part affects all the rest. It is a vast tissue of reciprocal activity" (Cooley, 1918:28). Moreover, *"Self and other do not exist as mutually exclusive social facts,"* nor was the individual strictly self-seeking (Cooley, 1902:126).

Cooley concluded that the "imaginations which people have of one another are the *solid facts* of society, and . . . to observe and interpret these must be the chief aim of sociology." Thus, not only must society be studied "by the imagination . . . but . . . the *object* of study is primarily an imaginative idea or group of ideas in the mind" (1902:121, 122). Sociologists therefore have to "imagine imaginations."

Two of Cooley's contributions to understanding social life are his theory of the development of the self in relation to others and of primary groups that shape individuals. He also contributed to sociological methodology through the use of statistics.

The Self   Cooley's "mentalistic" understanding of social life was stimulated by his reading of William James. James maintained that the self can be known, and that the known self is plural—that is, a number of selves that appeared in response to the individuals and groups one encounters. For example, as a student reading this text you have a self that is different from the self presented to your parents, and the self you present to your parents is different from the self presented to your close friends or a grocery clerk, and so on. But all these "selves" are part of you as an existing person. James envisaged the self as an "internal conversation" between an "I" and a "Me" (Levine, 1995:255). The "self for the parents," then, is the result of an internal conversation, or set of ideas and beliefs about this self that you and your parents have developed over the years. James's ideas formed the foundation for both Cooley's and Mead's work.

According to Cooley, the individual gains a stable view of self by seeing how others view him or her. Cooley insisted that the analysis of the self is not an abstract philosophical exercise. The "I" is not the self or ego used by moralists but an "empirical self . . . that can be apprehended or verified by ordinary observation" (1902:168). Sociological concepts, for Cooley, must be anchored in the real social world of interacting individuals. Sociology, he believed, can contribute to the precise, scientific process that human beings pursue in testing ideas and techniques, to human beings' adaption to their social and material environments, and to how human beings view themselves.

The essence of what the sociologist seeks to understand is the **mental-social complex**—the human mind with all of its "socially developed sentiments and understandings" (Cooley, 1930:295). The mental-social complex is not directly observable or amenable to exact measurement. However, it can be observed in the way people express themselves in behavior—in the "symbols of communication, in gesture, voice, words, and the written symbols which are preserved unchanged for ages" (1930:297). Cooley thought such symbols could be recorded and measured. From communication, then, the "I" emerges (Cooley, 1902:127).

The sense of self is therefore developed in reference to others. Cooley called this social self the "reflected or **looking-glass self.**" You understand yourself as you understand what others think or imagine you to be (Cooley, 1902:119). The looking-glass self has three elements: "the imagination of our appearance to the other person; the imagination of his judgement of that appearance, and some sort self-feeling, such as pride or mortification." The last element is the most critical, because feeling pride or shame is not simply a reflection of the self but the "imagined effect of this reflection upon another's mind" (1902:184–185).

The development of the looking-glass self was based on Cooley's observations of his third child and her gradual assertion of "I." As he recorded, learning "I" is a problem because it seems impossible that this can be learned by direct imitation. When "I" is used by one child, it does not have the same referent as when another child uses it. Unlike the word "apple," which is "an apple to all, . . . 'I' is different for every user of the word." Cooley suggested that the meaning of "I" is grasped when the child becomes aware of "self-feeling accompanying the use of 'I', 'me' and 'my' by others" and this awakens one's "own self-feeling, already existing in an inarticulate form." The child sympathizes with the words and "reproduces them in his own use" and they "come to stand for a *self-assertive feeling or attitude*, for self-will and appropriation" (Cooley, 1930:230, 231). Cooley recorded that his daughter used "I" to address an audience "usually with some emphasis—and its purpose is to impress upon that audience the power (I make go), the wish (I go play sand-pile), the claim (my mama), the service (I get it for you) of the speaker" (1930:232).

Society exists in an individual's mind because of interactions with many other individuals, so that "self and society are twin-born . . . and the notion of a separate and independent ego is an illusion" (Cooley, 1909:5). Cooley claimed that Descartes was incorrect in his assertion *"cogito ergo sum,"* as self-consciousness cannot be separated from, or assumed to precede, social consciousness. Self-consciousness and social consciousness are mutually sustaining. Consequently, Descartes could have said "'We think,' *cogitamus*, on as good ground as he said *cogito*" (Cooley, 1909:20). Social life is an organic whole, as Cooley's primary group concept further illustrates.

Primary Groups   Cooley defined **primary groups** as those characterized by "intimate face-to-face association and cooperation." They are fundamental

> in forming the social nature and ideals of the individual. The result of intimate association, psychologically, is a certain fusion of individualities in a common whole, so that one's very self, for many purposes at least, is the common life and purpose of the group. (Cooley, 1909:23)

The most significant primary groups to Cooley were the "family, the play-group of children, and the neighborhood or community of elders." Cooley believed

these groups are universal, "belonging to all times and all stages of development." Because primary groups are the major, universal groups, they form the
basis of "what is universal in human nature and human ideals" (1909:24).

If primary groups are critical to human social and moral development, and
to solidarity with others, then any threat to an individual's contact with significant primary groups will result in problems for the individual and society. Thus,
it is very important that the child not be deprived of consistent, long-term contacts in the early years. Social development of orphaned children often demonstrates the truth of this point, as the case of adopted orphans from some East
European countries after the fall of communism illustrates.

Like Durkheim, Cooley recognized that the problems of industrialization
and urbanization have a lot to do with the absence of, or deficiencies in, primary groups. Cooley's analysis of the tenement house gangs of early-twentieth-
century cities sounds familiar to us today: "In crowded neighborhoods, where
there are no playgrounds and street sports are unlawful, the human nature of
these gangs must take a semi-criminal direction" (1909:49). According to
Cooley, the "crowding and aggressive commercialism" in modern cities, coupled
with inhuman conditions such as child labor, could be alleviated by the development of new forms of primary association.

Thus, the primary group is not all positive for Cooley. It is usually a "competitive unity, admitting of self-assertion and various appropriative passions,"
but these tendencies are controlled by the common spirit. An individual may be
ambitious, but that ambition includes a "desired place in the thought of others,
and he will feel allegiance to common standards of service and fair play"
(1909:23–24).

At the same time, ideas of love, freedom, and justice also had their origins in
primary groups. These ideas are not uniform across societies and may vary
"with race, with the general state of civilization, and with the . . . institutions
that may prevail." Primary groups, however, "need to be watched and cherished
with very special care" so they do not decay or disappear, because they are the
basis on which higher imaginations, "moral unity," and "brotherhood" are built
(1909:33).

Statistical Methods in Sociology   Cooley worked briefly as a statistician,
and he was conscious of the value of statistics to sociology. But statistics could
not substitute for "social sympathy and imagination." Cooley likened the statistician to the cook who "neither supplies the food nor consumes it, but is a specialist on the intervening process." In his view, the exact methods of statistics
need to be complemented by "sympathetic observation and interpretation." In
using a questionnaire, for example, the "first duty of the user is to dramatize the
play of thought and feeling that takes place between the person that puts the
question and the person who answers it if it is to have any scientific value"
(1930:303).

Cooley did not believe that sociology should or could become like physics.
He saw sociology as resting on interpretation involving a complex of "native
ability, factual knowledge, social culture, and training in a particular technique"
to provide "imaginative reconstructions." He concluded that behavior can be recorded and handled statistically, but there is no way to avoid the ultimate inter-

pretive question: "What does it mean?" (Cooley, 1930:298). For Cooley "interpretation is all" because "untouched by the magic of a sufficiently powerful and trained imagination, data play dead" (1909:vii).

Nature of Society, Humans, and Change

Cooley admitted that his definition of society was broad, but he claimed that any other definition had to include the whole range of experience (1902:134). He defined **society** as a *"relation among personal ideas"* (1902:119). Everyone's imagination is a "special phase of society," and the "mind or imagination as a whole . . . is the *locus* of society in the widest possible sense" (1902:134). Cooley maintained that "all life hangs together in such a manner that any attempt to delimit a part of it is artificial" (1902:135).

Society is not, for Cooley, a Durkheimian "reality" standing apart from and above individuals. Society and individuals were not separable, but "simply collective and distributive aspects of the same thing." (1902:135).

Humanness, or **human nature,** to Cooley, is found in communication. Without it the mind remains in an "abnormal and nondescript state neither human nor . . . brutal." Communication is not simply speech, but includes gestures, facial expressions, tone of voice, as well as "writing, printing, railways, telegraphs, telephones, and whatever else may be the latest achievement in the conquest of space and time" (Cooley, 1909:61, 62). If Cooley were alive today, he would include the Internet and e-mail as communicative devices with meaning for personal and social life.

Primary group communication also makes us human, according to Cooley. Individuals do not "have" human nature at birth; they acquire it in "fellowship, and it decays in isolation." Thus, human nature is not simply an individual attribute, but is *"group nature . . .* a relatively simple and general condition of the social mind." Cooley concluded that family and neighborhood life are essential to the genesis of human nature. People realize this when they recall their own experiences and extend them through sympathetic observation (1909:29–31).

As for **social change,** Cooley held the Darwinian notion that growth and development characterize humans and societies. But for Cooley, evolution was more a philosophy and a faith than a method (Reck, 1964:xxxiv).

Individuals and society change together—physically, psychologically, and morally—and the change is inevitable and irreversible (Hinkle, 1966:xviii). But change and progress are the result of conflict in which "each individual, class or institution seeks to realize its own idea of good" (Cooley, 1909:199). Cooley understood such conflict in Hegelian dialectical terms: "Differences are resolved and integrated (but retained) in a new relation, a new unity. They are not constantly extinguished, as the Darwinian version of the struggle for existence and the survival of the fittest might suggest" (Cooley, 1918:xxxi). Rather, conflict and cooperation are "phases of one process which always involves something of both" (Cooley, 1918:39). In addition, change is not caused by a single factor, such as economics, as Marx and socialists believed (Cooley, 1909:255).

Cooley saw society as a "psychical whole" and social change in terms of growth in the individual of an ever-expanding we- or group-feeling, involving sympathy and understanding for others (Reck, 1964:xxxiv). Expansion of we-feeling or connection is accomplished through improved communication. "Enlargement of consciousness" strengthens the public will, and this leads to the "brotherhood of man in modern democracy" on an ever-increasing scale (Cooley, 1909:194). The harmony and altruism Cooley foresaw resulting from the extension of the public will would offset the social and psychological costs of modern industrial society because it would make social change more rational and economical.

Behind Cooley's optimism regarding change was a religious sensibility (Reck, 1964:xxxvi). Cooley believed that democracy was of the "same nature as Christianity," and although many reject religion, they are "Christian in feeling" because of the "deeper sense of common life." Democracy and Christian selfless-ness must first be established in the foundational primary group, the "happy family" (Cooley, 1909:52).

Class, Gender, and Race

Class, gender, and race were important aspects of Cooley's thought, with class and race being interconnected. He compared class and caste, and saw the race problem in the United States as a problem of caste formed by hereditary physi-cal differences. Two principles are fundamental to the formation of class in Cooley's view: heredity and competition. The principle of heredity is linked more to caste, the principle of competition to class.

Class   Cooley saw **caste,** or rigid inequalities between groups in society, as perpetuated by three conditions: "likeness or unlikeness in the constituents of the population; . . . the rate of social change . . . and . . . the state of communi-cation or enlightenment" (1909:217). A caste system persists in populations that are relatively homogeneous in physical characteristics and where intergroup communication is limited. Classes replace castes when members of society are less similar and when communication increase.

A more open and free society promotes divisions based on competition rather than heredity and marked a transition from caste to **class** society. Social class is not, however, a single phenomenon for individuals. Cooley maintained that there are "likely to be several kinds of classes overlapping one another, so that men who fall in the same class from one point of view are separate in an-other" (1909:248). This distinction may be pertinent to you as students. Your family antecedents may identify you as working class, but your college educa-tion is already preparing you for a different class position. This conception of so-cial class differs markedly from that of Marx.

Cooley believed that class consciousness promoted community or "we-feel-ing," but it had to be a consciousness that pursued the right social ends of "jus-tice and kindness" (1909:242). He suggested that modern industry provided ample opportunity for "ambitious young men" to move into the capitalist class, but that this should not obscure the "encroachment of slavery on an unguarded flank." With "bad housing, insecurity, excessive and deadening work, child la-bor and the lack of any education suitable to the industrial masses," some effec-tive class organization was imperative for the working class. Trade unions were not a complete answer, because "as soon as a man shows that marked capacity which would fit him to do something for fellows, it is ten to one that he accepts a renumerative position, and so passes into the upper class" (1909:275).

Cooley believed that class war was unlikely in the United States, but not so improbable in Europe, where economic classes were often castes and democracy was comparatively absent. In the United States he believed that class conflict would be relatively mild, as the various parties estimated their strengths in the "economic, social and moral situation, and so establish a *modus vivendi*" and avoid violent revolution (1918:273).

Class consciousness in the working classes of modern industrial societies was important, in Cooley's view, because without it "men become isolated, degraded and ineffective" (1909:242). Such consciousness was a means for the improvement of social conditions—but this beneficial collectivity did not extend to racial castes.

Race   Cooley was not sure that social change and democracy would "overcome the caste spirit when fostered by obvious physical and psychical differences" (1909:218). The entrenchment of racial caste in the United States illustrated the difficulty. Cooley believed that differences in "cranial and facial type may reasonably be supposed to mean *something*," however unfair the interpretation of these differences may have been (1918:274–275). The bias accompanying physical differences made it almost impossible to determine how much was due to biology and how much to culture.

Cooley maintained that, "in theory," a society composed of different race groups could cooperate with equality and goodwill (1918:279). But in such societies, in practice, one race had always dominated the other(s).

In his discussions of race, Cooley wavered between a separatist argument based on biology and a humanist argument that focused on universal brotherhood. Arguing from the former, he suggested there were "excellent grounds of national policy for preventing [different races'] mingling in large numbers in the same state" because "race antagonism weakens the common spirit, that moral unity, that willing subordination of the part to the whole, that are the requisite to a healthy national life" (1918:280). From this perspective, Cooley saw no reason why the United States and Australia should not avoid a caste problem by restricting Asian immigration, or why Asian nations should not discourage Western colonies (1918:280).

Restricting immigration, however, did not touch upon internal race problems. Cooley noted that thoughtful whites justified the subordination of blacks on the basis that "race *is* an organic whole—bound together by hereditary and social connection" and the "integrity of the white race and . . . civilization . . . requires Negro subordination." He suggested that this argument was "probably sound" if the two races were regarded as "distinct organisms" and was "perhaps better sociology than the view that every one should be considered solely on his merits as an individual." But he noted that this argument also represented "caste arrogance," because it did not recognize a spiritual brotherhood between races (1909:219). The idea that the black man is "fundamentally a man like the rest," Cooley concluded, should not be denied. "Science, religion, and the democratic spirit all give [the Negro] the right to it; and the white man cannot deny it to him without being false to his own best self" (1909:220).

Cooley's ambiguous views on race were in many ways typical of progressive or *liberal* white reformers at the turn of the century. His views on gender, like those of many other classical sociologists you have met, were similarly conventional.

Gender   Gender differentiation in that first primary group, the family, is natural, according to Cooley. From the outset, girls are more conscious of their looking-glass self—"they care more obviously for the social image, study it, reflect upon it more, and so have even during the first year an appearance of subtlety, *finesse*, often of affection, in which boys are comparatively lacking" (1902:202). Boys' imaginations are occupied with things rather than people, and they have a stronger, more complex ego than girls. A woman is more dependent on the good opinion of others. As a result, a woman needs to "fix" upon a person "in whose mind she can find a stable and compelling image of herself by which to live." This image is a source of strength; if it is not found, the woman may become a "derelict and drifting vessel" in contrast to a man who has a "greater power of standing alone" (1902:203). And although the sex instinct expresses the need to exert power for both men and women, Cooley maintains that in men this is a "masterful passion," whereas for women it is a "need to be appropriated or dominated" (1909:203–204).

In words reminiscent of Comte and Durkheim, Cooley believes that men are "more rational and stable" and should be the source of leadership in order to keep women's emotionality in check. Nevertheless, women were critical to the production of moral unity in society. Women are the ones who are "inspired by sympathy with children and with the weak and suffering classes" (1909:364).

An important aspect of the transformation of I-feeling into we-feeling was women's maternal instinct. Cooley had reservations about the turn-of-the-century women's movement, especially with regard to marriage and the welfare of the race, because it might inhibit women's we-feeling. He saw much that seems "anarchical and reckless . . . in feminist tendencies," but acknowledged that this might be because society is in a transitional state. Women when trained and trusted might be more sensible, since they are not likely to reject "any real wisdom that the male mind may be able to contribute" (1918:216).

Other Theories and Theorists

It was the we-feeling that Cooley, as a humanist, wished to see prevail in society at large. Moral unity was, for Cooley, the "mother . . . of all social ideals" (1909:35). Social change, or progress, was found in the growth of sympathy and understanding—that is, we-feeling—through improved communication. Communication promoted democracy, broke down caste, and "wipes out conventional distinctions," leaving only those that were functional for the organic whole (1909:192–193).

The transformation of I-feeling into we-feeling on a large scale is at the heart of Cooley's ethical stance with respect to sociology. "A social science which is not also, centrally, an ethical science is unfaithful to its deepest responsibility, that of functioning in aid of general progress" (Cooley, 1930:258).

A vital contribution of sociology to the progress of social democracy was the demonstration of community and communication in primary groups. Public opinion, emerging out of "attention and discussion," is critical to a vigorous democracy. Cooley believed that this would be made easier by modern technological innovations—transforming through communication the representative republic originally framed in the Constitution into a fully functioning democracy involving all people.

Critique and Conclusions

Like Max Weber, Cooley insisted that sociological knowledge required not simply analysis of observable behavior, but insight into the meaning of that behavior to those involved. In pursuit of this end, Cooley used his own mind and imagination as the starting point for his sociological observations. He was the prototype "armchair sociologist." Although this description has often been applied derisively, Cooley's "introspective analysis" remains an indispensable part of present-day sociology, "while the labors of many fact gatherers are long forgotten" (Coser, 1977:330).

G. H. Mead, to whom we turn next, characterized Cooley's idea of society as mental rather than scientific. Mead was influenced by Cooley's ideas on the interactive, communicative nature of society, and the idea that the self was created from such interactions, beginning in attachment to small, primary groups, through which links to larger social structures are established.

George Herbert Mead (1863–1931)

George Herbert Mead was born at South Hadley, Massachusetts. His father, a clergyman, was appointed to the Chair of Homiletics (the art of preaching) at Oberlin College in Ohio in 1870. In 1881 Mead's father died, leaving his family in dire straits. To make ends meet, Mead's mother taught at Oberlin, and she later became President of Mount Holyoke College. Mead waited tables to earn his board at Oberlin, where he graduated in 1883. He taught school for a while, then worked as a railroad construction surveyor in the northwestern United States and Canada, while continuing to tutor in the winter months. In 1887 Mead decided to return to college and enrolled at Harvard to study philosophy.

At Harvard, Mead became interested in the work of the philosopher Josiah Royce, Hegelian idealism, and William James's pragmatic philosophy—influences that remained important throughout his career. Mead also read Darwin, which fueled his disenchantment with the religiosity of his father and the religious atmosphere at Oberlin and made him receptive to the works of Royce and James. Mead found Royce's work "intoxicating" because it demonstrated that "philosophy was no longer the handmaiden of theology, nor the textbook for formal logic and puritan ethics" (Mead, 1964b:168). Nonetheless, the Christian principles that Mead absorbed from his parents and at Oberlin influenced him throughout his life (Coser, 1977:342).

In 1888, Mead went to study in Germany, where he became interested in the work of physiological psychologists. In 1891, he returned and became an instructor in the Department of Philosophy and Psychology at the University of Michigan. There he met both Cooley and John Dewey. In 1893, Dewey went to the University of Chicago as Chair of the Department of Philosophy, and he invited Mead to join him. Mead and Dewey remained lifelong friends. Mead particularly admired Dewey's ability to combine academic research and political life (Shalin, 1988:924).

Mead remained at the University of Chicago for the rest of his life. Chicago was an ideal location for an academic with progressive reform ideas, because the university encouraged faculty interest in social problems and Chicago was a microcosm of the sort of problems that *rapid industrialization, urbanization,* and *mass immigration* generated at the turn of the century. Much of what we now have as Mead's writing was, in fact, sets of lectures compiled by his students.

Mead was typical of the liberal or progressive reformers who were the children of Protestant ministers. They endorsed reform but had faith in science and education, rather than religion, to achieve the needed social transformations (Crumden, 1982).

Mead's wife was a feminist, and he "marched in social protest against women's disenfranchisement and had many suffragists stay at his home" (Deegan, 1988:209). One of Mead's doctoral students, Jessie Taft, wrote her thesis in 1913 on "The Woman Movement from the Point of View of Social Consciousness." Taft wanted to be a professor, but academic barriers to women were formidable. With Mead's help, in 1934 she became Director of the School of Social Work at the University of Pennsylvania, where she remained until her retirement in 1950 (Deegan, 1991:386).

Mead's endorsement of women's rights involved not only his wife, but his daughter-in-law, Irene Tufts Mead, as well. In 1910 she solicited his advice about whether she should attend medical school or follow her friends' advice and volunteer for public and mental health groups. Despite the fact that she had a young child, making attending medical school difficult, Mead maintained that "worthwhile things are difficult" and a "woman as well as a man should have training for a social calling apart from family life, this for the sake of the best family life but principally for the independence of mind and self which everyone legitimately craves" (quoted in Rosenberg, 1982:137). This was unusual advice for a middle-class married woman to receive at the turn of the century, especially from her father-in-law.

Mead's Central Theories and Methods

Several background strands led to the formulation of Mead's ideas: pragmatism, Darwinism, the experimental method, and social psychology, as well as his philosophical training. They shaped his ideas about the way individuals become integrated into society and, like Cooley, about the nature and role of communication.

German Idealist Tradition   Mead took from Hegel the idea that consciousness and society were dialectically emergent phenomena. Like Marx, Mead also replaced Hegel's "Spirit" that constantly overcame its alienation with "universal society in which all social potential would be realized in a unified world." The characteristic of social development for Mead was individuals realizing themselves "in their opposition to one another"; those "oppositions are the starting point for the development of a new social order" (1938:655). More generally, from German idealism Mead took the idea that the development of the self requires reflexivity—that is, the ability of an individual (the subject) to be an object to himself as a result of "taking the attitudes of others who are involved in his conduct" (1964b:283–4). This idea is at the heart of Mead's concept of the generalized other.

Darwin and Evolution   The general idea of evolution was important to Mead, but it was Darwin's idea of random variations that Mead found most useful. To Mead, Darwin's key point was the idea of constant pressure leading "to the selection of those variants which are better adapted to the conditions under which they must live" (Mead, 1934:11). In the realm of humans, random variations allow for unpredictability and indeterminism in the course of social evolution. The adaptive mechanism is the reflective consciousness of human beings, who adapt, rather than simply react, to their environment. The self and society are therefore adaptive and subject to evolutionary processes. These processes, in turn, depend on communication.

Symbolic Communication   One of the physiological psychologists Mead met in Germany, Wilhelm Wundt, had discussed gestures as signs and symbolic communication. Symbolic communication is the use of signs, such as gestures, to convey meaning. When the gesture is more than a reflex action that stimulates a response in the other, it becomes a **significant symbol**. A significant symbol is any gesture that has an idea behind it, such that the symbol "answers to the meaning in the experience of the first individual and . . . also calls out the meaning in the second individual" (Mead, 1964a:157).

Making self an object contributes to symbolic communication in two ways, according to Mead: First, "the individual indicates things and their character to others, and second, . . . the stimulus of which he makes use is one to which he tends to respond in the same fashion as that in which the others respond" (1938:371–372). The self, then, is a social object dependent on communication, especially the communication of symbols and gestures.

Mead extended Wundt's idea of gestures as significant communication to the "conversation of gestures" (1964a:161). This point is illustrated in the example of a dog fight, in which each dog's action is a stimulus for the other dog; as the act is "responded to by the other dog; it in turn, undergoes change" (1964a:154). This is a conversation of gestures, though not **significant gestures**. Gestures only become significant when there is an attitude behind them. In the case of an aggressive dog attacking another dog, the observer cannot say that the animal "means it in the sense that he has a *reflective* determination to attack" (1964a:157, emphasis added). The dog fight can be compared to the action of someone shaking a fist. In this case, a plausible assumption would be not only that the gesture indicates a hostile attitude but that there is some idea behind it (1964a:157). When the gesture has an idea behind it, and when it arouses that idea in the other individual, we have a significant symbol.

Mead indicated that the conversation of gestures can be not only external, or between discrete individuals, but also internal, or "between a given individual and himself." Both involve the individual's "taking the attitude of the other in his gestures" (1964a:159). And it is only with significant symbols that mind or intelligence is possible. Significant symbols are the basis of language, which, in turn, enable humans to express meaning. From verbal language and gesture emerged the mind and the self (1964a:195). In other words, "mind arises through communication . . . and not communication through mind" (1964a:161–162).

Mead's "perfected social intelligence" is a social ideal to be achieved as human beings increase their reflexivity through symbolic communication. The ability to objectify oneself results from "taking the attitudes of others who are involved in his conduct" and thus "becoming an object for himself" (1964b:283–284). This "other," then, is not specific but general.

The Generalized Other   Mead believed that human biology provides the capacity for developing mind and self, but that only in social interaction do we become "human." The self develops only when we take into account others' actions and reactions. This idea, close to Cooley's looking-glass self, is central to Mead's conception of the **generalized other** which involves a person's ability to objectify the self by "taking the attitudes of others" toward her or his conduct (1964b:283–284).

The capacity to take the role of others develops in two stages. In the **play stage,** the child takes the role of a few significant others, such as parents. For example, when playing with a doll, "he responds in tone of voice and attitude as his parents respond to his cries and chortles" and in doing so, "he calls or tends to call out in himself the same response that he calls out in the other" (Mead, 1964a: 285). The play stage represents relatively simple role-taking because one role at a time is played and the relationship between roles is not clearly understood.

The **game stage** involves the ability to understand connections between roles. At this stage, the child must "not only take the role of the other . . . but must assume the various roles of all participants in the game, and govern his action accordingly" (Mead, 1964b:285). When this stage is reached, the child is able to exercise some control over self, and over others' reaction to that self. The character of a game is that "every act in the game is determined and qualified by all other acts," and "this is expressed in the rules of the game, and implies in each individual a generalized player that is present in every part that is taken" (Mead, 1938:374). In the game stage, the child learns to "function in the organized whole, and thus tends to determine . . . his relationship with the group to which he belongs" (Mead, 1934:160). The game stage begins the ability to take the role of the generalized other.[1]

---

[1]Mead (1964a:218) points out that inanimate objects as well as other people can take the role of generalized other to the extent that the individual's response to the object(s) is a social response.

Part of one's response to the generalized and internalized other is the conscience—the behaviors and attitudes about which one feels guilty or for which one punishes oneself. The conscience provides a practical or pragmatic way for human beings to adapt to their environment or generalized other.

Pragmatism   Mead's concept of the conscience was based on the pragmatism of William James and John Dewey. According to William James and John Dewey, ideas are the result of humans' adaptation to their environments, and the meaning of "truth" is determined by the practical results of such adaptations. Consciousness therefore has a "transitive character" according to the nature of experience(s). Because meaning constantly emerges in relation to social action, the stimulus-response model developed by John Watson is limited. This is why Mead called his approach social behavorism. Social psychology was, for Mead, "behavioristic in the sense of starting off with observable activity," but it was not "behavioristic in the sense of ignoring the inner experiences [or self] of the individual" (1964a:121–122).

Human beings reflect on the meaning of a stimulus before reacting. Meaning depends on the purpose of the act, the context in which it is performed, and the reactions of others to the act. As James noted, the self is both knowing and known. According to Dewey, it is out of reflexive action(s) in problematic situations that humans constructed morality, which is a group or societal phenomenon. It is the "social aspect of the selves of all individual members taken collectively." Ethical ideals and ethical problems represent the outcome of the "conflict between the social and the asocial . . . aspects of the individual self" (1964a:274, 275). As "truth" and ethical standards are social creations, they are not fixed for all time. Different problematic situations in different cultures give rise to different ethical solutions, and different consciences.

The Scientific Method in Sociology   In his 1923 essay "Scientific Method and the Moral Sciences," Mead stated that the *Scientific Method* carries the assumption that the social world, like the physical world, is governed by laws that the sociologist or reformer may discover.

> The intelligence which exhibits itself in the solution of problems in natural science is of the same character as that which we . . . should apply in dealing with our social and moral problems because it is the same intelligence which enters into and controls the physical world and which deals with the problems of human society. . . . It is this frank acceptance of human society as part of the natural order that scientific method demands when it is applied to the solution of social problems. (1964b:264)

However, unlike the physical scientist, who stands apart from the object of investigation, the sociologist is part of the "forces that are being investigated," and for this reason reflective consciousness is critical (1964b:4). Reflective consciousness enables the investigator to recognize problems requiring change. But the investigator should tackle a problem not in terms of some utopian plan, but as something to be solved in the present. Mead maintained that this pragmatic attention to present difficulties is compatible with the nature of the universe, which is "continually readjusted according to problems arising in the consciousness of the individuals within society" (1964b:209). Any "vision on the mount," setting out a future ideal society, was, for Mead, "pernicious," anti-democratic, and doomed to failure (1964b:5).

The scientific method was compatible with democracy, in Mead's view. Science demanded that all the facts be taken into account. Democracy also sought to consider all opinions and values in formulating policies that would provide maximum satisfaction for all social needs. Although science could not legislate values, it could illuminate the consequences of positions and actions proposed by democratic policymakers (1964b:210). Science is a "great secular adventure" that advanced society by constant adjustments to the environment—physical or social—and with every adjustment "society and its individuals have changed in like degree" (1964b:266).

Nature of Society, Humans, and Change

Because of Mead's emphasis on the development of the self and mind, there has been a tendency to overlook his views on the nature of society. But according to Mead, mind and self only develop in society, and society itself is changed by individuals. This dialectical interdependence between society and the individual is predicated on communication and on individuals' ability to understand one another. The development of mutual understanding is, in Mead's view, the great adaptive advance separating humans from the rest of the animal world.

Humans are able to undertake collective actions through communication, and the key to human communication is the ability to take the role of the other. The ability to take "the same attitude toward himself that the community takes" usually ensures that the individual recognizes "duties as well as . . . rights" and will "admonish himself as others would" for any failings. The evolution of society is the result of communication through which different individuals participate in common activities (1964a:35, 36).

Mead maintained that social evolution is always in the direction of greater size and complexity. Social evolution cannot be reversed and, in Mead's view, should not be, because evolution also involves enlarged, more altruistic minds and actions.

Humans   The essential condition for the development of the mind is, according to Mead, "that the individual in acting in reference to the environment should, as part of that action, be acting with reference to himself, so that his action would include himself as object" (1938:367). When the self objectifies itself, the individual has attained self-consciousness. Self-consciousness can be glimpsed in children's play when children refer to themselves as Dick or Jane, as in "Jane (or Dick) now does so-and-so."

Mead believed that human beings are only human when a reflective mind takes the self as an object. Thus, there are no minds or selves apart from society. Reflection allows humans to work together, to envisage a future, to imagine objects and situations that are not physically present, and to plan future behavior toward those objects and situations. Mind and self are not inborn, but develop from social experience and activity, most especially the activity of taking the role of others, including the generalized other. This concept returns us to society, since the generalized other is one's "organized community or social group" (1964a:218).

Three comments seem in order here. First, our discussion of humans and society has interwoven them, since they were not separated by Mead, nor did he consider either primary. Second, Mead saw societies as differing in what they viewed as good or bad, so he considered cultural values to be relative, not absolute. Thus, neither human nature nor society is good or bad, except in relation to its own norms and behaviors. Third, he saw humans as pliable, meaning that human nature can be altered.

The generalized other, according to Mead, exerts social control over the attitudes and behaviors of individuals, thereby ensuring a certain predictability in social life. This predictability is not complete, however—individuals can and do act spontaneously—hence the distinction between the "I" and the "Me."

The I, the Me, and Social Change   The self that emerged from taking the attitude of others Mead called the **"Me."** The "Me" represents the attitudes of others that the self is aware of, and to which the "I" responded (1964a:230). The "Me" contains the social knowledge of roles, structures, values, and beliefs and their implications for social action. The "Me" represents self-control as the "expression of the 'Me' against the expression of the 'I'" (1964a:238–239). To use a "Freudian expression, the 'me' is in a certain sense a censor," or superego (Mead, 1934:210).

The **"I,"** on the other hand, is the creative, imaginative part of the self, which Mead believed is particularly evident in artists. An artist's emphasis on the unconventional is an example of the assertion of the "I." In the symbiotic relationship between the "I" and the "Me," the "Me" usually prevails, but impulsive or uncontrolled behavior can occur in which the "Me" does not determine the expression and actions of the "I."

Mead also suggested that on unusual occasions the "I" and "Me" may not be distinct. This occurs in highly emotional collective situations, such as on religious or patriotic occasions, when there was a "peculiar sense of exaltation." In these contexts, the "reaction one calls out in others is the response which one is making oneself" (1934:273).

According to Mead, all individuals sought self-expression, especially when feeling confined, as by routine work. Routinization prompted individuals to seek ways to express themselves—to express the "I." In a modern industrial society of "functional . . . differentiations" that are opposed to "individual needs and ends," hobbies, leisure pursuits, and even "goofing off" were critical to the "I" and the health of the individual (1934:310).

Because of the ongoing interactions of the "I" and the "Me," Mead argued, society was never static but always changing—"a universe which may be continually adjusted according to the problems arising in the consciousness of individuals" (1964b:208–209). Mead, as a pragmatist and a progressive, was pointing out that social reform cannot be predicated on some ideal, utopian model, but is necessarily tailored to the needs and interests of the individuals involved. For this reason, the sociologist as scientist was important to any social reform.

Class, Gender, and Race

Mead was sympathetic to socialism, and many of his ideas paralleled those of Marx (Shalin, 1988:929). Both saw the dehumanizing effects of industrialism and capitalism, and both believed that science and technology have the potential to transform this situation.

Class   Whereas for Marx only class revolution could abolish the inequities of capitalism, Mead believed that democratic, liberal reforms could solve those problems. Mead talked about "institutionalizing revolution," meaning that revolutions can be effected by "strictly constitutional and legal" methods (Shalin, 1988:931). Democracy could allow a peaceful transformation through the use of progressive legislation.

Mead recognized that U.S. democracy is far from perfect, because unrestricted laissez-faire capitalism creates a large, nominally free, but deprived underclass. For this reason Mead, along with other Progressives such as Dewey, stressed the need for both education and economic changes to alleviate capitalism's worst excesses and to restore human dignity to the deprived. A key to this restoration is taking "the role of the other" by those more fortunate. On this count socialism was significant to Mead because it opposed the utilitarian view of the asocial human who acts without regard for others. When the utilitarian view prevailed, even in a democracy, individuals would act selfishly and "injustice and human misery" would continue (Shalin, 1988:938).

Gender   Mead was not simply an ivory-tower theorist, he was also a social activist, and much of his published work concerned social reform issues and practical politics.[2] Among these concerns was an interest in the status of women, as noted earlier. And his theoretical concepts—"the self, the other, the generalized other, mind, society, institution, international-mindedness"—are, for the most part, nonsexist (Deegan, 1988:208).

Mead, as well as Dewey and other pragmatists and progressives, worked closely with the sociologist Jane Addams at Hull House, a settlement house that developed programs to assist the poor. Hull House, however, offered more than social assistance: Addams and the other settlement workers, including Charlotte Gilman for a short period, undertook social surveys, "gathered statistics, investigated factories and industries, conducted health examinations, examined sanitary conditions, and lobbied for legislative and political reform" (Deegan,1991:39). Mead supported, intellectually as well as practically, Addams's applied sociological work.

Race   Mead did not address directly the exclusion of African Americans from mainstream U.S. society (Shalin, 1988:947). His views, from his pragmatist phi-

---

[2]Commentators on Mead usually state that he published very little and that the bulk of the published work consists of the compilation of graduate student notes. For example, Strauss (in Mead, 1964a:vii) states that in his lifetime Mead published only a few papers. But Mead's publications were more pragmatic and applied sociological works than purely theoretical efforts.

losophy of history, stressed the importance of experimental science as the means to "change the environment within which society exists, and the forms and institutions of society itself" (Mead, 1938:508). One scientific technique that Mead believed would be of benefit in transforming society was **eugenics**. Mead argued that "biology and psychology" had discovered the "valuable traits and types which could with intelligent selection be encouraged and rendered permanent." Consequently, for those "human beings who are most distant from us" by virtue of "social caste, economic status, race, and differences of culture and civilization," their intolerable social conditions are susceptible of intelligent control through eugenics (1938:510–511).

Mead's endorsement of eugenics must be interpreted historically. The horrors of the Nazi regime and more recent genocidal practices in the interest of "ethnic cleansing" based on eugenics were still to come. Furthermore, in Mead's view, race prejudice was an "unthinking emotional attitude based on an equally unthinking sense of group superiority." This may have been functional in the past to reinforce group solidarity, but it was now obsolete. To Mead, what eugenics offered was control over prejudice through the "careful and scientific application of the intelligence test" (1938:510).

Other Theorists and Theories

Mead was indebted to the ideas of many other scientists and philosophers, including Cooley's theory of mind, self, and society. This debt is seen in Mead's essay, "Cooley's Contributions to American Thought" (1964a:293–307). Mead agreed with Cooley's rejection of Cartesian dualism—individual versus society, mind versus body, egoism versus altruism. He endorsed Cooley's view that the "stream of consciousness is the carrier of both the self and society, and each can be seen to be dependent upon the other for its evolution in experience" (1964a:296).

Mead, however, criticized Cooley's view that external reality is only to be found in the mind of the individual. Mead contended that if reality appears in the imagination, then it must already have an existence apart from that imagination. That is, for others to appear in one's imagination they must have a prior, objective existence.

For Mead, then, **society** is the product of reflexive individuals' taking account of others, and mind and self can only develop in society. Thus, there is a dialectical relation between individuals and society: society emerges from individual action at the same time that the individual is a product of society. Society's basis is the **social act**, which he defined as "one in which one individual serves in his action as a stimulus to a response from another individual" (1964b:123).

Albert Einstein and Relativity   Mead found Einstein's work important in illustrating the relativity of perspectives. That is, any individual action is variable in terms of time, space, and past experiences. More generally, relativity meant that the social was an emergent phenomenon, and "emergent life changes the character of the world just as emergent velocities change the character of masses" (Mead, 1932:65). Thus, for Mead, the determinism of early positivism was replaced by indeterminacy. Science, including social science, must take into account the multiplicity of perspectives on reality.

Reform and Science   As noted previously, Mead the philosopher, sociologist, and scientist was also the hands-on liberal reformer. His reformist activities were informed by a belief that moral issues were not about right or wrong, but about the "possibility of acting so as to take into account as far as possible all the values involved" (1938:465). Taking account of values required the scientific method. Mead insisted that the progressive reformer must face social problems like a scientist and formulate a "working hypothesis" to be tested and applied, recognizing that the solution might need to be changed or revised in the future. The reformer/scientist had a "method and a control in application, not an ideal to work towards" and his "foresight does not go beyond the testing of his hypothesis" (1964b:3).

Humanism and Conflict   Despite his insistence on the relativity of all values, Mead endorsed democracy and international-mindedness. Mead believed that the latter would prevail, although he recognized that hostility, war, competition, and conflict were at least as normal as peace and cooperation.

Like Simmel, Mead recognized that conflict might promote social cohesion. Mead pointed out that the "solid South is a product of common hostility to the Negro" and the "Ku Klux Klan is a deliberate manufacture of compact groups by the use of racial and religious antipathies." Other institutionalized conflicts such as organized labor and employers' associations also "preserve their solidarity . . . by the mechanism of hostility" (1964b:369). Internationally, the First World War was an example both of the unifying nature of conflict and of the difficulty in promoting international-mindedness.

Mead suggested that until national-level conflicts were overcome, international-mindedness would be elusive, and the current crop of tribal and ethnic conflicts seems to endorse this point. But Mead pointed out that the same psychological mechanism that promoted solidarity in conflict groups—the recognition of common interests and identities—might promote national- and international-mindedness. What the sociologist and reformer must do is analyze this mechanism without getting "caught in its meshes," so as to be able to provide a scientific solution (1964b:356). The key was to transform self-interest into collective, altruistic interest. The "ideal or ultimate goal of human social progress—is the attainment of a universal human society in which all individuals would possess a perfected social intelligence" and an "interlocking interdependence of human individuals upon one another" (1934:310).

Critique and Conclusions

Cooley and especially Mead laid the foundations for the **symbolic interactionist** theoretical perspective—the understanding of interaction based on communication through the use of symbols. Mead's followers promoted this perspective in competition with the structural functionalism dominating U.S. sociology at mid-century (see Chapter 14). Mead's work was also important to various sociological specialties: the labeling theory of deviance, Erving Goffman's dramaturgical approach (see Chapter 20), role- and reference-group theory, child-development and socialization studies, and the sociology of knowledge.

Both Mead and Cooley stressed the need to preserve and enlarge democratic freedoms, though Mead was more involved than Cooley in the promotion of reforms. Both theorists believed that the success of reform efforts depends on the use of scientific methods, with the sociologist having a great contribution to make. Sociological methods could evaluate all claims by allowing the participants to have input. However, the exact nature of any future society could not be specified because "every generation has to accomplish democracy over and over again" and any utopian formula may "turn into a straitjacket" (Shalin, 1988:945).

Mead suggested that although the world "comes to us from the past" and "possesses and controls us," we can "possess and control the world we discover and invent. This is the world of moral order . . . a splendid adventure if we can rise to it" (1964b:266). Such optimism was less apparent in the work of Sigmund Freud.

Sigmund Freud (1856–1939)

Sigmund Freud was born in the small Moravian town of Freiberg in 1856. His family was Jewish, and his father was a wool merchant. His mother was his father's second wife, and he had two older half-brothers from the previous marriage. One of these sons had children of his own very close to Freud's age.

The family moved to Vienna in 1860, where Freud entered the University in 1873 to study medicine. In 1876 he became a neurological researcher at Ernst Brucke's physiology laboratory. He spent most of his time examining the nervous system, first in fish and then in humans. During this period Freud met Josef Breuer, a physician and physiologist, who became a friend and later a collaborator on the work *Studies in Hysteria* (1895).

Freud graduated in medicine in 1881 and began work at the Psychiatric Clinic in the Department of Nervous Diseases at the General Hospital in Vienna. Biographers have claimed that the move from Brucke's laboratory was occasioned by the fact that Freud had fallen in love with Martha Bernays, and he realized he needed to make more money if he hoped to marry her. Freud continued his research in cerebral anatomy, but began to concentrate on nervous disorders.

In 1885 he went to Paris to study at the Pathological Laboratory of Jean Charcot. Freud was particularly interested in Charcot's use of hypnosis to cure hysterical paralysis, and was also interested in Charcot's contention that sexual issues were always at the root of hysteria. After returning to Vienna from Paris, Freud set up a private practice, and was able to afford to marry Martha in 1886. He experimented with hypnosis but found that the effects were short-lived; however, he did accept Charcot's belief that neuroses and other mental aberrations were sexually motivated.

Freud's reputation became international, and supporters of his psychoanalytic theories increased in numbers. However, he was never without critics, especially those offended by his emphasis on sexuality. Freud traveled widely, but remained a fixture in Vienna until 1938. The takeover of Austria by the Nazi regime made it imperative that Freud, as a famous Jew, find asylum. It was inevitable that he and his family would be a target, and indeed his apartment and office were searched by Nazi brown shirts. Freud and his family moved to England, where he died in 1939.

Freud's Central Theories and Methods

Freud's theories are well known, if not always well understood. They have inspired numerous references in popular culture—for example:

> They fuck you up, your mum and dad.
> They may not mean to, but they do.
> They fill you with the faults they had
> And add some extra, just for you. (Larkin, 1974:30)

Freud, a trained medical scientist, saw psychoanalysis as a science dealing with the psychic energy of the mind and personality. For Freud, mind and body could not be separated: The operations of the mind arise out of instinctual forces that in turn cause varieties of human behavior. More specifically, the causes of maladjustments or neuroses lie in the unconscious, rather than in the conscious mind. For example, in *The Psychopathology of Everyday Life* (1904), Freud examined "errors" such as slips of the tongue or pen, obsessive behaviors, forgetting familiar names and places, and mislaying objects. These he saw as clues to the existence of an unconscious and to the unacknowledged desires in the unconscious that governed such behaviors.

Freud began with the assumption that a scientific explanation of mental illness requires looking at physical and chemical changes in the body. He later came to believe that explanation must take into account human motives as well as instincts and drives. Freud believed that the psychoanalyst must uncover the unconscious factors hidden beneath the behaviors and communications of the patient, and help the patient understand these factors. The basic personality structure, its topography, and conflict resolution are important parts of Freud's theory, as is his view of gender. Equally important for our purposes is his theory of culture and society, or social control.

Basic Personality Structure   Freud postulated that the personality combined the id, superego, and ego.

The **id** is the source of psychic energy, which strives for pleasure and gratification. It has no concept of time, causality, or control. It seeks immediate discharge of love, hate, aggression, and other instinctual drives. If the id were in control, noted Freud, there would be no civilization and no adulthood. The infant is all id.

The **superego** is both the means of and the result of socialization. It includes the moral norms that govern conduct, the prescriptions and proscriptions (do's and don'ts) that a culture seeks to teach an individual. It is the censor of and guide to actions. It is almost synonymous with conscience, except that it also includes the ideal self. The incorporation of the superego's demands causes the individual to feel remorse and guilt.

The **ego** is the conscious intelligence that "referees" or is the executor between the id and superego. It is the "reality" principle, involving thinking, reasoning, and choosing. It has a sense of time, making it possible for the individual to delay gratification. In the healthy individual, the ego strikes a balance between impulse and control—id and superego. While the work of the ego is sometimes conscious, more often than not it is unconscious.

Levels or Topography of the Personality   The struggles among id, superego, and ego take place at three "levels": conscious, preconscious, and unconscious.

The **conscious** level is that of which we are immediately aware. What are you thinking of as you read these words? Freud's ideas, or noise outside, or the fact that you are hungry and finding it hard to concentrate? We are only aware of a small number of things at any one moment.

The **preconscious** is that which can be summoned forth by memory. If I ask you to remember what you had for lunch yesterday or what you did on your 15th birthday, you can call it to mind, or bring it from the preconscious to the conscious level. Thousands upon thousands of bits of information are in the preconscious, available "for the asking."

The **unconscious** is that large body of struggles, events, experiences, wishes, drives, and fears that you simply cannot dredge up by yourself. Most of the fear-inducing portions of our experience are in the unconscious, and in order to deal with such problems we must become conscious of these deep-seated issues. That is where psychotherapy comes in: The work of psychoanalysis or therapy is to help the individual bring these problem to the surface, or into consciousness, so they can be dealt with.

Conflict Resolution   When we are able to deal with conflict on the conscious level, we make a rational choice about whether to act upon an urge or to control it. Many conflicts, however, are unconscious, and they may be set aside, or repressed, rather than solved. Freud talked about the **defense mechanisms** individuals use in order to avoid dealing with their id/superego struggles. One is **sublimation**, transforming an undesirable id striving into an acceptable social outlet. For example, he suggested, one exercises or engages in an artistic endeavor as a way to expend psychic energy. This is one of Freud's terms that has become part of our everyday speech.

Another defense mechanism is **rationalization**—proposing consciously acceptable motives for what you have done or want to do. Rationalization is reminiscent of Pareto's derivations, or justifications—not reasons—for our actions. Freud discussed other defense mechanisms, but these two examples are sufficient to indicate how they work. They are, as the word suggests, defenses, not solutions. They do not resolve the problems they attempt to deal with; they merely deflect or repress them. We turn now to Freud's ideas that have implications for society and culture.

Instincts and Civilization   Until Freud was almost 60 years of age, he concentrated on the personality. However, in the last 23 years of his life he turned his attention to culture and society. In 1935, in the postscript to his

Autobiography, he made a remarkable comment on his change during the previous two decades:

> My interest . . . after making a long detour through the natural sciences, medicine and psychotherapy, returned to the cultural problems which had fascinated me long before, when I was a youth scarcely old enough for thinking. (Freud, 1935:20)

He began with the idea that the mind is the repository of **instincts.** Instincts represent the demands of the body on the mind, and are prime motivating forces for behavior. In Freud's view, there are two basic types of instincts: the sexual, **Eros,** and the aggressive or death instinct, **Thanatos** (1933:103). Eros is associated with eroticism and self-preservation, Thanatos with aggression and destruction. Freud concentrated on Eros, especially as manifested in sexual drives, in the early years, but later on Thanatos took on more significance. However, Eros and Thanatos "seldom—perhaps never—appear in isolation, but always mingle with each other" (1930:98).

It is these two basic instincts that, according to Freud, "make human communal life difficult and threaten its survival" (1933:110). **Civilization** controls both sexual and aggressive instincts—it is the superego in the culture. Freud asserted that "civilization is to blame for a great part of our misery, and we should be much happier if we were to give it up and go back to primitive conditions," in which the id had free reign. All human beings seek happiness, or pleasure, but this goal is unattainable, so humans ordinarily are both controlled and unhappy (1930:44, 28). Human suffering has three sources: "from our own body, which is destined to decay and dissolution, . . . from the outer world, which can rage against us with the most powerful and pitiless forces of destruction; and finally from our relations with other men." The unhappiness from "this last origin we find perhaps more painful than any other" (1930:28). Civilized unhappiness, as Freud saw it, was both a cultural and an individual phenomenon, involving coercion and control.

Coercion/Control   Karl Marx, you recall, argued that the proletariat or working class was oppressed and exploited by the bourgeoisie—that is, the haves oppressed the have-nots. He and Engels argued that private property corrupted human nature. To Freud, however, civilization was not just wealth or property and its control. If private property were abolished, aggression would still appear in human relations.

Marx, in Freud's view, ignored the fact that everyone, not just the have-nots, was oppressed by civilization or superego controls. If society oppresses us all, then the only alternative is that proposed by the anarchist, not the Marxist. Class oppression, then, was not as important as the opposition between civilization and every individual. And one element in society's coercion, according to Freud, was religion.

Religion   Religion, according to Freud, meets human beings' need for comfort and their need to avoid feelings of helplessness. However, he considered it an illusory solution that would be discovered to be a fraud. Human beings' memory of the origins of society lay in a mythic past.

In *Totem and Taboo* (1913), Freud related the origins of religion and civilization to the myth of the murdered primeval father. He believed his views on the origins of civilization and religion were confirmed in the work of both Darwin and Durkheim. Darwin had speculated that precivilized men had lived in groups or hordes under the control of one strong male. Durkheim (Chapter 4) had illuminated the connection between the control of the dominant male, the worship of the totem and the taboo preventing sexual relations among those belonging to the same totemic group. The **totem** is the bird or animal with whose characteristics a society identifies closely.

Freud suggested that in "Darwin's primal horde" one strong male, the primal father, "keeps all the females for himself and drives away his sons as they grow up." The result was that the sons "came together, killed and devoured their father and so made an end to the patriarchal horde" (1913:141). This cannibalism was the first totemic meal, and the "repetition and . . . commemoration of this memorable and criminal deed" were the "beginning of so many things—of social organization, of moral restrictions and of religion."

After the sons had satisfied their father-hatred, Freud theorized, they identified with him by eating him. Their "affection" for him resurfaced, and a "sense of guilt made its appearance," so that the "dead father became stronger than the living one had been." The sons' expiation of their guilt was achieved by "forbidding the killing of the totem, the substitute for their father; and they renounced its fruits by resigning their claim to the women who had now been set free" (1913:142, 143). Renunciation of these women was pragmatic. The brothers were rivals for the possession of the women when the father was eliminated, so if they were to live together, they had no alternative but to institute a law against incest.[3] Thus, the two major taboos of totem religion and the Oedipus complex (to be discussed later)—murder and incest—were established.

According to Freud, then, society is based on "complicity in the common crime," and religion on "the sense of guilt and the remorse attaching to it" (1913:146). God is therefore "nothing other than an exalted father," and an individual's relation to God parallels his relation to his biological father. Freud concluded that the "beginnings of religion, morals, society and art converge in the Oedipus complex" (1913:156).

Nature of Society, Humans, and Change

In introducing Freud's major themes, we have already become familiar with his view of the nature of society and humans. Here we add to those ideas.

Society   Freud's theory about the nature of society or civilization had to do with the way in which basic instincts were controlled. Since Marx's class-based solution was inadequate, what could be done about the discontents that everyone suffered from in civil society (Freud, 1930)? There was no solution, but a partial solution would be to give more freedom to nondestructive id impulses,

---

[3] Freud suggested that there may have been a brief intermediate period of matriarchy after the murder and before the brothers were able to join together and restore patriarchy.

such as consensual sex. However, Freud never pushed this partial solution to the point that some of his disciples did.

Like Thomas Hobbes, Freud suggested that civilization did not free the individual; on the contrary, individual freedom was "greatest before any culture." Civilization induced guilt in the individual for the persistence of those impulses that had to be controlled or denied. It was therefore incorrect to equate civilization with "the path by which man is ordained to reach perfection" or freedom (1930:61). Like Pareto, moreover, Freud was an elitist: "It is just as impossible to do without control of the mass by a minority as it is to dispense with coercion in civilization" (1927:10). Thus, Freud saw individuals as controlled by civilization, and any given society as controlled by its elite.

Human Nature   To Freud, human nature included the id strivings we have noted, which were present from birth. Human development was a matter of dealing with these strivings or impulses. Freud argued that individuals were driven by the id until society, civilization, and culture implanted in them the controls necessary for group life. He did not say that human nature was bad, just that it was based on id impulses.

Social Change   For Freud control of instinctual desires was the problem for civilization. Modern society required a great deal of renunciation, and this meant that social change might involve progress or a return to barbarism. Eros and Thanatos were permanent fixtures, whatever the stage reached by civilization, and cultural evolution was always the "struggle between Eros and Death, between the instincts of life and the instincts of destruction" (1930:103).

In 1932 Albert Einstein asked Freud if there was any way to deliver mankind from the menace of war. In his response, Freud pointed to the impossibility of suppressing "humanity's aggressive instincts" and indicated that the only solution might be to try to divert them into "a channel other than warfare." He suggested the "counter-agent," Eros, be used to increase feelings of "community, identification," and goodwill among men on the order of "love thy neighbour as thyself" (Freud, 1968:93, 94). Consistent with his elitism, Freud suggested that because men are divided into the "leaders and the led," society should be "at greater pains . . . to form a superior class of independent thinkers, unamenable to intimidation and fervent in the quest for truth, whose function it would be to guide the masses" toward an ideal community in which "every man subordinates his instinctive life to the dictates of reason" (1968:94). Thus, the rejection of destructive ends and impulses was Freud's remedy for war.

For Freud, the "best hope for the future" was that the "intellect—the scientific spirit, reason—may in . . . time establish a dictatorship in the mental life of man." He was cautiously optimistic that the scientific advances of the previous century would continue and that the "dominance of reason will prove to be the strongest uniting bond among men" (1933:171).

Class, Gender, and Race

In his essay "The Question of a Weltanschauung?" Freud discussed the work of Karl Marx. He was impressed with Marx's stress on the "decisive influence which the economic circumstances of men have upon their intellectual, ethical and artistic attributes" (1933:178). But to Freud, economic motivation was not the only significant societal cause; psychological factors were equally decisive. Humans' "self-preservation instinct, their aggressiveness, their need to be loved, their drive towards obtaining pleasure and avoiding unpleasure" were always present. Consequently, the origins of the class structure lay in the "struggles which, from the beginning of history, took place between human hordes," and social distinctions were originally between "clans or races," not economic classes. The triumph of one group over another resulted from "psychological factors, such as the amount of constitutional aggressiveness" reinforced by "firmness of the organization within the horde, and by material factors, such as the possession of superior weapons." In this picture of early humanity, Freud saw "no sign . . . of a natural law or of a . . . [dialectical] evolution" (1933:177).

In practical terms, Freud saw the Marxism practiced in the Soviet Union as having an "uncanny likeness" to the regime it had displaced. It had developed a "self-contained and exclusive character," or worldview, and "created a prohibition of thought which is just as ruthless as was that of religion in the past." Thus, although science and technology were the motors of socialist development, and "practical Marxism has mercilessly cleared away all idealistic systems and illusions, it has itself developed illusions which are no less questionable and unprovable" (1933:180).

Despite these criticisms, Freud did see the Russian experiment as a "message of a better future." He believed that only time would tell whether the message was accurate or premature (1933:181).

Gender   Freud's view of gender began with human sexuality. All infants, he claimed, seek bodily satisfaction and pleasure. Initially human infants experience sexual pleasure in diffuse and nongendered ways, such as suckling the breast or being fondled and caressed. The sexual instinct progresses through oral (ages 1–2), anal (3–4), and phallic (5–6) stages. It is at the phallic stage that sexuality becomes gender specific. At this stage the **Oedipus complex** occurs, and the child is socialized into the cultural prescriptions for masculinity and femininity.

Freud derived the concept of the Oedipal complex from Sophocles' play *Oedipus Rex*. In the play the oracle tells Oedipus's father, Laius, that his son will kill him. Laius sends his son away to be killed, but Oedipus survives. He returns when older and kills his father, without knowing it is his father. After the murder, Oedipus marries the widow—his mother. When he discovers what he has done, Oedipus blinds himself. His crimes are the two taboos of totemism: murder of the father and incest with the mother.

Freud maintained that the Oedipus complex is a cultural universal, and the instinctual desire that Oedipus consummated is basic to all human beings early in life when the mother is the central love object for both boys and girls. It is at the phallic stage that the desire for the mother takes on a different meaning for boys and girls.

At this stage, according to Freud, sexual desire for the mother brings with it the fear of castration for the boy. Desiring the mother challenges the rights and power of the father. Fear of castration is overcome when the boy identifies with the father and renounces his desire for the mother. The "Oedipus complex is abandoned, repressed and, in normal cases, destroyed and a severe superego is set up as its heir" (Freud, 1933:129). The boy then enters patriarchal culture—the realm of morality, order and control, culture or civilization.

The process is different for girls, argued Freud, because they discover they lack a penis, and thus can never "have" their mother. Girls "feel seriously wronged, often declare that they want to 'have something like it too,' and fall victim to 'envy for the penis'" (1933:125). Girls believe they may eventually grow a penis, but finally give up this hope. The girl blames her mother for bringing her into the world without a penis, and mother is abandoned. The girl then turns to the father as love object, in the hope that he will give her a penis. This desire is normally translated into a desire for the father's child, a baby taking the place of a penis (1933:128). Later the desire will become focused on other males. Unlike the boy, the girl does not entirely sever association with mother, because accepting her lack is to identify with her mother. At the same time, the mother is to blame and this, in Freud's view, accounts for the devaluation of women by other women, as well as by boys and men.

When the girl turns to her father for a penis/baby, in Freud's theory, she enters her Oedipal stage. However, unlike the boy, she lacks the critical component that resolves the boy's Oedipal complex—overcoming the castration fear. So girls stay locked into the Oedipus complex for "an indeterminate length of time; demolishing it late and . . . incompletely" (1933:129). Thus, the girl's superego is formed differently and less adequately:

> I cannot evade the notion (though I hesitate to give it expression) that for women the level of what is ethically normal is different from what it is in men. Their superego is never so inexorable, so impersonal, so independent of its emotional origins as we require it to be in men.
>
> Character traits which critics of every epoch have brought up against women—that they show less sense of justice than men, . . . are less ready to submit to the great exigencies of life, . . . are more often influenced in their judgments by feelings of affection or hostility—all these would be amply accounted for by the modification in the formation of the superego. (Freud, 1977:342)

Freud's belief in girls' weak superego is important, because he believed that the superego is the repository of culture and is only fully developed with the resolution of the Oedipus complex. So, for Freud, women were never as civilized or cultured as men (see Sydie, 1987).

Bisexuality, in Freud's theory, is fundamental for infants and is expressed as a choice between active (masculine) and passive (feminine) pleasures. During the oral and anal stages, pleasure and pain are the same for both sexes. The **libido** or id impulse is theoretically gender neutral, but Freud suggested that "more constraint has been applied to the libido when it is pressed into the service of the feminine function, and that—to speak teleologically—Nature takes less careful account of its . . . demands than in the case of masculinity." This difference is because the accomplishment of human goals has been entrusted to men's aggressiveness, and may be independent of women's consent (Freud, 1933:131).

Later, Freud suggested, the psychological and physiological differences between men and women appear: women have a weaker ego, greater narcissism, and a stronger need to be loved. In addition, the "predominance of envy" in women's mental life "is related to their lesser sense of justice; and their lesser capacity for sublimating their instincts than men" (1933:132, 134). Freud concluded with the observation that

> a man of thirty strikes us as a youthful, somewhat unformed individual, whom we expect to make powerful use of the possibilities for development opened up to him by analysis. A woman of the same age, however, often frightens us by her psychical rigidity and unchangeability. Her libido has taken up final positions and seems incapable of exchanging them for others. (1933:134–135)

Freud thus justified the subordinate position of women in terms of their being "less civilized." Men undertake the "work of civilization" requiring that they sublimate their instincts, while women "represent the interests of family and sexual life" (1930:73). Women's opposition or weaker tie to civilization means that monogamy and sexual fidelity, which formalize women's subordination, are necessary. Special controls on women are required to protect civilization from their potentially dangerous sexual libido. The triumph of patriarchy represents the "victory of spirituality over the senses . . . a step forward in culture, since maternity is proved by the senses whereas paternity is a supposition based on deduction" (1930:145–146).

Having established the origins of, and necessity for, patriarchal dominance, Freud then admitted that his account is "incomplete and fragmentary" and does not always sound friendly to women (1933:135). This seeming qualification, however, must be balanced by the recognition that psychoanalysis viewed the pleasure principle, of which sexuality is the prime manifestation, as the source of both gender differences and social life.[4]

Race   In *Moses and Monotheism* (1939), Freud looked at the relations between Judaism and Christianity, suggesting that anti-Semitism has its origins in Judaism itself. Moses is the central figure in the establishment of Judaism, but Freud claimed that the biblical Moses is a combination of two men—an Egyptian who introduced circumcision as a mark of consecration to the new God, and another man, a Midianite, who introduced the vengeful God, Yahweh. The combination of the ideas of the two men produced the one powerful and bloodthirsty God of Judaism and, later, Christianity.

Freud believed that the Egyptian Moses was killed by the Jews, who refused to admit to the crime. As in the murder of the primal father by his sons, the murder of Moses remained part of the unconscious collective memory. This

---

[4]Despite Freud's views on women, he had many women friends and many women in the early years became psychoanalysts, including Freud's daughter, Anna. Anna Freud remained loyal to her father's memory, but some of the women analysts, such as Karen Horney and Melanie Klein, criticized his work and suggested that Freud had overlooked critical cultural factors that would explain female behavior.

memory led to a feeling of guilt that Jews attempted to mollify with the development of Christianity. A Son of God, innocent himself, sacrificed himself and thereby took over the guilt of the world.

It had to be a son, in Freud's theory, for the sin had been murdering the father (1939:110). Mosaic religion was a "Father religion," and Christianity became a Son religion—a rival of the old Father religion. Christianity gave up the Jewish idea of a chosen and circumcised people and also took over such symbolic rites as a mother goddess (Mary) and polytheism (the saints), from other religions (1939:112).

The roots of anti-Semitism, according to Freud, lay in the accusation "You killed our God" (1939:114). The "jealousy which the Jews evoked in other peoples by maintaining they were the first-born, favourite child of God the Father" remained. This arrogance, combined with the Jews' marking their "aloof position" with circumcision, brought to Christians the memory of the "dreaded castration idea and of things in their primeval past" that they would rather forget, thus explaining the persistence of anti-Semitism (1939:116).

Jewish self-confidence was resented especially by Christians, whose conversion was recent and who remained "barbarically polytheistic" underneath the "thin veneer of Christianity." Christians projected their "grudge against the new religion which was forced on them" onto the source of that religion, so that "hatred for Judaism is at bottom hatred for Christianity, and it is not surprising that in the German National Socialist revolution this connection . . . finds such clear expression in the hostile treatment of both" (Freud, 1939:117). Whether Christian or Jewish, religion in Freud's view is a "collective neurosis" with murderous consequences in the twentieth century.

Other Theories and Theorists

As evidence for his theories, Freud used his own and other analysts' case studies as well as literature. An interesting combination of case study, literature, and historical records is Freud's psychosexual analysis of Leonardo da Vinci. The basis for the study was Leonardo's own description of a childhood memory. Leonardo recalled that while he was in his cradle a vulture appeared and "opened my mouth with his tail and struck me many times with his tail against my lips" (Freud, 1947:33–34). Freud interpreted this memory as tied to Leonardo's illegitimate birth, his upbringing by his natural father and stepmother, and his ambiguous sexuality attested to by contemporaries.

More important, Freud saw this memory as the key to Leonardo's art. To Freud, Leonardo's art was a sublimation of his homosexual desire. In his later years, when he met a woman "who awakened in him the memory of the happy and sensuously enraptured smile of his mother," he produced the Mona Lisa, Saint Anne, "and other mystic pictures . . . characterized by the enigmatic smile" (Freud, 1947:115–116).

Whether Freud's account of Leonardo's psychosexual experiences and their relation to his art is convincing or not, the basis for this analysis—the reality of repressed sexual desires in the unconscious—has become an assumed truth for psychotherapy. In Chapter 16 you will find Freud's ideas used and modified by some of the critical theorists of the Frankfurt School.

Critique and Conclusions

Freud's work has been the subject of both adulation and criticism. On the one hand, adulation has led to a school of thought and practical treatment based on his views of human impulses and personality. On the other hand, critics have several complaints. The first is that psychoanalysis itself has become a religion, with Freud as the leader. It demands an initiation—a requirement for entry into the psychoanalytic ranks is to be analyzed—and an uncritical acceptance of certain ideological positions.

A second criticism has to do with the scientific status of psychoanalysis. Psychoanalysis does not satisfy the requirement that scientific theories must be testable and, in principle, falsifiable (Popper, 1959). In essence, there is no way to demonstrate psychoanalysis to be false because it claims to explain everything.

Furthermore, the unconscious is, by definition, unobservable. When therapeutic claims have been tested in clinical trials using control groups, the numbers who recover through psychoanalysis are not noticeably different from those who recover without such intervention.

Not surprisingly, feminist theorists have been particularly critical of Freud's ideas on the development of "normal" feminine and masculine identities. Some have argued that Freud's theory may have been culturally specific to a few late-nineteenth-century hysterical Viennese women. Other feminists have rejected the idea of a biological basis for gender differences—anatomy, they say, is not destiny (de Beauvoir, 1952). Still others have focused on the significance of the mother, not the father, in the development of both masculine and feminine identities (Chodorow, 1978; Dinnerstein, 1976). These critics claim that mothering produces male dominance, and some have even questioned why boys do not have "breast envy" instead of girls' envying the small aggressive male organ—the penis.

Freud's ideas have been subjected to various modifications. Jacques Lacan (1958) and others have argued that the medical use of psychoanalysis concentrates on the individual and ignores the neuroses that may be built into society's norms. They have criticized psychoanalysis as a status quo conservative ideology that seeks to adjust the individual to society. Lacan and other European theorists would prefer to employ psychoanalytic theory as a means for the critical analysis of modern society.

Finally, it is interesting to note that what Freud once called a "detour" became the basis for Freudianism—both as a school of thought and an object of criticism. His theoretical treatment of the oppressive nature of civilization, as well as his elitism, faded into the background.

Final Thoughts

This has been a long and intense chapter, covering three theorists of the mind, self, and personality in society. Cooley and Mead were primarily interested in the social construction of the self, while Freud added the instinctual and unconscious components. Cooley and Freud theorized gender differences as innate, while Mead did not.

The common thread in the work of all three is the development of the self, especially in modern society. Their focus is different from that of most theorists introduced in the first 12 chapters, whose concern was the nature of society, not the individual. But in subsequent chapters you will find some theorists trying to incorporate the complex self as an agent into their discussions of social structures.

References

Appignanesi, Lisa, and John Forrester. 1992. *Freud's Women*. New York: Basic Books.
Bocock, Robert. 1983. *Sigmund Freud*. London: Tavistock Publications.
Chodorow, Nancy. 1978. *The Reproduction of Mothering*. Berkeley: University of California Press.
Cooley, Charles Horton. 1902/1983a. *Human Nature and the Social Order* (Philip Reiff, Ed.). New Brunswick and London: Transaction Books.
———. 1909/1983b. *Social Organization: A Study of the Larger Mind*. New Brunswick and London: Transaction Books.
———. 1918/1966. *Social Process* (Roscoe C. Hinkle, Ed.). Carbondale: Southern Illinois University Press.
———. 1930. *Sociological Theory and Social Research* (Robert Cooley Angell, Ed.). New York: Henry Holt.
Coser, Lewis A. 1977. *Masters of Sociological Thought*. New York: Harcourt Brace Jovanovich.
Crumden, Robert M. 1982. *Ministers of Reform: The Progressives' Achievement in American Civilization 1889–1920*. New York: Basic Books.
de Beauvoir, Simone. 1952. *The Second Sex* (H. M. Parshley, Trans.). New York: Alfred A. Knopf.
Deegan, Mary Jo. 1988. *Jane Addams and the Men of the Chicago School, 1892–1918*. New Brunswick and London: Transaction Books.
———. (Ed.). 1991. *Women in Sociology*. New York: Greenwood Press.
Dinnerstein, Dorothy. 1976. *The Mermaid and the Minotaur: Sexual Arrangements and Human Malaise*. New York: Harper & Row.
Freud, Sigmund. 1904/1965. *The Psychopathology of Everyday Life* (Alan Tyson, Trans.; James Strachey, Ed.). New York: W. W. Norton.
———. 1913/1950. *Totem and Taboo* (James Strachey, Trans.). London: Routledge & Kegan Paul.
———. 1927/1957. *The Future of an Illusion* (J. W. D. Robson-Scott, Trans.; James Strachey, Ed.). New York: Doubleday Anchor.
———. 1930/1951. *Civilization and Its Discontents* (Joan Riviere, Trans.). London: Hogarth Press.
———. 1933/1965. *New Introductory Lectures on Psychoanalysis* (James Strachey, Trans. and Ed.). New York: W. W. Norton.
———. 1935. *Autobiography* (James Strachey, Trans.). New York: Standard Editions.
———. 1939. *Moses and Monotheism* (Katherine Jones, Trans.). New York: Vintage Books.
———. 1947. *Leonardo da Vinci: A Study in Psychosexuality* (A. A. Brill, Trans.). New York: Random House.
———. 1963. *General Psychological Theory* (Philip Rieff, Ed.). New York: Collier Books.
———. 1968. *Civilisation, War and Death* (John Rickman, Ed.). London: Hogarth Press.
———. 1977. *On Sexuality*. Harmondsworth, England: Penguin.

Freud, Sigmund, and J. Breuer. 1895/1956. *Studies on Hysteria*. London.

Hinkle, Roscoe C. 1966. "Introduction." In Charles Horton Cooley, *Social Process* (pp. xi–lxiv). Carbondale: Southern Illinois University Press.

Lacan, Jacques. 1958/1982. "The Meaning of the Phallus." In Juliet Mitchell and Jacqueline Rose (Eds.), *Feminine Sexuality: Jacques Lacan and the Ecole Freudienne*. London: Macmillan.

Larkin, Philip. 1974. *High Windows*. London: Faber & Faber.

Levine, Donald N. 1995. *Visions of the Sociological Tradition*. Chicago: University of Chicago Press.

Masson, J. 1984. *The Assault on Truth: Freud's Suppression of the Seduction Theory*. London: Faber & Faber.

Mead, George Herbert. 1932. *The Philosophy of the Present* (Arthur E. Murphy, Ed.). Chicago: Open Court Publishing Company.

———. 1934. *Mind, Self and Society*. Chicago: University of Chicago Press.

———. 1938. *The Philosophy of the Act* (Charles W. Morris, Ed.). Chicago: University of Chicago Press.

———. 1964a. *On Social Psychology* (Anselm Strauss, Ed.). Chicago: University of Chicago Press.

———. 1964b. *Selected Writings* (Andrew J. Reck, Ed.). New York: Bobbs-Merrill.

Popper, Karl. 1959. *The Logic of Scientific Discovery*. London: Hutchinson.

Reck, Andrew J. (Ed.). 1964. "Introduction." In George Herbert Mead, *Selected Writings* (pp. xiii–lxii). New York: Bobbs-Merrill.

Reiss, Albert J., Jr. (Ed.). 1968. *Cooley and Sociological Analysis*. Ann Arbor: University of Michigan Press.

Rosenberg, Rosalind. 1982. *Beyond Separate Spheres*. New Haven, CT: Yale University Press.

Shalin, Dmitri N. 1988. "G. H. Mead, Socialism, and the Progressive Agenda." *American Journal of Sociology, 93*, 913–951.

Sydie, R. A. 1987. *Natural Women, Cultured Men: A Feminist Perspective on Sociological Theory*. Toronto: Methuen.

Young-Bruehl, Elisabeth (Ed.). 1990. *Freud on Women: A Reader*. New York: W. W. Norton.

SECTION VII

Twentieth-Century Functionalism and Beyond

As we saw in the chapters on Spencer and Durkheim, an important approach to sociological theory has been to examine the issues of order and integration in society, and to seek answers to questions such as What does it do? What needs does it meet? How does it work?

Chapter 14 picks up the themes of societal integration and functional analysis as they were expanded upon by Talcott Parsons and Robert K. Merton in the middle third of the twentieth century. Parsons developed various schemes—the pattern variables, AGIL—to organize his thinking on social action and on the social system. Later he turned his attention to modernization (also see Chapter 18), agreeing with those writers who were convinced that the whole world would eventually accept Western culture.

Merton was a student of Parsons, but attempted to avoid the straitjacket of order and function by introducing ideas such as latent function and dysfunction. Still alive and writing at the turn of the twenty-first century, Merton has dealt primarily with middle-range or lower-level theories, instead of the grandscale, society-wide theories of the Parsonsian kind. Parsons and Merton dominated sociological theory at midcentury, and thus provide the baseline for the second half of this volume.

In Chapter 15 you will meet two theorists who may very well be the most prolific writers since Herbert Spencer. Niklas Luhmann's work on social systems outgrew his discipleship to Parsons, and he wrote at length about trust, power, risk, and reflexivity as well. Anthony Giddens, whose "structuration" theory has parallels to structure-functionalism, also wrote on the topics just listed, as well as modernization and others. Luhmann died only recently, and Giddens is still active as a theorist. Thus, both made their theoretical contributions in the last third of the twentieth century.

Chapter 14

Twentieth-Century Functionalism
Parsons and Merton

Andra Lyons can't explain how she raised four children alone on a $5-an-hour job pumping gas. She only knows it's been a numbing struggle. . . . Her hardships are familiar to neighbors on the St. Regis Mohawk reservation, where roughly half the 13,000 residents lack full-time jobs and per capita income is $14,000, two-thirds of the national average.

But with today's opening of the $30 million Akwesasne Mohawk Casino, Lyons believes the Mohawks' luck is turning.

"We've needed something like this for a long time," says Lyons, who trained for weeks to become a card dealer at the casino.

But the Mohawks do expect gambling to have the same . . . impact it did for the Oneidas, who have pulled themselves out of poverty and used their new wealth to start other businesses, buy back ancestral lands and build homes. . . . Some opposition to gambling remains on the reservation.

Still, no one expects another outbreak of the violence that roiled St. Regis almost a decade ago, when two men were killed.

Almost a dozen casinos operated illegally then, . . . run for the profit of their owners, not the tribe. (Kates, 1999)

What does it do? What and whose needs does it meet? What is its purpose? How does it work? What function does it perform? These are the questions raised by functional analysis. It is important to note that the previous quotation makes no moral judgment regarding gambling. It speaks only to the issue of what function it performs, what needs it meets and will meet, and for whom. Perhaps the legal casino will meet an economic need for the tribe, while the illegal ones were beneficial (functional) for a few owners.

The larger issue within which such questions arise concerns the integration of society by means of consensus, or agreement on how its needs will be met. Order, integration, structure, and function are issues that first arose in the work of Herbert Spencer and Emile Durkheim (Chapters 3 and 4). Now you find them full grown in Talcott Parsons and Robert K. Merton, central figures in U.S. sociology and sociological theory during the middle third of the twentieth century.

Talcott Parsons (1902–1979)

Charles Camic (1991) has done a great service by bringing to light the early years of Parsons's productive life, from 1923 until the publication of *The Structure of Social Action* in 1937.[1] Talcott was the youngest of five children. His father was a "social gospel" Protestant and a professor at Colorado College; his mother was a progressive and a suffragist (Camic, 1991:x). Wrongly dismissed by the college, his father took the family to New York City, where he worked for the YMCA for a year, and then became President of Marietta College in Ohio.

In New York, Parsons spent his last two years of high school at the Horace Mann School for Boys, "which was affiliated with Columbia Teachers College and renowned at the time for making available 'the very best American education had to offer to high-ability children who planned academic and professional careers'" (Camic, 1991:xi, quoting Cremin, Shannon, and Townsend,1954:104). From Horace Mann he went to Amherst College, which at the time was undergoing a transformation that would turn it into one of the leading liberal arts and intellectual environments in the United States. Parsons at the time was sympathetic with the Russian Revolution and the British Labor Party, but above all he was thinking broadly about politics and society (Camic, 1991:xiv).

When Parsons entered college he was leaning toward the natural sciences, with secondary interests in philosophy and the social sciences. In his junior year, a course on institutional economics completed his conversion from biology to social science. When he graduated from Amherst in 1924, Parsons spoke at commencement on social and economic reform in the United States.

He spent the next year at the London School of Economics (LSE), where he became familiar with what he called the "antecedents of modern industrial society" (Parsons, 1962:888). While there, he also learned of and appreciated the British social anthropologist Bronislaw Malinowski's view of societies as systems of interconnected parts. More influential, however, was his acquaintance with the sociology of L. T. Hobhouse, whose viewpoint incorporated social philosophy and the various institutional specialties (religion, economics, politics) into a large field called sociology. To Parsons, this meant that sociology should include the institutional economics he had learned at Amherst.

Though his family might have preferred him to come home after his year at LSE, he proceeded to Heidelberg, Germany, to work on his PhD, and while there spent a summer studying in Vienna. His time in Germany brought to Parsons's attention the work of Max Weber, especially *The Protestant Ethic and the Spirit of Capitalism*. He also became acquainted with Weber's wife Marianne, an important scholar in her own right (see Chapter 7), and several young German thinkers.

---

[1] For the complete treatment of Parsons's early work, see Camic, 1991:ix–lxix.

While working on his dissertation, he went back to Amherst as an instructor, and in the summer of 1927 he returned to Heidelberg to receive his degree.

In the fall of 1927, Parsons was appointed as a nonfaculty instructor in the Economics Department at Harvard, the center of orthodox social scientific thought in the United States at the time (Camic, 1991:xxiii). For the next ten years, his project was threefold.

First, in debt to Weber, he wrote essays on capitalism and its origins. Suggesting that some social scientists had gone too far toward a progressive, genetic interpretation of society and Marx had gone too far toward a purely economic theory, Parsons showed a clear preference for Weber's unwillingness to simplify in either of these direction. A subagenda was to introduce historically based German social science to the individualistic, rationalistic, pragmatic outlook of U.S. sociologists such as G. H. Mead. Before 1930 it was already clear that Parsons believed a higher synthesis would emerge, incorporating both German and Anglo-American contributions (Camic, 1991:xxvi). Although the synthesis was not yet available, Parsons himself expected to be the one to provide it.

A second theme of Parsons's early work was a theory of action. This was not to be the individualistic/rationalistic outlook of many of his colleagues, but was to involve recognition of religious motives, of social regulation and norms, of goals and choices, and of society as a system of interrelated elements. During the early 1930s he was still struggling to bring together a synthesis of such elements.

His third early theme Camic called "The Fundaments of Analytic Sociology" (1991:liv). Parsons described these fundaments in a 1933 letter. Though no element is more fundamental than any other, "action" and "value" are essential. Next, the various aspects of society are inseparably tied together in a single indivisible whole. Third, in the attempt to be analytically objective, one must not ignore the problem of the "subjective" (recall Weber on this). These complexities—action, value, unity, objective, and subjective—were essential parts of Parsons's developing thought from the mid-1930s on (Camic, 1991:lv).

An important aspect of Parsons's background concerns his early experiences at Harvard. Though privileged to study with Joseph Schumpeter and other esteemed Harvard economists, it is noteworthy that Parsons himself spent the nine years from 1927 to 1936 "lower in rank than an untenured assistant professor" (Camic, 1991:xl). Not on the tenure track in economics, Parsons was recommended to the budding Sociology Department because of his obvious sociological interests. The result was a three-year position as a faculty instructor in sociology. However, two great barriers lay ahead. The first was a lack of enthusiasm on the part of the Sociology Department Chair, Pitirim Sorokin, himself a renowned theorist, who was not impressed by Parsons's kind of synthesis. The second resulted from the retirement of Harvard's president, and his succession by a distinguished chemist. The new president decided that appointments at the lower levels had become mediocre, and he determined to make retention and tenure more difficult to obtain. Parsons continued for six years as an instructor, with no change in rank. Having seen his father dropped from Colorado College and President Meiklejohn fired by Amherst, his anxiety and his bitterness were understandable.

Late in 1935, Parsons's materials were finally circulated to the tenured sociology faculty. These materials included his early essays and writings and most of the chapters of the book that made his early reputation, *The Structure of Social Action* (1937). Again Sorokin's reaction was mixed, but with the support of other professors, Parsons finally received an advance to Assistant Professor in 1936, though still without tenure. When Parsons received an attractive offer from another university, he was retained by Harvard with a promise of tenure in two more years (Camic, 1991:xliv). As you can see, success did not come easily or quickly for Talcott Parsons. But his ability and confidence kept him working and pursuing his goals.

Parsons's Central Theories and Methods

Parsons was a "grand-scale" theorist, somewhat in the mold of Herbert Spencer. Like Spencer, he was a more than a functionalist, not all of his theoretical insights fitting comfortably within that framework. He was extremely prolific, and was a master at collaborating with other notable scholars of his time. We will begin with a few comments on his style.

First, as William Mitchell has commented, there is no hint of "wit, satire, or other literary devices in the writings of Parsons. He who would like to be entertained, amused, inspired, moved, or given flashing insights is well advised not to consult Parsons" (1967:17). No anger (à la Marx), passion (à la Du Bois), or iconoclasm (à la Veblen) is found in Parsons.

Second, he was a notoriously poor writer. His defense, of course, would be that the complexity of the social world demands complex language. However, when needed complexity is coupled with a Germanic sentence structure, it makes for hard going. At the end of an edited volume devoted to Parsons's ideas, in which the murkiness of his writing was often noted, he was given the opportunity to defend himself. His response was itself one of his most obscure writings. Is the complexity necessary? Is his work worth the effort? Those questions will be held until the end of our discussion.

Third, after his first book, Parsons footnoted sparingly, referring mainly to his own writings or those of his students (Mitchell, 1967:17).[2] In this he was reminiscent of Pareto, though perhaps not as extreme.

At a 1961 symposium on Parsons's theories, one sociologist expressed his fear at trying to summarize a theory still being written and revised. "Like Birnam Wood, . . . it moves: Parsonian theory in the late 1950s differs in some important respects from that of a decade ago" (Devereaux, 1961:2). Another comment put a more positive spin on Parsons's changing ideas: "The zest with which he responds to the stimulation of others' ideas and the rapidity with which the salient features of these are incorporated into the snow-balling of his work reveal the scientist's quest for knowledge no matter where it may lead" (Loomis and Loomis, 1961:365). Although his ideas did change over the span of his productive life, his goal was to cover, as completely and generally as possible, the major dimensions of social life and society.

---

[2]There are exceptions to Parsons's tendency not to footnote. For example, his 13-page paper on "The Present Status of Structural-Functional Theory in Sociology" (1975) concluded with three pages of footnotes.

Parsons's primary concern throughout his life was the problem of order in society. Many critics have claimed that this focus caused Parsons to virtually ignore conflict and change. Yet it is also possible to argue that since the conditions or variables affecting order were his concern, he must have at least recognized the possibility of disorder.[3] "The problem of 'order,' so fundamental for Parsons, could not even be a problem if it were not contingent on conflict," or disorder (Mitchell, 1967:37).

Some themes, such as social action and systems, ran through virtually all of Parsons's writings, from the early essays until his death. And although his theoretical position changed, as already noted, the central issues that interested him were continuous for more than four decades.

Social Action   Parsons's view of social action changed or expanded during his scholarly life. Don Martindale (1960) perhaps overstated the change as one from "Social Behaviorism" to "Macrofunctionalism," but there is no question that at about the time of World War II, Parsons expanded his action framework. Let us look first at his action framework in *The Structure of Social Action* (1937) and other prewar writings

Social action, wrote Parsons, is (1) voluntaristic, or a matter of making choices; (2) subjective, or based on internal orientations and responses; and (3) at least partially governed or limited by the norms and values of one's culture (1937:43–51). These three factors explained not only rational social action, but much irrational as well.

In developing his voluntaristic or choice-based theory, Parsons rejected, but to some extent incorporated, the insights of positivists, of classic economists, and of cultural idealists. Devereaux (1961) has explained clearly what Parsons was trying to accomplish. Positivism was unacceptable because it did not allow enough freedom of choice. Classic economics models were elegant, but did not fit the real social world. Idealism placed too much emphasis on the spirit, or ethos, and relativity of cultures, making comparison virtually impossible. In Parsons's pre–World War II work, then, social action involved an actor, with goals, choosing between alternatives, and influenced by norms and values.

The beginning of the expansion of Parsons's social action theory can be seen in a 1945 essay, where he stated that "the structure of social systems cannot be derived directly from the actor-situation frame of reference. It requires functional analysis of the complications introduced by the interaction of a plurality of actors" (Parsons, 1945, in 1954:229). Thus, social action take place not only between actors but also within a social system.

Had Parsons changed his mind and abandoned individual actors, or simply expanded his attention to include the context within which social action occurred? Apparently it was the latter, because in 1951 he stated that action is "behavior oriented to the attainment of ends in situations, by means of the normatively regulated expenditure of energy" (Parsons and Shils, 1951:53). Modes

---

[3]Parsons has been accused of not only paying attention primarily to order, but valuing order to the exclusion of the sorts of conflict or struggle that Marx and DuBois saw as absolutely necessary. We will say more about this in the "Critique" section.

of orientation or motivation for individual actions include the cognitive, cathectic, and evaluative (Parsons and Shils, 1951). These terms are close to the everyday meanings of thinking, feeling, and valuing or willing.

Parsons believed that his expanded theory of action was broad enough to include consensual and conflictive, rational and irrational action. But it would be unwise to separate his expanded action theory from the contextual aspects found in his systems theory.

Systems Theory   A **system**, in Parsons's theory, is a complex unit of some kind, with boundaries, within which the parts are connected, and within which something takes place. Parsons distinguished three systems: the cultural, the personality, and the social (Parsons and Shils, 1951). The cultural system includes the values and norms that influence the individual's choices. The personality system involves individuals' motivations and need-dispositions that govern, along with the norms, the choices they make. The social system is based on the interrelations between actors. These three systems are not reducible to each other; thus, the social system is not merely an aggregate of individual personalities, nor is it determined merely by the cultural norms that govern it. It is worth noting that of the three systems, the only one that received book-length treatment by Parsons was the social system (1951)—a reminder that society was Parsons's primary focus of attention. Within the social system, Parsons looked at roles, equilibrium, and pattern variables.

1, The simplest unit of a social system is a **role**. The nature of social roles is seen most clearly in Parsons's analysis of the simplest social system— the relationship between two actors, ego and alter. Each has an orientation toward the other, involving shared goals and values. (A problem arises, we should add, if ego and alter have divergent goals and values). Role reciprocities between actors result not only from the values and norms of the culture, but also from long-term or patterned interactions between them resulting from their personalities and preferences. Such patterns become more or less stable or "institutionalized," meaning that they are governed by rules, or even by habits. So we have "social action" taking place between actors playing roles within a "system" having boundaries that separate it (more or less) from other systems and from its environment.

2. Once we accept the system principle, several additional issues arise. Besides roles, another system concern is **equilibrium**. Some readers of Parsons see him as saying that in social systems equilibrium is the basic condition. Even though it may sound that way, one of Parsons's later writings indicated that equilibrium or order is an empirical question, or a variable. The concept of equilibrium, he wrote,

> is a fundamental reference point for analyzing the processes by which a system either comes to terms with the exigencies imposed by a changing environment, without essential change in its own structure, or fails to come

to terms and undergoes other processes, such as structural change, dissolution as a boundary-maintaining system (analogous to biological death for the organism), or the consolidation of some impairment leading to the establishment of secondary structures of a "pathological" character. . . . Whether maintenance actually occurs or not, and in what measure, is entirely an empirical question. (Parsons, Shils, Naegele, and Pitts, 1961, vol. 1:37)

3. Besides roles and equilibrium, another systemic issue for Parsons was what he called the **pattern variables**. Looking at individual choices from a macro-cultural perspective, Parsons and Shils (1951) noted that different cultures guide individuals toward one or the other of a set of dichotomous choices. Though he did not use Durkheim's or Weber's terms, Parsons noted that one set of choices is dominant in the mechanically solidary or traditional society, while the other usually occurred in the organically solidary or bureaucratic (modern) society. These choices or variables are listed in Exhibit 14.1.

Exhibit 14.1   Dichotomous Choices

Traditional Society	Modern Society
Affectivity	Affective neutrality
Collectivity (Selfless)	Self (Selfish)
Particularistic	Universalistic
Quality (Ascription)	Performance (Achievement)
Specificity	Diffuseness

Source: Parsons and Shils, 1951:172–183.

Let us examine these dichotomies one at a time.

Affectivity/Affective Neutrality. Are the actors emotionally involved or not? Are they immediately gratified or disciplined—that is, under control? This reminds one of Sigmund Freud's distinction between an individual's id gratification and ego control. Modern or "civilized" society, according to Freud, generally demands the latter.

Collectivity/Self. Do the actors choose in favor of group or community interests, or are they oriented by what is "best for number one." Here we have the assumption that modern industrial societies are characterized by greater individualism.

Particularistic/Universalistic. Do the actors orient to different "alters" according to particular characteristics, or do they treat everyone alike? In traditional society, according to Parsons, alter is treated differently depending on whether she or he is a relative or royalty or has some other favored status, is an acquaintance or a stranger (à la Simmel). In modern society one is expected to treat customers or clients or job applicants alike, or in terms of universalistic criteria.

Quality/Performance. Does the actor interact with other people according to who they are in relation to the actor, or according to what they have accomplished? The modern bureaucratic actor, in Parsons's view, is concerned with what people have accomplished, not who they are, or who their parents were.

Specificity/Diffuseness. Is the actor's obligation to others diffuse, or general, or is it restricted to the specific function they perform? As Weber noted, the bureaucrat is obliged to be an expert only in a specific role, whether teaching a course or bagging groceries or making quilts, and the relationship to "alter" is restricted to that role and function.

Several issues arise immediately regarding these dichotomous choices. First, is this an exhaustive list of culturally determined potential choices? It seems that, at least at the beginning, Parsons and Shils would have answered yes. Second, are these choices really dichotomous? Although Parsons called them pattern variables, he treated them as if they were opposing choices. This might hold for the macro-perspective, meaning that a specific culture or society is dominated by one choice or the other. From the standpoint of the individual, however, it would seem that variation in intensity of commitment would make it possible to choose one side under certain conditions and the other side under other circumstances, or to feel more or less strongly about one's choice. Third, are the five dichotomies equally important? Parsons himself seemed to indicate that two choices are most important in distinguishing modern from traditional societies: universalism-particularism and achievement-ascription (Mitchell, 1967:71, 107). One set of choices, we might say, is "functional for," or more appropriate to, one type of society and the other set for the other type of society. Using the language of functionalism leads us to a fourth major issue under Parsonsian system theory: the functional problems that a society or social system must solve.

4. The functional problems or dimensions of system structure and process are an aspect of Parsons's thought that changed over the years. One of his latest and clearest expositions of these problems is in his 1961 essay, "General Theory in Sociology." All social systems, he asserted, "are organized, in the sense that they are structurally differentiated, about two major axes" (1961:5). One axis is the internal-external—the relationships among the subparts of the system, and the relationships between the system and the environment or other systems. There are parts of a social system whose function is to solve internal problems, and other parts intended to solve external problems. The other axis is instrumental-consummatory—Parsons's way of saying means-ends. Some structures function in terms of a society's means or processes, and others according to its ends or outcomes. Parsons admitted that he has had some "difficulty in stabilizing both conceptualization and terminology in this field" but went on to present "the best formulation I have been able to attain to date" (see Exhibit 14.2; Parsons, 1961:6, 7).

Exhibit 14.2   AGIL Scheme of Social Systems

	Instrumental	*Consummatory*
External	A (Adaptive Function)	G (Goal-Attainment Function)
Internal	L (P)* (Pattern-Maintenance and Tension-Management Function)	I (Integrative Function)

Source: Parsons, 1961.

*Parsons usually discussed Pattern maintenance (P) as "Latent" Pattern maintenance (L). Why this is latent, rather than recognized and intended, Parsons did not make clear.

In relation to the external world, the means are aimed toward adaptation, while the ends are the attainment of the system's goals. In relation to the system itself, the means involve pattern-maintenance and the management of tensions (conflicts), and the internal end is integration, or smooth functioning. Since these are problems that a system must solve, it is obvious that Parsons recognized the possibilities of lack of adaptation, non–goal attainment, tension and conflict, and nonintegration. However, as we have said, his focus was order or equilibrium, not disorder.

Parsons himself wrote, in a lengthy footnote, about the relation between this AGIL(P) scheme and the pattern variables presented earlier:

> Readers familiar with the "pattern-variable" scheme but not with the present scheme of four functional problems and two axes by means of which they are classified may wonder about the relation between the two schemes. In the present analysis I do not use pattern-variable terms because I think the new scheme is a more generalized one from which the scheme of pattern variables can be derived. . . . What the newer scheme does is to consolidate, except for the self-collectivity variable, the other four pattern variables into a set of four rather than eight categories. The self-collectivity variable I interpret to be a special case of the external-internal axis. The categorization for the instrumental-consummatory axis is new. (1961:7)

This note illustrates Parsons at both his self-declared clearest and at his murkiest. He leaves it for the reader to connect the four pattern variables with the cells in the 2 × 2 AGIL table. And he leaves us to explicate what he means by self-collectivity as a special case. Self, presumably, means an internal orientation not to the system but to the individual him- or herself; collectivity, then, must mean an orientation that is external to the self and focuses on the system or community. This is a good example either of lack of clarity in Parsons's thinking or of his inability to communicate to the reader what was perfectly clear to him.

What makes the four problems an exercise in functional analysis is that they are intended to explain what a system must *do* to attain and maintain equilibrium—or, if you will, to operate or function.

Nature of Society, Humans, and Change

Two good sources on Parsons's view of the nature of the social world and on his ideology are Black's (1961) edited volume and Mitchell's (1967) look at Parsons from a political science perspective. We have already seen Parsons's emphasis on order in society. To this, Mitchell adds that the four functional problems are important to Parsons because of his view of *human nature*. A human being, to Parsons, "is an optimizing animal in terms of the gratification he seeks . . . but is faced with an environment which, at any given time, is characterized by scarcities of facilities, resources, and rewards" (Mitchell, 1967:60; Parsons and Shils, 1951:120, 197–201). Furthermore, the functional problems are real problems for human nature and society; they may be coped with, but not completely solved. In fact, to Parsons, the four problems can not be simultaneously and optimally resolved (Parsons and Smelser, 1956:46–47).

Parsons also noted that, because of scarcity, the choices we make involve costs or trade-offs. However, having the capacity to learn, humans are capable of making better choices as time goes by. Humans change, and so does society. Most change, however, is not revolutionary; it involves strain, followed by the social system's attempt to re-equilibrate as painlessly and quickly as possible, and as closely as possible to the previous equilibrium. According to Robin Williams (1961:88), Parsons's analysis of change requires identifying its sources, identifying the affected interests, specifying what has changed, how, and how much; and relating change to the functional problems. Because of his emphasis on order and equilibrium, Parsons saw change in the system as basically disruptive and, therefore, both minimized and undesirable (Parsons, 1951).

Ideologically, it is generally agreed that Parsons was a political liberal. Order, effectiveness, and participation are important values, and his essay on "McCarthyism" (Parsons, 1955) illustrated his concern with the potential excesses of a supposedly free system. However, while he believed McCarthyism to be an illness, he did not understand why Marx and C. Wright Mills (Parsons's contemporary) considered the capitalist power elite also to be an illness.

Why do so many readers of Parsons see him as a status quo conservative, or as having a conservative, rather than a liberal, bias (Hacker, 1961:290)? First, his early book *The Structure of Social Action* (Parsons, 1937) analyzed the social science of Marshall (a conservative economist), Durkheim, Weber, and Pareto. Durkheim and especially Pareto have been viewed as status quo conservatives. Even when Parsons later incorporated others into his writing, they included Freud, whose theory of society is both elitist and based on social control, but not Marx. Thus, the radicals played almost no role in Parsons's writings.

Second, although Parsons wrote about a great variety of issues, most of them concerned leaders rather than followers. He wrote about professionals, but not their clients: the therapist, not the patient, the educator, not the student. The working classes seldom appeared in his writings.

Third, even stronger evidence of his status quo conservative ideology can be found in some of his specific comments: "The role of the economy in American society and of the business element in it is such that political leadership without prominent business participation is doomed to ineffectiveness and to the perpetuation of dangerous internal conflict" (1960:247). In other words, the business elite aid capitalism in avoiding conflict. Again, in reviewing Mills's book *The Power Elite*, Parsons wrote:

> I think we can, within considerable limits, regard the emergence of the large firm with operations on a nationwide basis as a "normal" outcome of the process of growth and differentiation of the economy. Similarly, the rise to prominence within the firm of specialized executive functions is also a normal outcome of a process of growth in size and in structural differentiation. (1954:182)

Thus, differentiation and managerialism are normal, as Spencer and Durkheim claimed. Parsons was hardly critical of the "captains of industry," as Veblen was, or of the "power elite," like Mills.

Finally, Parsons's "conception of the political system as functionally oriented toward *system* goal-attainment, rather than simply being a tool of the upper classes or of those who wield power, strongly suggests a somewhat conservative viewpoint" (Mitchell, 1967:183). Mitchell concludes:

> Parsons tends to line up with those who believe that man is religious and needs religions, that societies are natural, organic products of evolutionary growth, that man is a creature of instinct and emotion as well as reason, that men are unequal, and that class differentiation, hierarchy, leadership, and differentials in power are all inevitable. . . . Parsons views man's potentials and limitations with neither delight nor regret. The same may be said of his estimate of human institutions. (1967:183–184, 187)

Parsons, then, was certainly not among the radicals who viewed *human nature* as good and *society* as bad and in need of complete overhaul (revolution). He viewed much of what exists in social systems as at least inevitable, if not good.

Class, Gender, and Race

Class   To Parsons, class inequality or "stratification is to an important degree an integrating structure of the social system" (1954:329). But what about class conflict, which Parsons admitted did occur, given the scarcity of rewards? Class conflict developed because (1) a competitive job system means that some people are losers; (2) people resist authority in organizations; (3) those in power sometimes exploit others; (4) conflicting ideologies emerge and exist; (5) attitudes and values vary across classes; and (6) the promise of equal opportunity will not be fulfilled (Hacker, 1961:297). Notice Parsons was not saying that equal opportunity has not occurred so far, but that it *will not* occur. Thus, Parsons saw both inequality and strain as inevitable.

It is important to note that Parsons spoke of strata, not classes. He pointed to widespread consensus on occupation as the primary criterion of stratification, and on the ranking of occupations (Parsons, 1940). According to one commentator, Parsons

> identified the amounts of skill, required education, and authority over others as being potentially associated with the ranking of a position. Parsons's primary emphasis, however, was upon economic reward and

value consensus. Thus, his major answer to the question of what accounts for an occupation's rank is: "the more highly valued jobs are the best paid." (Abrahamson, 1978:59, quoting Parsons, 1940:857)

So, even inequality is functional for society, and is based on consensus regarding what and who should be more highly valued and rewarded.

Gender   Parsons's view of gender is most clearly expressed in his collaborative book on family and socialization (Parsons, Bales, Olds, Zelditch, and Slater, 1955). The beginning point for this portion of Parsons's thought was his discovery of Robert Bales's research on leadership in small, task-oriented groups. Bales had found that in most such groups two types of leaders emerge: the task leader and the social-emotional leader. The task leader is the individual having the best ideas and urging the group to complete the task. The social-emotional leader is the one who keeps the group from falling apart, or from rebelling against the task leader. Bales, incidentally, had also found that in a small fraction of cases the same person was able to play both roles—that is, having ideas but also cracking jokes, sometimes at their own expense (Bales, 1949).

Parsons found Bales's results applicable to family relations. He and his coauthors reported that the task leader in families around the world is ordinarily the male or father, and the social-emotional leader is the female or mother. For Parsons, the male "task" is economic provision, while the role of holding the family together is played by the female(s). He argued that this arrangement is functional for the social and economic system because it provides a free-floating male labor force that follows the needs of the job market. It is functional for the family because only one family member, the male, provides economically, while the women and children follow the male. And it is functional or appropriate for the two genders because it is consistent with their basic personalities.

Miriam Johnson, in her feminist review of Parsons's gender theory (Parsons, 1942a), excused his views as being simply descriptive, not prescriptive (Johnson, 1989:116). However, Parsons pointed out that women who follow a "masculine pattern" and seek careers would, if their numbers increase, cause profound alterations in the family's structure. And since absolute equality would be incompatible with family solidarity, it seemed that Parsons was not just describing the family in 1949. Rather, given his emphasis on equilibrium, he considered such profound alterations to be a bad thing.

The Parsons/Bales view has been criticized on several grounds. First, cross-cultural research has found that in some societies women provide from 60 to 90 percent of what is eaten, which calls into question the generalization of male as provider. Second, the definition of the family's "task" has been debated. If the family's task is to raise well-adjusted children, then who is most likely to be the task (or socialization) leader? Might it not be the mother? Third, many feminists, from Gilman to Dorothy Smith (see Chapter 22), have questioned the Freudian notion that gender differences are biologically based, and that the Parsonsian gender distinctions are innate and are functional for society (Smith, 1990).

Race   In his World War II writings on fascism and Nazism, Parsons (1942b) referred to racial antagonisms as having a negative effect by increasing tensions within a social system, and in the world of nation-states. Though never becoming an important theme, he later expanded on race as a factor in group tensions. It is clear that, unlike his conservative view of power and gender, he did not see racial tensions as natural outcomes of evolution, but as problems to be solved.

Other Theories and Theorists

Power Relations   Given Parsons's conservative view of the social system, it is not surprising that he saw power as an essential integrative element. He used Hobbes's definition of power as "a man's present means to any future good," but added one qualification: "that such means constitute his power, so far as these means are dependent on his relations to other actors; the correlative is the obligation of alter to respect ego's rights" (Parsons, 1951:121). Power, according to Parsons, is both generalizable and quantifiable in social systems.

To Parsons, the two primary subsystems of power are economy and politics. Economic power is best understood through exchange, with the most obvious means of exchange being money—as in the everyday expression "purchasing power" (Parsons, 1951:124). The other subsystem that directly involves power is the political, which is primarily a matter of influence over outcomes or goals. Economic power, then, is primarily a matter of means, while political power focuses on ends (recall the AGIL scheme in Exhibit 14.2).

Parsons noted both the functional significance and potential misuse of power. Since the power of one actor is always relative to that of another, he observed,

> power can readily become the focus of disruptive conflicts. Finally, . . . force in *one* primary context, namely that of the *prevention* of undesired action, is an ultimately effective means, and force is inherently linked to territorial location because it is a *physical* means. This complex of facts is of such crucial functional significance to social systems that it is safe to say that no paramount integrative structure of a society could perform that function effectively unless it were intimately tied in with the control of power relations in general and force in particular. (1951:162)

Even technology, Parsons noted, is a facility that is useful for carrying out power relations in a social system. Thus, as with conflict, Parsons did not ignore power, but rather located it within his systemic framework as an integrative mechanism that is sometimes misused.

Modernization Theory   In his later writings, Parsons turned his attention increasingly to modernization theory. With the pattern variables Parsons had indicated that modern societies make certain characteristic choices. By 1971, he had joined those who were arguing that the entire world is moving toward the Western model. As a neo-evolutionist, Parsons saw modernization as a worldwide goal, with subgoals of industrialization, economic development, and political independence (Parsons, 1964, 1966, 1971). All this will lead to a unified world system, with shared "modern" values. In Chapter 18 of this volume you will find an expanded discussion of twentieth-century evolutionary and modernization theory.

As we have seen, Parsons borrowed from and expanded on those whose theories he found useful, but ignored those, such as the radicals, with whom he disagreed. This is again reminiscent of Herbert Spencer, who produced a comprehensive system of thought, while ignoring most of his antagonists.

Critique and Conclusions

Parsons—and functionalism in general—have been criticized on two grounds. First, he did not account for survivals or dysfunctional "leftovers" from a bygone day. Second, he did not allow much room for dissensus and conflict. Actors, according to Parsons, comply with each other's expectations because they want to (consensus) and because one's expectation is another's obligation (complementarity). Not wanting to comply and not sharing consensus on roles and obligations may lead to conflict, but as Gouldner (1970) has pointed out, this possibility has little place in Parsons's theory.

Parsons's action theory has been criticized as providing a conceptual framework but "not a theory or even a set of theories" (Mitchell, 1967:47). While acknowledging that much of Parsons's effort was spent on (often obscure) conceptualization, we might defend him by pointing out that once we have waded through the terminology and accepted his presuppositions, his thought leaves little in society unaccounted for. Action takes place between actors influenced by society's norms and their personalities; the social system has problems to solve if it is to continue ordered and in equilibrium; one of its tools is power; and the goal of much of the world is to become industrialized at the expense of its traditional cultures. We may argue that all of this results from an ideology that gives too much emphasis to order and its desirability, but it is hard to argue that it is simply incomplete.

We have criticized much of Parsons's theory as we have gone along, including his incomplete treatment of change, his conservative ideology, and his views on gender. As Mitchell commented in 1967, "when a sociologist wishes to debate, question, criticize, or rebel, it is usually Parsons who becomes the target. One often establishes his position by reference to Parsons" (189). This appraisal continued to be accurate through the 1970s.

However, Mitchell made two other observations that were even more insightful, even prophetic. Parsons, noted Mitchell, had not produced a great empirical work, such as those carried out by Durkheim or Marx.[4] "Nor has there been a study equivalent to Durkheim's *Suicide*. The fact that Parsons has not guided his energies in that direction is not important in itself, but it will probably somewhat diminish his reputation" (1967:191).

The second comment on Parsons is found in Mitchell's Preface: "I doubt very much that we are yet in a position to attain a really profound analysis of the man and his work. The passage of time is a prerequisite to such understanding"

---

[4]It could be argued that Parsons's writings about hospitals, universities, and the military were, in fact, empirical studies—especially his paper on the mental hospital (1957), which included interview data. But the criticism that he never did a major empirical work still holds.

(1967:ix). And what has the passage of time done to Parsons? From the late 1970s through the 1980s, his reputation diminished substantially, kept alive by thinkers such as Jeffrey Alexander. But in the 1990s, Camic republished the early essays, including a lengthy biographical statement, and other theorists, such as Anthony Giddens and Niklas Luhmann (see Chapter 15), either re-sponded to or built upon Parsons's work.

Robert K. Merton (1910–)

Robert King Merton was born in 1910 in a South Philadelphia slum. In 1994, at the age of 84, he gave a useful autobiographical statement titled "A Life of Learning" (Merton, 1994).

The son of Jewish immigrant parents, Merton early manifested a love of learning, and spent much time at a nearby Carnegie library. He also became ac-quainted with Leopold Stokowski's world-renowned Philadelphia Orchestra, at-tending concerts for 25 cents (1994:343, 345). Thus, observed Merton, this supposedly deprived South Philly slum provided him with "every sort of capi-tal—social capital, cultural capital, human capital, and above all, what we may call public capital—that is, with every sort of capital except the personally finan-cial" (1994:346).

By the age of 14, Merton was a fairly proficient magician, with Harry Houdini as his role model. Houdini had changed his name from Ehrich Weiss, and Meyer Schkolnick decided that such a change was appropriate for him as well. And so Meyer Schkolnick became Robert Merlin, after King Arthur's fa-mous magician, and—after being reminded that this was a bit hackneyed—Rob-ert Merton. Five years later Meyer Schkolnick's name was legally changed to Robert King Merton (1994:348).

Merton earned a scholarship to Temple University, where he happened into a sociology class taught by George E. Simpson, the translator of Durkheim. Simpson saw to it that Merton attended an annual meeting of the American So-ciological Society, where Merton heard and met Pitirim Sorokin of Harvard. Merton followed his degree from Temple by daring to apply to Harvard, where Sorokin was chair. But, Merton recalled, "it was not the renowned Sorokin who most influenced my sociological thinking there; instead, it was a young instruc-tor with no public identity whatsoever as a sociologist. Talcott Parsons had then published only two articles" (1994:350). Working with Parsons and with a his-torian of science named George Sarton, Merton completed his PhD in 1936. From there he went to Tulane, where he spent two years, before joining the fac-ulty at Columbia University in New York City.

Parsons influenced Merton's theoretical stance, and, as noted previously, the two were the leading U.S. functionalists from the 1930s into the 1970s. How-ever, it was when he went from Tulane to Columbia that Merton began what he called an "improbable collaboration":

> Paul Lazarsfeld and I may have been the original odd couple in the domain
> of social science. He, the mathematically-minded methodologist, inventor
> of powerful techniques of social inquiry such as the panel method and

latent structure analysis; I, the confirmed social theorist albeit with something of an empirical bent, insisting on the importance of sociological paradigms. (1994:354)

These two became colleagues in 1941 at the Bureau of Applied Social Research at Columbia University, where they collaborated until Lazarsfeld's death in 1976.

Merton recalled that he finally convinced the mathematician that the field of sociology really existed, while "Paul's abiding concern with research methods rubbed off on me and once resulted in a codification of what I called the focussed interview," later to become the "focus group" (1994:355; Merton and Kendall, 1946). Thus, Merton stood firmly planted in both the theoretical and empirical worlds, and some of his most insightful writing was on the relation between the two (Merton, 1946). At his retirement, he became a professor-at-large and Emeritus Professor of Columbia. In the year 2000, he turned 90.

Merton's Central Theories and Methods

Parsons was gratified by Merton's apparently growing appreciation of Parsons's efforts at grand-scale theory-building (see Parsons, 1961:3). However, Merton saw his own work as contributing in two multifaceted theoretical directions: middle-range theorizing and specification of functional analysis.

Theories of the Middle Range   Between grand-scale theory and the "fishing expeditions" of raw empiricists can be found theories that deal with a specific subportion of social life. Merton defined **middle-range theories** as those "that lie between the minor but necessary working hypotheses that evolve in abundance during day-to-day research and the all-inclusive systematic efforts to develop a unified theory that will explain all the observed uniformities of social behavior, social organization, and social change" (1968:39).

Such theories are in the style of Durkheim's *Suicide* and Weber's *Protestant Ethic*, and much of Merton's work was of that kind. Merton may have appreciated his mentor Parsons's theories, but considered most grand-scale theorizing to be at least premature, if not ill-conceived (Hunt, 1961). Merton wrote about deviance, role sets, political machines, and medical student attitudes; we will look briefly at the first two of these.

One of the studies that helped to make Merton's reputation was his analysis of **deviance**. Using, but altering, Durkheim's concept of anomie and the functionalist's distinction between means and goals, Merton reported four kinds of deviance; his fifth category was conformity, or the acceptance of the culture's dominant means and ends. The individual who accepts the society's goal of monetary success and strives through education and hard work to attain it, is a conformist, not a deviant at all.

The first type of deviant in Merton's analysis is the innovator—a person who accepts the goal of success but uses an alternate, or nonestablishment, means of attaining it, such as selling drugs. The second, opposite type is the ritualist—one who uses the accepted means, but rejects the goal, such as the educated person who rejects success in favor of becoming a monk. These two, innovator and ritualist, are characterized by anomie, because means and goals are inconsistent.

Merton's third type of deviant is the retreatist, who rejects both society's goals and the means of attaining them. This individual may be a drug addict, may be mentally ill, or may simply live in a hollow tree, but is clearly an outsider. The final type of deviation based on means and goals is rebellion—the substitution of another set of means and goals for the culture's dominant ones. Merton's scheme has been used to account for class, racial, and ethnic deviance, and has continued to be used and qualified in the half-century since it first appeared.

Role-sets, as Merton described them in 1957, are multiple role expectations that are parts of the same position or status. For example, a high school student plays various roles vis-à-vis his or her teachers, adviser, parents, and other students. As is typical with Merton, such specification makes it possible to explain conflict, as one set of expectations—for example, getting along with other students by not being a "curve-raiser"—conflicts with another set of expectations, such as making teachers and parents happy by getting good grades.

Role-set analysis clarifies not only conflicting expectations, but also inequities. If one were to list the role-sets related to the status of mother and compare it with that of father, one might discover the former to be overburdened.

> For example, does the school nurse always phone the mother when the child is sick, even when both parents work? By virtue of being a mother, is she, and not the father, automatically involved in role relationships with the school nurse? And if demands are unequal, what are the likely consequences? (Wallace and Wolf, 1986:59)

This is one of the ways in which Merton's middle-range specifying of functional theory allows for the conflict and inequities that seem to be missing from Parsons.

Specifying Functionalism   While middle-range theories are of interest, for the purposes of this chapter Merton's contributions to functional analysis are more important. Merton recognized that, as noted early in this chapter, most functionalists answer questions such as "What does it do?" or "What purpose does it serve?" This, to Merton, is oversimplified.

Merton's first specification was the distinction between manifest and latent functions. The same action or structure may perform either or both such functions. The **manifest function** is the observed or intended outcome; the **latent function** is the unintended or unrecognized result. Other sociological observers, noted Merton, had "from time to time distinguished between categories of subjective disposition ('needs, interests, purposes') and categories of generally unrecognized but objective functional consequences ('unique advantages,' . . . 'unintended . . . service to society,' 'function not limited to conscious and explicit purpose')" (1968:116).

An example of the value of this distinction is a reanalysis of Durkheim's treatment of religion, with religion serving the manifest function of solving the human quest for ultimate meaning and the latent function of providing social identity and solidarity. Another example, referred to by Merton, was Veblen's *Theory of the Leisure Class*, where accumulation of material possessions had the manifest function of making life more comfortable and the latent function of providing status and prestige.[5]

What does this distinction accomplish? First, according to Merton, it clarifies "the analysis of seemingly irrational social patterns," or patterns that only make sense when seen in terms of their latent consequences. Second, it can help draw attention "to theoretically fruitful fields of inquiry." Third, it contributes to the sociology of knowledge, helping us understand how we know what we know. Finally, it "precludes the substitution of naive moral judgments for sociological analysis" (1968:119–126). Merton thus recognized the tendency of functionalism to slide from "What is is functional" into "What is is good."

Merton's second specification of functional analysis is found in the concept of dysfunction. The danger of functional analysis is its focus on structure and equilibrium. Even though, as noted earlier, Parsons referred to strains and tension management, he never attempted to incorporate them into his model of order and system. Merton, however, noted that aspects of culture and society may have "consequences which lessen the adaptation or adjustment of the system" (1957:105). Bureaucratic rules, for example, while presumably intended to increase efficiency by making things run smoothly, may be dysfunctional when they lead to "red tape" and an inability to make rational decisions.

Another use of the concept of dysfunction relates to the question "functional for whom?" Functionalists such as Parsons often assumed, without direct reference, that the need met is societal or systemic. Merton, however, noted that, to take our opening example, a casino may be functional for a rich owner while being dysfunctional for the Native American tribe. Racial discrimination may be functional for the race that controls power but extremely dysfunctional for the racial minority. Not all the parts of a social system or its culture are integrated, or work together for the good of the whole. Thus, in the same way that the manifest/latent distinction seeks to escape moral judgments, recognition of dysfunction as a structural possibility helps the observer to escape a status quo conservative stance (Merton, 1975).

Merton's third specification of functionalism is found in his view of functional alternatives. The true-believing functionalist is likely to argue that a given structure or portion of a system is functional because it is the solution to some need of the system (perhaps A, G, I, or L). It exists because it must—because it is essential or necessary. Merton, however, noted that although a structure may exist because it solves some problem, it is hardly indispensable. Thus, for example, a political machine in a big city may be functional for immigrants who do not know how to solve their own problems. But the same need could be met by education for the immigrants and taxation of the well-to-do. By turning structures into analyzable variables, into alternatives instead of indispensables, Merton has again escaped the status quo conservative trap.

Yet all this does not imply that Merton was simply a critic of functionalism. His approach to theory was still to ask the functionalist questions of ends and

---

[5] Veblen was hardly a functionalist, and Merton's use of him indicates a willingness to go "outside the camp" in order to expand and clarify functionalist assumptions and simplifications.

means, structure and consequence. Merton himself gave us a summary paradigm, or guiding framework, for what should be analyzed in functional terms: (a) items to which functions are imputed; (b) concepts of subjective dispositions (motives, purposes); (c) concepts of objective consequences (functions, dysfunctions); (d) concepts of the unit served by the function; (e) concepts of functional prerequisites; (f) concepts of mechanisms through which functions are fulfilled; (g) concepts of functional alternatives; (h) concepts of dynamics and change; (i) concepts of structural context; (j) problems of validation of functional analysis; and (k) problems of the ideological implications of functional analysis (1946:50–54). One can readily see from this list that Merton had broadened functionalism, not abandoned it.

Methods/Research/Problems   We have already noted that, while working with Paul Lazarsfeld, Merton (with Patricia Kendall) wrote a methodological piece on the focused interview. Although he was never totally oriented to methods, some of Merton's most insightful pieces concerned the relation between research and theory, and the issue of problem-solving in sociology. His lengthy treatment of the interplay between research and theory is found in his collection of writings *Social Theory and Social Structure* (1968). Among his main points were (1) that different research methods are necessary for different empirical problems; (2) that research may lead to empirical generalizations, but fall short of direct theory testing; and (3) that empirical research is useful for much more than the testing of hypotheses drawn from a general theory. In short, Merton pointed out the necessary but complex links between theory and research. Merton's paper on "Problem-Solving" (1961), again showed that he had one foot firmly planted in the empirical world of research and the other in the world of middle-range theories and theoretical complexity.

In introducing a volume of papers on the current state of sociology, Merton (1961) asked, What is a sociological problem, and how does one find or formulate it? His answer was multifaceted. First, one may find it by specializing, or by becoming "more and more interested in less and less"—that is, in a smaller and smaller portion of the social world. Second, one may seek to correct errors or emphases. An overemphasis on psychological explanations, for example, led to Durkheim's sociological analysis of suicide. Third, a recurring problem may come to one's attention simply because it has never been answered adequately. Fourth, there may be conceptual obstacles to overcome. Race, class consciousness, gender, and family may all need a certain amount of reconceptualization. Du Bois, for example, noted problems with what he called the "race concept." Fifth, inconsistent or contradictory "facts" or findings may call for new data, and new theory to explain them. Finally, a real-world problem may come to the attention of both the researcher and the theorist. It might be the authoritarian personality, identified in Nazi Germany in the 1930s (see Chapter 16), or the "cooling-out function" in education—convincing college students that they don't belong there. Numerous such sociological problems are identified simply by living in the world and observing it (Merton, 1961:xxxiii–xxxiv).

For Merton, then, theorizing was central, but it requires methodology, research, and problem identification, not just an armchair or an ivory tower.

Nature of Society, Humans, and Change

As Parsons had stated, society is a system, with a structure and parts. However, to Merton it is not in equilibrium, with the parts contributing to the good of the whole. Rather, it consists of manifest and latent functions, even dysfunctions, and, as such, is a mixture of elements, including conflict as well as order. Merton argued, then, that functionalism is not necessarily inherently conservative in its view of society.

Though he did not devote much attention to human nature, Merton made one important observation: Human nature is neither inherently good nor bad, but is changeable. It is only, he said, "with the rejection of social fatalism implied in the notion of unchangeable human nature that the tragic circle of fear, social disaster, and reinforced fear can be broken" (1948:200). He was referring to racial inequality, noting the importance to change of believing that it is possible. Clearly, Merton was a believer in changeable human nature, behavior, and attitudes.

To Merton, then, change is possible and often desirable, though that is the sort of value judgment he sought to avoid. Reading between the lines, it seems that to Merton change is best approached within the established order, by liberal means, rather than by revolution.

In terms of ideology, it should be obvious by now that Merton did not see himself as a status quo conservative. However, the questions he asked about structure and function, needs, ends, and means come from that tradition. Despite his liberalism, Merton did not completely escape the criticisms to which functional theorists such as Parsons opened themselves.

Class, Gender, and Race

Class, gender, and race were not the central topics in Merton's work. However, one of his earliest writings dealt with class. In discussing anomie and deviance, he noted that the unskilled may lack "legitimate means for becoming successful" (1938:677). Their response will be either to reject the dominant goal, or to find alternative (deviant) means for achieving it. Thus, Merton suggested, lower-class individuals are likely to "innovate," and the lower-middle classes to "conform." However, when the national ideology extols freedom and opportunity for all, it leaves some individuals with a sense of failure, even if "the cards were stacked against them." Merton's analysis of class, then, was related for the most part to his discussion of deviance.

Gender was even less a focus of Merton's attention, showing up only once in his essay on insiders and outsiders. Treating women and African Americans as out-groups, Merton noted how difficult it is for the women's movement to draw on both white and black women, and how difficult it is for black liberation movements to unite both men and women (Merton, 1972:30). With no further comment on women's liberation, Merton again avoided any sort of ideological comment on gender.

Race, like gender, was dealt with in the essay on insiders and outsiders. However, Merton also discussed race in his commentary on the self-fulfilling prophecy, which will be discussed later (Merton, 1948:183–201). He began the discussion of insiders and outsiders by noting that education is not enough to change race relations. Furthermore, a racial group may be criticized and punished for being either successful *or* unsuccessful. Thus, African Americans may be seen as inferior, so that resources are not "wasted on them," so that they continue to be less successful, which demonstrates their inferiority. Or Jews may be punished for too much success, as they were in Nazi Germany. Institutional change, not education alone, is necessary to combat ethnic and racial prejudices (Merton, 1948:200). Merton, then, saw racial inequality as a problem to be solved, not as an inevitable aspect of society.

Other Theories and Theorists

Merton's middle-range theories covered a wide variety of topics, making it impossible to introduce but a few of the more interesting and useful ones.

Self-Fulfilling Prophecy   The "self-fulfilling prophecy" was one of Merton's phrases that has been incorporated into everyday speech. Merton began with a quote from W. I. Thomas in 1928: "If men define situations as real, they are real in their consequences" (Thomas and Thomas, 1928:572). Carrying this idea further, Merton argued that if we define something as real, and act upon it, it will in fact become real.

The first illustration he presented concerns the folding of a bank. A rumor, however started, that a bank cannot cover the deposits of its customers, if acted upon will become real. No bank ever has all the money at hand that has been credited to accounts, because it reinvests most of it. Thus, "despite the comparative liquidity of the bank's assets, a rumor of insolvency, once believed (and acted upon) by enough depositors, would result in the insolvency of the bank" (Merton, 1948:184–185).

Another illustration pertained to African Americans' being kept out of unions because they are defined as "scabs" or strikebreakers. Because (in 1948) they were not allowed into the unions and needed work, they then *became* strikebreakers (Merton, 1948:187). Thus, a belief, when acted upon, may become true or factual.

Plausibility and Truth   One of Merton's most insightful comments is found in a footnote to his "Notes on Problem-Finding in Sociology" (1961). The relation between the plausible and the true, wrote Merton, leaves the sociologist

> with some uncomfortable alternatives. Should his systematic inquiry only confirm what had been widely assumed—this being the class of plausible truths—he will of course be charged with "laboring the obvious." . . .
> Should investigation find that widely held beliefs are untrue—the class of plausible untruths—he is a heretic, questioning value-laden verities. If he ventures to examine socially implausible ideas that turn out to be untrue, he is a fool, wasting effort on a line of inquiry not worth pursuing in the first place. And finally, if he should turn up some implausible truths, he

must be prepared to find himself regarded as a charlatan, claiming as knowledge what is patently false. (Merton, 1961:xv–xvi)

Dealing with society, about which everyone has some knowledge and many opinions, leaves the researcher and theorist open to all these possible responses.

Critique and Conclusions

Merton, then, is a theorist, researcher, and thinker about the world in which he lives. He has attempted, through many years of productive scholarship, to help us appreciate the complexities of society, and the functions performed by its various aspects. His functionalism is broad-based, and he has been able to escape many of the criticisms faced by other conservative functionalists, from Spencer to Parsons.

One scholar whose criticism Merton has not escaped, however, is Randall Collins. Merton's deviance theory, according to Collins (1981), had two advantages: first, it drew on (and altered) Durkheim, a central figure in mid-twentieth-century American sociology, and second, it rode the wave of the "great juvenile delinquency scare" of the 1950s. According to Collins, then, it was more popular than creative.

Collins's second criticism is a broad indictment of Merton's corpus of work. Merton's lack of attention to stratification and classes exemplified, in Collins's view, what was weakest in American sociology at the time. Consistent with the "great Communist scare" of that time, intellectuals such as Merton helped to drive sociology as far as possible away from Marxism. Lacking a serious theoretical and ideological dialogue, the discipline was weak and, in many ways, simply reflective of U.S. ideology. Collins's argument with Merton, and even more so with Parsons, is that, despite the interesting issues raised, the answers given lack dynamism, excitement, and dialogue.

Final Thoughts

In 1959, at the height of the dominance of functionalist theory in U.S. sociology, Kingsley Davis published a most instructive paper. In it he argued, in agreement with Merton, that a functionalist does not have to believe that everything that exists meets a need, is indispensable, or is in a system where all the parts work for the good of the whole. All that the functionalist needs to conclude is that things are interrelated, and that society is integrated or "working" (functioning) most of the time. In this sense, Davis suggested, every sociologist is a functionalist. Sociology *is* functionalism, because sociology starts from the premise that societies are real and, therefore, are integrated (Davis, 1959).

If Davis is right, then functionalism is not a theory at all, but merely a set of premises that sociologists—and non-sociologists—accept, and within which we all operate. In reading the present volume, you may want to keep Davis's point in mind, and ask yourself to what extent he has correctly stated, or overstated, the case.

References

Abrahamson, Mark. 1978. *Functionalism*. Englewood Cliffs, NJ: Prentice-Hall.

Bales, Robert Freed. 1949. *Interaction Process Analysis: A Method for the Study of Small Groups*. Reading, MA: Addison-Wesley.

Black, Max (Ed.). 1961/1976. *The Social Theories of Talcott Parsons*. Carbondale: Southern Illinois University Press.

Camic, Charles. 1991. *Talcott Parsons: The Early Essays*. Chicago: University of Chicago Press.

Collins, Randall. 1981. *Sociology Since Midcentury*. New York: Academic Press.

Cremin, Lawrence, David Shannon, and Mary Townsend. 1954. *A History of Teachers College: Columbia University*. Morningside Heights, NY: Columbia University Press.

Davis, Kingsley. 1959. "The Myth of Functional Analysis as a Special Method in Sociology and Anthropology." *American Sociological Review, 24,* 757–772.

Devereaux, Edward C. 1961/1976. "Parsons' Sociological Theory," In Max Black (Ed.), *The Social Theories of Talcott Parsons* (pp. 1–63). Carbondale: Southern Illinois University Press.

Gouldner, Alvin W. 1970. *The Coming Crisis of Western Sociology*. New York: Basic Books.

Hacker, Andrew. 1961/1976. "Sociology and Ideology." In Max Black (Ed.), *The Social Theories of Talcott Parsons* (pp. 289–310). Englewood Cliffs, NJ: Prentice-Hall.

Hunt, Morton M. 1961, "How Does It Come to Be So? " [Profile of Robert K. Merton]. *New Yorker, 36,* 39–63.

Johnson, Miriam M. 1989. "Feminism and the Theories of Talcott Parsons." In Ruth A. Wallace (Ed.), *Feminism and Sociological Theory* (pp. 101–118). Newbury Park, CA: Sage.

Kates, William. 1999, April 11. "Casino Opening Gives Mohawks Hope." *Wisconsin State Journal*, p. 6A.

Loomis, Charles P., and Zona K. Loomis. 1961. *Modern Social Theories*. Princeton, NJ: D. Van Nostrand.

Martindale, Don. 1960. *The Nature and Types of Sociological Theory*. Boston: Houghton Mifflin.

Merton, Robert K. 1938. "Social Structure and Anomie." *American Sociological Review, 3,* 672–682.

———. 1946. *Social Theory and Social Structure*. New York: Free Press.

———. 1948/1996. "The Self-Fulfilling Prophecy." In Piotr Sztompka (Ed.), *Robert K. Merton: On Social Structure and Science* (pp. 183–201). Chicago: University of Chicago Press.

———. 1957. "The Role Set: Problems in Sociological Theory." *British Journal of Sociology, 2,* 106–120.

———. 1961. "Notes on Problem-Finding in Sociology." In Robert K. Merton, Leonard Broom, and Leonard S. Cottrell (Eds.), *Sociology Today: Problems and Prospects* (pp. ix–xxxiv). New York: Basic Books.

———. 1968. *Social Theory and Social Structure* (3d ed.). New York: Simon and Schuster.

———. 1972. "Insiders and Outsiders: A Chapter in the Sociology of Knowledge." *American Journal of Sociology, 77,* 9–47.

———. 1975/1996. "Functional Analysis in Sociology." In Piotr Sztompka (Ed.), *Robert K. Merton: On Social Structure and Science* (pp. 96–100). Chicago: University of Chicago Press.

———. 1994/1996. "A Life of Learning." Philadelphia: American Council of Learned Societies. Reprinted in Piotr Sztompka (Ed.), *Robert K. Merton: On Social Structure and Science* (pp. 339–359). Chicago: University of Chicago Press.

Merton, Robert K., and Patricia L. Kendall. 1946. "The Focused Interview." *American Journal of Sociology, 51,* 541–557.

Mitchell, William C. 1967. *Sociological Analysis and Politics: The Theories of Talcott Parsons.* Englewood Cliffs, NJ: Prentice-Hall.

Parsons, Talcott. 1937. *The Structure of Social Action.* New York: McGraw-Hill.

———. 1940. "An Analytic Approach to the Theory of Stratification." *American Journal of Sociology, 45,* 841–862.

———. 1942a/1954. "Age and Sex in the Social Structure of the United States." In *Essays in Sociological Theory* (pp. 89–103). Glencoe, IL: Free Press.

———. 1942b. "Some Sociological Aspects of the Fascist Movements." *Social Forces, 21,* 138–147.

———. 1945/1954. "The Present Position and Prospects of Systematic Theory in Sociology." In Talcott Parsons, *Essays in Sociological Theory* (pp. 212–237). New York: Free Press of Glencoe.

———. 1951. *The Social System.* New York: Free Press.

———. 1954. *Essays in Sociological Theory* (rev. ed.). New York: Free Press of Glencoe.

———. 1955. "'McCarthyism' and American Social Tension: A Sociologist's View." *Yale Review, 44,* 226–245.

———. 1957. "The Mental Hospital as a Type of Organization." In Milton Greenblatt, Daniel J. Levinson, Richard H. Williams (Eds.), *The Patient and the Mental Hospital* (pp. 108–129). New York: Free Press of Glencoe.

———. 1960. *Structure and Process in Modern Societies.* New York: Free Press of Glencoe.

———. 1961. "General Theory in Sociology." In Robert K. Merton, Leonard Broom, and Leonard S. Cottrell (Eds.), *Sociology Today: Problems and Prospects* (pp. 3–38). New York: Basic Books.

———. 1962. "Richard Henry Tawney (1880–1962)." *American Sociological Review, 27,* 888–890.

———. 1964. "Evolutionary Universals in Society." *American Sociological Review, 29,* 339–357.

———. 1966. *Societies: Evolutionary and Comparatives Perspectives.* Englewood Cliffs, NJ: Prentice-Hall.

———. 1971. *The System of Modern Societies.* Englewood Cliffs, NJ: Prentice-Hall.

———. 1975. "The Present Status of Structural-Functional Theory in Sociology." In Lewis A. Coser (Ed.), *The Idea of Social Structure: Papers in Honor of Robert K. Merton* (pp. 67–83). New York: Harcourt Brace Jovanovich.

Parsons, Talcott, Robert F. Bales, James Olds, Morris Zelditch, and Philip E. Slater. 1955. *Family, Socialization, and Interaction Process.* New York: Free Press of Glencoe.

Parsons, Talcott, and Edward Shils (Eds.). 1951. *Toward a General Theory of Action.* Cambridge, MA: Harvard University Press.

Parsons, Talcott, Edward Shils, Kaspar D. Naegele, and Jesse R. Pitts. 1961. *Theories of Society* (2 vols.). New York: Free Press of Glencoe.

Parsons, Talcott, and Neil J. Smelser. 1956. *Economy and Society.* New York: Free Press of Glencoe.

Smith, Dorothy. 1990. *The Conceptual Practices of Power: A Feminist Sociology of Knowledge.* Boston: Northeastern University Press.

Thomas, W. I., and Dorothy Swaine Thomas. 1928. *The Child in America.* New York: Alfred A. Knopf.

Wallace, Ruth A., and Alison Wolf. 1986. *Contemporary Sociological Theory: Continuing the Classical Tradition.* Englewood Cliffs, NJ: Prentice-Hall.

Williams, Robin. 1961. "The Sociological Theory of Talcott Parsons." In Max Black (Ed.), *The Social Theories of Talcott Parsons* (pp. 64–99). Englewood Cliffs, NJ: Prentice-Hall.

Chapter 15

Systems, Structuration, and Modernity
Luhmann and Giddens

Nicholas Luhmann and Anthony Giddens are two encyclopedic sociological theorists of the late twentieth century. Although they differed in their responses to Talcott Parsons—Luhmann outgrew him and Giddens rejected him—they have much in common besides the volume of their writings. Neither was willing to simplify the complexity of the social world. Both addressed issues of social structure—Luhmann writing about social systems, and Giddens about the process of structuration. Both discussed problems of trust, risk, power, and reflexivity. And, because of their differences, it is interesting to compare them with each other and with the functionalists who preceded them in Chapter 14. Let us introduce them.

> *Luhmann:* Luhmann's social theory is a systemic supertheory. . . . [His] basic attitude towards the world is one of ironic distance. His . . . vision of the world is one of wonder. . . . Luhmann's social theory offers a systemic analysis of the social ordering of chaos. . . . Luhmann literally demoralizes the world. He has given up hope and given away the normative foundations of social criticism. (Vandenberghe, 1999:2)

> *Giddens:* Low-probability, high-consequence risks will not disappear in the modern world, although in an optimal scenario they could be minimized. . . . Relatively *small-scale* events, such as the dropping of atomic bombs on Hiroshima and Nagasaki or the accidents at Three Mile Island or Chernobyl, give some sense of what could happen. (Giddens, 1990:134; italics added)

The modern world consists of complex systems (Luhmann), but is not too bad a place (Giddens). It is not a Parsonsian functional system, with the parts working together as they do in an organism; it consists of numerous relatively independent systems—religious, political, economic, educational, and so on—and of people who think about themselves and their actions (Luhmann).

Looked at optimistically, that same world is moving toward global democracy, with individuals having the power to make things happen, and with the dropping of atomic bombs being but small-scale negative events (Giddens).

In this chapter we will meet the German, Niklas Luhmann, and the Britisher, Anthony Giddens.

Niklas Luhmann (1927–1998)

Max Weber, as you saw in Chapter 7, never sought to simplify the complexity of the social world into single-factor descriptions or explanations; he did, however, attempt to make that complexity as understandable as possible. Niklas Luhmann not only saw the modern world as complicated—more so than during Weber's time—but mirrored it in his writing. The words are complex, the thoughts are complex, and his works are almost prohibitively so. He used a flexible and abstract set of concepts and propositions that could be combined in many different ways (Luhmann, 1984:xix).

The difficulty of reading Luhmann involves much more than its having been translated from German: The ideas are abstract, the sentences include new or little-known words, and they string together numerous concepts. However, it is not just his sentences that are complex—so is the overall structure of his works. Books such as *Social Systems* (1984) have no natural starting point—any order of chapters is equally reasonable and acceptable. Have you ever read a book in which it didn't matter where you started, or in what order you read the chapters? Not likely. But this is true of Luhmann's work.

Luhmann himself acknowledged that "Complicated conceptual relationships of this kind may intimidate sociologists"—and, we might add, students.[1] However, he claimed, it was not possible to convert the book "into a thoroughly plausible statement" (1984:488). Modern society is complex, and Luhmann was unwilling to simplify for the sake of accessibility. Thus, as we begin, it is logical to ask, is Luhmann "worth it"? The answer, however, must come at the end—not at the beginning—of our journey.

Niklas Luhmann was born in 1927 in Luneburg, Germany. In 1949, he completed a law degree at the University of Freiburg/Breisgau, and subsequently practiced law (Poggi, 1979:vii). However, he became disillusioned with the repetitive nature of much in the legal profession, and joined the civil service in Saxony. This he also found less than fulfilling, and during his free time he read Descartes, Kant, and the functionalist theories of Bronislaw Malinowski and A. R. Radcliffe-Brown (Knodts, 1995:xiii). His own theoretical development took place as a result both of his reading and of his civil service work on post–World War II German reparations.

---

[1]Not meaning to scare the reader away, here is one sentence from *Social Systems*: "At this functional point in the theory, the concept of ideality enters to guarantee apodictically the unconditional repeatability of thoughts, and thus the enduring richness in content of transcendental 'life'" (Luhmann, 1984:263). Got it? If not, you are not alone!

By 1960, Luhmann's administrative duties began to get in the way of his intellectual interests, and he sought and received a leave to spend a year (1960–1961) studying with Talcott Parsons at Harvard. On his return to Germany, he took an academic position at the School of Administrative Science at Speyer, where he began to expand his theoretical position beyond that of Parsons, based largely on his studies in cybernetics and biology.

The world of Luhmann's time included the rise and fall of Germany in World War II, its occupation by foreign troops during his early adulthood, and his resulting lack of confidence that modern society is a better place to live. As one commentator has observed, the way in which his

> "optimism of the intellect," is countered by a "pessimism of the will" can be seen in his almost cynical appreciation of the defeat of the Third Reich. Unlike Habermas,[2] who described himself without irony as a typical product of postwar re-education, Luhmann provocatively declares that he remembers only one thing about the liberation—that American soldiers beat him up and stole his watch. (Vandenberghe, 1999:2)

Luhmann taught in various settings from 1965 to 1968, when Helmut Schelsky invited him to join the sociology faculty at Bielefeld. The problem was that Luhmann had no formal degree in sociology. So he proceeded to get two of his early publications accepted in lieu of a degree, and in 1968 he followed Schelsky to Bielefeld, where he taught and later was Emeritus Professor until his death.

Much of Luhmann's early reputation was based on criticism of the already famous Habermas's liberal ideology. But Luhmann's later productivity was truly amazing. He wrote 40 books and 350 journal articles, a feat which he attributed to his system of cross-referenced file cards. He once stated that he spent more time "arranging and rearranging his system of file cards than writing books" (Vandenberghe, 1999:1). One reason that Luhmann is not well known in the English-speaking world may be the sheer difficulty and complexity of his systems theory. One commentator describes Luhmann's mode of presentation as "non-linear":

> One can enter the theory by a multiplicity of conceptual gates—such as complexity, contingency, system, environment, meaning, communication, self-reference, openness through closure, and so forth—but as one can never be sure to be on the right track, it is often tempting to go for the next exit. In this respect, the theory resembles more a labyrinth (or maze) than a highway to a happy end. (Vandenberghe, 1999:1)

Another commentator suggests a second reason why Luhmann may not be well known in the English-speaking intellectual world. In his work, Luhmann drew on formal logic, cybernetics, and biology, not just on the social sciences.

---

[2]Jurgen Habermas is an important contemporary German critical theorist who deals with language, and who published and debated with Luhmann. He will be discussed in Chapter 16.

Such interdisciplinary work crosses the typical intellectual boundaries, while modern scientific knowledge is compartmentalized by discipline and department. The result is that inter- or cross-disciplinary conversations and work are either ignored (being considered to be someone else's), or fragmented, dealt with like the blind men and the elephant—one inadequate piece per discipline (Savard, 1999:1). For the same reason, however, another commentator suggests that "because of the truly universal scope of his published work, Niklas Luhmann seems richly to deserve his growing reputation as the most original German sociologist since Max Weber" (Holmes and Larmore, 1982:xxxvi–xxxvii).

Luhmann's Central Theories and Methods

Luhmann's self-introduction in *The Differentiation of Society* summarizes his two most important theoretical interests:

> In recent years, I have worked on two theoretical projects that cross-fertilize one another. On the one hand, I have pursued a general theory of social systems. . . . On the other hand, I have worked extensively on a theory of modern society. We can no longer define society by giving primacy to one of its functional domains. (1982: xi–xii)

We will examine each of these themes in turn.

Systems Theory   What is a **system**? One familiar example is the solar system, which consists of a star—the Sun—with a cluster of planets revolving around it. Several of these planets also have moons around them. It is, then, a set of inter-related parts all focused on and guided by their relation to a single center. This is the sort of system that Spencer and Parsons used to characterize society.

Two other well-known systems are the interstate highway system and the telephone system. Each of these consists of interconnected parts, but neither has a single center around which it revolves. Rather, one can enter at any point and be connected to the rest. In the United States, the phone "system," while interconnected, is actually a number of subsystems, or separate carriers. And while a highway system and a telephone system are relatively independent of each other, they are both means of keeping in touch, or communicating. Telephone lines are often near highways, because a highway makes it possible to reach a telephone line to repair it. The common denominator in such systems, then, is independence with interconnectedness.

While reading Malinowski and Radcliffe-Brown and studying with Parsons, Luhmann became interested in the theory of systems. In the early stages of his theoretical development, Luhmann's view of the social system was not very different from that of Parsons. Social systems, in Luhmann's early work, consisted of real actions based upon shared meanings or interpretations. These actions and interpretations are, in turn, the result of expectations, both for one's own behavior and that of others. Such expectations are likely to be stable and consistent, or institutionalized and consensual. Thus, norms, roles, and institutions are the heart of the study and understanding of social systems (Poggi, 1979:xiii–xiv).

Words such as *systems, actions, norms,* and *institutions* are already familiar from the work of Parsons and Merton and the functionalists who preceded them. However, while indebted to Parsons, Luhmann "believes that Parsons always overestimated both the existence and the necessity of shared value commitments in modern society." Part of Luhmann's project was to explore "'alternatives to normative integration,' that is to say, ways in which modern society has maintained . . . forms of order and orderly change *without* relying on society-wide consensus about communal purposes," or relying on society-wide interconnectedness (Holmes and Larmore, 1982:xvii).

Social systems, according to Luhmann, consist primarily of communication networks. Even **socialization**, or the growth of the individual into her or his society and culture, is a result of communication: "All socialization occurs as social interpenetration; all social interpenetration, as communication" (1984:243). The gap in systems theory, claimed Luhmann, has only recently been filled with a theory of the media of communication (1982:350). Recalling G. H. Mead (Chapter 13), Luhmann argued that systems are based on shared meanings, and shared meanings are always the result of communication. However, his departure from Parsons began when he argued that, although there are systems in the modern world, there is not a single overarching and integrated system striving for equilibrium.

Modern Society   From the beginning of his career, and increasingly later on, Luhmann emphasized two points about contemporary society: "the drastic intensification of societal complexity" and "the increasing external differentiation of the societal subsystems" (Poggi, 1979:xv). The first point means that modern society has no central institution. Aware of Marx's argument for a shift from the primacy of politics to the primacy of economics in the modern industrial world, Luhmann argued that there is *no* primary, or central, institution—politics or economics. To him modern society more closely resembles the telephone system than the solar system. As Luhmann's translators put it, "Today, a gradual process of increasing differentiation has brought into being a type of society that is relatively stable even though it has no single center and no subsector that can claim unchallenged supremacy" (Holmes and Larmore, 1982:xv). This idea is of concern to economists, and even more so to political scientists, who have fiercely criticized Luhmann's concept of a centerless or headless society (Savard, 1999:4).

His second point is that modern society is not a single social system with related parts, but several systems, including some commonly recognized institutions—such as law, religion, communication media, education, politics, and economics—and other systems consisting of organizations, personalities, and/or interactions. To Luhmann, each of these is a system, with the other systems as its environment. Society is like the telephone system and the interstate highway system: each is part of the other system's environment. The concepts of system and of function "no longer refer to 'the system' . . . but to the relationship between system and environment. . . . Everything that happens belongs to a *system* (or to many systems) and *always at the same time* to the *environment of other systems*" (Luhmann, 1984:176–177).

Luhmann's second point, about system "compartmentalization," must not be overstated. The telephone system is, after all, part of the same larger social system as the highways, and Luhmann did believe that modern society is characterized by a high degree of interdependence among social sectors. Compartmentalization was thus a relative term: Compared to preindustrial and early industrial societies, modern society exhibits much less consensual, communal, or societal solidarity. In fact, Luhmann's translators suggested,

> If we redefine the unity of society or social integration as "resistance to disintegration," it even becomes plausible to interpret compartmentalization as a palliative rather than as a threat. In one sense, at least, [this] is a mechanism for enhancing social integration. By localizing conflicts, a highly "parcelized" social order can prevent crises from spreading like brushfire from one social sector to another. In other words, or so Luhmann would have us believe, the "absence of a common life" is hardly a cause for unmitigated grief, since it may well ensure that society as a whole does not flare up like a box of matches. (Holmes and Larmore, 1982:xvi)

Thus, to continue with our analogy, when an accident occurs on the highway, the telephones are not usually affected; rather, they may be used to call for help. And when telephone lines are down, the repair truck uses the highways to go to the source of the problem. Again, a ship may be compartmentalized, so that if water enters one compartment, it can be closed off and the ship does not sink.

Trust   Luhmann's most readable work may well be his essay on trust. People put their **trust**, according to Luhmann, "in the self-evident matter-of-fact 'nature' of the world and of human nature every day," and "the necessity of trust can be regarded as the correct and appropriate starting point for the derivation of rules for proper conduct" (1979:4). Thus, we trust that a car will not lose a wheel at full speed, that a bridge will hold our car, and that the mechanic who worked on our car is knowledgeable and trustworthy. The more complex the world is, the more necessary is trust. Trust, wrote Luhmann,

> strengthens the capacity . . . for understanding and reducing complexity: it strengthens states as opposed to events and thus makes it possible to *live and to act with greater complexity in relation to events.* In terms of a well-known psychological theory, trust increases the "tolerance of uncertainty."
> This effect is not to be confused with instrumental mastery over events. (1979:15)

Mastery does not require trust, because we ourselves are determining the outcome. Ignorance, however, may require trust just as much as familiarity justifies it. We may be ignorant of the workings of an automobile, but we entrust it to a knowledgeable mechanic. "Familiarity is," wrote Luhmann, "a precondition for both trust and distrust" (1979:20). The more we know about another person (or system), the more we believe her (it) to be trustworthy or not. Thus, "familiarity and trust are . . . complementary ways of absorbing complexity": Familiarity is based on past experience, and trust on a willingness to take risks in the future (Luhmann, 1979:19).

The complexities and differential system functions of modern society demand trust, but also allow for distrust. On the system level,

> trust depends on the inclination towards risk being kept under control and on the quota of disappointments not becoming too large. If this is correct, then one could suppose that a system of higher complexity, which needs more trust, also needs at the same time more distrust, and therefore must institutionalize distrust, for example in the form of supervision. (Luhmann, 1979:89)

A large organization may have a time clock for its workers to punch in, and a floor supervisor to see to it that the work is being done. In other words, a complex world involves interpersonal and system trust and distrust. However, distrust, unless it is institutionalized—built into the rules—can be extremely exhausting or burdensome. It may "absorb the strength of the person who distrusts to an extent which leaves him little energy to explore and adapt to his environment in an objective and unprejudiced manner" (Luhmann, 1979:72).

Integrity is another word for trustworthiness. In a governmental body, for example, certain members are considered to have "personal integrity," while others are not. In addition, people may not trust an entire governmental body, causing them neither to vote nor to believe what politicians tell them. Such mass lack of trust can also be seen in relation to other subsystems of society. People trust in the value of money, and in the institutions or systems that administer it. But such system trust may be undermined by a rapid devaluing of a currency or by a bank's being unable to cover the withdrawals of its patrons (see Luhmann, 1979:50). The result of such an event may be system mistrust, resulting in a run on one or many banks.

One may trust an institution or another person for certain purposes but not for others. For example, one trusts that a bank is handling one's money well, but may not accept the bank's advice on how to invest it. Or one can "accept without question the opinion of one's colleague about a technical matter but nevertheless not risk lending him money 'personally'" (Luhmann, 1979:91).

Luhmann summarizes the role of trust in the complex modern world as follows:

> Trust reduces social complexity by going beyond available information and generalizing expectations of behavior in that it replaces missing information with an internally guaranteed security. It thus remains dependent on other reduction mechanisms developed in parallel with it, for example, those of law, of organization and, of course, those of language, but cannot, however, be reduced to them. Trust is not the sole foundation of the world; but a highly complex but nevertheless structured conception of the world could not be established without a fairly complex society, which in turn could not [function] without trust. (1979:94)

Risk   Living in the modern world requires not only trust but also the taking of risks, a subject that Luhmann examined in detail. We seek to make decisions that reduce risk;[3] we seek to ensure safety and security. In Luhmann's view, however, the best we can do is to normalize or accept it, and to calculate the likelihood of accident (1993:76).

Luhmann made an important distinction between **risk** and **danger**: We may make a decision in which we calculate or accept the risk involved; or we may be in a dangerous environment. Perhaps the simplest way to distinguish these two is to say: "I take a risk," or "I am in danger." Thus, if I drive 100 miles per hour, I am taking a risk, but I am also putting passengers and other drivers in danger. Smoking can be seen as a form of risk-taking, while asbestos in a ceiling is a danger.

Important areas involving risk and danger include technology, politics, economic life, and organizational behavior. Regarding technology, Luhmann suggested that more "than any other single factor, the immense expansion of technological possibilities has contributed to drawing public attention to the risks involved" (1993:83). Risky technologies may cause confidence to evaporate. For example, after World War II the danger of atomic and hydrogen bombs caused many people to try to reduce their danger by building "fallout shelters." Likewise, unknown technological complexities caused a fear of potential Y2K computer breakdowns.

With respect to politics, leaders may make risky decisions that bring the populace into danger. However, the closed nature of the political system—even in a supposed democracy—causes people to feel helpless about reducing risk through their own choices; they simply "leave it up to the leaders." With power, then, comes the risk of making mistakes (Luhmann, 1979:161). In addition, personified evil makes it possible to externalize blame for the dangers we feel incapable of lessening. Thus, in the Western world it has been useful to identify Mao Tse-tung, Idi Amin, Noriega, Khaddafi, Saddam Hussein, Slobodan Milosovic, and others as the risk-takers who have put us in danger (Luhmann, 1993:162, 171). However, new external threats must continually be identified, because over time the previously identified persons lose their usefulness as external personifications of evil and, therefore, danger.

In the realm of economics, Luhmann offered the analogy of the immune system, whose job it is to control disease. Deflation and inflation in the economy are immune system responses to fluctuations in money supply, demand, and so on. They are not harmless—they do affect individuals and businesses—but they are intended to reduce the risk of even greater variations (1993:177). In organizations, leaders continually make risky decisions: Should we expand, should we change to email from face-to-face contact, should we drop a line of goods, and so on. "The task of leadership would then . . . consist in weighing opportunities against risks" (1993:199).

Before writing his lengthy essay on risk, Luhmann presented in his 1984 book on *Social Systems* the following summary statement regarding modern-day risk:

> To be sure, we still have not been able to produce a theory of modern
> society. But we have experience enough with such things as: technology

---

[3]Today we attribute too much to decisions, even when the decision makers can't even be identified. One way risk is reduced psychologically (but not in reality) is to say to ourselves "they know what they are doing" (Luhmann, 1993:119).

and ecology; the volatility of international investments; . . . indispensable yet problematic political differentiation into "states," with war as the result; the acceleration of structural change; the dependence of notions of society on highly selective mass media; the demographic consequences of modern medicine; careers as the main form of the [mobile] integration of individuals and society; . . . with the consequence that the future affects the present above all in the form of risk. (1984:xlii)

Modern society, then, is so complex and so differentiated into subsystems that we live with a high level of both risk and danger, and we seek to reduce these by trust and by the control of distrust.

Power   Power, as noted above, places upon the individual or organization the responsibility of making risky decisions that may put others in danger. Luhmann's discussion of power followed to a great extent that of Weber. **Power,** he noted, has both personal and system characteristics. It may or may not involve the use of physical force or violence, but "the possibility of the use of violence *cannot be ignored* by the person affected." Power is asymmetrical, organized, and often centralized (Luhmann, 1979:149). Like the other aspects of life in modern systems, power requires communication: It is transmitted by communication, while at the same time communicating about itself—that is, about the power being asserted.

Luhmann saw power as more central to modern systems than Parsons admitted, and more open to misuse. In fact, Luhmann reminded us of a critical version of Vilfredo Pareto, suggesting that the twentieth century was one that "surpasses all others in the extent and efficiency of the misuse of power." Luhmann was not referring to Marx's "creaming off of surplus value by the ruling class," but to making risky decisions, obstructing needed actions by others, communicating faulty information about one's purposes, and ignoring obvious dangers (1979:162).

One complicating factor, of course, is the differentiation of society into semi-independent subsystems. It is simply impossible, Luhmann believed, even for a state—much less an educational or religious organization—to take actions that determine outcomes for everyone in a society. Power, like function, is fragmented. Although power is an important aspect of social systems, it is checked or limited by societal differentiation.

To summarize briefly, Luhmann might say that a normal or structured part of life in modern society is trusting those (persons, organizations) with power so as to reduce risks or to take risks that do not place us in unnecessary danger.

Autopoiesis   Perhaps the most difficult part of Luhmann's theoretical apparatus is what he called **autopoiesis**. The simplest definition is self-reference, or perhaps self-consciousness within one's context (Luhmann, 1984:487). With this concept, Luhmann was suggesting that human beings do not act blindly, simply on the basis of habits and norms. Rather, they are aware of their choices, of their contexts or systems, and of their environment. When I decide to go to a particular movie, for example, I am conscious of other choices I might make, such as staying home and watching TV; of what my friends are doing; of what is outside my social system, such as recreational activities I have never tried; and perhaps even of other societies that do not have such recreational activities.

The idea of self-reference enabled Luhmann to avoid the reduction of social life to the analysis of systems or norms. Self-reference, then, is at the heart of his view of social action. His theory of action includes not just the unconscious and systemic, but the self-aware, or conscious, choices that humans make. Because we live only in the present, we are continually reproducing our social worlds or systems. This self-referential reproduction, however, "would not be possible without an anticipatory recursivity" (Luhmann, 1984:446–447)—by which he meant expected response or anticipated outcome. Later in this chapter we will confront a somewhat different version of autopoiesis, or self-awareness, in Giddens's view of reflexivity.

Nature of Society, Humans, and Change

From the Middle Ages into the nineteenth century, according to Luhmann, the world was seen as a moral place. While human perfection was the goal, *human nature* was seen as both good and evil. But this optimistic view had within it a contradiction:

> Doesn't it define the nature of humanity and its actions in a contradictory way: good and bad? . . . Materialists, moralists, utilitarians, and Rousseauists in turn called this nature good. They based their optimism on perfectibility. But this solution rests on an obvious theoretical mistake. "Good" is discussed on two different theoretical levels: within the disjuncture of good/bad and on the meta-level of nature. (Luhmann, 1984:380)

If human nature is good and perfectible, how can it also be both good and bad? Luhmann himself answered this question for the nineteenth century: Human perfection was considered socially realizable, but this "did not deny that this could founder on the general corruptibility of all nature" (1984:211). So while the goal was perfection and moral good, human nature as seen in the nineteenth century was in reality dichotomous.

In terms of ideology, then, Luhmann clearly rejected the oversimplified radical nineteenth-century idea that humans were good and society was bad. The human being "is no longer the measure of society. This idea of humanism cannot continue. Who would seriously and deliberately want to maintain that society could be formed on the model of the human being" (1984:213)?

As for progressive, or liberal, and conservative thought, Luhmann recognized the existence of both in the modern world. Anything that exists, observed Luhmann, can become a theme for change in the hands of reformers or progressives, while "any proposal for change can be countered by questioning the reasons for it and by arguing for what already exists" (1979:144). Nothing in political or social life tells us which is correct.

> Whoever is in favor of something which might plausibly be characterized as "authority" or "domination" is **conservative**. Whoever wants to be "emancipated"—especially if he wants to foist "emancipation" on others—is **progressive**. Representatives of monopoly capitalism appear to be conservative. Representatives of . . . capital monopolism consider themselves progressive. (Luhmann, 1982:167, bold added)

Recalling the chapter's opening quote, Luhmann has been viewed by some as non-moral in his view of society (Vandenberghe, 1999:2). However, others see him as leaning toward the more conservative views of his mentor, Parsons. His translators commented, "While no reader of Luhmann's work can fail to notice his ironic detachment and skepticism, neither is it possible to overlook his basic commitment to the overall advantages of functional differentiation" (Holmes and Larmore, 1982:xxxvi). Because of his emphasis on systems and functional differentiation, then, Luhmann may be interpreted as having conservative leanings, but he was hardly as conservative as Parsons.

A final word on Luhmann's ideology concerns values. Human beings evaluate people, things, and systems that matter to them. If these values are guided by an overview of the world, these values are ideological. "Values become ideological once this selective function in the orientation of action becomes conscious and is used in turn to evaluate values"—one's own or other people's (Luhmann, 1982:97).

What, then, was Luhmann's view of change? According to Luhmann, neither Parsons's theory of equilibrium nor the Darwinists' theory of evolutionary stages was, in fact, a theory of change. Luhmann characterized his own theory not as one of stable equilibrium, but as one of renewal and change—not static, but concerned with dynamic stability or instability (1984:49). Change can be planned or unplanned, but it is continuous. It can strengthen systems, alter them, or terminate them. Systems, according to Luhmann, are restless; and they are restless about their own restlessness. This can lead to self-destabilization, even to the point of self-destruction (1984:50).

Although Luhmann was critical of the evolutionary theories of developmental stages, he was in many ways an evolutionist. Much of his book *The Differentiation of Society* (1982) dealt with the way society has evolved toward greater and greater functional differentiation, and toward more and more independent subsystems. Sociocultural evolution involves the increasing complexity of society, but, claimed Luhmann, this is not a theory. It does not explain why differentiation has occurred, only that it has (1982:244).

Luhmann did not view massive and long-term social changes as necessarily requiring people's moral approval or disapproval (1982:364). Much, but not all, change up to the present can be covered by his terms "functional and system differentiation."[4] His view of change was clearly not an idealized, and certainly not a radical, one. He commented, for example, that we can "always moralize about the problem of unequal distribution. But we cannot actually advance

---

[4]Luhmann's translator summarized the many forms of differentiation mentioned in *The Differentiation of Society* (1982) as follows: (1) the privatization of religion; (2) the rise of territorial nation-states, with increasingly bureaucratic administrations; (3) the separation of property ownership and the social acceptability of individual profit-seeking; (4) the approval of "curiosity" as a legitimate motive for the pursuit of knowledge; (5) the release of art from civic and religious functions; (6) constitutional limits on political power; (7) marriage based on passionate love and personal choice, and the shrinkage of the basic kinship unit; (8) the birth of universal and compulsory public schooling; and (9) the shift in the basis of legality from immutable "natural law" to formal procedures for changing legal codes in an orderly way (Holmes and Larmore, 1982:364).

from unequal to equal distribution." Moralizing, to Luhmann, had ideological, not empirical, functions (1982:234–235). In his caustic way, he noted that the

> future is expected to bring about the communist society, an ecological disaster, emancipation from domination, or *l'homme integral*[5] extolled by Sartre and Merleau-Ponty. This, no doubt about it, is the future that cannot begin. It remains a present future and (at the very least) an infallible sign that social critics are on the scene. (1982:280)

To Luhmann, then, *human nature* was neutral, or, perhaps, unknown. Ideology was used by individuals and groups to guide their lives, but it, too, could be analyzed sociologically. And finally, change was ubiquitous and perhaps evolutionary, but hardly governable, at least not by ideology, and certainly not to be approved of or criticized.

Class, Gender, and Race

Class Luhmann had little to say about gender and race, but he did provide some insights into class. He saw no chance "that a rebellion of the unpropertied classes against property owners could result in the utter abolition of the *difference* between owning and not owning" (1982:358). Much of Luhmann's attention to class, in fact, was focused on criticizing Marx's oversimplified view of both present and future. However, he also noted the alternate basis for hierarchy: "the fact that some persons are of better 'quality' than others and that they take precedence." This idea, noted Luhmann, had been superseded as society changed from stratified to differentiated (1984:468). In other words, in modern society, he argued, different does not mean better or worse—it simply means different(iated). Yet this does not mean that equality exists, or ever will. It simply means that hierarchy is not inherited; it is earned within one or more subsystems of society.

Was Luhmann critical of inequality, or what he called "stratified differentiation," in modern society? The following comment shows another reason why Luhmann is often identified as ideologically conservative: "Both empirical research and the critique of stratification, because of their moralistic preoccupations with domination, exploitation, and a general asymmetry in the distribution of life chances, have lost sight of this genuinely positive contribution of stratiform differentiation" (1982:264). Thus, Luhmann hardly had a theory of class or stratification, but simply said it existed, it would continue to exist, and it performed some positive functions for the modern world.

Gender and Race On gender and race, Luhmann said surprisingly little—surprising because of the sheer volume and scope of his writings. One important point is what he did not do: He did not carry functional differentiation to the point of Parsons's gender differentiation, with males as task leaders and females

---

[5]*"L'homme integral"* is the unified or integrated or complete human being desired by these French philosophers.

as social-emotional leaders. While most of his theory seemed to focus on male behaviors and characteristics, he did not indicate that his theory of systems, trust, and so on, was not applicable to females as well.

Luhmann noted what he called "the archaicism of race," as it was treated in the ancient world. Again, one can only infer from what he did not say. He did not indicate that race is an important factor in modern societal subsystems, and this would seem to be a serious oversight. But we must refrain from reading too much into what is missing from his writings.

Other Theories and Theorists

It has been impossible to introduce Luhmann's ideas without discussing Parsons and Marx. We have noted several times that Luhmann's systems theory began in and then outgrew that of Parsons. His debt to his mentor is made clear: "Parsons' theory is a milestone. . . . It has been the only attempt to begin with *a number of equally important functions* and then *to give a theoretical deduction of them*" (Luhmann, 1982:59).

Parsons never stated the importance of value consensus and normative orientation as strongly as his critics claimed he did, but according to Luhmann, order was overstated by Parsons. Luhmann's criticisms of Parsons involved the issues of functional primacy, complexity, and double contingency. Parsons posited primary and secondary functions; the primary ones involve mainly economics and politics. For Luhmann, however, there is no subsystem, such as the economic or political, that determines what occurs in the other systems. Rather, each subsystem is at least somewhat autonomous, and performs functions considered more or less important by a society.

The issue of complexity should be apparent by now. Schemes such as Parsons's AGIL are much too simple to deal with the subsystems of the modern industrial world (Luhmann, 1982:60). Finally, double contingency is the key factor by which Luhmann's theory of action goes beyond that of Parsons. For Parsons, social action takes place within the social system, as individuals (and whole societies) make choices governed by norms, the pattern variables, and so on. Double contingency, like autopoiesis, means that the individual thinks about the choices she or he makes, and about the contingent or reactive choices of others, or of a subsystem, to those choices. In other words, reflection makes choosing and acting much more complex than Parsons saw them. Thus, much of Luhmann's reaction to Parsons is simply that his work was too neat, unfinished, and did not go far enough (1982:47).

Luhmann's criticism of Emile Durkheim resembles one of the criticisms he raised regarding Parsons: We do not "begin with normative presuppositions. Nor, like Durkheim or Parsons, do we view the concept of norms as the ultimate explanation of the facticity or possibility of social order pure and simple" (1984:325). He also found Durkheim frustratingly oversimplified, in concepts such as organic solidarity and collective consciousness, and accused him of locking away "complex relational problems in compact concepts" (1982:17). Luhmann himself, as we have seen, was unwilling to simplify for the sake of clarity or readability.

Luhmann saw Max Weber's faults as different from those of Parsons. Parsons was too system-oriented, while the "concept of system plays no important role in Weber's terminology. 'System' seems to have been inconsequential for the development of Weber's concepts of action, social action, social relation, and association" (Luhmann, 1982:41). However, he agreed with Weber that social groups consist of social actions. "It follows automatically that persons are never entirely incorporated into a social system" (1982:42). For Luhmann, then, interactional systems and social systems are separable, instead of the former simply being a subpart of the latter. Luhmann saw Weber as underemphasizing the importance of the system, and Parsons as overemphasizing it.

One further point concerns Weber's view of bureaucratic structures. Luhmann—and others—criticized Weber for outlining the characteristics of bureaucracies without doing justice to the complex interactions and behaviors within them. As Luhmann put it, "the actual difficulties of behavior and decision-making in bureaucratic organizations and the problems of making compromises between complex, competing demands within a relatively broad temporal horizon do not get discussed" (1982:46).

In his essay on trust, Luhmann referred to Merton's self-fulfilling prophecy. Distrust, noted Luhmann, "has an inherent tendency to endorse and reinforce itself in social interaction" (1979:74). In other words, if we do not trust people, we treat them as, and perhaps even make them, untrustworthy. Without referring directly to him, Luhmann also repeated an insight of Georg Simmel. In a sharply differentiated society, it is difficult to "combine a plurality of roles into a coherent life story" (Holmes and Larmore, 1982:xxi). Simmel had noted a century earlier that the modern individual sometimes plays roles that reinforced each other, but often simply "pigeonholes" incompatible behaviors. Luhmann added that "in extreme cases there are people, or social systems, who earn trust simply by remaining fixedly and immovably what they are" (1979:61). This is, to use David Riesman's language, the inner-directed individual, or John Wayne type, who has consistent, internalized orientations, and does not adjust to the expectations of group or setting.

Luhmann, finally, spoke to many of the same issues as Anthony Giddens, the focus of the final portion of this chapter.

Critique and Conclusions

Luhmann may be, as one translator put it, "the most original German sociologist since Max Weber" (Holmes and Larmore, 1982:xxxvii). His central theoretical principles were (1) increasing functional and structural differentiation, (2) noncentralized, semi-independent, societal subsystems, and (3) their combined outcome in complexity. Under the umbrella of systems theory, he introduced trust, risk, power, and autopoiesis—the self-awareness and self-consciousness of both individuals and systems. The modern person or group, that is, does not act just to satisfy church, government, or employer, but weighs alternatives and others' potential responses before acting. This, of course, is not entirely healthy; it reminds us of the idea of "future shock," or decision-making overload. "One of the psychological difficulties of living in modern society," admitted Luhmann, was "the disorienting abundance of choices that threaten to inundate the individual" (Holmes and Larmore, 1982:xxii).

One of the two major criticisms of Luhmann is that he never reduced the complexity of the modern world for the sake of readability. All his work was complex, but especially his "nonlinear" book on *Social Systems*. His insights seem worth grappling with, but they are almost randomly assembled, use extremely abstract concepts, and utilize few illustrations to increase the reader's understanding.

The second criticism is that Luhmann's conservatism was only partially concealed. He was highly critical of Marx, emphasized functions and systems, and argued that social inequality is permanent and performs some positive functions. Even though he was concerned about overload and future shock, critics and radicals see him as analytically beclouding his acceptance of and support for the *modern, industrial, capitalist world*.

Many of Luhmann's theoretical insights mirror, complement, and in some cases disagree with, those of the British theorist Anthony Giddens. We turn now to Giddens, and will close the chapter with comparisons of the two.

Anthony Giddens (1938–)

If any other contemporary theorist comes close to being as productive as Luhmann, it is Anthony Giddens. He has produced 31 books, now published in 22 languages, and more than 200 articles and reviews ("Anthony Giddens: Meet the Director," 1999:1). He is better known than Luhmann not only in the English-speaking world, but in most of the scholarly world.

Giddens was born in 1938 in North London. He was the first member of his family to go to the university, graduating from Hull in 1959. He completed his M.A. at London School of Economic in 1961, after which he taught at Leicester until the late 1960s. From there he went to Simon Fraser in Canada, and then to the University of California at Los Angeles (UCLA). He was at UCLA during the Vietnam War protests of the late 1960s, and his glimpse of U.S. sociology and life broadened his European view of the world of class and authority. From there he went to Cambridge, where he was a sociology lecturer, reader, and then professor from 1970 until 1997 ("Anthony Giddens: Factfile," 1999:1). At that time he became Director of the London School of Economics and Political Science, where he is at the present time.

In 1985 Giddens founded and became director of the Polity Press, which is still in operation. In 1999 he gave the Reith lectures on the BBC. He is often referred to as Britain's developer of "left-of-center politics," and as Tony Blair's guru ("Anthony Giddens: Meet the Director," 1999:1).

Giddens's first three books were on Weber, Durkheim, and the major nineteenth-century theorists, including Marx ("Anthony Giddens: Publications," 1998:1). This was hardly an atypical way to begin a career in theory, but by the mid-1970s Giddens had begun to evolve his own theoretical position, beginning with a focus on structuration. Thus, Giddens became known at first for his treatment of the "classics," before accepting the challenge of producing original contributions to sociological theory.

Giddens's Central Theories and Methods

Structuration   After his work on the nineteenth-century social theory classics, the heart of Giddens's work until the late 1980s was structuration:

> Every process of action is a production of something new, a fresh act; but at the same time all action exists in continuity with the past, which supplies the means of its initiation. *Structure thus is not to be conceptualised as a barrier to action, but as essentially involved in its production:* even in the most radical processes of social change which, like any others, occur in time. (Giddens, 1979:70)

Note that **structuration** actually describes an action: "to structurate" or "to do or produce structure." Giddens placed great emphasis on individual action: "As a leading theorem of the theory of structuration, I advance the following: *every social actor knows a great deal about the conditions of reproduction of the society of which he or she is a member*" (1979:5). As one commentator explains: "The theory of structuration is an attempt to overcome the dualism that he sees as plaguing other theories—a dualism that gives priority either to actors or to social structures. . . . Structures are created by humans, but they, in turn, constrain and enable human action" (Kivisto, 1998:148).

Giddens, then, was trying to bring the individual back into social theory. Calling his theory a "non-functionalist manifesto," Giddens argued that any theory that treats social systems as ends in themselves is invalid (1979:7), and he claimed he was trying to recover the subject or actor without lapsing into subjectivism or nonobjectivism (1979:44). Arguing that both subject and object—individual and system—exist, Giddens emphasized the "fundamentally recursive character of social life" and "the mutual dependence of structure and agency" (Giddens, 1979:69). **Recursivity** is feedback, or conscious concern with outcomes or results. Thus, it parallels Luhmann's idea of autopoiesis—self-reflection or self-consciousness.

Giddens argued that structure-functionalism ordinarily treats structure as constraint, or as opposed to freedom, and as based on agreement or consensus on the rules or norms that constrain individuals. While Giddens was perhaps overstating the constraining nature of order in functionalism, he wanted to emphasize order not as a barrier to action, but as in interplay with the actor—as a mixing of freedom and constraint (1979:70). Even the rules of interaction are reconstituted through action and interaction. Giddens, then, reconceptualized the duality of the social world from "individual and society" into the relation between "agency and structure" (Giddens, 1984:162).

To summarize many of the main points of the theory, as expressed in various sources, Giddens emphasized (1) human *agency*, or the rational/deciding actor; (2) *reflexivity*, which is not merely self-consciousness, but is "the monitored character of the ongoing flow of social life"; and (3) *structure*, or the continually reconstructed result of rules, resources, and agency (see Giddens, 1982:15–16, 1984:2–3, 376–377).

Modernity   Giddens's second major concern, though less theoretical than structuration, is what he calls "late *modernity*." This has been his major interest since the beginning of the 1990s. By modernity, Giddens refers

> to the institutions and modes of behavior established first of all in post-feudal Europe, but which in the twentieth century increasingly have become world-historical in their impact. "Modernity" can be understood as roughly equivalent to "the industrialized world," so long as it be recognised that industrialism is not its only institutional dimension. (1982:15–16)

It is important to note that Giddens speaks of "late modern" society, not post-modern or post-industrial society. By this means he emphasizes historical continuity and change, rather than disjuncture (Kivisto, 1998:147).

Giddens's distinguishes between **capitalism**—a highly competitive system of production with labor markets operating on a global scale—and **industrialism**, which refers to the use of machine technology to control and transform nature (Kivisto, 1998:149). Besides industry, the most recognizable feature of this late modern world is the nation-state. In addition, though not to the same extent as Luhmann does, Giddens notes the importance of communication in tying the modern world together (Giddens, 1982:24).

The modern world has made possible survival, even "the good life," for an increasing proportion of its population. The nation-state provides the opportunity for democracy, for individual agency within a complex world. In *Beyond Left and Right* (1994) and *The Third Way* (1998), Giddens asserts that old "left" ideas are out of date, while those of the "right" are contradictory and even dangerous. His social democratic (liberal) "third way" is not just a theory but an action program, aimed at rekindling political activism and idealism (1994). The retreat of the gods and of tradition, he argues, has freed organizations and movements in the modern world for "reflexive self-regulation," meaning that we can contemplate and then make our own history (1984:203).

The subparts of Giddens's theory of modernity include distanciation, power, trust, and risk. **Distanciation** refers to the fact that relationships are no longer tied to specific locales. While this has been true since the invention of Morse code and the airplane, it is infinitely more so at the turn of the twenty-first century than ever before, thanks to the computer. AT&T introduced the slogan "Reach out and touch someone," and in the age of e-mail it takes only a few seconds to touch someone in Singapore, Sweden, or South Africa (Kivisto, 1998:149).

An important aspect of Giddens's theory of both structuration and modernity is **power**, or agency—the capacity to make decisions and do things (1979:69). Power is not a resource; the media are resources, and so are social connections (1984:10, 1982:39). Power both constrains and enables. Power as constraint is not force, it is restriction of choice. In other words, even without the power that goes with domination, individuals in the modern world still have a certain amount of power (or control) over the choices they make (1984:176, 257–262).

Power, then, is not only domination, but also "transformative capacity," or the ability to make things happen (1979:91). Thus, to Giddens, the modern world is "empowering," because it has freed people from the strictures of traditional, preindustrial society.

Giddens argues that the reason orthodox (structure-functional) theory does not explain social action is that it ignores the importance of power—both individual and structural (1979:253). To Giddens, power or capability is the central feature of social action, so if constraint, even by norms, is the focus of a theory, it makes it impossible to understand action.

Like Luhmann, Giddens also refers to trust and risk. As with Luhmann, trust is required in the modern world because we know so little about the systems with which we have to deal. Giddens defines **trust** as "the vesting of confidence in persons or in abstract systems, made on the basis of a 'leap of faith' which brackets ignorance or lack of information" (1991:244).

The issue that Giddens raises that is most closely related to Luhmann's theory concerns **risk**. To Luhmann, you will recall, risk involved politics, economics, technology, and other aspects of life in a highly complex and differentiated modern society. Giddens emphasizes even more than Luhmann the agency or "choice" aspect of risk. An actor may calculate the risk involved in a certain conduct in terms of sanctions "being actually applied, and may be prepared to submit to them as a price to be paid for achieving a particular end" (1979:87). For example, in the movie *A Few Good Men*, a U.S. Marine takes food to a fellow soldier who is being punished, consciously taking the risk that he too will be sanctioned if his "good deed" is found out. It is discovered, and he is expelled from the Marine Corps, having run the risk by doing what he considered right.

However, a second part of Giddens's view of risk goes beyond Luhmann's. Human beings continually try to calculate future risk. In a rapidly changing modern society, individuals attempt to lessen risk through planning. A good example is health or life insurance. Giddens calls this "colonization of the future." Thinking in terms of risk may be uncomfortable, but because nothing can be taken for granted, many individuals make decisions aimed at risk reduction and peace of mind (Giddens, 1991:133–134).

Giddens lists four risks that are more or less specific to the late modern world: (1) the surveillance, governmental and otherwise, that none can escape; (2) escalation of military power resulting in the risk of nonsurvival of the species; (3) the potential of the collapse of economic growth, because of capitalism's erratic qualities (recall Joseph Schumpeter's similar concern of 60 years ago); and (4) the ecological and environmental limits that constrain capitalism (1990:55–63). He points out that

> Low-probability, high-consequence risks will not disappear in the modern world, although in an optimal scenario they could be minimized. . . .
> Relatively small-scale [sic] events, such as the dropping of atomic bombs on Hiroshima and Nagasaki or the accidents at Three Mile Island or Chernobyl, give some sense of what could happen. (1990:134)

The Self   Giddens has devoted considerable attention to G. H. Mead's theory of the self. Although hardly an original insight, Giddens notes that Mead's view of the "I," "me," and "self" is reflexive, but their origin is not made clear. More important, Mead's theory does not situate the reflexive and reflective individual within the differentiated larger society. Giddens addresses the influence of the self on others, society, and even global strategies (1991:214). He believes that agency and structuration fill the gap in Mead's social-psychological theory.

In fact, Giddens's view of the modern self is quite different from those of Cooley, Mead, and Freud, discussed in Chapter 13. In his books on self-identity (1991) and intimacy (1992), he discusses the connections between modern life and the individual. The individual exists within a structure but is also agent, meaning that the self must be created. In Giddens's view, the late modern world gives "rise to new mechanisms for forging self-identities, with the self being both object and agent in the process" (Snow and Heirling, 1992:847). One further issue in self-creation is self-actualization, or the effort to make oneself into what one wishes to be. To Giddens, self-actualization is possible because of reflexivity, or self-reflection, but is also a goal that is often impossible to attain.

Intimacy in the late modern world is often a matter of one's internal state, not constrained by external factors or demands such as the necessity of parenthood or some other role. Whether a "pure" relationship is or can be altogether satisfying is an empirical question (Giddens, 1992:3). The pure nature of relationships also causes them to be exceptionally breakable or fragile.

In summary, then, the modern world involves both human agency and constraint, which together are close to the definition of structuration. That world includes distanciation, power, trust, risk, and the created self.

The Nature of Society, Humans, and Change

From Giddens's discussion of the almost overwhelming risks of modern life, one might assume that he is a pessimist regarding the future. However, as a liberal, he sees these risks as possibilities, not problems or inevitabilities. He sees the labor, peace, and environmental movements as guaranteed neither of success nor of failure. Giddens's liberalism has been described as "plausible utopian realism" (Kivisto, 1998:151).

Despite Giddens's apparent optimism regarding human agency, he does not define *human nature* as good, and certainly not as perfectible. Speaking in the same way as the twentieth-century evolutionists, Giddens notes "human control over nature." This, he says, is actually "the emergence of an internally referential system of knowledge and power." The result is that the world is now, for the most part, a created environment, consisting of humanly structured systems. Note, however, that he refers to "human control over nature," not "control over human nature" (1982:144). Though not seeing human nature as good, he views it positively enough that an increase in human agency or choice is seen as a good thing, and as capable of producing positive results in the late modern world.

Change, Giddens suggests, can be brought about through human agency. It is not evolutionary, in the sense of natural selection, or adaptation, or stages, but it is ubiquitous—the modern world can be defined as a world of change. As we have already noted, Giddens is sympathetic with—even positive toward—this late modern world of human agency and structuration. But, surprisingly, there are times when he sounds a little like Max Weber—that is, critical of the changing world. "The sheer sense of being caught up in massive waves of global transformation is perturbing. . . . Understanding the juggernaut-like nature of modernity goes a long way towards explaining why, in conditions of high modernity, crisis becomes normalised" (Giddens, 1991:183–184). In addition, modernity creates tensions for the self: unification versus fragmentation, options versus powerlessness and meaninglessness, personal versus commodified experience, and authority versus uncertainty (1991:201). Thus, the criticism that Giddens sees the modern world "through rose-colored glasses" is at least an overstatement.

Giddens's ideology, as noted previously, is distinctly liberal and social democratic. In fact, he treats ideology as virtually synonymous with conservatism: "the capability of dominant groups or classes to make their own sectional interests appear to others as universal ones" (1979:6). Viewing himself as a liberal and critical theorist, he is also opposed to any social thought, Marxist or otherwise, that treats capitalism as evil and in need of overthrow. In summary, Giddens believes in the efficacy of human thought and action, and sees the modern world as a mixture of freedom and structure, with both negative characteristics and positive possibilities.

Class, Gender, and Race

Class Giddens makes it clear that, in his view, "Marx's assessment of the endemic character of class conflict in capitalism is closer to contemporary industrial reality than the views which Durkheim offered" (1982:122). He agrees with Marx's view of the contradictory nature of capitalist classes, "entangled in the asymmetrical relations between class division and social or welfare rights," and that the "buying and selling of time, as labour time, is surely one of the most distinctive features of modern capitalism" (1984:144).

However, Giddens is not a Marxist. Speaking of rule by the bourgeoisie, he asserts, "we cannot today be content to leave their positive features unanalyzed" (1982:176, 178). In addition, he argues that "all social actors, no matter how lowly, have some degree of penetration of the social forms which oppress them" (1979:72). Classes are not isolated; interaction between them occurs. Even humor, he observes, can be used against the rulers in order to lessen the burden of disadvantage (1979:72). Whether humor speaks to Marx's serious issues of oppression and exploitation is at least questionable. And Giddens's emphasis on agency, even that of the oppressed, is a far cry from Sigmund Freud's argument that we are all oppressed by civilization.

Gender As for gender, Giddens notes that modern society has dichotomized reason as a male characteristic, and emotion as female. "The identifying of women with unreason, whether in serious vein (madness)[6] or in seemingly less

---

[6]You may recall (Chapter 11) that Charlotte Gilman's divorce and giving up of her baby were considered signs of madness or insanity—a label often given a female who did not fit the late-nineteenth/early-twentieth-century gender stereotype.

consequential fashion (women as creatures of caprice), turned them into the emotional underlaborers of modernity" (1990:200). Men, as the rational gender, were seen as the logical actors in and controllers of both the extrafamilial, or larger, society and the internal society of family.

Not only was the world of rationality and politico-economic activity viewed as male, but feminism as a movement was oriented primarily toward opening that sphere to women. "Women's identities were defined so closely in terms of the home and the family that they 'stepped outside' into social settings in which the only available identities were those offered by male stereotypes" (Giddens, 1991:216). Seeing no place for emotion in his theory, Giddens fails to recognize that feminism-humanism also seeks to open emotional life to the male. As a part of his theory of modern society and its opportunities, however, Giddens is not surprised by women's seeking of new freedoms and opportunities. Change is ubiquitous, and gender roles are being freed.

Race Although Giddens has written at some length about class and gender, he has said little about race. He has used ethnic segregation to illustrate how a social pattern results from individual motives and activities—the end result, ghetto-like areas, being an unintended consequence (latent function) of a large number of intentional individual behaviors (1984:13). But he has given little further attention to race or ethnicity as a factor in the late modern world.

Other Theories and Theorists

Perhaps more than any other recent theorist, Giddens has commented on other sociological theorists. Comte, Marx, Weber, Durkheim, Mead, Parsons, Merton, and even Luhmann are all either referred to directly or their ideas used. He criticized Auguste Comte for trying to use science, including social science, to "generate a moral ethos" that could replace traditional beliefs (1991:74–75). Humans, as active creators of society, are no longer likely to simply react to revelation or believe in their own creations.

We have already seen Giddens's sympathy with and disagreement with Marx, and his concern with the incompleteness of Weber's view of bureaucracy. These reactions, however, were hardly original with Giddens. He criticized Durkheim, and later Parsons, for overemphasizing the importance of constraint and order in social structure, to the neglect of agency and enablement. As Giddens puts it, "One person's constraint is another's enabling" (1984:170–176).

Having already indicated the problem with Parsons's structure-functionalism, we should note some of Giddens's responses to Robert Merton. Merton's notions of latent functions and unintended consequences may make sense of apparently irrational conduct, but "to suppose that such a demonstration of a functional relation provides a reason for the existence of a practice is mistaken" (Giddens, 1984:12). Such an argument may satisfy the observer, but it is not necessarily an explanation for behavior.

Recalling Merton's discussion of why sociological findings are ignored, Giddens observed that this is usually not because they are too outlandish or unexpected, but because they are too well known and familiar. "Where social research reveals that what actors believe about the conditions of their own action, or other features of their society, are in fact the case, its findings will necessarily appear banal or unilluminating." But, as Merton stated, when findings show commonsense beliefs to be wrong, social science can appear revelatory (Giddens, 1979:249).

Critique and Conclusions

Several commentators have argued that Giddens's attention to agency as well as structure is an important addition to contemporary theorizing. Structure-functionalism focused so completely on function and order as to virtually negate any sort of human control. Giddens, according to Kivisto (1998), "has played and will continue to play a singularly important role in the ongoing act of examining and reflecting on the human condition in the contemporary world" (152).

However, not all evaluations of Giddens's work are so favorable. Stjepan Mestrovic's recent book on Giddens's theory is extremely critical. Some of his criticisms, as of Giddens's view of women and his view of the modern world, are greatly overstated. However, two criticisms deserve mention. The first concerns Giddens's emphasis on human agency, and the second is on Giddens's optimistic view of the modern world.

According to Giddens, "Every competent member of every society knows a great deal about the institutions of that society: such knowledge is not *incidental* to the operation of society" (Giddens, 1979:71). As a participant, this knowledge is greater closer to one's day-to-day activities, rather than further away (Giddens, 1979:250). Both Luhmann and Mestrovic, however, question this assumption. According to Luhmann, citizens today are overwhelmed with information they are too busy, or too stressed, to analyze. They lose interest in the political sphere, feeling powerless to affect it, and even in their own milieu they feel incapable of controlling its complexities (Savard, 1999:3). Mestrovic (1998) adds that "most people seem to feel helpless concerning the course of world events, . . . yet they are comforted by Giddens' observations that they can still feel empowered and exercise agency in local milieux" (149). And Snow and Heirling (1992) wonder "exactly what proportion of humanity . . . Giddens really address[es]"—that is, how many people in today's world actually feel and act like effective agents.

According to Mestrovic (1998:109),

> Giddens fails to explain the miracle by which human agents communicate with each other; he fails to explain how agents come to perceive social structure; and he fails to explain the origins of the agent's *faith* that his or her actions will result in specific consequences. For Giddens, all these aspects of agency and structure are seemingly self-begotten, which is not an adequate sociological explanation.

Thus, more likely than a sense of agency and control, people today feel a sense of fatalism, even apathy, about making an impact on others or on their environment (Mestrovic, 1998:206).

Giddens's theory is of a rational world in which individual actors are effective, and in which emotion and suffering apparently have little place. Although he recognizes the presence of "low-probability, high-consequence risks," such as nuclear obliteration, he seems to minimize such "relatively small-scale events" as the bombing of Hiroshima and Nagasaki (1990:134). This concerns Mestrovic greatly, and his response is full of emotion:

> After five years of dialogue, negotiation, and touting of Western human rights standards, the West essentially let the Serbs keep the spoils of their genocide in Bosnia. It is incumbent upon Giddens to explain how this was possible despite all his lofty theorizing about dialogue, reflexivity, democracy, and globalization. (1998:142)

Had he written a year later, Mestrovic might have added that the eventual response of bombing would hardly fit Giddens's view of a rational world either.

Final Thoughts

Mestrovic's final criticism of Giddens might be raised regarding Luhmann as well. Mestrovic noted

> the trouble Giddens's readers have in trying to understand him, decipher his jargon, and agree on what he means. Yet the new leisure class is satisfied with this lack of clarity, for it means that those who say they have read and understood Giddens have achieved an honor reserved for the very few. (1998:216)

Readability is not a criterion on which all the theorists we have reviewed in this volume necessarily rank high. But, as we asked at the beginning, are Luhmann and Giddens "worth it"? The answer is yes, on several grounds.

First, they are quite contemporary—more so than mid-twentieth-century writers such as Parsons and Merton—and as such have not tried to reduce the complexity that confronts us at the beginning of the twenty-first century. Whether that world is made up of headless subsystems as Luhmann proposed, or is as alterable and democratically viable as Giddens argues, the reader may decide. Likewise, we must think about reflexivity and risk in today's world.

Second, Luhmann and Giddens are not simply conservative and liberal, respectively. Neither is, or should be, that easy to label. Much of Luhmann's thought is demoralized, if not pessimistic, as well as conservative, while Giddens at times comes across as conservative instead of liberal.

Third, as a result of all this, Luhmann and Giddens form an excellent bridge to the radical, change, and modernist theories that lie just ahead.

References

"Anthony Giddens: Factfile." 1999. Internet: www.lse.ac.uk/Giddens/factfile.htm.
"Anthony Giddens: Meet the Director." 1999. Internet: www.lse.ac.uk/Giddens/meet.htm.

"Anthony Giddens: Publications." 1998. Internet: www.lse.ac.uk/Giddens.publications.htm.

Giddens, Anthony. 1979. *Central Problems in Social Theory: Action, Structure and Contradiction in Social Analysis*. Berkeley: University of California Press.

———. 1982. *Profiles and Critiques in Social Theory*. Berkeley: University of California Press.

———. 1984. *The Constitution of Society*. Berkeley: University of California Press.

———. 1990. *The Consequences of Modernity*. Stanford, CA: Stanford University Press.

———. 1991. *Modernity and Self-Identity: Self and Society in the Late Modern Age*. Cambridge: Polity Press.

———. 1992. *The Transformation of Intimacy*. Stanford, CA: Stanford University Press.

———. 1994. *Beyond Left and Right*. Cambridge: Polity Press.

———. 1998. *The Third Way: The Renewal of Social Democracy*. London: Polity Press.

Holmes, Stephen, and Charles Larmore. 1982. "Introduction." In Niklas Luhmann, *The Differentiation of Society* (pp. ii–xxxvii). New York: Columbia University Press.

Kivisto, Peter. 1998. *Key Ideas in Sociology*. Thousand Oaks, CA: Pine Forge Press.

Knodts, Eva M. 1995. "Foreword." In Niklas Luhmann, *Social Systems* (pp. i–lii). Stanford: Stanford University Press.

Luhmann, Niklas. 1979. *Trust and Power* (Howard Davis, John Raffan, and Kathryn Rooney, Trans.). New York: John Wiley & Sons. (Two essays originally published in 1973 and 1975.)

———. 1982. *The Differentiation of Society* (Stephen Holmes and Charles Larmore, Trans.). New York: Columbia University Press.

———. 1984/1995. *Social Systems* (John Bednarz, Jr. Trans.). Stanford, CA: Stanford University Press.

———. 1993. *Risk: A Sociological Theory* (Rhodes Barrett, Trans.). New York: Walter de Gruyter.

Mestrovic, Stjepan. 1998. *Anthony Giddens: The Last Modernist*. London: Routledge.

Poggi, Gianfranco. 1979. "Introduction." In Niklas Luhmann, *Trust and Power* (Howard Davis, John Raffan, and Kathryn Rooney, Trans.). New York: John Wiley & Sons.

Savard, Nelly. 1999. "Niklas Luhmann: The Political Section of His Theory." http://www.webb.net/sites/sociocyberforum//n_savard1.html

Snow, David A., and Joseph Heirling. 1992. "The Beleaguered Self." *Contemporary Sociology, 21*, 846–848.

Vandenberghe, Frederic. 1999. "Niklas Luhmann, 1927–1998." http://Rp/biog/94luhmn.

Criticism, Marxism, and Change

In the previous section we looked at the more-or-less "official" twentieth-century conservative capitalist theory and ideology of functionalism, followed by Luhmann's and Giddens's expansions on and deviations from this theme. Now we come to three chapters emphasizing criticism and change.

The two great European wars of the twentieth century and the Great Depression of the 1930s increased Marxists' confidence in the demise of capitalism. However, critics of the Soviet Union's Stalinist socialism also raised question about whether the Soviet model was the one to follow. In addition, many of Marx's principles, such as the labor theory of value, increasing misery of the poor, and the final revolution, were being criticized by both bourgeois economists and those sympathetic to Marxism.

Starting in the 1930s, the Frankfurt (or Critical) School, described in Chapter 16, was in dialogue with both capitalism and Marxism. Rejecting Marxist determinism and Russia's bureaucratic and totalitarian regime, this school of thought—including Max Horkheimer, T. W. Adorno, Erich Fromm, Herbert Marcuse, and others—reduced the role of economics by integrating it with political questions. In addition, criticism was broadened to include psychologized—Freudian—versions of alienation, working-class fragmentation, and even family issues (Bottomore, 1983).

Jurgen Habermas, a second-generation critical theorist, discussed the twin crises in rationality and legitimation, the former resulting from economic contradictions and the latter from a loss of popular loyalty. Together, according to Habermas (1973:49), these result in a crisis of motivation, leading to noncommitment or noninvolvement. The Frankfurt school, then, is critical of twentieth-century Western capitalism as well as of simplified classical Marxism.

The rise and fall of Russian communism, coupled with dramatic events in Western Europe, led to serious theoretical discussions and disagreements among committed Marxists. Those whose views are presented in Chapter 17 include

Nicos Poulantzas, Louis Althusser, Raya Dunayevskaya, and Erik Olin Wright. Among the issues they raise are the following: (1) Of what does societal influence or dominance consist? Is it more than control of the means of production? (2) Is Soviet socialism Marxist at all, or is it a form of state capitalism, only slightly different from that of the Western nations? (3) What is the nature of the modern nation-state? (4) What is the difference between twentieth-century monopoly capitalism and the entrepreneurial capitalism about which Marx wrote? (5) Is history predetermined toward the final revolution, is it full of contradictions unique to specific times and places, or is it a result of rational choices made by Giddens-type "actors"?

In short, then, what is the condition of Marxism at the turn of the twenty-first century, after the fall of Soviet communism and the apparent victory of capitalism's "new world order"? Erik Olin Wright, an academic Marxist, has avoided throwing the theoretical and analytical Marxist "baby" out with the Soviet "bathwater." During the 1990s, Wright spoke to many of the questions raised by the Soviet Union's collapse, and his work gives a clear view of Marxism at present.

Chapter 18 focuses on change from a world perspective. Evolutionary optimism, which seemed to disappear with World War I, reappeared, especially in the United States after World War II. The Marshall Plan and other U.S. initiatives were based on the belief that the rest of the world wants to be "just like us"—and will be, with our help. However, not all evolutionary thinking was that optimistic, nor that simplistic, as illustrated in the work of Elman Service.

Chapter 18 also introduces the "world system" theory of Immanuel Wallerstein, who notes that the peripheral parts of the world are not necessarily developing or catching up with Western industrialism—nor do they necessarily want to—but the world is a single system. At the close of Chapter 18, Theda Skocpol introduces nonevolutionary and non-Marxist views of revolutionary change. What conditions give rise to revolutions, and what are their outcomes?

Thus, by the time you complete these three chapters, you will have examined critical views of both capitalism and Marxism, as well as current theories of social change.

References

Bottomore, T. B. 1983. "Frankfurt School." In T. B. Bottomore (Ed.), *A Dictionary of Marxism* (pp. 182–188). Oxford: Blackwell.
Habermas, Jurgen. 1973. *Legitimation Crisis*. London: Heinemann.

Chapter 16

Critical Theory
The Frankfurt School and Habermas

A persistent hope for many of the Marxist theorists you have encountered so far was that the proletariat would eventually come to their senses and overthrow capitalist society. By the 1920s, a number of Western theorists had started to despair that this would ever occur. In fact, the 1917 socialist revolution in the semifeudal Russian state seemed to call into question the original Marxist analysis of capitalism. Many social theorists felt a return to the drawing board was in order to try to discover why the revolution was delayed, despite the persistence of inequality and alienation, and what could be done to alter the situation in order to usher in the change to a new socialist state. This was the central focus for the work of the theorists examined in this chapter.

Some social theorists have maintained their optimism about an eventual socialist transformation despite the revelations of less desirable or equitable conditions under former socialist regimes in the twentieth century. But in the view of many Western social theorists at the beginning of the twenty-first century, capitalism seems to have won, and they see little point in pursuing an old, discredited nineteenth-century dream of an equitable, planned society. However, the view from many of the countries in Africa, or Central Asia, or the Russian Republic itself, as well as among the dispossessed in capitalist states, is less celebratory about the triumph of capitalism. Consequently, it is worth considering the explanations offered by the critical theorists as to why the twentieth-century proletariat failed to transform the world as well as reflecting on the possibility that a revolutionary class can still be identified in the twenty-first century.

The Institute of Social Research

The Institute of Social Research at the University of Frankfurt was established in 1921. This was a period of turmoil and instability in Germany and in Europe in general. Despite these conditions, the revolution anticipated by many Marxist theorists did not occur. What did transpire was an increasing conservatism that in Germany culminated in the misnamed National Socialist regime.

The establishment of the Institute was made possible by an endowment from a wealthy German ex-patriot, Hermann Weil, who lived in Argentina. Weil had made his fortune shipping grain to Europe. His son, Felix Weil, was sent to the University of Frankfurt, where he obtained a doctorate in political science. While at Frankfurt, Felix Weil became associated with various radical groups, and he conceived the idea of an independent research institution for Marxist studies and the study of anti-Semitism (Jay, 1973:31–32). Felix Weil persuaded his father to endow the Institute, and Felix himself was associated with the venture until the onset of World War II, when he returned to Argentina to look after the family business.

In the 1930s, anti-Semitism was increasingly evident in Germany, fueled by the National Socialist fascists. One of the major research tasks for the Institute was the analysis of anti-Semitism as well as research into social and cultural conditions for an emancipated, equitable society. The Institute's financial independence was fortuitous when, in the 1930s, the Jewish members of the Institute were forced into exile. The Institute relocated to Columbia University in 1934 under the directorship of Max Horkheimer. Thus, the "revolutionary and Marxist" research Institute resettled in "the center of the capitalist world, New York City" (Jay, 1973:39).

Various theorists were associated with the Institute in addition to Max Horkheimer, including Theodor Adorno, Herbert Marcuse, Leo Lowenthal, Friedrich Pollock, Karl Wittfogel, Walter Benjamin, and Erich Fromm. The work of these theorists was voluminous and comprised a number of perspectives. For example, Lowenthal was interested in literature, Adorno in music, Pollock in the intersection of capitalism and the state, and Fromm in a synthesis of Marxism and psychoanalysis. Although everyone associated with the Institute shared a critical Marxist perspective, they did not embrace a singular theoretical stance or necessarily endorse a common view of revolutionary practice. Consequently, the reference to these critical theorists as the **Frankfurt School** is somewhat misleading because they did not represent a singular focused group (Held, 1980:15).

Max Horkheimer became director of the Institute in 1930. At his installation he emphasized that the Institute would be a place where "philosophers, sociologists, economists, historians, and psychologists must unite in a lasting working partnership . . . to pursue the great philosophical questions with the most refined methods" (Held, 1980:33). The Institute's major research focus was on alienation and domination in modern capitalist society. The Institute's research was to be **supradisciplinary** not interdisciplinary. That is, research and theoretical approaches were to transcend separate disciplinary positions to create a "supradisciplinary social theory" (Kellner, 1989:7).

The supradisciplinary nature of the research was framed by the conviction that Marxist theory was an "open-ended, historical, dialectical theory that required development, revision, and modification precisely because it was . . . a theory of contemporary socio-historical reality which itself was constantly developing and changing" (Kellner, 1989:11). The Institute's researchers saw their task as urgent because of the emergence of fascism and the lack of working-class revolutionary fervor despite the recurrent crises of capitalism.

The reassessment of Marxist theory and practice focused especially on the question of the revolutionary consciousness of the working class. Horkheimer, Adorno, and Marcuse had reached the conclusion in the 1930s that the traditional Marxist focus on a revolutionary working class had to be reformulated because false consciousness had such a grip on that class, penetrating the "innermost layers of human personality," that class-based or even individual emancipatory action was impossible in the immediate social and political context (Agger, 1979:14). This pessimism about the revolutionary potential of the working class persisted especially after the onset of World War II.

After the Nazis came to power in 1933, Horkheimer, along with other Jewish faculty members, was dismissed from the University of Frankfurt. The collection of brilliant minds at the Institute was dispersed. Most of the theorists at the Institute had Jewish backgrounds, and most of them thought of themselves as assimilated. Whatever their beliefs about assimilation, they were abruptly disabused of the notion with the rise of National Socialism, and most of the Institute members wisely chose exile. They left for Geneva, France, Great Britain, and the United States.

Max Horkheimer went to New York, where he was joined by Pollock and Adorno. Fortunately, the private endowment from the Weil family allowed the Institute to remain relatively financially secure during the years of exile and its initial reconstitution in New York. In essence, Horkheimer, Pollock, and Adorno represented the Institute during the years of exile. In the 1940s, the three went to Los Angeles and remained there until their return to Frankfurt in 1950. Other Institute exiles found various positions. Marcuse, for example, worked for the Office of Strategic Services and the State Department, after which he went to Brandeis in 1954 and then to the University of San Diego in 1965.[1]

In this chapter we concentrate on the work of Horkheimer, Adorno, Marcuse, and Fromm. The outline of their ideas sets the foundation for the examination, later in the chapter, of a contemporary critical theorist, Jurgen Habermas.

The Critical Theorists of the Frankfurt School

> We had set ourselves nothing less than the discovery of why mankind,
> instead of entering into a truly human condition, is sinking into a new a
> new kind of barbarism. (Adorno and Horkheimer, 1944:xi)

Max Horkheimer (1895–1973)   Max Horkheimer's father was a manufacturer in Stuttgart, and Horkheimer had commercial training before doing his military service. As part of that training, with his friend Friedrich Pollock, he went to Brussels and London in the years 1913–1914 to learn French and

---

[1]One of the theorists who went to France, Walter Benjamin, committed suicide after the outbreak of World War II and the establishment of the puppet fascist regime in Vichy France.

English.[2] After 1918 he attended the universities of Munich, Freiburg, and then Frankfurt, where he obtained his doctorate in 1922 with a thesis on Kant. He became a lecturer in 1925 at the Institute for Social Research, and in 1929 he was appointed to the new chair of Social Philosophy at the Institute. He became director of the Institute in 1930.

Theodor Wiesengrund-Adorno (1903–1969) Theodor Wiesengrund-Adorno was born in Frankfurt, the son of a successful Jewish merchant. His mother had had a successful singing career prior to her marriage, and the name Adorno was from her side of the family. She was the daughter of a German singer and a French army officer, and her father's background was Corsican and Genoese. Apparently in response to Pollock's concern that there were too many Jewish-sounding names on the Institute's roster, Adorno dropped the Wiesengrund part of his name when he was in the United States (Jay 1973:22).

His mother's sister was an accomplished concert pianist who lived with the family, and Adorno's family encouraged him to take up the piano and study composition at an early age. This interest in music continued in his theoretical work on the nature of the culture industries in capitalist society (Adorno, 1984). Adorno attended the University of Frankfurt and obtained his doctorate with a thesis on Husserl's phenomenology in 1924. In 1925 he went to Vienna to study composition with Alban Berg, and it was here that he came to appreciate the atonal experiments of Schönberg. He returned to Frankfurt in 1928 and in 1931 became associated with the Institute, becoming a full member in 1938.

Herbert Marcuse (1898–1979) Herbert Marcuse was born in Berlin to a prosperous, assimilated Jewish family. In 1918, after his military service, he was associated with the Social Democratic Party and the revolutionary Soldiers Council in Berlin. In 1919, he left the Social Democratic Party in protest over what he saw as the betrayal of the proletariat (Jay, 1973:28).

Marcuse went on to study philosophy at the universities of Berlin and Freiburg and obtained his doctorate in 1923 with a thesis on literature. Marcuse then spent six years as a bookseller and publisher in Berlin, returning to Freiburg in 1929 to study with the philosophers Husserl and Heidegger. He left Freiburg in 1932 largely because of political differences with Heidegger, whose right-wing views clashed with Marcuse's Marxist views. On Husserl's recommendation, however, he became a member of the Institute in 1933.

Erich Fromm (1900–1980) Erich Fromm was born in Frankfurt and was brought up in an intensely religious household (Jay, 1973:88). His Orthodox Jewish parents both came from families of rabbis. In his early twenties, Fromm,

---

[2]Pollock accompanied Horkheimer and Adorno into exile in New York, and he was indispensable in maintaining the viability of the Institute despite the dispersal of most of its members. In particular, Pollock was responsible for "arranging the mundane details of their lives to allow Horkheimer the maximum time for his scholarly pursuits" (Jay, 1973:7).

along with Leo Lowenthal, who also became associated with the Institute, was active in a religious group formed around Rabbi Nobel at the largest Frankfurt synagogue. Fromm's orthodoxy lessened after his analysis in 1926 in Munich, although he never renounced his religion (Jay, 1973:89).

Fromm's doctorate, under Alfred Weber at Heidelberg, was on *Jewish Law: A Contribution to the Sociology of the Jewish Diaspora*. It was at Heidelberg that Fromm met Freida Reichmann, a Jewish psychoanalyst, who later became his wife. Fromm went on to train at the Berlin Psychoanalytic Institute and opened his own practice in 1927. In 1929 the Frankfurt Institute of Psychoanalysis was opened, and Fromm and his wife both became lecturers at the new Institute. In 1930, Fromm became director of the Social Psychology section at the Institute of Social Research. His interest in combining Marx and psychoanalysis appealed to Horkheimer and others. But by 1940 Fromm's association with the Institute came to an end, largely because of Horkheimer's disagreement with Fromm's criticisms of Freud.

Central Theories and Methods of the Frankfurt School

The theoretical backgrounds of the various members of the Institute were varied, but for most of them the work of Hegel (filtered through the work of Georg Lukacs), Marx, Weber, Nietzsche, and Freud was important. The critical stance involved the development of theory that described and analyzed the present society in relation to its past and, in doing so, enabled those who were oppressed to realize the forces that caused their oppression. In addition, the analysis would show how this oppression could be overcome with new, emancipatory conceptualizations and practices.

The critical theorists were concerned with the way in which the promise of Enlightenment rationality had been subverted in modern society. The major problem for modern society was, according to Horkheimer, the fact that "Reason has liquidated itself as an agency of ethical, moral, and religious insight" (1947:18). Reason had become rationalization that, as Max Weber had pointed out, led to a bureaucratized, controlling state rather than a liberated, equitable society.

Reason and Objectivity   Horkheimer distinguished between objective and subjective reason. **Objective reason** referred to reason as an instrument for determining social ends. Objective reason was a "force not only in the individual mind but also in the objective world—in relations among human beings and between social classes, in social institutions, and in nature and its manifestations" (1947:4).

Subjective reason was simply concerned with "means and ends, with the adequacy of procedures for the purposes more or less taken for granted and supposedly self-explanatory." Subjective reason is instrumental reason, and it "attaches little importance to the question whether the purposes as such are reasonable," just, or equitable (1947:3). Consequently, when the subjective version of reason holds there is no "reasonable" basis upon which to make ethical choices, "The acceptability of ideals, the criteria for our actions and beliefs, the leading principles of ethics and politics, all our ultimate decisions are made to depend upon factors other than reason" (1974:7).

The focus on subjective, or instrumental, reason as evidenced in positivist science meant that reason could be as easily used by the Nazi extermination industry as by institutions concerned with the elimination of poverty and suffering. Subjective or instrumental reason involved elevating the scientific "classification of facts and the calculation of probabilities" as the only "authority." In terms of subjective reason, the "statement that justice and freedom are better in themselves than injustice and oppression is scientifically unverifiable and useless," as meaningless as the statement that "red is more beautiful than blue" (Horkheimer, 1947:24).

The critical theorists maintained that disinterested, objective research was impossible because facts and values could not be separated and the researcher was always a part of the social situation being investigated. More specifically, positive methods were rejected on the basis that positivism's "exclusive faith in mathematics" was "philosophical technocracy" (Horkheimer, 1947:59). Horkheimer and Adorno maintained that positivism saw the world only in terms of "facts and things" and failed to connect these facts and things with social, and individual, needs and desires (Horkheimer, 1947:82).

Critical theory, on the other hand, not only understood the "various facts in their historical development" but also saw through the "notion of fact itself" as an historical and thus relative phenomenon. The "so-called facts ascertained by quantitative methods, which positivists are inclined to regard as the only scientific ones, are often only surface phenomena that obscure rather than disclose the underlying reality" (Horkheimer, 1947:82). The task of the critical theorist was to reveal the real conditions underlying the "facts" and, in doing so, provide a blueprint for an alternative, emancipatory reality.

The analysis of social conditions was an ethical enterprise for critical theorists. Horkheimer maintained that the Kantian ethical universals of duty and good will were abstractions that did not address the changing social context of human needs. Human nature is "continuously influenced and changed by a manifold of circumstances," and there is "no formula that defines the relationship among individuals, society, and nature for all time" (Horkheimer, 1935:152–153). The only ethical ideal should be happiness, because human beings "cannot escape from the longing for happiness and the fear of death" (Horkheimer, 1935:155).

Horkheimer believed that the transition from the hopeful promise of Enlightenment objective reason into modern subjective, instrumental reason was not an accident and could not "arbitrarily at any given moment be reversed" (1947:62). Hegel had pointed out that reason changed historically, and although this was a progressive dialectical change toward freedom, this was not guaranteed. As Marcuse pointed out, the central category of the dialectic was negation (1960:449). Negation could mean that the "unreasonable becomes reasonable and, as such, determines the facts; in which unfreedom is the condition of freedom, and war the guarantor of peace" (Marcuse, 1960:vii).

Reason, in modern society, was instrumental in "sustaining injustice, toil, and suffering"; at the same time, the exercise of reason was still the best hope for the future (Marcuse, 1960:450). For example, Marxian theory took shape "as a critique of Hegel's philosophy . . . in the name of Reason," and in modern society it was only through constant critique that "Reason," and thus individuals, could come to understand the contradictions of social life and devise ways to transcend them (Marcuse, 1960:xii–xiii).

Emancipatory Theory   Like Marx, the critical theorists emphasized that theoretical critique was not simply a way of making sense of the "facts"; it was also a way of helping individuals to see and understand what "is" and in doing so see what "might be." Methodologically, critical theory overcame the breach between theory and practice, ideas and reality, and in this way was true to its Marxist heritage.

Marx had pointed out that capitalism was a "union of contradictions. It gets freedom through exploitation, wealth through impoverishment, advance in production through restriction of consumption," so that the "very structure of capitalism is a dialectical one: every form and institution of the economic process begets its determinate negation and the crisis is the extreme form in which the contradictions are expressed" (Marcuse, 1960:311). If enlightenment and progress means "freeing . . . man from superstitious belief in evil forces, in demons and fairies, in blind fate—in short the emancipation from fear—then denunciation of what is currently called reason is the greatest service reason can render" (Horkheimer, 1947:187). **Negative critique** "salvage[s] relative truths from the wreckage of false ultimates" (Horkheimer, 1947:183) and leads to the understanding of these contradictions because it rejects "the absolute claims of prevailing ideology" as well as "the brash claims of reality" by demonstrating their relativity (Horkheimer, 1947:182).

Theoretical critique was seen as a necessary but not sufficient condition for revolutionary change. Although theory remained primary—as Marcuse (1960: 322) put it, "Practice follows the truth, not vice versa"—change required an agent. But for the Institute theorists, finding an agent under the conditions of monopoly capitalism was a problem. The alienation of the proletariat envisaged by Marx seemed to have been subverted by the ability of capitalism to satisfy an abundance of needs. The result was an "increasing distance between the consciousness of the working class and the critical individual who acts in its name" (Benhabib, 1986:157). The absence of revolutionary working-class consciousness, the entrenchment of monopoly capitalism, and the consolidation of the authoritarian state generated increasing pessimism about the possibility of emancipatory transformation in the immediate future.

Critical theorists pointed out, however, that although capitalism might satisfy many proletariat needs, increased consumption did not necessarily translate into human satisfaction and happiness, and it certainly did not compensate the proletariat for the alienation of their labor power. Capitalism, and especially monopoly capitalism, regulated consumption according to what was profitable, not according to human needs. Capitalism duped consumers into believing that they were exercising real choices among items and that these items would satisfy their needs.

Although the consumer is, so to speak, given his choice, he does not get a penny's worth too much for his money, whatever the trademark he prefers to possess. The difference in quality between two equally priced popular items is usually so infinitesimal as the difference in the nicotine content of two brands of cigarettes. (Horkheimer, 1947:99)

Even if the consumer suspected that the choice was an illusion, this would not guarantee the production of revolutionary consciousness because of the pervasiveness of reification. **Reification** refers to the process of domination whereby the products of human labor take on the appearance of things external to, and uncontrollable by, human beings. For example, economic fluctuations are often blamed on the operation of "the market." But the market is not some abstract, inevitable force; it is *people* making decisions about money, commodities, and trade.

Georg Lukacs, a friend of Max Weber, had earlier developed the theory of reification. In *History and Class Consciousness* (1922), Lukacs suggested that the proletariat were prisoners of bourgeois ideas that encouraged the belief that capitalism and alienated labor were "natural"—that is, an inevitable part of abstract market forces that individuals could not control. Consequently, for Lukacs, it was the task of vanguard intellectuals to overcome this reification by educating the proletariat as to their "real" position in the relations of production and showing how the proletariat could control their destiny.

To the critical theorists, reification was both an objective process, being a part of the exchange relations of capitalism, and subjective because it was embedded in belief and understanding. Reification was false consciousness that was "self-inflicted alienation"—the alienation that a person and social class did to themselves (Agger, 1979:150). Consequently, it was the duty of critical theory to help generate revolutionary consciousness and practice among the proletariat.

Fromm and Freud   Simple economic determinism was not the motor of revolutionary transformation. Culture, or ideology, embedded in the consciousness, also played an important part in producing distorted personalities who reproduced the conditions of domination. This realization made Freud's work useful to critical theory because it provided an explanation for false consciousness as well as an explanation for the authoritarian personality types of modern society. Freud's libido theory also held out the promise that total domination might be subverted by the fact that basically human beings desire freedom (Alford, 1987:26).

Erich Fromm was central to the incorporation of Freud into the work of the critical theorists. Fromm maintained that psychoanalysis was compatible with Marxian historical materialism because it uncovered the unconscious forces controlling behavior. Irrational behavior had its origins in social life—in religion, customs, politics, and education.

Marxists have usually assumed that what works behind man's back and directs him are economic forces and their political representations. Psychoanalytic study shows that this is much too narrow a concept. Society

consists of people . . . equipped with a potential of passionate strivings. . . .
This human potential as a whole is molded by the ensemble of economic
and social forces characteristic of each given society. These forces . . .
produce a certain social unconscious, and and certain conflicts between the
repressive factors and given human needs which are essential for sane
human functioning (like a certain degree of freedom, stimulation, interest
in life, happiness). . . . revolutions occur as expressions of not only new
productive forces, but also of the repressed part of human nature, and they
are successful only when the two conditions are combined. (1965:37–38)

The psychoanalytic focus on the family was important to critical theory because it was through the family that a society put its stamp on the individual
personality. Specifically, it was through the family that society reproduced the
class structure. In addition, it was the family that produced the authoritarian
personality type that underlay anti-Semitism.

Investigations into the way in which economic and political structures affected the psychic life of individuals resulted in the Institute projects *Studies on
Authority and Family,* conducted in Germany in the 1930s, and *Studies in Prejudice,* conducted in the United States in the 1940s. The work *Dialectic of the Enlightenment,* by Adorno and Horkheimer (1944), also explored the social and historical basis for the development of the authoritarian personality and the origins
of fascist society.

Nature of Society, Humans, and Change

Modern Capitalist Society   The critical theorists focused primarily on the
nature of modern Western society and the historical development of capitalism.
A key transformation was seen to be the replacement of individual competitive
capitalism with monopoly and state capitalism. With state capitalism replacing
liberal capitalism after World War II, the critique of society could no longer be
simply a critique of political economy.

It is no longer the norms of a bourgeois public sphere, of the liberal marketplace and of the liberal state, practicing the rule of law, to which critique
can appeal. . . . Emancipatory norms are no longer immanent in public and
institutional structures. Instead, they have to be searched for in the unre-
deemed utopian promise of culture, art, and philosophy (Adorno), or in the
deep structures of human subjectivity that revolt against the sacrifices
demanded by an oppressive society (Marcuse). (Benhabib, 1986:180–181)

The transformation to state capitalism is marked by the development of
mass culture and the extension of social domination into the psychological as
well as the economic experiences of human beings. It represents the triumph
of instrumental rationality that Weber discussed. **Instrumental rationality** is
concerned only with matching effective means to selected goals and thus acts
as a mechanism of repression in modern society. This dehumanized exercise is
contrasted with a rationality, or reason, that is concerned with the human

values of happiness and justice. Horkheimer remarked that even after the defeat of fascism, the

> hopes of mankind seem to be farther from fulfillment today than they were even in the groping epochs when they were first formulated by humanists. It seems that even as technical knowledge expands the horizon of man's thought and activity, his autonomy as an individual, his ability to resist the growing apparatus of mass manipulation, his power of imagination, his independent judgement appear to be reduced. Advance in technical facilities for enlightenment is accompanied by a process of dehumanization. (1947:vi)

Weber's fears about a bureaucratized, impersonal world of "icy darkness" seemed to the critical theorists to have been realized, making it difficult to conceive of ways in which emancipatory change could be effected.

The irony is, as both Marx and Weber understood, that technological "progress" enabling human beings to control the natural world becomes "progressive enslavement" as technology and science become the singular determinants of human needs (Marcuse, 1964:144).

> The fallen nature of modern man cannot be separated from social progress. On the one hand the growth of economic productivity furnishes the conditions for a world of greater justice; on the other hand it allows the technical apparatus and social groups which administer it a disproportionate superiority to the rest of the population. . . . Even though the individual disappears before the apparatus which he serves, that apparatus provides for him as never before. (Adorno and Horkheimer, 1944:xiv)

In the early years the critical theorists subscribed to Marx's idea that technology could be harnessed for the satisfaction of human needs in a positive rather than a negative manner, but in the aftermath of the Holocaust this optimism was abandoned.

> The real individuals of our time are the martyrs who have gone through infernos of suffering and degradation in their resistance to conquest and oppression, not the inflated personalities of popular culture, the conventional dignitaries. . . . The anonymous martyrs of the concentration camps are the symbols of humanity that is striving to be born. The task of philosophy is to translate what they have done into language that will be heard, even though their finite voices have been silenced by tyranny. (Horkheimer, 1947:161)

The technological expertise the Nazis brought to bear on the elimination of whole sectors of humanity was produced by "modern" human beings. It seemed that in modern society, "conscience and personal responsibility decline 'objectively' under conditions of total bureaucratization . . . where the functioning of the apparatus determines—and overrides—personal autonomy" (Marcuse, 1970:50). The "fallen nature of modern man cannot be separated from social progress," and even though the "individual disappears before the apparatus which he serves, that apparatus provides for him as never before. In an unjust state of life, the impotence and pliability of the masses grows with the quantitative increase in commodities allowed them" (Adorno and Horkheimer, 1944:xiv–xv).

Horkheimer pointed out that the modern celebration of the "individual" is ironic. The Enlightenment dream of "machines doing men's work has now come true," but it is "also true that men are acting more and more like machines" (1974:26). False needs, satisfied by the culture industry and the increasing proliferation of commodities, extend the reach of capitalist domination. For example, the "real you" is defined in relation to the clothes you wear, the car you drive, even the toothpaste you use. Fromm (1955:133) pointed out, "We drink labels. With a bottle of Coca-Cola we drink the picture of the pretty boy and girl who drink it in the advertisement, we drink the slogan of 'the pause that refreshes'. . . least of all do we drink with our palate." Individuality is subverted by technology in the "one-dimensional society" of enslaved consumers and mass culture audiences (Marcuse, 1964). Freud's insights on subjectivity were important to critical theory because of the decline of autonomous individuality, and with it the possibility of critical reflection on society that might lead to emancipatory practice.

Human Nature   Human beings are inseparable from society because the individual "is *real* only as part of the whole to which he belongs. His essential determination, his character and inclination, his avocation and view of the world all have their origin in society and in his destiny in society" (Horkheimer, 1947:9–10). The isolated individual is an illusion: "The most esteemed personal qualities, such as independence, will to freedom, sympathy and the sense of justice, are social as well as individual virtues." Consequently, the "emancipation of the individual is not an emancipation from society, but the deliverance of society from atomization . . . that may reach its peak in periods of collectivization and mass culture" (Horkheimer, 1947:135). As society changes, individual personalities change, and the "realization that young men and women today are, at bottom, different even from what they were at the beginning of the century" means that the notion of an unchangeable human essence must be discarded (Horkheimer, 1947:13). Human needs, "including sexuality," have an "historical character" (Marcuse, 1970:59).

The significance of the historical nature of human nature lay in the way repressive social forces penetrated the psyche. In advanced industrial societies, these repressive forces penetrated ever more deeply, leading to the "obsolescence of the role and autonomy of the economic and political subject" (Marcuse, 1970:59). Specifically, it was the loss of a "personal private realm" that weakened the "consciousness and conscience" and thus decreases the autonomy and rationality of the individual (Marcuse, 1970:50).

Adorno and Horkheimer used Homer's epic of Odysseus's voyage from Troy to Ithaca, which illustrated man's domination of nature, to trace modern psychic repression. They pointed out that domination of nature was necessary for man to become human, but it also marked the beginnings of man's self-repression (1944:46). A key event in Odysseus's voyage was his escape from the lure of the Sirens. Odysseus had to pass between Scylla and Charybdis while listening to the song of the Sirens. Scylla and Charybdis had the right to capture whatever came between them. They were assured of their prize because no mariner could resist the seductive songs of the Sirens. The Sirens represented the sensuous, natural world—the world of the Freudian id. Odysseus cunningly found a way to resist the temptation of the Sirens. He put wax into the ears of his rowers so they could not hear the songs and had himself bound to the mast so that he could hear the songs but could not succumb to the lure. Odysseus "has found an escape clause in the contract, which enables him to fulfill it while eluding it" so that he "as subject need not be subjected" to the Sirens (1944:59).

Odysseus was able to dominate nature, but at the price of repressing his own instinctual inner nature. He was therefore the prototype of the bourgeois whose deferment of pleasure was critical to the success of rational capitalism. Odysseus's strategy also reinforced his domination over his men, who could not hear the songs and who had to rely on Odysseus's judgment. "The oarsmen . . . are each yoked in the same rhythm as the modern worker in the factory," and their impotence, like that of modern workers, was not simply a "stratagem of the rulers, but the logical consequence of the industrial society into which the ancient Fate . . . has finally changed" (1944:37). In the long run, the taming of nature resulted in a "bourgeois commodity economy," and the conditions were established for a "new barbarism" (1944:32).

The repression of instinctual nature, necessary for individual and social progress, resulted in a transition from what Freud called the **pleasure principle** to the **reality principle** (Marcuse, 1966:12).

Pleasure principle	Reality principle
Immediate satisfaction	Delayed satisfaction
Pleasure	Restraint of pleasure
Joy (play)	Toil (work)
Receptiveness	Productiveness
Absence of repression	Security

The result of the transition was that the "curse of irresistible progress" became "irresistible regression" (Adorno and Horkheimer, 1944:36).

Adorno and Horkheimer became increasingly pessimistic about the possibility of any collective emancipatory project after the 1940s. Marcuse (1966), however, suggested that instinctual repression allied with supremely efficient technological rationality could be a source of liberation. That is, too much repression would invariably mean an eventual rebellion against those repressive forces.

Social Change   Marcuse suggested that Freud's libidinal repression was not a singular, static phenomenon, but varied in relation to changes in society. In modern society, repression is excessive. Basic repression has been superceded by surplus repression. **Surplus repression** occurs because capitalism can produce an abundance that can liberate humans from scarcity, but "the closer the real possibility of liberating the individual from the constraints once justified by scarcity and immaturity, the greater the need for maintaining and streamlining these constraints lest the established order of domination dissolve" (Marcuse,

1966:85). Surplus repression is repression in the interest of domination rather than in the interest of the development of civilized human beings.

Surplus repression can be undermined by the fact that the "quantitative reduction in labor time and energy leads to a qualitative change in human existence" and the "expanding realm of freedom becomes truly a realm of play" (Marcuse, 1966:222–223). In time the "distinction between rational and irrational authority, between repression and surplus-repression, can be made and verified by individuals themselves." If this distinction is not made currently, this "does not mean they cannot learn to make it once they are given the opportunity to do so" (Marcuse, 1966:225).

The escape from the "iron cage" can be accomplished by a **great refusal**—the refusal to "buy into" the consumer society. Marcuse believed that this refusal would not be made by the proletariat because they have been co-opted by the ability of advanced capitalism to satisfy consumption needs and produce the semblance of the "good life" (Marcuse, 1964:18). The great refusal will be made by the "substratum of the outcasts and outsiders, the exploited and persecuted of other races and other colors, the unemployed and the unemployable" who exist outside democratic society and whose opposition is "revolutionary even if their consciousness is not" (1964:256). It is when these individuals started "refusing to play the game" that the "beginning of the end" is in sight (1964:257).

Marcuse was hopeful that the various counterculture movements of the 1960s indicated the beginnings of the great refusal. For Marcuse, love and sexual freedom were the routes to social transformation. As individuals come to recognize the excessive rationalization of society, there would be a reversion to childhood polymorphous sexuality that modern, post-Oedipul genital sexuality represses. The body would become an "instrument of pleasure," and this would hasten the disintegration of "the monogamic and patriarchal family" (Marcuse, 1966:201). Marcuse's optimistic forecast of sexual revolution as the motor of social transformation was made before STDs and AIDS were recognized as serious problems.

Adorno, Horkheimer, and even Marcuse realized that "transformation is objectively necessary but the need for it is not present among precisely those social strata who are defined as agents of transformation" in Marxist theory (Marcuse, 1970:99). Nonetheless, resistance was imperative, whether it took the form of a great refusal or some other form, because the "new fascism . . . will be very different from the old fascism." The new fascism will undermine democracy by repressive legislation, supported by the masses, that will "cut back . . . existing civil and political liberties" (Marcuse, 1970:100). Some theorists today maintain that this is precisely what has occurred in the late twentieth century in Western societies and that the vital sociological question remains, who can resist? If it is not the working class, maybe resistance can emerge from feminists and racial minorities.

Class, Gender, and Race

Class   The critical theorists recognized the class divisions in modern society but provided no systematic analysis of class (Kellner, 1989:229). They were more concerned with the way in which Marxian class politics had been subverted by psychological as well as economic repression. A key institution in psychological repression was the family. Fromm pointed out that the family was the "medium through which the society or the social class stamps it specific structure on the child, and hence the adult. *The family is the psychological agency of society*" (1988:483).

The research *Studies on Authority and the Family*, undertaken by the Institute in the 1930s, examined the nature of the family and the psychic repression it generated under industrial capitalism. Critical theorists pointed out that the family was not a natural, unchanging form, but changed in response to external social and historical conditions. The patriarchal, bourgeois family was the particular form developed in relation to the needs of industrial capitalism. It was the ideals of this family form that tended to prevail and entrench subjective domination.

Studies on Authority and the Family was based on an empirical study of the attitudes and beliefs of German workers. Three thousand questionnaires were distributed to workers asking them their views on "the education of children, the rationalization of industry, the possibility of avoiding a new war, and the locus of real power in the state" (Jay, 1973:116).

An important methodological innovation was used in this research. The answers were recorded verbatim and then analyzed "the way a psychoanalyst listens to the associations of a patient"—that is, key words were taken as an indication of the "underlying psychological reality beneath the manifest content of the answers" (Jay, 1973:117). The study revealed discrepancies between beliefs and personality traits. The research found that approximately 10 percent of the respondents exhibited authoritarian characteristics, and about 15 percent anti-authoritarian views, with the majority being highly ambivalent.

Horkheimer and Adorno found that under state capitalism the patriarchal, bourgeois family was the foundation for the authoritarian personality. The Oedipal conflict, involving the rejection of the mother in favor of the father's authority, was the means for the child to learn to accept the authority of society. The "rational" adaptation of the child to the father's authority was internalized to produce a strong ego and superego, or conscience, adapted to the needs of capitalist society.

> The self-control of the individual, the disposition for work and discipline, the ability to hold firmly to certain ideas, consistency in practical life, application of reason, perseverance and pleasure in constructive activity could all be developed, in the circumstances, only under the direction of the father whose own education had been won in the school of life. (Horkheimer, 1982:101)

It is clear that the child referred to was a male child. In the early stages of capitalist, bourgeois society, the authority of the father provided the son with an object against which to rebel. This rebellion produced individual autonomy and the ability to resist domination. However, with the transformation of liberal, entrepreneurial capitalism to state capitalism, the father's economic power and family authority declined. The child still experienced the Oedipal complex but came to realize that the father did not embody total power and authority. The child then sought a father-substitute in order to develop a strong, autonomous self. But the only father-substitute was the abstract authority of instrumental reason, with the result the child became the "mass individual, a heteronomous social atom who is narcissistic, materialistic, and sadistic" and unable to resist domination (Jagentowicz Mills, 1987:98). The child learned that not "the father but the playmates, the neighbors, the leader of the gang, the sport, the screen are the authorities on appropriate mental and physical behavior" (Marcuse, 1970:52).

The foundations for capitulation to an authoritarian, fascist leader were found in the psychic fallout from these transformed family relations. From their research into the family lives of German workers, the critical theorists concluded that the "German working class would be far less resistant to the right-wing seizure of power than its militant ideology would suggest"—a conclusion borne out by the general enthusiasm for National Socialism (Jay, 1973:117).

Gender   Horkheimer and Adorno focused on the problems for the male child in state capitalist families. The mother, "as representative of nature," was, in the early stages of bourgeois capitalism, a source of security and comfort for the male child. Women in general were "the enigmatic image of irresistibility and powerlessness" (Adorno and Horkheimer, 1944:71–72). The mother provided a refuge from the father's authority, and her unconditional love was a source of emotional sustenance that provided the child with a vision of an alternative, utopian reality—a vision of instinctual Eros in contrast to rational authority, the pleasure principle as opposed to the reality principle.

This idyllic situation, according to the critical theorists, changed as women entered the productive sphere and many of their socialization tasks were taken over by other institutions. The mother ceased to offer a refuge from the authoritarian world of the father because she became more and more like a man. For Adorno and Horkheimer, as well as Marcuse, this was a negative step. For example, Marcuse believed that the feminine principle, based on the "promise of peace, of joy, of the end of violence" natural to women, was the foundation for emancipation of both men and women (1972:77).

The celebration of the feminine principle was a blind spot in the work of the critical theorists. The principle merely restated the gender dichotomies that support capitalist patriarchy (Jagentowicz Mills, 1987:116). The mother might represent the promise of liberation for sons, but this promise did not extend to daughters. Daughters, in the Freudian account, had to reject the mother in favor of the father in order to develop a mature femininity. At the same time, like their mothers, daughters must embody the same liberatory promise for men.

There was some nostalgia for the nineteenth-century bourgeois family among the critical theorists. They saw the destruction of this family form as the destruction of the sphere of love, and thus of any possibility of resistance to the instrumentality of mass society. But the emotional support it offered its male members obscured the damage this family form did to mothers and daughters. Adorno and Horkheimer concluded that "Fatherlessness creates a mass individual or an authoritarian personality" but a motherless society meant a "loss of a vision of the future lived in freedom," a society "without love or hope" (Jagentowicz Mills, 1987:109). A motherless society was one that was primed for anti-Semitism, and for racism in general.

Race   Horkheimer and Adorno argued that "race is not a naturally special characteristic" but was a potent sign in certain social contexts (1944:169). Anti-Semitism, for example, projected repressed fears and wants onto the despised other, most especially the fear of impotence in the face of overwhelming social and economic forces. They saw Nazism as a "psychological problem, but the psychological factors themselves have to be understood as being molded by socio-economic factors" (Fromm, 1941:208).

In capitalist society, anti-Semitism was economically important to the bourgeoisie because it concealed the nature of domination in productive relations. Adorno and Horkheimer pointed out that Jews had historically been denied access to manufacturing so they often found their livelihood in commercial and financial enterprises. Thus, "commerce was not their vocation but their fate" (Adorno and Horkheimer, 1944:175). The actual nature of productivity in these occupations was often concealed, and the merchant and banker appeared to profit on the backs of productive workers. They were, however, simply middlemen who concealed the reality of the capitalist manufacture's appropriation of surplus wealth. The Jew became the "bailiff of the whole system and takes the hatred of others upon himself" (1944:174). Under monopoly capitalism, wealth was concentrated in the hands of a few and the middleman role became redundant. The Jew, however, remained a handy scapegoat for the resulting economic problems that monopoly capitalism produced.

Jews, and others who were similarly stigmatized, were easy targets for persecution. They could be used to expiate the social dislocations of capitalism as well as the unconscious antisocial forces that were barely repressed under systems of instrumental domination.

In the 1940s, a large study dealing with prejudice, and specifically with anti-Semitism, was launched in the United States.[3] *Studies in Prejudice* was a five-volume collaborative work, with Adorno and the members of the Berkeley Public Opinion Study Group, R. Nevitt Sanford, Daniel Levison, and Elsie Frankel-Brunswik, as the main researchers. Horkheimer was the overall coordinator of the project. The main theoretical underpinning for the discovery of the subjective manifestations of prejudice came from psychoanalysis.

The studies employed both qualitative techniques, such as interviews, and quantitative techniques. The five studies were *Dynamics of Prejudice*, which examined the personality traits and prejudicial attitudes of war veterans; *Anti-Semitism and Emotional Disorder*, which consisted of case studies of psychotherapy patients who demonstrated anti-Semitism; *Prophets of Deceit*, which examined the techniques of mass persuasion; *Rehearsal for Destruction*, which described the historical origin of anti-Semitism in Germany; and *The Authoritarian Personality*, which examined the correlations between prejudice and personality traits.

---

[3]The study was funded by the American Jewish Committee.

The Authoritarian Personality (Adorno et al., 1950) was specifically concerned with outlining the personality traits of the potentially fascist individual. Extensive questionnaires and interviews were conducted, and an F scale was developed that measured anti-Semitism and antidemocratic attitudes. The study concluded that prejudiced individuals had distinctive personalities as a result of their socialization. Prejudiced, antidemocratic personalities came from authoritarian families in which conformity was the rule, discipline was strict but often arbitrary, and any deviations from rigidly held but conventional values were severely punished. The authoritarian personality had a strong resemblance to the sadomasochistic personality discussed by Fromm in the earlier *Studies on Authority and the Family.*

The Authoritarian Personality revealed the familial psychosocial dynamic of authoritarianism and prejudice, but "the authoritarian family did not produce authoritarian children solely because of what it did—provide a model for arbitrary domination—but equally for what it could not do—protect the individual against the claims made on his socialization by extra-familial agencies" (Jay, 1973:247). As Fromm (1955:237) pointed out, "Fascism, Nazism and Stalinism have in common that they offered the atomized individual a new refuge and security. These systems are the culmination of alienation." Prejudice was a persistent social problem because the authoritarian personality type was as much a product of society at large as it was of family dynamics.

Adorno concluded *The Authoritarian Personality* with the observation that if "fear and destructiveness are the major emotional sources of fascism, *eros* belongs mainly to democracy" (Adorno et al., 1950:976). Education, therefore, had to be tied to democratic politics if prejudice was to be curtailed.

After the second World War, Horkheimer reflected on the situation of German Jews and concluded that the trauma of the Nazi era had yet to be overcome. He believed that protection from repeating the past lay in knowledge of that past and, more important, in education that made individuals "critical in the face of demagogy" so that they could distinguish "demagogy from a truly rational politics" (1974:117–118).

Other Theories and Theorists

We have concentrated on four key members of the Institute because of space limitations, but several other important theorists were associated with the Institute in its early years. Among them were Leo Lowenthal and Walter Benjamin, who were interested in a sociology of literature; Karl Wittfogel, whose interest was in comparative sociology; Karl Mannheim, who developed the sociology of knowledge; and Paul Lazarsfeld, who became important to communications research in U.S. sociology. In addition, Adorno produced a considerable amount of work on art and culture, specifically critiques of mass culture.

The major focus for the diverse work of the critical theorists was on **domination** in capitalist and, during the war years, fascist society. They suggested that because domination penetrated into the innermost core of the personality, domination was often unrecognized and unrealized. This made it difficult to conceptualize how the world should be; that is, it made it difficult to mount a rational critique of the present and formulate possibilities for an emancipated future.

Critique and Conclusions

A major criticism of the critical theorists is that they simply replaced economic analysis with cultural analysis and, in doing so, weakened, if not eliminated, the possibility of revolutionary praxis on the part of the proletariat. But the critical theorists from the outset maintained that the former political economy (base) and culture/ideology (superstructure) division no longer held in twentieth-century society. The two were critically interconnected, and it was the interconnections that made emancipation difficult. The focus on ideology, culture, and the damaged psyche in a capitalist society was part of a continuing concern with how capitalism changed historically and how the impulse to a better world could be promoted. After the 1930s, however, Adorno and Horkheimer became pessimistic about the possibility of radical transformation, and neither participated in any direct way with the radical student protests of the 1960s.

Another criticism of critical theory is that it remained a philosophical, unscientific enterprise that did not come to grips with the "real" conditions of modern repression and domination. This criticism has some validity, but it should be recalled that the immediate postwar situation of the original Institute members could not, and did not, approximate those of the 1930s origins. After the Institute's reconstitution in Germany, the work of critical theory remained focused on revealing the structures of domination underlying the seeming benevolence of state capitalism. This focus influenced the work in the critical theoretical tradition of students such as Jurgen Habermas.

Jurgen Habermas (1929–)

Jurgen Habermas was born in Gummersbach, near Düsseldorf, and grew up during the Nazi regime and the Second World War. The early experience of the Nazi era had a profound effect on his thinking. As a teenager, Habermas was shocked by the Nuremberg trials and the "discovery of the horrors of the Nazi regime" (Bernstein, 1985:1). In the 1950s he became concerned about the "continuities between the Nazi regime and the emergent West German state" (Outhwaite, 1994:2). His work has been a search for a social framework that can ensure that fascism will not reappear.

Habermas studied philosophy at Göttingen, Zurich, and Bonn. He obtained his doctorate from Bonn in 1954. For a couple of years he was a journalist, and from 1956 until 1959 he was Adorno's assistant at the Frankfurt Institute. In 1961 he was appointed professor of philosophy and sociology at the University of Heidelberg. He returned to the Institute in 1964, where he assumed Horkheimer's chair in philosophy and sociology.[4] In 1971 he assumed the directorship of the new Max Planck Institute for the Study of the Conditions of

---

[4]Horkheimer had not been very supportive of Habermas when he was a student. Kellner (1989:207) suggested that this was because Horkheimer became more conservative after his return to Germany and he found Habermas's work too left wing. Adorno, however, did support Habermas for the Chair position.

Life in the Scientific-Technical World. He returned in 1982 to the Chair of Sociology and Philosophy at the University of Frankfurt, where he remained until his retirement.

Habermas's Central Theories and Methods

Charting the intellectual influences on Habermas is a daunting task because of his encyclopedic knowledge of contemporary philosophical and social theories (Outhwaite, 1994:5). Central to his work, however, have been the theorists of the Frankfurt Institute and the classical theorists, Marx, Freud, and Weber. His main focus is on transforming the negative critique of original critical theory into a positive program for emancipatory practice.

Communication   Like his critical theory predecessors, Habermas is concerned with reformulating Marxian theory in the light of twentieth-century social changes, and most especially in light of the expansion of state power into all spheres of social life. Habermas expands Marx's conception of humanity by adding **language** (communication) to **work** (labor) as a distinct feature of species-being.

The introduction of language as a significant part of human development led Habermas to concentrate on how undistorted communication might be possible and how it could lay the foundation for emancipatory practice. **Distorted communication** is the equivalent of Marx's false consciousness. **Undistorted communication** refers to the conditions under which social goals and values can be discussed on a rational, egalitarian basis so that a consensus can be reached on the ends and values to be pursued. Undistorted, rational communication only occurs when the "peculiarly constraint-free force of the better argument" prevailed (1984: 1:26).

Habermas's model for undistorted communication is psychoanalysis. In Freudian psychoanalysis the patient is encouraged, through a process of self-reflection, to become aware of previously repressed needs. Recovery (freedom) results from the patient's recognition of this self-imposed repression. As with the psychoanalyst, the role of the critical theorist is to assist the repressed to recognize and understand their collective, social situation and, as a result, formulate emancipatory practices. Habermas regards this endeavor as particularly important today because of the extent to which science and technology distort communication in the interest of technological rationalization and the political reinforcement of repression.

Domination and Communication   In his analysis of current forces of domination, Habermas turned to Weber's analysis of purposive-rational action. Habermas extended Weber's recognition of the penetration of purposive-rationality in the economy to the knowledge spheres of science, art, and political/legal/moral theory. His main point was that purposive-rationality penetrates everyday practices, especially everyday communications, and contributes to the loss of meaning in everyday life. In a modern society governed by purposive-rationality, everything "has a price." Everything can be justified in rational, means-end terms. As a result, the normative sphere is sidelined, or even made obsolete, and emotional desires and subjective intuitions are relegated to the irrational sphere.

But Habermas claimed that it was possible to find a way out of the "disenchantment" of modernity through the construction of an ideal speech community. The **ideal speech community** presupposes that (1) all individuals capable of speech can participate in the debate; (2) all individuals have equal rights to give their reasons for their stated position; and (3) no individual can be denied the right to participate in the debate. These are the necessary and universal conditions for the ideal speech community because they guarantee that the force of better (rational) argument will prevail.

The ideal speech community is Habermas's way of maintaining critical theory's injunction to link theory and practice. The ideal speech community connects with Marx's idea that ideology can be understood as distorted communication (Held, 1980:277). The ideal speech situation is therefore politically important in providing the foundation for the full realization of human needs and interests. The very nature of communication in the ideal speech community is one of mutual trust and comprehension rather than the achievement of rational, instrumental ends.

Positivism and Communication   According to Habermas, a critical part of modern distorted communication, and hence domination, is the value placed on science and technology. Like his critical theory predecessors, Habermas maintained that science and technology were not neutral or objective procedures without any evaluative weight. Habermas recognized that science in the early nineteenth century was a progressive force, but by the twentieth century science, in its positivist form, had become a form of ideological domination. Positive science became a means for the manipulation of both the natural and social world in the interest of technical rather than social progress. Furthermore, Habermas claimed that science was "no longer understood as *one* form of knowledge"; rather, knowledge was now identified as science (1971:19).

"Scientism"—the belief that all problems have a technical solution apart from any political or moral considerations—is the new ideology of advanced capitalism. The individual becomes powerless in the face of technical experts, whose presumed efficiency in solving social and economic crises is presented as being in the best interests of the individual. The result is "the depoliticization of the mass of the population" as "reified models of the sciences . . . gain objective power" over individuals' self-understanding (Habermas, 1970:374). For example, the advertisers' catchphrase "Studies show . . ." acts as a powerful persuader of a commodity's value, or recommendation for certain behaviors as desirable. Critical reflection and protest are eliminated by the idea that experts know best.

Habermas claimed that the dominance of technological rationality and positivist science over all spheres of life was not an inevitable process, although ideologically it might be presented as such (1976:11). Habermas saw science as having an instrumental place in modern society, freeing individuals from the constraints of external nature, but argued that this place must be balanced by a politics that was enlightened and emancipatory. A basic distinction needed to be made between rational-purposive action, on the one hand, and communicative action taking account of values and beliefs, on the other.

The interrelationship of productive forces and normative structures is, in Habermas's view, important to the legitimation problems of the state. Habermas is particularly concerned with the legitimacy of the state in advanced capitalist societies because of the state's special position in its "role as corporate actor, not only making decisions affecting the whole society, but doing so in the name of society itself" (Wuthnow, Hunter, Bergesen, and Kurweil, 1984:218). These decisions are, in fact, in the interests of elites, but this is obscured by the ideological appeals to technical expertise.

Nature of Society, Humans, and Change

Society   Habermas analyzed the historical nature of the steering problems and crises in four types of society: primitive, traditional, capitalist, and postcapitalist. In the postcapitalist designation, Habermas included "state-socialist societies—in view of their political-elitist disposition of the means of production" (1976:17). With the exception of primitive societies, he considered all of the societal types to be **class societies**.

Steering problems were those that involved system integration and social integration. Habermas defined **social integration** as "*life-worlds* that are symbolically structured" (1976:4)—normative structures concerned with integration and pattern maintenance (Talcott Parsons's terminology). **System integration** referred to controlling or "steering performance of a self-regulated *system*" (1976:4). System integration involved adaptation and goal attainment.

According to Habermas, crises occurred (1) when "members of a society experience structural alterations as critical for continued existence and feel their social identity threatened"; and (2) when social integration is "at stake, that is, when the consensual foundations of normative structures" are impaired and society becomes "anomic" (1976:3). Habermas's evolutionary model of social change departed from the Marxist emphasis on the economy to stress the importance of normative legitimations in the process of social change.

Primitive societies were based on a kinship system, with age and sex as the "organizational principle." In this type of society, change occurred as a result of external factors that undermined "familial and tribal identities" (Habermas, 1976:18). The usual sources of social change were "demographic growth in connection with ecological factors—above all, interethnic dependency as a result of economic exchange, war, and conquest" (1976:19).

In **traditional** societies, the basic organizational principle was "*domination* in political form." The centrality of the kinship system characteristic of primitive society gave way to the "power and control of the state" (1976:19). In traditional societies, differentiation and functional specialization began to appear. Social change or crises occurred as a result of the "contradictions between validity claims of systems of norms and justifications that cannot explicitly permit exploitation, and a class structure in which privileged appropriation of socially produced wealth is the rule." The result was "heightened repression" in order to maintain system integration, but such repression led to "legitimation losses, which for their part result in class struggles." These struggles could, over time, lead to "the overthrow of the political system and to new foundations of legitimation—that is, to a new group identity" (1976:20).

When looking at capitalist societies, Habermas distinguished between **liberal capitalist** society and **organized** or **advanced capitalist** society. The organizational principle of liberal capitalism is *"the relationship of wage labor and capital,* which is anchored in the system of bourgeois civil law" (1976:20). In this type of society, "economic exchange becomes the dominant steering medium" and the state's power is limited to "(a) the protection of bourgeois commerce in accord with civil law (police and the administration of justice); (b) to the shielding of the market mechanism from self-destructive side effects (for example, legislation for the protection of labor); (c) to the satisfaction of the prerequisites of production in the economy as a whole (public school education, transportation, and communication); and, (d) to the adaptation of the system of civil law to needs that arise from the process of accumulation (tax, banking, and business law)" (1976:21).

The key transformation in liberal capitalist society, according to Habermas, is the "uncoupling," or separation, of the economic system from the political system. This separation allows for a sphere in "bourgeois society that is free from traditional ties and given over to the strategic-utilitarian action orientations of market participants" (1976:21). The result is that the "relations of production can do without traditional authority legitimated from above" (1976:22).

But when legitimacy rests on the operations of the market, Habermas argues, the inevitable fluctuations of the market become a threat to social integration. These fluctuations, with their consequences of increased unemployment and/or inflation, make the inequities of economic relations clearly evident despite the ideology that the marketplace is a meeting place of equals. "Economic crisis is immediately transformed into social crisis; for, in unmasking the opposition of social class, it provides a practical critique of ideology of the market's pretension to be free of power," and this critique threatens social integration (1976:29).

The crisis in liberal capitalist systems differs from that in previous social types because the conflicts take on the "appearance of natural catastrophes" and lose the "character of a fate accessible to self-reflection," acquiring the "objectivity of inexplicable, contingent, natural events" (Habermas, 1976:30).

The transformation of liberal capitalism to organized or state-regulated capitalism occurs with the rise of multinational corporations. The state, observes Habermas, is increasingly called upon to intervene in the economy because of the steering problems caused by economic fluctuations. As a result, the distinction between the economic and political systems tends to disappear when, for example, the state offers subsidies to industry, sets up job creation schemes, and offers tax relief to attract industry.

The "re-coupling," or interdependence, of the economic and political systems increases legitimation problems for the state. But, argues Habermas, the legitimation problem is not solved democratically with the "genuine participation of citizens in the process of political will-formation," which might reveal the "contradiction between administratively socialized production and the continued private appropriation and use of surplus value" (1976:36). The contradiction is concealed by making the administration independent of the democratic political system. Consequently, the needs and desires of the citizens can be ignored, especially when the administration claims to be exercising scientific expertise in the "best interests" of the citizens. The result is democracy in form only (1976:37).

Economic/political interdependence is unstable, however, because the manipulation of the normative structure often has unintended effects of highlighting meanings and norms previously taken for granted. Turning the spotlight on these meanings and norms subjects them to public scrutiny, and the resulting public discussion and discontent raise the possibility that change will be demanded (Habermas, 1976:47–48). That the state will have legitimation problems is almost guaranteed because, according to classical free enterprise ideology, the state is damned if it does intervene in the economy but, given the inevitable social problems, the state is damned if it does not intervene (Wuthnow et al., 1984:220).

Legitimation crises can only be avoided, in Habermas's view, by the development of new ways of reaching normative consensus through communicative competence. **Communicative competence** refers to the everyday world of taken-for-granted assumptions that structure understanding of how the world is and how individuals can act in that world. Communication is different from instrumental action. In modern society, however, the taken-for-granted assumptions are increasingly tied to the rationalization of the everyday world because of the reliance on technical rules and scientific knowledge. For example, marriage becomes a contract; family members seek legal redress against each other; education is tied to employment; universities are required to act like businesses; and political debate becomes 30-second sound bites of slogans fueled by vast sums of campaign "donations" (Waters, 1994:165).

Rationalization is in competition with understanding, and social relations are "regulated only through money and power" (Habermas, 1984, 2:154). But "money and power can neither buy nor compel solidarity and meaning" (1984, 2:363). The construction of an ideal speech community to reclaim the right of citizens to determine their own fate becomes imperative, in Habermas's view, in the face of the loss of meaning caused by the rationalization of everyday life.

Humans Communicative competence, to Habermas, is bound up with identity formation. Habermas turned to George Herbert Mead's idea that reason is based on the communicative relations between individuals. That is, identity can only develop in interaction with others, and individuals know themselves only through the eyes of others (1984, 1:390).

Socialization is therefore the internalization of a society's grammatical as well as normative rules governing communication. This internalization occurs, according to Habermas, in four stages of cognitive and moral development.

- The **symbiotic** stage occurs in the first year of life, when the child's dependency means a lack of differentiation from the surrounding world of people and objects.

- The **egocentric** stage begins when the child learns to distinguish self from the surrounding environment of people and objects but judges the significance of that environment in terms of his or her own needs and desires.

- The **sociocentric-objectivist** stage, from about age four to adolescence, involves the child's learning to differentiate the environment of people and objects using complex and abstract symbols and categories. At this stage, the child learns to distinguish objects from their symbolization, and her or his understanding from the understanding of others.

- The **universalistic** stage involves the ability to think abstractly and to reflect critically on the self and its place in the world. At this stage, autonomy, especially from the immediate agents of socialization, is achieved. Also at this stage, altruism prevails as individuals transcend their private needs and desires to take account of communal needs and goals.

Socialization produces "individuals." However, individual identity does not occur as a result of individual efforts, claims Habermas, but as a result of intersubjective recognition (1990:130). In the stages of development, therefore, the most significant one is the development of cognition, the egocentric stage. Cognition is the basis for the development of competent communicative abilities, which in turn produce intersubjective recognition. Communication is therefore not simply about reaching understanding; it is also about social interaction and social integration. Communication involves interactions that "develop, confirm, and renew" an individual's group membership and personal identity. Communication involves not only social interaction and integration but also "processes of interpretation in which cultural knowledge is 'tested against the world'" (Habermas, 1984, 2:139).

According to Habermas, human beings organize themselves in terms of **knowledge-constitutive human interests** as a result of their work and symbolic communication about work activities (1971:311). Three types of knowledge interests guide human action:

- **Technical interests** give humans control over nature and are represented in the social organization of work.

- **Practical interests** enable human beings to act in relation to common traditions and rest on language competence.

- **Emancipatory interests** have to do with power and the need to free human beings from domination by abstract, hypostatized powers.

All of these interests depend on communication. But for the third, emancipatory interest, to be an effective critique of domination, argues Habermas, the communication must meet certain validity criteria.

When individuals communicate, they make validity claims that are either accepted or rejected. Three types of **validity claims** determine whether a communication is understandable:

- An objective scientific claim that the communication is true.

- A normative claim that the communication is in accordance with legal requirements and social norms.

- A subjective, ethical claim that the communication sincerely expresses the individual's feelings.

The intention in communication is to reach a consensus about validity claims, and this is achieved when all speakers have an equal, unconstrained access to the dialogue so that the "force of the better argument" prevails (Habermas, 1984:26).

Habermas recognized that communication could be systematically distorted, either consciously or unconsciously. But whether the communication represents conscious lying and manipulation or unconscious delusion, both speaker and audience assume that the claims made are true, right, and sincere.

Communication and Change For Habermas, the key to social change lies in the development of the ideal speech situation. The ideal speech situation is not a physical place. It is an outline of the "necessary but general conditions for the communicative practice of everyday life" that will enable the participants to realize "concrete possibilities for a better, less threatened life, on *their own* initiative and in accordance with *their own* needs and insights" (1989:69). The ideal speech community is not simply a "talking shop" of endless discussion and interpretation. Emancipatory critique is not arbitrary, but rests on the rational justification of normative statements.

New social movements represent one of the ways in which the ideal speech situation might materialize. Habermas regards contemporary social movements, such as the environmental movement, the peace movement, the gay rights movement, and the women's movement, as sources for emancipatory transformation. These movements are quite unlike the class conflicts of labor and capital because they are concerned with the quality of life, self-realization, and normative expectations. These movements not only protest the domination of capital and state power, but they also develop alternative practices to the rationalized, technological world ruled by money and power.

Habermas's ideal speech situation presupposes that if the correct procedural norms are followed, consensus will be possible because reason will prevail. The outcome will be defensible because it is true, right, and sincere. A key requirement for this ideal situation is that all the participants be free and equal and genuinely desire to reach rational agreement on the issue(s) involved. These requirements may be problematic when race and gender are taken into account, at least in the short term.

Class, Gender, and Race

Class Habermas argues that capitalist society has changed so drastically that the "two key categories of Marxian theory, namely class struggle and ideology, can no longer be employed as they stand" (1971:107). Advanced, state-regulated capitalism suspends class conflict by buying off the workers with improved access to goods and services. The probability that the stark differences between the owners of capital and the nonowners will become more obvious, promoting a revolutionary consciousness among the dispossessed, is circumvented by the glitter of consumer society.

Class distinctions persist, but according to Habermas, they are not central to social conflict. Conflict in modern society involves underprivileged groups who are not classes as such and certainly do not represent the majority in the society. The disenfranchisement and pauperization of groups such as single mothers or homeless youth, "no longer coincides with *exploitation*, because the system does not live off their labor." Although these groups may "react with desperate destruction and self-destruction," as long as they are marginalized from other, more privileged groups in the society, there is little possibility that their protests will translate into general revolutionary action (1971:110). In fact, the state may use these groups to consolidate its power by encouraging potential allies to see them as social misfits, lazy bums, and welfare cheats.

Like the earlier critical theorists, Habermas has abandoned the proletariat as a potentially emancipatory force, and he has problems finding another group to replace them. He also tends to overlook the situation in non-Western countries and the possibility that emancipatory transformation may arise as a result of the obvious inequities of global capitalism. He has suggested that the only truly revolutionary group in Western societies is the women's movement (1971:112).

Gender   Habermas has actually said little about gender in his work, overlooking the gender implications in relations between public and private institutions in capitalist societies. For example, the public economic sphere is linked in Habermas's account to the private sphere of the nuclear family. Exchanges between the family and the economy are "channeled through the 'roles' of worker and consumer." Similarly, the public sphere of politics is linked with the administration system of the state, and the exchanges between the two are linked through the "role" of citizen and, "in late welfare state capitalism, that of client" (Fraser, 1989:123). These "roles" are, however, gendered. For example, the child-rearing role is generally a feminine role that is unpaid but produces the next generation of workers and consumers. Similarly, the role of citizen is frequently compromised by the fact that it is women as single mothers, for example, who comprise the majority of the clients of state welfare.

Critical theory generally needs to be more attuned to the issues of gender. Most especially, the possibility of the emancipatory transformation through the ideal speech situation envisaged by Habermas requires a consideration of the way in which women's voices and opinions can be heard when there has been little change in gender relations. As Fraser (1989:137) puts it, "From a feminist perspective, there is a more basic battle line between the forms of male dominance linking 'system' to 'life world' *and us*."

This battle line is not eased by Habermas's observation that the "historical legacy of the sexual division of labor, to which women were subjected in the nuclear bourgeois family, . . . gives them access to virtues, to a set of values that are both in contrast and complementary to the male world and at odds with the one-sided rationalized praxis of everyday life" (1987, 2:394). Separate but equal, with the suggestion that women's moral superiority can usefully temper male rationality, is hardly a revolutionary or emancipatory observation.

Race   Habermas's work has similar problems of omission with respect to race. Habermas has addressed the issue of race largely in the context of immigration and citizenship issues regarding "guest" workers in Europe. He sees the right-wing opposition to these workers as resting on the idea that they threaten national identity—that different cultural values, religious beliefs, and ethnic identities challenge conceptions of citizenship. Habermas's call for civic-minded debate about social issues is thus compromised by the conflict between legal and ethnic conceptions of citizenship (Pensky, 1995:90).

As Warnke (1995:140) has pointed out, the possibility of normative consensus on issues such as "liberty, equality, sanctity of life, and human rights in general" as a result of participating in the ideal speech situation can still be "impeded by power, wealth, race, or gender" and the coexistence of different cultures. Habermas has not successfully addressed these issues to date.

The importance of these issues can be seen in the vote of a Swiss suburb in March 2000 on the acceptance or rejection of recent immigrant requests for citizenship. In a process that approximated the full information requirement of Habermas's ideal speech community, the voters were give a booklet containing information on the salary, tax status, background, and hobbies as well as family photographs of the individuals seeking citizenship. Out of fifty-six families, only four, all of Italian origin, were accepted. Those rejected were largely of Yugoslavian origin ("Who's Swiss? City Votes Against Most Foreigners," 2000).

Other Theories and Theorists

Habermas's consistent focus throughout his work has been on the relation among reason, modernity, and democracy, with the aim of providing an outline of an emancipated, rational society. Habermas himself has stated that his "research program has remained the same since about 1970" (1993:149). He has pursued the development of a theory of communicative action as the means to continue critical theory's injunction to connect theory and practice.

Critique and Conclusions

The work of Habermas and the earlier critical theorists is predicated on the idea that theory was central to the practical transformation of society. But for Habermas and earlier critical theorists, the revolutionary agent of such transformation was difficult to identify. Critical theory stresses the "importance of fundamental transformation which has little basis in social struggle" but tends to lose sight of "important social and political struggles both within the West and beyond it—struggles which have changed and are continuing to change the face of politics" (Held, 1980:399–400). For example, it is difficult to imagine the possibility or the conditions for the beginnings of free, unconstrained dialogue and discourse among the current ethnic and racially based contenders in Africa, South America, the Balkans, the Middle East, and Asia, let alone the members of politically extreme parties and movements in Western democracies. In fact, Habermas's optimistic, evolutionary assumption that moral consciousness evolves and that norms and values become more universalistic seems unconvincing in the face of the barbarism of the past century.

Habermas's ideal speech community assumes a singular public sphere rather than a multiplicity of publics and carries the implication that democratic politics revolves around a unitary state. But the voices of women, gay activists, and racial and ethnic minorities that are often excluded from formal political structures of debate and dialogue suggest the need to recognize the multiplicity of public spheres. Furthermore, individuals discuss a lot of things in public contexts that do not resemble Habermas's "classical Enlightenment sphere." Such public discussions, taking place in "churches and self-help groups, among filmgoers and on talk-radio, among parents waiting for their children after school dances," are about "childbearing and childrearing, marriage and divorce, violence of various sorts"—everyday topics of immediate concern to the body politic (Calhoun, 1996:460).

Axel van den Berg (1980:476) is scathing in his judgment of the critical theorists, claiming "they have chosen the comfortable heights of philosophical abstraction and obscurity far away from the daily concerns of the rabble" and that "to expect any public support for a philosophy whose only distinction is its sheer obscurity, for a notion of reason lacking all substance, for a utopia without any indication of its features or feasibility has absolutely nothing to do with emancipation of any kind." In fact, however, Habermas's intentions are somewhat more modest than the grand utopian solution against which van den Berg takes aim.

Habermas sees critical theory that is true to its Marxist origins as providing the means to analyze the abstractions of social life that conceal the real relations of exploitation and domination. To accomplish this, the analysis must concentrate on the "grammar of forms of life" (Habermas, 1984, 2:576). Habermas sees critical theory as therefore true to the origins of sociology.

> *Sociology* originated as a discipline responsible for the problems that politics and economics pushed to one side. . . . Its theme was the changes in social integration brought about within the structure of old-European societies by the rise of the modern system of nation states and by the differentiation of a market regulated economy. Sociology became the science of crisis par excellence; it concerned itself above all with the anomic aspects of all the dissolution of traditional social systems and the development of modern ones. (1984, 1:4)

Critical theory's importance remains clear, in Habermas's view, because the legacy of National Socialism lives on in European neoconservatism and neo-Nazism (1989).

Final Thoughts

Sociology, as a critical theoretical enterprise, still has a place in the twenty-first century. The global crises that threaten the freedom of citizens, the fragility of democratic institutions in the face of global market forces, and the various siren calls for ideological purity in the name of a race, religion, or nation, all need to be critically and publicly analyzed. Sociology is a critical resource at the individual level also in its analysis of the everyday/everynight threats to human dignity and self-esteem. There are no guarantees, no "ultimate redemption" guaranteed by the "laws of history," but redemption remains, as Habermas puts it, a "practical hypothesis" from which a critical sociology can start (McCarthy, 1989:xiv).

References

Adorno, Theodor. 1984. *Aesthetic Theory* (C. Lenhardt, Trans.). London: Routledge and Kegan Paul.

Adorno, Theodor, Else Frenkel-Brunswik, Daniel J. Levison, and R. Nevitt Sanford. 1950. *The Authoritarian Personality*. New York: Harper.

Adorno, Theodor, and Max Horkheimer. 1944/1979. *Dialectic of Enlightenment*. London: Verso.

Agger, Ben. 1979. *Western Marxism: An Introduction*. Santa Monica, CA: Goodyear Publishing Company.

Alford, Fred, C. 1987. "Habermas, Post-Freudian Psychoanalysis and the End of the Individual." *Theory, Culture and Society, 4*(1), 3–29.

Ashenden, Samantha. 1999. "Questions of Criticism: Habermas and Foucault on Civil Society and Resistance." In Samantha Ashenden and David Owen (Eds.), *Foucault Contra Habermas*. London: Sage.

Benhabib, Seyla. 1986. *Critique, Norm, and Utopia*. New York: Columbia University Press.

Bernstein, Richard J. (Ed.). 1985. *Habermas and Modernity*. Cambridge, MA: MIT Press.

Calhoun, Craig. 1996. "Social Theory and the Public Sphere." In Bryan S. Turner (Ed.), *Social Theory* (pp. 429–470). Oxford: Blackwell.

Delanty, Gerard. 1997. "Habermas and Occidental Rationalism: The Politics of Identity, Social Learning, and the Cultural Limits of Moral Individualism." *Sociological Theory, 15*(1), 30–59.

Fraser, Nancy. 1989. *Unruly Practices: Power, Discourse and Gender in Contemporary Social Theory*. Minneapolis: University of Minnesota Press.

Fromm, Erich. 1941. *Excerpt from Freedom*. New York: Holt, Rinehart and Winston.

———. 1955. *The Sane Society*. New York: Holt, Rinehart and Winston.

———. 1960. *The Fear of Freedom*. London: Routledge and Kegan Paul.

———. 1965/1981. *On Disobedience and Other Essays*. New York: Seabury Press.

———. 1979/1980. *The Greatness and Limitations of Freud's Thought*. New York: Harper and Row.

———. 1988. "The Method and Function of an Analytic Social Psychology." In Andrew Arato and Eike Gebhardt (Eds.), *The Essential Frankfurt Reader* (pp. 477–496). New York: Continuum.

Habermas, Jurgen. 1970. *Towards a Rational Society* (Jeremy J. Shapiro, Trans.). London: Heinemann.

———. 1971. *Knowledge and Human Interests* (Jeremy Shapiro, Trans.). Boston: Beacon Press.

———. 1974. *Theory and Practice* (John Viertel, Trans.). London: Heinemann.

———. 1976. *Legitimation Crisis* (Thomas McCarthy, Trans.). London: Heinemann.

———. 1984. *The Theory of Communicative Action* (vol. 1) (Thomas McCarthy, Trans.). Boston: Beacon Press.

———. 1987. *The Theory of Communicative Action* (vol. 2) (Thomas McCarthy, Trans.). Boston: Beacon Press.

———. 1989. *The New Conservatism* (Shierry Weber Nicholsen, Ed. and Trans.). Cambridge, MA: MIT Press.

———. 1990. *Moral Consciousness and Communicative Action* (Christine Lenhardt and Sherry Weber Nicholsen, Trans.). Cambridge, MA: MIT Press.

———. 1993. *Justification and Application: Remarks on Discourse Ethics* (Ciaran P. Cronin, Trans.). Cambridge, MA: MIT Press.

Held, David. 1980. *Introduction to Critical Theory*. London: Hutchinson.

Horkheimer, Max. 1935/1993. *Between Philosophy and Social Science* (C. Frederick Hunter, Matthew S. Kramer, and John Torpey, Trans.). Cambridge, MA: MIT Press.

———. 1947. *The Eclipse of Reason*. New York: Oxford University Press.

———. 1974. *Critique of Instrumental Reason*. New York: Seabury Press.

———. 1982. *Critical Theory: Selected Essays*. New York: Continuum.

Jagentowicz Mills, Patricia. 1987. *Woman, Nature and Psyche*. New Haven, CT: Yale University Press.

Jay, Martin. 1973. *The Dialectical Imagination: A History of the Frankfurt School and the Institute of Social Research 1923–1950*. Boston: Little, Brown.

Kellner, Douglas. 1989. *Critical Theory: Marxism and Modernity*. Baltimore: Johns Hopkins University Press.

Lukacs, George. 1922/1968. *History and Class Consciousness*. Cambridge, MA: MIT Press.

Marcuse, Herbert. 1960. *Reason and Revolution*. Boston: Beacon Press.

———. 1964. *One-Dimensional Man*. Boston: Beacon Press.

———. 1966. *Eros and Civilization*. Boston: Beacon Press.

———. 1970. *Five Lectures: Psychoanalysis, Politics, and Utopia*. Boston: Beacon Press.

———. 1972. *Counterrevolution and Revolt*. Boston: Beacon Press.

McCarthy, Thomas. 1989. "Introduction." In Jurgen Habermas, *The Structural Transformation of the Public Sphere* (pp. xi–xiv) (T. Burger and F. Lawrence, Trans.). Cambridge: Polity Press.

Outhwaite, William. 1994. *Habermas: A Critical Introduction*. Stanford, CA: Stanford University Press.

Pensky, Max. 1995. "Universalism and the Situated Critic." In Stephen K. White (Ed.), *The Cambridge Companion to Habermas* (pp. 67–94). Cambridge: Cambridge University Press.

van den Berg, Axel. 1980. "Critical Theory: Is There Still Hope?" *American Journal of Sociology, 86,* 449–478.

Warnke, Georgia. 1995. "Communicative Rationality and Cultural Values." In Stephen K. White (Ed.), *The Cambridge Companion to Habermas* (pp. 120–142). Cambridge: Cambridge University Press.

Waters, Malcolm. 1994. *Modern Sociological Theory*. London: Sage.

White, Stephen K. (Ed.). 1995. *The Cambridge Companion to Habermas*. Cambridge: Cambridge University Press.

"Who's Swiss? City Votes Against Most Foreigners." 2000, March 13. *Globe and Mail,* pp. 1, 3.

Wiggershaus, Rolf. 1994. *The Frankfurt School* (Michael Robertson, Trans.). Oxford: Polity Press.

Wuthnow, Robert, James Davison Hunter, Albert Bergesen, and Edith Kurweil (Eds.). 1984. *Cultural Analysis*. Boston: Routledge and Kegan Paul.

Chapter 17

Marxism Since 1930
Poulantzas, Althusser, Dunayevskaya, and Wright

Struggles for freedom continue, whether by workers experiencing near depression levels of unemployment, women confronting attacks on their right to control their own bodies and minds, black people and other minorities combating resurgent racism, or youth protesting environmental destruction, militarism and a decaying educational system. . . .

How, then, can it be that despite the persistence of such aspirations for freedom, we are witnessing a breakdown in the effort to articulate a concept, a goal, an *idea* of human liberation that speaks to the realities of our time?

Part of the reason lies in the fact that all too many revolutionaries failed to grasp the *class* divide separating Marx's Marxism from its absolute opposite, Communist totalitarianism. (Hudis, 1992:viii)

What has become of Marxism at the turn of the twenty-first century? Did it die with the Soviet Union? Is it on the defensive, regrouping, purifying, or explaining its theory? Is it still waiting for capitalism to self-destruct, or is it merely an academic discourse? In this chapter we will attempt to speak to these issues as we follow Marxist theory and practice from Lenin's death to the twenty-first century. We will begin with a brief review of Marxism, as presented in Chapters 5 and 6, then discuss a series of theoretical issues, and close the chapter with a look at Erik Olin Wright's contemporary Marxism.

An outstanding two-volume work, *A History of Marxian Economics*, edited by Howard and King and published in 1992, summarized classical orthodox Marxism-Leninism. By 1900, the central pillars of Marxism were three: First, capital was being concentrated in ever larger and more powerful economic units. This led "to a rising rate of exploitation and to the relative (if not absolute) immiseration of a rapidly increasing and class-conscious proletariat." Second, "economic crises were inescapable under capitalism and would tend to become more severe." This resulted not just from exploitation, but from the inherent contradictions within capitalism. "Third, and as a consequence of all this, capitalism itself was ripe for replacement." A corollary to this third proposition was that "socialism offered a viable, and in every way preferable, alternative to the capitalist mode of production" (Howard and King, 1992:387).

Somewhat later, in the writings of Lenin and Luxemburg, a fourth claim was advanced: "Theories of imperialism asserted that the struggle for economic territory was the fundamental impulse behind the political and military rivalries of the various capitalist states" (Howard and King, 1992:387). The other addition to Marxism in the early twentieth century was the existence of an avowedly Marxist state—the Soviet Union.

Marxism from 1930 to 1980

Since 1930, many important world events have needed interpretation: the Great Depression of the 1930s in the United States and much of the world, the Second World War, the political independence of former colonies, the spread of transnational corporations, and the eventual fall of Marxism in the Soviet bloc countries. "Uneven development entailed the underdevelopment of backward and dependent, or Third World, regions and not . . . their rapid assimilation as more or less equal partners in the world system" (Howard and King, 1992:388). Thus, the language used to describe Third World countries changed from "developing" to "underdeveloped."

In addition, the safeguards produced by capitalism itself—such as the federal reserve system—have at least called into question the potential severity of economic crises. Although the crisis principle has not been completely rejected, it is being debated by Marxists today. Likewise, the notion that capitalism is ripe for overthrow also seems questionable. This is not simply because of the capitalist world's military might, which Marx and Engels recognized, or because of **false consciousness**—the identification of the oppressed with the system that oppresses them. It is also because capitalism continues to "deliver the goods." Even relative immiseration is hard to recognize in the advanced capitalist countries, though it can certainly be found in the Third World (Howard and King, 1992:388).

As for capitalist conflicts and socialism's readiness to take over (as it supposedly did in Russia), two issues have arisen. On the one hand, U.S. economic and military dominance after 1945 produced a new (capitalist) world order, and on the other hand, the Stalinist model of socialist development failed to live up to its own Marxist ideology, in Russia and elsewhere (Dunayevskaya, 1958; Howard and King, 1992:389). In the face of all these changes, critics have been only too eager to announce Marxism's demise.

In this chapter we will examine at length some of the major currents in Marxism since 1930, closing with Erik Olin Wright's "no frills" Marxism in which ideology and utopia are minimized. Wright's analytical Marxism is important because it embodies a broad spectrum of today's academic Marxism, the "Left Academy," which in the past 30 years has attempted to give Marxism intellectual credibility, while not succumbing either to the glorification of communist states or to defeatism in confronting the capitalist world order.

Central Theories and Methods of Post-1930s Marxism

In this section we will examine several important Marxist theoretical concepts developed during the period between 1930 and 1980, approximately in the order in which they appeared. Several of them, such as hegemony, in the 1930s, and the state and structuralism, in the 1960s, were discussed in ways that emphasized their complexity. Next, the concept of state capitalism sought to explain the non-Marxist nature of the Soviet Union and Eastern Bloc states, while the concept of monopoly capitalism built on Thorstein Veblen and Lenin in demonstrating the large-scale, neo-imperialistic nature of modern capitalism. We will close this section with several miscellaneous but valuable Marxist insights.

Hegemony **Hegemony** is leadership, or authority. According to Marx, throughout human history hegemony has been determined by control of the means of production and exploitation of the workers. For Vilfredo Pareto (Chapter 9), such hegemony was a matter for the political ruling elite. However, the key figure in an expanded twentieth-century Marxist understanding of hegemony was Antonio Gramsci, an Italian who lived from 1889 to 1937. Gramsci joined the Italian Communist Party in 1913, and throughout the rest of his life was a dedicated Marxist revolutionary. He was in prison for more than a decade at the end of his life, having questioned Mussolini's fascist control over Italy. He was also critical of Stalin's government in Russia, and, of course, of capitalism. While in prison, he produced his most important theoretical writings, despite long periods of ill health (Gramsci, 1937).

For Gramsci, hegemony was not just structural domination through economics or politics. It was a combination of political, intellectual, and moral leadership (Mouffe, 1979:179), meaning that it involved superstructure or ideology and private institutions as well as politics. While dictatorship may or may not be one element, wrote commentator Jacques Texier, Gramsci's formulations were important

> precisely because they stress the unity of consensus and dictatorship. This is the case with the definition of the **integral state** as follows: "State = political society + civil society, in other words, hegemony protected by the armour of coercion." A social group exercises its hegemony over subordinate social groups which accept its rule so long as it exercises its dictatorship over the hostile social groups which reject it. (Texier, 1979:64, quoting Gramsci, 1937:263)

Hegemony, then, is exercised through the commitment of those who are persuaded and through control of any opposition.

The hegemonic apparatus of a society includes, according to Gramsci, "schools, churches, the entire media and even architecture and the names of streets" (1937:332). Hegemony, then, involves persuasion or consensus, as well as coercion. Leadership and power have to be explained as they function in the "real world," not in some simplified economic or political portion of it (Paggi, 1979:138). And hegemony in the real world involves creation of a higher synthesis, a general interest or collective will (Mouffe, 1979:184, 194). Note that Gramsci was not saying that the hegemony of those in power is the general interest, but that it incorporates ideology, institutions, and power in order to appear that it is.

What can the working classes do to offset such broad-scale hegemony by the bourgeoisie? In Gramsci's view, it is

> vital for the working class not to isolate itself within a ghetto of proletarian purism. On the contrary, it must try to become a "national class," representing the interests of the increasingly numerous social groups. In order to do this it must cause the disintegration of the historical bases of the bourgeoisie's hegemony by disarticulating the ideological bloc by means of which the bourgeoisie's intellectual direction is expressed. (Mouffe, 1979:197)

This process is much more complex and difficult to effect than the working-class uprising described and preached by early Marxists. Gramsci thus sought to reincorporate ideological issues into the Marxist discussion of bourgeois control and proletariat revolution.

State Capitalism   In the early twentieth century, Luxemburg criticized Lenin's centralized Russia (see Chapter 6). But by the 1940s, Marxist criticisms of the Soviet Union as not having lived up to its supposed embodiment of communist thought had increased dramatically. If Stalin's totalitarian regime exemplified Marxism in action, capitalist ideologues needed to do very little to discredit it, except to point out its characteristic failings. In the early 1940s, Raya Dunayevskaya, formerly the Russian-language secretary to Leon Trotsky, began to describe the Soviet Union not as a Marxist state, but as "State-Capitalism." This was, of course, 50 years before Russia gave up the trappings of Marxist ideology in favor of capitalism.

When Dunayevskaya began writing about the Soviet Union, it was still being held up by Marxists as an example—albeit an imperfect one—of a Marxist state. Even during the radical activity of the "New Left" in the 1960s, criticism of Russia was often muted. Peter Hudis, in introducing Dunayevskaya's book, wrote that the '60s radicals were convinced that their effectiveness would make it possible to pick up Marxist theory on the way to the revolution. "This skipping over of theory," noted Hudis, "only made it easier for the New Left to fall into the trap" of glorifying a nation-state "masquerading as Communism, since the Stalinist rulers continued to use 'Marxist' language" (Hudis, 1992:xx).

When Lenin's Bolshevik party took over the government as the vanguard of a proletarian dictatorship, he claimed that he was carrying out Marxist doctrine. When he instituted the New Economic Policy of a mixed economy as a necessity, he argued that it would eventually wither away into true communism. And when Stalin transformed the Soviet Union into a bureaucratized totalitarian state, he defended the necessity of "purification"—of getting rid of the misguided.

However, Dunayevskaya claimed in the 1940s that the Soviet Union was never really Marxist, and certainly not communist. To understand it, she suggested, one had to combine the realities of (1) Lenin's party dictatorship, (2) Russia's mixed economy, and (3) Stalin's bureaucratic totalitarian state, while (4) ignoring the Marxist "smoke-screen." Dunayevskaya carried out a meticulous analysis of the Russian economy in 1942–43 and carried it further in 1946–47 (Dunayevskaya, 1951:35–82). In these analyses, she noted the ownership of property by the state, the surplus value being extracted by the state intelligentsia, the "fight for profit," and the class system of the Soviet Union. Connecting her analysis back to Marx's *Capital* (Volume 3), she concluded that the Soviet Union was simply **State-Capitalism**, far removed from Marx's theory. The Soviet bureaucracy was, in fact, the "bodyguard of capital," making it an "absolute contradiction" between theory and practice. Such state-capitalism was not the highest stage of capitalism in its contradictions; it was "the *transformation* of monopoly capitalism into its opposite" (Dunayevskaya, 1951:98).

On this view, the Soviet Union did not *become* capitalist at the beginning of the 1990s; it simply confessed to what it already was. It had been a combination of socialism and capitalism since its inception, and had become more so during Stalin's time.

Monopoly Capitalism and Imperialism   Two key figures in twentieth-century U.S. Marxism were Paul Baran and Paul Sweezy. Both were born in 1910, the former in Russia and the latter in New York City. They met in the early 1940s at Harvard, and began their long collaboration. The centerpiece of their collaboration was the best-selling book *Monopoly Capital*, which appeared in 1966, two years after Baran's death.

The first major issue for Baran and Sweezy concerned underconsumption and waste. Observing a lengthy post–World War II growth in capitalist production, Baran, and later Sweezy, reported that capitalism's problem is that so much of its productive capacity is wasted on the military (recall Luxemburg), on advertising, and on product differentiation. Despite Marx's observation about capitalism's need for new, esoteric goods and services, Baran saw much of the supposed boom as using up or wasting profits. Recalling Veblen's discussion of waste (Chapter 10), Baran and Sweezy criticized capitalism for wasting instead of promoting a higher standard of living for the masses.

As the economic boom of the 1940s and 1950s began to wane, and especially as former colonies became politically independent, Baran and Sweezy turned their attention to underdevelopment in the Third World. Using terms such as *neo-imperialism* and *neocolonialism*, Baran noted that economic neo-imperialism has "effortlessly replaced colonial [political] control and brought about sustained underdevelopment. Surplus continues to be drained off, principally through the repatriation of profits from foreign" investments in the Third World (Howard and King, 1992:171). Even the class structures of such peripheral societies, which are primarily proletarian, are products of neo-imperialism. Advanced capitalist societies dominate not only by investment, but by their control of technological expertise and of money through the World Bank, International Monetary Fund, and other sources. **Monopoly capitalism** includes all of this.

Though it was not central to their argument, Baran and Sweezy took note of racism when they connected Third World peoples with the marginalized peoples of the advanced capitalist societies. Looked at worldwide, they observed that race is highly correlated with class, meaning that the revolution, when it comes, will involve both.

Sweezy's Marxist enthusiasm eventually changed its focus from Eastern Europe and Russia to Cuba. Although Baran died too soon after the Cuban revolution to follow Sweezy's lead, it is possible he might never have done so. Baran's "traditional Marxist contempt for the peasantry" and his allegiance to heavy industry as central to the socialist revolution might have kept him from ever viewing the Third World as a primary locus of revolution (Howard and King, 1992:175). In fact, unlike Dunayevskaya, Baran was so impressed by the command or socialist economies of Russia, Eastern Europe, and China that at his death he was still convinced that neither capitalist reform nor peasant uprising could accomplish what could be done by a centrally planned industrial politico-economic system.

Once North American Marxism turned away from the underconsumption argument, in only "two respects did the ideas of Baran and Sweezy have a more permanent impact upon Marxian economics throughout the world. This was in their treatment of armaments expenditure . . . and in their theory of underdevelopment in the Third World" (Howard and King, 1992:124).

The last important issue in monopoly capitalism is imperialism and the multinationals. Present-day Marxism takes two views of capitalism and development. The older view, found in some parts of Marx's own writing, is that capitalism creates the material preconditions for a better (socialist) society, as well as the class forces that will bring it about. This is the classical Marxist position stating that society must pass through a capitalist phase on the way to socialism. The second, more recent, view is that "it is precisely the failure of capitalism to generate economic development that makes revolution necessary," especially in the Third World (Brewer, 1980:16). This second position is found in the work of Immanuel Wallerstein, who argues, as we will see in Chapter 18, that capitalism is now a world system, with some nations at the core and others on the periphery. (On these two versions of Marxism, see Blomstrom and Hettne, 1984:33–38.)

An important feature of imperialism today, as Baran and Sweezy noted, is the multinational or transnational corporation—a result of the centralization and then the internationalization of capital. Manufacturing where there is cheap labor, and distribution close to the markets, make it rational to locate enterprises in more than one setting, sometimes in several advanced societies, and sometimes also in less developed countries. Some have argued that multinationals indicate a lessening of the importance of the nation-state. However, Anthony Brewer and Nicos Poulantzas assert that, although national economies may be less relevant, "this is quite different from arguing the irrelevance of the national governments as a site of class conflict, of political integration, and of a state apparatus that has at its command more potent weapons than those of monetary and fiscal policy" (Brewer, 1980:279). In short, "capital that operates internationally needs the support of a home state to protect its interests" (1980:280).

Marx and Engels wrote at a time of relative peace among the advanced capitalist nations. Engels, for example, witnessed the Berlin conference of 1885, in which Africa was carved up into colonies by the European powers. Lenin and

Luxemburg, on the other hand, wrote during World War I, when these same nations were at each other's throats. The present "world order" under U.S. dominance seems to again represent capitalism's "peaceful" hegemony, with conflicts concentrated largely in the Third World or involving ethnic rivalries.

Before the turn of the twentieth century, transport improved, organizational forms made the international flow of capital easier, and the international transfer of technology became possible. A century later, the computer has advanced the technology of communication even more dramatically, potentially making core dominance—economic and military—over the periphery easier than ever. However, underdevelopment does not necessarily support or strengthen neo-imperialism. The other two potential outcomes are increasing capitalist development in the periphery, or socialist/communist revolution.

So far, we have looked at Gramsci's theory of hegemony, Dunayevskaya's view of the Soviet Union as state capitalism, and twentieth-century monopoly capitalism as expressed particularly in economic neo-imperialism. We come now to Poulantzas's view of the state in relation to Marxism.

Poulantzas and State Power   Nicos Poulantzas was born in Athens and in 1968 joined the faculty at the Sorbonne in Paris. Perhaps more than any other late-twentieth-century Marxist, Poulantzas developed a Marxist theory of the state. Although his thousands of words on this subject were not always consistent, it is possible to bring together and summarize his key ideas: "as his work developed during the 1970s, Poulantzas increasingly emphasized the nature of the state as a system of *strategic selectivity* and the nature of political struggle as a field of *competing strategies for hegemony*," or dominance and control (Jessop, 1990:221).

Marx's and Engels's theory of the state was primarily that it is the mechanism (structure) whereby the owners of the means of production rule a society. Others had treated the state as little more than the expression of control in a society, or, as Gramsci put it, an expression of both political and ideational hegemony. For Poulantzas the **state** is even more complex:

> a *strategic field and process* of intersecting power networks, which both articulate and exhibit mutual contradictions and displacements. . . . This strategic field is traversed by tactics which are often highly explicit at the restricted level of their inscription in the State: they intersect and conflict with one another, finding their targets in some apparatuses or being short-circuited by others, and eventually map out that general line of force, the State's "policy," which traverses confrontations within the State (1978:136)

Poulantzas went on to say that these tactics are not merely detachable and oppositional parts. They exhibit a unity of state power, which is both unified and contains inconsistencies. One, but only one, of the inconsistencies involves class interests, to which we shall return. To follow Poulantzas, we must discard the view of the state as completely unified.

Demonstrating his ability to explain complexity, Poulantzas noted that the state is more than a combination of repression and ideological false consciousness. Even fascist or totalitarian societies must control unemployment and introduce social legislation to meet the needs of the population (1978:31). In fact, Poulantzas argued that even from the micro-political standpoint, much state behavior is incoherent and chaotic (1978:135).

Furthermore, the state apparatus includes more than state power: it includes everything from the postal service to the road system. Such services are not, of course, independent of power, because those in power need such mechanisms themselves. "Thus, while all the State's actions are not reducible to political domination, their composition is nevertheless marked by it" (1978:14). In summary, then, for Poulantzas the state was neither completely unified nor free-standing. It was, rather, a complex mixture of class and group struggles, including ideological and economic issues, interest group goals and desires, services, and cross-national connections.

Poulantzas (1978) also laid out the relations among state, nation, language group, and class. Noting that there was no Marxist theory of the nation, he argued that the nation, defined by its territory, preceded both capitalism and the modern state. Moreover, it will outlast capitalism: The state will wither away, but not necessarily the nation. Language groupings overlap imperfectly with the state, although modern "nation-states" work very hard—legally and otherwise—to construct national languages. Whether it be Hindi in India or English in the United States, there are state- and power-based reasons for constructing a dominant language, a language of government and education.

The state and its power, then, were Poulantzas's central theoretical interest. Breaking out of the mold of both dogmatic Marxism and Louis Althusser's structuralism (discussed next), he was willing to deal with complexity, to admit that state, power, and economic classes overlap but are not synonymous. This was a major contribution to Marxist thought.

Althusser's Marxist Structuralism   Defining **structuralism,** Edith Kurzweil asserted that "ultimately all social reality" is "the interplay of the as yet unconscious mental structures" (1980:4). Based primarily on the work of the French anthropologist Claude Levi-Strauss, structuralism was adopted by French psychoanalysts, linguists, sociologists, and even Marxists. It dominated French scholarship from the 1950s into the 1970s, and even though it waned after that, structuralist language continued to be used.

Most of Louis Althusser's Marxist structuralism was published in the 1960s, especially in two books: *For Marx* (1965) and, with Etienne Balibar, *Reading Capital* (1968). A key aspect of Althusser's thought was separating Marx's writings into four periods: "1840–1844: the Early Works; 1845: the Works of the Break; 1846–1857: the Transitional Works; and 1857–1883: the Mature Works" (Althusser, 1965:35). In so doing, Althusser was able to downplay the importance of Marx's early humanistic concerns—"alienation, the abstraction (in the Hegelian sense) that unites the opposites, the negation of the negation"—and simplified economic determinism (Althusser, 1965:199). The "mature Marx," according to Althusser, should be the focus of attention and theory 100 years after Marx's death.

Of what did the mature Marx consist, according to Althusser? Society is a "structured whole," consisting of complex mental and physical conditions. This complexity includes the contradictions of which Marx spoke. These contradictions constitute the

> conditions of existence. As an example, take the complex structured whole that is society. In it, the "relations of production" are not the pure phenomenon of the forces of production; they are also their condition of existence. The superstructure is not the pure phenomenon of the structure, it is also its condition of existence. (Althusser, 1965:205)

Such complexity includes structures of dominance or hegemony (a concept for which Althusser gave Gramsci credit), uneven development, economics, politics, and superstructure or ideology (Althusser, 1965:114, 217). Calling himself a scientific Marxist rather than a structuralist, Althusser rejected humanistic Marxism, simplified "upside-down" Hegelianism, the notion of the inevitable revolution growing out of capitalism, historically specific Marxism related to a single time and place (such as Italy in the 1930s), and, as we have noted, simple economic determinism. He also rejected the notion of mental continuity (Levi-Strauss) and of change growing out of equilibrium (functionalism). Rather, he argued that the structural complexity and unevenness of capitalism must be understood and not simplified, and the revolution must be prepared for and organized (Kurzweil, 1980:36).

According to François Dosse, it was Poulantzas's 1968 work on power and the state that brought Althusser to the attention of the French intelligentsia and other Marxists. Poulantzas argued that Althusser's insights included criticism of two "misreadings of Marx: the one historical, and the other economist." The historical mistake was in a simplified viewing of social class as the subject of history. Class is but one portion of societal complexity, one bearer of social structure. The other misreading of Marx reduced classes to relations of production. Poulantzas, expanding Althusser into the realm of power and the state, had, according to one commentator, "the merit of proposing a new way of thinking about power conceived of as a vast and encompassing strategic realm, a far more complex approach than the usual references to a state-class instrument" (Dosse, 1967:173).

Althusser's attempt to both purify and complexify Marxism began to wane almost as soon as it became popular. French demonstrations and riots in 1968 received little support from Althusser, which left him open to criticism by other French Marxists. Even more important, in 1974 Althusser wrote *Elements of a Self-Criticism*. In this book, he stated that he had overemphasized ideology or the structure of ideas: "Our 'flirtation' with structuralist terminology certainly went beyond acceptable limits" (1974:57).

What, then, was Althusser's contribution? "By complexifying Marx's work, paying the price of a system of rigorous, synthetic [structural] thinking that wanted to totalize, Althusser managed to stave off Marxism's decline—a random spark . . . [in a] century in which Marxism was to lose itself in its fatal destiny, in the tragedy of totalitarianism" (Dosse, 1967:188).

Technology, Functionalism, Rational Choice: G. A. Cohen and Others In Chapter 5, we noted that one oversimplification of Marx leads to economic or technological determinism. G. A. Cohen, in his analytic and quasi-functionalist reformulation of historical materialism, comes close to this oversimplification.

Central to history, according to Cohen, are productive forces and technological change, founded on three premises: (1) humans are somewhat rational; (2) human history is one of scarcity; and (3) human intelligence enables us to improve our situation (1978:152). As a whole, this means that human beings have the capacity to solve scarcity problems. Production is only one pole of the solution, however; distribution is the other.

The other two elements in Cohen's thinking, both of them tied to the three premises noted above, are functionalism and rational choice. To Cohen, class oppression, not just differentiation, is necessary to the growth of surplus, because some people have to make other people work. The nonproducers have to see to it that the producers produce a surplus. At early historical stages, the surplus was not yet such that all could survive comfortably. It is only at what Cohen called "stage 4" that the surplus is sufficient for redistribution to be "functional" for everyone's comfortable survival.

Cohen spent two full chapters of his book explaining functionalism in general and then Marxist functionalism. The functional explanation of a societal ritual, for example, might explain what it does for a people, without stating that some other ritual might not meet the same need (Cohen, 1978:276). Thus, one can state the function of something without explaining it by referring to its function (1978:283). Cohen, like Robert Merton, questioned whether functional explanation is inherently ideologically conservative. Cohen argued that not only class oppression but class conflict may be historically functional, in the sense of meeting an important societal need for change and equality.

As for rationality, Cohen is one of several rational choice Marxists. Sometimes referred to as "analytical Marxism," this strand of theorizing begins with Cohen's premise that humans are at least somewhat rational. This school of thought, which arose and grew in the 1970s and 1980s, has three main features:

> First, rational choice Marxists have shown a concern for rigour and clarity to a degree unusual in Marxian theory. . . . Second, . . . the concepts and ideas of non-Marxists have figured prominently, and especially those of analytical philosophy, mathematical model-building, modern psychology and neoclassical economics. . . . Although critical . . . of Marx's central claims, rational choice Marxists have frequently demonstrated that much of his analysis is correct, and that this can be demonstrated by using non-Marxian theory.
>
>   Third, there is a pronounced tendency to deduce Marxian propositions about socio-economic systems from the rational behaviour of decision-makers. It is this feature which makes analytical Marxists also rational choice Marxists. (Howard and King, 1992:335)

Cohen, John Roemer, and Jon Elster are important figures in this school of Marxist thought. However, Cohen has contributed little except his statement of the principle of rationality. Roemer, whose major concern is not history but values and ethics, argues that the distribution of property is more central to capitalism than is labor exploitation (Roemer, 1986). It is property and, as Cohen noted, technology about which choices are made, and on which capitalism is based. Roemer and Elster both depart from Marx in their **methodological individualism**, meaning that explanation is always in terms of individual, rather than class or nation-state, actions. Such micro-level explanation, depending on the choices individuals make in society, is said to be the foundation for understanding societal action and change.

Since Roemer reduces explanation to the individual level, one is left to wonder if theory or explanation actually requires one further reduction—to the biological level. Of course, Marxists do not make this final reduction. Besides, Roemer and Elster do not consistently reduce explanation to the individual, and Elster notes that individual decisions are often governed by Darwinian evolutionary processes and group norms (Elster, 1985, chap. 1).

However, these theorists argue that structuralist explanations, like those of Louis Althusser and Nicos Poulantzas, restrict individual choice to the point that it is virtually inconsequential. Cohen's writing, discussing as it does both functionalism and rational choice, bridges the gap between societal structures and the individual will, showing that neither should be carried so far as to become a caricature. It is worth noting that these theorists seldom refer to Marxists other than Marx himself, and they often correct his logic. Finally, Chapter 21 will expand on the theme of rational choice as an important late-twentieth-century non-Marxist theoretical position.

This section has covered a broad spectrum of twentieth-century Marxist perspectives. Dunayevskaya criticized the Soviet Union as not being Marxist at all, but as state capitalism. Baran and Sweezy carried the theory of monopoly capitalism and imperialism beyond Veblen's and Lenin's early-twentieth-century views. Gramsci presented his complex view of hegemony, which was then employed by Althusser in his structuralist theory, and by Poulantzas in his theory of state power. Finally, Cohen and others added technological determinism, functionalism, and rational choice to Marxist thought.

Nature of Society, Humans, and Change

Marxism has been consistent over the past 150 years in its views of society and change. *Capitalist society* is seen as exploitative and coercive. However, according to Gramsci and Althusser, its exploitation is a complex mix of political domination, control over economic production and property, and ideological hegemony. Its oppressive character means that it requires change—a change involving revolution, not just gradual, continuous evolution. Present-day Marxists disagree on the likelihood, location, and timing of the revolution, but they continue to argue for its necessity.

It is much too simple to say that Marxists today believe that human nature is good. Rather, human nature, according to Gramsci, is the "complex of social relations." This, he says,

> is the most satisfying answer because it includes the idea of becoming . . .
> and because it denies "man in general." Indeed, social relations are expressed by various groups of men which each presupposes the others and
> whose unity is dialectical, not formal. Man is aristocratic in so far as man is
> a serf, etc. (1937:355)

In other words, *human nature* is defined by one's membership in society, in relation to other humans. This is somewhat reminiscent of Cooley, Mead, and even Merton.

To Althusser, human nature is freedom. "It is the essence of man just as weight is the essence of bodies" (1965:224). Thus, the oppression of humans goes against human nature. Existence under capitalism is "man dispossessed, alienated." Liberal reform is not enough; human nature requires "the revolt of man against his inhuman conditions" (1965:226). The essence of humanity is freedom, which can only be achieved by the overthrow of an inhuman, oppressive society.

Class, Gender, and Race

Class, gender, and race have all been important to Marxists, generally in descending order of importance.

Class   As a major issue in Marxist theory, class was referred to often in the "Central Theories" section of this chapter. Here we will look at class in the writings of Poulantzas, for whom this topic was a second major focus of attention (after state power).

Poulantzas disagreed with classic Marxism that classes can be "in-themselves" and later become "for-themselves." Classes are, by their nature, for themselves; that is, they are self-aware, and exist only in and for the class struggle (Poulantzas, 1974:14). Furthermore, much of the state apparatus (though not all) is also a function of class. This apparatus includes repression (police, prisons, army); ideological institutions (religious, media, educational, entertainment); conservative trade unions; and even monogamous bourgeois families (recalling Engels). Of course, the most direct aspects of class domination are the elements that Marx himself discussed: means and relations of production.

Poulantzas noted, as did Joseph Schumpeter (Chapter 10), that individuals occupy places within a class structure. However, while Schumpeter's interest was in how aptitude determines one's class position, for Poulantzas individual position is secondary to the reproduction and continuation of the class system itself (Poulantzas, 1974:28–29).

The single most important contribution of Poulantzas to class theory is found in his discussion of the **petit bourgeoisie.** You will recall that in classic Marxism the petit bourgeoisie were the owner-workers, who both own and work their own means of production. However, according to Poulantzas, the new petit bourgeoisie are what non-Marxists might call the lower middle class. This group results from the decomposition in capitalism of the role of entrepreneur into two separate roles: creator-owner, on the one hand, and clerks and service workers, on the other. These wage earners lack both ownership and control, and the criterion used to distinguish them is the lack of power and authority, in Max Weber's sense of those terms. What they have in common with the old petit bourgeoisie is that they are neither bourgeoisie nor proletariat.

One criticism of Marxism is that the rise of the middle class means that Marx's two-class opposition is not just incomplete, but wrong. Poulantzas, however, uses "group" instead of class for the petit bourgeoisie, continuing to emphasize the Marxist struggle between proletariat and bourgeoisie.

What happens to the petit bourgeoisie? Marx assumed that the old petit bourgeoisie would eventually be driven out in the competition with big capitalism, ending up in the proletariat. As for the new petit bourgeoisie, Poulantzas's conclusion is that a few will move up into the bourgeoisie, while most will fall into the proletariat. He reminds us of Michels's point about the ideology of mobility: "the ideology of 'promotion' and of 'climbing' up into the bourgeoisie. . . . This upward transfer is in fact very restrained, but it continues to feed the illusions and hopes that these agents have for themselves and especially for their children" (Poulantzas, 1974:284). The majority, as in the case of the old petit bourgeoisie, end up in the working class or proletariat.

We have seen that for Poulantzas the state is more than a "tool" of the ruling class, and classes are more complex than the classic twofold division. However, struggle is still central to understanding classes, and the final revolution is still to be worked and hoped for. Is Poulantzas optimistic about the future? Does he believe in the revolution's inevitability? We will examine this important issue in "Final Thoughts" at the end of this chapter.

Gender   Poulantzas makes several important comments on gender, especially in *Classes in Contemporary Capitalism* (1974). Class barriers impose inequalities on certain groups of people—old and young, but especially on women. The complexity of their position results from the fact that they are influenced by both a class and a gender division of labor. Women, he argues, are double victims of their position both as nonproductive, or domestic, workers and as exploited members of the workforce. "It is well-known how detrimental a factor it can be for the struggles of women . . . that their wages may be thought of in the family apparatus as simply providing a little extra for housekeeping," not as breadwinner, but as supplementer (1974:306).

Another insight on gender is his observation of the difference between what happens when working-class men are upwardly mobile and when working-class women are upwardly mobile. Male workers, notes Poulantzas, "who leave the working class go chiefly into the 'independent' sector," or bourgeoisie, "while female workers move above all into . . . the petty bourgeoisie," becoming clerks and service workers (1974:319). And these workers, in turn, are more likely to be "downsized" by automation/computerization.

While Poulantzas hardly provides a complete theoretical explanation for patriarchy or for women's subordinate role in the societal and familial division of labor, his Marxist concern with inequality is expressed in his recognition that women face gender-based, as well class-based, difficulties (see Jessop, 1990: 238–239).

Raya Dunayevskaya (1981) wrote at greater length than did Poulantzas on women under capitalism. Speaking first about Rosa Luxemburg, she observed: "Luxemburg rightly refused to be pigeonholed by the German Social-Democracy into the so-called Woman Question, as if that were the only place she belonged" (1981:89). For twenty years, she noted, Luxemburg and Clara Zetkin worked closely. Zetkin chose to concentrate on organizing working-class women, while Luxemburg focused on more general Marxist issues.

Luxemburg and Zetkin played leadership roles in the Stuttgart Women's Conference of 1907. While they supported women's suffrage, they made it clear that the larger issues were the general strike and the revolution itself. Thus, while "everything merged into the proletarian revolution, . . . always thereafter, woman as revolutionary force revealed its presence" (Dunayevskaya, 1981:95). Luxemburg understood the important role of women in the revolution—a role that could not be played in the patriarchal world of her time.

Dunayevskaya did more than indicate Luxemburg's support for the liberation of women. She spoke to the issue herself at the beginning of the 1980s in her appropriately titled essay, "The Task That Remains to Be Done: The Unique and Unfinished Contributions of Today's Women's Liberation Movement" (1981:99–112). Fifty years after Luxemburg's contribution to the woman question, Dunayevskaya noted that the women's liberation movement of the 1960s not only opposed capitalistic patriarchy but also "directed the male-chauvinist epithet at the male left" (1981:99). In other words, male radicals themselves were rightly accused of sexism. In many countries around the world, noted Dunayevskaya, spokeswomen began to enunciate the need to involve women both before and during the organizing phase of the revolution.

What happened in Russia was certainly not good enough: To assume that the revolution led by the Bolshevik party would somehow, in the long run, take care of women's needs and problems automatically was to make a serious error. According to Dunayevskaya, as we have seen, that first workers' state turned into its "opposite, the state-capitalist monstrosity we know today" (1981:109).

Women's liberation, then, is an important Marxist issue. The oppression of women is explained by patriarchal structures and attitudes, both in the capitalist world and in radical organizations.

Race   Race is an issue that Marxists often speak of tangentially, as being subsumed under class. However, Dunayevskaya introduced her discussion of women's liberation with an essay titled "An Overview by Way of Introduction: The Black Dimension" (1981:79–87). She began the essay with references to Mary Wollstonecroft (1792; see Chapter 1) and to an African American woman, Maria Stewart, who spoke thus in 1831:

> O ye daughters of Africa, awake! awake! arise! No longer sleep nor slumber but distinguish yourselves. Show forth to the world that ye are endowed with noble and exalted faculties. . . . How long shall the fair daughters of Africa be compelled to bury their minds and talents beneath a load of iron pots and kettles? (Dunayevskaya, 1981:79)

Tracing the history of black women in the United States through the nineteenth and into the twentieth century, Dunayevskaya noted that they had been ignored throughout much of Western history. This was true not only in the United States; "take Africa, whose history, especially as it concerns women, has hardly been touched" (1981:84). So the revolution, as it spreads, must involve women and the nonwhite races, as well as the working class. We will see more on African American women in the writings of Patricia Hill Collins (Chapter 22).

Other Theories and Theorists

We have introduced Poulantzas's and Dunayevskaya's ideas on classes, gender, and race. A few insights on other topics are also worth noting.

Besides the ideology of upward mobility, Poulantzas referred to another issue that concerned Michels: reformist and conservative unions, particularly trade unions. Like Michels, he criticized them as anything but revolutionary, hardly representing working-class needs and interests (Poulantzas, 1978:225).

Poulantzas also commented on the similarities among political parties in modern nation-states:

> These parties never offered a real political alternative to the reproduction of capitalism; yet they made it possible to choose between centres that formulated bourgeois policy in different ways. Today, they differ over little more than the aspect of administrative-executive policy that should be popularized. (1978:230)

The differences are not simply fictitious, but—whether Tories and Labor in Britain, or Republicans and Democrats in the United States—they certainly do not represent clear-cut ideological cleavages.

Both Poulantzas and Luxemburg criticized Lenin—though not as strongly as did Dunayevskaya—as having laid the groundwork not for rank-and-file democracy, but for the exact opposite. Without general elections, Lenin's organization of the Soviet Russian state led directly to Stalin's bureaucratization (Poulantzas, 1978:253). The popular masses remain outside the state looking in, with even the practice of representative democracy leaving the masses far from the seats of power. Thus, mass movements and infiltration of government by the working class are important, and both are difficult to effect (Poulantzas, 1978:259).

Poulantzas had much to say about the possibilities and limitations of U.S. global hegemony. Writing in 1974, he concluded that the European nations, Japan, and the Vietnam War had all conspired to weaken U.S. dominance. (Whether he would have said the same thing 25 years later is questionable.) However, he added that 60 percent of all foreign investments come from the United States. He also noted that U.S. dominance of the computer industry has made for worldwide standardization—an insight that today could be expanded to include CNN, movies, and other aspects of U.S. culture disseminated around the world (Poulantzas, 1974:66). Hegemony, as Gramsci pointed out, is not restricted to multinational corporations and military interventions; it includes a great variety of cultural elements, all of which serve to spread capitalist products and ideas.

Critique and Conclusions

Our criticisms and conclusions regarding Marxism will be held until the end of the chapter, after we have introduced Erik Olin Wright's theoretical contributions that begin the twenty-first century. In his analytic and academic approach, Wright argues that Marxism has not been defeated by the transition of Eastern Europe's "quasi-Marxist" states to avowed capitalism. In fact, as you will see, his contributions to Marxist theory increased during the 1990s, after the breakup of the Soviet Union.

Marxism Now: Erik Olin Wright (1947–)

Erik Olin Wright was born in 1947 in Berkeley, California, to an academic family. He completed BA degrees at Harvard and at Oxford and a PhD in sociology at the University of California, Berkeley. Since 1976 he has been on the sociology faculty at the University of Wisconsin–Madison, except for one year as a visiting professor at Berkeley.

Wright has been a productive Marxist scholar for more than twenty years, but his important recent works are three books published in the 1990s, since the collapse of the Soviet Union and the East European bloc of communist countries: *Reconstructing Marxism* (1992, with Levine and Sober), *Interrogating Inequality* (1994), and *Class Counts* (1997).

In his 1994 book, Wright speaks of what has been called the "crisis of Marxism": (1) the above-mentioned changes in countries formerly ruled by nominally communist parties; (2) the lack of coherent programs for change in communist, socialist, and social democratic parties in the capitalist world; (3) the exit of intellectuals from Marxism toward liberalism or post-Marxism; and (4) the decline in consensus among Marxist intellectuals over the core principles of Marxism (1994:175). Wright's task, then, as he sees it, is to "contribute to this reconstruction of Marxism as a theoretical framework for radical social science." He believes "that the Marxism which will emerge from the present period of theoretical transformation will not only be more powerful theoretically than the Marxism of the heyday of the New Left, but will also be of more political relevance" (1994:175–176, 179).

Wright is an analytical Marxist who is also an empirical and an academic Marxist. His empiricism is clearly stated in his most recent book:

> Research pushes social theory forward in two basic ways. Where there is a controversy between contending theoretical claims about some problem, research potentially can provide a basis for adjudication between the alternatives. . . . The goal of research can [also] be to find interesting surprises, anomalous empirical results that go against the expectations of a theory and thus provoke rethinking. (1997:519–520)

His goal in this book is to try to convince non-Marxists that class analysis is useful, and to convince Marxists that quantitative analysis is useful (1997:546).

Wright's primary focus of attention is classes, to which we will turn later. First, however, we will discuss his analytic and antireductionist approaches to Marxist thought.

Wright's Central Theories and Methods

Wright's contributions to Marxist theory are in midstream, and can be expected to continue into the twenty-first century. However, we will begin this discussion with his antireductionism.

Antireductionism   Wright and his coauthors contrast their approach with **methodological individualism**, which is "the view that all social phenomena are best explained by the properties of individuals who comprise the phenomena" (Wright, Levine, and Sober, 1992:108). Though critical of it, they believe that Jon Elster's (1985) book *Making Sense of Marx* is the most insightful one written by an individualist. Elster seeks explanation only at the individual level, and argues that radical holism or "methodological collectivism" is teleological and lacking in credibility. Likewise, Wright and his colleagues question Althusserian structuralism, asserting that "structures cause structures and individuals are only 'supports' of social relations" (1992:114).

Wright and his coauthors are **"antireductionists,"** meaning that not all phenomena can or should be reduced to the individual level. Their approach, they believe, is a good one if Marxism seeks to deal with the real—that is, the empirical—world. In other words, antireductionists have room for both irreducible social- or structural-level phenomena and for micro- or individual-level explanations (1992:124, 127).

Analytical Marxism   Analytical Marxism was spurred by a London conference in 1979, the year of Poulantzas's death, that included Cohen, Elster, and Roemer—a group Wright joined in 1981. Wright argues that four specific commitments justify considering Analytical Marxism as a distinct "school" of contemporary Marxist thought. First is its commitment to conventional scientific norms. Second is an emphasis on systematic conceptualization, especially of core concepts. Third is a concern with fine-grained specification of the steps in the theoretical linking of concepts, whether they are about causal processes in explanatory theories or about logical connections in constructing normative theories. Finally, attention is paid to the intentional action of individuals within both types of theories (Wright, 1994:181–182).

Marxism has often been hostile to conventional science; even what has been called "scientific socialism" has abused the canons of science (for example, Althusser's work). Wright believes that if Marxism aspires to be more than an ideology, to be a genuine social scientific perspective, it must engage relevant data from empirical research. But what makes Analytical Marxists "Marxist"? (1) Their questions come from the Marxist tradition; (2) their agenda (such as Wright's research on class) is Marxist; (3) their language is Marxist; and (4) they share a core normative orientation to Marxism (Wright, 1994:192–193).

One of the subfields of Analytical Marxism to which Wright does not subscribe, and which has caused much controversy among contemporary Marxists, is the rational choice model discussed earlier in this chapter, especially in the work of Roemer. This view states that, at the very least, Marxist theory should incorporate as one element a concern with conscious choice (Roemer, 1981, 1982). Wright does not ignore such choice, but he does not use it as a prime explanatory tool.

Nature of Society, Humans, and Change

Wright is committed to the Marxist view of societal inequality and exploitation. He is also committed to research on class as a (not the) factor explaining the nature or characteristics of society. He does not, however, hold to a firm belief in a postcapitalist socialist/communist world. These issues are treated at length in his 1994 book.

Wright cites three conceptual nodes within Marxism's view of society: class analysis; a theory of historical trajectory, or the direction of history; and an emancipatory theory and ideology. Marxism, Wright summarizes, "is above all about using *class analysis* to understand the political processes for the realization of *historically* possible *emancipatory* goals" (1994:239).

Human nature is mixed, and change is necessary, but not inevitable. In all that Wright says about society, class is the central concept. He agrees ideologically with much that Marxists have said about the ills of capitalism, but he is not an optimistic Marxist—not convinced of the feasibility, much less the inevitability, of the final revolution or cure. As an empirical researcher, Wright argues that the motivator is the reduction of the class factor in society, not classlessness; he emphasizes the process, not an ideal endpoint (1994:245). To this we will return in the concluding section.

Class, Gender, and Race

Class   It is impossible to discuss Erik Olin Wright's view of society without raising the issue of class. Class analysts, according to Wright, can study anything they want: religion, war, crime, cultural tastes, and so on. However, the dependent variable is history, and the emancipatory ideology is the vision of a classless society in which exploitation has been eliminated. Thus, says Wright, "Marxism as class emancipation identified the disease in the existing world. Marxism as class analysis provided the diagnosis of its causes. Marxism as the theory of historical trajectory identified the cure" (1994:240). Few Marxists today, notes Wright, believe that class is the sufficient cause explaining capitalism, and even fewer believe that the historical trajectory is toward socialism as the result of capitalism's development, ills, and contradictions.

Traditional Marxist treatments of classes, in Wright's view, have suffered from two problems: They have been too abstract and too macro—meaning that they have viewed classes in structural terms, but have not mapped class in the lives of individuals. He sees three potential foci of attention within class analysis: structure, formation (how they come into being), and individuals within the class struggle. Wright emphasizes structure and individuals-in-classes (1994).

Class is the empirical and theoretical subject of his latest book, the 500-plus page cross-national analysis titled *Class Counts* (1997), in which he analyzes structure, change, permeability, consciousness, gender, and race. We will begin with the first two, then move on to gender and race.

With regard to class structure, Wright notes that if the only criterion used is relation to the means of production, 85–90 percent of most developed countries are in one class. Therefore, he sees the need to include skills and authority in the definition. These, of course, are similar to the criteria Poulantzas used to define the new petit bourgeoisie. Looking at cross-national data, Wright concludes that all three dimensions are appropriate for defining class structure, though authority is not as independent, nor its boundary as clear, as the other two. At present, Wright sees a total of six locations in class relations: capitalist, petty bourgeoisie, expert managers, experts (such as scientists and engineers), nonskilled managers, and workers (1997:24, 525–526).

The "middle class" are those who are in a contradictory structural location. In some ways they are exploiters, and in some ways exploited. While this is reminiscent of Poulantzas's discussion of the petit bourgeoisie, Wright does not indicate that the middle class will eventually end up in either the bourgeoisie or the proletariat (1994:251).

In discussing class change, Wright notes that the working class in the United States declined in the last third of the twentieth century, and the decline appears to be accelerating. Some would argue, he says, that this is an indication of deproletarianization, while others would argue from a global perspective that "the transnational character of capitalism in the world today makes it inappropriate to study" class transformations "within single national units." Wright's data seem to point to the second explanation, which, of course, is consistent with those who have claimed that the working classes of the developed countries are actually among the exploiters—that is, part of the international bourgeoisie (1997:108–109).

So what are the chances that change will lead to a classless society? In his 1994 book, Wright gives the arguments against such an outcome, and then those that support it. First, the arguments against:

1. Incentives and sanctions [are] needed for efficiency of complex economies.

2. Skepticism about the possibility of democratic control of the means of production in large firms.

3. Information problems make centralized planning of production impossible. (1994:218–219)

Support for the possibility of eliminating class inequities rests on the following arguments:

1. Incentives need not threaten classlessness, especially when public goods replace the need for some private consumption.

2. More education, fewer work hours, and other reforms make democratic control more possible.

3. Market mechanisms could allocate capital with a strong state neutralizing the classist effects. (1994:219)

As we have noted, Wright is not completely convinced of the validity of the second set of arguments, or of the potential for a classless society.

Gender and Race Wright adds both gender and race to his analysis of class, recognizing that some Marxists argue that both of these can be subsumed under, or reduced to, class.

In *Interrogating Inequality* (1994), Wright compares the premises of Marxist and feminist emancipation:

> Marxists have often treated the viability of communism—a society without class oppression—as problematic; . . . . Feminists generally take it for granted that social life does not *require* male domination; Marxists are

forced to defend the claim that social life under conditions of developed technology does not need some form or other of class domination. . . . One hundred years ago it was quite different. Radical class theorists took it as obvious that class inequality and domination were becoming increasingly unnecessary and could be superseded in a post-capitalist society. . . . Feminists in the last century, on the other hand, rarely envisioned a society without a quite substantial gender division of labor and even gender inequality. (1994:211, 220)

Gender, notes Wright, is seen by some as reducible to class, by some as reciprocal to class, or as a sorting mechanism for class, or as a linkage to class, or as causally related to class (1997:243–247). His empirical analysis of gender and class adds much to our understanding of these potential relationships. Labor force participation in the six countries he studied does little to explain gender involvement in household tasks. Though Wright was not the first to discover this, whether women have high-status jobs, low-status jobs, or no jobs, they do the large majority of housework. "Feminists," notes Wright, "have long argued for the autonomy of gender mechanisms in explaining the production and re-production of male domination," and that is in fact what his data show for the United States, Canada, the United Kingdom, Norway, Sweden, and Japan (1997:304).

Wright's insights into gender and class are reinforced when race is added to the data mix. In 1992 he noted that functionalist Marxists, such as Cohen, usually translate non-class interests, such as race, into class interests. Whites, it is said, have class "'interests' in dominating blacks," and this is explained by bourgeois interest in dominating workers (Wright et al., 1992:75). However, his six-country data show that "race is a salient feature of the social structure only in the United States." His U.S. sample contained no black capitalists, only one black small employer (a woman), and only a handful of black petty bourgeoisie (all men) (Wright, 1997:67).

What happens when employer/authority/expertise are combined and related to race and gender? Wright finds that in the United States 33% of white males are in this "privileged" class location, compared to 12.5% of white women, 8.4% of black men, and 3% of black women. Looked at from the working-class perspective, Wright's data show that 87% of black women 77% of black men, 67% of white women, and 51% of white men are in the extended working class. In short, today's U.S. working classes are mostly women and racial minorities (Wright, 1997:69).

A word on class consciousness by race and gender is instructive. The anti-capitalism of the black working class is much greater than that of the white working class, while gender differences in class consciousness are negligible. This can be explained, Wright believes, by the fact that the black experience of slavery in the United States heightened racial consciousness, while the sharing of households by men and women makes for more of a common cross-gender expression of class. One further insight from Wright's data is that gender inequality and consciousness are greater in countries where class inequality is less and where racial inequality is not a factor (1997:544).

Wright's conclusion is that the independent effects of race and gender seem to mean that the struggle for equality in these two ascribed statuses is worth pursuing within capitalism, rather than strictly as a subpart or by-product of the class struggle (1997:545).

Other Theories and Theorists

Wright, of course, responds to some of Marx's ideas, as well as those of recent Marxists, such as Roemer. However, he offers a lengthy evaluation and critique of Cohen's reconstruction of historical materialism. The notion of the long-term nonviability of capitalism, endorsed by Cohen, is based on the labor theory of value and on the tendency of the rate of profit to fall. However, this trend is debatable, according to Wright's data. A more likely basis for internal contradiction in capitalism is its ultimate inability to keep the social connections and organization of workers from leading to their acting as a class. But Wright questions whether a "radical egalitarian alternative" might not be possible, rather than Cohen's (and Marx's) revolutionary outcome (Wright, 1994:229).

As have others, Wright notes that class consciousness depends to a great extent on the individual's perception of his or her future class situation. This, of course, recalls again Michels's argument that the ideology of mobility reduces class antagonism, because individuals believe that they can make the system work for them.

Finally, Wright refers to Giddens, Theda Skocpol, and Ann Orloff. Giddens (see Chapter 15) argued that there is no fundamental dynamic in society that explains its trajectory. Although Wright is hardly a "true believer," he does emphasize class as a central component of history and change. Skocpol (see Chapter 18) and Orloff argue that the emergence of social insurance is explained by the institutional capacities of states, but Wright believes that a 100-year period would show that classes and other Marxist dynamics can explain social insurance at least as well as the action of the capitalist state.

Critique and Conclusions

Though we will not try to summarize all the issues raised in this chapter, concluding comments on Wright and Poulantzas are in order. Wright's own conclusion is that "it is unlikely that fine-grained assessments of the relative importance of different causes can be made" (Wright et al., 1992:174). Class is a cause, but not *the* cause, for society's structures and for individual choices—pervasive, yes; primary or single, probably not. His empirical work has turned Marxism into measurable variables instead of dogmatic dichotomies. And Wright's task is hardly complete, as he himself admits.

Where does Wright's work leave Marxism at the turn of the twenty-first century? Is it in crisis because of the collapse of avowedly Marxist governments, or because of its historical failure thus far to truly emancipate according to its dogma? That seems at least partially correct. But as a scientific and theoretical perspective from which to analyze international neocolonialism, technology, the role of the state, and the class factor, it is very much alive.

Bob Jessop, the main biographer and critic of Poulantzas, claims that Poulantzas never utilized either Althusser's structuralism nor Michel Foucault's micro-power perspective (see Chapter 23) to the extent that they would have been useful to him. Whether he would have done so had he lived longer is only conjecture. Despite Poulantzas's complex views of the state and classes, Jessop concludes that he "failed to develop an adequate account of hegemonic strategies, to consider their relation to accumulation, and to connect them to the process of class formation. He continued to refer to hegemony and its crises as if these involved processes of class leadership" (1985:326). While these points may be correct, it is perhaps unfair to complain about the loose ends left dangling by Poulantzas at his death at the age of 43.

Final Thoughts

Though they do not agree on all major points, Marxists agree on the exploitative and oppressive nature of the capitalist world order. But the complexity and hegemony of that world is daunting. Dunayevskaya criticized the Soviet Union as 70 years of state capitalism, not Marxist socialism. Gramsci, Althusser, and Poulantzas addressed the complexity of capitalist hegemony, seeing it as difficult to combat. Baran and Sweezy showed how large-scale capitalism controls the world through neocolonialism. And the personal stories of Althusser and Poulantzas are disturbing, as we shall see. A powerful commitment can also mean a profound discouragement.

What about the future—the final revolution? In 1974 Poulantzas stated that we "must rid ourselves once and for all of the illusions . . . that an objective proletarian polarization of class determination must necessarily lead in time to a polarization of class positions" (1974:334). Four years later he stated this position even more strongly. History, he asserted, has provided us no example of a successful experience of the democratic or revolutionary road to socialism, but only "negative examples to avoid and some mistakes upon which to reflect" (1978:265). Does this mean it is impossible?

> Maybe. We no longer share that belief in the millennium founded on a
> few iron laws concerning the inevitability of a democratic-socialist revolu-
> tion. . . . What is more, optimism about the democratic road to socialism
> should not lead us to consider it as a royal road, smooth and free of risk.
> (Poulantzas, 1978:265)

Just how pessimistic was Nicos Poulantzas about the revolution required to bring justice and equality to the world he was committed to changing? All we know is that a few months after writing the above, in 1979, he gave up the fight and committed suicide. A year later, Althusser ended a life of depression and intellectual uncertainty by killing his wife, spending the last ten years of his life in an asylum. On the other hand, Marxists today, such as Erik Olin Wright, are optimistic about the value of Marxist analysis and categories, and continue to contribute greatly to understanding and explaining capitalism— even though Marx's own optimism about the final revolution is hardly reflected in his followers today.

References

Althusser, Louis. 1965/1969. *For Marx*. London: Allen Lane/Penguin Press.

———. 1974. *Eléments d'autocritique [Elements of Self-Criticism]*. Paris: Hachette.

Althusser, Louis, and Etienne Balibar. 1968/1970. *Reading Capital*. London: New Left Books.

Baran, Paul, and Paul Sweezy. 1966/1970. *Monopoly Capital*. Harmondsworth, England: Penguin.

Blomstrom, Magnus, and Bjorn Hettne. 1984. *Development Theory in Transition: The Dependency Debate and Beyond: Third World Responses*. London: Zed Books.

Brewer, Anthony. 1980. *Marxist Theories of Imperialism: A Critical Survey*. London: Routledge and Kegan Paul.

Cohen, G. A. 1978. *Karl Marx's Theory of History: A Defense*. Princeton, NJ: Princeton University Press.

Dosse, François. 1967/1997. *History of Structuralism*. Minneapolis: University of Minnesota.

Dunayevskaya, Raya. 1951/1992. *The Marxist-Humanist Theory of State-Capitalism*. Chicago: News and Letters.

———. 1958/1971. *Marxism and Freedom: From 1776 Until Today* London: Pluto Press.

———. 1981/1991. *Rosa Luxemburg, Women's Liberation, and Marx's Philosophy of Revolution*. Urbana: University of Illinois Press.

Elster, Jon. 1985. *Making Sense of Marx*. Cambridge: Cambridge University Press.

Gramsci, Antonio. 1937/1971. *Selections from the Prison Notebooks*. London: Lawrence and Wishart.

Howard, M. C., and J. E. King. 1992. *A History of Marxian Economics: Vol. 2. 1929–1990*. Princeton, NJ: Princeton University Press.

Hudis, Peter. 1992. "Introduction." In Raya Dunayevskaya, *The Marxist-Humanist Theory of State-Capitalism* (pp. i–xxvi). Chicago: News and Letters.

Jessop, Bob. 1985. *Nicos Poulantzas: Marxist Theory and Political Strategy*. London: MacMillan Publishers.

———. 1990. *State Theory: Putting Capitalist States in Their Place*. University Park: Pennsylvania State University Press.

Kurzweil, Edith. 1980. *The Age of Structuralism*. New York: Columbia University Press.

Mouffe, Chantal (Ed.). 1979. *Gramsci and Marxist Theory*. London: Routledge and Kegan Paul.

Paggi, Leonardo. 1979. "Gramsci's General Theory of Marxism." In Chantal Mouffe (Ed.), *Gramsci and Marxist Theory* (pp. 113–167). London: Routledge and Kegan Paul.

Poulantzas, Nicos. 1974. *Classes in Contemporary Capitalism*. London: New Left Books.

———. 1978. *State, Power, Socialism*. London: New Left Books and Verso.

Roemer, J. E. 1981. *Analytical Foundations of Marxian Economic Theory*. Cambridge: Cambridge University Press.

———. 1982. *A General Theory of Exploitation and Class*. Cambridge, MA: Harvard University Press.

———. 1986. *Analytical Marxism*. New York: Cambridge University Press.

Texier, Jacquies. 1979. "Gramsci, Theoretician of the Superstructures." In Chantal Mouffe (Ed.), *Gramsci and Marxist Theory* (pp. 48–79). London: Routledge and Kegan Paul.

Wright, Erik Olin. 1994. *Interrogating Inequality*. New York: Verso.

———. 1997. *Class Counts: Comparative Studies in Class Analysis*. Cambridge: Cambridge University Press.

Wright, Erik Olin, Andrew Levine, and Elliot Sober. 1992. *Reconstructing Marxism*. London: Verso.

Chapter 18

Sociocultural Change: Evolution, World System, and Revolution
Service, Wallerstein, and Skocpol

One of the issues we have been concerned with throughout this volume is macro-theories of change. Spencer and Sumner presented social evolutionary theory, emphasizing the survival of the fittest, and societal change from homogeneity to heterogeneity—also known as differentiation or specialization. Durkheim described such differentiation as an increasing division of labor—a change from mechanical to organic solidarity. Marx and his followers depicted the "underside" of capitalist exploitation and oppression of workers, arguing for the necessity of an anticapitalist revolution to bring about the necessary changes. Pareto claimed that nothing important *ever* changes. The struggle for power and the human motives behind this struggle are always the same. Of course, technology changes, and so do the rationalizations we use for what we are doing or what we want, but the basic nature of society and humans is always the same. Parsons and the functionalists argued that change does take place, but it is usually minimal and with a view to reinstating the former equilibrium as closely as possible.

We focus in this chapter on three twentieth-century perspectives on change, using one U.S. theorist as the center point of each discussion, but bringing in others as needed. We begin with Elman Service and the various elements of evolutionary thinking today, including modernization theory. Then we look at Immanuel Wallerstein's world system theory, as a reaction to modernization theory, and also introduce its critics. Finally, we examine Theda Skocpol's non-Marxist theory of revolution, comparing it briefly with other non-Marxist theories.[1]

---

[1]In this chapter we cannot introduce all the theories of cultural and social change that might interest you. However, in this footnote we touch briefly on two.

There is a kind of theory that uses personality and family to explain change toward development and modernization. Everett Hagen (1962) argues that race, religion, climate, urbanization, and environment are all causal, but are preceded in their effects

Twentieth-Century Evolutionism: Elman Service (1915–)[2]

Looking back at nineteenth-century thinking, we recall that the dominant belief in Europe was not just in biological evolution, but in social and cultural evolution as well. In the 1800s, wrote V. Gordon Childe,

> "progress" was an accepted fact. Trade was expanding, the productivity of industry was increasing, wealth was accumulating. Scientific discoveries promised a boundless advance in man's control over Nature, and consequently unlimited possibilities of further production. Growing prosperity and deepening knowledge inspired an atmosphere of unprecedented optimism throughout the Western world. (Childe, 1936:9)

Both Lewis Henry Morgan and Edward Tylor, writing independently in 1871, saw "technology, science, and material culture generally, as undergoing a progressive, cumulative evolution, independent from religion and 'intellectual and moral' progress" (Service, 1971:8).

According to Robert Nisbet (1969), the key elements of classic or nineteenth-century social evolutionary thinking were the following:

1. Change is *natural*. It is as much a part of a social entity—whether a civilization, an institution, or a cluster of cultural elements—as is structure or equilibrium.

2. Though not an observable fact, change is *directional*. It has a beginning, a middle, and an end—or, metaphorically, birth, growth, and death.

---

by a change in personality. This change, in turn, is influenced by social structure, parental behavior, and childhood. Most traditional societies produce an authoritarian personality, but some produce an innovative one, which leads to change. David McClelland's (1962) argument is close to Hagen's. Of the various characteristics related to change, McClelland argues, a need for achievement (n-ach) is central. N-ach results from societal contacts and comparisons, giving rise to entrepreneurship and the desire for improvement or betterment. Each of these is a subtheory of modernization, but they seem to beg the question of what causes traditional families and societies to produce such personalities.

Godfrey and Monica Wilson's 1958 book, *Analysis of Social Change*, is neither an economic nor a psychological theory of change, but a demographic one. Change occurs when there is either an increase or decrease in the scale or density of a society. This can be a result of inadequate space (exhaustion of land supply), conquest by (or of) a society, or various other causes.

Three comments are necessary: First, these theories are more complex than we have indicated. Second, they are versions of modernization theory, which dominated the 1950s and 1960s. Third, they are not incompatible with other theories presented in this chapter, but seem to require explanations that push the causal chain further back toward the individual.

[2]We have selected Service, rather than V. G. Childe, Leslie White, or Marshall Sahlins, for discussion in this chapter not because he is necessarily the most creative, but because he introduces a broader spectrum of issues than the others. Also, Service confronts several unique evolutionary problems that connect him to other theorists in this volume. Like Erik Olin Wright in the previous chapter, Service raises the important contemporary issues in his particular school of thought.

3. Change is *immanent*. It is internal to societies, their structures and cultures, and not ordinarily induced from the outside.

4. Change is *continuous*, consisting of small gradations or steps within a single series. The problem with this, of course, was that Darwin's geological evidence found gaps and apparent reversals in the record, and so did accounts of peoples. Nonetheless, nineteenth-century writers tended to assume natural, continuous, incremental change.

5. Change is *necessary*. There is logical necessity in evolution and progress. Not only conservative thinking, but some of Marx's early arguments, despite the language of revolution, were based on the necessity of change through capitalism to socialism.

6. Finally, nineteenth-century evolutionists believed in *uniform causes*, traceable to a beginning point in natural history, rather than to a cataclysm, crisis, or God-directed event. (Nisbet, 1969:166–188)

All this changed in the twentieth century. During and after World War I, many European thinkers lost confidence in evolutionary progress. In addition, the Depression of the 1930s and worldwide discontent affected European sociological theorizing. Within the social sciences themselves, two non- (sometimes anti-) evolutionary viewpoints spread. One was that of Franz Boas, Robert Lowie, and other U.S. cultural anthropologists who stated that civilization involves a variety of elements, some borrowed, some internal, and some "leftovers." Thus, culture is a "planless hodgepodge, [a] thing of shreds and patches" (Lowie, 1920, quoted in Service, 1971:149). In praising Lowie's book, *Culture and Ethnology*, one reviewer wrote: "The theory of cultural evolution [is] to my mind the most inane, sterile, and pernicious theory in the whole . . . of science" (quoted in White, 1960:v).

The other nonevolutionary viewpoint is found in the writings of Malinowski and Radcliffe-Brown, British social anthropologists, who argued in the 1920s and 1930s that explanation comes from getting inside a society and its culture and understanding the current interrelations of its parts, and not from concerning oneself with its history. Thus, for more than 30 years nonevolutionary thinking dominated the West—a result of world upheaval, Lowie's "fragmentary" cultural perspective, and British functionalism.

Elman Service was born in 1915. In his 1975 book, he recounts his intellectual history:

> The problem of the origins of civilization and primitive states has been a preoccupation of mine since I simultaneously discovered anthropology and Marxism in the late 1930s. . . . I eventually became dissatisfied with Marxism and, I hope, with all forms of "systematic" thought. (1975:xvi)

Service explains that in the 1940s, at the University of Michigan, Leslie White's evolutionary teaching and writing helped him focus his long-term interests. To this was added the influence of Julian Steward at Columbia, with whom Service did graduate work in the late 1940s. He then returned to the University of Michigan, where he did his early scholarly work with Marshall Sahlins.

Service's Central Theories and Methods

Despite Childe's brief 1936 book, published in Britain, only in the 1950s was there any noticeable shift of opinion toward an evolutionary outlook again. Following World War II, European thinking continued to be pessimistic, but optimistic evolutionary thought reemerged in the United States, as a result of victory without internal destruction, and in the nonwhite world, as a reaction against the dominance of Western nations and the white race (Service, 1971:9).

Cultural Evolutionism   By 1959, there were already two major distinctions within twentieth-century cultural evolutionary thought. One was between directed and nondirected evolution; the other was between supra-historical and historical evolution.

In the nineteenth century, the dominant view was clearly that evolution was **nondirected**—a "natural," or uncontrolled, process. Evolution results from competition, from natural selection or the survival of the fittest, or else (according to Charlotte Gilman and L. F. Ward) from cooperative adaptation, with competition as secondary. White (1949) agreed, arguing that culture determines what people do, not vice versa. He gave little credence to free will, claiming that if one person does not synthesize cultural elements in a new way, someone else will. Thus, White agreed with Herbert Spencer and William James that history is not the story of the doings of great individuals, but of cultural and social forces, neither guided by human endeavor, nor headed toward a predetermined goal.

Although it may seem only a matter of emphasis, Childe titled his 1936 book *Man Makes Himself*. The main difference, according to Childe, between biological and cultural/social evolution is that humans can look back, can think through problems, and can even imagine and then construct or **direct** future evolution. "Changes in culture and tradition can be initiated, controlled, or delayed by the conscious and deliberate choice of their human authors and executors" (1936:21). It is the brain, in Childe's view, that makes humans different from other animals and makes it possible for humans to control their own cultural evolution (1936:28).

Others, such as Charles Erasmus in his 1966 book *Man Takes Control*, later took the same position. They argued that cultural, especially technological, evolution is not a natural process, but is guided by the thought and action of specific human beings. The building of a "better mousetrap" or a better computer is not a matter of the natural selection of elements, but results from human thought, planning, and development.

Throughout his scholarly career, Service agreed with White and the "social forces" or nondirected school of evolution, rather than with Childe and Erasmus. For example, in 1975 he quoted favorably Max Gluckman's view of the rise of Shaka to power among the Zulu in South Africa. While Shaka may have been endowed with military genius, his "rise to power was probably also a result of tides that had been running in the life of the African peoples for two centuries," including population growth, emigration, crowding of land, and contact with Europeans (Gluckman, 1960:158). Later Service generalized this point: Individuals make decisions and do things, but we "welcome, for the more general purposes of this book, a sophisticated grasp of the structural leverages and constraints that plot the actors' actions in general ways" (Service, 1975:164).

The second important distinction is between unilinear and multilinear, or supra-historical and historical, evolution. The dominant position on this issue remains, as it was in the nineteenth century, **unilinear**—the idea of a single path along which human societies, cultures, and technology have moved and are moving. Complexity, cross-cultural differences, and even speed of change are irrelevant to the overall course of human history. Also called "universal" or "general" evolution, this view sees a "passage from less to greater energy transformation, lower to higher levels of integration, and less to greater all-around adaptability" (Sahlins and Service, 1960:38).

Although this is the dominant position, Julian Steward, one of Service's teachers, introduced the multilineal concept. Noting that diffusion or borrowing has often been used to explain how cultural elements got from one part of the world to another, Steward disagreed. Why, he asked, would not the same environmental conditions give rise to the same inventions and adjustments independent of one another, without the necessity of culture contact? The **multilinear** view, first, "postulates that genuine parallels of form and function develop in historically independent sequences or cultural traditions. Second, it explains these parallels by the independent operation of identical causation in each case" (Steward, 1955:14).

It is possible that Childe and White as unilinear and Steward as multilinear evolutionists are not in substantial disagreement. Childe spoke of urban civilization, with its cultural characteristics, as "not simply transplanted from one centre to another, but . . . in each an organic growth rooted in the local soil" (Childe, 1936:135). Service, referring to his teachers White and Steward, declared: "I never felt that the two approaches were incompatible" (Service, 1962:viii).

In 1959, a symposium was held on "Principles of Culture Evolution." The outcome was the 1960 volume *Evolution and Culture* written by several scholars, including Sahlins and Service, who served as editors. In this small work they solved the debate by simply saying that evolution is both. That is, the two writer/editors utilized the concepts of **general** and **specific** evolution. By specific they meant historically specific, which included Steward's notion of independent origins (Sahlins and Service, 1960:38).

Two years later, however, Service claimed that the "general" and "specific" distinction was basically Marshall Sahlins'. He added that some of his own ideas "were precipitated out of discussions (and arguments) with Sahlins, with whom I have been collaborating off and on for some time" (Service, 1962:viii). By 1975, when he published his most important book, Service was still interested in the history of specific societies, but only as they contributed to a general understanding of the origin and development of civilization and the state.

Civilization and the State   Childe (1936) claimed that the first civilizations originated in what he called an "urban revolution." Its important aspects included specialists, such as craftsmen and priests, food surplus from the countryside, public buildings, a ruling class, writing, arithmetic, long-distance trade, and controlled force—the state (Service, 1975:7).

In his 1962 book, *Primitive Social Organization*, Service argued that urbanization itself had to be explained, and that the primary change was from agricultural tribes to centralized chiefdoms. This centralization, he observed, took place in environments consisting of dramatically different climates in fairly close proximity. A seacoast, a fertile lowland, and highland forests might be characterized by fishing, agriculture, and animal hunting, respectively. At first people were nomadic, moving from region to region as seasons changed. However, Service proposed, at some point certain individuals settled "in the middle," and traded the mountain and seacoast produce between the now-settled peoples, keeping some for themselves. The outcome, in these climatically varied parts of the world, was "specialization in production and redistribution of produce from a controlling trade center. The resulting organic base of social integration made possible a more integrated and differentiated society, and the increased efficiency in production and distribution made possible a denser society" (1962:144).

Thus, Service's argument was that in Central America, China, and elsewhere, environmental or climatic diversity and productive specialization gave rise to redistribution, which in turn gave rise to urban agglomerations. He stated this point again in 1975: "A chiefdom in good working order seems to be held together because it can accomplish the above functions [specialization, worship, etc.] well, especially redistribution—here, in fact, is the organismic model of society so beloved of the classical sociologists" (1975:79).

But by that year (1975), his explanation was changing and becoming more complex. Looking at a variety of societies around the world, he argued that

> those of the New World were unrelated to those of the Old World. This is a most significant fact, for it affects our perspective. Were it one single development that spread to the other areas by conquest, diffusion, emulation, or whatever, then the problem would be "historical"—that is, our concern would be simply, what happened? When? But since it happened several times independently we immediately wonder, even if it only happened twice, . . . what *causes* or repetitive *processes* were at work. (1975:5)

Was this general evolution a result of economic redistribution, as he had argued previously? No. Political "power organized the economy, not vice versa." Administration came first; it included economic redistribution, but much more than that. These first governments, argued Service, "seem clearly to have reinforced their structure by doing their economic and religious jobs well—by providing benefits—rather than by using physical force," or being acquisitive (1975: 8). When violence was used, it was against either "princes" or other pretenders to power, or else against external forces. In fact, he says, "neither urbanism nor state violence is a necessary factor in the *development* of civilization" and the state (1975:185). This, of course, is very different from Lenin's and Poulantzas's views of the state.

The stages of evolution included the hunting-gathering band, the agricultural tribe, the diversified chiefdom, and finally the state, whose functions included religious leadership, economic redistribution, class control (à la Marx), specialization (à la Durkheim), bureaucracy (à la Weber), and control of force if necessary. Viewing this evolution in terms of leadership or authority, it is from the agricultural big-man, to the traditional chiefdom, to the bureaucratized and civilized state. This, Service reminds us, coincides with Weber's three types of authority: charismatic (big-man), traditional, and rational-legal or bureaucratic (Service, 1975:306).

Another of Service's concerns was the fall, as well as the rise, of societies and states. Although the terminology of growth and decay is metaphoric, there is no question that societies go through some such process. Adaptation is functional up to a point, fostering adjustment to and even control over one's environment. However, "there are both positive *and* negative aspects of adaptation to environment. . . . More adaptation equals less adaptability" (Service, 1975:319). Here Service referred, as he had in 1971, to Thorstein Veblen's efficiency principle, described as "the penalty of taking the lead" (Veblen, 1915). Thus, "newly civilized societies of the frontier have an increasing evolutionary potential that the original center steadily loses in the very act of successfully dominating [and adapting to] its own local environment" (Service, 1975:314). This might be labeled the "leap-frog" principle.

For Service, then, evolutionary explanation includes (1) the primacy of beneficial administration, (2) economic redistribution, (3) specialization, and (4) evolutionary potential in inverse relation to successful adaptation. Together these are the prime factors in explaining the rise of civilizations as well as the fall of specific societies. Service, like Weber, recognized that the real world is much more complex than such principles: "Numerous other factors are ultimately involved in the actual history of the rise and fall of a civilization. Disease, fire, flood, drought, earthquakes, overpopulation, soil depletion—who knows what else?—may have been involved in the fall of real societies." But, he argued, "such findings would have no bearing on the general relevance of the administration/adaptation/potentiality factor in evolution" (Service, 1975:322).

Nature of Society and Humans

Since change is the theme of this chapter, we will leave it out of this heading. As for society and humans, complexity is again the theme.

> Human beings do have varying abilities directed and powered by different motives and values (ideally they would be self-serving at the same time that they are socially useful); but the high offices and positions of power, wealth, and authority as institutional *structures* are real, too, and we need analysis of their evolution and functional connections and purposes. Both radical and conservative positions are important and interesting and in our case it would be nice to know the rulers' ego-structures as well as the social structure. (Service, 1975:288)

However, "to guess at the underlying motives and personalities of leaders, and then offer the guess as an explanation, is to be reductionistic. . . . Let us then, at this point, desist from Hobbesian or Rousseauian guesswork about the bad and good in human motives" (1975:289). Furthermore, although we believe that our explanation of the origin and rise of civilization, the state, and society, may be fairly accurate, we must not assume that the study of origins "somehow reveals that entity's *true nature*" (1975:286).

In short, Service was unwilling to hazard a guess as to the goodness or badness of either human nature or society. Once again, we must conclude that he believes complexity allows for neither simplification nor reductionism.

Class, Gender, and Race

With his focus was on evolutionary change at the societal level, Service did not speak to issues of class, gender, and race. Even when he used the term *class*, it referred not to the Marxist or Weberian socioeconomic categories, but to traditional Australian kinship divisions or moieties (Service, 1971:115–133).

Other Theories and Theorists

Closely related to evolutionary thinking is modernization theory. Sahlins and Service hypothesized, in 1960, why evolutionary theory was reviving: "Is it because we now find ourselves observing a world-wide conflict between older, entrenched social orders and once-lowly and dominated peoples whose awakening has made 'progress' again the slogan of the day?" (1960:2). The answer in the 1960s was clearly yes. The political independence of former colonies, their push for economic development, and the Western societies' economic "evangelization" and neocolonialism were seen in the writings of Talcott Parsons, Daniel Lerner, and others as leading to "modernity," or stated in terms of process, "modernization" (Janos, 1986:42; Lerner, 1958). "Heavily influenced by the evolutionary theory, American social scientists conceptualized modernization as a phased, irreversible, progressive, lengthy process that moves in the direction of the American model" (So, 1990:261).

What, precisely, is this **modernity,** viewed by the West as giving it the status of a worldwide "vanguard" (to use Lenin's term)? Nisbet defined it as "technology, industrialism, democracy, secularism, individualism, equalitarianism, and, for a few, socialism. Counterposed to these were the attributes of *traditionalism* or . . . 'backwardness' or 'primitivism,'" including kinship, religion, and ruralism (1969:191). The expected changes, then, included moving from small-scale to large-scale societies, from simple to complex technology, and from personal to impersonal or anonymous relationships. In theories about worldwide evolution, terms used interchangeably included "civilized," "modern," and "developed."

Just how dominant was such evolutionary thinking, when applied to worldwide change? One volume, *Modernization: The Dynamics of Growth*, published in 1966, included the writings of 25 Western scholars (Weiner, 1966). The underlying assumption was that, over time, the rest of the world would become "just like us." Modernization was not only an evolutionary theory, it was an action program. Advisers were sent to various parts of the world to oversee change, development, and Westernization. Capitalists, critics (such as Veblen), and Marxists all agreed that the world was headed toward large-scale capitalism. However, capitalists saw it as the end or completion of the process, while Marxists saw it as the semi-final stage, to be followed by the worldwide revolutionary overthrow of capitalism.

Critique and Conclusions

Service used his "leap-frog" approach to change in hypothesizing about the future. He believed that the country most likely to leap over the United States and the West is China. To do so, however, it must choose not to simply allow itself to be incorporated in a subordinate role to the West-dominated world order (Service, 1975:323–324). Were he writing 25 years later, he might conclude that China is already foregoing this opportunity and opting for Western influences.

Modernization theory of the 1950s–1970s was basically a subbranch of twentieth-century evolutionary theory. It included as a major value judgment the concept of progress. Sahlins and Service defined progress as "improvement in 'all-around adaptability.'" Speaking of cultures, they asserted that the higher forms "are again relatively 'free from environmental control,' i.e., they adapt to greater environmental variety than lower forms" (1960:38). And, other evolutionists added, higher forms adapt their environment to meet their needs. Nisbet noted that belief in such progress "calls plainly for a gigantic act of faith." But, he added, most of us cannot live without such faith (Nisbet, 1969:223).

Nisbet remarked in 1969 that the theory of social evolution had been a justification for the ascendancy of the West, and that, aside from empirical research, the theory had changed little since the 1800s (1969:202). In the final quarter of the twentieth century, however, both the definition of modernity and the belief in progress have been questioned. Much recent thinking on modernization has given a more positive role to tradition and suggested a complex relationship between tradition and modernity. In fact, the language of multilinealism is now being used to describe differentiated paths into the so-called "modern world" (So, 1990:86–87). At the beginning of the twenty-first century, the notion of uniformity or a single path is being criticized by Immauel Wallerstein and others.

Other doubts have also been raised. Sahlins and Service spoke of the "passage from less to greater energy transformation, lower to higher levels of integration" (1960:38). But how does the evolutionist or modernization theorist deal with the using up of energy sources, polluting of the environment, and ever-increasing inequalities both within and between societies? These issues must be ignored if the term "progress" is to be used. Marx and Engels, of course, warned that these were inherent characteristics of capitalism; but observers have so far been able to overlook them in the light of ever-increasing productivity, at least in the advanced capitalist societies.

The term "advanced capitalist societies" leads us to alternative theoretical views regarding economic development and evolutionary progress. After some 20 years, evolutionary modernization theory was challenged by dependency, underdevelopment, and world-system theories.

World System Theory: Immanuel Wallerstein (1930–)

Much of the background for world system theory is the same as that for evolutionary and modernization theory. The post–World War II period of U.S. confidence in a single path to development waned and was followed by several alternate attempts to explain what was happening in the world.

Immanuel Wallerstein began in the 1960s as an Africanist and Marxist (So, 1990:171) and has taught for many years at the State University of New York at Binghamton. His research in Africa convinced him that interdependence was such that a society or state could not be understood in isolation. Noting the economic difficulties being faced by the newly independent African countries, he attacked the central features of modernization theory: reification of the nation-state, belief in a single path to development, and disregard for the "development of transnational structures that constrain and prompt . . . diverse as well as parallel paths" (Skocpol, 1994:55–56). He proposed an analytic framework that is worldwide, with the nation-state as but "one kind of organizational structure among others within this single social system" (Wallerstein, 1974:7).

In introducing Wallerstein's world system, we should note that he has never abandoned the Marxist view of exploitation and oppression. He does not, however, speak of a final revolution, and his analysis of oppression does not focus on classes within nation-states, but primarily on the world capitalist system.

Wallerstein has stated more than once that he is doing "world-system analysis," not writing world system theory. However, his efforts at explanation from this perspective justify treating it as a theory.

Wallerstein's Central Theory and Methods

Wallerstein's multivolume historical project is still in progress. He began in 1974 with *The Modern World System*, a treatment of the emergence of capitalist agriculture and a European-dominated world economy in the sixteenth century. That his view involves change is seen in an essay published the same year, "The Rise and Future Demise of the World Capitalist System."

According to Wallerstein, three factors were essential to the establishment of a world economy during and after the sixteenth century:

> an expansion of the geographical size of the world in question, the development of variegated methods of labor control for different products and different zones of the world economy, and the creation of relatively strong state machineries in what would become the core-states of this capitalist world-economy. (1974:38)

Why did the world capitalist system emerge in Europe, instead of China, or, earlier, in Rome? In the sixteenth century, says Wallerstein, China had a population and technology equivalent to Europe's, and was equally involved in exploration. However, as a political empire, China's centralization discouraged entrepreneurship, and its focus (as Rome's had been) was control of people, rather than Europe's concern with space and resources (1974:63). This is, in short, the "structural advantage" of world economy over world empire (1974:179).

Since then the world has increasingly become a single system, with an international division of labor. As one commentator describes Wallerstein's orientation, "the focus of political inquiry shifted from the narrower Durkheimian concept of the division of labor within a society to the division of labor on a larger, global scale and, as a corollary, from the concept of social stratification to stratification among national societies" (Janos, 1986:71). This modern world system, notes Wallerstein, is capitalist, meaning that it "is based on the priority of the ceaseless accumulation of capital. Such a system is necessarily inegalitarian, indeed polarizing, both economically and socially" (1999:87).

According to Wallerstein, at the outset this was an economic system with fairly independent subparts, not a political empire. However, it became a system in which different world regions played different roles, and still do. The **core** comprises those economic interests and nation-states that control productive activities. They have money to invest, expect a large return on investment, involve a free-floating labor force, and exploit the resources of the periphery. The **periphery** is the opposite. For much of its history it was neither economically nor politically independent. Its resources are controlled by the core, and its labor supply is controlled by either its own bourgeoisie or that of the core, or both. By trading with the core at a disadvantage, "the peripheral ruling class contributes to regional income disparity and undermines its own political position in the international system" (Janos, 1986:77).

The **semiperiphery** is the "halfway house" between the other two, but it is more than that. It serves as a buffer between core and periphery, keeping the system from disintegrating. It is also a location to which production is transferred when costs increase in the core (for example, Mexico and Indonesia). It has capital of its own, but is nevertheless dependent on the core for much of its infrastructure.

An interesting question is how a nation moves from periphery to semiperiphery, or even from semiperiphery to core. Wallerstein speaks of three mechanisms for moving from periphery to semiperiphery. The first is "seizing the chance," when an aggressive state "takes advantage of the weakened political position of core countries and the weakened economic position of domestic opponents of such policies" (1979:76). The second is "by invitation," when a transnational corporation simply moves into a less developed part of the world, and in so doing brings that area into the semiperiphery (1979:80). The third, riskiest approach is "self-reliance"—distancing one's economy from the world system, perhaps by nationalizing a resource, thereby chancing both the loss of foreign investment and core pressure for reincorporation into the periphery (1979:81).

Wallerstein makes no secret of the fact that much of his analysis continues to have a Marxist orientation. He uses Marx's terminology of exploitation, mode of production, conflict, bourgeoisie, and so on. The four Marxist ideas that Wallerstein finds useful are class struggle, polarization, the socioeconomic determination of ideology, and alienation as an evil to be eliminated (1995:226–231). Worldwide class distinctions are between states as well as within them. Exploitation is an international phenomenon, but it is also overt in the periphery, "where the elites exercise and institutionalize it in order to extract surplus from their own populations and thereby to import luxuries" (Janos, 1986:76).

The mark of the modern world, says Wallerstein, "is the imagination of its profiteers and the counter-assertiveness [docility, fatalism] of the oppressed." However, exploitation "and the refusal to accept . . . [it] as either inevitable or just constitute the continuing antimony of the modern era, joined together in a dialectic which has far from reached its climax in the twentieth century" (1974:357).

At the same time, Wallerstein notes the inadequacy of Marxist analyses of racial, ethnic, and gender struggles (1995:228). And he adds that his view of the avowedly socialist countries is quite un-Marxist: He sees them as semiperipheral, seeking access to the core. This view seems to have been corroborated by the collapse of the Soviet Union, the changes in Eastern Europe, and these countries desired incorporation into the capitalist "new world order." However, Wallerstein does not agree with Dunayevskaya's view that these countries have always been covertly capitalist. In fact, he speaks of 1917 to 1991 as "the period in which there were states governed by Communist, or Marxist-Leninist, parties." In his view, the Russian revolution of 1917 was actually "one of the first, and possibly the most dramatic, of the national liberation uprisings in the periphery and semi-periphery of the world-system" (1999:7, 11).

Wallerstein and others have written thousands of pages on his world system analysis, but let us attempt to summarize its major tenets: (1) The division of labor and of classes is a worldwide phenomenon. Although Marx and Engels noted this in the *Manifesto*, Wallerstein details its historical development, observing the expansion of the capitalist system, especially in the twentieth century. (2) Economics is the predominant factor, not politics. Political divisions serve economic needs, and political dominance may even thwart development. (3) The world system is made up of three types of units: core, semiperiphery, and periphery. Although these are agglomerations of nation-states, they are more regional than national. (4) Change is continuous, but it is neither Marxist nor a matter of modernization. It is not unidirectional, or even directional, and is not likely to be revolutionary, in the traditional sense of the word. We will return to this issue later.

Nature of Society, Humans, and Change

Wallerstein is, in many ways, a disillusioned Marxist. On the positive side, he gives capitalism credit for having created the world system, since, "for all its cruelties, it is better that it was born than that it had not been" (1974:357). On the negative side, however, capitalism "has been more exploitative (that is, extractive of surplus labor value) and destructive of life and land, for the vast majority of persons located within the boundaries of the world-economy, than any previous mode of production in world history" (1984:9).

It is the vigor of capitalism that exacerbates its contradictions. Capitalists are successful at amassing profit, and in so doing they continue to increase the inequities of the world they control. Wallerstein's criticism of this social world or society, however, is not necessarily opposed to a view of human nature as good.

Echoing Marx's "to understand in order to change," Wallerstein argues that "our intellectual responsibilities are moral responsibilities" (1984:113). Social scientists—that is, those most capable of understanding capitalism and its world system—are those most responsible for making the world a better place. Without action, the social scientist becomes irrelevant. Stated positively,

> social science really does have something to offer the world. What it has to offer is the possibility of applying human intelligence to human problems and thereby to achieving human potential, which may be less than perfection but is certainly more than humans have achieved heretofore. (1996:24)

In Wallerstein's view, the *world capitalist system* and its human alienation are essentially evils in need of correction. The intellectuals (Marx) or the social scientists (Wallerstein) can and must do something about it, not because they are perfect, or even good, but because they understand. We will return to the role of the social scientist in the section on "Other Theories."

Wallerstein presented his views on social change at the opening of the Third Portuguese Congress of Sociology in 1996 (Wallerstein, 1999:118–134). He began with the opening sentences of his 1995 book: "Change is eternal. Nothing ever changes." He explained this theme as follows: "That change is eternal is the defining belief of the modern world. That nothing ever changes is the recurrent wail of all those who have been disabused of the so-called progress of modern times" (1999:118).

Looking at technology, it is obvious that planes circle the globe, keeping up with time zones; we e-mail friends in Sweden or Singapore, and receive a response in minutes; a sale of stocks in Tokyo affects Wall Street a few hours later. At the same time, we are being told that the modern world is in terminal crisis, that we may soon resemble the fourteenth century more than the twentieth-first, that our infrastructure "may go the way of the Roman aqueducts" (1999:119). Technological change, yes, but progress? There are those, says Wallerstein,

> who look back on the multiple hunting and gathering bands that flourished . . . as structures in which humans worked many fewer hours per day and per year to maintain themselves than they do today, whose social relations were infinitely more egalitarian, and that operated in an environment that was far less polluted and dangerous. . . . The past ten-thousand years may therefore be said to constitute one long regression. (1999:119)

Not surprisingly, Wallerstein claims that neither the language of change nor of non-change is valid as stated; nor is the language of progress. A deceptive way of looking at change is in terms of functionalism. If a system is working well, it is described as superior in its functioning; if it dies, it is because it was inferior in its functioning (Wallerstein, 1999:126). However, these statements are tautological, or circular.

The major changes that have taken place in the twentieth century are, according to Wallerstein, (1) the self-determination of nations, especially resulting from decolonization—although political freedom has not been coupled with economic freedom, and certainly not with democracy; (2) a dramatic growth in economic capability or productivity, resulting in increased inequality rather than more equal distribution (1995:269); (3) the rise and fall of avowedly Marxist nation-states, which, in their time, did not live up to their own ideology.

Where is the world headed in the future? In his post-USSR book (1995) Wallerstein made predictions about the period 2000–2025. Japan, the United States, and the European Economic Community will continue to form a powerful core economy, while "the overall share of the South," meaning the population below the Equator, "in world production and world wealth will go down," with a decline in their health, education, and other social indicators. The North-South confrontation "will be at the center of the world political struggle from now on" (1995:20, 24). Wallerstein was unwilling to predict a favorable outcome, stating the changes that *should* take place, but not assuming they will.

Change, in Wallerstein's view, should be approached by looking at systemic, historical, and social change, but not looking for progress. The change from feudalism to capitalism was systemic and historical. However, the replacement of the Ming Chinese empire by the Manchu was not a systemic change, or a change in essential form. And, says Wallerstein, although we are going through a systemic transformation at present, it is not clear what this will mean in terms of long-term social change (1999:133).

Liberalism dominated the world system during the middle third of the twentieth century. Liberalism emphasizes liberty; democrats want equality. The demand for democracy, according to Wallerstein, "is stronger than it has been at any time in the time of the modern world-system" (1999:98). Liberal reformism—the managing of change by competent people, as seen in the social programs of Scandinavia and to a lesser extent in the United States—is on the defensive in the face of conservative pressures to reduce government spending and increase private control. Whether the result will be a new growth of fascism or new kinds of radical movements, Wallerstein is not sure.

Class, Gender, and Race

Class   Not surprisingly, as a quasi-Marxist, Wallerstein considers class to be a crucial analytic category. Using a somewhat broader, even vaguer, definition than Marx, Wallerstein defines classes as "groups that have a common relationship to the economy" (1984:8). He seeks to explain "why, in the history of the capitalist world-system, the bourgeoisie and proletariats have often defined their class interests in status-group terms and expressed their class consciousness in national/ethnic/religious forms" (So, 1990:229). The reason, says Wallerstein, is that class represents an antinomy [opposition], as a dialectical concept should. On the one hand, class is defined as relationship to the means of production, and hence position in the economic system which is a *world*-economy. On the other hand, a class is a real actor only to the extent that it becomes class-*conscious*, which means to the extent that it is organized as a *political* actor. But political actors are located primarily in particular national *states*. (1979:196)

But, according to Wallerstein, the existence of national economies within the world system is more rhetoric than reality. Classes are "real" in the world economy, not in nation-states. Since class consciousness is produced by and for nation-states, most of it is a false or fake consciousness, to use Marxist terminology (Wallerstein, 1984:8). "Hard-hat" workers support their flag and government, unaware that their common interest is actually at the sub- or supranational class level. Wallerstein also notes, as have Michels and others, the way in which the prospects for upward mobility weakened any sense of class solidarity in the early twentieth century (So, 1990:192). Thus, international classes, national false class consciousness, and the ideology of mobility are Wallerstein's main contributions to the discussion of class.

Gender   Wallerstein notes that in the twentieth century, "those oppressed by racism and sexism insisted on claiming the rights that liberals said they theoretically had" (1995:155). But capitalist liberalism, he suggests, may actually be an oxymoron: Liberals assert human rights and a belief in equality, while living in and supporting a world system that is, and always will be, based on inequality (1995:160–161). In other words, much of what poses as gender equality is rhetoric, not action intended to reduce or wipe out the oppression of women.

However, says Wallerstein, feminism is a real challenge not just to liberalism, but to the classic sociology of Marx, Weber, and Durkheim. Both the world and the world of knowledge have been male biased in many ways. As Gilman noted (Chapter 11), the perspective of women has been ignored. But, adds Wallerstein, feminism is not a united viewpoint: White women, women of color, and Third World women often have decidedly different interests and goals.

Race   Wallerstein has written a considerable amount about race and ethnicity in the world capitalist system. In his analysis, race and ethnicity are tools used by the capitalist world economy for two purposes: (1) to justify and enforce unequal benefits from the world system, and (2) to keep the working classes from uniting (Campbell, 1999:12). **Ethnicities** (nations, peoples) are actually social constructs; they are shaped, reshaped, created, and destroyed as they are found to be useful or detrimental to individual or societal goals (Wallerstein, 1984:20). An ethnic Meru professor at the University of Nairobi was once asked if he was both Meru and Kikuyu—a larger ethnic category under which the Meru are sometimes subsumed. His answer was: "When it is to my advantage, I am Kikuyu; when it is disadvantageous, I am just Meru." Even the terminology used serves a purpose:

> To the extent that these "peoples" are defined by themselves (and by others) as controlling or having the "moral" right to control a state-structure, these "peoples" become "nations." To the extent that a given "people" is not defined as having the right to control a state-structure, these people become "minorities" or "ethnic groups." (Wallerstein, 1984:20)

In other words, not only national class consciousness and identification, but ethnicity, nation, minority, and even race are to some extent concocted, and therefore false, labels.

Quijano and Wallerstein (1992:551) note that during slavery, African Americans were kept legally in inferior positions. However, in the postslavery period, ethnicity was not sufficient to maintain the advantages of whites, especially white males. A large amount of upward mobility made informal boundaries insufficient to maintain the ethnic/racial hierarchy. Thus, racism, both prejudicial and discriminatory, was institutionalized to reinforce ethnic stratification. Then, with formal changes toward equality, advantage continued for those in the upper strata of society, with less need for explicitly racist controls.

Some have argued, notes Wallerstein, that because of busing and reverse discrimination, we now live in a world of multiculturalism. In his view, however, we have barely scratched the surface of historic racial/ethnic inequities. "Blacks, women, and many others are still getting the short end of the stick, by and large, whatever the marginal improvements here and there" (1999:100).

Race and ethnicity apply to the entire world economy. They are not the only categories used to divide people, but they are significant; if anything, they are becoming more important in maintaining the world system. And, as noted above, ethnicity is flexible enough to be changed to meet the occupational and social needs of those in control (Wallerstein, 1987:386). As one commentator has pointed out, Wallerstein's "analysis of race is quite consistent with his previous assertions about the nature of science and society" (Campbell, 1999:15). To Wallerstein, it is important that race be examined in the context of the world system. As a social construct, it is central to the power and economic relations of the world, and—as in the case of gender—an understanding of race is necessary for those who would change society.

Other Theories and Theorists

So far in this chapter we have looked at evolutionary modernization theory and world system theory. To these two we need to add theories of dependency/underdevelopment/dependent development—that is, theories that have questioned both the evolutionists and Wallerstein's world system.

Dependency Theory   While Wallerstein was developing his world perspective, beginning with Africa, dependency theory arose in and focused on Latin America. There are many parallels between Wallerstein's early work and the Latin American dependency theory of Andre Gunder Frank—a most important "voice from the periphery" (Blomstrom and Hettne, 1984).

Earlier we noted that modernization was not just a theory but an action program, aimed by the United States especially at Latin America. Alvin So (1990) has described how this gave rise to dependency theory:

> The dependency school first arose in Latin America as a response to the bankruptcy of the program of the U.N. Economic Commission for Latin America (ECLA) in the early 1960s. . . . Many populist regimes . . . tried out the ECLA development strategy of protectionism and industrialization through import substitution in the 1950s, and many Latin American researchers had high hopes for a trend toward economic growth, welfare, and democracy. However, . . . in the early 1960s, Latin America was plagued by unemployment, inflation, currency devaluation, declining terms of trade, and other economic problems. Popular protests were followed by the collapse of popular regimes and the setting up of repressive military and authoritarian regimes. (1990:91)

In 1969, Frank wrote an influential paper, "The Sociology of Development and the Underdevelopment of Sociology," in which he criticized American writers on modernization. He characterized such change as "(1) empirically untenable, (2) theoretically insufficient, and (3) practically incapable of stimulating a process of development in the Third World" (Blomstrom and Hettne, 1984:50).

Arguing particularly with Talcott Parsons's pattern variables,[3] Frank asserted that the developed nations are often less universalistic, less based on achievement, and not as functionally specific as Parsons would lead us to believe; likewise, the underdeveloped nations are not as particularistic or ascriptive as this theory claims (Frank, 1969). Also, according to Frank, "underdevelopment was not an original stage, but rather a created condition; to exemplify he points to the British deindustrialization of India," as well as the negative effects of the European invasion of Africa and Latin America (Blomstrom and Hettne, 1984:52). In other words, contact with and oppression by Europe "underdeveloped" the Third World.

Fernando H. Cardoso joined Frank and others in spelling out the theoretical principles of the dependency school. As we have noted, much of their earliest thought paralleled very closely Wallerstein's world system perspective. A summary of dependency theory must include the following: (1) Obstacles to development arise not so much from a lack of capital or skills, but from the international division of labor; that is, they are external, not internal. (2) Surplus is transferred from underdeveloped to developed countries, so that the former lack the surplus necessary to develop. (3) Self-reliance and dissociation from the developed nations offer the only path to development (Blomstrom and Hettne, 1984:76).

---

[3]As discussed in Chapter 14, these pattern variables are (1) diffuseness–specificity, (2) affectivity–affective neutrality, (3) particularism–universalism, (4) ascription–achievement, and (5) self-orientation–collectivity orientation. According to Parsons, the first of each is found in traditional societies, and the second in modern, industrial societies. Furthermore, the worldwide change toward modernization is toward the second of each pair (Parsons, 1966:22–23).

During the 1970s and 1980s, dependency theory was both criticized and made more complex. Some societies were seen as characterized by national control of their own development, having produced their own technological expertise and goods internally.[4] Others were seen as having "export enclaves," or centers linked to the developed world, and still others as simply underdeveloped. These types were explained and further specified according to various configurations of politics (fascist, socialist, democratic), of resources (many/few, diverse/specific), of technological capability and training, and of available capital.

Knowledge and the Future   Wallerstein spent the 1990s analyzing the future of both society and social science. He claims that the next 50 years will see more upheavals in both the periphery and the core. Just where today's world system will be in AD 2050 he is unwilling to predict. As for social science, Wallerstein argues that we must do two things: (1) break down so-called disciplinary barriers, and (2) accept the responsibility of proposing changes that will make the world a better place. The task of social science, he concludes, is greatest precisely

> when the historical social system is . . . furthest from equilibrium, when the fluctuations are greatest, when the bifurcations are nearest, when small input has great output. This is the moment in which we are now living and shall be living for the next twenty-five to fifty years. (1999:217)

Critique and Conclusions

Although it would be interesting to go into dependency/underdevelopment theory in greater detail, the point has been made that multiple theories of world economics and economic change now exist. In summary, the four major schools of thought are (1) the modernization school, focusing on the "developed" societies and aimed at making the rest of the world "just like us" by bringing them along a single evolutionary path; (2) the Marxist view, discussed in the previous chapter, focusing on capitalist exploitation, imperialism, and the eventual socialist revolution; (3) Wallerstein's quasi-Marxist world system view, which sees the world as a three-tiered system, with oppression and contradictions but little hope of an overall revolution to correct its ills and inequalities; and (4) the underdevelopment/dependency view, which focuses on the Third World and proposes a more complex relationship among the factors making for economic change.

To return now to world system theory, Marxist critics have argued that Wallerstein does not explain as well as Marx did the transition from feudalism to capitalism. They have also rejected his focus on production for the market, rather than on relations of production. Finally, they assert that "class is afforded only a peripheral role in Wallerstein's conceptual apparatus, and is therefore,

---

[4]For example, Anthony Brewer wrote, "I see no reason why an independent capitalist class should not be formed on the basis of export-led industrialization or copying of techniques" (1980:289).

like the mode of production, of little importance [to Wallerstein] as an analytical tool" (Blomstrom and Hettne, 1984:188–189). Some critics simply state that Wallerstein provides a world stratification analysis, not a class analysis.

In response to these critics, Wallerstein and his followers have "conceded that the concept of 'world-system' is merely a research tool, that the world-system perspective can be used to study local historical developments, and that social class should be conceptualized as a dynamic historical process" (So, 1990:230).

Another criticism of Wallerstein is that his theory has only one new idea: that the world is a single system. Everything else he presents is either borrowed or is (often massive) descriptive detail. A final, quite intricate criticism comes from Theda Skocpol, whose theory of revolution is the focus of the third section of this chapter. Wallerstein responds directly to her criticism, but we will save their exchange until we have looked at Skocpol's theory.

Revolution: Theda Skocpol (1947–)

So far in this chapter on change, we have examined evolutionary theory and theories of world system and development (or the lack thereof). We turn now to non-Marxist theories of revolution, especially that of Theda Skocpol.

In the early 1970s, as the Vietnam War was winding down, Theda Skocpol was a politically involved graduate student at Harvard. "The times certainly stimulated my interest in understanding revolutionary change," she says. "And it was during these years that my commitment to democratic socialist ideals matured" (Skocpol, 1979:xii).

After finishing her degree at Harvard, Skocpol remained as a member of the nontenured faculty from 1975 to 1981. From 1981 to 1985, she taught sociology and political science at the University of Chicago, before returning to Harvard as Professor of Sociology, subsequently becoming jointly tenured in the Harvard Department of Government.

Skocpol studies both sociology and comparative history, and her dissertation compared the French, Russian, and Chinese revolutions. This became the focus of her first pathbreaking book, *States and Social Revolutions* (1979).

Skocpol's Central Theories and Methods

Skocpol was influenced by Barrington Moore's 1966 book on democracy and dictatorship, which we will look at under "Other Theorists" below. However, her viewpoint is very much her own, and involves understanding the state as well as revolutions.

The State   A **state**, says Skocpol, is not simply created and manipulated by a dominant class, nor is it just an arena for socioeconomic or class struggles.

> It is, rather, a set of administrative, policing, and military organizations headed, and more or less well coordinated by, an executive authority. Any

> state first and fundamentally extracts resources from society and deploys
> these to create and support coercive and administrative organizations. . . .
> These fundamental organizations are at least potentially autonomous from
> direct dominant-class control. (1979:29)

In fact, Skocpol asserts, while performing its own functions the state may even create conflicts of interest within the dominant class. "The state normally performs two basic sets of tasks: It maintains order, and it competes with other actual or potential states" (1979:30).

Skocpol's non-Marxist view of the state is interesting when compared with those of Nicos Poulantzas and Elman Service. Poulantzas, though a committed Marxist, also noted that the state was, from time to time, an independent actor in the capitalist world—related to the ruling class, but not to be analytically subsumed under it (Poulantzas, 1978; Skocpol, 1979:28). Service's view of the origin of the state was that it was primarily an administrative structure, whose task was to organize and control a region, with economic redistribution occurring later and secondarily. Thus, there is much similarity among the three, and all contrast in some degree with orthodox Marxism.

States, according to Skocpol, are actual organizations whose primary functions are to control their populations, collect taxes, and recruit for the military. Given these functions, "international military pressures and opportunities can prompt state rulers to attempt policies that conflict with, and even in extreme cases contradict, the fundamental interests of a dominant class." A state must deal both with its own class-divided socioeconomic structures and with an international system of other states. If a state deals efficiently with these primary functions, it will be considered legitimate by most people within its territory (Skocpol, 1979:31).

Revolution   Why study revolutions, and why discuss them in this volume? Skocpol claims that they "deserve special attention, not only because of their extraordinary significance for the histories of nations and the world but also because of their distinctive pattern of sociopolitical change" (1979:4). And change is what this chapter is about.

> **Social revolutions** are defined as rapid, basic transformations of a society's
> state and class structures; and they are accompanied and in part carried
> through by class-based revolts from below. Social revolutions are set apart
> from other sorts of conflicts and transformative processes above all by the
> combination of two coincidences: the coincidence of societal structural
> change with class upheaval; and the coincidence of political with social
> transformation. (Skocpol, 1979:4–5, bold added)

Rebellions, in contrast, do not result in structural change, and neither do riots.

Where and why do revolutions take place? According to Skocpol, "Modern social revolutions have happened only in countries situated in disadvantaged positions within international arenas" (1979:23). The causal factors include (1) an organized landed class that can stand up to the state; (2) peasant discontent with both land and state policies; and (3) a rigid leadership, such as a hereditary monarchy, and/or a state under pressure from other stronger nations. According to Skocpol, these are the conditions that held in France in the 1780s and in Russia and China in the twentieth century. Political crises emerged in all three countries because their old regimes were unable to implement basic reforms, and because of external pressures from Britain, Germany, and Japan, respectively.

Inflexibility and external threat are only part of the explanation. Peasant revolts, argues Skocpol, "have been the crucial insurrectionary ingredient in virtually all successful social revolutions to date," certainly in those of France, Russia, and China (1979:113). Here Skocpol draws a distinction between serfs who work on large estates and those who farm their own land. The latter, she says, are much more likely to be able to organize and revolt. Thus, the original propositions in her theory of revolution were (1) external threat, (2) state rigidity and weakness, (3) fairly independent and discontented communities, and (4) peasant insurrection. Skocpol later summarized her 1979 position as follows:

1. State organizations are central to social revolutions because they can only occur when administrative and coercive powers break down.
2. International/world historical context is crucial because context has often created the precipitating crisis/breakdown.
3. A structural, non-voluntarist approach is necessary because purposive action alone does not create and structure a revolution—it is no use trying to explain revolutions in terms of mass psychology or class interests or ideological leadership. (1994:7–9)

However, while Skocpol was writing her 1979 book, the Shah of Iran was toppled, and it was incumbent on her to explain the Iranian revolution from her theoretical perspective.

What should I say about a massive old-regime state whose bureaucracies and armies crumbled *without* first facing defeat in war or strong military competition from abroad? Even more pressing, what should I say about a revolution that apparently was "made"—quite deliberately—by urban social movements, in the absence of either peasant revolts or a rural guerrilla movement? (1994:17)

External threat and peasant discontent seemed to be missing from the Iranian revolution. However, external influence through multinational oil companies and through the Shah's acceptance of Westernization may have played the same role as a military threat. More important, she later wrote, "I became convinced that this social revolution, like others, occurred through a conjuncture of state weakness and popular revolts rooted in relatively autonomous communities" (1994:17). That these communities were urban instead of rural simply broadened her theory, reducing peasant insurrection to a subspecies of autonomous-community discontent. That the Shi'a Islamic clerics took control and made the Iranian government into a conservative Islamic state is not very different from Lenin's Bolsheviks taking control in Russia after the state had already been overthrown/fallen.

As noted earlier, Skocpol rejects a factor that has been treated as central in some other theories. Ideological hegemony is often important in postrevolutionary society, she argues, but it does not provide a predictive key to either the occurrence of revolution or the postrevolutionary organizational activities of the revolutionaries (1979:170). Her analysis emphasizes "the clear importance not only of political consolidation but also of state structures in determining revolutionary outcomes" (1979: 163–164).

Skocpol recognizes that there are failed or unsuccessful revolutions, such as those in England in the seventeenth century and Germany in the mid-1800s. Her argument is that these revolutions failed because the monarchy (the state) was strong and flexible enough to withstand internal and external pressures, and that enough power was delegated to the landlords that they were able to withstand peasant discontent (1979:140).

Finally, Skocpol discusses common postrevolutionary features. One is the creation of a centralized, bureaucratized state; a second is the loss of old upper-class control and privilege; a third is the transformation of the class structure (1979:161). However, she notes that, despite similar causal factors, the results are different because the revolutions occur in different world-historical contexts. In other words, she is more willing to theorize about causal factors than about common consequences (1979:233–234).

Social Policy   In the past decade, Skocpol's work has moved from revolutions to social policy. Four theories, she suggests, have been offered to explain social policy programs in Western societies. First is the logic of industrialism approach, which argues that cities and industrial development have forced societies to do something about the problems produced thereby. A second theory is based on national values. Belief in independent versus group action in problem solving is used to explain differences in the speed with which industrializing, urbanizing societies develop social policies. Third, welfare capitalism theory argues that social policy is a result of ideological divisions between conservatives and liberals, who disagree on the extent to which social insurance measures should be instituted by corporations themselves. Finally, the political class struggle approach is based on the ruling class's "doing good things" for those in need in order to keep the class structure under control—as Marx posited (Skocpol, 1995:17–18).

Nature of Society, Humans, and Change

Skocpol makes no judgments either about human nature or about society. And her theory avoids the rational radicalism of Rousseau and those who followed him, who claimed that through ideology and human thought one could envision, and then construct, a better world.

Skocpol's entire theory pertains to one kind of change: the dramatic, radical overthrow and rebuilding of a society's structures. She does not argue that there are no other forms of change, or even that there is a single combination of factors leading to revolution (recall her discussion of Iran).

Class, Gender, and Race

Although Skocpol is not primarily a theorist of class, much has already been said about her view of the relationship between class and revolution. Classes and class conflict are not the "prime movers" in revolutions, though they may be actors. According to Skocpol,

> class forces, whether capitalist classes that retain control over strategic means of production and economic linkages, or popular classes whose revolts or military mobilization contribute to the revolutionary struggle, are bound by ties of conflict and cooperation, command and mobilization to the dynamic and partially autonomous activities of states and state builders. (1979:291–292)

Thus, classes play a complex role in revolutionary activity, but to Skocpol, unlike Marx, they are not the prime movers in society.

Skocpol says little about race and gender in her theory of revolutions. However, in her recent work on social policy she speaks briefly to each of these factors. In discussing the U.S. War on Poverty, she notes the importance of race as an issue that is sometimes treated as unique, and sometimes subsumed under class or poverty (1995:251).

Skocpol's discussion of gender and social policy (1995:72–135) focuses on explaining the differences between British and U.S. social policies. Calling them paternalistic and maternalistic, respectively, she shows how British policies have been for the most part subsumed under labor movements. In the United States, in contrast, women were excluded from party politics, resulting in separate movements on their own behalf (1995:114–135). This distinction is reminiscent of the contrast between Beatrice Webb's socialist but nonfeminist activity in Britain and C. P. Gilman's clearly feminist writing and action in the United States.

Other Theories and Theorists

Current theories of revolution, according to Skocpol, can be divided into four categories: Marxist, aggregate-psychological, systems/value consensus, and political conflict (1979:8–9). All these theories are voluntarist, meaning that revolution is seen as the result of beliefs, consciousness, and planning on the part of individuals and groups. None of them, notes Skocpol, recognizes the state as an actor and reactor, and all ignore "*inter*national structures and world-historical developments" (1979:14). The Marxist theory, involving class consciousness and the actions of revolutionaries, we are already familiar with. Let us here look briefly at some of the others.

The theory that most influenced Skocpol's ideas was that of Barrington Moore. Moore's *Social Origins of Dictatorship and Democracy* (1966) was quasi-Marxist and in direct opposition to the single-path theory of modernization (Blomstrom and Hettne, 1984:21). For Moore, the two key factors that explain the recent histories of the world's societies are commercial transformation and violent revolution (or lack thereof). These two factors can combine in any of four ways, with the following results: "Commercialization and revolution together breed democracy; commercialization without revolution results in fascism; revolution without commercialization leads to communis[m]; . . . and, finally, the absence of both commercialization and revolution is the harbinger of political stagnation and decay" (Janos, 1986:61). Revolutions from above ordinarily result in bourgeois democracy, while those from below are more likely to produce socialism/communism.

Moore's fairly simple and straightforward theory left several loose ends dangling. First, commercialization was treated as either synonymous with or precedent to industrialization. But the discussion of dependency and underdevelopment, you will recall, indicated that it is possible to have large-scale commercial/market activity without industrialization, resulting in dependence on the more industrialized societies. Second, commercialization and revolution, while resulting in bourgeois democracy in France and the United States, has produced other outcomes—such as a socialist/capitalist mix or a semiperiphery position—at other times and places.

Lest we become too critical of Moore's simple and elegant theory, however, Skocpol reminds us that in the mid-1960s there were two primary views of the world: Marxism and modernization. To Moore's credit, he broke social scientific thinking out of this dichotomous debate.

A second view of revolution is that people become angry and frustrated and, as a result, bring about change (Gurr, 1970). This frustration-aggression school of thought opposes, but is analogous to, the theory of development/modernization that says personality and achievement orientation of individuals modernize societies (see footnote 1). The problem with frustration-aggression theory is that so many different life circumstances can give rise to feelings of frustration and relative deprivation. "To extrapolate from sums or proportions of individual attitudes to the occurrence of structural transformations . . . is to accept a naive additive image of society and its structure" (Portes, 1971).

A third approach, the ideology school of thought, argues that a well-worked-out set of alternative ideas leads to organization and then to change (Johnson, 1966). One of Skocpol's major debates has been with Bill Sewell, who represents the ideological school. Looking primarily at the French Revolution, Sewell argues that Skocpol has over-reified the concept of structure. The Enlightenment, says Sewell, contradicted the ideology of the Old Regime, insisting on natural law rather than divinity and revelation, and universalism rather than the ideology of privilege. After coexisting peacefully for a time, ideological oppositions were polarized by economic crisis, leading eventually to revolutionary upheaval (Sewell, in Skocpol, 1994:176–178). In this view, ideology is a causal focus for revolution that cannot simply be subsumed within structural analysis. Though it is more complicated than this, Skocpol's response is that it is a matter of emphasis: For her, structure is more important, while for Sewell, ideology is primary.

A fourth approach is the political-conflict perspective, best articulated by Charles Tilly. Tilly criticized other theorists for concentrating "on individual attitudes or on the condition of the social system as a whole" (Tilly, Tilly, and Tilly, 1975:488). Political violence, including revolution, "tends to flow directly out of a population's central political processes, instead of expressing diffuse strains and discontents within the population" (1975:436). Mobilization of discontent, or political conflict, is the focus of Tilly's ideas. However, one is left wondering what it is that mobilizes discontent. Is it class interest, or group frustration, or something else?

It should be noted that not all of these theories are mutually exclusive. Frustration might be channeled within existing structural divisions, or ideology might reinforce class interests. So let us move to our conclusions, first on Skocpol and Wallerstein, and then on the chapter as a whole.

Critique and Conclusions

One of the more interesting debates involving those discussed in this chapter has been between Wallerstein and Skocpol. Skocpol was asked to contribute to a review symposium on Wallerstein's *Modern World-System* (1974), and she took the opportunity to again think through her own ideas in relation to his. Her major criticisms were of his focus on economics to the exclusion of politics, and his focus on the world system to the exclusion of states and regional subdivisions.

> Wallerstein's insistence on a world-historical approach to development was to be welcomed, . . . but not his economic reductionism or his teleological treatment of the whole world as a single seamless "system." . . . I advocated the analysis of states as administrative and military organizations embedded in international geopolitical systems of military competition. (Skocpol, 1994:12)

Comparative-historical studies of states and regions seem to Skocpol most useful in making appropriate comparisons. She is also critical of Wallerstein's attempted explanation of the rise of capitalism in the fifteenth and sixteenth centuries; earlier we noted that his view of origins is indeed the weakest part of his theoretical framework. Skocpol also argues that Wallerstein, while rejecting modernization theory, makes some of the same mistakes in treating certain changes as inevitable; he is, after all, quasi-Marxist and, as such, views the world as having traveled along a certain socioeconomic path. But having said all this, it is obvious that Skocpol's major criticism is that Wallerstein deemphasizes national class divisions and nation-states too much.

By way of response, Wallerstein argues that Skocpol's notion of states as having a life of their own misperceives their character. All institutions, including states, have staffs and rules that give them a life of their own. However, this "life" is used for various purposes by its members and those who support it. It is not independent of other parts of a regional and world system. In other words, the state is not unimportant, but as part of an explanatory framework it must be subsumed under the larger, more important world structure (Wallerstein, 1984:30–35). And, he might have added, he does not represent the world system as seamless, but as comprising three subparts playing different but complementary roles.

Once again, then, it may be a matter of emphasis, with Skocpol's primary unit of analysis being the state, but not simply as an independent actor, and Wallerstein's primary unit being the world economic system, while recognizing that its subparts include nation-states. It is worth noting that Skocpol's dependent or outcome variable is revolution, whereas Wallerstein's is world economic change. Wallerstein and Skocpol, of course, would argue that the difference is much more than emphasis—that their central variables are in fact the beginning point for understanding the changing social world in which we live.

Final Thoughts

We have covered a large amount of theoretical material in this chapter. First, we have examined evolutionary theories of change, including the "modernization" idea that the whole world should and will develop toward the Western/European model. And while modernization theory is clearly questionable, some of Service's evolutionary insights into the origins of states and redistributive networks seem correct.

In the second part of the chapter, we looked at Wallerstein's world system approach, which he painted with such broad strokes that it was (like Marx's ideas) bound to have loose ends. Skocpol's questioning of Wallerstein's ignoring the state, Wallerstein's weak explanation of the origins of capitalism, and the dependency/underdevelopment view of stagnation and world antagonisms have left some questioning much of Wallerstein's framework. Then, in the final section, we became acquainted with Theda Skocpol's theory of revolutions, and compared it with several other such theories.

The overall concern of this chapter has been change—evolutionary, developmental, and revolutionary. Some explanations (Marxist, Wallerstein) have treated the entire world as an economic system, while others have reduced it to personality characteristics. Many changes are in fact incremental, resulting from small internal alterations in technology or organization; they are handled with as little social change as possible, in order to get back to equilibrium, or "business as usual." Others are revolutions on a massive, perhaps even worldwide, scale. You might find it interesting to try combining several theories that are complementary instead of contradictory. We have already noted, for example, how Service's theory of the origin of the state can be combined with Skocpol's on the role of the state in revolutions. The rest is up to you.

References

Blomstrom, Magnus, and Bjorn Hettne. 1984. *Development Theory in Transition: The Dependency Debate and Beyond: Third World Responses*. London: Zed Books.

Brewer, Anthony. 1980. *Marxist Theories of Imperialism: A Critical Survey*. London: Routledge and Kegan Paul.

Campbell, Mary E. 1999. "An Exploration of the Theories of Immanuel Wallerstein." Unpublished paper.

Childe, V. Gordon. 1936/1951. *Man Makes Himself*. New York: Mentor Books.

Erasmus, Charles J. 1966. *Man Takes Control*. Minneapolis: University of Minnesota Press.

Frank, Andrew Gunder. 1969. *Latin America: Underdevelopment or Revolution*. New York: Monthly Review Press.

Gluckman, Max. 1960. "The Rise of a Zulu Empire." *Scientific American, 201,* 157–168.

Gurr, Ted Robert. 1970. *Why Men Rebel.* Princeton, NJ: Princeton University Press.

Hagen, Everett. 1962. *On the Theory of Social Change.* Homewood, IL: R. D. Irwin.

Janos, Andrew C. 1986. *Politics and Paradigms: Changing Theories of Change in Social Science.* Stanford, CA: Stanford University Press.

Johnson, Chalmers. 1966. *Revolutionary Change.* Boston: Little, Brown.

Lerner, Daniel. 1958. *The Passing of Traditional Society.* New York: Free Press.

McClelland, David. 1962. *The Achieving Society.* Princeton, NJ: Princeton University Press.

Moore, Barrington, Jr. 1966. *Social Origins of Dictatorship and Democracy: Lord and Peasant in the Making of the Modern World.* Boston: Beacon Press.

Nisbet, Robert A. 1969. *Social Change and History: Aspects of the Western Theory of Development.* New York: Oxford University Press.

Parsons, Talcott. 1966. *Societies: Evolutionary and Comparative Perspectives.* Englewood Cliffs, NJ: Prentice-Hall.

Portes, Alejandro. 1971. "On the Logic of Post-Factum Explanations: The Hypothesis of the Lower-Class Frustrations as the Cause of Leftist Radicalism." *Social Forces, 50,* 26–44.

Poulantzas, Nicos. 1978. *State, Power, Socialism.* London: Verso Editions.

Quijano, Anibal, and Immanuel Wallerstein. 1992. "Americanity as a Concept, or the Americas in the Modern World-System." *International Social Science Journal, 44,* 549–557.

Sahlins, Marshall D., and Elman Service. 1960. *Evolution and Culture.* Ann Arbor: University of Michigan Press.

Service, Elman R. 1962. *Primitive Social Organization: An Evolutionary Perspective.* New York: Random House.

———. 1971. *Cultural Evolutionism: Theory in Practice.* New York: Holt, Rinehart, and Winston.

———. 1975. *Origins of the State and Civilization: The Process of Cultural Evolution.* New York: W. W. Norton.

Skocpol, Theda. 1979. *States and Social Revolutions.* New York: Cambridge University Press.

———. 1994. *Social Revolutions in the Modern World.* Cambridge: Cambridge University Press.

———. 1995. *Social Policy in the United States.* Princeton, NJ: Princeton University Press.

So, Alvin Y. 1990. *Social Change and Development: Modernization, Dependency, and World-System Theories.* Newbury Park, CA: Sage Publications.

Steward, Julian H. 1955. *Theory of Culture Change: The Methodology of Multilinear Evolution.* Urbana: University of Illinois Press.

Tilly, Charles, Louise Tilly, and Richard Tilly. 1975. *The Rebellious Century, 1830–1930.* Cambridge, MA: Harvard University Press.

Veblen, Thorstein. 1915. *Imperial Germany and the Industrial Revolution.* New York: The MacMillan Company.

Wallerstein, Immanuel. 1974. *The Modern World-System: Capitalist Agriculture and the Origins of the European World-Economy in the Sixteenth Century.* New York: Academic Press.

———. 1979. *The Capitalist World-Economy.* New York: Cambridge University Press.

———. 1984. *The Politics of the Capitalist World-Economy.* Cambridge: Cambridge University Press.

———. 1987. "The Construction of Peoplehood: Racism, Nationalism, Ethnicity." *Sociological Forum, 2,* 373–388.

———. 1995. *After Liberalism.* New York: The New Press.

———. 1996. "Social Science and Contemporary Society: The Vanishing Guarantees of Rationality." *International Sociology, 11,* 7–25.

———. 1999. *The End of the World As We Know It.* Minneapolis: University of Minnesota Press.

Weiner, Myron (Ed.). 1966. *Modernization: The Dynamics of Growth.* New York: Basic Books.

White, Leslie A. 1949. *The Science of Culture.* New York: Farrar, Straus and Giroux.

———. 1960. "Foreword." In Marshall D. Sahlins and Elman Service (Eds.), *Evolution and Culture* (pp. v–xii). Ann Arbor: University of Michigan Press.

Wilson, Godfrey, and Monica Wilson. 1958. *Analysis of Social Change.* Cambridge: Cambridge University Press.

SECTION IX

Transitions and Challenges

A number of late-twentieth-century views have challenged the Durkheim-Marx-Weber core of sociology. Two of these—feminism and Freudianism—were already active in theoretical circles by the turn of the twentieth century (see Chapters 11 and 13, respectively). In the next five chapters, we will introduce our own set of transitions and challenges, beginning with a review of mid-twentieth-century sociology in Chapter 19.

Chapter 19 notes the hegemony of structural-functional thinking at mid-century (see Chapter 14) and the strong belief within sociology that value-free knowledge is possible. This was questioned by Alvin Gouldner and C. Wright Mills from a Marxist perspective, and by the 1960s it was also challenged by student and "New Left" protests. In addition, outstanding Third World, feminist, and African-American thinkers were challenging the marginalization of women and minorities.

The four challenges introduced (or reintroduced) in Chapters 20–23 are: symbolic interactionism (Chapter 20), rational choice and exchange (Chapter 21), feminism (Chapter 22), and Michel Foucault's view of power, sex, violence, and science, along with its feminist critics (Chapter 23). Finally, although it is not part of Section IX, Chapter 24 will present a recapitulation and some final thoughts.

Chapter 20, on symbolic interactionism, picks up where George Herbert Mead left off in his theoretical treatment of the development of the self, and of the use of symbols in interpersonal communication. You will meet briefly the disciple of Mead who coined the term "symbolic interactionism"—Herbert Blumer. Next is Erving Goffman, who was both indebted to and distinct from the Mead-Blumer tradition. His dramaturgical approach explained interaction as analogous to behavior on a theatrical stage, in which "appropriate" lines are delivered, with "backstage" behavior being less scripted. Goffman also studied total institutions, such as asylums and prisons, in which individuals live their entire lives. The other major figure you will meet in Chapter 20 is Arlie Hochschild. Her work on emotions adds to the hyperintellectualized version of symbolic interactionism presented by the male scholars. And her application to family is an important part of her work.

Chapter 21 introduces rational choice and exchange theories, focusing on James Coleman's version of each. "I think, therefore I choose or decide" and "I think, therefore I choose what is in my best interest" are simplified versions of these two theories. The notions of making rational decisions and of maximizing one's profit are old ideas, but they are important in current theorizing. Those who disagree argue either from the premise that humans are irrational and emotional, or else from Pareto's view that humans are rationalizers, not rational.

Chapter 22 picks up feminist issues where we left them with Gilman and Webb in Chapter 11. As we noted in that chapter, male scholarship did an effective job of obliterating females from the core of sociological theory. By the 1970s, many feminists and female sociologists were active, often having to rediscover the answers produced a half century or more earlier—but also asking new questions. Dorothy Smith and Patricia Hill Collins are the central figures in this chapter.

One issue that arose in the 1960s and 1970s was that the radical movements of that period kept women "in their place," playing secondary roles. Smith sought to bring women's experience into what must be explained, and she has helped to clarify both the similarities and differences between women's and men's lives in today's world. Collins adds an important dimension to the discussion by comparing not only women's experience with men's, but black women's experience with white women's. Her insights draw together many earlier concerns of Gilman, Du Bois (Chapter 12), the Marxist Dunayevskaya (Chapter 17), and recent feminists.

Chapter 23 presents a serious expression of doubt regarding the traditional core of sociology. Foucault represents a number of sociologists who have questioned the very meaning of the texts we read. What is sociological knowledge, and what is its relation to power? Does power simply create so-called "knowledge"? Even more than those who raise issues of irrationality and rationalization, Foucault seeks to explain punishment, violence, and madness in today's world—meaning that we live in anything but a rational modern world. Feminist scholars have seen Foucault in two ways: On the one hand, they appreciate his interest in discipline and punishment as referring to much of women's historical experience; on the other hand, they are not convinced that his treatments of sex and pleasure comprehend women's lives.

Chapter 19

Mid-Twentieth-Century Sociology

The late 1950s and 1960s have, in historical hindsight, been regarded as significant years of momentous changes in the social and cultural life of most Western societies. From Elvis and an explosion of popular culture to a proliferation of experimental transformations in the arts in general; from mechanical worlds to the wired worlds of media and microchip; from love and marriage connected like a horse and carriage to "free," experimental, and cosmic love and later, with the prevalence of AIDS, dangerous love; from political reformism/conformity to the politics of protest and violence; from "father knows best" to the rise of the feminist movement—the period has marked critical changes, most especially in embodying a general "crisis of authority" and "movements of dissent" (Owram, 1996:171).

A major part of the transformation was related to the baby boom that altered, numerically and culturally, most Western societies. The idea of radical transformations that affected all aspects of social life has given the period its historical "identity" in the West. Of course, in the same time period, many non-Western societies were neither peaceful nor conformist, and the independence movements in Africa were defining non-Western events. What set the Western world apart was the scale of the changes and challenges that the baby boomers generated. Among those changes and challenges we can include the questioning of sociological orthodoxy, especially the idea of a structural-functionalist hegemony so important in North American sociology.

Ideological Disputes

As you saw in Chapter 1, sociological theory tries to understand and explain what goes on between people. By the 1960s, this exercise had become a fragmented, fractious enterprise. The internal sociological disputes over theory and methods were often played out in the meetings of various national and international sociological associations as well as in the pages of journals and reviews.

A frequent accusation used by the protagonists was that their opponent's stance was "ideological." This accusation usually meant that the opposing position was either radical (even revolutionary) or conservative (or possibly neo-fascist). The accusations of ideological bias were complicated by the political upheavals of the era in various parts of the world. Sociological radicals were implicitly (and in some cases explicitly) associated by their opponents with radical political aims and even accused of associating with, or at least condoning, so-called terrorist organizations such as the Black Panthers. Conservative sociologists were associated, again implicitly if not explicitly, with repressive state and corporate institutions and were often accused of being tools of the military-industrial complex (Mills, 1959).

We have pointed out that ideological content is part of any theory and its presence does not necessarily invalidate the theory. But in many of these disputes over the "correct" way to theorize and practice sociology, ideology as bias was the weapon of choice to invalidate an opponent's stance. The dissatisfaction with the dominant sociological paradigm took a "quasi-ideological form" in the 1960s when "system theory, particularly the Parsonian variety, was seen simply as providing justification for the conservative impulse dominating the post-war period" (Friedrichs, 1970:25).

In hindsight we can recognize that many of the debates were "tempests in an academic teapot" and that the presumed practical political importance of sociology's and sociologists' "taking a stand" was overdrawn. For example, the opposition of a considerable number of sociologists to the Vietnam War provided moral comfort but had little practical effect on the nature and duration of the war. The disputes did, however, highlight the fact that sociology has always been "political" in the sense of assuming that the discipline could in some way make a difference to society. This assumption has often meant that sociology has been "an 'oppositional science' despite its establishment as an academic subject" (Shils, 1985:175). What was important in the 1960s were the new sociological directions that spun off from many of the disputes, and it is these new directions that comprise the content of the rest of this volume.

To understand the various theoretical positions that have characterized sociology in the second half of the twentieth century, some discussion of the debates and disputes is useful. The vicissitudes of these debates will be discussed under the headings of facts and values, macro/micro perspectives, feminism and feminist theory, and race relations, recognizing that in fact the debates overlapped these divisions.

Facts and Values

In Howard Becker's 1960 presidential address to the American Sociological Association, he insisted that "There is no substitute for remaining in close touch with the empirical evidence, with the 'damned facts'" (Becker, 1960:809). The post–World War II sociological generation in the United States had been carefully trained in empirical research methods and were "dedicated to the gospel that value judgments were to be described and not made" (Friedrichs, 1970:77). This stress on research methods, especially statistical research, was less prevalent in European circles and in Britain. Empirical work, like that of the Webbs (see Chapter 11), remained outside the university context, being largely undertaken by government departments. In most cases, sociology in Europe and Britain was more social philosophy than empirical research (Bulmer, 1985:5).

But the view that it was empirical evidence, purged of any evaluative content, that formed the bedrock of the sociological enterprise was already the subject of contention in the U.S. sociological community in the 1950s. Alfred McClung Lee and Elizabeth Briant Lee, Alvin Gouldner, C. Wright Mills, and Robert S. Lynd were some of the dissenters from the idea of a value-free sociology. The dissent was muted at first by the institutional dominance of the value-free perspective. In a 1953 recording played at the annual American Sociological Association meeting, containing advice from 20 former presidents on the nature of the sociological enterprise, only one, Harry Pratt Fairchild, "mentioned a concern for social justice." All of the others stressed "the need for a value-free science" (Galliher and Galliher, 1995:27).

Mid-twentieth-century sociology in North America was dominated by a small set of theoretical positions (Collins, 1981:1). Collins characterized the sociological profile for North America at that time as functionalism—the "main pretender to being general theory"—with social change taking the form of an "ethnocentric evolutionist developmentalism" and, at the micro level, the "narrow positivism of social behaviorism" or the "loyal opposition of symbolic interactionism." Kingsley Davis, in his presidential address to the American Sociological Association in 1959, asserted that sociology equaled functional analysis.

The most influential of the functionalist theorists was Talcott Parsons (see Chapter 14). Parsons's *The Social System* (1951) was a key text in establishing the paradigmatic status of system and functionalism, which were "deemed by the well-informed professional to represent sociological orthodoxy in the 'fifties'" (Freidrich, 1970:19). Hinkle (1994:336) asserts that by 1950 the "ascendance of structural functionalism seemed to be assured" and various alternative theoretical orientations from the past had become residual.

The general indifference to alternative sociological perspectives in U.S. sociology in the 1950s was, according to Hinkle, the result of the institutionalization of the discipline in the academy. Gouldner (1963:45) saw the problem more specifically as the compulsive trend to transform an institutionalized sociology into a "profession." In a discussion of Parsons's paper "Sociology as a Profession," Gouldner remarked that Parsons's description had been rejected by E. C. Hughes. Hughes (1963:45) claimed that the American Sociological Association was not a "professional but, rather, a learned society." Gouldner, however, pointed out that professionalism seemed to have taken hold, resulting in "the growth of technical specialists" and a "diffusion of the value-free outlook to the point where it becomes less of an intellectual doctrine and more of a blanketing mood" (Gouldner, 1963:48).

Value-free Sociology

The push for professionalism and value-free sociology and the codification of sociological orthodoxy as structural functionalism were accompanied by an increase in the numbers of sociology students in the 1940s and in the membership of the American Sociological Association, which grew from 1,651 in 1946 to 3,241 in 1950. The entrenchment and expansion of sociology within academia consolidated the idea that the only viable sociological enterprise was a **scientific** enterprise and that it was "statistically-oriented, qualified empiricist neo-positivism" that formed the "legitimating criteria (or norms) for undertaking valid sociological research" (Hinkle, 1994:62).

In a review of the state of sociology in the 1950s, Lipset and Smelser proclaimed the "complete triumph since World War I of the new 'scientific sociology'" (1961:40). George Lundberg (1961:40) stated confidently that, like physical scientists, social scientists could produce scientific knowledge with "impersonal, neutral, general validity for whatever purposes man desires to use it." Lundberg went on to point out that the "services of *real* social scientists," as value-free scientists, "would be as indispensable to Fascists as to Communists and Democrats, just as are the services of physicists and physicians" (Lundberg, 1961:57).

The claims to value neutrality did not go unchallenged. Gouldner pointed out that the segregation of reason and passion (or sociological scientific techniques and social ethical positions) *"warps reason by tingeing it with sadism and leaves feeling smugly sure only of itself and bereft of a sense of common humanity"* (1963:51, emphasis in the original). Despite such criticisms, the majority of North American sociologists believed that the discipline had made progress toward becoming a science of society.

The triumphalism of North American commentators on the state of the discipline at that time was only minimally echoed in other sociological centers such as Europe, Asia, Britain, and South America, but there was *seeming* consensus on the nature of the sociological enterprise as necessary, worthy, and scientific. Structural and functional perspectives were current in other sociological centers, but they were often given national interpretations that had to do with the particular development of sociology in those centers. A significant divergence from the structural/functional perspective was the retention of a Marxist or conflict perspective in European sociology, and C. Wright Mills at Columbia was a persistent critic of North American sociology from the 1950s. Mills's *The Sociological Imagination* (1959) critiqued structural functionalism and abstract empiricism and contrasted these perspectives with what he saw as the more sociologically relevant European critical tradition.

Nonetheless, in both the European and North American context, there was a "widely shared dream that sociology could and would produce the objective truth of modern society" (Lemert, 1992:65). Lundberg (1961) asked the question "Can Science Save Us?" and concluded that, yes, science—both natural *and* social science—could alleviate physical and social problems. There were no other alternatives to placing "faith in social science" for "social solutions" (1961:134).

This "agreeable" sociological atmosphere was to undergo considerable disruption as the decade of the 1960s progressed. As Friedrichs (1970:25) euphemistically remarked, sociology "entered a time of troubles." This period resembled the crisis stage that Kuhn (1970) saw as the "necessary prologue to the emergence of a new paradigm." The time was ripe for a transformation of the nature, grounds, and methods of sociology. It was the value-free, scientific claim that was a target for young "dissenters."[1] A particular focus for opposition was the theoretical hegemony of Parsons's structural functionalism (Alexander, 1987:111).

Protests and Challenges

The claims of *any* scientific enterprise to be the agent of progress, social well-being, and in the West at least, democracy had come under increasing scrutiny in the aftermath of World War II and Hiroshima. The irony of sociology's adoption of the "value-free posture . . . informed by the image of natural science" was that the claim was "at least a generation out of date," as most Western spokesmen for natural science saw "creative work in science as riddled by personal, idiosyncratic factors" (Friedrichs, 1970:137).

In the 1960s, the discussions and dissent over sociology as a value-free science became more evident and insistent. The internal sociological malaise was situated in, and affected by, the more general social and political upheavals of the decade. The mid-sixties saw protests aimed at postindustrial society and the upheavals of "race, poverty and the Vietnam War" (Eisenstadt and Curelaru, 1976:335). Much of the protest was centered in universities and colleges, fueled by the huge increases in postsecondary student populations.

Among the radical protesters, "from Berkeley and New York to Paris and Berlin," sociology students were usually in the forefront, if not the leaders, of student protest and revolts (Collins, 1981:316). Lipset and Ladd (1972) showed that sociologists in general were more predisposed to political radicalism than other members of the professoriate. Janowitz (1972:114) reported that, on the central issues of the 1960s—the Vietnam War, race relations, and civil liberties— data collected for the Carnegie Commission of Higher Education showed that "sociology professors had the highest concentration of 'left of center' attitudes on these related issues." A large proportion of the more radical sociologists were young graduates and newly minted doctorates rather than the structural-functional old guard in North America or the old left-leaning partisans in Britain and Europe.

The radicalism of this period has often been subsumed under the term New Left. The description does not refer to any singular, specific political party or movement, but refers more generally to the fact that the ideas of Marx and Lenin, as well as Mao, were regarded as relevant to the necessary, revolutionary, global struggle against the forces of any entrenched institutional repression.

---

[1]Friedrichs (1970:24) pointed out that Bell's "end of ideology" thesis was dated by the revolutionary events of the 1960s almost as soon as it appeared in 1960.

The Marx who was relevant was not, however, the Marx of class conflict but the Marx of alienation. For the whole counterculture, "of which the New Left was a part, the whole notion of existential angst was essential" (Owram, 1996:230). Indeed, many of the radicals of the 1960s maintained a tenuous, usually remote, relationship with the members and organizations of the traditional "working class." For example, Maoists maintained that the more interesting and necessary tactics were motivating and assisting peasant uprisings.

What these interrelated movements, ideologies, and activities meant for sociology was a more eclectic approach to what counted as a foundational theoretical past. For North American sociology in particular, it meant a more systematic incorporation of Marx's work into the sociological mainstream after its subterranean existence in the 1950s in various conflict theories. Part of the reason for the neglect of Marx in North American sociology had to do with the political tenor of the times, in particular the postwar reaction to Stalin and McCarthy's witch-hunts for communists in U.S. government service. In North American sociology, it was New Left sociologists, using Marx's legacy, who criticized structural functionalism by accusing it of neglecting the socially significant forces of "inequality, power, coercion, conflict and change" (Turner and Turner, 1990:168).

Marx's work had always been important to European and British sociology, but the nature of that importance was reinterpreted, focusing on the "humanist" Marx, the "young" Marx, or the Hegelian legacy in Marx's work. Freud also found a new audience as an important theorist of sex/gender constructions that differed from the previous clinical, psychiatric utilization of his work. Freud's new audience was, however, a radically critical audience of new-wave feminists.

The radicalism of sociology students and young faculty encountered resistance. In some cases, military force was used to quell student protests. From the 1964 free-speech agitation at Berkeley to the Paris student riots in May 1968, including numerous strikes and occupations at universities and colleges around the world, civil disobedience was met with increasing intolerance by established state authorities. The use of force to control and contain the protests was partly in response to the increasing violence of the protests themselves, as the romanticism of "flower power" gradually gave way to the Realpolitik of, for example, the guns and bombs of the Weathermen, the Red Brigade, and the Front de la Libération du Quebec.

Negative reactions and resistance were also found in the various institutional supports for academic sociology—the journals, association meetings, and faculty committees. The central concern was the future course of the discipline, especially the issue of value-free sociology. Some of the tenor of the debate can be gleaned from some of the American Sociological Association presidential addresses of the late 1960s and 1970s.

Presidential Addresses

In his 1964 presidential address, George C. Homans criticized the structural functional perspective that had been dominant "for a whole generation" but which, in his view, "had run its course, done its work, and now positively gets in the way of our understanding of social phenomena" (Homans, 1964:809). Homans's main criticism was that structural-functional explanations were not in fact scientific, largely because they failed to provide explanations for empirical relations. According to Homans, the perspective did not take "the job of theory seriously enough," and it never "produced a functional theory that was in fact an explanation" (1964:818). More specifically, as the title of his address, "Bringing Men Back In," indicated, the structural functional focus on the social system at the expense of social action produced a theory that "appeared to have no actors and mighty little action" (1964:817). Homans's own theoretical perspective, which concentrated on the nature of social action in terms of rational choice, is discussed in Chapter 21 of this volume.

The growing chorus of criticism of the structural functional perspective, and of the work of Talcott Parsons in particular, continued, and a pluralism of perspectives developed. Some of the fiercest critics were feminists, who saw Parsons's work as the codification of patriarchal attitudes and practices. For example, Betty Friedan (1963:121–123) took Parsons to task for his promotion of the segregation of sex roles as "functional" to the maintenance of the patriarchal status quo. Other departures from the mainstream paradigm included ethnomethodology and phenomenological sociology as well as feminist sociology.

The resulting pluralism was not greeted with delight by all members of the sociological community. Coser's presidential address in 1975, titled "Two Methods in Search of a Substance," was a critique of both ethnomethodology and the search for technical precision at the expense of theory. In Coser's view, these two developments were representative of the "growth of narrow, routine activities" that produced "sect-like, esoteric ruminations," and together they reflected "crisis and fatigue within the discipline and its theoretical underpinnings" (Coser, 1975:691). Despite the seeming difference, even antagonism, of the two methods, Coser detected a common thread in their "preoccupation with method" that led to the "neglect of significance and substance." Coser maintained that sociology would be judged in terms of the "substantive enlightenment" it was able to bring to the "social structures in which we are enmeshed and which largely condition the course of our lives." If this was neglected, sociology would forfeit its birthright and degenerate into "congeries of rival sects and specialized researchers who will learn more and more about less and less" (Coser, 1975:698).

Coser was not alone in his criticism of sociological pluralism, especially as represented by the methodological debates around statistical research and theoretical significance.[2] Gouldner, in *The Coming Crisis of Western Sociology* (1970), had also launched an attack on the theoretical mindlessness of statistical research and the limitations of structural functionalism, as well as ethnomethodology—which he characterized as psychedelic anarchism. Collins (1981) maintained that Gouldner's focus on Western sociology was somewhat misleading, however. It did not address other traditions such as Marxist or neo-

---

[2]The idea that mathematical functions should be developed to express social relationships and thus establish sociology as a genuine scientific enterprise was promoted by a small number of sociologists in the early years. See, for example, Dodd (1942).

Weberian conflict theory, phenomenology, or the "European idealist-historicist tradition," so that in Collins's view, a more apt title for the book would have been "The Crisis of Functionalist Theory" (Collins, 1981:317).

The debunking of the value-free proposition, exemplified by structural-functionalist perspectives and the instrumentalism of "pure" empiricism, was deemed vital because, according to the critics, social and political conditions of the late1950s and 1960s made sociology vulnerable to manipulation by pragmatic, but often unscrupulous, politicians. Galliher and Galliher (1995:28–32) have documented some of the positions taken by prominent sociological advocates of value-freedom on the McCarthy era, fascism, and racism. For example, Parsons helped U.S. military intelligence and the State Department find university appointments for "experts on the Soviet Union, who had assisted the Nazi government during WW II," and Edward Shils thought the Vietnam War was justified and expressed regret that "it had to be halted without success."

The way in which the presumed neutrality of statistical "facts" could make sociological work amenable to misuse by nonsociologists was the subject of Alfred McClung Lee's 1976 presidential address. Lee's election had been the result of a write-in campaign, and the "candidacy of such an anti-establishment candidate was aided by the widespread alienation generated by the war in Viet Nam" (Galliher and Galliher, 1995:113). Lee had long been opposed to the idea of value-freedom, seeing it as simply moral bankruptcy on the part of sociologists. He and his wife, the sociologist Elizabeth Briant Lee, founded the Society for the Study of Social Problems in 1951 and, in 1976, the Society for Humanist Sociology. Their concern was that sociology address "real life problems of peace, equality and social justice" (Galliher and Galliher, 1995:126).

Lee's address was titled "Sociology for Whom?" His answer was a "sociology for the service of humanity" (1976:925). Lee had always been concerned that strict empiricism and a value-free perspective would simply prepare sociologists "for employment by social manipulators" (1973:36). He maintained that the "great challenge of social science is the development and wide dissemination of social wisdom and social action techniques that will enable more and more people to participate in the control and guidance of their group and their society" (1973:6). In Lee's view, the integrity of sociology and its founding principles was at stake.

Lee's concern reflected Peter Blau's disquiet, expressed in 1974. Blau had warned that the "growing concentration of resources and powers in large organizations and their top executives poses a serious threat of structural consolidation in contemporary society" that was fundamentally "incompatible with democracy, which depends on checks and balances to protect the sovereignty of the people." Blau's conclusion was that the "challenge of the century" was to "find ways to curb the power of organizations in the face of their powerful opposition, without destroying in the process the organizations and democracy itself." The alternative, he believed, was that "democratically instituted recurrent social change" would be replaced by "alternate periods of social stagnation and revolutionary upheaval." In his view, the "threat is serious, and the time is late" (Blau, 1974:633–634).

Ethical Sociology

The call for sociological ethical responsibility exemplified what Friedrichs has called the "prophetic stance" characteristic of some earlier positions in U.S. sociology, found in the work of, for example, Pitrim Sorokin, Robert S. Lynd, and C. Wright Mills. A key feature in the work of these sociologists was a "critical diagnosis of existing social institutions combined with a highly optimistic image of the contribution that sociology might make to a more intelligent reordering of human affairs" (Friedrichs, 1970:74). Most of these sociologists did not involve themselves directly in the political realm, but their position was akin to that endorsed by Max Weber who, as we saw in Chapter 7, pointed out that although party politics had no place in research or the classroom, this did not mean that sociologists should adopt a posture of moral indifference to the events of their time. Indeed, indifference could be dangerous in that it supported established powers by default and produced a sociology in which "research is typically utilitarian and consideration of ethics is proudly eschewed," and there is no concern for the subjects who are studied (Galliher and Galliher, 1995:176).

An ethical sociology is important, but as Becker and Horowitz (1972:64) pointed out, "radical rhetoric or ideological posture does not inevitably result in politically useful sociological work." Furthermore, ideology is no substitute for "cogent, empirically verified knowledge of the world as a basis for effective action." In their view, there was, sociologically speaking, no substitute for the "damned facts." But this does not mean that factual investigations are, or ever could be, devoid of values, or that the "facts" exist apart from interpretation. More recently, Sica has suggested that "sociological work of the highest order began as, and continues to be, an exercise in *applied ethics*" and the "self-abnegating "scientist," aloof from values or political freight, fools no-one anymore" (1997:3).

The debates and disputes that characterized the 1960s and early 1970s were often bitterly fought, but the result was constructive in pushing theoretical and research enterprises in new directions. Levine (1995:271–272) lists 18 different approaches that are currently pursued in sociology, some of which are new departures on old themes, such as ethnomethodology, structuralism, phenomenology, sociobiology, rational choice theory, and world systems theory. The proliferation of approaches, characterized by different presuppositions about the nature of the social, has often been simplified by the idea of a macro/micro divide (Ritzer, 1983). The divide refers to some theorists' concentration on the "macro" level of total social systems while others concentrate on the "micro" level of analysis of social action and social relations.

Macro/Micro Perspectives

The macro/micro (or in European sociology, structure/agency) conceptualization was a shorthand way of acknowledging the multiparadigmatic character of sociology. In *The Structure of Scientific Revolutions*, originally published in 1962, Thomas Kuhn defined **paradigms** as "universally recognized scientific achievements that for a time provide model problems and solutions to a community of practitioners" (1970:57). Paradigms define "what should be studied, what questions should be asked, how they should be asked, and what rules should be followed in interpreting the answers obtained" (Ritzer, 1983:7).

Kuhn's work criticized the traditional idea that progress in the physical and natural sciences was cumulative and that each scientific breakthrough was based on previous scientific work in the manner implied by Isaac Newton's comment, "If I have seen further, it is because I stood on the shoulders of giants." Kuhn maintained that, although accumulation of knowledge in "normal science" did occur and progress was made, the more significant breakthroughs were the result of scientific revolutions. **Normal science** he defined as research "based upon one or more past scientific achievements, achievements that some particular scientific community acknowledges for a time as supplying the foundation for its further practice" (1970:10). Dominant paradigms, or common frames of reference, enable normal science to accumulate knowledge, but at some point the paradigms prove insufficient to explain all that needs explaining.

Kuhn pointed out that all science is continually confronted with exceptions and anomalies that cannot be explained in terms of the dominant paradigm. Initially, scientists either ignore these anomalies or attempt to incorporate them into the established paradigm. When the anomalies persist and it becomes apparent that the established paradigm cannot explain them, the foundations for a scientific revolution are established.[3] When anomalies cannot be overlooked or denied, the scientific discipline enters a state of crisis. Dissent increases within the scientific community, until the old paradigm is rejected and a new one takes its place. Such revolutions, or paradigmatic shifts, are usually the work of young scientists, less bound by tradition, who are able to formulate new conceptualizations that make better sense of the evidence (the facts) and thus transform the way in which the subject matter, or scientific "reality," is perceived and understood.

Sociology and Paradigm Conflicts

Sociology is also characterized by paradigmatic conflicts. The facts/value debate, for example, was a paradigmatic debate about the role of the sociologist and the subject matter of sociology. Another paradigmatic divide concerns the appropriate object, or unit of analysis, for sociology. Should the sociologist study society, as Durkheim suggested, or should the appropriate unit of analysis be the interactions and symbolic meanings of social actors, as advocated by Mead and Cooley? That is, is sociology the **macro** study of total social systems and their structures and institutions, or is it the study of **micro** social interactions with an emphasis on the autonomy of the social actor?

---

[3]Kuhn points out that the anomaly "appears only against the background provided by the paradigm," and the fact that "a significant scientific novelty so often emerges simultaneously from several laboratories is an index both to the strongly traditional nature of normal science and to the completeness with which the traditional pursuit prepares the way for change" (1970:65).

The institutionalization of the macro/micro dichotomy occurred at the Tenth World Congress of Sociology, held in Mexico in 1983. The title for the conference was "Macro- and Micro-Sociological Analysis." The general tenor of the Congress was to try to heal the divide and lay to rest the idea that there were two separate theoretical pursuits in sociology. Many of the papers delivered at the Congress saw the dichotomy as resulting from "partisan, selective and one-sided readings of the classics" (Eisenstadt and Helle, 1985, 1:3).

Despite the efforts of scholars at the World Congress, the dichotomy tended to linger on in sociological discourse and sociological textbooks. One reason was that, as you have seen in the previous chapters, classical sociologists often used different paradigms, and these subsequently became the basis for overgeneralized differentiations among the theorists and their theories. For example, Durkheim's focus on social facts is often contrasted with Weber's verstehen approach. Durkheim's insistence on the distinction between sociology and psychology, with sociology having a subject matter all its own, has also been used to justify the macro/micro division. Similarly, Durkheim or Spencer's focus on social systems may be contrasted with Simmel's focus on the intricacies of social interaction.

The division of the work of the classical sociologists into rigid macro/micro categories often misrepresents their work. For example, Simmel's (micro) studies of the forms and types of interaction are complemented by his monumental (macro) analysis of the history and development of monetary systems. In the 1960s, however, the division seemed entrenched, as did the often acrimonious relations between "interactionists" and "system" theorists over the "correct" unit of sociological analysis.

Some of the acrimony was related to the entrenchment of sociology in the academy and the boom in sociology enrollments, with the consequent competition for legitimacy and students (and their fees). Lemert (1992:66) suggests that the divisions were apparent in the 1950s and early 1960s, but there was a "mutual nonaggression pact by which the parties agreed simply to keep silent about their differences" for the "greater good of sociology." By the late 1960s, the pact fell apart. "Differences were not just allowed but passionately desired," and "ethnomethodology, constructionism, phenomenology, critical theory, Marxisms of various kinds were the rage in many departments, at least among graduate students. Some survived; some did not. But none had any particular intention of respecting official orthodoxy other than their own" (Lemert, 1992:66).

Contemporary Paradigmatic Divisions

Despite our belief that the macro/micro dichotomy is a misguided division of the sociological endeavor, we use it here because it remains descriptive of the divided focus of much contemporary sociological work and, despite the valiant efforts of many contemporary theorists, the desired synthesis seems elusive. In 1984, Collins still saw sociology split into "separate cocoons that scarcely occupy the same intellectual universe." He singled out statistical sociology in particular, claiming that it "makes no concessions of intelligibility toward outsiders and shows almost no interest in linking up with larger theoretical concerns" (Collins, 1984:330). Collins maintained that it was a mistake to regard statistics as "neutral method," arguing that "statistics is not method but theory" or rather, "*substantive theory* of how chance processes operate in the social world" (1984:331). Collins also saw "anti-positivists" militantly promoting their own programs of "interpretive, historical, Marxist, structuralist, or ethnomethodological sociology" and condemning their "positivist opponents *in absentia*" (Collins, 1984:330–331).

In 1990, Turner and Turner (1990:139–140) called sociology an "impossible science" because any synthesis of the various paradigms remained elusive. They saw the lack of synthesis as resulting from the encouragement of "enormous intellectual diversity" by the American Sociological Association (ASA) during the expansive years of the 1960s. Turner and Turner suggested that the problem became serious when student enrollments and financial support began to decline in the 1970s. The fragmented sociological community and the ASA did not have the control or resources to cope with the decline by reorganizing the discipline or mobilizing the "profession toward a more coherent conception of itself as a discipline" (1990:140). Their conclusion was that "it will be difficult for American sociology to become theoretically unified like the natural sciences" (1990:171).

Turner and Turner's pessimism can be qualified by Kuhn's point that no scientific endeavor remains static or is more than briefly unified in its understandings of the content and methods appropriate to its subject matter. Indeed, the vitality of much physical and natural science in the later twentieth century would appear to be the result of a variety of competing paradigms, and the same applies to late-twentieth-century sociology.

The search for synthesis/coherence/unity is itself an ideological project. Scientific revolutions rejuvenate, and the proliferation of perspectives might just as well be seen, in Kuhn's terms, as a "pre-paradigm shift" in which "several schools compete for the domination of a given field." Over time, however, a "post-paradigm" period emerges, the number of schools is reduced, and a "more efficient mode of scientific practice begins" (Kuhn, 1970:178). Thus, Turner and Turner's "impossible science" is probably only a temporary phenomenon.

Indeed some of the more recent theoretical work attempts to bridge, if not eliminate, the various divides as well as incorporate extrasociological disciplinary perspectives. Two sociological developments that address and attempt to bridge these divides are feminist sociological theory and theories of race and colonialism.

Feminism and Feminist Sociological Theory

A student of sociology in the 1950s would have assumed that the discipline, like most other academic pursuits, was almost entirely a masculine activity. This assumption was accurate with respect to the academy. Despite the increased number of women students in sociology graduate programs from the late 1950s on, and despite, as we have already seen, the significant contributions of women in the past to the establishment of sociology, research and academic appointments remained masculinist.

Women's Marginality

The situation for women in the sociology department at Berkeley was representative of most sociology departments prior to the 1960s. From 1948 through 1970, the university hired no women in tenure track positions, although between 1952 and 1972 one-third of its graduate students were women (Orlans and Wallace, 1994:6). In 1940, before the establishment of the department of sociology at Berkeley in 1946, Dorothy Swaine Thomas (1899–1977) was hired as a lecturer in rural sociology on the understanding that she would eventually chair the department of sociology when it was established. Thomas's reception at Berkeley was less than cordial among male sociologists; Nisbet was particularly opposed to her potential leadership of the department, claiming that Thomas was "personally and professionally . . . a menace to a liberal arts college" (Murray, 1979:72). Despite this opposition, Thomas became the first woman elected president of the American Sociological Society (now the ASA) in 1952. When the department was formed and Thomas was excluded, she left for the University of Pennsylvania, where she remained until her retirement in 1974.

Similarly, Deegan (1995:325) noted that the sociology department at the University of Chicago had a total of 11 untenured and thus marginal, female faculty members between 1892 and 1960. The first woman to obtain tenure at the University of Chicago was Evelyn Kitagawa in 1975. Deegan's figures are particularly telling because it was at the University of Chicago that North American sociology really became recognized as an academic discipline. The first sociology graduate program was established at the University of Chicago in 1892, and in the early years, from 1892 to 1920, women made significant contributions to the department.[4]

The marginality of women at the University of Chicago and Berkeley was echoed in other sociological centers, despite the important contributions made by many women to the establishment of the discipline. Morgan (1980) listed 117 women sociology graduates from North American colleges and universities in the nineteenth century, but noted that only 6 of the 117 obtained academic positions. The marginality of women sociologists was not simply their failure to obtain academic positions; their work was also overlooked in books and discourses about the sociological canon. For example, Charlotte Perkins Gilman (see Chapter 11) was regarded as a utopian novelist rather than an important sociologist.

A similar historical amnesia affected European women sociologists. Harriet Martineau (see Chapter 2) wrote the first methods text for sociology and introduced Comte's work to the English-speaking world with her translation and condensation of his six-volume *Cours de philosophie positive* into two volumes in

---

[4]Mary Jo Deegan (1991) has produced a valuable reference book documenting the lives and work of 51 women sociologists, from Harriet Martineau (1802–1876) to more contemporary sociologists such as Dorothy Smith and Alice Rossi. In addition, she lists 64 other significant women sociologists whose biographies are not included in the book. The numbers are impressive, especially as Deegan's work does not include the women sociologists who would have been part of the graduate cohorts of the 1970s.

1853, yet her contributions have, until recently, been overlooked. Marianne Weber's sociological work is usually overlooked, especially when that of her husband is discussed. And in Britain, Beatrice and Sydney Webb, who formed a lifelong sociological team and were prime movers in the establishment of the first social science institution, the London School of Economics (LSE), in 1895, did their own sociological work outside the academy. In fact, there were no women sociologists of any note in Britain before the late 1950s. When sociology at LSE began to expand in 1950 with the enrollment of 12 graduate students, only one was a woman—Olive Banks, who went on to a distinguished career at the University of Leicester (Halsey, 1985:152).

The absence of women from the new sociological institutions in the late nineteenth and early twentieth centuries is all the more remarkable when you recall that this was the period of the first women's movement and, as you have seen in previous chapters, many of the classical sociologists had something to say about women and the "woman question."

The marginality of women in the institutionalization of sociology in North America in the 1950s was attributable partly to their role as wives and mothers and partly to institutional impediments, such as nepotism rules, that made it impossible for faculty wives to obtain faculty positions—other than temporary, part-time, and untenured positions. More insidious was the invisibility of women's contributions to their husbands' publications. Many women sociologists were effectively coauthors of their husbands' work, but many did not receive recognition in print. An exception was Alfred McClung Lee, who included his wife, Elizabeth Briant Lee, as coauthor of *The Fine Art of Propaganda* (1969). This acknowledgment was, as one commentator observed, "almost unheard of at the time . . . even if the woman did most of the writing and research" (Galliher and Galliher, 1995:57).

The invisibility of women and their intellectual contributions was not peculiar to sociology. Spender (1982) noted that men had often claimed credit for the intellectual labor of women, or had discredited the scholarship because of the sex of the author rather than on the basis of the content of the work. The result was that the legacy of women's intellectual work was lost, and women were often in the position of "reinventing the wheel." This was certainly the case in the early years of the second women's movement, when women researchers began to look into the archives and to unearth the work of women in the past, only to discover that many of the issues they currently identified and confronted had been addressed by their foremothers, often in the same terms. In the 1960s, feminists in the academy began to challenge this masculine hegemony.

Feminist Transformations

The process of recovering women's social realities, as well as women's past sociological contributions, began in conjunction with the second women's movement in the 1960s. As you have seen in previous chapters, classical sociologists frequently had a great deal to say about women's roles and behaviors, but in twentieth-century text summaries and evaluations of their work, their comments on women as well as on race were usually omitted. The elimination of these often misogynist comments on women by the classical theorists tended to reinforce the idea that the development of sociology was a heroic male quest.

The initial feminist transformations of sociology were directly connected with the women's movement. As one feminist sociologist noted, "The women's movement has struggled to make women's voices heard in universities and colleges, and within academic disciplines," and researchers "took seriously in practice and in theory the universality lent our project by the category 'women'" (Smith, 1999:16, 18). For second-wave feminist sociologists, experience was privileged as a source of knowledge. The claims of objectivity, or a value-free science, were rejected as unattainable and, when pursued, productive of distorted knowledge and oppressive practices.

The origins of the second wave of feminism were in the various political protest groups of the New Left, the civil rights movement, and colonial liberation movements. The feminist movement was also fueled by the increased population of female students in colleges and universities. Many of these female graduates became the young, educated suburban housewives whose discontent Betty Friedan called the "problem with no name." Friedan (1963:13) found that the "dream image" offered American women, which was believed to be the envy of women "all over the world"—the suburban housewife—was profoundly unsatisfying to many of these women. Women were discovering that they were, as Simone de Beauvoir (1961:xvi) put it, the "Other":

> Thus, humanity is male and man defines woman not in herself but as relative to him: she is not regarded as an autonomous being . . . she is simply what man decrees; thus she is called "the sex," by which is meant that she appears essentially to the male as a sexual being. For him she is sex—absolute sex. . . . She is defined and differentiated with reference to man and not he with reference to her; she is incidental, the inessential as opposed to the essential. He is the Subject, he is Absolute—she is the Other.

The "problem with no name" was not confined to suburban housewives; women in the New Left movements were confronted with a similar experience. As Lydia Sargent (1981:xii) observed, "They were doing important, valuable work: stopping a war, fighting for civil rights; they were taking risks, learning and growing." But movement women also knew that the "men in the movement (and in some cases the women) saw women's function and legitimacy primarily through their participation in traditionally 'feminine' ways, i.e., as movement wives, mothers, sisters, mistresses, secretaries, maids, waitresses, nurses, and sex objects." The discovery of persistent inequities, even in movements devoted to freedom and equality, and the realization that change would have to start with women themselves, produced a variety of women's movements devoted to the analysis of women's conditions and the search for social change.

The early movements were often dominated by young women students, and especially young women sociologists. What they discovered was that the sociological subject was normatively a white male, with women, as well as blacks, making an appearance in restricted contexts of marriage and family or race relations. When women were included in sociological accounts, the information was often ideological rather than based on careful empirical investigation. Broverman and associates, for example, documented the double standard that prevailed in judgments of mental health. From a clinical point of view, a "healthy" woman accepted the behavioral norms for her sex, although these same norms were considered unhealthy for a competent, mature adult. The norms governing healthy adult behavior matched those that defined the healthy, mature *male* (Broverman, Broverman, Clarkson, Rosenkrantz, and Vogel, 1970).

Women's Issues

The identification of women's issues under the general rubric that the "personal is political" began to transform traditional sociological content, methods, and theoretical perspectives. The feminist recognition of the political significance of "private" matters helped a demographer, Harriet Presser, generate a "research agenda that reflected both my personal experiences and my political concerns." This research agenda had the effect of enhancing her "commitment to the field," which in turn helped to "broaden the field itself" (1994:142). For Presser, the personal was not only political "but also professional."

For many other young women sociologists, the "everyday world" became "problematic," which generated studies of sex/gender social divisions (Smith, 1987). Ann Oakley, for example, did a sociological analysis of housework as work. Her *Sociology of Housework* (1974) documented women's dissatisfaction with the nature and conditions of housework that paralleled, in many respects, the dissatisfactions expressed by male assembly-line workers. Oakley's work was initially greeted with disbelief by mainstream, mostly male, sociologists, for whom the idea that housework was work, only differentiated from their own studies of work by being unpaid, was absurd and certainly unsociological!

The women's movement linked together the inequities of home and work and brought women's concerns into the political arena. Housework, sexuality, and "daily life in the community and the family" were seen as "sites of struggle and consciousness" and, therefore, as significant issues for sociological research (Rowbotham, 1992:273). More important, feminist research was not research *on* women, but research *for* and *by* women.

As the access to the sociological establishment remained difficult for women, they set about forming their own networks, associations, and publishing outlets, just as Gilman had done 60 years earlier. Several journals devoted to feminist research were established, many of them interdisciplinary in nature and focused on social change. An example of interdisciplinarity and the productive results of the crossing of boundaries is the journal *Signs: Journal for Women in Culture and Society*, first published in 1977.

Mainstream sociology was slow to recognize the profound transformation that feminist research involved for a comprehensive analysis of the nature of the social. But as you will see, in most contemporary theory, feminism is having an impact on the discipline, if only in making sex/gender issues theoretically important and not easily relegated to "nature." Beginning in the early 1970s, courses and research on gender have burgeoned. In these developments, the interrelationship of theory and practice—so central to the initial stages of the feminist movements, historically and in the present—has been retained in the theoretical focus and empirical research of feminist sociologists.

The early focus on "women" as an undifferentiated social category quickly gave way to the recognition of differences among women, and the resulting debates have been a source of considerable intellectual and practical progress and change. For many women sociologists, feminism, and the scholarship it has generated, has been personally significant in their lives and careers. For many academic and professional women, second-wave feminism has been the most intellectually challenging and exciting development of the twentieth century, whether in sociology or any other discipline.

Feminist Sociology and Race

For disadvantaged women, especially women of color, feminism has occasionally been a source of support in the pursuit of social change, but in other ways it has been seen as an impediment. The early feminist movements tended to be dominated by young, white, Western, middle-class women and to reflect the lives and aspirations of these women. Women of color and lesbian women often felt excluded not only from the movements but also from the feminist sociological work.

The invisibility of race in the early feminist movements was akin to the invisibility of women and blacks in the early consolidation of sociology. Historically, the relation of white feminists to racism has been ambiguous. As you recall, Gilman and Webb (see Chapter 11) expressed racist sentiments. The fact that most pre–Civil War white women advocates of equal rights for women in the United States were abolitionists does not mean, in bell hooks's view, that they were antiracist (1981:124). Hurtado maintains that "white feminist theory has yet to integrate the facts that for women of color, race, class, and gender subordination are experienced simultaneously and that their oppression is not only by members of their own group but by whites of both genders" (1994:138–139).

Women of color have faced a persistent dilemma in opposing inequalities of race and gender. Opposition to the dominance of white society involves a particular opposition to white men, who have historically exploited women of color in more brutal and unthinking ways than their exploitation of white women. But women of color also have to contend with the ambiguity of identifying with men of color in their collective oppression. The recognition that these same men are themselves implicated in a patriarchal culture means that women of color experience a double subordination.

It was not only in the context of feminism that race became a salient sociological issue in the post–World War II years. In the 1960s especially, race relations became a focal point in the perceived "failure" of mainstream sociology to address the critical issues of the day.

Race and Colonialism

Women and racial minorities may have been topics of sociological research, but the "perspectives of sociology—its basic premises, concepts, and explanations—reflected the experience, social interests, and values of predominantly White, middle class men" (Seidman, 1994:97). Politically, according to Seidman, the "exclusion of an African-American and feminist perspective . . . made sociology more acceptable because it was more in line with the mainstream of liberal America." He suggests that the "painless institutionalization of sociology" in the United States was accomplished by excluding those "movements and perspectives that were threatening to middle America, e.g., feminism, Black nationalism, socialism, sexual radicalism" (1994:98).

British and European sociology always had, at least marginally, a socialist perspective. However, feminism, sexual radicalism, and nationalism in relation to colonial empires were relegated to the sociological sidelines in British and European as well as North American sociology.

The 1950s and 1960s saw a proliferation of liberation movements nationally and internationally. The nationalist movements against colonialism in Africa, Asia, and Latin America were paralleled by internal racial conflicts that were especially violent in the United States. Frantz Fanon's *The Wretched of the Earth* (1963) was a powerful and influential account of the psychopathology caused by racism and colonialism. Fanon concluded that shaking off colonial oppression meant repudiating the white, European philosophical heritage of the Enlightenment and formulating indigenous solutions to social problems and inequities. Fanon was appealing to indigenous Algerian rebels against French colonial rule, but his work resonated internationally. He called on the rebels to "Leave this Europe where they are never done talking of Man, yet murder men everywhere they find them" (1963:252). In the 1960s, "the term 'racist' became, with 'fascist,' the ultimate epithet . . . replacing the increasingly ineffectual term 'communist'" (Owram, 1996:167).

Black Militancy

For African Americans, the independence of many African states by 1960 fueled impatience with their own second-class standing in the United States. C. Eric Lincoln (1961:9–10) remarked that "Many Negroes for whom Africa seemed as remote as the planet Jupiter" began to find themselves "exhilarated and encouraged by the emergence of black national states in the once 'dark' continent." The assimilationist position of the National Association for the Advancement of Colored People (NAACP) was overshadowed by the increasing militancy of the Black Muslim movement and its pursuit of an independent, segregated Black Nation in the late 1950s.

Militancy increased with the formation of the Black Panther party, whose goal was to "exert organized force in the political arena" to satisfy the needs and desires of black people and whose leaders spoke of "political power growing out of the barrel of a gun" (Cleaver, 1969:84–85, quoting Huey P. Newton). The motto of the Black Panther party, taken by Huey Newton from Mao Tse-tung's *Little Red Book*, stated, "We are advocates of the abolition of war; we do not want war; but war can only be abolished through war; and in order to get rid of the gun it is necessary to pick up the gun" (Cleaver, 1969:89).

The Black Panthers were the revolutionary offshoot of the Black Power movement of Malcolm X and the security force, the Fruit of Islam, set up to protect (as well as discipline) the members of the Black Muslim Nation. The militancy of young black men became even more evident after the death of Malcolm X, who was shot in 1965. There was some justification for the increasingly violent tenor of the protests, given the violence of state forces in reaction to peaceful protests, sit-ins, and voter registration in the southern states.

The increasingly violent response of young black men was at odds with the longstanding integrationist policies of the NAACP. Martin Luther King had delivered his "I Have a Dream" speech in Washington, DC, in August 1963, and in 1964 Congress passed the Civil Rights Act and the Voting Rights Act. The militant Stokely Carmichael, however, claimed that by 1964 it had become clear to many young blacks that nonviolent demonstrations and the passage of laws did nothing to alleviate the underlying poverty and despair of the majority of the black population. In 1965, one of the most violent demonstrations erupted in the largely black community of Watts in California (1969:93).

Carmichael regarded the civil rights movement as a "bourgeois" movement. He maintained that it did not address the international issue of U.S. colonial domination, which was of critical concern to the Black Power movement. Carmichael pointed out that white society calls blacks "niggers," Spanish-speaking people "spics," Chinese "chinks," and Vietnamese "gooks." This dehumanization justified colonial and neo-colonial enslavement, exploitation, and oppression. Furthermore, enslavement was made easier because the oppressed began to "believe in [their] own inferiority" (Carmichael, 1969:97). Carmichael's solution was not simply the destruction of racism but also the destruction of economic exploitation represented by imperialistic capitalism. Black Power meant that blacks had to see themselves as "part of the Third World; that we see our struggle as closely related to the liberation struggles around the world" against white imperialism (1969:101–102).

Sociology and Race

In the academic sociological community, reactions to the protests and violence were ambiguous. Robert E. Park had studied race relations in the 1930s and had recognized that all "national minorities" would want to "control and direct their own destinies" in situations of oppression (1950:114). But Park's work was itself a minority effort. In 1961, John Howard Griffin published *Black Like Me*, an account of his (a white man's) sojourn in the southern United States disguised as a black man. The book was a powerful sociological account of the character of racism and its social and cultural consequences. The book also garnered African American criticism of a white man in "blackface."

Griffin's book did not become influential in mainstream sociology, which tended to examine race through the lens of the functions of social conflict. Himes, whose work was characteristic of this approach, examined what he called the rational conflict responses of black Americans to social abuses (1966). But the conflict he examined focused on relatively peaceful acts of protest and political action; he ignored the violent conflicts more characteristic of that period. In fact, Himes's analysis was a form of bourgeois sociology that matched Carmichael's indictment of the NAACP.

A more divisive controversy arose within the sociological community in response to James Coleman et al.'s 1975 report *Trends in School Segregation, 1968–73*. The report claimed that the racial desegregation of white schools through compulsory busing had resulted in a white flight to the suburbs. The result was that racial imbalance in the schools—which the busing was intended to combat—had increased rather than decreased. This report came as a shock, given that in 1966 Coleman had reported test results showing positive effects of racial desegregation. However, several sociologists questioned the nature and interpretation of the statistical evidence in the 1975 report.

Among the critics was Alfred McClung Lee who, as president of the American Sociological Association, raised questions about the findings and asked for an investigation. The ASA council rejected the request for an investigation, but several critical responses essentially called into question the way in which the data had been interpreted. Most especially, the critics focused on the political conclusions drawn from the supposedly value-free report of statistical trends. These critics maintained that it was "false to assume that the use of statistical techniques would automatically take care of the value questions" (Galliher and Galliher, 1995:122–123) and concluded that "the allegedly value-free social scientist was not so value-free after all" (1995:120). Galliher and Galliher (1995:122–123) report that Coleman was "hurt" and "stunned" by the criticisms of what he claimed were issues of "scientific fact," and for a number of years he dropped his membership in the ASA. The Coleman/Lee controversy illustrated the dilemmas generated by opposing views on the ethical and scientific responsibilities of sociologists, especially when important political issues are involved.

Race relations were the subject of sociological concern, but it was a concern that seemed to be generated "after the fact." In 1963, Everett Hughes asked, "Why did social scientists—and sociologists in particular—not foresee the explosion of collective action of Negro Americans toward immediate full integration into American society?" (1963:879). Hughes's answer was that sociologists had failed to use their sociological imaginations because "our conception of social science is so empirical, so limited to little bundles of fact applied to little hypotheses, that we are incapable of entertaining a broad range of possibilities, of following out the madly unlikely combinations of social circumstances" (1963:889). More generally, Hughes argued that the very professionalization of sociology was responsible, limiting creative sociology and curbing "that utopian imagination which can conceive of all sorts of alternatives to the way things are" (1963:890). He encouraged sociology to be more "playful," to break out of the straightjacket of academic sociology and be open to new, innovative perspectives.

The variety of different perspectives, the interdisciplinary collaborations, and a renewed emphasis on comparative, historical research that emerged from the turbulent decades of the 1960s and early '70s, which we examine in the rest of this volume, certainly broke out of the straitjacket in interesting ways.

Final Thoughts

Both gender and race, as well as the international legacy of colonialism, brought into clear view the divisions that had animated sociology from its inception. During the 1960s and early 1970s, the divisions were often generational, pitting young against old, and fought in the public domain as well as in the academic context. In sociology, themes of "conflict, power, diversity, and inequality" became almost as prevalent as the former stress on integration and shared belief systems characteristic of structural functionalist theory (Seidman, 1994:133).

But mainstream academic sociology did not turn totally "outward to engage public life, it turned inward to focus on the making of scientific knowledge" (Seidman, 1994:133). The maverick spin-offs already mentioned, such as ethnomethodology, phenomenology, and gender and cultural studies, attempted to retain the classical sociological conception of the discipline as an objective theoretical enterprise as well as a socially responsive and responsible one. Consequently, in the 1990s, "theory in American sociology has never encompassed such a range of diversity," although some perspectives have "only a fringe existence" (Hinkle, 1994:341).

The "new" directions are often critical reassessments and reinterpretations of past classical sociological work. These classical theoretical supports are generally used as foundations in an attempt to bridge—or, more hopefully, to transcend—the sociological divisions and conflicts that became so clear in the disruptive period of the 1960s and early 1970s. In the rest of this volume, we will examine the trends in late-twentieth-century sociology in terms of the search for at least a temporary agreement in theory and practice, given the inescapable multiparadigmatic, and ultimately political, nature of the sociological enterprise.

References

Abrams, Philip. 1968. *The Origins of British Sociology, 1834–1914.* Chicago: University of Chicago Press.

Alexander, Jeffrey C., 1987. *Twenty Lectures: Sociological Theory Since World War II.* New York: Columbia University Press.

Becker, Howard. 1960. "Normative Reactions to Normlessness." *American Sociological Review, 25,* 803–810.

Becker, Howard S., and Irving Louis Horowitz, 1972. "Radical Politics and Sociological Research: Observations on Methodology and Ideology." *American Journal of Sociology, 78*(1), 48–66.

Bell, Daniel. 1960. *The End of Ideology.* Glencoe, IL: Free Press.

Bendix, Reinhard. 1970. "Sociology and the Distrust of Reason." *American Sociological Review, 35,* 831–843.

Blau, Peter M., 1974. "Parameters of Social Structure." *American Sociological Review, 39,* 615–635.

Bourdieu, P., and J. C. Passeron. 1970. *Reproduction: In Education, Society and Culture.* Beverley Hills, CA: Sage.

Broverman, I. K., D. M. Broverman, F. E. Clarkson, P. Rosenkrantz, and S. R. Vogel. 1970. "Sex-Role Stereotypes and Clinical Judgments of Mental Health." *Journal of Consulting and Clinical Psychology, 34,* 1–7.

Bulmer, Martin. 1985. "The Development of Sociology and of Empirical Social Research in Britain." In Martin Bulmer (Ed.), *Essays on the History of British Sociological Research.* Cambridge: Cambridge University Press.

Carmichael, Stokely. 1969. "Black Power and the Third World." In Tariq Ali (Ed.), *The New Revolutionaries: A Handbook of the International Radical Left.* Toronto: McClelland and Stewart.

Clark, Terry. 1973. *Prophets and Patrons: The French University and the Emergence of the Social Sciences*. Cambridge, MA: Harvard University Press.

Cleaver, Eldridge. 1969. "Letter from Jail." In Tariq Ali (Ed.), *The New Revolutionaries: A Handbook of the International Radical Left*. Toronto: McClelland and Stewart.

Coleman, James S., Sara D. Kelly, and John A. Moore. 1975. *Trends in School Segregation, 1968–73*. Washington, DC: The Urban Institute.

Collins, Randall. 1981. *Sociology Since Mid-Century*. New York: Academic Press.

——— (Ed.). 1984. *Sociological Theory*. San Francisco: Jossey-Bass.

Coser, Lewis A. 1975. "Two Methods in Search of a Substance." *American Sociological Review, 40*, 691–700.

de Beauvoir, Simone. 1961. *The Second Sex*. New York: Bantam Books.

Deegan, Mary Jo. 1987. "An American Dream: The Historical Connections between Women, Humanism, and Sociology, 1890–1920." *Humanity and Society, 11*, 353–365.

——— (Ed.). 1991. *Women in Sociology*. New York: Greenwood Press.

———. 1995. "The Second Sex and the Chicago School." In Gary Alan Fine (Ed.), *A Second Chicago School? The Development of Postwar American Sociology* (pp. 322–364). Chicago: University of Chicago Press.

Dodd, Stuart S. 1942. *Dimensions of Society*. New York: Macmillan.

Eisenstadt, S. N., with M. Curelaru. 1976. *The Form of Sociology: Paradigms and Crises*. New York: John Wiley and Sons.

Eisenstadt, S. N., and H. J. Helle, 1985. *Perspectives on Sociological Theory. Volume 1: Macro Sociological Theory. Volume 2: Micro Sociological Theory*. London: Sage.

Fanon, Frantz. 1963. *The Wretched of the Earth*. New York: Grove Press.

Friedan, Betty. 1963. *The Feminine Mystique*. Harmondsworth, England: Penguin.

Friedrichs, Robert W. 1970. *A Sociology of Sociology*. New York: Free Press.

Galliher, John F., and James M. Galliher. 1995. *Marginality and Dissent in Twentieth Century American Sociology*. New York: State University of New York Press.

Gouldner, Alvin W. 1963. "Anti-Minotaur: The Myth of a Value-Free Sociology." In Maurice Stein and Arthur Vidich (Eds.), *Sociology on Trial*. Englewood Cliffs, NJ: Prentice-Hall.

———. 1970. *The Coming Crisis of Western Sociology*. New York: Basic Books.

Griffin, John Howard. 1961. *Black Like Me*. Boston: Houghton Mifflin.

Halsey, A. H. 1985. "Provincials and Professionals: The British Post-War Sociologists." In Martin Bulmer (Ed.), *Essays on the History of British Sociological Research*. Cambridge: Cambridge University Press.

Himes, Joseph. 1966. "The Functions of Racial Conflict." *Social Forces, 45*, 1–10.

Hinkle, Roscoe C. 1994. *Developments in American Sociological Theory, 1915–1950*. New York: State University of New York Press.

Homans, George C. 1964. "Bringing Men Back In." *American Sociological Review, 29*, 809–818.

hooks, bell. 1981. *Ain't I a Woman? Black Women and Feminism*. Boston: South End Press.

Hughes, Everett C. 1963. "Race Relations and the Sociological Imagination." *American Sociological Review, 28*, 879–890.

Hurtado, Aida. 1994. "Relating to Privilege: Seduction and Rejection in the Subordination of White Women and Women of Color." In Anne C. Herrman and Abigail J. Steward (Eds.), *Theorizing Feminism: Parallel Trends in the Humanities and Social Sciences* (pp. 136–154). Boulder, CO: Westview Press.

Janowitz, Morris. 1972. "Professionalization of Sociology," *American Journal of Sociology, 78*, 105–135.

Kuhn, Thomas. 1970. *The Structure of Scientific Revolutions* (2nd ed.). Chicago: University of Chicago Press.

Lee, Alfred McClung. 1973. *Toward Humanist Sociology.* Englewood Cliffs, NJ: Prentice-Hall.

———. 1976. "Sociology for Whom?" *American Sociological Review, 41,* 925–936.

Lemert, Charles. 1992. "Subjectivity's Limit: The Unsolved Riddle of the Standpoint." *Sociological Theory, 10,* 63–72.

Levine, Donald N. 1995. *Visions of the Sociological Tradition.* Chicago: University of Chicago Press.

Lincoln, C. Eric. 1961. *The Black Muslims in American,* Boston: Beacon Press.

Lipset, Seymour Martin. 1972. *Rebellion in the University: A History of Student Activism in America.* London: Routledge and Kegan Paul.

Lipset, Seymour Martin, and Everett Carl Ladd, Jr. 1972. "The Politics of American Sociologists," *American Journal of Sociology, 78*(1), 67–104.

Lipset, Seymour Martin, and Neil J. Smelser (Eds.). 1961. *Sociology: The Progress of a Decade.* Englewood Cliffs, NJ: Prentice-Hall.

Lundberg, George. 1961. *Can Science Save Us?* New York: Longmans, Green.

Madge, John. 1962. *The Origins of Scientific Sociology.* New York: Free Press.

Mills, C. Wright. 1959. *The Sociological Imagination,* New York: Oxford University Press.

Morgan, J. Graham. 1980. "Women in American Sociology in the Nineteenth Century." *Journal of the History of Sociology, 2,* 1–34.

Murray, Stephen. 1979. "Resistance to Sociology at Berkeley." *Journal of the History of Sociology, 2,* 61–84.

Oakley, Ann. 1974. *The Sociology of Housework.* New York: Pantheon Books.

Orlans, Kathryn P. Meadow, and Ruth A. Wallace (Eds.). 1994. *Gender and the Academic Experience.* Lincoln: University of Nebraska Press.

Owram, D. 1996. *Born at the Right Time.* Toronto: University of Toronto Press.

Park, Robert E. 1950. *Race and Culture.* Glencoe, IL: The Free Press.

Parsons, Talcott. 1951. *The Social System.* New York: The Free Press.

Presser, Harriet B. 1994. "The Personal Is Political *and* Professional." In Kathryn P. Meadow Orlans and Ruth A. Wallace (Eds.), *Gender and the Academic Experience* (pp. 141–156). Lincoln: University of Nebraska Press.

Ritzer, George. 1983. *Contemporary Sociological Theory.* New York: Alfred A. Knopf.

Rowbotham, Shiela. 1992. *Women in Movement.* London: Routledge.

Sargent, Lydia (Ed.). 1981. *Women and Revolution.* Montreal: Black Rose Books.

Seidman, Steven. 1994. *Contested Knowledge: Social Theory in the Postmodern Era.* Cambridge, MA: Blackwell.

Shils, Edward. 1985. "On the Eve: A Prospect in Retrospect." In Martin Bulmer (Ed.), *Essays on the History of British Sociological Research.* Cambridge: University of Cambridge Press.

Sica, Alan. 1997. "Ethical Culture." *Perspectives, 19*(1), 1–3.

Smith, Dorothy. 1987. *The Everyday World as Problematic: A Feminist Sociology.* Toronto: University of Toronto Press.

———. 1999. *Writing the Social.* Toronto: University of Toronto Press.

Spender, Dale. 1982. *Women of Ideas and What Men Have Done to Them.* London: Ark Paperbacks.

Turner, Stephen Park, and Jonathan H. Turner. 1990. *The Impossible Science.* Newbury Park, CA: Sage.

Chapter 20

Symbolic Interactionism
Blumer, Goffman, and Hochschild

The theorists discussed in the earlier chapters of this volume might be classed as "grand theorists" in the more classical, or traditional, form. The theorists discussed in this and the following two chapters represent important divergences and qualifications to the grand theory tradition. However, these theorists still owe debts to the classical grand theorists, as well as to the structural functional and critical theorists of the twentieth century. We begin in this chapter with a general overview of the interactionist tradition and a short exposition on the work of Herbert Blumer, and then move on to discuss the work of Erving Goffman and Arlie Hochschild.

The Interactionist Tradition

The interactionist tradition has been associated with the work of a varied group of sociologists described as the "Chicago School," including George Herbert Mead, W. I. Thomas, and Robert E. Park. Mead's social psychological approach was foundational for the interactionist tradition, but the empirical work of Thomas and Park in urban and race relations generated the critical methodological characteristics of the tradition. Field research, ethnographic studies, interviewing, case histories, documentary sources, and ecological analysis were used in a variety of important studies that emerged from the sociology department at the University of Chicago during the early years of the twentieth century. These methods remain important to any current interactionist research.

One of the strengths of the Chicago "school" in the early years was the encouragement of interdisciplinary links. Although the term "school" has "connotations of clique or cult," this was not the case for the Chicago sociologists. Interdisciplinarity was encouraged by the "interest in local research on the city of Chicago" and the "pragmatist orientation widely diffused through the university" (Bulmer, 1984:190). Robert Park, for example, was particularly interested in adopting ideas from a variety of disciplines to help in his research (Bulmer, 1984:215).

The overriding character of early interactionist research was its empirical nature and its pragmatic focus. Interactionism was a radical sociology that attempted to provide the means for people to improve their lives (Deegan and Hill, 1987:xi). This focus was quite unlike that of most classical sociologists, for whom "first- or even secondhand acquaintance with the contemporary world was not seen as a necessary requirement for fruitful sociological generalization," and empirical work, such as census taking and social surveys, were not the major concern (Bulmer, 1984:5). It was assumed that social surveys and social research were different enterprises. Survey research was seen as primarily focused on social problems and social planning, whereas social research had a broader focus, formulating "hypotheses or propositions about social action" and attempting to produce "theories and laws to explain social phenomena" (Bulmer, 1984:65).

In the early twentieth century, Chicago sociologists set a precedent with an impressive body of empirical work. A new direction was established for American sociology. Theorists became more aware of the vital importance of the empirical research. Some of the important work produced during the early years included Thomas and Znaniecki's *The Polish Peasant in Europe and America*, Johnson's *The Negro in Chicago*, and a whole series of empirical urban studies such as *The Hobo*, *The Gold Coast and the Slum*, *The Gang*, *The Taxi-Dance Hall*, *The Natural History of a Delinquent Career*, and *Social Factors in Juvenile Delinquency*. All of these works, focusing on the social problems of the city, were major contributions to the development of specialized fields such as criminology, the sociology of the family, the sociology of social problems, and urban sociology (Bulmer, 1984:89).

Some critics have suggested that interactionism is good at empirical research but bad at theory. Others contend that the early Chicago school "successfully bridged the gap between, and combined together, theory and empirical research" (Bulmer, 1984:224). The theorists we discuss in this chapter certainly combined the two approaches.

Blumer sets out the terms of the interactionist tradition, Goffman extends the tradition in important ways, and Hochschild continues the innovative research tradition, building on Goffman's work in her examination of the sociology of emotions.

Herbert Blumer (1900–1987)

It was Herbert Blumer who coined the term **symbolic interactionism**. Blumer's work focused on the ways human beings took control of their lives, as "acting people" in a society that is a "complex of ongoing activity" (Blumer, 1969:85). The two parts—symbol and interaction—produce meaningful interaction. That is, interaction involves giving social objects symbolic value. Social objects can be anything—physical objects, animals, history, language, ideas, emotions—as well as self and other people. According to Blumer (1969:80), the individual in all of his or her everyday acts "is designating different objects to himself, giving them meaning, judging their suitability to his action, and making decisions on the basis of the judgment." People interpret and act on the basis of symbols.

Symbols are abstract meanings attached to things, people, and behavior so that they can have different meanings for different individuals. The important point is that individuals consciously and creatively evaluate, make decisions, and act. Whether the evaluation, decision, and action are "functional" or even ethically commendable is not necessarily an issue. However, given the legacy of George Herbert Mead, there is an assumption that individuals will progress toward a more democratic society and that this progress will be helped by sociology.

Interaction involves the self engaged in communicating with self: selecting, checking, suspending, regrouping, and transforming meanings in terms of the social context and the individual's intentions and interests (Blumer, 1969:5). But for Blumer, the most significant feature of all "human association is that the participants *take each other into account*" as a basis of conduct (1969:194). Society is a "complex of ongoing activity" involving collectively initiated "joint actions" (Blumer, 1969:85). **Joint actions** are "constituted by the fitting together of the lines of behavior of separate participants" as, for example, in a trading transaction, family dinner, wedding, games, or war (1969:70). Joint actions have a history that is "orderly, fixed and repetitious" because the participants have a common definition of the situation (1969:71).

Social interaction is an interaction between people, not between roles. "It is ridiculous," argued Blumer, "to assert, as a number of eminent sociologists have done, that social interaction is an interaction between social roles" (1969:75). Roles may affect, in some degree, the "direction and content of action," but "this is a far cry from asserting action to be a product of roles" (1969:75).

Blumer took the position that social structures, like roles or status, are important but not determinant in the way that structural functionalists maintain. In his view, "grand theory" that "orders the world into its mold" provides little information about the nature of social life (1969:14). For Blumer, sociology involves examining and interpreting the empirical evidence in order to develop an inductive understanding of human behavior and human society.

In summary, the premises of symbolic interaction are as follows: (1) "human being act towards things on the basis of the meaning things have for them"; (2) "the meaning of such things is derived from, or arises out of, the social interaction one has with one's fellows"; and (3) "these meaning are handled in, and modified through, an interpretative process used by the person in dealing with the things he encounters" (Blumer, 1969:2). Individual and joint actions are framed by historical and cultural meanings, but there is always room for creativity and improvisation. It is "the social process in group life that creates and upholds the rules, not the rules that create and uphold life" (Blumer, 1969:19).

Blumer's methodology was inductive. "The isolation of relations, the development of propositions, the formulation of typologies, and the construction of theories are viewed as emerging out of what is found through constant observation of that world instead of being formed in an *a priori* fashion through deductive reasoning from a set of theoretical premises" (Blumer, 1975:62). This approach to research is qualitative rather than quantitative. It begins with an **exploratory stage,** in which the investigator looks closely at a "sphere of life that is unfamiliar and hence unknown to him" in order to develop a research focus. Once the research focus is achieved, the investigator moves to the **inspection stage,** which involves an "intensive focused examination of the empirical content of whatever analytical elements are used for purposes of analysis" (1969:43). The investigator uses **sensitizing concepts** that "suggest directions along which to look," which in turn will lead to **definitive concepts** that provide "prescriptions of what to see" (1969:148–149).

Blumer's theoretical and methodological focus provides a part of the background to the work of Erving Goffman. However, Goffman did not claim membership in any "school." Goffman himself "did his best to avoid being classified . . . even to the point of declaring a belief in conceptual eclecticism" (Burns, 1992:6). According to Fine (1990:121), however, although Goffman never labeled himself a symbolic interactionist, if he is excluded from the perspective "we exclude our soul."

The link with interactionism lies in Goffman's analysis of the "interaction order" and his development of a theory of face-to-face interaction. Goffman's focus also extended the symbolic interaction tradition in his examination of patterns, or rules of social interaction that apply in a variety of situations. In Goffman's ASA presidential address, he pointed out that "pedestrian traffic rules can be studied in crowded kitchens as well as in crowded streets, interruption rights at breakfast as well as in courtrooms, endearment vocatives in supermarkets as well as in the bedroom" (1983b:2). In this development of a theory of the **interaction order,** Goffman moved beyond and away from the interaction roots exemplified by the Chicago school.

Erving Goffman (1922–1982)

Erving Goffman was born in Manville, Alberta, Canada, in 1922. He graduated from the University of Toronto in 1945 and went to the University of Chicago for graduate work in sociology and social anthropology. He obtained his master's degree in 1949. His master's thesis was a "protracted and ultimately vain attempt to use statistics to understand an audience's responses to a then popular American radio soap opera called 'Big Sister'" (Manning, 1992:7).

Goffman's subsequent work was a drastic departure from the quantitative focus of his master's thesis. One of his pieces, "On Cooling the Mark Out" (1953), published prior to his PhD dissertation, foreshadowed his subsequent work. In this essay, Goffman studied the art of the con man and illustrated the procedures the con artist used to reconcile people to their realization that they had been conned. "Cooling out" refers to the efforts of the con artist to control the anger of the "mark" (the person who has been "taken") in order to defuse the risk of police intervention or other forms of retaliation on the part of the person who has been wronged.

Goffman pointed out that being conned is not an unusual event that only happens to gullible people. Everyone, at some time, is a potential mark. Any venture runs the risk of failure and thus the loss of self-esteem. When this happens, repair work is necessary to restore "face"—that is, to restore the image of the self and thus restore social order. This examination of the ostensibly "trivial and commonplace, or peripheral or bizarre" as a means to reveal the nature of "normal behavior" in society as a whole was to remain Goffman's style and method (Burns, 1992:16).

Goffman's PhD thesis was based on fieldwork on a remote Shetland Island. The thesis was initially conceived of as a participant observation study of the social structure of the island. Goffman's "cover" for his stay on the island was an interest in agricultural techniques. He also worked as a part-time dishwasher at the island's one hotel. Shortly after his arrival, Goffman became fascinated by the various stratagems and rhetorics used by the islanders in their interactions among themselves and with strangers and visitors. The island was a small, barren place, with only 300 families as permanent residents. Everyone lived in almost constant sight of one another. This provided Goffman with an ideal social microcosm in which to study face-to-face interactions. His PhD study of social interaction and self-presentation, titled "Communication Conduct in an Island Community" (1953), was published in 1959 as *The Presentation of Self in Everyday Life*.

In 1954 Goffman became a visiting scientist at the National Institute of Mental Health in Bethesda, Maryland. As a ward orderly at the hospital, Goffman did participant observation research on the interactions among patients, doctors, and administrators, recorded in his work *Asylums* (1961a). In 1957 he joined the Department of Sociology at Berkeley, and in 1968 he moved to the University of Pennsylvania, where he remained until his early death at age 60.

Goffman's Central Theories and Methods

Goffman's work was the observation and analysis of individual conduct "as an attribute of social order, of society, not as an attribute of individual persons" (Burns, 1992:23). Goffman was indebted to, but stood apart from, the interactionist, and later symbolic interactionist, tradition fostered at the University of Chicago. In addition to the heritage of George Herbert Mead at Chicago, Goffman was also influenced by Everett Hughes, who is best known for his studies of occupations. Hughes's view that "basic patterns of behavior and institutional structures were best looked for in the analogies which underlie seeming incongruities"—such as finding out about doctors by studying plumbers, or prostitutes by studying psychiatrists—was applied to great effect in Goffman's early essay "On Cooling the Mark Out" (Burns, 1992:11). Goffman also used Hughes's concept of "total institution" in his study of mental hospitals.

The influence of W. Lloyd Warner, a social anthropologist, was also significant to Goffman's work (Collins, 1986:109). Goffman's graduate work was in social anthropology as well as sociology, and he was Warner's research assistant at Chicago when Warner was working on his analysis of social stratification. As an anthropologist, Warner maintained that more was known about the ceremonies and rituals of tribal peoples than about modern urban individuals, and he set out to chart the ceremonies and rituals of status in modern American society (Collins, 1986:109). In his early work, Goffman combined Warner's social anthropology with the Chicago empirical tradition to produce his own "studies of the rituals of everyday life" (Collins, 1986:110).

Goffman was concerned with the composition of the "self" at the "micro" level of social action and interaction. However, he also placed these interactions within a more "macro" moral context. In Goffman's view, "universal human nature is not a very human thing. By acquiring it, the person becomes a kind of construct, built up not from inner psychic propensities but from the moral rules that are impressed on him from without" (1967:45). He focused on the individual as a product of social interaction, not on the individual whose existence predated society.

For Goffman, the connection between the individual and society was through ritual. Goffman's use of ritual was indebted to Emile Durkheim (see Chapter 4); he argued that the "self" in modern society becomes a sacred object in the same way that the collective symbols of more primitive societies operated in Durkheim's *The Elementary Forms of Religious Life*. The "self" as "sacred object . . . must be treated with proper ritual care and in turn must be presented in a proper light to others" (1967:85). The rituals of modern social life that individuals perform for each other, to maintain "civility and good will on the performer's part" and acknowledge the "small patrimony of sacredness" possessed by the recipient, are "stand-ins" for the power of supernatural entities described by Durkheim (Goffman, 1961b:62). As Goffman (1967:95) put it, "Many gods have been done away with, but the individual himself stubbornly remains as a deity of considerable importance."

Among the classical theorists, Goffman was also influenced by Georg Simmel (see Chapter 8). Like Simmel, Goffman looked at the details of everyday life not simply as illustrations or data for theoretical abstractions but to provide an accurate description of the social world. Simmel's concept of "pure sociation" established the study of interaction as basic to sociological analysis. Goffman continued this tradition in his insistence that face-to-face interaction comprised an autonomous area of sociological analysis. "My concern over the years has been to promote acceptance of this face to face domain as an analytically viable one" (1983b:1).

Goffman's methods of incorporating the Simmelian micro level of interaction and the macro-level analysis of Durkheimian ritual behavior have been described as empirically eclectic: a "bricolage" (Fine, 1990:124). For example, in *Behavior in Public Places*, Goffman noted that the data he used came from "a study of a mental hospital . . . some from a study of a Shetland Island community . . . some from manuals of etiquette, and some from a file where I keep quotations that have struck me as interesting" (1963:4). His approach was basically **inductive**, identifying the ways in which individuals in a variety of social contexts accomplished interaction. Goffman thus paid attention to speech as well as silence, and to "bodily appearance and personal acts" such as "dress, bearing, movement and position, sound level, physical gestures such as waving or saluting, facial decorations, and broad emotional expression," selecting his material in a seemingly unorganized manner (1963:33).

Goffman's seemingly eclectic methods were not really new, unusual, or unorganized; they represented basic sociological methods, if sociology is understood as the interpretation of "events, actions, reported experiences" that are a part of everyday life. Sociological discoveries are thus not about the "discovery of previously unknown facts," but about "re-ordering what is already known" (Williams, 1988:73).

For Goffman, reordering starts from a "small observational base" and moves toward "more and more comprehensive conceptual frameworks for the description of that base" (Williams, 1988:73). Using this procedure, Goffman's methodology was "simultaneously theoretical and empirical." That is, he proceeded to "borrow, beg and build concepts," seeking the "interrelationship between them" and at the same time making discoveries "consisting of new ways of organizing data" (Williams, 1988:82). For example, in observing the ways in which individuals attempt to control the impressions they make on others in any interaction, Goffman used drama as a metaphor, describing such impression management as a "performance" involving "stage-craft and stage management" (1959:15).

Goffman cautioned, however, that the **dramaturgical** approach was "in part a rhetoric and a maneuver" and that the language of the stage was a "scaffold . . . [that] should be erected with an eye" to being demolished (1959:254). Goffman was careful to make a distinction between theoretical abstractions and the real world to which they referred. Conceptual abstractions are "exhaustible where reality is not," and there is no "simple correspondence . . . between the knowable and the real such that the former directly reflects the latter" (Williams, 1983:101).

The theater metaphor was a handy means of illustrating the "structure of social encounters" that occur in all social life (Goffman, 1959:254). As a means to illuminate the nature of social life, drama has been used by a number of other theorists in the Western social theory tradition, beginning with Plato. Although Goffman used this metaphor, he did not regard it as inevitable or universal in all interactions. The idea that people "behave *as if* they are scripting their own roles" was, however, insightful and theoretically significant (Fine, 1990:124). Goffman claimed that sociology did not provide "a ready framework" that could order the sort of data he examined. Although "many of these data are of doubtful worth, and my interpretations . . . may certainly be questionable," he maintained that "a loose speculative approach to a fundamental area of conduct is better than a rigorous blindness to it" (1963:4).

Goffman acknowledged the criticism that sociology had produced little of value in its short career and that sociologists might well trade what they had produced "for a few really good conceptual distinctions and a cold beer." However, he maintained that sociologists should not trade in their calling, but instead should "sustain in regard to all elements of social life a spirit of unfettered, unsponsored inquiry, and the wisdom not to look elsewhere but ourselves and our discipline for this mandate" (1983b:17).

Nature of Society, Humans, and Change

Society as Frame   In *Frame Analysis*, Goffman stated that he was concerned with "the structure of experience individuals have at any moment of their lives" and made "no claim whatsoever to be talking about the core matters of sociology—social organization and social structure" (1974:13). This does not mean, however, that Goffman or interactionists generally ignore society and social structures. Goffman's position was that the nature of society and its structures or institutions is discovered in the behaviors of individuals. This theoretical perspective is consistent with Durkheim's definition of social fact: "every way of acting, fixed or not, which is general throughout a given society, while existing in its own right, *independent of its individual manifestations*" (quoted in Burns, 1992:25). As Goffman (1967:43) suggests, "If persons have a universal human nature, they themselves are not to be looked to for an explanation of it. One must look rather to the fact that societies everywhere, if they are to be societies, must mobilize their members as self-regulating participants in social encounters."

According to Goffman, society frames interaction, but interaction is not dependent on macrostructures. Furthermore, interaction can have a transformative impact on social structures. The key point in Goffman's work is that he rejected the classical sociological opposition between the individual and social structure that still retains credibility in current sociological theory. For Goffman, "individual and social structure are not competing entities"; they are "joint products of an interaction order sui generis" (Rawls, 1987:138).

Goffman saw the interaction order as a "substantive domain in its own right" and argued that "isolating the interaction order provides a means and a reason to examine diverse societies comparatively, and our own historically." He noted that all of us spend time "in our daily life . . . in the immediate presence of others" and all that we do is *"socially situated."* This social situatedness gives rise to "indicators, expressions or symptoms of social structures such as relationships, informal groups, age grades, gender, ethnic minorities, social classes and the like," and these "effects" should be treated as "data in their own terms" (1983b:2). The "forms of social life" that these effects illustrate can be "catalogued sociologically" to expose the intrinsic nature of "interactional life," or the distinctive features of face-to-face interaction. Furthermore, social structures are "dependent upon, and vulnerable to, what occurs in face-to-face contacts" (1983b:246).

Although social structures "don't 'determine' culturally standard displays," such as rituals and ceremonies, they do "help select from the available repertoire of them" (1983b:251). Thus, there is a "loose coupling" between interaction and social structure. As an example, Goffman notes that a small number of males, "such as junior executives, . . . have to wait and hang on others' words" in a manner similar to that of women involved in informal cross-sexed interaction (1983b:252). This observation of cross-gender similarities allows Goffman to formulate a role category of subordination that "women and junior executives (and anyone else in these interactional circumstances) share." But this subordinate "role . . . belongs *analytically* to the interaction order, which the categories women and junior executives do not" (1983b:252).

Goffman does not provide any clear definition of society or social structure other than to point to their constructed and "framing" nature. **Frames** are basic background assumptions that enable us to understand what is going on in any encounter or situation. These prior assumptions make sense of the situation and the interaction and enable the individual to respond appropriately. Frames are the organizational principles that define everyday situations (1974:11). There are two kinds of frames: natural and social.

Natural frames refer to events in the physical world that do not seem to involve human intervention, such as the weather.[1] **Social frames** are the basic understandings individuals bring to any interaction that provide the means to comprehend the motives, intentions, and desires of others. Social frameworks are not simply an understanding of the other's actions; they also involve an appraisal of those actions as to their "honesty, economy, safety, elegance, tactfulness, good taste, and so forth" (1974:22). Frames anchor social life and make it predictable most of the time. But frames can be undermined, and it is when they are undermined that we become aware of them. For example, Goffman points to media stories of visits from aliens or demonstrations of levitation as being outside the conventional beliefs about reality, and thus illuminating the taken-for-granted, everyday assumptions that frame behavior.

The predictability of everyday life is based on primary frameworks, but that predictability can be precarious. Primary frameworks can be "keyed"; that is, they can be transformed into something different. A **key** is defined as a "set of conventions by which a given activity, already meaningful in terms of some primary framework, is transformed into something patterned on it but is seen by the participants as something quite else" (1974:43–44). For example, sports and some games involve the keying of combat into a more restrained, less consequential activity.

Keying transforms experiences, but it is not always or necessarily a benign transformation. Keying can also involve fabrications such as hoaxes, illusions, satire, "frame-ups," and so on, in which some people are "in the know" and others are duped. Fabrications undermine frames and make people uneasy, and in this respect they can produce social disruptions and disorder. Direct fabrications, if they are harmful to the duped, can usually be countered, but indirect fabrications are more troubling. Indirect fabrications occur when an individual claims that a definition or a rumor told to another is untrue, but the recipient of the information refuses to believe that it is a lie (1974:107).

These discussions of frames and fabrications are part of Goffman's attempt to illustrate the nature of the "self" and the way in which that self has some modicum of security in social interaction. Individuals are able to progress through their everyday lives on the basis that the self they present to others in any particular situation will be accepted by others as a sincere and competent "me" that the "I" reacts to, usually creatively.[2]

Goffman moved from a central concern with the "self" as dramatic performance to the analysis of the structures and strategies of interaction in his later works, *Strategic Interaction* (1969) and *Frame Analysis* (1974). In these studies, Goffman moved from more concrete analysis of self to "more abstract analysis

---

[1]The weather *seems* to be an example of the extra-human, but of course the activities of human beings, such as clear-cutting of forests or using ozone-depleting fuels, do affect the weather.

[2]Goffman's debt to G. H. Mead is evident here, especially Mead's conception of the knowledgeable creativity of human beings.

of principles that organize our experience" (Lemert and Branaman, 1997:lxxiv). *Frame Analysis* is an investigation of the "organization of experience"—what occurs when individuals ask themselves and others, "What is going on here?" (1974:153). Goffman is not dealing here with the "structure of social life" but with the "structure of experience that individuals have at any moment of their social lives." The film *Rashomon* is an ideal representation of such framing. When individuals believe they understand "what is going on," they will "fit their actions to this understanding and ordinarily find that the ongoing world supports this fitting" (1974:158).

The organizational premises of everyday life are what Goffman calls the "frame of the activity," and everyday life contains many "quickly changing frames." For example, "a man finishes giving instructions to his postman, greets a passing couple, gets in his car, and drives off" (1974:161). All of these activities are "framed" in different ways, although they are performed sequentially. The instruction "belongs to the realm of occupational roles," and the greeting is "part of the ritual order in which the individual can figure as a representative of himself." Although all these various activities could be "subsumed under the term 'role'—for example, the role of suburbanite— . . . that would provide a hopelessly gross conceptualization" of what was going on (1974:161).

The frames within which individuals organize experience are cultural constructs, prefabricated by the society or cultural group. They "buttress" in real life "what people understand to be the organization of their experience," so that actions are performed "self-fulfillingly" (1974:162). People develop a "corpus of cautionary tales, games, riddles, experiments, newsy stories, and other scenarios which elegantly confirm a frame-relevant view of the working of the world" and then "comport themselves so as to render this analysis true" (1974:162–163). Thus, there is no original behind the frame.

Humans as Performers   In *The Presentation of Self in Everyday Life*, Goffman used the theatrical metaphor of performance to illustrate how human beings present themselves in their various social roles in face-to-face interactions with others. According to this analysis, individuals play parts, and observers are "asked to believe that the character they see actually possesses the attributes he appears to possess, that the task he performs will have the consequences implicitly claimed for it, and that, in general, matters are what they appear to be" (1959:17).

The individual is both performer, who fabricates impressions in the "all-too-human task of staging a performance," and a character, "typically a fine one, whose spirit, strength, and other sterling qualities the performance was designed to evoke" (1959:252). The **impression management** that is involved in the presentation of a self is not intrinsic to the individual, but derives from "the whole scene of his action" that hopefully convinces the audience of the self being presented. Thus, a "correctly staged and performed scene leads the audience to impute a self to a performed character, but this imputation—this self—is a *product* of a scene that comes off, and is not a *cause* of it" (1959:252). The self "as a performed character, is not an organic thing—the product of some intrinsic nature —with a specific location, whose fundamental fate is to be born, to mature, and to die; it is a dramatic effect arising from the scene that is presented, and the characteristic issues, the crucial concern, is whether it will be credited or discredited" (1959:252–253).

Goffman suggests that the presentation of a performance involves front and back stage behaviors. **Front stage** refers to actions that in a "general and fixed fashion . . . define the situation for those who observe the performance" (1959:22). The props to maintain the front include physical settings; personal possessions such as "clothing; sex, age, and racial characteristics; size and looks; posture; speech patterns; facial expressions; bodily gestures; and the like" (1959:24). **Back stage** is a place "where the impression fostered by the performance is knowingly contradicted as a matter of course" (1959:112). It is the place in which the performer "can relax; he can drop his front, forgo speaking his lines, and step out of character" (1959:112). As an illustration, Goffman quotes Simone de Beauvoir on women's relationships in the absence of men: "With other women, a woman is behind the scenes; she is polishing her equipment, but not in battle; . . . she is lingering in dressing-gown and slippers in the wings before making her entrance on the stage." A woman prepares back stage for her confrontation with men, in which she is "always play-acting; she lies when she makes believe that she accepts her status as the inessential other" and at all times with her "husband or with her lover, every woman is more or less conscious of the thought: 'I am not being myself'" (quoted in Goffman, 1959:113).

Maintaining the separation of front and back stage is important for impression management. This separation is found in all areas of social life—for example, the bedroom and the bathroom are "places from which the downstairs audience can be excluded. Bodies that are cleansed, clothed and made up in these room can be presented to friends in others" (1959:123). But the separation can break down, and when it does, it can result in "embarrassment and dissonance" and seriously undermine the credibility of the previous performance.

Impression management, whether successful or unsuccessful, involves an audience that also has a stake in ensuring a successful performance. Consequently, in some cases where the performance slips or something unexpected occurs, the audience may attempt to "save the day" by ignoring the faux pas or providing excuses for the untoward behavior. However, there are situations in which the audience makes the successful performance of a role difficult, as Goffman illustrated in *Asylums* (1961a) and *Stigma* (1965).

In his dramaturgical approach in *The Presentation of Self in Everyday Life*, Goffman suggests that the performer has considerable control over the image of the self, but in *Stigma* this control is compromised. Whatever the stigma— "abominations of the body" or "blemishes of individual character," usually inferred from records of "mental disorder, imprisonment, addiction, alcoholism, homosexuality, unemployment, suicidal attempts, and radical political behavior," or the "tribal stigma of race, nation, and religion"—there is likely to be a gap between an individual's virtual and actual social identity. **Virtual identity** refers to what an individual is supposed to be in the eyes of others—the "character we impute to the individual." **Actual identity** refers to the "category and attributes" an individual can be "proved to possess" (1965:2, 4).

Social identity is spoiled when there is a discrepancy between the virtual and the actual identity, as is often the case for individuals with a stigma. Indeed, many "normals" believe that "the person with a stigma is not quite human" and will practice various forms of discrimination that, unthinkingly or not, reduce the stigmatized individual's life chances (1965:5). The stigmatized individual also tends to "hold the same beliefs about identity" as the "normals." As a result, the stigmatized individual perceives "that whatever others profess, they do not really 'accept' him and are not ready to make contact with him on 'equal grounds'" (1965:7).

Goffman's point in discussing the ways in which stigma affects social identities, along with the various interactional practices used to conceal, accommodate, or even flaunt stigma, is that all individuals at some point are subject to stigma. He suggested that possibly the only nonstigmatized individual in U.S. society was a young male "married, white, urban, northern, heterosexual Protestant father of college education, fully employed, of good complexion, weight and height, and a recent record in sports." Any male who "fails to qualify in any of these ways is likely to view himself—during moments at least—as unworthy, incomplete, and inferior" (1965:128). In sum, "stigma management is a general feature of society," and Goffman suspected that the "role of normal and the role of stigmatized are . . . cut from the same standard cloth" (1965:130). Furthermore, as "interaction roles are involved, not concrete individuals," in many instances "he who is stigmatized in one regard nicely exhibits all the normal prejudices held towards those who are stigmatized in an another regard" (1965:138).

The stigmatized are not without resources to resist their typification, as Goffman demonstrated in his study of asylums. Asylums, like prisons, concentration camps, nunneries, or monasteries, are **total institutions**—that is, they are totally, or almost totally, closed to the outside world. The closure, bureaucratization, and rationalization of everyday life characteristic of such institutions diminish the identity, the "self," of the inmate. The new inmate of such institutions confronts a "series of abasements, degradations, humiliations and profanations of self" designed to produce a "self" that the institution can deal with and control.

In total institutions, the self is "systematically, if often unintentionally, mortified" (1961a:55). Various indignities are constantly visited on the inmates, such as having to ask for the most mundane things. For example, asking permission to use the toilet or the telephone may result in teasing or having "the request denied" or being "questioned at length, ignored, or put off" by those in authority (1961a:41).

> In a total institution, minute segments of a person's line of activity may be subjected to regulations and judgments by staff; . . . Each specification robs the individual of an opportunity to balance his needs and objectives in a personally efficient way and opens up his line of action to sanctions. The autonomy of the act itself is violated. (1961a:38)

Individuals in total institutions make a primary adjustment to the organization when they identify and cooperate with the organizational demands and become "normal" or "programmed" members. However, individuals may also make secondary adjustments that "represent ways in which the individual stands apart from the role and the self that were taken for granted for him by the institution" (1961a:189). Individuals may use the resources of the institution in creative ways to reestablish the self and claim some autonomy and status. Goffman suggests that this "underlife" of the institution, by which "participants decline in some way to accept the official view of what they should be putting into and getting out of the organization and, behind this, of what sort of self and world they accept for themselves" represents a "movement of liberty" (1961a:305). For example, he observed that mental hospital inmates created "free places" for themselves, such as the woods on the hospital grounds that were used as a cover for illicit drinking or for playing poker. Free places enabled the inmates to escape, for a short time, the surveillance of the staff and affirm a personal sense of self in the face of institutional impositions.

This analysis of the production and constitution of the self in total institutions again illustrates the central concern found in all of Goffman's work: the self as a dramatic performance accomplished in the context of, and constrained by, social expectations or rituals of social life. Whatever the constraints, however, social interaction is creative action, and this is the key to the issue of social change.

Social Change   Goffman does not address the issue of social change directly; there are no accounts of dramatic or revolutionary social change in his work. But his discussions of the ways in which individuals "modify their conduct in many normatively guided ways" (1963:243) provide a clue to the nature of social change. It is from the multiplicity of everyday social interactions that the "gossamer reality of social occasions is built" (1963:247), and social change effected.

The reproduction and transformation of social institutions is accomplished through the creative interactions of individuals. All social interaction entails risk or "fatefulness." Risky or fateful activity is "activity that is both problematic and consequential," and although such fatefulness is minimized as much as possible in any social context, "the human condition is such that some degree of fatefulness will always be found" (1967:164). As Giddens (1984:139) observed, social changes "of a deep-rooted kind, by their very nature, involve alterations in the character of day-to-day social practices." The rituals of social interaction control and contain the unexpected and disruptive, but they are never totally successful, and it is from these disruptions that social change occurs.

Class, Gender, and Race

Goffman only referred obliquely to issues of class and race. He did point out that his focus on the "nature of personal experiencing" had political implications and that they were "conservative ones" (1974:157). He acknowledged that the analysis of personal experiences does not "catch at the differences between the advantaged and the disadvantaged classes" and in fact could be said "to direct attention away from such matters." Like the critical theorists, Goffman believed that "he who would combat false consciousness and awaken people to their true interests has much to do, because the sleep is very deep." His work was not intended "to provide a lullaby but merely to sneak in and watch the way people snore" (1974:158).

Goffman was more forthright in his discussions of gender. He pointed out that sex differences are assumed to be invariable and, therefore, significant. But, in his view, sex differences are only significant because the culture makes them so. For example, the fact that women can breast-feed and men cannot is a "temporary biological constraint" that is "extended culturally" to encompass a whole complex of rights and duties that are sex typed.

In *Gender Advertisements*, Goffman maintained that gender relations in Western society reproduce parent-child relations. When a male confronts a female or a subordinate male, "some mitigation of potential distance, coercion, and hostility is quite likely to be induced by application of the parent-child complex." This means that, "ritually speaking, females are equivalent to subordinate males and both are equivalent to children" (1979:5). This effect originates in the "home training of the two sexes" (1977:202).

Children acquire normative gender interaction patterns because of the differential treatment by parents depending on the sex of the child. In North American family life, Goffman observed, "whatever the economic or class level and however well or badly off a female sees she is when compared to children in other families, she can hardly fail to see that her male sib, equal to her when compared to children in other families and often equal, too, in regard to ultimate claims upon the family resources, is yet judged differently and accorded different treatment for herself by their parents" (1977:202–203).

Goffman pointed out that the differentiation of the sexes is a cultural artifact produced by the "interactional field." He gives the example of "toilet segregation," which is "presented as a natural consequence of the difference between sex-classes, when in fact it is rather a means of honoring, if not producing, this difference" (1977:205). Gender is displayed in ritual ways, and the presumed "naturalness" of the displays is often anchored by comparisons with animal life. But Goffman (1977:214–215) maintained that the animal analogy as "a source of imagery" was simply a "cultural resource." The animal kingdom only provides "mimetic models for gender display, not necessarily phylogenetic ones" (1977:214–215).

Male and female "human nature" is the "capacity to learn to provide and read depictions of masculinity and femininity and a willingness to adhere to a schedule for presenting these pictures and this capacity they have by virtue of being persons, not females or males" (1977:224). Thus, according to Goffman, "one might just as well say there is no gender identity. There is only a schedule for the portrayal of gender." Why gender is selected as primary rather than some other attribute is "an open question," but gender "in close connection with age-grade, lays down more, perhaps, than class or other social divisions an understanding of what our ultimate nature ought to be and where this nature ought to be exhibited" (1977:225).

Gender is thus constructed in the rituals of everyday interaction, and the sociologist's task is not to uncover "real, natural expressions, whatever they might be," but to illustrate the "capacity and inclination of individuals to portray a version of themselves and their relationships at strategic moments" (1977:223). Nothing "biological or social-structural" lies beneath the expressions of femininity and masculinity, although these same expressions "function socially . . . to support belief that there is an underlying reality to gender" (1977:226).

However, the recognition of the cultural construction of masculinity and femininity does not provide any easy political answer to sexism. Goffman pointed out that gender stereotypes "run in every direction, and almost as much inform what supporters of women's rights approve as what they disapprove" (1977:225). He believed that the problem with any social change in gender relations was that the very actions and relations that denote male domination are also the expressions that define the "gentlest, most loving moment." Unlike other disadvantaged groups, who can "turn from the world to a domestic scene where self-determination and relief from inequality are possible, the disadvantage that persons who are female suffer precludes this" (1977:226). The home is not a refuge from gender hierarchy and inequality, but rather the place in which such hierarchy is reaffirmed. Indeed, the "gentling of the world" as a result of the extension of the parent-child complex of "intimate, comfortable practices" is what produces female subordination (1977:226).

Changes in gender relations cannot be effected simply by altering institutional structures. Attention must be paid to the variety of everyday, taken-for-granted interactions that denote gender power relations. Goffman's somewhat pessimistic conclusion with respect to change in gender power relations has been criticized by Burns (1992:236), who contends that Goffman's caution regarding the significance of structural changes is contradicted by the historical evidence. Burns claims that the "partial emancipation gained by women's movements over the past century and a half is surely the result of the direct assault on 'structural arrangements,'" and the "greater liberty, more social acceptance on an equal footing with men . . . have all *followed* the gains registered in structural reforms" (1992:236).

In fact, both Goffman and Burns are correct. Structural changes have mitigated some of the disadvantages women experience, but the household division of labor remains skewed even in the most professedly egalitarian relationships. Many studies have indicated that housework remains primarily a female task, especially after the birth of the first child (Meissner et al., 1975; Coltrane, 1989; Hochschild, 1989). Furthermore, the occupational locations of women and men indicate that the gender rituals of everyday life are indeed hard to change.

Other Theories and Theorists

In later years, Goffman moved into the analysis of conversation. In this analysis, he maintained that meaningful, or "felicitous," conversation depended on the sharing of a common stock of knowledge. Correct speech, or "talk," is essential if the speaker is to demonstrate sanity and a well-meaning attitude toward the other. "Felicity's Condition" (1983a) refers to the "requirement to demonstrate the sanity behind our actions"—the common rule that underlies all face-to-face interaction (Manning, 1992:93). All communication must address the "other's mind, that is, . . . the other's capacity to read our words and actions for evidence of our feelings, thoughts, and intent" (1983b:192).

Goffman's interest in conversational analysis links up with the work of the ethnomethodologists, such as Dorothy Smith, whose work is examined in Chapter 22. However, Goffman's major focus, even in conversational analysis, remained a fascination with the self as performance and strategic impression management (Lemert and Branaman, in Goffman, 1983:lxiii).

Critique and Conclusions

Goffman's work cannot be easily "placed" in any one theoretical tradition. Goffman himself maintained that such genealogies were sterile exercises that detracted from an engagement with sociological practices and debates. His work was and remains a constant source of renewal in many different directions for sociological theory, as you will see in subsequent discussions in this volume.

Goffman's major achievement was to direct the attention of sociology to the significance of the "infinitely small, to the things which the object-less theoreticians and concept-less observers were incapable of seeing and which went unremarked because they were too obvious." As a result, the "guardians of positivist dogmatism assigned Goffman to the "lunatic fringe" of sociology." This judgment has proved erroneous, as Goffman has become "one of the fundamental references for sociologists, and also for psychologists, social psychologists and socio-linguists" (Bourdieu, 1983:112).

In his ASA presidential address, Goffman described his work as the promotion of the "face-to-face domain as an analytically viable one—a domain which might be titled . . . the *interaction order*—a domain whose preferred method of study is microanalysis" (1983b:2). His work was an important corrective to the seeming dominance in U.S. sociology of the structural functionalist orthodoxy. Anthony Giddens (1984), however, has pointed out that sociological analysis still needs to bridge the divide between the micro and the macro, between face-to-face interaction and social structures; he claimed that his own structuration theory was an attempt to use Goffman's work, as well as that of ethnomethodologists, to close the divide. Goffman's work was particularly valuable to many feminist sociologists, as you will see in Chapter 22.

Arlie Russell Hochschild (1940–)

Arlie Hochschild entered graduate school at Berkeley in 1962 and completed her MA and PhD there. She taught at the University of California at Santa Cruz for two years and then returned to Berkeley, where she is currently a professor of sociology.

Hochschild has recorded her ambivalence about her graduate studies and the problems she faced by attempting to combine graduate study, an academic job, and child care during the late 1960s and early 1970s. Like many other women graduate students at the time, she found few female role models in academia. At Berkeley there were no female professors other than Gertrude Jaeger, who was a lecturer, although "one fifth of the graduate students were women, hoping one day to become professors" (Hochschild, 1994:136).

Hochschild records that in 1968 the women graduate students began to meet and talk about their problems, both academic and personal, questioning the "basic concepts in sociology and trying to picture what sociology would look like if women's experiences counted as much as men's" (1994:136). The women's caucus that emerged out of the initial meeting was duplicated during that period at other universities and in other disciplines. The central theme for all of them was to take women's experience "and the public perceptions of that experience seriously." It was this perspective that led Hochschild to make the study of emotions central to her work.

Hochschild indicates that her focus on emotions was inspired by the "collective consciousness" of the second women's movement and by Goffman's work. Goffman's "focus on the have-nots of dignity" and "the poetry in his viewpoint" were important, but she was also aware that his description of the social world was from a male point of view. Although Hochschild did not take courses from Goffman during her period at Berkeley, she did come to know him through his visits to a Berkeley faculty study group after he had moved to Pennsylvania. Hochschild sent him some of her articles, and he responded with "trenchant comments and warm human support"; indeed she described his responses as akin to "God himself calling" (1994:137)!

Hochschild's Central Theories and Methods

Hochschild's work on emotions has extended Goffman's work in important ways. First, she has expanded on his studies of embarrassment and shame to incorporate a whole range of emotional responses. Second, she examines the outward signs of emotional response and work as Goffman did, but unlike Goffman, she also examines the inner emotional life of the self. Goffman looked at the emotions registered in social situations, but according to Hochschild, ignored the self as "subject of emotive experience"—the self that "introspects or dwells on outer reality without a sense of watchers" (1983:216). In contrast to Goffman, Hochschild is interested in "how people try to feel," rather than how "people try to appear to feel" (1979:560).

Freud has also had an impact on Hochschild, although she finds his work wanting. In contrast to Goffman, Freud "proposed a self that could feel and manage feeling," but in Hochschild's view, Freud's work was limited by his singular focus on anxiety. Hochschild is interested in how people "consciously feel" and not, "as for Freud, how people feel unconsciously" (1979:560).

Hochschild proposed looking at both the "social and psychological side" of emotion by asking how "institutions control how we 'personally' control feeling" rather than simply looking at how "institutions influence personality." She points out that emotion is the most important "biologically given sense" because it provides the means to know how to act in the world and, more important, enables us to understand self in that world—it is an "orientation toward *action*" and also "an orientation toward *cognition*" (1983:219).

Hochschild's first major work, *The Managed Heart* (1983), was a study of the emotional labor required by two occupations, flight attendant and bill collector. The two occupations represent opposite poles of emotional labor. Flight attendants are asked to feel "sympathy, trust, and good will" toward their clients, whereas bill collectors have to feel "distrust and sometimes positive bad will" (1983:137). The study of the two occupations was a mixture of interviews, participant observation, and documentary analysis. Her general focus was on the links between "feeling rules, emotion management, and emotive experience" as a corrective to the "tacit assumption" in social psychology that "emotion because it seems unbidden and uncontrollable, is not governed by social rules" (1979:551).

Class, Gender, and Race

Goffman (1961b:23) pointed out that individuals control "psychological states and attitudes" because they are aware of the general rule that "one enter into the prevailing mood in the encounter." In other words, people manage their emotions. Emotion management assumes that individuals are "capable of feeling, capable of assessing when a feeling is 'inappropriate,' and capable of trying to manage feelings" (Hochschild, 1979:557). The sociology of emotions is therefore concerned with the "theoretical junctures—between consciousness of feeling and consciousness of feeling rules, between feeling rules and emotion work, between feeling rules and social structure" (1979:560). It is concerned with **emotion work** and **emotion management**.

There are two general types of emotion work: "*evocation*, in which the cognitive focus is on a desired feeling which is initially absent" and "*suppression*, in which the cognitive focus is on an undesired feeling which is initially present" (Hochschild, 1979). These types of emotion work are managed by three general techniques: "*cognitive*: the attempt to change images, ideas, or thoughts in the service of changing the feelings associated with them"; "*bodily*: the attempt to change somatic or other physical symptoms of emotion"; and "*expressive* emotion work: trying to change the expressive gestures in the service of changing inner feeling" (1979:562). These three techniques are often found together in practice.

Emotion work is usually accomplished without too much conscious effort; it is when feelings do not fit the situation that individuals become conscious of the "work" involved in emotion. There are guidelines, or social "feeling rules," about the appropriate fit between a situation and displayed emotion. For example, it is expected that people will be sad at funerals, happy at weddings. These feeling rules are "implicit in any ideological stance" and often become clear when the definition or meaning of situations change. For example, Hochschild points to the different feeling rules that traditionally were ascribed to men and women on the assumption that they have different natures. Women were supposed to be more sensitive and emotional in contrast to manly stoicism.

Hochschild points out, however, that these ideological assumptions about men and women have been transformed to some extent by the feminist movement, which has attempted to change gender-based feeling rules. For example, when the "same balance of priorities in work and family now ideally applies to men as to women," women can "as legitimately (as a man) become angry (rather than simply upset or disappointed) over abuses at work, since her heart is supposed to be in that work and she has the right to hope, as much as a man, for advancement." Similarly, "a man has the right to feel angry at the loss of custody if he has shown himself the fitter parent" (1979:567).

Class   Hochschild does not discuss class directly, but her discussion of emotional labor is connected to class distinctions. Hochschild distinguishes emotion work and emotion management from emotional labor. **Emotional labor** refers to the commoditization of emotion work—the "management of feeling to create a publicly observable facial and bodily display." This labor is "sold for a wage and therefore has exchange value," in contrast to the use value of emotion work and management (1983:7). The smile and solicitous demeanor of the flight attendant is an essential part of the job. And just as the assembly-line worker can be estranged from work and self, so the emotional laborer can suffer estrangement. But whereas the alienating labor of the assembly line can be mitigated by the emotional sanctuary of the home, estrangement resulting from emotional labor is not easily left on the job.

The physical laborer and the emotional laborer are both "subject to rules of mass production. But when the product—the thing to be engineered, mass-produced, and subjected to speed-up and slowdown—is a smile, a mood, a feeling, or a relationship, it comes to belong more to the organization and less to the self" (1983:198). Emotional labor "becomes a public act, bought on the one hand and sold on the other," and feeling rules are "no longer simply matters of personal discretion, negotiated with another person in private but are spelled out publicly . . . in training programs, and the discourse of supervisors" (1983:118–119). As a result, "there is much less room for individual navigation of the emotional waters" (1983:119). In jobs that require emotional labor, the strain that often results from feeling, and feigning feeling, results in "emotive dissonance."

Emotional labor, with its accompanying emotive dissonance, is most characteristic of the middle classes and women. Women, especially middle-class women, are expected to, and in fact do, manage feeling more than men. Hochschild indicates that some working-class jobs, such as prostitution or personal service, also require emotion work, but generally emotional labor as opposed to physical labor is much less prevalent in working-class than in middle-class jobs. Furthermore, middle-class parents tend to control their children through appeals to and management of feeling, in contrast to working-class parents who tend to control their children through management of behavior. Consequently, "middle class parents prepare their children for emotional management" and emotional labor more than working-class parents do (1979:570–571).

Gender   Hochschild states that because women in general still "depend on men for money," one of the ways of repaying their debt is to do "extra emotion work—*especially emotion work that affirms, enhances, and celebrates the well-being and status of others*" (1983:165). Because the "world turns to women for mothering . . . this fact silently attaches itself to many a job description" (1983:170). Hochschild looked at the gender characteristics of standard occupational groups in the U.S. Census and found that of the twelve major occupational groups, six required emotional labor. The six groups were professional and technical workers, managers and administrators, sales workers, clerical workers, and service workers. In these six occupational categories, women were "overrepresented . . . about half of all working women hold such jobs," whereas men were "underrepresented; about a quarter of all working men are in emotional labor jobs" (1983:234–235).

The gender discrepancy in emotion work and emotional labor was an important part of the problems Hochschild observed in her next project: an examination of the way in which dual-career or dual-job couples handle their domestic and child-rearing responsibilities. In *The Second Shift* (1989), Hochschild reported her study of more than 50 dual-career or dual-job couples. She also focused in depth on the strategies of ten of the couples in the management of their home and work responsibilities. She found that although women may have changed, workplaces have "remained inflexible in the face of the family demands of their workers" and, on the home front, "most men have yet to really adapt to the changes in women." The result has been a "stalled revolution" (1989:12).

Most of the couples maintained a compromise between "traditional and egalitarian ideals" of domestic and paid labor, but generally the women assumed far more of the burden of the "second shift" than did the men. Hochschild noted that many married men made a single action the "substitute for a multitude of chores in the second shift." The man offered a "token"—for example, "Evan took care of the dog"—which came to symbolize his contribution to the second shift. But Evan, like the other men in the study, had the "male norm" on their side: Because men "out there" did even less than they were doing, their wives should feel "lucky" that they did what they did, no matter how minimal (1989:47, 51).

Hochschild observed a cycle that tended, over time, to reinstate women's "traditional" responsibilities for most domestic and child-rearing work—the "backstage stage" work. Men are expected to (and do in the general case) "put more of their 'male' identity in work" so that their "work time is worth more than female work time—to the man and to the family" (1989:254). The greater "worth of male work time makes his leisure more valuable, because it is his leisure that enables him to refuel his energy, strengthen his ambition, and move ahead at work." The result is that "his aspirations expand. So does his pay. So does his exemption from the second shift" (1989:254).

The lack of "backstage support" women experienced for their paid labor, in contrast to men, raised the "emotional price of success impossibly high" for most women (1989:256). The emotional price women paid in the burden of the second shift became clearer when, in a later study, Hochschild examined the family and work arrangements in an organization that had instituted "family-friendly" policies. The corporation, called Amerco in her study *The Time Bind* (1997), had introduced flextime, job sharing, and parental leave, and ran an excellent day-care center for employees' children.

Hochschild discovered that of the family-friendly policies, "only flextime, which rearranged but did not cut back on hours of work, had any significant impact on the workplace" (1997:26). In general, the majority of workers, both men and women, worked more hours. In addition, the "best-paid employees—upper-level managers and professionals—[were] the least interested in part-time work or job sharing," and few men "at any level expressed interest in part-time work" (1997:28). The "first shift (at the workplace)" tended to take more and more time, with the result that the "second shift (at home) becomes more hurried and rationalized" (1997:214). Generally, the more that work—with its "deadlines, its cycles, its pauses and interruptions"—shapes the lives of workers, the more "family time is forced to accommodate to the pressures of work" (1997:45). Child care was especially difficult, and parents held out the hope that "quality time"—that is, "scheduling intense periods of together-ness"—could compensate for the loss of time and possible loss of quality in the parent-child or family relationship. However what quality time usually entailed was simply "transferring the cult of efficiency from office to home" (1997:50).

Hochschild observed that juggling domestic, especially child-care and spou-sal, relations often produced difficulties and conflict, largely for women. She found that problems at home upset women more than problems at work, and that both types of problems upset women more than men. Many of her respon-dents, both women and men, indicated that work, in contrast to the home, be-came a "haven" as a "tired parent flees a world of unresolved quarrels and un-washed laundry for the reliable orderliness, harmony, and managed cheer of work" (1997:44). Hochschild found, however, that women, more than men, sought support mechanisms at work where they could complain about domes-tic, spousal, and child-care problems and seek solutions from coworkers. Furthermore, work as the "haven" from domestic turmoil seemed to pro-duce longer hours on the job the more domestic responsibilities increased. Hochschild noted that single parents at Amerco averaged 45 hours a week—hourly female single parents 43 hours and hourly single male parents 48 hours a week. Women with children in dual-earner marriages averaged 51 hours a week, and men with children in dual-earner marriages averaged 53 hours a week (1997:261, fn. f).

The "third shift" of emotional work that resulted from the compression of the second shift was especially difficult for women. Generally, the "time-starved mother" was forced into choosing between "being a good parent and buying a commodified version of parenthood from someone else" (1997:232). The "commodification of home life" in turn tended to make "children's pro-tests" worse. Generally, the children's "resentment, resistance, passive acquies-cence . . . frustrations . . . stubborn demands or whining requests," resulting from the "damage done by the reversal of worlds," caused considerable emo-tional turmoil, especially for mothers (1997:218). This third, "unacknowl-edged" shift of emotional work, carried mainly by mothers, reinforced the feel-ing that "life at home is hard work" compared to life in the workplace.

In the traditional focus on cognition and behavior, Hochschild argues, soci-ology has ignored a critical dimension of social life—emotions. Hochschild's work seeks to correct this critical blind spot in sociological research. Her work demonstrates that emotional display is learned behavior, and points to the im-portance of emotion work in "bridging . . . traditional interactionist concerns with self and situation" (Fine, 1990:134). In addition, Hochschild makes an im-portant contribution to bridging the micro/macro divide in her studies on the organization of "feeling work" in social institutions.

Other Theories and Theorists

After Blumer, suggests Fine (1990:119), interactionism could generally be divided into two perspectives. The first perspective, following Mead, focused on the "self." This perspective was social psychological with a "heavy overlay of cognitive imagery." To some extent, Hochschild's work falls more in this tradition. The second focus owed more to the Park and Thomas survey research tradition at Chicago, with its concentration on a "situation." This perspective was micro sociological, with "strong ties to social and cultural anthropology and a focus on 'behavior,' not 'cognition.'" Goffman's work is more attuned to this second perspective. However, neither Hochschild nor Goffman can be totally subsumed under either of these perspectives.

Recent work in the interactionist tradition is more diverse, involving combinations of these foci. In fact, some theorists claim that the interactionist perspective is not limited to micro sociological analysis, but can also deal with macro issues. The main areas in which interactionists have contributed in recent years are "(1) self and identity theory; (2) dramaturgy, accounts and presentation of self; (3) collective behavior and collective action; (4) culture and art; (5) sociolinguistics approaches ; and (6) social problems theory" (Fine, 1990:121).

Critique and Conclusions

The work of Hochschild and others on emotion extends the focus of interactionism in important ways. As Hochschild has noted, the work of Mead and Blumer on "conscious, active and responsive gestures" might have been even more fruitful if they had also attended to the "importance of feeling" (1979:555).

The social psychological focus of interactionism takes seriously the premise that people are active, creative interpreters of their social worlds. In this sense, interactionsim stands in contrast to the formulation of the abstract "actor" of "grand theory." But although interactionism may be contrasted with grand theory, it is nonetheless important to such theory. The focus on the micro relations of social life, and the inductive and qualitative nature of the methodology generally employed, provides a rich source of data and raises important, usually overlooked, issues that can put the proverbial "meat" on the bones of abstract theoretical constructions.

Final Thoughts

Interactionism has been associated with phenomenology and ethnomethodology on occasion, but these approaches represent a somewhat different view of what constitutes the sociological object. Interactionism is *"at its core* social and relational, whereas the phenomenological approach emphasizes the individual construction of the world, a world of discrete and separate actors" (Fine, 1990:139). The ethnomethodological approach also differs, focusing more on conversational analysis. Phenomenological sociology and ethnomethodology also represented challenges to the structural functional tradition in American sociology, and we touch on these approaches in Chapter 22.

References

Blumer, Herbert. 1969. *Symbolic Interactionism: Perspective and Method*. Englewood Cliffs, NJ: Prentice-Hall.

———. 1975. "Comments on Parsons as a Symbolic Interactionist." *Sociological Inquiry, 45*, 59–62.

Bourdieu, Pierre. 1983. "Erving Goffman, Discoverer of the Infinitely Small." *Theory, Culture and Society, 2*(1), 112–113.

Bulmer, Martin. 1984. *The Chicago School of Sociology*. Chicago: University of Chicago Press.

Burns, Tom. 1992. *Erving Goffman*. London: Routledge.

Collins, Randall. 1986. "The Passing of Intellectual Generations: Reflections on the Death of Erving Goffman." *Sociological Theory, 4*, 106–113.

Coltrane, Scott. 1989. "Household Labor and the Routine Production of Gender." *Social Problems, 36*, 473–491.

Deegan, Mary Jo, and Michael R. Hill (Eds.). 1987. *Women and Symbolic Interaction*. Boston: Allen & Unwin.

Drew, Paul, and Anthony Wooton (Eds.). 1988. *Erving Goffman: Exploring the Interaction Order*. Cambridge: Polity Press.

Fine, Gary Alan. 1990. "Symbolic Interactionism in the Post-Blumerian Age." In George Ritzer (Ed.), *Frontiers of Social Theory* (pp. 117–157). New York: Columbia University Press.

Giddens, Anthony. 1984. *The Constitution of Society*. Cambridge: Polity Press.

Goffman, Erving. 1953/1997. "On Cooling the Mark Out: Some Aspects of Adaptation to Failure." In Charles Lemert and Ann Branaman (Eds.), *The Goffman Reader* (pp. 3–20). Oxford: Blackwell Publishers.

———. 1959. *The Presentation of Self in Everyday Life*. Garden City, NY: Doubleday Anchor Books.

———. 1961a. *Asylums*. Garden City, NY: Doubleday Anchor Books.

———. 1961b. *Encounters: Two Studies in the Sociology of Interaction*. Indianapolis: Bobbs-Merrill.

———. 1963. *Behavior in Public Places*. New York: Free Press of Glencoe.

———. 1965. *Stigma: Notes on the Management of Spoiled Identity*. Englewood Cliffs, NJ: Prentice-Hall.

———. 1967. *Interaction Ritual: Essays on Face-to-Face Behavior*. Garden City, NY: Doubleday Anchor Books.

———. 1969. *Strategic Interaction*, Philadelphia: University of Pennsylvania Press.

———. 1974. *Frame Analysis*. New York: Harper Colophon Books.

———. 1977/1997. "The Arrangement between the Sexes." In Charles Lemert and Ann Branaman (Eds.), *The Goffman Reader* (pp. 201–227). Oxford: Blackwell Publishers.

———. 1979. *Gender Advertisements*. Cambridge, MA: Harvard University Press.

———. 1981. *Forms of Talk*. Philadelphia: University of Pennsylvania Press.

———. 1983a. "Felicity's Condition." *American Journal of Sociology, 89*, 1–53.

———. 1983b/1997. "Frame Analysis of Talk." In Charles Lemert and Ann Branaman (Eds.), *The Goffman Reader*. Oxford: Blackwell Publishers.

———. 1983c. "The Interaction Order." *American Sociological Review, 48,* 1–17.

Hochschild, Arlie Russell. 1979. "Emotion Work, Feeling Rules, and Social Structure." *American Journal of Sociology, 85,* 551–573.

———. 1983. *The Managed Heart: Commercialization of Human Feeling.* Berkeley: University of California Press.

———, with Anne Machung. 1989. *The Second Shift.* New York: Viking.

———. 1994. "Inside the Clockwork of Male Careers." In Kathryn P. Meadow Orlans, with Ruth A. Wallace (Eds.), *Gender and the Academic Experience.* Lincoln: University of Nebraska Press.

———. 1997. *The Time Bind.* New York: Henry Holt.

Lemert, Charles, and Ann Branaman (Eds.). 1997. *The Goffman Reader.* Oxford: Blackwell Publishers.

Manning, Philip. 1992. *Erving Goffman and Modern Sociology.* Stanford, CA: Stanford University Press.

Meissner, Martin, et al. 1975. "No Exit for Wives: Sexual Division of Labor and Cumulation of Household Demands." *Canadian Review of Sociology and Anthropology, 12,* 424–439.

Rawls, Ann Warfield. 1987. "The Interaction Order Sui Generis: Goffman's Contribution to Social Theory." *Sociological Theory, 5,* 136–149.

Scheff, Thomas J. 1986. "Micro-Linguistic and Social Structure: A Theory of Social Action." *Sociological Theory, 4,* 71–83.

Williams, Robin. 1983. "Sociological Tropes: A Tribute to Erving Goffman." *Theory, Culture and Society, 2,* 99–102.

———. 1988. "Understanding Goffman's Methods." In P. Drew and A. Wooton (Eds.), *Erving Goffman: Exploring the Interaction Order.* Cambridge: Polity Press.

Chapter 21

Rational Choice and Exchange
Coleman

> What is "rationality"? Often the term is used in a purely evaluative sense: decisions I make are "rational"; those of which I disapprove are not. Occasionally, we adopt a broader perspective, and judge rationality not just in terms of approval but in terms of the "best interests" *of the person making the decision*—"best interests" as defined by *us*. Thus, for example, some of Adolf Hitler's decisions may be viewed as rational and others are irrational, despite the fact that we may disapprove of all of them. (Dawes, 1988:7–8)

In the 1600s, René Descartes said "Cogito ergo sum," translated as "I think, therefore I am." In this chapter, two claims are made: "I think, therefore I choose," and "I think, therefore I choose what benefits me." The first reflects rational choice theory, which comes primarily from a psychological tradition. The second represents exchange theory, which is based on both psychology and economics.

Rational choice involves making a decision based on (1) one's current assets, or capability of "following through"; (2) the possible consequences of one's choice; and (3) if the consequences are uncertain, evaluation of outcomes in terms of probabilities (Dawes, 1988:8). Does my choice "make sense" or not?

It is rational to act in one's own best interest. That is, it is rational to try to maximize one's gain or profit and minimize one's loss or cost. An example from exchange theory will help:

> Suppose that two men are doing paper-work jobs in an office. According to the office rules, each should do his job by himself or, if he needs help, he should consult the supervisor. One of the men, whom we shall call Person, is not skillful at the work and would get it done better and faster if he got help from time to time. In spite of the rules he is reluctant to go to the supervisor, for to confess his incompetence might hurt his chances for promotion. Instead he seeks out the other man, whom we shall call Other for short, and asks him for help. Other is more experienced at the work

than is Person; he can do his work well and quickly and be left with time to spare, and he has reason to suppose that the supervisor will not go out of his way to look for a breach of the rules. Other gives Person help and in return Person gives Other thanks and expressions of approval. The two men have exchanged help and approval. (Homans, 1961:31–32)

In this example, "Person" needs help and it is rational to seek it, but it could be costly to seek it from his supervisor. "Other" sees it as rational to give the needed help, because he believes his shared expertise is appreciated and is bound to come to the attention of the supervisor. For the supervisor it is rational to ignore his own rule, because "Other" is able to give adequate help to Person, thus saving supervisor's time for other tasks. Thus, the exchange is rational; it involves help in exchange for respect and approval.

Elements of these theories can be traced back to John Stuart Mill and Jeremy Bentham in the nineteenth century, as well as several thinkers in the second half of the twentieth century. In this chapter we will begin with the work of James Coleman, who speaks to both rational choice and exchange. Then we will bring in Mancur Olson, Peter Blau, George Homans, and others under the heading of "Other Theorists."

James S. Coleman, 1926–1995

James Coleman studied with Paul Lazarsfeld and Robert K. Merton at Columbia University and received his PhD in 1955. He taught at the University of Chicago for three years and then founded the Department of Social Relations at Johns Hopkins, where he served until 1973. At that time he returned to the University of Chicago, where he spent his last 22 years as University Professor. His scholarly career, noted *Footnotes*,[1]

> was devoted to the creation and utilization of social science methodology and theory to study social phenomena and to illuminate major issues in public policy. His main contributions lay in sociological theory—including the analysis of social change, collective action, and rational choice—mathematical sociology, the sociology of education, and public policy. Exceptional ability, fertile imagination, and the courage to go against received opinion and to bear sometimes vicious attacks marked his distinguished career. ("Jim Coleman," 1995:1)

The variety of Coleman's interests is seen in his major publications: *Union Democracy* in 1956 (with S. M. Lipset and Martin Trow), *The Adolescent Society* (1961), *Introduction to Mathematical Sociology* (1964), *Power and the Structure of Society* (1974), *Individual Interests and Collective Action* (1986), and his magnum opus, *Foundations of Social Theory* (1990), which is the focus of this chapter.

---

[1]*Footnotes* is a journal of the American Sociological Association that discusses sociology meetings, issues within the discipline, and from time to time obituaries of important sociologists.

The *Foundations* book brings together many of Coleman's earlier themes in a single volume. It begins with 530 pages on rational choice and exchange theories, followed by 130 pages on modern society and social policy implications, and then closes with a 275-page application of mathematical models to the theory presented in the first 500-plus pages.

Coleman's Central Theory and Methods

Throughout Coleman's career he was interested in both theory and methods. We will begin this section with his theory, and will close with a few words on his methods.

Rational Choice and Exchange   Theory is best, maintained Coleman, when it does *not* stay at the system level, as Emile Durkheim's theory does. "An explanation based on internal analysis of system behavior in terms of actions and orientations of lower-level units is likely to be more stable and general than an explanation which remains at the system level" (Coleman, 1990:3). The "lower-level units" to which he refers are individual actors, which are Coleman's primary focus of attention. In addition, there are what he calls "corporate actors," involving multiple individuals or groups, an example being a modern corporation (Coleman, 1990:421f).

Coleman, then, begins at the individual level, focusing on purposive action based on reasons for it. When I am asked why I did something, a possible response is "I had my reasons." The commonsense meaning of this is that I had an intended goal, and I perceived my behavior or action as contributing to that goal in specific and knowable ways (Coleman, 1990:13).

A frequent criticism of such a purposive view, Coleman admits, is that it is explicitly teleological, meaning that the end is used to explain the action-based means. This view considers individuals as purposive, responsible, rational actors. A part of the criticism is that individuals often act irrationally, even self-destructively. In response, Coleman asserts that social scientists have as their purpose an

> understanding of social organization that is derivative from actions of individuals and since understanding an individual's actions ordinarily means seeing the reasons behind the action, then the theoretical aim of social science must be to conceive of that action in a way that makes it rational from the point of view of the actor. (1990:18)

In other words, a rationality assumption on the part of an actor is necessary in order to understand (explain) the behavior. While Vilfredo Pareto would argue with this assumption, viewing reasons as excuses or rationalizations, we will begin by accepting Coleman's premise in order to understand his theory.

Very early on, Coleman introduced the concept of **exchange** into his theory of rational behavior. An important aspect of rationality involves the use of resources, or those elements that actors have available to use in exchange. System is based on interdependence, and interdependence is based on these two factors—rationality and exchange. "It is this structure, together with the fact that the actors are purposive, each having the goal of maximizing the realization of his interests, that gives the interdependence, or systemic character, to their actions" (1990:29). Coleman added, "Social relations between two persons are, of course, the building blocks of social organization" (1990:43).

Coleman was cognizant of the kinds of criticisms to which he was open. His first assumption, he admitted, is a rational actor who is purely self-interested and unconstrained by societal norms or rules. This, he believed, is a necessary beginning point, so that the genesis and maintenance of norms could be introduced later, along with moral codes and identification with collectives, as problematics rather than as givens. In the same way, corporate actors would be introduced only after individual actors were clearly understood.

What, then, are the various aspects of rational action on the part of individuals? Coleman began with types of resources. These include (a) resources that affect other actors; (b) personal attributes, such as skills and looks, valued by others; (c) and resources, such as money, that can be used in direct exchange (1990:33). Thus, even though exchange theory derives from economics, resources include much more than material goods, or money and property.

Three forms of **capital** (or accumulated resources) are **physical, human,** and **social**. "Physical capital is wholly tangible, being embodied in observable material form; human capital is less tangible, being embodied in the skills and knowledge acquired by an individual; social capital is even less tangible, for it is embodied in the *relations* among persons" (Coleman, 1990:304). Social capital includes trust and trustworthiness, which enable a group to accomplish much more than if they are lacking. Trust, as we have said before, is a resource that can depreciate over time if it is not maintained and renewed.

Another aspect of the behavior of rational actors involves rights to act. These rights include control over resources and **authority**, or the granting by others of those rights. The rights due to authority may be based on delegation or permission (such as when one parent grants the other the right to instruct and discipline their children), on normative legitimation (such as traditional authority because one is in the "royal line"), and even on force (as when slavery is treated as an acceptable part of a society's structure).

Legitimation raises an important distinction between **principal** and **agent**, or controller and controlled. Though not always based on legitimate authority or the right to act, there are in society some who control the exchange process and others who are "under control." Recalling Marx's discussion, the working class under capitalism are seen as exchanging their labor for an income, but without sufficient control to keep the capitalists from extracting surplus labor value. The rationality of their behavior is based on the premise that such controlled labor is preferable to no job at all. Of course, Marx would argue that rational behavior would lead them to overthrow the system that controls and exploits them.[2]

Recalling Luhmann's and Giddens's discussions (Chapter 15), Coleman argues that another important aspect of rationality and exchange involves trust.

---

[2]Mancur Olson discusses Marx's view from a rational choice perspective; we will look at this analysis under "Other Theorists."

Trust is necessary when there is time asymmetry in an exchange. In the lower classes, notes Coleman, help is often given when another person is in need, with no expected time for "returning the favor." The giver trusts the receiver of help to reciprocate if or when the need arises; thus, this trust is based on *potential* reciprocity, not on a known condition or time of its expression. Trust, of course, can be lost as well as gained, as when an individual no longer trusts his or her spouse, because of deviant or untrustworthy behavior.

After introducing resources, rights, and trust to his rational/exchange theory, Coleman introduces **norms**—behavioral prescriptions and proscriptions. "Social norms . . . specify what actions are regarded by a set of persons as proper or correct, or improper or incorrect" (rational or irrational).

> They are purposively generated, in that those persons who initiate or help maintain a norm see themselves as benefiting from its being observed or harmed by its being violated. Norms are ordinarily enforced by sanctions which are either rewards for carrying out those actions regarded as correct or punishments for carrying out those actions regarded as incorrect. (Coleman, 1990:242)

Norms may be **conjoint** or **disjoint**. Conjoint norms are those accepted by and beneficial to everyone; disjoint norms are those that are rewarding to or practiced by some people (or groups of people) and punishing to or ignored by others. For example, the gender "double standard" is a disjoint norm that says women must restrict sexual activity while men are granted sexual freedom. Disjointness may also be seen in the old idea that a man may seek to engage in sexual behavior with a woman, while looking for a long-term relationship with a woman who has not so engaged. Furthermore, those with power or in control may have the freedom to violate a norm. During wartime, for example, money may make it possible for some to hoard scarce goods, even though there is a norm that says "Don't hoard."

Coleman readily admits that a theory grounded in rational (purposive) choice has difficulty dealing with the process whereby norms develop and become internalized. However, he maintains that this problem is no more difficult than that of the functionalist who tries to explain norms as based on societal purposes at the level of the social system (1990:292). In Coleman's theory, an important aspect of the development of norms involves coping with the limited resources of an environment (such as what is considered edible or inedible), while their internalization has to do with socialization, or the passing along of norms from one generation to the next.

Coleman summarizes his rational/exchange theory up to this point as follows:

> Actors are seen as beginning with resources over which they have some (possibly total) control and in which they have interests. Social interdependence and systemic functioning arise from the fact that actors have interests in events that are fully or partially under the control of other actors. The result of the various kinds of exchanges and unilateral transfers of control that actors engage in to achieve their interests is . . . the formation of social relationships having some persistence over time. Authority relations,

relations of trust, and consensual allocations of rights which establish norms are the principal ones that have been examined here. (1990:300)

Thus far, Coleman's theory has focused on individual actors and their interrelations. However, the introduction of norms begins the transition to the supra-individual level. Norms, after all, may be enforced collectively, rather than by one individual or another. The official expression of norms Coleman calls a **constitution**—in effect, the formal expression of a society's rationality. While this concept is not restricted to what we usually think of as a constitution, Coleman uses the common meaning to illustrate it: "The U.S., Polish, and French constitutions were perhaps the first constitutions of nation-states that had as an ideological base a social contract among equal citizens" (1990:327).[3]

So as not to be limited to individual behaviors, Coleman moves from the constitution to the **corporate actor.** A corporate actor includes more than one individual, often a principal and agent, but is more than simply multiple individuals. It is a group actor, or actors, exemplified by a corporation's owning another corporation or subsidiary. Here Coleman comes close to reifying the group level, a difficulty that he finds in Durkheim. But he tries to distinguish his view from Durkheim's by speaking of both corporate rationality and corporate authority at the level of organization—be the organization a church, corporation, or nation-state. There is, furthermore, a supra-individual control and exchange of resources, with the corporate actor mirroring the individual actor.

Coleman closes out his theoretical development with a discussion of the **self**. The self-conscious actor is able to think introspectively and decide upon rational action; such an actor may be a person or may be corporate. An important distinction is made here between subjective and objective interests. Does the self always understand what is in her or his best interest? Those in control often act as if the answer is no. After all, an outside source, such as the state, may intervene in private affairs, or on behalf of a weaker party to an interaction—the excuse being that "it is for your own good" (Coleman, 1990: 512).

This completes Coleman's rational/exchange perspective, but leaves him raising once again (as the reader might) the issue of deviations from rationality. Such deviations, he claims,

> do not substantially affect the theory developed here. To put it another way, my implicit assumption is that the theoretical predictions made here will be substantially the same whether the actors act precisely according to rationality as commonly conceived or deviate in the ways that have been observed. (1990:506)

Once again, Coleman briefly summarizes both his theory and its difficulties:

> The theory of rational action or purposive action is a theory of instrumental rationality, *given* a set of goals or ends or utilities. If a theory of internal change of actors is to be justifiable or consistent with the basic principle of

---

[3]It is perhaps noteworthy that the Code of Hammurabi is a variety of constitution that can be traced back to the Mesopotamian River basin more than four millennia ago.

action, it must do what appears to be impossible: to account for *changes* in utilities (or goals) on the basis of the principle of *maximization* of utility. (1990: 516)

Coleman later describes a perfect social system as one in which actors are rational

and in which there is no structure to impede any actor's use of resources at any point in the system. In economists' terms there are no transaction costs. Free rider problems do not exist, for actors are able to use their resources to induce others with like interests to contribute to the common good. (1990:719)

The "free rider" concept will be explained in the next section; other elements of Coleman's theory, and its relation to other theorists, will be introduced in the "Other Theories" section.

Methods   In a book of readings on *Rational Choice Theory* (Abell, 1991), it is argued that this is the best theory from which to develop systematic deductive models. A number of researchers have developed testable propositions and used sophisticated statistical techniques to study relative deprivation, free ridership, collective action, the prisoner's dilemma, and so on (Kosaka, Marwell and Ames, Oliver and Marwell, Heckathorn, in Abell, 1991:291–304, 329–380).

Coleman himself, as noted earlier, devoted many pages of his book to carrying out such analyses. While this may not be the only operationalizable theory in this volume, that is certainly one of its goals and major strengths.

Nature of Humans, Society, and Change

James Coleman was a socially active social scientist who believed the world could be changed for the better by those who understood it. He did not believe in a perfectible human nature, nor in a perfectly rational world. He was, however, a humanist in the classic sense of the term. He was engaged, as a social scientist, with the issues of his day.

Like most of the great sociologists of the nineteenth and early twentieth centuries, Coleman's commitment to his field was moral. For him, social science could not be justified merely as an intellectual exercise. Rather, it had to prove its worth by showing policy-makers how to design legislation and institutions that would be beneficial to society. ("Jim Coleman," 1995:8)

Coleman's social concern was evident in what came to be known as the "Coleman Report," which indicated that lower-class black children in the United States benefited from attending integrated schools. This finding was one of the primary bases for busing to achieve school desegregation, and was not an altogether popular conclusion.

Coleman also spoke of the social responsibility of corporate actors. He noted that major stockholders are likely to be more socially responsible, because they carry out and receive credit for civic or philanthropic activities while small stockholders do not. The small stockholder is likely to be a **"free rider,"** sharing in the benefits of corporate policies and responsibility without contributing to them in any direct way (1990:575).[4]

Change, to Coleman, is both factual and prescriptive. Much of his book speaks of changes that have already occurred in the social world. Primordial structures, such as the family and community, have given way to purposive structures, such as bureaucratic organizations. "The constructed social environment," Coleman noted, "consisting of purposive corporate actors and their agents, constitutes a large part of the social environment of most persons in modern societies" (1990:614). It is because of the dominance of such organizations, including multinational corporations, that Coleman believed a theory of rational exchange to be appropriate for today's world.

Like Max Weber, Coleman was concerned about the effect of purposive organizations on human life. Such organizations can handle those functions that can be bought and sold, but not those that cannot. The result is that relationships, even child rearing, are undermined by the organized society. But why cannot nation-state legislation simply create structures to replace the primordial or traditional ones that have been lost? Coleman argued that the multinational organization of corporate life is even beginning to make nation-states irrelevant, and their legislatures ineffectual.

What, then, were Coleman's prescriptions for change? Sounding somewhat like Immanuel Wallerstein, he argued that prescriptions must come from applied research and theory. The new social science must be dedicated to the task of replacing what has been lost, and improving what remains. Coleman believed that the beginning point is an understanding of the rational and exchange character of human relationships as they exist today (Coleman, 1990:664).

Class, Gender, and Race

Although rational choice theory can be applied to class, gender, and race, Coleman did not do so; the index at the back of his 993-page tome includes none of them. However, it is possible from some of his earlier writing to conclude that he was concerned about racial inequalities, though less about the position of women in society. Some feminist critics have argued that his theory is inadequate to handle gender issues. Later we will note how others have used the exchange perspective in family relations.

Other Theories and Theorists

Although Coleman's book has been the focus of our introduction to both rational choice and exchange, we will now back up to the 1960s and add other insights on these two theories. On rational choice theory, we will refer to Mancur

---

[4]The "free rider" idea is sometimes expressed in everyday speech as just being "along for the ride," meaning that one is going somewhere without doing anything to further the trip. See Marwell and Ames (1981).

Olson, Russell Hardin, and others; for exchange theory, we will use George Homans, Peter Blau, and others.

Rational Choice Theory   As already indicated, rational choice theory can be traced to the nineteenth century, and even earlier. However, we will begin with Mancur Olson and his work *The Logic of Collective Action*, published in 1965.

Rational behavior, according to Olson, is not necessarily selfish or unselfish. Rational simply means that "objectives, whether selfish or unselfish, should be pursued by means that are efficient and effective for achieving" them (1965:65). As an example of rationality, Olson notes that it is rational for union members to be in favor of attendance at union meetings, while not attending themselves. This is because a large turnout is helpful in achieving group goals, while attendance by any one member of a large organization has little effect on outcomes (1965:86–87).

Olson also pointed out exceptions to rational behavior. Situations in which behavior cannot be explained by rational choice include (1) acting on the basis of an emotional response or ideological commitment, as exemplified by cult members who believe in the cataclysmic end of the world,[5] and (2) working for an obviously "lost cause," which may require a psychological instead of an economic/rational explanation (1965:12, 161).

The notion of working for a lost cause brings us back to Olson's comments on whether or not Marx was a rational choice theorist. "Marx," noted Olson, "sees self-interested individuals and self-interested classes acting to achieve their interests." Many critics have attacked Marx for emphasizing self-interest and rationality too much. According to Olson, however,

> It is *not* in fact true that the absence of the kind of class conflict Marx expected shows that Marx overestimated the strength of rational behavior. On the contrary, the absence of the sort of class action Marx predicted is due in part to the predominance of rational utilitarian behavior. *For class-oriented action will not occur if the individuals that make up a class act rationally.* (1965:105)

Instead, Olson argued, it is rational for people to focus on their own individual interests, because they will benefit from any class action whether or not they participate, and it is not rational to risk life or property for a struggle in which one's individual contribution may have little effect, or even a negative personal outcome. Marx, then, is a rational choice theorist because he expects the class revolution to be successful—although those who believe it to be impossible or personally costly see him as irrational.

Russell Hardin, in his 1982 book on *Collective Action*, agrees with Coleman and Olson that not all behavior can be explained by a theory of rational choice. Extrarational motivations may include moral sentiments, such as those governing the environmental or civil rights movements (Hardin, 1982:104, 108). A possible response to this view is that such involvements may be totally rational

---

[5]Of course, while they seem out of touch with reality, it is always possible that at some point they will be right (rational) and the rest of us will be wrong.

if we believe it is important to attempt to shape world historical events. In addition, it is rational to work for the environment if we believe that lack of such a concern will eventually lead to the irrational destruction of our world; and it is rational to be morally committed to civil rights if we believe that the world of race and ethnic relations must change or else experience some sort of cataclysm.

Hardin's book adds two more important qualifications to Coleman's version of rational choice theory. First, it is important to remember that choice is not static; it is a dynamic process. Some choices take time, and the conditions governing them change. For example, while one is deciding on the purchase of a home, an illness may occur that makes it irrational to buy at that time, or makes it rational to buy something smaller. Also, one choice often leads to another, so that rationality requires thinking ahead to multiple or serial decisions (Hardin, 1982:13).

Second, bringing exchange theory into his discussion of rational choice, Hardin notes that rational choices are often asymmetrical. The asymmetry of costs and benefits from a collective good may be such as to cause two persons to make rational but opposing choices (Hardin, 1982:67–68). For example, good schools are a collective good that is more beneficial to a family with young children than to an elderly couple. Or a good music program in school may be seen as much more beneficial by one set of parents than by another. Thus, process and asymmetry are important additions to Coleman's theory.

Exchange Theory   To add to Coleman's discussion of exchange, we must go back to the 1960s and 1970s to the insights of theorists such as George Casper Homans, John Thibaut and Harold Kelley, and Peter Blau.

For Coleman, exchange was a subprinciple of rational choice: it is rational to seek profit and avoid cost. Earlier, however, Homans (1961) laid out a more complete exchange theory intended to provide the groundwork for understanding all of social behavior. His theory "envisages social *behavior* as an exchange of activity, tangible or intangible, and more or less rewarding or costly, between at least two persons" (1961:13).

Homans's theory was stated in terms of testable propositions.[6] One such proposition is "For all actions taken by persons, the more often a particular action of a person is rewarded, the more likely the person is to perform that action" (Homans, 2d ed., 1974:16). George Ritzer calls this Homans's "success" proposition, because reward results in repetition. A second proposition stated that a stimulus followed by a behavior that is rewarded will have the same result when it (the stimulus) occurs again (Homans, 1961:23). These two propositions describe the repetition effect of behavior rewarded by others, and the effect of a stimulus followed by a behavior rewarded by others.

A third proposition stated that if an individual sees an action as personally rewarding (rather than rewarded by others), it will be repeated (Homans, 1974:25). However, Homans qualified this with a fourth proposition, the effect of satiation: "The more often in the recent past a person has received a particular reward, the

---

[6]George Ritzer (1983:247–250) lists and discusses Homans's propositions in his chapter on exchange theory.

less valuable any further unit of that reward becomes for him [or her]" (1961:29). In other words, behavior that is rewarding, either to oneself or to others, is repeated—but only up to a point. Finally, when behavior does not receive the expected reward, or is punished unexpectedly, the response is anger—and the aggressor will find such aggression rewarding (1961:37).

While Homans's theory of profits or benefits and losses or costs was born in economics, he did not restrict it to material exchanges. He argued that "the principles of economics are perfectly reconcilable with those of elementary social behavior, once the special conditions in which each applies are taken into account. Both deal with the exchange of rewarding goods," with goods being defined broadly (1961:68). He defined "psychic *profit* as reward less cost" and argued that "no exchange continues unless both parties are making a profit" (1961:61). Although mutual profit is important to the continuation of interaction, however, each individual is primarily concerned about his or her own profit.

Homans briefly introduced rationality to his theory of exchange. It is not a hedonistic theory, Homans claimed. "So long as men's values are altruistic, they can take a profit in altruism too. Some of the greatest profiteers we know are altruists" (1961:79). It is, after all, rational to seek profit and minimize cost, even if the profit is psychic. Homans, whose aim was explanation, left rationality to a simple assumption: "All we impute to them in the way of rationality is that they know enough to come in out of the rain unless they enjoy getting wet" (1961:82). Thus, for Coleman, rationality is the primary explanatory principle, with exchange as a subelement; for Homans, explanation is based on principles of exchange, with rationality as a simple assumption.

Two years before Homans published his *Social Behavior*, Thibaut and Kelley (1959) presented a very similar theory of social exchange. A key factor in their theoretical propositions neatly ties together rational choice and exchange. They called it the "comparison level for alternatives" and explained it thus: A choice involves more than one alternative. When it involves the continuation or leaving of a relationship, the question is whether there is sufficient profit to continue. It is, after all, rational to maximize benefit in the choices one makes and in the relationships one has.[7]

Unlike Coleman, neither Homans nor Thibaut and Kelley spoke of corporate actors, focusing instead on what they considered to be the elementary (or individual) level of explanation. Peter Blau (1964) came much closer to Coleman's position, recognizing the possibility of organizational as well as individual exchanges. One commentator offers the following explanation of Blau's four-stage transition leading from the individual to social structure to change:

Step One: Personal exchange transactions between people give rise to . . .
Step Two: Differentiation of status and power, which leads to . . .
Step Three: Legitimation and organization, which sow the seeds of . . .
Step Four: Opposition and change.

---

[7]Reminiscent of Mosca's complaint that Pareto had plagiarized, Thibaut and Kelley believed that Homans had drawn much of his argument from their work. This issue was never resolved.

However, because large groups within a social structure involve persons who may never interact with one another, their connection is by means of shared norms and shared values, rather than direct exchange (Ritzer, 1983:252, 254).

One difference between Coleman and Blau is the same as that between Coleman and Homans: Coleman's focus was on rational choice, with exchange as a secondary issue; Blau's focus was on exchange.

> Not all human behavior is guided by considerations of exchange, though much of it is, more than we usually think. Two conditions must be met for behavior to lead to social exchange. It must be oriented toward ends that can only be achieved through interaction with other persons, and it must seek to adopt means to further the achievement of these ends. . . . In brief, social exchange may reflect any behavior oriented to socially mediated goals. (Blau, 1964:5)

For Blau, exchange theory was neither a matter of equal gain (recall Hardin) nor a "zero-sum game," in which the gains of some equal the losses of others. Individuals associate with one another, according to Blau, "because they all profit from their association. But they do not necessarily all profit equally, and even if there are no direct costs to participants, there are often indirect costs borne by those excluded from the association" (1964:15), as, for example, when two members of a group pair up, to the exclusion of other potential suitors.

How does trust fit into Blau's theory of exchange? Blau used "trust" in a somewhat different way from Coleman. To Coleman, you will recall, trust is ordinarily a matter of differential timing: one person benefits now while the other trusts that she or he will (or may) benefit later. To Blau, **trust** accrues from long-term or stable obligations: "Since trust is essential for stable social relations, and since exchange obligations promote trust, special mechanisms exist to perpetuate obligations and thus strengthen bonds of indebtedness and trust" (1964:99). Trust of the sort described by Blau is, of course, crucial to family—especially marital—relationships.

Power enters into Blau's exchange theory in the following way: Suppose, he says, a person is frequently in need of services from an associate to whom he or she has nothing to offer in return. What are the alternatives?

> First, he may force the other to give him help. Second, he may obtain the help he needs from another source. Third, he may find ways to get along without such help. If he is unable or unwilling to choose any of these alternatives, however, there is only one other course of action left for him; he must subordinate himself to the other and comply with his wishes, thereby rewarding the other with power over himself as an inducement for furnishing the needed help. (1964: 22)

In other words, a result of unequal exchange is the power of one individual over another. From the standpoint of the benefactor, "overwhelming others with benefactions serves to achieve superiority over them" (1964:111). And, as Coleman stated, legitimated power is defined as authority.

One of Blau's major contributions to exchange theory was his presentation of certain dilemmas, as in the following example: What does one have to do, asked Blau, to be incorporated into a group? An individual's endeavors to impress the rest of the group with his outstanding qualities in order to prove himself attractive to them and gain their social acceptance simultaneously poses a status threat for these others that tends to antagonize them. The very outstanding qualities that make an individual differentially attractive as an associate also raise fears of dependence. (1964:318)

Another exchange dilemma noted by Blau has to do with incompatible goal states. Actions designed to attain one goal may impede the accomplishment of a second goal. Or one requirement for accomplishing a goal may interfere with another requirement for achieving the same objective or goal. An example would be a love relationship between two professionals, such as academicians, that may be extremely rewarding to them, but may make it difficult for them to pursue their individually desired professional goals of obtaining tenured positions.

Other Issues   Before we turn to critiques and conclusions, let us bring rational choice and exchange to bear on two additional issues: gender and family, and revolution.

Although Coleman did not discuss gender and family as an exchange issue, Ivan Nye and others have applied exchange theory to family relationships, showing how such resource exchanges as good looks for money or status for race occur. Such analyses have often been based on traditional gender-role stereotypes, such as the male breadwinner/ female homemaker distinction.

Coleman wrote at length about revolutions, as did Blau before him. In his chapter on "Revoking Authority," Coleman began with a question: Does revolution occur when conditions are getting worse? His answer was that impoverishment leads to passivity and apathy, not revolution. Instead, revolts against nations or institutions occur when things are getting better, and when control is being relaxed. In the nineteenth century this phenomenon had been noted by Alexis de Tocqueville:

> It is not always when things are going from bad to worse that revolution breaks out. On the contrary, it more often happens that, when a people which has put up with an oppressive rule over a long period without protest suddenly finds the government releasing its pressure, it takes up arms against it. (1860:176–177)

Although this may seem irrational, Coleman maintained that it could be explained by rational choice theory. He first introduced the frustration theory of revolution (discussed briefly in Chapter 18). This theory, noted Coleman, begins with the premise that frustration results when reality falls short of expectations. But when things are in fact getting better, expectations rise even more rapidly than objective conditions. This explanation is highly individualistic, and therefore in all probability incomplete, though it is, of course, individuals who become frustrated (Coleman, 1990:473, 479).

Thus, rising expectations and accompanying frustration are, according to Coleman, inadequate for explaining revolutions. Power theories, by contrast, state that those opposed to a regime see small changes (improvements) made by an administration as an indication that they (the opposition) are winning. This gives them a sense of power, and they double their efforts. In addition, they may take this opportunity to mobilize the uncommitted, who may—if made aware—see the advantage of joining the revolution.

But what is rational about the choice to revolt? Coleman put it this way:

> If revolutionary activity and support for the revolutionary activity of others are regarded as rational actions, it becomes evident that such activity will be more likely to occur as those who have an interest in seeing the authority system replaced come to have a belief that they will succeed. (1990:480)

Thus, power theory is generally compatible with Coleman's position. Coleman noted that revolutionary activity ordinarily involves but a small portion of a population, with the majority simply being bystanders, going about their daily lives.

In developing his theory, Coleman asked what the reasons are for the revolutionary involvement of any given individual. Speaking in exchange terms, he saw three sets of benefits. First, there are the objective benefits expected if the regime changes. These, of course, may be independent of an individual's commitment; that is, there will be "free riders." The second set of benefits depends on both involvement and success. Since material benefits are in scarce supply, they will go primarily to those whose participation was important to the revolution's success. These Mancur Olson (1965) called "selective incentives." The third type of benefits results simply from participation, regardless of the revolution's success or failure. Participation benefits are of two kinds: benefits or satisfactions from being involved with one's friends, particularly in the service of an ideology to which all are committed; and the internal reward that comes from "doing the right thing," from trying to make one's society (or world) a better place (Coleman, 1990:493–494). The pursuit of such benefits was, to Coleman, rational.

Blau's chapter on "Opposition" raises some of the same issues regarding revolutions from his exchange perspective. Isolated victims of oppression are helpless, even passive in terms of action. However, as outrage and hostility are communicated to others, a social consensus emerges that legitimates the feelings and absolves the individual of guilt feelings for nonnormative attitudes. At this point a revolutionary ideology may be adopted, which turns consensual outrage into a noble cause. And pursuit of such a cause is rewarding enough that the committed are willing to pay the costs of risky action. Unlike Coleman, however, Blau emphasizes relative rather than absolute deprivation—on the part of the very poor, who feel left out of their society's benefits, and of the lower middle class, who see their superiority over the workers being threatened by labor movements (Blau, 1964:251). Thus, for Blau, revolts are a matter of—to use Thibaut and Kelley's term—the comparison level of alternatives.

Applications   Coleman was greatly concerned with the application of theory to social life. The applied tradition goes back at least to Jean-Jacques Rousseau in eighteenth-century France, who believed that human understanding could be brought to bear on society's ills and inadequacies. If, wrote Coleman,

> there is no effect of social research or social theory on society's functioning, then sociologists must seriously question their purpose. If the examination

shows that there are effects, whether or not they bias functioning, then guidance is provided for optimal institutionalization of applied social research. (1990:649)

Coleman did see a danger that application conceived too narrowly might become merely a service to the powerful, which today means large corporate actors. But conceived

> more broadly, this new social science becomes science that extends its knowledge to the understanding of how power comes to be distributed and accumulated in society, and to the understanding of how natural persons can best satisfy their interests in a social system populated with large corporate actors. (1990:651)

Critique and Conclusions

We must summarize and critique not only Coleman's ideas, but those of the other theorists, such as Homans and Blau, who have helped us understand rational choice and exchange.

Peter Abell, in introducing his book *Rational Choice Theory* (1991), stated his belief that this theoretical position is based on

> the almost complete failure of the established theoretical traditions—be they marxist or non-marxist, functionalist or non-functionalist, inter-actionist or non-interactionist, structuralist or non-structuralist—to provide a framework for the systematic deductive modeling of that complex realm called "social reality." (Abell, 1991:ix)

Like Abell, Coleman and Blau are "true believers." However, Coleman and Blau pointed out the limitations of rational choice and exchange theory as well—rather than waiting for their critics to do so. Coleman stated that for "a number of reasons, this approach is not completely satisfactory. It does not deal well with socialization, internalization," or changes in the springs of action. And it does not explain deviations from rationality that result from being out of touch with reality, weakness of will, preference reversals, force, or fear. In addition, he admitted that his attempts to deal with corporate actors fell short of success.

> From one perspective a corporate actor is a system of action containing actors, resources, and events, and leading to outcomes. But considered as an actor with a utility function, this same system is . . . an unanalyzed entity. Although the actions of a corporate actor would seem to correspond to outcomes of indivisible events in a system of action, these two perspectives have not been made consistent. In other words, there has not been made explicit any means of mapping between event outcomes in a system of action and utility functions . . . for that system of action considered as a corporate actor. (Coleman, 1990:932)

Thus, Coleman admitted that it was difficult to speak of a corporate actor without reifying the system level, which he saw as a problem with Durkheim, and which he sought to avoid doing in his own theory.

Blau also discussed these limitations, or aspects of social life that exchange theory had difficulty explaining. In addition, he noted the opposite problem. If all behavior, whether economic, interpersonal, altruistic, or anonymous, can be explained post hoc in terms of individual profit or gain, has anything actually been explained? As Blau put it, it is "tempting to consider all social conduct in terms of exchange, but this would deprive the concept of its distinctive meaning. People do things for fear of other men or for fear of God or for fear of their conscience, and nothing is gained by trying to force such action into a conceptual framework of exchange" (1964:89).

While Coleman and Blau both admitted the problems with rational choice and exchange theories, a most interesting debate between Talcott Parsons and Homans also contributes to this discussion.

Parsons versus Homans   The functionalist Parsons and the exchange theorist Homans had an ongoing debate when they were colleagues at Harvard. Parsons maintained that "Homans is under obligation to show how his principles can account for the principal structural features of large scale social systems" (1964:216). According to Ritzer (1983:251), Parsons "concluded that even if Homans were to try to do this, he would inevitably fail, because social facts are variables capable of explaining, and being explained, without reference to Homans's psychological principles."

Homans, on the other hand, argued that Parsons-type social facts are not explanatory. To theorists such as Durkheim and Parsons, Homans issued the following challenge:

> Let them therefore specify what properties of social behavior they consider to be emergent and show, by constructing the appropriate deductive systems, how they propose to explain them without making use of psychological propositions. I guarantee to show either that the explanations fail to explain or that they in fact use psychological propositions, in however disguised a form. (Homans, 1971:376)

In short, then, Homans would say that Parsons does not explain structure at the societal level, and Parsons would say that Homans does not explain structure at the psychological (or economic) level (Ritzer, 1983:252). Or, we might say, Homans believes that Parsons has explained nothing, and Parsons would say that Homans explains little of sociological importance.

Blau According to Ritzer   What of Blau and Coleman, who seek to use rational choice and exchange to explain not only individual behaviors, but corporate or group actors as well? Ritzer offers the following criticism of Blau:

> Although Blau argued that he was simply extending exchange theory to the societal level, in so doing he twisted exchange theory beyond recognition. He was even forced to admit that processes at the societal level are fundamentally different from those at the individual level. In his effort to extend exchange theory, Blau managed only to transform it into another theory congruent with the social facts paradigm. Blau seemed to recognize that exchange theory is primarily concerned with face-to-face relations. (Ritzer, 1983:256)

Although Blau may have recognized this limitation, he continued to apply exchange theory to the group level.

Coleman According to Neil Smelser   Neil Smelser is a functionalist in the mold of Parsons. His review of Coleman's book, therefore, parallels Parsons's response to Homans. Smelser states at the outset that Coleman's magnum opus "is the most ambitious effort ever to build a general sociology on the basis of the individualistic, utilitarian, rational-actor, voluntarist assumptions enunciated in classical economics and democratic theory" (Smelser, 1990:778). Coleman, notes Smelser, moved between the micro and macro levels, never simply treating the latter by aggregating individuals. Coleman himself, Smelser reminds us, made very explicit which theories he did *not* prefer: (1) those based on external forces, such as technology; (2) those explaining change by means of cultural values; (3) functionalism; (4) normative, or oversocialized, explanations; and (5) structural explanations, such as Weber's treatment of bureaucracy.

Coleman, says Smelser, recognized that irrational behaviors occur, but did little of theoretical value with that recognition. Coleman explained away much irrationality: "Much of what is ordinarily described as nonrational or irrational is merely so because the observers have not discovered the point of view of the actor, from which the action *is* rational" (Coleman, 1990:18). According to Smelser, once we enter Coleman's realm of individual self-interpretation, we have opened the door to the problem of unique self-understanding and non-generalizability (Smelser, 1990:780). To this we might add that we also enter Pareto's trap, wherein the individual is assumed to rationalize and justify her or his motives and behaviors.

Smelser then speaks as a functionalist (like Parsons): Perhaps the most important problem with rational choice theories is that they tend to forget "that the free economic agent and the free citizen are themselves in, and products of, a specific complex of cultural values and institutions" (1990:781). Smelser does admit that ours is in fact the kind of quasi-rationalized society about which Coleman is theorizing. While Smelser also criticizes many of Coleman's historical references and his applied concerns, it is the theory itself with which we are concerned.

Final Thoughts

As we saw in Chapter 15, Stepjan Mestrovic criticized Anthony Giddens for overemphasizing human agency. Many humans do not see themselves as effective agents, because they are not; they are more likely to feel powerless. Here we are left with the same sort of dilemma. Just how rational are humans? And how much of modern life do Coleman's rational choice and exchange perspectives actually explain? Harrison Whyte, in the same symposium where Smelser's review is found, concludes with a most important point: Rational choice, in

> economics or political science or in Coleman's work, is a sensible and rational basis for model building, but only where the intervening constructs of preference and goal can be known and are stable—which is to say, where little change and turbulence is going on, little institutional change or shift in style. In short, rational choice will serve well where there is not much to

predict, and even then only perhaps in a society where goal-directed activity is part of socialization. (Whyte, 1990:788)

Coleman's final response to all these criticisms is easy to predict. Goal-directed activity *is* a large part of socialization today, as we are taught how to live purposefully in a rationally organized world. Besides, Coleman would say, Whyte is wrong to think that rational choice and exchange theory cannot handle change and turbulence. My book, Coleman might say, shows how to explain revolutions, collective behavior (mobs, panics, rumors, and the like), and other apparent turbulence and change. Rationality, agency, beneficial choices or not—this is one of the theoretical positions whose advocates and critics are extremely clear-cut in their opposing presuppositions and arguments.

References

Abell, Peter. 1991. *Rational Choice Theory*. Aldershot, England: Edward Elgar.

Blau, Peter. 1964. *Exchange and Power in Social Life*. New York: John Wiley.

Coleman, James S. 1961. *The Adolescent Society: The Social Life of the Teenager and Its Impact on Education*. Westport, CT: Greenwood Press.

———. 1964. *Introduction to Mathematical Sociology*. New York: Free Press of Glencoe.

———. 1974. *Power and the Structure of Society*. New York: Norton.

———. 1986. *Individual Interests and Collective Action: Selected Essays*. Cambridge: Cambridge University Press.

———. 1990. *Foundations of Social Theory*. Cambridge, MA: Belknap Press.

Dawes, Robyn M. 1988. *Rational Choice in an Uncertain World*. San Diego: Harcourt Brace Jovanovich.

Hardin, Russell. 1982. *Collective Action*. Baltimore: Johns Hopkins University Press.

Homans, George Casper. 1961/1974. *Social Behavior: Its Elementary Forms*. New York: Harcourt, Brace & World.

———. 1971. "Commentary." In Herman Turk and Richard Simpson (Eds.), *Institutions and Social Exchange* (pp. 363–376). Indianapolis: Bobbs-Merrill.

"Jim Coleman Leaves Legacy of Excellence." 1995, May/June. *Footnotes*, pp. 1, 8.

Lipset, Seymour Martin, Martin A. Trow, and James S. Coleman. 1956. *Union Democracy: The Internal Politics of the International Typographical Union*. Glencoe, IL: Free Press.

Marwell, Gerald, and Ruth Ames. 1981. "Economists Free Ride, Does Anyone Else?" *Journal of Public Economics, 15*, 295–310.

Olson, Mancur. 1965. *The Logic of Collective Action: Public Goods and the Theory of Goods*. Cambridge, MA: Harvard University Press.

Parsons, Talcott. 1964. "Levels of Organization and the Mediation of Social Interaction." *Sociological Inquiry, 34*, 207–220.

Ritzer, George. 1983. *Contemporary Sociological Theory*. New York: Alfred A. Knopf.

Smelser, Neil J. 1990. "Can Individualism Yield a Sociology?" [Review of Coleman, *Foundations of Social Theory*]. *Contemporary Sociology, 19*, 778–783.

Thibaut, John W., and Harold H. Kelley. 1959. *The Social Psychology of Groups*. New York: John Wiley and Sons.

Tocqueville, Alexis de. 1860/1955. *The Old Regime and the French Revolution* (S. Gilbert, Trans.). Garden City, NY: Doubleday.

Whyte, Harrison C. 1990. "Control to Deny Chance, But Thereby Muffling Identity" [Review of Coleman, *Foundations of Social Theory*]. *Contemporary Sociology, 19*, 783–788.

Chapter 22

Feminist Sociological Theory
Smith and Collins

Sark Women Gain the Right to Inherit Property

After more than 400 years, women finally have gained the right to inherit property in this tiny island. After a year of meetings to allow the island's inhabitants to have their say, the 52 mainly unelected rulers of Sark . . . voted . . . to change the law governing the transfer of land. Sark, between Britain and France, is the smallest independent state in the Commonwealth, and has been described as the last bastion of feudalism in the modern world. A committee is being formed to review the whole constitution, which allows wife-beating if the husband uses a stick no thicker than his finger and does not draw blood. (*Edmonton Journal*, November 26, 1999)

The above report comes as a surprise at the end of the twentieth century in Western society. It certainly gives pause to any feminist celebration that women have "come a long way" and achieved equality, at least in the West, during the twentieth century. It is a sobering note to the optimism of the feminist movements of the 1960s.

Sociology and Feminism

In Chapter 19 we discussed the social context in which the contemporary women's movements arose. Feminist theory was a concomitant development of the movement, because both were predicated on the assumption that theory and practice must go hand in hand: "The personal is political."

For many young female sociologists, the impact of the movement was emancipating. Lillian Rubin (1994:241) recalled the impact it had on her life and work, shattering "the paradigms that until then had dominated our personal, social, and intellectual worlds." For Alice Rossi (1988:45), an awareness of gender inequity came after a "jolting experience of sex discrimination" in 1962. Rossi was fired by the principal investigator of a study that Rossi had "designed, supervised the field-work for, and was happily analyzing." She had drafted a proposal for funds from the National Science Foundation to continue the project, and when it was approved, the principal investigator "decided the study was a good thing he wished to keep to himself" (1988:45). Sheila Rowbotham (1973:24) recalled the development of her feminist consciousness resulting from her realization, in the revolutionary ferment of 1968, that the "culture which was presented as 'revolutionary' was so blatantly phallic."

A part of the excitement for many women was the realization that their contemporary issues and concerns had been central to those of the women's movements of the nineteenth and early twentieth centuries. Many young feminists found to their "astonishment" that some of the pioneers of the earlier movements, such as Dora Russell and Rebecca West, were still alive (Spender, 1983:6). Spender noted that ignoring these women and not profiting from their experiences meant that post-sixties feminists "contributed to their invisibility" and "played a role in the denial of women's existence and strength" (1983:6).

Most of the young feminist sociologists were part of a relatively privileged group of women who had access to higher education, but, as Juliet Mitchell (1971:21) remarked, it is never "extreme deprivation that produces the revolutionary." Revolutionaries (as we saw in Chapter 21) come from groups who, although not absolutely deprived, nevertheless feel deprived in the light of what they have been promised or assume that they should obtain. The 1960s and 1970s were eye-opening decades for young women activists who found that, despite their contributions to civil rights and the antiwar movement, they were still "victims of male sexism" (Bernard, 1989:24). Women found that in "groups dedicated to human liberation, they were second-class members—useful at the typewriter, in the kitchen, and in bed, but expected to leave policy making to the men" (Deckard, 1983:326).

Academic women formed a significant proportion of the 1960s feminist movements' membership in its early stages, and invariably their feminist consciousness affected their academic work and interests. At the same time, their critical approach to traditional academic theories was also intended to inform movement practice. As Eichler (1992:134) pointed out, "Women's studies courses would not have come into existence without the women's movement." The movement was also a "clear recipient of benefits" of knowledge and data compiled by academics that allowing "activists to carry on the struggle."

Feminism in the academy mounted critiques of the masculine theoretical canon in what Bernard has called the "Feminist Enlightenment" (1989:25). This "Enlightenment" revealed sexism as an "invisible paradigm" that colored all aspects of women's lives. The attempt to transform, in revolutionary ways, traditional academic theory and practice met with mixed success. In sociology, feminism has had little impact on the core theoretical perspectives (Stacy and Thorne, 1985). The reason for the "missing feminist revolution in sociology," Stacy and Thorne argued, had to do with the continuing dominance of functionalist theoretical conceptions and positivist methodology, the social organization of the discipline, and the "ghettoization of feminist insights" (1985:306). Feminism seems to have had more impact in anthropology, history, and literature because these fields have strong interpretive traditions, in contrast to the positivist epistemology of sociology, political science, economics, and psychology (1985).

The relationship between sociology and feminism continues to be a fractious one.[1] The interdisciplinary character of feminist theory challenges traditional academic boundaries and their foundational assumptions, most especially the modernist dichotomies that distinguish masculine/feminine and maintain that these differences are "natural" and unchangeable. These dichotomies and assumptions have been particularly significant in classical sociological theory, as you have seen in previous chapters.

Criticism of gender dichotomies as "natural" has always informed feminist writings; it was central to Simone de Beauvoir's *The Second Sex,* one of the influential texts for the contemporary women's movement. De Beauvoir insisted that there was no "natural" or fixed human essence. What is assumed to be male or female is a social construction. Furthermore, the social construction of the female is in reference to the male: She is the second sex to his first place, "He is the Subject, he is Absolute—she is the Other" (1974:xix). Women generally did not contest their subordinate position because it was assumed to be "natural" and unchangeable. But de Beauvoir maintained that, although biology is important, it did not "establish for her a fixed and inevitable destiny." As she put it, "One is not born, but rather becomes, woman" (1974:36).

In examining gender inequality, de Beauvoir rejected explanations from biology, psychoanalysis, and Marx. She maintained that in all of these theoretical traditions, women were not presented as subjects in themselves but simply as objects for men, and most especially as sexual objects: "she is sex—absolute sex, no less" for men (1974:xix). More generally, the male was the political and economic subject of modernity whose rationality and objectivity were "natural facts" that justified the maintenance of the separate gendered spheres of home and work. Epstein (1988:233) pointed out that dichotomous thinking still prevails, especially in daily life, but also among "great scientific minds," and when comparisons are made, the characteristics assigned to men are always ranked higher.

Marxism and Feminism

One of the central debates among feminists in the 1970s revolved around the relationship between feminism and Marxism. To recap our discussion in Chapter 5, Marxist analysis assumed that women's subordination to men was a result of their absence from the productive process. Consequently, women did not control property but were themselves property. Only when women entered paid labor did they enter into productive class relations. It was assumed that the entry of women into paid labor would contribute to the eventual triumph of the proletariat revolution, so that after the revolution women's subordination to men would be eliminated. This solution was problematic from the outset because the basis for social organization was supposedly found, according to Marx,

---

[1]In a fairly recent sociology text, Alan Swingwood's *A Short History of Sociological Thought* (1991), there is no mention of feminism, and "gender" and "sex" do not appear in the index.

in the "production and *reproduction* of immediate life" (Marx and Engels, 1845–1846:17).

Feminists had long maintained that any changes in productive relations must be matched by changes in reproductive relations if there was to be any equality between the sexes. These changes were unlikely when Marxism found the origin of class divisions in the family, "where the wife and children are the slaves of the husband" from the moment that monogamous sexual relations were established (Marx and Engels, 1845–1846:21). This view of family relationships, especially the ambiguous status of domestic labor as having only use value rather than the exchange value of "productive" paid labor, was contested by many feminists. For example, Dalla Costa and Jones (1973:7) maintained that domestic labor was productive labor because it produced and reared the next generation of workers. Consequently, domestic labor represented the "hidden source of surplus labor."

Many feminists maintained that the "woman question" for Marxists had never been a "feminist question." The feminist question is directed at "male dominance over women," whereas Marxist analysis looks at "the relationship of women to the economic system, rather than that of women to men" (Hartmann, 1981:3–4). Because patriarchy combined with, and reinforced, capitalist exploitation and oppression, it made more sense to talk about capitalist patriarchy than simply a capitalist system (Eisenstein, 1979:22).

The key to patriarchal oppression, according to Eisenstein, is the control men assert over women's sexuality and reproduction. Men have "chosen to interpret and politically use" the idea that sex differences are "natural," biologically determined differences to subordinate women (1979:25). Marxist analysis has been as guilty as any other analysis of social relations in using the idea of "natural" differences to ignore or sideline women's position and concerns. As a result, women "should not trust men to liberate them after the revolution, in part, because there is no reason to think they would know how; in part, because there is no necessity for them to do so" (Hartmann, 1981:32). Harding (1981:159) concluded that "women are now the revolutionary group in history" and that it was women who must now address the "man question" and surmount the resistance of men to feminist theory and practice.[2]

Not all feminists rejected Marxist analysis in toto, but most agreed that, like other emancipatory theoretical analyses, it was deeply flawed when it came to the analysis of sex and gender relations. Like any knowledge system, including sociology, it was understood as "particularistically biased in the direction of the male experience of the world." Therefore, all "accepted social science knowledge should be reevaluated to take account of all the actors and relations involved in the multidimensional production of social life" (Lengermann and Niebrugge-Brantley, 1990:318). For example, the idea of the "actor" has been central to sociological theorizing but, as Wallace (1989) pointed out, prior to a feminist sociology, few sociologists ever "picture the 'actor' mentioned by so

---

[2]Not all feminist social theory was radical in focus; liberal feminism that continued the nineteenth-century traditions was also another important theoretical stance. For a discussion of the distinctions, see Jaggar (1983).

many theorists as anything but male." Indeed, Homan's 1964 ASA presidential address, "Bringing Men Back In," was an "affirmation of the actor as male" (Wallace, 1989:7).

Theory and Practice

Feminist theory did retain the critical Marxist stance that stressed theoretical knowledge must be generated and used for emancipatory practice. Feminist sociology is understood as a critical enterprise on three counts:

- It takes a woman-centered perspective.
- It interrogates the core concepts and assumptions of sociology from this perspective.
- It asks how social change can be effected to produce a more humane social world.

Feminist sociology theory strengthens the "critical emphasis in sociology" by its insistence that "sociological work be critical and change-oriented, not only towards society . . . but also towards sociology itself" (Lengermann and Niebrugge-Brantley, 1990:318).

This emancipatory thrust of a feminist sociology seemed to be a more coherent project in the early years. The assumption was that a *cause* of women's oppression could be found and that, whatever the particular cause, it could be found "at the level of the *social structure*." In addition, "the idea of *oppression* . . . seemed to have self-evident application" (Barrett and Phillips, 1992:2). With some consensus on these points, feminist debates revolved around where to place the "explanatory weight." Was women's oppression "located in the sphere of work or the sphere of the family? In the realm of production or the realm of reproduction?" What weight should be given to "structures of patriarchy (or sometimes the sex/gender system) versus capitalism; and to either of these structural accounts versus social roles, or psychologies of power" (Barrett and Phillips, 1992:4)?

By the decade of the 1990s, it was clear that any feminist sociological consensus had fractured. This was a consequence of the "impact of black women's critique of the racist and ethnocentric assumptions of white feminists"; more nuanced analyses of the earlier simplistic sex/gender distinction, with more attention to psychoanalysis, the mothering experience, and the variety of sexual desire and practice; and the "appropriation and development of post-structuralist and post-modernist ideas" (Barrett and Phillips, 1992:4–5). All of these more recent developments are characterized by interdisciplinary perspectives and a critical rejection of the "master" narratives and discourses of modernity.

Master Narratives

Two important master narratives that were subjected to feminist sociological critique were structural functionalism, especially as exemplified in the work of Talcott Parsons, and positivism.

As you have seen in Chapter 14, Parsons distinguished between instrumental and expressive roles and tied them to gender roles in the occupational and family realms. Parsons claimed that women's primary focus on the expressive roles of domesticity and child care, and men's primary focus on occupational roles, were "functional" adaptations. Women's family roles suited women's nature and were functional because they eliminated "any competition for status . . . between husband and wife which might be disruptive of the solidarity of marriage" (Parsons, 1954:192). Indeed, the "broadly humanistic values such as 'good taste' in personal appearance, house furnishings, cultural things like literature and music" were functionally equivalent in Parsons's view to the husband's "competitive occupational achievement" (1954:192).

Feminist reactions to Parsons pointed to the negative aspects of this idea of separate spheres and to the fact that this family pattern was historically and culturally specific. Rossi (1964:615) pointed out that motherhood, as a full-time occupation for adult women in a nuclear family, appeared for the first time in human history among middle-class women in the 1940s and 1950s, primarily in North America. In addition, the dichotomized roles do not apply in practice. Domestic and child-care work, for example, involves instrumental as well as expressive components. Generally, structural functional theory was critiqued as conservative, especially in Parsons's stress on the importance to social system stability of dichotomized sex-role compliance.[3]

The instrumentality that Parsons attributed primarily to men was a part of the feminist critique of positivism. Feminists suggested that positivist research methods that stressed the objectivity of the researcher reflected a particularly masculine view of the world. Positivism's idea of the "god-like" position of the researcher was rejected (Stanley and Wise, 1983:113). The idea that social reality can be "objectively constituted" and that there was "one true 'real' reality" that the emotionally uninvolved researcher can objectively find was debunked (Stanley and Wise, 1983:113). Similarly, the subject/object dichotomy, in which what is studied becomes an "object," is rejected along with the assumption that scientists are "experts in other people's lives" (1983:114).

Feminists insist that "*women* should define and interpret our experiences, and that women need to *re-define* and *re-name* what other people—experts, men—have previously defined and named for us," thus breaking the positivist "power relationship which exists between the researcher and the researched" (Stanley and Wise, 1983:144). The two theorists examined in this chapter— Dorothy Smith and Patricia Hill Collins—specifically address these methodological issues in their suggestions for sociological practice.

All of the issues discussed above remain important in current feminist sociology. What emerged from the contemporary women's movement and the work of feminist scholars were more critical and comprehensive analyses of

---

[3]It should be noted that not all feminist sociologists rejected Parsons's work entirely. Miriam Johnson (1989:116) suggested that Parsons's "evolutionary framework and his early analyses of the family can serve as a useful framework to understand feminist thinking and the changes associated with it."

social life, because gender became a pivotal concept in feminist research. In addition, feminist criticisms of traditional, positivist methodology that privileged the researcher as an uninvolved, objective observer have produced innovative and more inclusive research practices that emphasize a process of mutual discovery for all the participants. In this regard, feminist sociology attempts to honor the goal of empowering research subjects.

These methodological and theoretical innovations are still not universally welcomed or acknowledged in the profession. In 1990, Turner predicted that the future of sociology would be a positivist future because positivist sociology was "on the verge of developing laws and models that are the equivalent of those in the natural sciences." Turner believes that in the near future, "when the bankruptcy of much current 'theory' is recognized," positivist sociologists will finally realize "Comte's original vision for a 'social physics'" (Turner, 1990:388–389).

Turner's prediction represents a narrowly focused view of the sociological enterprise and in no way applies to the much broader social theoretical focus of feminist theory. Feminist theory is not confined by traditional academic boundaries, including the boundaries between arts and sciences. Feminist methodological and theoretical critiques of knowledge construction apply equally to the physical, biological, and social sciences, as well as to the whole range of specializations under the rubric of philosophy, arts, and languages.

The work and lives of the two sociologists that we consider in this chapter illustrate the cross-disciplinary nature of feminist theory. Obviously, they have been selected from a very large pool of feminist social theorists. Consequently, the perspectives they advance do not represent all of the perspectives that animate feminist social theory in general or feminist sociological theory in particular, but their work has been pivotal to many of the theoretical and methodological debates among feminist sociologists.

Dorothy Smith and Patricia Hill Collins both focus on the "situated knowledge" of women in their theoretical and methodological approaches. They are both concerned with the actual activities and knowledge of subjects in relation to, or as a result of, social and ideological structural constraints. They are also linked in another way. In 1993, the American Sociological Association conferred the Jessie Bernard Award on Dorothy E. Smith and Patricia Hill Collins. The Association stated that both scholars had transformed sociology by extending the "boundaries . . . to include the standpoint, experiences, and concerns of women; together they have extended the boundaries of gender scholarship to include the intersection of race, class, and gender"; and both scholars "seek to empower women through a dialectic of theory and practice" (American Sociological Association, 1993:13).

Dorothy E. Smith (1926–)

Dorothy Smith obtained her BA degree in sociology in 1955 from the London School of Economics (LSE). She met her husband at LSE, who was there on a GI bill, and after she got her degree they married and went to Berkeley. She records that as an undergraduate she had been an "independent and autonomous person" and had delighted in her "discovery of the life of the intellect," but that the "combination of Berkeley and marriage took that delight and autonomy away" (1994:46).

Her years as a graduate student, wife, and mother in Berkeley, although often unhappy, did provide her with the foundation for feminist sociology. In Berkeley she came to realize that she occupied two realms. The realm of academia was a "world organized textually . . . and organized to create a world of activity independent of the local and particular," but when she went home, she "entered a different mode of being," the mode of a mother with two small children that was a local and particular world (1987:6).

Erving Goffman supervised her 1963 PhD at Berkeley. She remained at Berkeley as a lecturer between 1964 and 1966, after which she went to the University of Essex (1966–1968), the University of British Columbia (1968–1976), and finally to the Ontario Institute for Studies in Education in Toronto, where she is currently a Professor Emeritus.

In her biographical essay, Smith records the beginnings of a feminist consciousness resulting from her experiences as a graduate student and, later, lecturer at Berkeley. She recalled deciding, when she was a lecturer, to tell women graduate students about some of the realities she had come to know of women's situation at Berkeley. "I thought they shouldn't be as naïve as I had been. That meeting was my first political move in this still-hidden women's movement that I didn't know I was a part of" (1994:48). When Smith was at Berkeley, there were more than 40 male faculty members in the sociology department and "one or two transitory women" on "temporary appointments" (1987:7).

> It was a male world in its assumptions, its language, its patterns of relating. The intellectual world spread out before me appeared, indeed I experienced it, as genderless. But its apparent lack of center was indeed centered. It was structured by its gender subtext. . . . Within the discourses embedded in the relations of ruling, women were the Other. (1987:7)

Like other women sociologists, Smith recognized that the discourse of sociology in which she had been trained was a discourse that expressed, described, and provided the working concepts and vocabulary for "a landscape in which women are strangers" (1987:52).

It was this "rupture in consciousness—the line of fault" that generated her feminist sociology. Her feminist focus was combined with Marxism in "trying to discover and trying to understand, the objective social, economic, and political relations which shape and determine women's oppression in this kind of society" (1977a:12). It was from these varied experiences that Smith began to formulate her intention to make a "sociology from the standpoint of women" that would treat the taken-for-granted everyday world as problematic (1987:8).

Smith's Central Theories and Methods

Smith's concern was to develop a sociology *for*, rather than *about* women. In this enterprise, she indicated, certain thinkers were influential in the development of her theoretical perspective—most notably, George Herbert Mead, Maurice

Merleau-Ponty, Karl Marx, and Harold Garfinkel (1987:8–9). But although the work of these theorists can be seen as influential in the development of her ideas, Smith has stated that she is not a "symbolic interactionist, nor a phenomenological sociologist, nor a Marxist sociologist, nor an ethnomethodologist" (1987:9).

Her sociology, Smith asserts, is designed to be "capable of explicating for members of the society the social organization of their experienced world, including in that experience the ways in which it passes beyond what is immediately and directly known, including also, therefore, the structure of a bifurcated consciousness" (1987:89). Smith's key focus on the "actual activities of actual people" is a "method developed from a conjunction of the materialist method developed by Marx and Engels . . . and Garfinkle's ethnomethodology. Both of these ground inquiry into the actual ongoing activities of actual individuals" (Smith, 1989:38, fn. 6).

A **bifurcated consciousness** refers to two different ways of "knowing, experiencing, and acting—the one located in the body and in the space that it occupies and moves into, the other passing beyond it" (1987:82). From the standpoint of women, the subject is located in a "material and local world," a world "directly experienced from oneself as centered (in the body) on the one hand and a world organized in the abstracted conceptual mode, external to the local and particular places of one's bodily existence" (1987:84). This is in contrast to a world "organized in the abstracted conceptual mode, external to the local and particular places of one's bodily existence" (1987:84). The abstract, conceptual mode is a masculine mode that sociology, conceived of as a scientific discipline, participates in. The "ethic of objectivity and the methods used in its practice" separate the knower from the known, especially from the "knower's interests, 'biases,' . . . that are not authorized by the discipline" (1990a:16).

However, to develop a sociology from the **standpoint of women** (or subjects in general) who are "located materially and in a particular place does not involve simply the transfer from one conceptual frame to another." Nor does it mean "renunciation of the rational, conceptual, scientifically rigorous method or procedure" in favor of locating a "distinctive 'female' in the subjective, emotional side, so that the alienative intellectual practices of sociology are eliminated rather than transformed." This is because the two sides of the bifurcated consciousness are not equal. The only way to enter the "abstracted conceptual mode of working" is to pass through, and make use of, the "concretely and immediately experienced"—a fact that "official" sociology obscures and ignores (1987:86).[4]

Once it is recognized that knowledge starts from the materiality of the everyday world, then sociology has a basis that begins not in "discourse but in the actual daily social relations between individuals" (1987:98). Methodologically, a sociology that begins from "where people are in the world" reverses the usual procedure of starting with a "conceptual apparatus or theory drawn from the

---

[4]Smith takes her theoretical cue here from Merleau-Ponty, who pointed out that all human beings try to make sense of their world. Consequently, theorizing must start with the ordinary, everyday experiences of those worlds.

discipline" (1987:89). Smith contends that the sociological assumption that the everyday world is "unformed and unorganized" until the sociologist's conceptual framework selects, assembles, and orders it, is the way in which sociology obscures its complicity with the forces of domination (1987:89–90).

Reversing the methodological approach is critical because the "everyday world is neither transparent nor obvious"; social relations are organized from "elsewhere" (1987:91–92). A sociology for women is concerned with exposing the way "our own situations are organized and determined by social processes that extend outside the scope of the everyday world and are not discoverable within it" (1987:152). Consequently, beginning with the standpoint of women does not mean a "sociology concerned exclusively with the world of women's experience or with the subjectivity of the sociologist herself." It means a "search for a sociology that does not transpose knowing into objective forms in which the situated subject and her actual experience and location are discarded," and it gives subjects the ability to grasp "the social relations organizing the worlds of their experience" (1987:153). That is, it produces a sociology that empowers those who are the subjects of sociological interest by revealing the real relations governing their everyday world.

A sociology from the standpoint of women is an "investigation and explication of how 'it' actually is, of how 'it' actually works," whatever the methods used—"observation, interviewing, recollection of work experience, use of archives, textual analysis, or other" (1990b:160). The key questions to ask are "How does it happen to us as it does?" and "How is the world in which we act and suffer put together?" (1987:154).

But investigating the "problematic of the everyday world does not involve substituting the analysis, the perspectives and views of subjects, for the investigation by the sociologist." Women, or any subjects, may be "expert practitioners of their everyday worlds," but the "extralocal determinants" of experience do not "lie within the scope of everyday practices." It is the discovery of these "extralocal determinants"—the structures underlying what appears to be "real"—that is the "sociologist's special business" (1987:161). Sociology from the standpoint of women explores and explicates what the subject does not know— "the social relations and organization pervading her world but invisible in it" (1992:91).

Smith points out that taking the standpoint of women always involves a sociology in the making, "unlike sociologies that seek to generate a totalizing system" (1992:91). It aims to produce sociological accounts that can tell subjects "how it works" rather than producing "unitary, absolute, or final truth" (1992:94). Smith's sociology is thus a "*method of inquiry*, always ongoing, opening things up, discovering," having relevance for the "politics and practice of progressive struggle, whether of women or of other oppressed groups" (1992:88). A feminist method of sociological inquiry must, in Smith's view, "go beyond . . . interviewing practices and . . . research relationships to explore methods of thinking" in order to produce sociological texts that "preserve the presence of actual subjects while exploring and explicating the relations in which our everyday worlds are embedded" (1987:111). Consequently, texts and discourse are particularly important to Smith's sociology. She sees them as the primary means in modern societies of structuring everyday worlds and maintaining, as well as concealing, relations of domination.

Smith's examination of the contours of modernity and capitalism in terms of texts, discourse, and objectivity started with a Marxist framework. Smith initially considered Marxism the only method that addressed the particularities of the everyday/everynight in terms of social and economic processes. However, she found the engagement with Marxism a "painful and difficult experience" because of the rejection of feminism by many Marxists (1977a:12). Smith recognized that initial feminist confrontations with political Marxists in the 1970s produced important insights into gendered class and race relations, but women's standpoint was not explicitly taken into account.

Smith's conception of women's standpoint as a critique of ruling ideological practices reformulates Marx's use of the standpoint of labor as the means to critique capitalism. She points out that it is women's work that underpins the "abstracted conceptual mode of ruling" done by men (1987:81). Whether in the home or in paid labor, women mediate the abstract, conceptual actions of men and the "actual, concrete forms on which it depends," especially in the corporate capitalist world (1987:83). The mundane home work of maintaining healthy bodies and minds and the workplace activities of ensuring space, time, and resources for the production of abstract conceptualizations in the form of reports, memos, strategic plans, and the like are all largely the work of women *for* men. Women are corporate capitalism's housekeepers at home and in paid labor.

Women have been drawn into paid labor in large numbers under corporate capitalism, but this has not produced gender equality as Marx and Engels expected. Smith suggested that the "bifurcation of the world into public and private spheres" has not diminished; on the contrary, it has taken on new dimensions unforeseen by Marx or Engels (1977b:19). The increasingly abstract, objectified reality produced by texts and communicative modes are what govern, regulate, produce, and reproduce social relations. These texts and communications— whether books, television, plays, soap operas, art, or the Internet—produce the "images, vocabularies, concepts, knowledge of and methods of knowing the world" that are "integral to the practices of power" (1975:354). These abstractions embody the relations of ruling in modern society (1990b:122). By **relations of ruling**, Smith refers not simply to political organizations but to all of the various institutions that rule, manage, and administer society. And these institutional locations are largely the work of men supported by the invisible, but necessary, work of women.

Nature of Society, Humans, and Change

Society   Smith has no formal definition of "society." In her work, the social is always the actual practices of human beings who are understood as "expert practitioners of their everyday worlds" (1987:161). The social practices of actual people in their everyday/everynight worlds comprise society.

The practices that produce and reproduce social relations are not "fixed relations between statuses but . . . an organization of actual sequences of action *in time.*" If social processes are seen as "ongoing activities of actual people," then attention must be paid to what has formally been regarded as "subjective or as cultural phenomena," such as discourse, texts, and ideology (1990b:160). It is these forms that produce the "internally coordinated complex of administrative, managerial, professional and discursive organization that regulates, organizes, governs, or otherwise controls our societies" (1989:38).

These organizations are not "monolithic," Smith argues, but they are "pervasively interconnected" because they are characteristically and essentially "textually mediated" (1999:49). From birth, we are all subjected to a textual record that multiplies throughout our lives—licenses, registrations, medical files, school reports, tax records, and so on—and that is presumed to be an "objective" record of our self, our life. Sociology participates in the relations of ruling by producing some of the records that other organizations use to control and manipulate individuals (1990a:14). Concepts used by sociologists such as "mental illness, crimes, riots, violence, work satisfaction, neighbors and neighborhoods, motivation, and so on—these are the constructs of the practice of government" (1990a:15).

Texts are critical, in Smith's view, to the ruling apparatus's way of organizing, regulating, and directing contemporary society. In texts, power relationships are "abstracted from local and particular settings and relationships" in order to be reproduced in those very settings. Sociology has been an important part of the textual mediation of social reality that reproduces gender, class, and racial power relationships. The "texts of the relations of ruling—newspapers; television; census and economic reports; policy documents; the reports of commissions, tasks forces, ad hoc committees, and so forth—bring a virtual reality into the presence of the sociological reader" (1990a:54). The "social facts" the sociologist works with are thus already separated from the everyday, from the "subjective presence of individuals," and they are presented in a mode that fits the bureaucratic administrative hierarchy of the relations of ruling. Consequently, the world sociologists often "encounter and rely on is *already ideologically structured*" (1990a:57).

Smith illustrates the way in which sociological methods are ideological by the use of three "tricks":

> Trick 1. Separate what people say they think from the actual circumstances in which it is said, from the actual empirical conditions of their lives, and from the actual individuals who said it.
>
> Trick 2. Having detached the ideas, arrange them to demonstrate an order among them that accounts for what is observed.
>
> Trick 3. Then change the ideas into a "person"; that is, set them up as distinct entities (for example, a value pattern, norm, belief system, and so forth) to which agency (or possibly causal efficacy) may be attributed, and redistribute them to "reality" by attributing them to actors who can now be treated as representing the ideas. (1990a:43–44)

At the conclusion of the three tricks, the original subject and her actions have disappeared, only to reappear as an abstract, "objective" sociological account of the "actor." For example, in asking the interview question "Are single mothers a social problem?" the tricks might work in the following manner:

1. If the answer is recorded as "yes," despite any qualifications the respondent may have introduced in answering "yes," the response will be coded collectively and reported as a percentage.

2. The percentage of "yes" to "no" responses can then be tied to current social, or sociological, theories about ideal mothering.

3. The idea of the ideal mother can then be compared to the single mother—in the process constructing, in most cases, a negative picture of the individual single mother.

It is because the relations of ruling in society are obscured and mystified by the predominance of textual forms, Smith maintains, that an alternative sociology is so important—especially a sociology from the standpoint of women.

Humans   Throughout her work, Smith emphasizes the primacy of the subject who is "active in the same world as we are situated in as bodies" (1987:141). The problem she deals with in some detail is the difference between women and men in their ability to claim authority over their actions and over the explanations for those actions. The key to her focus here is Alfred Schutz's idea of **multiple realities**.

Schutz identified four realms of social reality: the realm of **directly experienced** social reality (*umwelt*); the realm of **indirectly experienced** reality (*mitwelt*); the realm of the **future** (*folgewelt*); and the realm of the **past** (*vorwelt*). All of these realms can be present at the same time in any particular activity for any individual. Smith is particularly concerned with the realms of direct and indirect experience in relation to gender differences.

The realm of direct experience of reality is the world of everyday, face-to-face encounters. The world of indirect experiences is the world of abstraction, in which personal life is suspended. The suspension of the personal, of the particular subject, is accomplished by organized theoretical practices that produce the move from "*knowing* to *knowledge*" (1990a:66).

Knowing is the subjective activity of a subject, but **knowledge** "discards the presence of the knowing subject" (1990a:66). This "objectification of knowledge is a general feature of contemporary relations of ruling," the organization of which is based on the work women do that enables the theorist to "forget" his bodily existence and needs. Just as the housewife takes care of the mundane realities of existence, the secretary does the same job at work.

In the gender relations of a corporate capitalist world, argues Smith, the indirect realm of knowledge, especially scientific knowledge—including sociological knowledge—is how the everyday world of women's knowing and practices is erased. Objective knowledge is a form of power that "breaks knowledge from the active experiencing of subjects and from the dialogic of activity or talk that brings before us a known-in-common object." It "subdues, discounts, and disqualifies our various interests, perspectives, angles, and experience, and what we might have to say speaking from them" (1990a:80).

According to Smith, understanding the nature and effect of "objective" knowledge is important to how human beings can be conceptualized as creative actors. For example, in the production of femininity in our society, Smith points out that it is important to look at a range of sources such as the "textual discourse vested in women's magazines and television, advertisements, the appearance of cosmetic counters, fashion displays and to a lesser extent books" (1990b:163). The "discourse" found in these diverse locations structures women's aspiration to perfection in the face of the always imperfect body. These discourses obliterate women as "autonomous subjects" at the same time as they require women's work in producing the required and desired appearance. Consequently, women are obliterated and then reintroduced as agents or subjects in the process of constructing the normative ideal of femininity (1990b:193). The "subject-in-discourse is deprived of agency," but the "subject-at-work behind her is active and skilled"—albeit active and skilled in reproducing her subordination to the ideological ideal of femininity (1990b:206).

As this example illustrates, attention to the actual activities of people reveals the ways in which they are participants in multiple realities and how, as participants, they may "give power to the relations that 'overpower' them" (1990b:161). Consequently, for Smith, a sociology that reveals the "organization and relations that are invisible but *active* in the everyday/everynight sites where people take up resistance and struggle" is a sociology that provides knowledge that "expands their and our grasp of how things are put together and hence their and our ability to organize and act effectively" (1992:96). It is a sociology that honors the knowledgeable human being and is relevant to the "politics and practices of progressive struggle, whether of women or of other oppressed groups" (1992:88). It is a sociology that deals with and contributes to progressive social change.

Social Change   The possibility of class and gender emancipatory transformations runs through all of Smith's work. It is through "doing sociology" in new ways that Smith sees the possibility of effecting change. What she wishes to establish is a sociology where "knowledge does not become a body of knowledge, where issues are not crystallized, where the conventions and relevances of discourse do not assume an independent authority over against its speakers and readers" (1987:22). However, Smith points out that she has "never seen resistance or opposition as beginning in theory, much less in sociology" (1992:96).

Smith points out that resistance and revolution need a "division of labor in which the production of knowledge plays an essential, though not a leading, part." Knowledge as "reflexive critique" has the power "to disclose just how our practices contribute to and we articulate with the relations that overpower our lives" (1990a:204). These disclosures provide a basis for reorganizing and transforming social relations.

As you saw above, Smith insists that the transformation of oppressive social relations in present-day society requires attention to the relations of ruling. It is in explicating the relations of ruling and the relations of capital, from the standpoints of the dispossessed, that sociologists can participate in "transforming oppressive relations" (1992:96).

Class, Gender, and Race

Class   Although gender is central to all Smith's work, initially her focus emerged out of a reformulated Marxist perspective. Smith points out that she is not concerned with being "faithful to Marx or to a Marxist tradition, but only to seize upon what it offers us as a means of exploring the dynamic relations in which our lives are caught up and which are continually at work in transforming the bases and contexts of our existence and our struggles" (1987:142). Just as the standpoint of labor reveals class relations, so the standpoint of women reveals gender relations. The standpoint of labor reveals that social class should not be "understood as a secret power behind our backs, determining how we think, how we understand the world, and how we act"; it should be understood as a "complex of social relations coordinating the activities of our everyday worlds with those of others with whom we are not directly connected" (1987: 135). Similarly, gender is not an innate, natural phenomenon but a complex of social relations that, like class, can be discovered in "routine, daily accomplishment" (1987:140).

In describing the contours of contemporary class and gender relations, Smith contrasts the nature of twentieth-century corporate capitalism with the more locally organized capitalism of the nineteenth century. In the nineteenth century, the market still seemed to be an external, impersonal force organizing social relations, "independent of the choices and wishes of individual capitalists," but control and administration of the enterprise were local and class relations were locally based (1987:75–76). By the end of the nineteenth century, these locally organized, individually owned enterprises began to give way to corporate enterprises controlled from some external center (1987:75).

The move from the local to the national, or even the global, enterprise involved a more "abstracted conceptual mode of organization" (1987:75). This mode includes the following characteristics:

- differentiation of the distinct functions—whether administration, management, or professional organization.
- System functions are primarily communicative and informational.
- Communication and information functions are increasingly dependent on "secondhand knowledge organized conceptually as 'facts.'"
- Organizing functions are dependent on "generalized systems of planning" in the same communicative, textual mode. (1987:75)

Contemporary corporate capitalism is thus very different from the nineteenth-century version. The ambiguity of ownership, the conceptual abstractions that administer the productive processes, and the interconnections of economic and political power make it a more difficult entity to challenge and transform, especially from the standpoint of women.

Smith points out that contemporary conceptions of class cannot be "identical to that of Marx and Engels, for the analytic capacity of such concepts is firmly articulated to the social relations of their time." However, a concept of class is still essential to understanding the nature of struggles for liberation and equality, especially the struggles of women. What is needed is a "political economy that will explore and display the properties and movement of the complex of powers, forces, and relations that are at work in our everyday/everynight worlds" (1999:44).

Gender   Smith explored the political economy of class in relation to gender in her 1977 article "Women, the Family and Corporate Capitalism." She looked at the alienation of the middle-class corporate manager and the way in which all the activities of his wife reinforced his alienation. The key distinction, according to Smith, is that the middle-class manager plays a **role** in contrast to the **job** of the working-class man. Although the working-class man is alienated from his labor and his wife's household labor is a personal service for the husband because he "owns the means of production on which she depends," nevertheless, when there is security of income and employment, then "making a home . . . becomes a common enterprise which is shared by husband and wife to which each contribute in different ways" (1977b:32). The relationship changes when the husband in unemployed and his position as "master in the home" is undermined. Thus, the working-class wife's dependence on her husband is a dependence on external economic arrangements over which neither the husband nor the wife has any control (1977b:30–31).

The alienation of the middle-class corporate manager is different because what is alienated is not "an object—not his product, but his activity" (1977b:25). Both worker and manager are alienated by the corporate enterprise, but for the manager it is "his ethical being, his motives, his strategies of thought and communication" that are appropriated, so that it is the "alienation of the person, not of the product" (1977b:26).

> The corporate structure requires of a manager that he subordinate himself and his private interests to the goals and objectives of the daily practices, and the "ethic" of the corporation. His *person* becomes relevant—the kind of person he is. Therefore non-functionally specific criteria—off-the-job criteria and information—become relevant. (1977b:32)

These off-the-job criteria involve the family, especially the wife, who must produce a home and family relationships that support his occupational status. Consequently, the middle-class family "becomes an enactment of the moral order legislated by the corporation" (1977b:33).

The image of the ideal family and the ideal family home is one that is produced by corporate enterprises—Martha Stewart, *Ideal Home, Homes and Gardens,* and the like. And the production of the appropriate home and family "image" is the work of the wife. Most especially, it is the wife who must provide emotional support and a "no-tension home" to ease the "injuries done to him in his occupational world." But this work produces "two double-binds" for the wife. First, supporting her husband in his role means in fact supporting the corporation that "violates him"; second, "insofar as the wife plays her own corporately-bestowed role of 'good homemaker,' she must maintain the image of the external order in the home." But the "imagined order" can make both her husband's success *and* his failure visible. Therefore, in order to be "a 'good wife' she must side with the external moral order against her husband" (1977b:39).

The public/private, work/family distinction affects both the working-class and middle-class wife, but whereas a working-class woman shares "in many ways the position of working-class men" to the relations of production, a middle-class woman's family and household labor is oriented to an external moral order of productive relations that alienate her husband and alienate her from her husband as well as from herself. Smith concludes that "monopoly or corporate capitalism" alienates both men and women of the middle classes, at the same time eliminating any "socio-economic basis for an autonomous selfhood" for women (1977b:46). The middle-class family is "subcontractual" and is "*for* the realization of the ruling-class moral order," in contrast to the working-class family which is "*for* its members" (1977b:33).

Race   Although Smith's work continues to explore the interrelationship of class and gender, she indicates that on the issue of race "I have not yet understood fully the intersection of racial oppression with the gender organization of the relations of ruling." Consequently, the "contradictions of class and racial oppression are still unsatisfied" in her work. She noted in *The Everyday World as Problematic* that such contradictions were "insistent presences speaking from beyond the text but not yet in it" (1987:8). Smith does point out that as women's issues are taken up and "accommodated to legal, administrative, and professional niches," if only in the margins, the "discourse of women" has tended to be the discourse of white women, excluding native and black women (1987:221).

Smith suggests that these exclusions can be seen in the "on-going actual activities of actual people" (1989:38), which reveal how "local and particular moments are entered into extended, generalized, and generalizing social relations." This understanding, in turn, exposes the "ideological practices" that are the "constituents of the relations of ruling" (1990a:204–205). In these ideological practices, the notion of "other" includes women, Native Americans, Asian, Hispanic, and African Americans and, at the same time, divides white women from the undifferentiated "others."

Other Theories and Theorists

Smith has always been concerned with the position of women in knowledge production, especially women in sociology. She points out that the emancipatory intentions of feminist sociology are at odds with the traditional complicity of sociology in the academy with ruling powers. "Social scientific knowledge represents the world from a standpoint in ruling relations, not from the standpoint of those who are ruled." Ruling relations are not monolithic, but generally there is enough control to ensure that the knowledge produced in the academy is "not oriented to the needs and interests of the mass of people, but to the needs and interests of ruling." Consequently, when leaks occur and loopholes appear, as they did in the 1960s and early 1970s, and those privileged with access to knowledge and knowledge production desert and "go over to the other side, their access is cut off" (1999:16).

Feminist critiques by the women's movements have been a particular challenge to the ruling hegemony of academic patriarchy. These challenges have not simply been a "matter of theory, but a matter of political practice" emerging out of activism on many fronts (1999:18). The initial reactions from within the academy were varied. In some cases, access to the academy was cut off; in other, more insidious ways, the critiques were marginalized and ignored as irrelevant or the work of the psychologically disturbed. Sociology was no more receptive than other disciplinary specialties. Laslett and Thorne (1992:60) have pointed out that a "wall of silence" still remains between "sociological theory and feminist theory," despite the fact that "feminists have more than kept their side of a potential conversation with sociological theorists." Nonetheless, "sociological theorists of virtually every school of thought have largely ignored the writings of feminists" (Laslett and Thorne, 1992:60).

Over time, the outright rejection of feminist critiques changed, and "women's studies" or even "gender studies" were incorporated into the academy. The result, notes Smith (1999), has been some success in "breaking down the radically one-sided character of the male-dominated discourses of the disciplines and sciences" and the creation of a "richness of critique and alternatives that is astonishing given the relatively brief period of our 'renaissance.'" But entry into the academy has also involved some cost, most notably the detachment from former linkages with "activism and organization outside the academy" (1999:20).

Smith is concerned that once feminists become "detached from independent sources of resistance and from the profoundly different take on the world they represent," then "feminism becomes professionalized" (1999:21). The "implicit political organization of the ivory tower university is still effective," and it is "not easy to go against it," although the recent agitation over "political correctness" suggests to Smith that feminists have been more successful than they realized (1999:26). The problem Smith points to for the future is how to "create active linkages with women working in sites outside the academy and to establish dialogue between the intra- and extra-academic" (1999:27). This is a critical task because "we know that there's desperation in society, and our social sciences don't know how to know this new and frightening world" (1999:27). But women know they have the "power and capacity to change," and this, in conjunction with the "hidden radicalism of the Enlightenment" still lurking in universities, provides Smith with hope for the future.

Critique and Conclusions

Dorothy Smith's work has generated a dialogue with various mainstream sociological theories. Smith has attempted to create an "insider's sociology, that is, a systematically developed consciousness of society from within, renouncing the artifice that stands us outside what we can never stand outside of" (1989:53). Such a sociology does not discard the "actual experience and location" of its subjects, but provides those subjects with "the means of grasping the social relations organizing the worlds of their experience" (1989:53). Smith's notion of "standpoint" does not "privilege a knower," but "shifts the ground of knowing, the place where inquiry begins." A sociology from the standpoint of women starts with the woman in her body who is "active; she is at work; she is connected with particular other people in various ways; she thinks, laughs, desires, sorrows, sings, curses, loves just here; she reads here; she watches television."

The "subject/knower of inquiry is not a transcendent subject but is situated in the actualities of her own living, in relation with others." The sociological inquiry Smith proposes is concerned with the social as "people's ongoing concerting and coordinating of activities" (1992:92).

Smith's sociology is not "a feminism and nothing but a feminism" (Lemert, 1992:68). Her method of inquiry can work as a place to begin an inquiry into anyone's experience—and that anyone could be "Afro- or Chinese or Caucasian Canadian, an individual from one of the First nations, an old woman or man, a lesbian or a gay man, a member of the ruling class, or any other man" (Smith, 1992:90). Indeed, one criticism of Smith's work is, How can we know whose experience is to count as important? And why is the knowledge of women, or any minority group, better than the sociologist's knowledge (Hekman, 1997)? Smith would respond that situated knowledge is better because it offers an explanation of the actual world the subjects inhabit. As to how to evaluate whose experience is to count, Smith points out that she makes "no claim to a unitary, absolute, or final truth" as the endpoint of her sociological work (1992:94). As she remarks, "Established sociology has powerful ways of writing the social into the text, which produce society as seen from an Archimedean point," but a sociology for women says, "You can't have that wish" (1992:94).

There is no "outside"; everyone, including the sociologist, is a participant. It is in this way that Smith responds to the criticism of her work by Patricia Hill Collins. Collins (1992:79) points out that the bifurcated consciousness, which allowed Smith to produce a "new angles of vision" on women and sociology, "demonstrates the power of knowledge created by one who stands outside the dominant discourse and who possesses local knowledge, namely knowledge growing from women's experiences" (1992:79). But Collins goes on the claim that Smith came to realize that "remaining on the line of fault leaves the inner circle unchanged because the rules of what constitutes sociology remain intact." Consequently, Collins suggests that Smith "chose to adhere to the rules" and do "theoretical sociology in a way that makes sense to members of the inner circle," as demonstrated in Smith's concern with text-mediated forms of power (1992:91).

Smith (1992:97) responds that her concern with text-mediated forms of power does not mean that "this is all there is to be done or indeed all that this method of inquiry makes possible," but only that it is a method that is "powerfully relevant to making change in our kind of society." Furthermore, Smith stresses that the so-called "outside positions" of "marginality, exclusion, suppressed and oppositional cultures and positions" are, in fact, "inside." There are "no modes of investigation other than those beginning from within" (1992:94).

It is from the inside that Collins begins in her explication of black feminist thought. Collins is particularly concerned with the silencing of women, especially African American women, who have been "silenced by not being allowed to speak the language they possess, at least in most public arenas" (1992:78). The alternative traditions women speak remain "invisible and unintelligible to existing sociological approaches," which can only be rectified by recognizing "diversity" and "the varied ways in which people create local knowledge to counteract objectifying knowledge" (1992:78).

We now turn to a brief examination of the work of Patricia Hill Collins. Collins has been centrally concerned with developing an "epistemological framework that can be used both to assess existing Black feminist thought and to clarify some of the underlying assumptions that impede the development of Black feminist thought" (Collins, 1990:202).

Patricia Hill Collins (1948–)

Patricia Hill Collins is currently a professor of African American studies and sociology at the University of Cincinnati. She earned her BA from Brandeis in 1969, her MA from Harvard in 1970, and her PhD from Brandeis in 1984.

Collins's central sociological concerns reflect her own experiences as a black female African American. This concern is expressed in her concept of the **outsider-within.** The outsider-within refers to the experience of being part of a society, or community or group, but at the same time set apart because of some personal attribute. The concept has similarities with Georg Simmel's idea of the stranger (see Chapter 8). Collins (1990:xi) illustrates the outsider-within position in her reflections on her own formative experiences. She recalls being "the 'first,' or 'one of the few,' or the 'only' African American and/or woman and/or working-class person in my schools, communities, and work settings." Although Collins felt that there was nothing wrong with being who she was, she came to the realization that others did not share this opinion. As a result, she reports that she "tried to disappear into myself in order to deflect the painful, daily assaults designed to teach me that being an African-American, working-class woman made me lesser than those who were not." In time she "became quieter and eventually was virtually silenced" (1990:xi).

In her book *Black Feminist Thought* (1990), Collins regains her voice with her own "self-defined standpoint." That voice is both "individual and collective, personal and political, one reflecting the intersection of my unique biography with the larger meaning of my historical times" (1990:xii). African American women in general have a "self-defined standpoint on their own oppression" that shows they have been "neither passive victims of nor willing accomplices to their own oppression." Collins's work explores the dimensions of this standpoint from the perspective of an outsider within the theoretical discourse of sociology (1989:747).

Collins's Central Theories and Methods

In *Black Feminist Thought*, Collins indicates that she draws on diverse theoretical traditions, "such as Afrocentric philosophy, feminist theory, Marxist social thought, the sociology of knowledge, critical theory, and postmodernism." However, she acknowledges that the "standard vocabulary of these traditions, citations of their major works and key proponents, and these terms themselves rarely appear in the text" because she regards the ideas, not the labels, as most important and, furthermore, she is concerned with placing "Black women's experiences and ideas at the center of analysis" (1990:xii). Instead of the usual transformation of an oppressed group's ideas and experiences into the language and conceptual framework of dominant groups, also discussed by Dorothy Smith, she seeks to present the multiple voices of those who are often silenced.

Like Smith, Collins maintains that "theory and intellectual creativity are not the province of a select few but instead emanate from a range of people" (1990:xiii). Black women's standpoint emerges from, first, their "political and economic status," which gives them a "distinctive set of experiences that offers a different view of material reality than that available to other groups"; and second, the "distinctive Black feminist consciousness concerning that material reality" that emerges out of those experiences (1989:747–748). Collins therefore uses a variety of sources, or "voices," in developing her argument. Musicians, poets, and writers, as well as political activists and scholars, are all represented in her work.

In Collins's view, the relationship between black women's standpoint and black feminist thought is a **dialectical** one in which the "everyday, taken-for-granted knowledge shared by members of a given group" is taken up by those "experts" who are part of that group who are able to articulate the taken-for-granted. By making the taken-for-granted clear, "experts" offer "Black women a different view of themselves and their world than that offered by the established social order" (1989:750). In this way, "Black feminist thought re-articulates a consciousness that already exists" and, in doing so, "gives African-American women another tool of resistance to all forms of their subordination" (1989:750). Collins points to a long history of black women intellectuals who merged intellectual work and activism—women such as Anna J. Cooper, Frances Ellen Watkins Harper, Ida B. Wells, and Mary Church Terrell, all of whom produced "analyses of Black women's oppression and worked to eliminate that oppression" (1992:29).

> Placing the ideas of ordinary African-American women as well as those of better-known Black women intellectuals at the center of analysis produces a new angle of vision on feminist and African-American concerns, one infused with an Afrocentric feminist sensibility. (1990:16)

Collins's major objective is to develop an epistemology that can "assess existing Black feminist thought and . . . clarify some of the underlying assumptions that impede the development of Black feminist thought." She believes this is necessary because "traditional epistemological assumptions concerning how we arrive at 'truth' simply are insufficient to the task of furthering Black feminist thought." Consequently, in the "same way that concepts such as women and intellectual must be deconstructed, the process by which we arrive at truth merits comparable scrutiny" (1990:17).

A definition of what constitutes black women's standpoint is complicated, notes Collins, by the complex relationships between "biological classification, the social construction of race and gender as categories of analysis, the material conditions accompanying these changing social constructions, and Black women's consciousness about these themes." She suggests that black feminist thought "consists of specialized knowledge created by African-American women which clarifies a standpoint of and for Black women." It therefore consists of "theoretical interpretations of Black women's reality by those who live it" (1990:22).

Collins stresses, however, that "ethnicity, region of the country, urbanization, and age combine to produce a web of experiences" that produce diversity among African American women. Consequently, it is "more accurate to discuss a Black *women's* standpoint than a Black *woman's* standpoint" (1990:24). In this respect, Collins sees her work as somewhat different from that of Smith. She claims that the "everyday" Smith examines is "individual, a situation reflecting in part the isolation of white, middle-class women," whereas her "everyday" is "collective as well as individual" because it reflects the "collective values in Afrocentric communities" and the "working-class experiences of the majority of Black women" (1990:40, fn. 5).

Methodologically, Collins rejects **positivist** epistemology, which she characterizes as "Eurocentric masculinist." In her view, distancing the researcher from the "object" of study, the elimination of emotions and ethics and values from the research process, and an adversarial approach to the establishment of truth claims cannot produce adequate knowledge of the black experience. Such an approach asks "African-American women to objectify themselves, devalue their emotional life, displace their motivations for furthering knowledge about Black women, and confront, in an adversarial relationship, those who have more social, economic, and professional power than they do" (1989:754).

Knowledge must include feelings, values, and interests, whether it is black female knowledge or knowledge generated by any other constituency. Collins's approach is to examine the "situated, subjected standpoint of African-American women in order to understand Black feminist thought as a partial perspective on domination." In this way, black women's standpoint can be related to "larger epistemological dialogues concerning the nature of the matrix of domination" (1990:236).

Nature of Society, Humans, and Change

Collins's views on society recognize the hierarchal relations of race, class, and gender. She identifies the core theme in black feminist thought as that of oppression. The legacy of struggle against oppression is central to black feminist understanding of society and self. In Western society, and in U.S. society especially, black women are, as Zora Neale Hurston pointed out, the "mules uh de world" (Collins, 1990:43).

Society Collins's work concentrates on the "society" of black experience that is different from but related to the "society" of Western whites. Collins points to an **Afrocentric** worldview that is distinct from and opposed to a Eurocentric worldview (1990:26). Although black people have been forced to adapt Afrocentric belief systems to the "institutional arrangements of white domination," nonetheless the persistence of this worldview has been "fundamental to African-American resistance to racial oppression" (1990:27).

The Afrocentric viewpoint is a collective, as opposed to an individualistic, orientation to social relations. For example, African American "community norms traditionally were such that neighbors cared for one another's children" (1990:120). When African Americans continue this tradition, they challenge "one fundamental assumption underlying the capitalist system itself: that children are 'private property' and can be disposed of as such" (1990:122). African Americans exist within multiple levels of domination, but an Afrocentric viewpoint, Collins believes, can be the basis for the empowerment of African Americans in general, and black women in particular.

Humans   Collins suggests that human beings may "experience and resist oppression on three levels: the level of personal biography; the group or community level of the cultural context created by race, class, and gender; and the systemic level of social institutions" (1990:227). All three levels are sites of domination and possible resistance. Most important, however, is the personal level of consciousness.

Each person has a "unique personal biography," notes Collins, and as "no two individuals occupy the same social space, . . . no two biographies are the same." In addition, "human ties can be freeing and empowering" or "confining and oppressive." Thus, the "same situation can look quite different depending on the consciousness one brings to it." It is at the level of "individual consciousness" that "new knowledge can generate change." Collins rejects the idea that domination only "operates from the top down by forcing and controlling unwilling victims to bend to the will of the more powerful superiors." The idea of top-down domination makes the "willingness of a victim to collude in her or his own victimization," or the persistent resistance of victims "even when chances for victory seem remote," difficult to explain. Black feminist thought, Collins maintains, challenges domination by emphasizing the "power of self-definition and the necessity of a free mind." That is, consciousness is understood "as a sphere of freedom" (1990:227).

The framework for African American women's power of self-definition is connected to their historical cultural context. Four critical aspects of Black women's experience provide the basis for their "difference" as well as for their resistance: concrete experience as a criterion of meaning; the use of dialogue in assessing knowledge claims; the ethic of caring; and the ethic of personal accountability.

In her discussion of the use of **concrete experience as a criterion of meaning**, Collins distinguishes between two types of knowing: knowledge and wisdom. Black women's survival depends upon knowledge of the "dynamics of race, gender, and class subordination" and "wisdom in assessing" that knowledge (1989:758). The distinction is "essential" because "knowledge without wisdom is adequate for the powerful, but wisdom is essential to the survival of the subordinate" (1989:759). Credibility is therefore tied to concrete experience rather than to knowledge gained from books or abstract speculations. In attaching value to the concrete, African American women invoke "not only an Afrocentric tradition, but a women's tradition as well" (1989:761).

Support for valuation of the concrete is centered in two institutions: black extended families and black churches. In these two institutions, "Black women experts with concrete knowledge of what it takes to be self-defined Black women share their knowledge with their younger, less experienced sisters" (1989:762). Sisterhood is a "model for a whole series of relationships" among African American women that black men, although "supported by Afrocentric institutions," cannot share (1989:762–763).

The valuing and evaluation of concrete experience is developed in dialogue. The **use of dialogue in assessing knowledge claims** is rooted in "an African-based oral tradition" and in the "knowledge-validation process of enslaved African-Americans." The importance of dialogue is exemplified in the interactive "call and response discourse mode" and the stress on the "active participation of all individuals" in the testing and validation of ideas in Black communication (1989:763). Again, the use of dialogue in the assessment of knowledge claims is a central dimension of black feminist epistemology as well as being, more generally, a "female way of knowing" (1989:765).

The **ethic of caring** is also central to the validation of knowledge. The ethic of caring "is rooted in a tradition of African humanism" that sees each individual as a "unique expression of a common spirit, power, or energy expressed by all life" (1989:766). This emphasis on individual uniqueness involves valuing **personal expressiveness**. Two other components are also important to the ethic of caring: **emotions** and **empathy** (1989:766). Emotion is a sign that the "speaker believes in the validity of an argument," and the capacity for empathy is important to making connection with the "other." Collins points to the convergence of "Afrocentric and feminist values in the ethic-of-care dimension of an alternative epistemology" but claims that, for white women, few institutions other than the family "validate this way of knowing," whereas for African American women, both family and church validate such knowledge (1989:768).

The **ethic of personal accountability** is also an Afrocentric as well as a feminist value. The ethic insists that individuals "develop their knowledge claims through dialogue and present those knowledge claims in a style proving concern for their ideas" and that they be accountable for such knowledge claims (1989:768). Thus, the assessment of any individual's knowledge claims is also an evaluation of the individual's "character, values, and ethics." In this way, the "Eurocentric masculinist belief that probing into an individual's personal viewpoint is outside the boundaries of discussion" is rejected. In sum, in Afrocentric feminist epistemology, "values lie at the heart of the knowledge-validation process such that inquiry always has an ethical aim." Central to such an aim, for Collins, are resistance and struggle (1989:769).

Social Change   According to Collins, the development of black feminist thought is a continuation of the African American tradition that emphasized the value of education as education for the entire race in order to "assist in the economic, political, and social improvement of the enslaved and later emancipated African-Americans" (1990:148). More specifically, educated black women saw their education as "something gained not just for their own development but for the purpose of race uplift" (1990:149).

Education has been particularly important to black women as a means of empowerment and political activism because of their traditional exclusion from, or suppression within, "organizations devoted to institutional transformation"

(1990:154). As a result, black women have attempted to create a "female sphere of influence" that "indirectly resists oppressive structures by undermining them" (1990:141). For example, a style of activism favored by black women in the pursuit of social change reflects a "belief that teaching people how to be self-reliant fosters more empowerment than teaching them how to follow" (1990:157).

Black women may not have been the leaders, but they have been active in institutional transformation in "civil rights organizations, labor unions, feminist groups, boycotts, and revolts" (1990:142). Generally, however, black women's activism has encompassed both spheres of influence and institutional transformation. Collins sees the dual nature of black women's activism as both "conservative and radical," especially in their maintenance of an Afrocentric culture (1990:144). She believes that African American women are more likely to use "strategic affiliation and reject ideology as the overarching framework structuring . . . political activism." This does not mean that black women "lack ideology but, rather, that our experiences as othermothers, centerwomen, and community othermothers foster a distinctive form of political activism based on negotiation and a higher degree of attention to context" (1990:160).[5]

The key to practical, emancipatory action is the idea articulated by Angela Davis of "lift as we climb"—that is, try to "guarantee that all our sisters, regardless of social class, and indeed all of our brothers climb with us" (quoted in Collins, 1990:158). However, Collins sees the "changing social class structure of African-American families and communities" as possibly changing the "shape and effectiveness of this long-standing Black women's activist tradition." For example, she suggests that many black college students, especially those attending white institutions, often fail to see the significance of their education for black "group survival" and institutional transformation (1990:160).

Class, Gender, and Race

As the previous discussion illustrates, issues of class, gender, and race are all interrelated in Collins's work.

Class   Collins points out that the primary sociological models of social class—status attainment and the conflict model—do not adequately explain black social class relations, especially black women's social class relations and experiences. **Status attainment** relies on identification of the occupational status of traditional male jobs, from which women's class position was supposed to derive. But black male unemployment rates, racial discrimination that provides only a narrow set of occupations for African Americans, and the "existence of household arrangements other than the two-parent nuclear families" make this model unsuitable to explain "Black social class dynamics" (1990:45).

Similarly, for the **conflict model,** the focus on paid labor, and especially on a particular type of paid labor—industrial factory jobs that many blacks, irre-

---

[5]The references to othermothers and centerwomen relate to Collins's point about the collective, communal nature of mothering in African American communities.

spective of gender, do not have access to—makes this model equally inadequate as an explanation of black social class. Only "placing women's work and family experiences at the center of the analysis" can provide a view of African American social class locations. Understanding the "intersection of work and family in Black women's lives is key to clarifying the overarching political economy of domination" (1990:45). Black feminist theory must therefore be concerned with the "changed consciousness of individuals" as well as the "social transformation of political and economic institutions" (1990:221).

Although all African American women "encounter the common theme of having our work and family experiences shaped by the interlocking nature of race, gender, and class oppression," the commonality and "racial solidarity" that these experiences generated in the past is increasingly strained as a significant black middle class appears in stark contrast to the poor, working-class women of the inner-city neighborhoods (1990:65). For Collins, reforging the traditional relationship of sisterhood is one of the important ways in which African American women can overcome the changing dynamics of class to involve all black women in political activism (1990:211).

Gender and Race   Gender and race cannot be separated in Collins's work. Only by seeing the everyday world through the "both/and conceptual lens of the simultaneity of race, class, and gender oppression and of the need for a humanist vision of community," argues Collins, can a "fundamental paradigmatic shift in how we think about oppression" be achieved (1990:221–222). Black feminist thought "reconceptualizes the social relations of domination and oppression" by replacing "additive models of oppression with interlocking ones" (1990:222, 225).

An interlocking model involves recognizing that although race, class, and gender have been the fundamental systems of oppression for African American women, other oppressions such as "age, sexual orientation, religion, and ethnicity" affect other groups. The key is to place the excluded group in the "center of analysis" and, in doing so, open up "possibilities for a both/and conceptual stance, one in which all groups possess varying amounts of penalty and privilege in one historically created system." Collins sees a "matrix of domination" so that, depending on the context, "an individual may be an oppressor, a member of an oppressed group, or simultaneously oppressor and oppressed" (1990:225).

The **matrix of domination** "contains few pure victims or oppressors" because each individual "derives varying amounts of penalty and privilege from the multiple systems of oppression which frame everyone's lives" (1990:229). It is by recognizing these multiple standpoints, and engaging in dialogue, that domination can be resisted. Because each group knows its knowledge is partial and thus "unfinished," each group is "able to consider other groups' standpoints without relinquishing the uniqueness of its own standpoint or suppressing other groups' partial perspectives" (1990:236).

Dialogue is a necessity to transcend difference and transform relations of domination. In Collins's view, black women's contributions to any dialogue are particularly important because being treated as an "invisible Other" gives black women their "peculiar angle of vision" and their "outsider-within status" (1990:94). Black feminist scholars, as outsiders-within academic discourse, also have an important part to play in challenging the "content of what currently passes as truth" and simultaneously challenging the "process of arriving at that truth" (1989:773).

Other Theories and Theorists

Collins criticizes the white academic depiction of black women as a strong ma-triarchs who "allegedly emasculate their lovers and husbands" (1990:74). In this interpretation, the "absence of Black patriarchy is used as evidence for Black cultural inferiority" and for black men's underachievement. But Du Bois (see Chapter 12) had earlier pointed out that "Black women's centrality in Black Families" was not a "*cause* of African-American social class status" but an "*outcome* of racial oppression and poverty" (1990:73). The notion of black matriarchy, Collins points out, diverts attention from the "political and economic inequality affecting Black mothers and children and suggests that anyone can rise from poverty if he or she only received good values at home" (1990:74).

The notion of the black matriarchal family is constructed in terms of the "mythical norm of the financially independent, white middle-class family organized around a monogamous heterosexual couple" (1990:165). Moreover, argues Collins, the presumed "deviance" of the black family is related to assumptions about unrestrained, animalistic black sexuality. By "labeling Blacks as sexually animalistic," Collins maintains, "whites in actuality aim to repress these dimensions of their own inner being" (1990:196). Collins is equally critical of the sexism of black men, but recognizes that it is often fueled by black men's acceptance of the white notion of a domineering black matriarchy.[6] What has to be recognized, she insists, is that sexuality and power on both the personal and the structural level reinforce the sex/gender hierarchy, which ensures the "smooth operation of race, gender, and class oppression" (1990:196).

Critique and Conclusions

Both Collins and Smith are centrally concerned with developing a theoretical stance that will be inclusive of groups previously excluded from abstract knowledge and knowledge production. In this aim, Collins is more successful than Smith. One of the major criticisms of Smith's work is that it is difficult for women outside the academy to comprehend because it remains situated in the language and form of sociological disciplinary specialization. bell hooks (hooks and West, 1991:72) points out that professionalization in the academy "limits those of us who want to speak to broader audiences," especially because editorial practices make all writing appear alike.

---

[6]For a discussion of the "myths" developed by black men, with the collaboration of some black women, that divest black women of power and freedom, see Barbara Smith (1983).

One further critique is related to the emphasis on experience. Grant (1993: 100) maintains that experience cannot "in and of itself, be the ground for an epistemology." There is "simply too much left unexplained," such as whose experience is to count as most important. For both Collins and Smith, the response to this criticism is essentially that the analysis of women's oppression provides a key to the "development of integrated analysis and practice based upon the fact that the major systems of oppression are interlocking" (Barbara Smith, 1983:xxxii). Furthermore, although the experiences of particular groups give rise to a plurality of knowledges, black women and white women share "a history of sexism and certain core experiences relating to female biology, sexuality, motherhood, and roles in the household and workplace" (Seidman, 1994:259).

Final Thoughts

Collins (1990:73) points out that "race, class, gender, and heterosexism" present major challenges to sociology, but despite "significant changes, the inner circle of sociological theory—its membership, epistemology, and theoretical frameworks—remains strangely untouched by the changes." The work of both Smith and Collins, and the multidisciplinarity of much feminist work in general, represent challenges to the "sanctity" of the theoretical inner circle. While both of them draw on a variety of theoretical traditions and are representative of the interdisciplinarity of feminist studies, both of them deal centrally with the issues that have concerned all sociological theorists. Both theorists are radical in their politics and their sociological focus.

The focus on these two sociologists in this chapter should not obscure the contributions to feminist social theory made in the past three decades by historians, political scientists, psychoanalysts, and anthropologists, as well as those in feminist literary studies and cultural studies, all of whom have presented important challenges to the theoretical hegemony that the classical, and in some cases the current, sociological tradition embodies. Some of the current feminist social theory from French feminists, from feminists influenced by Habermas and Foucault, and from new psychoanalytic perspectives will be touched on in Chapter 23.

References

American Sociological Association. 1993. "ASA Award Winners Reflect Broad Spectrum of Sociology." *Footnotes, 212*(7), 13.

Barrett, Michele, and Anne Phillips. 1992. "Introduction." In Michele Barrett and Ann Phillips (Eds.), *Destabilizing Theory* (pp. 1–9). Stanford, CA: Stanford University Press.

Bernard, Jessie. 1989. "The Dissemination of Feminist Thought: 1960 to 1988." In Ruth A. Wallace (Ed.), *Feminist Sociological Theory* (pp. 23–33). Newbury Park, CA: Sage.

Collins, Patricia Hill. 1989. "The Social Construction of Black Feminist Thought." *Signs, 14,* 745–773.

————. 1990. *Black Feminist Thought*. Cambridge: Unwin Hyman.

————. 1992. "Transforming the Inner Circle: Dorothy Smith's Challenge to Sociological Theory." *Sociological Theory, 10,* 73–80.

Dalla Costa, Mariarosa, and Selma Jones. 1973. *The Power of Women and the Subversion of Community*. Bristol, England: Falling Wall Press.

de Beauvoir, Simone. 1974. *The Second Sex*. New York: Alfred A. Knopf.

Deckard, Barbara Sinclair. 1983. *The Women's Movement*. New York: Harper and Row.

Eichler, Margrit. 1992. "Not Always an Easy Alliance: The Relationship between Women's Studies and the Women's Movement in Canada." In Constance Backhouse and David H. Flaherty (Eds.), *The Women's Movement in Canada and the United States* (pp. 120–135). Montreal and Kingston: McGill–Queen's University Press.

Eisenstein, Zillah. 1979. "Developing a Theory of Capitalist Patriarchy and Socialist Feminism." In Zillah Eisenstein (Ed.), *Capitalist Patriarchy and the Case for Socialist Feminism* (pp. 5–40). New York: Monthly Review Press.

Engels, Frederick. 1972. *The Origin of the Family, Private Property and the State*. New York: Pathfinder Press.

Epstein, Cynthia Fuchs. 1988. *Deceptive Distinctions: Sex, Gender, and the Social Order*. New Haven, CT: Yale University Press.

Friedan, Betty. 1963. *The Feminine Mystique*. New York: Dell.

Grant, Judith. 1993. *Fundamental Feminism: Contesting the Core Concepts of Feminist Theory*. New York: Routledge.

Harding, Sandra. 1981. "What Is the Real Material Base of Patriarchy and Capital?" In Lydia Sargent (Ed.), *Women and Revolution* (pp. 135–163). Montreal: Black Rose Books.

Hartmann, Heidi. 1981. "The Unhappy Marriage of Marxism and Feminism: Towards a More Progressive Union." In Lydia Sargent (Ed.), *Women and Revolution* (pp. 1–41). Montreal: Black Rose Books.

Hekman, Susan. 1997. "Truth and Method: Feminist Standpoint Theory Revisited," *Signs, 22,* 341–365.

hooks, bell, and Cornell West. 1991. *Breaking Bread*. Toronto: Between the Lines.

Jaggar, Alison M. 1983. *Feminist Politics and Human Nature*. Sussex, England: Harvester Press.

Johnson, Miriam. 1989. "Feminism and the Theories of Talcott Parsons." in Ruth A. Wallace (Ed.), *Feminism and Sociological Theory* (pp. 101–118). Newbury Park, CA: Sage.

Laslett, Barbara, and Barrie Thorne. 1992. "Considering Dorothy Smith's Social Theory: Introduction." *Sociological Theory, 10,* 60–62.

Lemert, Charles. 1992. "Subjectivity's Limit: The Unsolved Riddle of the Standpoint," *Sociological Theory, 10*(1), 63–72.

Lengermann, Patricia, and Jill Niebrugge-Brantley. 1990. "Feminist Sociological Theory: The Near-Future Prospects." In George Ritzer (Ed.), *Frontiers of Social Theory* (pp. 316–344). New York: Columbia University Press.

Marx, Karl, and Frederick Engels. 1845–6/1947. *The German Ideology*. New York: International Publishers.

McClure, Kirstie. 1992. "The Issue of Foundations: Scientized Politics, Politicized Science, and Feminist Critical Practice." In Judith Butler and Joan W. Scott, (Eds.), *Feminists Theorize the Political* (pp. 341–368). New York: Routledge.

Mitchell, Juliet. 1971. *Women's Estate*. Harmondsworth, England: Penguin.

Parsons, Talcott. 1954. *Essays in Sociological Theory*. Glencoe, IL: Free Press.

Rossi, Alice S. 1964 "Equality Between the Sexes: An Immodest Proposal." *Daedalus, 93*, 607–652.

———. 1988. "Growing Up and Older in Sociology: 1940–1990." In Matilda White Riley (Ed.), *Sociological Lives* (pp. 43–64). Newbury Park, CA: Sage.

Rowbotham, Sheila. 1973. *Woman's Consciousness, Man's World*. Harmondsworth, England: Penguin.

Rubin, Lillian B. 1994. "An Unanticipated Life." In Katheryn P. Meadows Orlans and Ruth A. Wallace (Eds.), *Gender and the Academic Experience*. Lincoln: University of Nebraska Press.

Schutz, Alfred. 1932/1967. *The Phenomenology of the Social World*, Evanston, IL: Northwestern University Press.

Seidman, Steven. 1994. *Contested Knowledge*. Oxford: Blackwell.

Smith, Barbara (Ed.). 1983. *Home Girls: A Black Feminist Anthology*. New York: Kitchen Table, Women of Color Press.

Smith, Dorothy E. 1975. "Ideological Structures and How Women Are Excluded." *The Canadian Review of Sociology and Anthropology, 12*, 353–369.

———. 1977a. *Feminism and Marxism: A Place to Begin, A Way to Go*. Vancouver: New Star Books.

———. 1977b. "Women, the Family and Corporate Capitalism." In Marylee Stephenson (Ed.), *Women in Canada* (pp. 17–40). Don Mills, Ontario. General Publishing.

———. 1987. *The Everyday World as Problematic: A Feminist Sociology*. Toronto: University of Toronto Press.

———. 1989. "Sociological Theory: Methods of Writing Patriarchy." In Ruth A. Wallace (Ed.), *Feminism and Sociological Theory* (pp. 34–64). Newbury Park, CA: Sage.

———. 1990a. *The Conceptual Practices of Power*. Toronto: University of Toronto Press.

———. 1990b. *Texts, Facts and Femininity*. London: Routledge.

———. 1992. "Sociology from Women's Experience: A Reaffirmation." *Sociological Theory, 10*, 88–98.

———. 1994. "A Berkeley Education." In Kathryn P. Meadows Orlans and Ruth A. Wallace (Eds.), *Gender and the Academic Experience*. Lincoln: University of Nebraska Press.

———. 1999. *Writing the Social*. Toronto: University of Toronto Press.

Spender, Dale. 1983. *There's Always Been a Women's Movement This Century*. London: Pandora Press.

Stacy, J., and B. Thorne. 1985. "The Missing Feminist Revolution in Sociology." *Social Problems, 32*, 301–316.

Stanley, Liz, and Sue Wise. 1983. *Breaking Out: Feminist Consciousness and Feminist Research*. London: Routledge & Kegan Paul.

Swingwood, Alan. 1991. *A Short History of Sociological Thought*. London: Macmillan.

Sydie, R. A. 1987. *Natural Women, Cultured Men*. Toronto: Methuen.

Turner, Jonathan. 1990. "The Past, Present, and Future of Theory in American Sociology." In George Ritzer (Ed.), *Frontiers of Social Theory* (pp. 371–391). New York: Columbia University Press.

Wallace, Ruth A. 1989. "Introduction." In Ruth A. Wallace (Ed.), *Feminism and Sociological Theory* (pp. 7–19). Newbury Park, CA: Sage.

Chapter 23

Knowledge, Truth, and Power
Foucault and Feminist Responses

Human knowledge and human power come to the same thing, because ignorance of cause frustrates effect. (Francis Bacon, *Novum Organum*)

Knowledge has always been linked to power, in the sense of having the power to have an effect on individuals or, more generally, on society. The fear of the village gossip, for example, was a fear of the gossip's presumed knowledge. The power of knowledge is even more important today with the proliferation of electronic systems that can store enormous amounts of data, recording the most intimate aspects of any individual's life. These data are stored in places that are accessible to governments and to those individuals, corporations, and institutions whose requests for such knowledge are deemed "legitimate," but the same data are often not accessible, or easily accessible, to the subjects who have contributed the information. This electronic capacity makes supposedly autonomous individuals into bureaucratic cases without control over the dispersal of knowledge about their lives and their intimate, inner being. Furthermore, there is often the suspicion that the "knowledge" stored in these sophisticated ways may be no more informed than the knowledge of the village gossip.

Michel Foucault's central concern was how knowledge related to power. He was especially concerned with charting how different regimes of knowledge shaped modern society. Foucault did not regard knowledge *as* power but as contributing in different ways, in different contexts, to the exercise of power. Foucault thus qualified Bacon's assertion that knowledge and power are like cause and effect. Knowledge itself does not provide any inevitable, predictable effects. Furthermore, power itself can produce knowledge. Foucault's concern is particularly timely given the way in which information about individuals is monitored, evaluated, and stored in modern society, effectively abolishing the classic Enlightenment distinction between a public and a private realm.

Michel Foucault (1926–1984)

Michel Foucault was born in Poitiers, France, to a prosperous bourgeois family. His father was a surgeon and obstetrician; his mother, who was independently wealthy, managed the household and her husband's medical practice. Foucault's adolescence was marked by the experience of World War II. He later recalled the fear he had felt about whether he would live through the bombing and, if he did, whether he would be German or French at the end of the war (Macey, 1993). Foucault, like many postwar intellectuals, felt it "intolerable to have a 'bourgeois' professional future as a professor, journalist, writer, or whatever," given the "urgency of creating a society radically different" from the one before the war (Trombadori, 1991:47). Foucault resisted his own bourgeois origins by rejecting the idea of following in his father's footsteps and becoming a doctor, despite a family tradition dictating that the eldest son study medicine. Foucault's defiance of his father's wishes resulted in a career that in fact encompassed the roles of professor, journalist, and writer.

Foucault attended the École Normale Supérieure, the training ground for the French cultural elite, and graduated with a philosophy degree in 1948. While there, he studied with Jean Hippolite, who taught Hegel, and with the Marxist, Louis Althusser. In 1950, Foucault joined the Communist party, supposedly at the urging of Althusser (Macey, 1993:37). However, it would seem that Foucault was not a very enthusiastic party member—no one recalled his attendance at any meetings—and by 1953 he had left the party (Macey, 1993:38).

In 1952 Foucault completed a diploma course in psychopathology at the Institut de Psychologie, and he was then hired at the University of Lille in the philosophy department to teach psychology to philosophy students. His teaching duties were light, and because "pastoral duties in a French university are traditionally so light as to be almost nonexistent, and staff–student relations tend to be formal, if not distant," Foucault had considerable time for other research and teaching (Macey, 1993:49). Foucault taught part-time at the École Normale Supérieure, and he was an unofficial intern at the major psychiatric hospital, Hôpital Sainte-Anne. In 1955 he went to the French Institute in Uppsala, Sweden, to teach French language and literature. Some years later, Foucault stated that he went to Sweden because it was "supposed to be a much freer country," but once there, he found that a "certain kind of freedom may have, not exactly the same effects, but as many effects as a directly restrictive society" (Kritzman, 1988:5). He left Sweden for Warsaw in 1958 to take charge of the University's Centre Français. Foucault was transferred to Hamburg as a cultural attaché in 1959 and returned to France in 1960 to become a professor at the University of Clermont-Ferrand in the Department of Philosophy.

In 1961 Foucault successfully defended his doctoral thesis, which was published as *Historie de la folie (History of Madness)*. Foucault remained at Clermont until 1966, when he went to Tunisia to teach philosophy at the University of Tunis. He returned to Paris in 1968 to teach philosophy at the new University of Vincennes. In 1970 Foucault was elected to the Chair in the History of

Systems of Thought at the most prestigious institution in France, the Collège de France.[1]

Foucault was often invited to lecture in North America, which he liked, especially California, finding the "intellectual life freer and more open than in France" as well as providing more opportunity to explore the "uses of pleasure," especially in the bathhouses of San Francisco (Macey, 1993:430). Foucault confessed that he preferred American to French food and declared a "good club sandwich with a coke. That's my pleasure. It's true" (Kritzman, 1988:12). Foucault visited San Francisco for the last time in 1983 and, according to Miller (1993:34), frequented the bathhouses despite the growing knowledge about, and fear of, AIDS. Foucault died in 1984. In his reflection on Foucault's death, Miller quoted from Foucault's *History of Sexuality*: "Sex is worth dying for" (1976:156).

Foucault's Central Theories and Methods

Foucault's work was not sociological in the North American sense of disciplinary specialization. His work ranged over a number of disciplines, including sociology, but also history, criminology, psychiatry, and philosophy. At the École Normale, his training was largely philosophical. Foucault recalled that when he was at the École, the philosophical currents were Hegel and phenomenology but that he had also become enthused about Nietzsche's work. Marx, Freud, and structuralism also figured in his training, but Foucault claimed that "I have never been a Freudian, I have never been a Marxist and I have never been a structuralist" (Kritzman, 1988:22). He described his intellectual training as based on a "pantheon of authors read 'against' Sartre and Hegel" (Macey, 1993:34). Foucault noted that prior to the 1960s, "France knew absolutely nothing . . . about the current Weberian thought" and critical theory, and the Frankfurt School was "practically unheard of" (Kritzman, 1988:26).

Foucault claimed that it was his reading of Nietzsche, along with other authors such as George Bataille, Maurice Blanchot, and Pierre Klossowki, that enabled him to "move away from [his] original university education" (1991:30). What interested him about these authors was that they did not construct systems but wrote from "direct, personal experience" (1991:30). By 1951, Foucault's intellectual interests were in the history of science, philosophy—especially Nietzschean philosophy—and psychology (Macey, 1993:35).

Foucault's interest in science had been stimulated by the work of George Canguilhem in biology and medicine. Canguilhem's work was predicated on the notion that "it is the abnormal which arouses theoretical interest in the normal" (quoted in Miller, 1993:60). Foucault's examinations of madness, prisons, and sexuality exemplify Canguilhem's view. Foucault was also influenced by the French philosophers of science, who stressed the idea that scientific "progress" was not some smooth accumulation of "truths" but resulted from conceptual

---

[1]The Collège is unique. It does not give degrees, and the 50 chairholders are elected by the other professors to "reward the most distinguished French practitioners in arts and sciences, from music to mathematics" (Miller, 1993:183). The only requirement is that the chairholders give an annual course of lectures, open to the public, in which they discuss their work in progress.

revolutions in how the world was understood. These conceptual revolutions produced demonstrable breaks or fault lines that transformed scientific disciplines (Miller, 1993:61).[2]

Foucault concluded that instead of "asking science to what extent its history has approached the truth (or impeded access to it)," science and scientific claims should be examined in the light of the idea that "the truth consists of a certain relationship that discourse and knowledge has with itself" (1991:62). That is, science and the scientist are historically situated, and there is no single "truth" but a "series of collective rational experiences" that construct the "knowing subject." Consequently, the scientist, as well as the research she or he produces, are part of the knowledge produced; they are both the "object" that is "known" (1991:63–64).[3]

Each historical age is characterized by particular forms of knowledge. Foucault called these particular knowledge forms an **episteme**, meaning sets of presuppositions that organize what counts as knowledge, truth, and reality and indicate how these matters can be discussed. For example, while the historian of science was busy determining "the constitution of scientific objects," Foucault would ask another question: "How does it happen that the human subject makes himself into an object of possible knowledge, through which forms of rationality, through what historic necessities, and at what price?" (Foucault, quoted in Lotringer, 1989:245).

Since the eighteenth century, the modern episteme has focused on the idea of the autonomous, rational subject—"Man"—as the subject *and* object of discourses about life and labor (Foucault, 1966:312). The "price" paid in making the human subject an object is control over that subject-become-object. This control is effected through the formulation of new kinds of knowledge about subjects as a result of the interrelated practices of documentation, surveillance, and confession. For example, in *Discipline and Punish* (1977), Foucault described how new kinds of scientific knowledge about the human body had given rise to new ways of controlling bodies.

> The human body was entering a machinery of power that explores it, breaks it down and rearranges it. . . . It defined how one may have a hold over other's bodies, not only so that they may do what one wishes, but so that they may operate as one wishes, with the techniques, the speed and the efficiency that one determines. Thus discipline produces subjected and practiced bodies, "docile" bodies. (1977:138)

Foucault's concern with knowledge was thus related to his concern with **power** and how it connects with **truth**. The background to Foucault's position is found in Nietzsche's analysis of good and evil in the *Genealogy of Morals*. Nietzsche argued that there was no essential, or original, definition of truth. Truth was an interpretation tied to the operation of power and domination.

---

[2]This perspective is very similar to that of Thomas Kuhn in his *The Structure of Scientific Revolutions* (1962), which, according to Miller (1993:61), is not surprising as Kuhn knew and admired the French historians of science.

[3]Foucault indicated that he came to this conclusion as a result of reading Nietzsche in conjunction with the philosophers of science.

Truth is therefore produced by power, and the consequences of the exercise of power are formulated as "truth."

> Power and knowledge directly imply one another . . . there is no power relation with the correlative constitution of a field of knowledge, nor any knowledge that does not presuppose and constitute at the same time power relations. (Foucault, 1977:27)

For example, government administrators "render phenomena (such as an expanding number of people) into objects (such as population) amenable to scientific study" at the same time that "scientific methodologies provide knowledge of these objects that render them amenable to government" (Simons, 1995:27–28).

"Truth," based on scientific discourse and the institutions producing such discourse, has the following traits, according to Foucault:

- "Truth" is centred on the form of scientific discourse and the institutions which produce it.
- It is subject to constant economic and political incitement (the demand for truth, as much for economic production as for political power).
- It is the object, under diverse forms, of immense diffusion and consumption (circulating through apparatuses of education and information whose extent is relatively broad in the social body).
- It is produced and transmitted under the control of a few great political and economic apparatuses (university, army, writing, media).
- It is the issue of a whole political debate and social confrontation ("ideological" struggles). (Foucault, 1980:131–132)

Power is also refigured in Foucault's discussions. The traditional understanding of power is that it is possessed by someone or something. Foucault suggests a different perspective on power. First, power is **exercised** rather than possessed. Second, power is not simply or inevitably **repressive** or **coercive** but can be **productive.** For example, in modern society power is exercised through the various practices and discourses that produce mad as opposed to sane people, or healthy as opposed to sick people, or "normal" as opposed to deviant people. Third, power does not flow from a **centralized source** but also flows from the **bottom up**— that is, from the multitude of interactions at the micro level of society.

Power is diffused throughout society. It is something that circulates: It is "never localised here or there, never in anybody's hands, never appropriated as a commodity or piece of wealth. . . . And not only do individuals circulate between its threads; they are also in the position of simultaneously undergoing and exercising power" (Foucault, 1980:98).

Central to the operation of power/knowledge/truth connections are discourses and texts. Foucault's emphasis on discourses and texts in the examination of epistemes, together with his conception of history as a series of ruptures and breaks rather than a unified, progressive totality, provides the basis of his methodology. He called his methodological procedures archaeology and genealogy.

Archaeology involves the study of discourses that set the conditions for what counts as knowledge in particular historical periods. It involves "comparison of one discursive practice with another and a discursive practice with the non-discursive practices (institutions, political events, economic and social processes) that surround it" (Sheridan, 1980:105). These practices determine, for example, what is "moral" or "scientific" and how the moral or scientific status of the object or event is to be described. The focus is on the type of knowledge produced in certain periods that generate a particular "object" that becomes the focus for disciplines—for example, sociology, biology, or medicine—and then becomes the knowledge of that discipline.[4] For example, in Chapter 1 we discussed the way in which "society" became an object of study in its own right and the variety of ways in which this new object became the linchpin of the new discipline of sociology.

Genealogy means tracing descent, and Foucault uses it to describe a different approach to historical research. Instead of assuming a discoverable causality for historical events, Foucault examines the contingency of historical objects. The focus is on the ruptures, transitions, and discontinuities that produce historical concepts and definitions. This involves tracing not only the historical "winners" but also the "losers" in the interplay of events. Contrary to Marx, Foucault sees no inevitable historical necessity for any particular events. Instead, he argues, the historian has to examine the possibility that what transpired could have been otherwise.

Archaeology is the "intellectual subconscious" of disciplines (Gutting, 1994:9). Genealogy is "**eventalization**"—that is, the investigation of history on the assumption that it need not have taken the course it did, that events were not "as necessary as all that." For example, it involves the recognition that it was not a "matter of course that mad people came to be regarded as mentally ill; it wasn't self-evident that the only thing to be done with a criminal was to lock him up" (Foucault, 1991:76). Eventalization means "rediscovering the connection, encounters, supports, blockages, plays of forces, strategies and so on which at a given moment establish what subsequently counts as being self-evident, universal and necessary" (1991:76).

Genealogy has three "domains" in Foucault's work:

- First, a historical ontology of ourselves in relation to truth through which we constitute ourselves as subjects of knowledge;

- Second, a historical ontology of ourselves in relation to a field of power through which we constitute ourselves as subjects acting on others;

- Third, a historical ontology in relation to ethics through which we constitute ourselves as moral agents. (Foucault, 1984a:354)

According to Foucault, all three domains were present in his first work, *Madness and Civilization*, "although in a somewhat confused fashion." Truth was studied

---

[4]Using the word *knowledge* to refer to the two procedures is somewhat confusing because of a translation problem. Foucault used *savior* and *connaissance*, both of which translate into English as knowledge. Foucault explained the difference this way: By *connaissance* I mean the relation of the subject to the object and the formal rules that govern it. *Savior* refers to the conditions that are necessary in a particular period for that type of object to be given to *connaissance* and for this or that enunciation to be formulated (Translator's note, Foucault, 1972:15, fn. 2).

in *The Birth of the Clinic* and *The Order of Things*, power in *Discipline and Punish*, and ethics in *The History of Sexuality* (Foucault, 1984a:352).

Foucault was not interested in proposing a "global principle for analyzing society" as other historians and sociologists had done. He was interested in the history of "the way things become a problem" and how the problem was constructed in discourse. As he put it, "my problem is to see how men govern (themselves and others) by the production of truth (I repeat . . . that by the production of truth I mean not the production of true utterances, but the establishment of domains in which the practice of true and false can be made at once ordered and pertinent)" (Foucault, 1991:79). This means that the certainties that sociologists have taken for granted, such as society as a sui generis entity, must be rejected as immutable truths, along with the idea of rationality as a natural human quality. This makes it somewhat difficult to use here the subheads "Society" and "Humans" that we have used in each chapter—a difficulty that Foucault would have found both amusing and obvious. Nonetheless, the following section is organized by those subheads, even if they are only contradicted by Foucault's work.

Nature of Society, Humans, and Change

Foucault does not have any conception of society as a definable structure or system. "Society" is the product of discourses and practices, especially those discourses and practices of the human or social sciences. Similarly, he rejects any timeless notion of the nature of human beings. According to Foucault, before the "end of the eighteenth century, *man* did not exist" (Foucault, 1966:308). That is, the idea of "Man" as both subject and object—as an individual who produces knowledge as well as that entity about which knowledge is produced—was not part of the discourses of truth prior to the eighteenth century.

The recent social constructions of "society" and "man" in the Western world has developed from a complex web of interconnections and conflicts in the social arena. To Foucault, the social arena is an historically situated and variable arena of power/knowledge, and the key to understanding society, humans, and social change lies in uncovering the power/knowledge grid. We will examine Foucault's *Discipline and Punish* first to illustrate how a variety of ideas and institutions gave rise to the notion of modern society as, ideally, a collection of disciplined, docile bodies.

Society   Foucault introduces *Discipline and Punish* with a description of a public execution in 1757 and a timetable of rules drawn up in 1837 for Parisian prisoners. The two descriptions represent two different forms of punishment and two different understandings of what constitutes a crime.

The description of the execution seems particularly horrific today, but at the time it was observed by many and calmly reported in its details by several observers. For example, the last part of the execution involved quartering, but "because the horses were not accustomed to drawing . . . instead of four, six were needed; and when that did not suffice, they were forced, in order to cut off the wretch's thighs, to sever the sinews and hack at the joints." But the spectators were "edified by the solicitude of the parish priest of St. Paul's who . . .

did not spare himself in offering consolation to the patient" (Foucault, 1975:3). Foucault claims that this form of punishment was "normal" until the eighteenth century, when torture and mutilation of the body, along with public executions, disappeared.

Public executions, and lesser forms of assault on the body such as amputation or branding, were both juridical and political acts. Prior to the eighteenth century, the law represented the sovereign's will. A crime was thus a personal attack on the sovereign and had to be publicly avenged in order to reassert/restore the power of the sovereign. A public execution demonstrated the power asymmetry between "the subject who has dared to violate the law and the all-powerful sovereign who displays his strength." Punishment had to be an exercise in terror in order to reinforce the belief, among the rest of the population, in the awe-inspiring power of the sovereign (Foucault, 1975:49).

By the nineteenth century, public punishment had virtually disappeared in Western societies. In fact, Foucault states, punishment became the "most hidden part of the penal process" (1977:9). Punishment became more "gentle" but more thorough, the object being to "punish less, but to punish more deeply in the social body" (Foucault, 1975:82). It was the prison that marked the transformation in the power and practice of punishment. The target of punishment became the body and soul of the prisoner, in an effort to remake the prisoner into an obedient subject. The prisoner is therefore subjected to the **discipline** of "habits, rules, order, and authority that is exercised continually around him and upon him, and which he must allow to function automatically in him" (1977:129). Discipline is reinforced by techniques of surveillance that constantly "see" and monitor behavior.

> The perfect disciplinary apparatus would make it possible for a single gaze to see everything constantly. A central point would be both the source of light illuminating everything, and a locus of convergence for everything that must be known: a perfect eye that nothing would escape and a center toward which all gazes would be turned. (1977:173)

The perfect model of such a disciplinary apparatus was Jeremy Bentham's plan for a Panopticon. The architecture of the Panopticon would enable a single observer, standing at the center of the cylindrical tower, to see each individual inmate in the cells ranged around the walls of the tower. The guard can see all, and all prisoners are conscious of their "permanent visibility," which in turn assures the "automatic functioning of power" (Foucault, 1977:201). The prisoners know they can be seen, but they do not know when they are being seen. As a result, prisoners will monitor or discipline themselves in case they are being observed. The "gaze" eliminates the need for "arms, physical violence, material constraints" because, under the gaze, each individual becomes his own "overseer . . . thus exercising this surveillance over, and against, himself" (1977:155). Although the Panopticon was never built, the panoptic principle was important in defining new power relations in everyday life. In fact, we live under the gaze of the all-seeing but remote eye of video cameras. We are captured on film in retail outlets, banks, and other public places in an ostensible effort to control crime.

Foucault argued that the panoptic principle of generalized surveillance had been gradually extended throughout society to form the **disciplinary society** (1977:209). From the eighteenth century on, the organization of prisons was complemented by the organization of workhouses for the poor, asylums for the mad, factories for the workers, and hospitals for the diseased, all devoted to disciplining the unruly bodies of the poor, the mad, the sick, and the underclasses. The modern disciplinary society was an historically constructed entity involving "economic, juridico-political, and . . . scientific" efforts (Foucault, 1977:218).

The disciplinary society was, in Foucault's view, a critical part of the transition of Western societies to modernity.

> If the economic take-off of the west began with the techniques that made possible the accumulation of capital, it might perhaps be said that the methods for administrating the accumulation of men made possible the political take-off in relation to . . . subjection. In fact the two processes—the accumulation of men and the accumulation of capital—cannot be separated. (1977:221)

The accumulation of men required a productive process capable of sustaining and using them, and "techniques that made the cumulative multiplicity of men useful accelerated the accumulation of capital" (1977:221). The conjunction of these processes required "docile bodies" who generally disciplined themselves as good citizens and diligent workers. The operation of power that produces docile bodies is obscured, however, by the "enlightened" modern assumption of the agency of the rational, autonomous individual.

A key aspect of the disciplinary society, Foucault observes, is the "reversal of the political axis of individualization" (1977:192). In feudal society, the more power and privilege a person possessed, the more the person was regarded as an individual. In modern disciplinary regimes, however, "as power becomes more anonymous and more functional, those on whom it is exercised tend to be more strongly individualized." For example, "the child is more individualized than the adult, the patient more than the healthy man, the madman and the delinquent more than the normal and the non-delinquent," and when one individualizes the "healthy, normal and law-abiding adult, it is always by asking him how much of the child he has in him, what secret madness lies within him, what fundamental crime he has dreamt of committing." All the "sciences, analyses, or practices employing the root 'psycho'—have their origin in this historical reversal of individuality." It is when the "sciences of man became possible" that the "new technology of power and a new political anatomy of the body were implemented" (Foucault, 1977:193).

Humans   Foucault's recognition of the fragmentation of the "individual" through the specialized disciplinary practices of the human and medical sciences, and the manner in which the autonomy of the individual has been compromised, is a critique of the Enlightenment concept of the rational, autonomous subject. When Foucault said "the concept of Man is a fraud," he did not mean that "you and I are nothing" (Hacking, 1986:39). What he meant was that the humanist celebration of the abstraction "Man" obscured the multitude of ways in which the subject is constructed. For Foucault, there is "no sovereign, founding subject, a universal form of subject to be found everywhere"; on the contrary, the subject is "constituted through the practices of subjection, or, in a more autonomous way, through practices of liberation . . . on the basis . . . of a number of rules, styles, inventions to be found in the cultural environment" (Foucault, 1988a:50–51).

The concept of Man, however, is necessary to the operation of a disciplinary society, as it provides the yardstick by which unruly minds and bodies can be controlled. The transformation of the "mad" illustrates this point.

In *Madness and Civilization*, Foucault points out that the construction of modern mental illness is quite different from earlier conceptions. Madness is thus historically contingent and not, as you might imagine, a universally recognized condition of unreason in contrast to reason. Furthermore, reason *as well as* madness is a social construction.

In medieval society, the madman, the fool, or the simpleton was regarded as the "guardian of truth" because "his simpleton's language which makes for no show of reason" was in fact "the words of reason" that revealed the truth (Foucault, 1964:14). It was in the seventeenth century that the understanding of madness began to change. Madness became identified with "poverty, . . . incapacity for work, . . . inability to integrate with the group." The transformation was linked to the new importance given to the "obligation to work, and all the ethical values that are linked to labor," as illustrated in Weber's *The Protestant Ethic and the Spirit of Capitalism*. Madness, which before had "floundered about in broad daylight: in *King Lear*, in *Don Quixote*," was now set apart and confined, "bound to reason, to the rules of morality and to their monotonous nights" (1964:64).

In the eighteenth century, madness as unreason resulted in the confinement of the mad: "Madness . . . became the paradoxical manifestation of non-being," and confinement was not to suppress but to "eliminate from the social order a figure which did not find its place within it" (Foucault, 1961:115). Confinement cements unreason as the "empty negativity of reason"; by confinement, "madness is acknowledged to be *nothing*" (1961:116). The confined were not simply the demonstrably disturbed but also disruptive people, such as beggars, vagrants, and prostitutes, whose behavior deviated from the bourgeois model of the moral, industrious citizen.

It was Freud who restored to medicine the "possibility of a dialogue with unreason" (Foucault, 1961:198). The psychiatric discipline was different from the medical discussion of "'diseases of the head' or 'nervous diseases' found in eighteenth-century medical treatises" (1961:179). Psychiatry emerged out of a "whole set of relations between hospitalization, internment, the conditions and procedures of social exclusion, the rule of jurisprudence, the norms of industrial labor and the norms of bourgeois morality, in short a whole group of relations that characterized for this discursive practice the formation of its statements. Psychiatry is another disciplinary practice" (Foucault, 1972:179).

According to Foucault, however, psychiatry retains the Enlightenment stamp, with its notion of a true, unified, and fixed self that can be uncovered by the confessional practices of psychoanalysis. Freud's analysis of the Oedipal complex was, in Foucault's view, another part of the power regime of modern society, reinforcing a normative conception of family and, more specifically, sexual identification and practice. In modern society, the key to a person's true self is believed to be sex: "We demand that sex speak the truth . . . and we demand that it tell us our truth, or rather, the deeply buried truth of that truth about ourselves which we think we possess in our immediate consciousness" (Foucault, 1976:69).

Sex as the Truth of Self   In the first volume of his *History of Sexuality*, Foucault traces the historical conjunction of sexuality, subjectivity, and truth. By the end of the eighteenth century, a "new technology of sex" had emerged. Sex became a state concern—a "matter that required the social body as a whole, and virtually all of its individuals, to place themselves under surveillance" (Foucault, 1976:116). Contrary to the assumption that the Victorians confined and repressed sexuality, Foucault states that sex was spoken of "*ad inifinitum*, while exploiting it as *the* secret" (1976:35). Sex was not confined to a "shadow existence" in the Victorian age only to emerge in the free-spirited 1960s; on the contrary, sex was a central preoccupation of the age.

The idea that the nineteenth-century advent of "modern industrial societies ushered in an age of increased sexual repression" must be abandoned. The evidence Foucault uncovers indicates that there was an "explosion of unorthodox sexualities," a "proliferation of specific pleasures and a multiplication of disparate sexualities" under modernity (1976:49). Even the term "sexuality" did not appear before the beginning of the nineteenth century (Foucault, 1986:3).

The new discourses and technologies of sex involved four strategies of "knowledge and power" that provided the means for a disciplinary control over sexual desire and practice (1976:103):

- The "*hysterization of women's bodies*" (1976:104). Women's bodies were understood to be "saturated with sexuality"; as a result, they were unstable bodies subject to hysteria. This discourse produced the "nervous woman"—a real medical category used, as you saw earlier, in the case of Charlotte Perkins Gilman.

- The "*pedagogization of children's sex*" (1976:104). All children indulged in sexual activity, but that it was seen as an activity "contra to nature." To protect children from the physical and moral dangers of sexual exploration, parents—and, more important, experts such as "educators, doctors, and eventually psychologists"—had to take charge of this "dangerous and endangered sexual potential." It is from this discourse that the myths about the dangers of masturbation arose.

- The "*socialization of procreative behavior*" (1976:104–105). Procreation became linked to the regulation of populations. State and medical experts encouraged the limitation or, alternatively, the proliferation of births in relation to their estimates of the "needs" of the society. Thus, the various financial inducements offered for procreation that societies have used, and continue to use, developed, as well as the provision of contraception for the limitation of births according to the "needs" of the social body. The "needs" were, and are, determined politically, using medical and demographic specialist information.

- The *"psychiatrization of perverse pleasure"* (1976:105). Sexuality became a "separate biological and psychical instinct," prone to anomalies that psychiatry normalized or pathologized, at the same time devising corrective technologies for the anomalies.

The four strategies produced four privileged objects of knowledge that were targets and anchor points for social control: the "hysterical woman, the masturbating child, the Malthusian couple, and the perverse adult" (1976:105).

With the modern transformation of sexuality, the individual became aware of the self as the subject of sexuality. For the "first time in history . . . biological existence was reflected in political existence," and power was exercised not simply over "legal subjects over whom the ultimate dominion was death, but with living beings" (1976:142–143). The four strategies produced what Foucault called **bio-power**—that is, "life and its mechanisms" were brought into the "realm of explicit calculations," and this knowledge/power conjunction produced an ability to transform human life (1976:143). At the "juncture of the 'body' and the 'population,' sex became a crucial target of power organized around the management of life rather than the menace of death" (1976:147). Prisons controlled individuals from the outside; the internalization of sexual norms and practices controlled individuals from the inside.

Foucault indicated that after completing the first volume of *The History of Sexuality* he had intended to trace the historical evolution of this knowledge/power connection up to the nineteenth century, but he realized that an important question remained: "Why had we made sexuality into a moral experience?" (1988a: 252). He turned to the investigation of how "for centuries, Western man had been brought to recognize himself as a subject of desire" (1984b:6). The second volume, *The Use of Pleasure*, investigates the way in which sexual practice was understood as an ethical practice in classical Greece (1984b:91).

Desire and the Ethical Subject   In classical Greece, the ethical domain demanded self-control, especially "dominion of self over self," in the face of acts "intended by nature," such as sex, and "associated by nature with an intense pleasure, and naturally motivated by a force that was always liable to excess and rebellion" (1984b:91). The ethical strictures in classical Greece emphasized austerity with respect to the body, marriage, and the love of boys (1984b:92). These strictures produced three techniques for self-control designed to produce the ethical subject: "dietetics, economics, and erotics" (1984b:251). **Dietetics** focused on the "right time" for sexual pleasure, taking into account the "variable states of the body and the changing properties of the seasons" (1984b:251). **Economics** involved conduct in marriage and family, including the "masculine art of governing a household—wife, servants, estate" (1984b:163). The "faithful" husband was not someone who renounced all sexual pleasure with others but one who "maintained the privileges to which the wife was entitled by marriage" (1984b:164).

Erotics referred to the moderation that should be exercised in relationships with boys. The love of boys generally involved an older man and a young boy, and was only condoned when it involved free citizens. What the relationship required was a delicate balance in which the older man was "master of his pleasure" but still made "allowance for the other's freedom." That is, love for the younger man must be balanced by the respect for the younger man's "future status as a free citizen." At the same time, the younger man must not respond to sexual urges of the older man because in doing so he made himself a passive sex object and thus unworthy of being a free citizen. Sex, as a test of self-control, did not mean "pure and simple abstention," but it did tend to stress the "ideal of a renunciation of all physical relations with boys" (1984b:252).

In the third volume, *The Care of the Self*, Foucault moves his investigation of the connection between sexuality and morality to the early Roman Empire. Foucault records a shift in emphasis from classical Greek ideas to a "greater importance accorded to marriage and its demands, and less value given to the love of boys" (1984c:36). The significance attributed to marriage began in the age of emperors, starting with Augustus. The change was connected to various economic and political transformations in the Empire, most notably a decline in the political significance of alliances among family groups in favor of the importance of close ties to the emperor. Marriage arrangements became "freer"— "free in choice of wife; free, too, in the decision to marry and in the reasons for doing so" (1984c:74). Marriage became more a "voluntary union between two partners," and a woman's "inequality diminished to a certain extent but did not cease to exist" (1984c:74). Foucault claims that the wife became more of a "companion to whom one opens one's soul" and marriage was more of a symmetrical relationship of "love, affection and mutual sympathy" (1984c: 179, 148).

The change in marital relations was connected with the development of a "culture of the self" that involved all aspects of daily life (1984c:59). A variety of practices, procedures, and recipes were "developed, perfected and taught," and included in these management practices was sexuality (1984c:59). Sexuality was both a pleasure and a danger. It was a danger because of the strength of uncontrolled passions and therefore must only be indulged in at appropriate times and with appropriate partners. It was an austere regime that played on the "haunting fear of the individual misfortunes and the collective ills that can result from disorderly sexual behavior" (1984c:64). There was a necessity, therefore, for a "rigorous mastery of desires . . . and the annulment of pleasure as the goal of sexual relations" (1984c:64).

Foucault's investigation of classical Greece and imperial Rome are contrasted with his analysis of Christian views on sex. Chastity and restraint were worthy virtues in the pre-Christian era, but it was in the Christian era that the idea of sin became connected to sexuality. This connection meant that individuals had to interrogate themselves as to their inner worth and constantly confess their transgressions. Christianity "prescribed as a fundamental duty the task of passing everything to do with sex through an endless mill of speech" (1976:21).

Foucault sees this policing of the sexual self in the confessional mode as eventually spreading to include all social relations: "one confesses one's crimes, one's sins, one's thoughts and desires, one's illnesses and troubles. . . . One admits to oneself, in pleasure and in pain, things it would be impossible to tell anyone else, the things people write about in books." The result is, "Western man has become a confessing animal" (1976:59). Sexuality as the truth of the person provides an avenue for the exercise of power. The sciences of medicine, psychology, demography, and sociology seize on the confessional body as an object of concern and manipulation (Merquior, 1985:121).

The last two volumes in the sexuality series are about the aesthetics of the self and body and mark a change in Foucault's perspective on the question of the subject. In these two works, the subject has agency, makes choices, and sets out goals (Shumway, 1989:154). But no *general* theory of the subject emerges. Foucault still maintained that human beings are different in different historical periods. "My objective . . . has been to create a history of different modes by which, in our culture, human beings are made subjects" (quoted in Drefus and Rabinow, 1983:20). This is why Foucault, following Nietzsche, saw the humanist concept of "Man" as a recent Western invention. He also indicated that ideas of autonomy, individual dignity, and self-determination were tied to the development of Western industrial capitalism and the development of a disciplinary society. These ideas are the means through which individuals become subjects *and* objects of knowledge and power.

A key question in the light of Foucault's rejection of any essentialist idea of the subject and the power/knowledge connection is how social change occurs. What is, or who is, the "motor" of social change?

Social Change   Foucault rejected any abstract, generalizing theory of social change. Ideas about causality, development, evolution, and the "spirit of the age" are rejected. What Foucault was interested in was an "analysis of *different types of transformation*" (1991:55). He examined **discontinuities** that demonstrated how the past was different from the present and that the present was not a product of some historical necessity. He rejected the Enlightenment idea of progress resulting from an inherent human rationality, just as he rejected the Marxian notion that progress can be achieved when human beings realize their basic material needs and capacities. In fact, Foucault maintained that "it is a bad method to pose the problem as: 'How is it that we have progressed?' The problem is: how do things happen?" keeping in mind that "what happens now is not necessarily better or more advanced, or better understood, than what happened in the past" (1980:50).

Central to how things happen, and thus how things change, is the operation of power. Power has a "capillary form of existence." It reaches "into the grain of individuals, touches their bodies and inserts itself into their actions and attitudes, their discourses, learning processes and everyday lives" (Foucault, 1980:39). In addition, power is seductive. It is not simply a "force that says no, . . . it traverses and produces things, it induces pleasure, forms of knowledge, produces discourse" (1980:119). Power should therefore be thought of as a "productive network which runs through the whole social body" (1980:119). Thus, it is not social classes, the state, or other institutional sites of power that are the prime movers in social change.

For Foucault, the question "Who exercises power?" cannot be answered apart from the question "How does it happen?" (1988b:103). Sociology can "show us who the bosses of industry are at present, how politicians are formed and where they come from," but even knowing who the decision makers are, "we will still not really know why and how the decision was made, how it came to be accepted by everybody, and how it hurts a particular category of person" (1988b:103–104). As Foucault pointed out, there is no *"one* knowledge or *one* power, or worse, *knowledge* or *power* which would operate in and of themselves. Knowledge and power are only an analytical grid" historically situated (1997:52).

Understanding power requires understanding the **strategies of power**—that is, all the ways in which decisions are made, accepted, and enforced (1988a:104). Power is never established for all time, because **resistance** is always possible. There are "no relations of power without resistances; the latter are all the more real and effective because they are formed right at the point where the relations of power are exercised" (1980:142). Among the important points of resistance are the "subjected knowledges"—that is, the "naïve" knowledge of the housewife, the mental patient, the poor, and the dispossessed that is disqualified by specialist, scientific knowledge regimes (1978:82). Counter discourses, such as feminism, are therefore ways in which power is resisted.

The key issue for Foucault was not to pinpoint some specific social/historical moment or event as pivotal in changing society, but to understand how the present has been constituted from a past of various, disparate events and ideas. In his essay "What Is Enlightenment?" Foucault indicated that the search for some principal cause of social change was replaced in his work by a genealogy that reassesses taken-for-granted notions of truth and looks for the "multiple determining elements" that eventually give rise not to a product as such but to an effect (1997:57). For example, in thinking about modernity, the question is not how does modernity come about, but how do individuals come to understand themselves as modern? Modernity is "an attitude rather than a period of history" (1997:113).

The question of modernity is tied to the Enlightenment linkage of reason and progress that remains, for Foucault, an important linkage and promise. The emancipatory promise can be sustained, in his view, by understanding "what we think, say, and do as so many historical events," thereby generating the possibility of "no longer being, doing and thinking what we are, do, or think" (1997:125–126). It was the task of specific intellectuals to provide the bases for these forms of understanding.

Foucault contrasts the **specific intellectual** with the **universal intellectual**, such as the Marxist vanguard intellectual, who claims to represent the enlightened consciousness of the dispossessed. Foucault remarked that the "role of the intellectual was not to tell others what they have to do"; rather, it is to "question over and over again what is postulated as self-evident, to disturb people's mental habits, the way they do and think things, to dissipate what is familiar and accepted, to reexamine rules and institutions and on the basis of this re-problematization (in which he carries out his specific task as an intellectual) to participate in the formation of a political will (in which he has his role as citizen to play)" (1988b:265). Foucault insists that the specific intellectual provides the tools of analysis, but "as for saying, 'Here is what you must do!,' certainly not" (1980:62).

The stakes are high, according to Foucault, because the growth of knowledge has always been accompanied by the growth of power. The key question is, "How can the growth of capabilities be disconnected from the intensification of power relations?" (1977:126).[5] Foucault does not have a precise answer to this question, but contrary to Habermas (see Chapter 16), Foucault did not believe that there could be a society without relations of power. The problem was "not of trying to dissolve them in the utopia of a perfectly transparent communication, but to give one's self the rules of law, the techniques of management, and also the ethics, the *ethos*, the practice of self, which would allow these games of power to be played with a minimum of domination" (1988b:18). The self-management that Foucault advocates, however, is somewhat problematic in the case of gender and race relations.

Class, Gender, and Race

Foucault's discussions of class, gender, and race are framed by his concern with the question of power.

Class For Foucault, power relations could not be adequately understood in terms of the dominance of the state, the nature of the class struggle, or the idea of capitalist exploitation. Foucault remarked that Marxist analyses of class struggle actually paid little attention to "struggle." Marxists, although not Marx himself, when speaking of class struggle as the "mainspring of history, . . . focus mainly on defining class, its boundaries, its membership, but never concretely on the nature of struggle" (1988b:123).

It was not the analysis of class power but the possibilities of resistance and struggle that interested Foucault. As he stated, his general theme was the "discourse of true and false" and the "formation of domains and objects and of the verifiable, falsifiable discourses that bear on them; and it is not just their formation that interests me, but the effects in the real to which they are linked" (Foucault, quoted in Burchell, Gordon, and Miller, 1991:85). For Foucault, then, the issue was not one of identifying class relations in the regime of power but of analyzing how those relations were formulated through discourses and practices. Foucault constantly questioned the idea of a universal subject—whether proletariat, abstract humanity, or Man—and the idea of a society free from power relations, asking instead how these ideas arose and what were their effects.

Foucault was skeptical about Marxism as a political blueprint for change that many French intellectuals endorsed in the postwar period. He regarded Marxism as a "dogmatic framework" that declined after the French student uprising of May 1968. One of the disillusioning features of the 1968 student rebellion was the lack of support from the proletariat. In fact, in Foucault's view, the French Communist party seemed to act as merely another repressive force. He maintained that the lesson learned from the events of 1968 was that "oppression associated with power could not be located within a single socio-political apparatus; it was dispersed in complex networks of social control that encompassed the

---

[5]Throughout his career, Foucault acted as a specific intellectual. He was involved in prison reform, gay rights, and support for Poland's Solidarity movement. He initially supported the Iranian revolution against the repressive regime of the Shah, until the evidence of human rights abuses by the new Islamic regime was revealed.

bureaucracy of an ossified revolutionary party" (Kritzman, 1988:x–xi). The "new political, new cultural interests concerning personal life" that appeared in the aftermath of these events, Foucault believed, made his own work more appealing (Foucault, 1988a:8).

In the context of Foucault's analysis of discourses and practices, his discussion of **bio-power**—that is, the regimes of discipline and population control—addresses most directly the question of class, gender, and race. According to Foucault, for example, the development of capitalism would not have been possible "without the controlled insertion of bodies into the machinery of production and the adjustment of the phenomenon of population to economic processes" (1976:141). Part of this process involved the gradual "moralization of the poorer classes" that took the form of "juridical and medical control of perversions, for the sake of a general protection of society and the race" (1976:16).

The moralization of the poor was connected with a form of bourgeois class consciousness in the eighteenth century that stressed the "affirmation of the body" (1976:16). The bourgeois "mechanisms of power are addressed to the body, to life, to what causes it to proliferate, to what reinforces its species, its stamina, its ability to dominate, or its capacity for being used" (1976:147). The cultivation of the ideal body was not simply "a matter of economy or ideology, it was a 'physical' matter as well" (1976:125). Important to the deployment of power over the physical body were the regimes of sexuality that defined the "normal" as opposed to the "perverse"; these were particularly important for the control of women and racial "others."

Gender   As Morris has remarked, "Foucault's work is not the work of a ladies' man" (1988:26). Although Foucault provided no distinctive discussion of gender, his work has nonetheless been useful to feminist social theory.

Foucault's work is particularly important for feminist theory in its repudiation of biological accounts of gender difference. As you have seen, his analysis in the first volume of *The History of Sexuality* pays attention to the way in which women's bodies were subjected to control and discipline in modern society. The modern link between expert, scientific knowledge and sexuality is based on the family as the "chief agents of the deployment of sexuality," supported by an array of medical, psychiatric, and educational specialists (1976:110). This regime gives rise to "new personages, . . . the nervous woman, the frigid wife, the indifferent mother—or worse, the mother beset by murderous obsessions—the important, sadistic, perverse husband, the hysterical and neurasthenic girls, the precocious and already exhausted child, and the young homosexual who rejects marriage or neglects his wife" (1976:111). But Foucault's interest in the sexualized subject was an abstract interest in the "human subject" and not focused on issues of gender inequities in modern society.

Foucault did make a brief comment on the women's movement in an interview. He stated that the "real strength of the women's liberation movement was not of having laid claim to the specificity of their sexuality and the rights pertaining to it, but that they have actually departed from the discourse conducted within the apparatuses of sexuality." He believed this departure resulted in a "displacement effected in relation to the sexual centering of the problem, formulating the demand for forms of culture, discourse, language and so on, which are no longer part of that rigid assignation and pinning-down to their sex which they had initially in some sense been politically obliged to accept in order to make themselves heard" (Foucault, in Gordon, 1980:219–220).

Race Bio-power is again important in Foucault's discussions of modern racism. Foucault pointed out that modern racism has a background in the aristocratic understanding of "blood." It was the "antiquity of its ancestry and the value of its alliances" that made blood the marker of caste distinction (1976: 124). Power "spoke *through* blood: the honor of war, the fear of famine, the triumph of death, the sovereign with his sword, executioners, and tortures; blood was *a reality with a symbolic function*" (1976:147). This aristocratic preoccupation with descent became a preoccupation with hereditary that found expression in the proliferation of "biological, medical, or eugenic precepts" (1976:124).

The dream of perfecting the species through the control of sex is the basis of modern racism's emphasis on the purity of blood to ensure the triumph of a race. The resulting "eugenic ordering of society, with all that implied in the way of extension and intensification of micro-powers, in the guise of unrestricted state control . . . was accompanied by the oneiric exaltation of superior blood" (1976:149). This exaltation implied the "systematic genocide of others" (1976:150). The expression of the symbolic importance of blood in eugenic programs justified the elimination of inferior traits and races; in this respect, "Nazism was doubtless the most cunning and the most naïve . . . combination of the fantasies of blood and the paroxysms of a disciplinary power" (1976:149). Ironically, Foucault maintains that the new forces of anti-Semitism began in socialist milieus with a "theory of degeneracy" that claimed the Jews were degenerate "firstly because they are rich, secondly because they intermarry" (1976:224). This theory is encountered in French "socialist literature down to the Dreyfus affair" and later in the "nationalist antisemitism of the Right," which adopted these themes pre-Hitler (1976:224).

Eugenics was a foundation for racist politics in many Western countries, but it was also an important part of the deployment of sexuality in respect to women and their bodies. It was mainly women who were, and still are, subject to control through sterilization, forced abortions, and detention in the interest of preventing the reproduction of the unfit and the degenerate. Again, Foucault does not discuss these specific gender consequences of the deployment of discipline and power over blood and bodies, but despite this omission, or perhaps because of it, many feminist theorists have appropriated his work. The appropriation has always been a critical one.

Other Theories and Theorists

Foucault edited two memoirs, one by Herculine Barbin (1978) and the other by Pierre Rivière (1975). The memoirs of Herculine Barbin were an example of the way in which bio-power becomes an "agent of transformation of human life" (1976: 143).

Herculine Barbin was a nineteenth-century hermaphrodite who lived as a girl for the first 20 years of her life. When it was discovered that she was a hermaphrodite, the doctors advised a sex change operation. It was the emphasis on precise categorization of "true" sexual identity that resulted in Herculine's being declared a man and forced to change. Despite the sympathy for her plight in the community, Barbin committed suicide. In Foucault's view, she was a victim of the new scientific medical passion for pinning down an exact, "true" sexual identity; in the past, "it was simply agreed that hermaphrodites had two" sexes (1978:vii).

The memoirs of Pierre Rivière concern his confession of the murder of his mother, sister, and brother. Rivière, a peasant, planned the murders carefully. He put on his Sunday clothes for the occasion and, after the act, wandered around the countryside and readily confessed when he was caught. He wrote his memoir in prison while awaiting trial, thus providing evidence against himself. At the trial, half of the experts—six lawyers and six doctors—considered Rivière insane, and the other half considered him sane. With a hung jury, Rivière was imprisoned rather than executed. He committed suicide some years later. The point that interested Foucault about this account was its demonstration of the confusion that attended the conjunction of medical and legal knowledge in the interest of social control in modern society. For Foucault, the case illustrated the ways in which unscientific beliefs constructed scientific knowledge of what was to be judged as "normal," which was then acted upon.

What is interesting about the two memoirs is that they are both confessional documents. In Foucault's view, psychoanalysis is the modern variant on the Christian injunction to confess, especially to confess the "truth" of sex. Two ideas—"that we must not deceive ourselves concerning our sex, and that our sex harbors what is most true in ourselves"—are central to the definition of what constitutes normality in modern society (1978:x). For feminists, however, the injunction to speak the truth of sex is a troubling issue when it is tied to the patriarchal idea of a "natural" sexual order.

Critique and Conclusions: Foucault and Feminist Social Theory [6]

Foucault stated that "man is an invention of recent date. And one perhaps nearing its end" (1966:328). Ricci asks "With the disappearance of man, what happens to women?" (1987:11). This is an important question because the rejection of the Enlightenment subject seems to have arrived most opportunistically. Hartsock asks, "Why is it that just at the moment when so many of us who have been silenced begin to demand the right to name ourselves, to act as subjects rather than objects of history, that just then the concept of subjecthood becomes problematic?" (1990:163).

Foucault's rejection of modernity and his critique of humanism at first glance seem an attractive position for feminists concerned with critiquing the androcentric Enlightenment ideas of "rational man" and "natural woman." Western humanism has, in fact, been "built on the backs of women and people of color" (Diamond and Quinby, 1988:xv). Diamond and Quinby (1988:x) suggest four points of convergence with Foucault and feminist theory:

---

[6]Although the focus in this section is on feminist critiques, philosophers, historians, political analysts, and psychiatrists have all mounted critiques of Foucault's work. See, for example, Dean (1994), Simons (1995), Gane and Johnson (1993), Goldstein (1994), and Davidson (1997).

- "Both point to the local and intimate operations of power rather than focusing exclusively on the supreme power of the state."
- "Both identify the body as a site of power, that is, as the locus of domination through which docility is accomplished and subjectivity constituted."
- "Both bring to the fore the crucial role of discourse in its capacity to produce and sustain hegemonic power and emphasize the challenges contained within marginalized and/or unrecognized discourses."
- "And both criticize the ways in which Western humanism has privileged the experience of the Western masculine elite as it proclaims universals about truth, freedom, and human nature."

But Foucault was not specifically concerned with the different effects of a power/knowledge regime on the dominated, such as women or racial and ethnic minorities. And although Foucault clarified the ways in which discourse was implicated in power relations, he did not take account of the "relations between masculinist authority and language, discourse, and reason," which means that language is never gender-free (Diamond and Quinby, 1988:xv).

Foucault's "neutral" analysis of discourses of power, truth, and sexuality is a masculine analysis. Seeing power, as he does, "everywhere and, at some level, as available to all, it can encourage us to overlook women's systematic subordination of other women, as well as systematic domination by men" (Ramazanoglu, 1993:10). Furthermore, if power is the "principle of *all* human relationships, then power cannot be seen *in itself* as a bad thing" (Grimshaw, 1993:55). Hartsock (1990:169) points out that if power is not a "single individual dominating others or . . . one group or class dominating others," because power is everywhere, then it would seem that "dominated groups participate in their own domination"—in other words, "blame the victim." But feminists need to distinguish between "malign and benign forms of power," and a critique of power requires some "independent critical stance or perspective" (Grimshaw, 1993:55). Foucault's work may contribute to "the feminist 'deconstructive' project" but "in the end offers nothing to the projects of articulating a vision of the future, a critical feminist ethics, or a coherent feminist politics" (Grimshaw, 1993:55).

Yeatman (1990:293) is even more critical of Foucault, contending that his "postmodern relativism reveals itself as the last-ditch stand of modern patriarchy." Ricci (1987:23) points out that "society did not wait for the invention of man" to repress or oppress woman. Foucault's jettisoning of an autonomous subject and his pluralities of power call into question feminist identity politics. Martin (1988:17) points out that Foucault's ideas, if taken to "their 'logical' conclusion, if made into imperatives rather than left as hypotheses and/or methodological provocations, could make the question of women's oppression obsolete." According to Martin, feminists must refuse a political stance "which pins us to our sex" and must "refuse to be content with fixed identities or to universalize ourselves as revolutionary subjects"(1988:16).

Not all feminists have seen Foucault's position on the issue of subjectivity and identity as problematic for feminist politics. Judith Butler suggests that the idea of the constructed subject does not preclude the possibility that the subject has agency. On the contrary, she believes construction is the "necessary scene of agency" (1990:147). The subject is a discursive production, and identities are unstable "fictions," which makes for a "subversion of identity." Butler maintains this instability allows for "new possibilities for gender that contest the rigid codes of hierarchical binarisms," especially as the insistence on an either/or gender identification invariably produces "failures"—the effeminate male, the assertive female, the lipstick lesbian (1990:145).

Butler does not suggest that the "political necessity to speak as and for *women*" should be abandoned, but that the term "women" should be understood as a "field of differences" that cannot be reduced to a single identity (1992:15). In fact, the very "rifts among women over the content of the term" represent the "ungrounded ground of feminist theory." Women's agency becomes possible when the term "women" is released from the "normalized, immobilized, paralyzed" position of subordination and becomes the basis for an ongoing "radical, democratic impetus of feminist politics" (1992:16).

Butler notes the importance to feminist politics of the way in which the dualities of bodies and sex maintain "reproductive sexuality as a compulsory order" (1992:17). The control over bodies and minds of individuals that is the mark of modern power/knowledge regimes is particularly invasive for women. In this context, Bartky (1988) uses Foucault's insights on modern power/knowledge regimes to illustrate how women's bodies are subject to disciplinary practices that produce the culturally approved face and figure. A range of practices are designed to produce a "body of a certain size and general configuration"; practices that elicit from the body a "specific repertoire of gestures, postures, and movements"; and practices that are "directed toward the display of the body as an ornamental surface" (1988:64). Diets, exercise, modest deportment, and attention to makeup and clothes mark the production of the feminine, but inferior, body. But the "disciplinary project of femininity is a 'setup'; it requires such radical and extensive measures of bodily transformation that virtually every woman who gives herself to it is destined in some degree to fail" (1988:71).

Despite persistent failure, women continue to seek perfect femininity because the work is undertaken for the male. A "panoptical male connoisseur resides within the consciousness of most women: they stand perpetually before his gaze and under his judgment" (Bartky, 1988:72). Consequently, the "top sergeant in this disciplinary regime of femininity" is not simply, or only, the law, parents, teachers, the media, or so-called "beauty experts," but "everyone and yet no one in particular" (1988:74). Resistance is, however, possible. As more women realize that their increasing "political, economic, and sexual self-determination" brings them "more completely under the dominating gaze of patriarchy," they are likely to resist (1988:82). For example, "dress for success" is an injunction that has a particular and restricting meaning for women. As women learn the consequences of these cultural messages, they develop "oppositional discourses and practices"—for example, women "pumping iron" who have little concern for the "limits of body development imposed by the current canons of femininity" (1988:83).

Despite the usefulness of Foucault's insights to many feminist theorists, others have had some grave reservations about his work. Foucault's observation that power is productive as well as prohibitive, that it is everywhere, that it is not the possession of any specific group or individual, and that it is capillary and constituted in the practices of the subjected has been seen as limiting for a feminist politics. If power is all-pervasive, how is resistance possible, and if it is possible, on what grounds can the resistance be mounted? As Fraser (1989:53) asks, "Why should we oppose a fully panopticized, autonomous society?" Relations of power/knowledge may change in ways charted by Foucault, but these changes seem merely to reaffirm "women's marginal status" (Ricci, 1987:24).

The problem with Foucault's analysis, contends Fraser (1989:32), is that "he calls too many different sorts of things power." She grants that cultural practices involve constraints, but the constraints are of a "variety of different kinds and thus demand a variety of different responses. Granted, there can be no social practices without power—but it does not follow that all forms of power are normatively equivalent nor that any social practices are as good as any other." Foucault seems oblivious to the "existence of a whole body of Weberian social theory with its careful distinction between such notions as authority, force, violence, domination, and legitimation," and his lumping them all under the label "power" results in "a certain normative one-dimensionality" (1989:32). Unlike Habermas, who was concerned with continuing the emancipatory promise of the Enlightenment, Foucault (whom Habermas called a "young conservative" because he was opposed to the project of modernity) elaborated a critique of humanism as inhumanism in practice. Foucault's critique has no obvious normative basis, which it needs if it is to be an effective critique.

Fraser maintains that Foucault "adopts a concept of power that permits him no condemnation of any objectionable features of modern society"; at the same time, his "rhetoric betrays the conviction that modern societies are utterly without redeeming features" (1989:33). For example, the regime of discipline and bio-power strikes the reader as objectionable, but why is this so? The objection, answers Fraser (1989:63–64), rests on the grounds that "(1) it objectifies people and negates the autonomy one usually prefers to accord them, and that (2) it is premised upon hierarchical and asymmetrical relations and negates the reciprocity and mutuality usually valued in human relations." These objections suggest that there may still be some emancipatory potential surviving in the humanism that Foucault has rejected (1989:64). Despite her criticisms of Foucault, Fraser does concede that he has "done more, perhaps, than anyone since Marx to expose and warn against the enormous variety of ways in which humanist rhetoric has been and is liable to misuse and co-option" (1989:65).

Foucault's work has been useful precisely because he articulated and documented the problems generated by the grand narratives of social theory that celebrated the "rational man" and placed a "natural," and inferior, woman (as well as racial and ethnic others) as the opposite, or object, to this Enlightenment subject. Sociology is both "a product of and active contributor to this categorical, dualistic, gender-permeated culture," as the dualistic concepts of "organic and mechanical solidarity, gemeinschaft and gesellschaft, . . . primary and secondary groups, capitalist and proletarian, achievement and ascription, universalistic and particularistic, micro and macro . . . hard and soft methodology" illustrate (Lendermann and Niebrugge-Brantley, 1990:333).

Using Foucault to address feminist issues, however, is not a simple matter. Ramazanoglu (1993:9–10) points out that Foucault's "deconstruction of power releases feminism from rigid conceptions of, for example, universal patriarchy, racism or heterosexism" and acknowledges the "multiplicity of difference" and "the end of 'woman' as a universal category." But Foucault's work carries the danger of reverting to "speaking in abstracted terms of deconstructed 'women,' because of the absence of . . . class, racism or gender as categories of power" (Ramazanoglu, 1993:10). The challenge for feminist social theory is to be constantly aware of the different, cross-cutting standpoints and interests, at the same time recognizing where common threads persist in the exercise of power. Foucault's work on discipline, docile bodies, bio-power, and the "gaze" are important contributions to this effort.

Soper (1993:29) suggests that Foucault has been "fortunate to have attracted the attention he has from feminists, since it is not clear that he has done much to deserve it." In fact, Soper reverses the connection, suggesting that the "deepest and most persistent impact on the *zeitgeist*" has been feminism and that the "Foucault-feminism connection" must be adjusted to reflect "not only what Foucault has to offer feminism, but also the interest Foucault has himself acquired in virtue of the feminist climate of his times" (1993:30). It is interesting that Foucault was writing at the same time that the second wave of feminism surfaced. His seeming indifference to the movement is all the more curious given the importance of the work of several French feminists such as Luce Irigaray, Julia Kristeva, and Helene Cixous. In fact, Cixous was a colleague of Foucault's during his tenure at the University of Vincennes and became a close friend (Macey, 1993:221).

In many ways, Foucault's work confirms and consolidates previous feminist critiques. Thus, Soper suggests, it is unwise to approach his work with too much deference. In fact, feminists need to retain considerable skepticism about notions of the "end of man" and Foucault's later emphasis on an aesthetics of self as a means of resistance. Foucault offers feminist social theory a critical method and the recognition that "dogmatic adherence to categories and assumptions as well as the elision of differences to which such dogmatism can lead" is what feminists must be ever alert to and try to avoid (Sawicki, 1991:29).

Final Thoughts

Foucault claimed that his work was a "history of the present" and the object of his studies was to "learn to what extent the effort to think one's own history can free thought from what it silently thinks, and so enable it to think differently" (1984c:9). The goal was a "history of truth" (1984c:11). What Foucault's work means for sociology is that the certainties of classical, and much contemporary, sociological theory are called into question—certainties that have proved, in practice as well as in theory, less than emancipatory for the majority of human beings, whatever the rhetoric addressed to post-Enlightenment "Man." Foucault's work has not been greeted with overwhelming interest in North American sociology, in contrast to other disciplines such as literary and cultural studies. This is not surprising, given his critique of concepts dear to the sociological tradition such as agency, social structure, evolutionary progress, and objectivity.

Foucault stated that "Truth is a thing of this world: it is produced only by virtue of multiple forms of constraint. And it induces regular effects of power. Each society has its regime of truth, its 'general politics' of truth; that is, the types of discourse which it accepts and makes function as true" (1980:131). Sociology has been part of the "general politics" of truth since the Enlightenment. To break out of the straitjacket of contingent "truths," sociology needs to practice "problematizing theory"; that is, sociology must analyze the "trajectory of the historical forms of truth and knowledge." When sociologists do this, they will disturb the "narratives of progress and reconciliation, finding questions where others have located answers" (Dean, 1994:4). In fact, Dean maintains, "After Foucault, no longer must sociological knowledge ground itself in truth" (1994:125). Whether or not Foucault's approach is as fruitful as Dean suggests for sociology, it is clear that the cross-disciplinary nature of his work and his unsettling of modernist "truths" have to be confronted by any sociological theory concerned, as it should be, with having practical and ethical relevance for the public, political sphere.

References

Bartky, Sandra Lee. 1988. "Foucault, Femininity, and the Modernization of Patriarchal Power." In Irene Diamond and Lee Quinby (Eds.), *Feminism and Foucault* (pp. 61–86). Boston: Northeastern University Press.

Burchell, Graham, Colin Gordon, and Peter Miller (Eds.). 1991. *The Foucault Effect: Studies in Governmentality.* Chicago: University of Chicago Press.

Butler, Judith. 1990. *Gender Trouble: Feminism and the Subversion of Identity.* New York: Routledge.

———. 1992. "Contingent Foundations: Feminism and the Question of Postmodernism." In Judith Butler and Joan W. Scott (Eds.), *Feminists Theorize the Political* (pp. 3–21). New York: Routledge.

Davidson, Arnold (Ed.). 1997. *Foucault and His Interlocutors.* Chicago: University of Chicago Press.

Dean, Mitchell. 1994. *Critical and Effective Histories: Foucault's Methods and Historical Sociology.* London: Routledge.

Diamond, Irene, and Lee Quinby (Eds.). 1988. *Feminism and Foucault: Reflections of Resistance.* Boston: Northeastern University Press.

Drefus, Hubert L., and Paul Rabinow (Eds.). 1983. *Michel Foucault: Beyond Structuralism and Hermeneutics* (2nd ed.). Chicago: University of Chicago Press.

Foucault, Michel. 1961/1965. *Madness and Civilization* (Richard Howard, Trans.). New York: Pantheon.

———. 1966/1970. *The Order of Things* (A. Sheridan, Trans.). New York: Random House.

———. 1972. *The Archaeology of Knowledge* (A. Sheridan, Trans.). London: Tavistock Publications.

———. 1973. *The Birth of the Clinic* (A. Sheridan, Trans.). New York: Vintage Books.

————. 1975. *I, Pierre Rivière, Having Slaughtered My Mother, My Sister, and My Brother . . . A Case of Parricide in the 19th Century* (Frank Jellinek, Trans.). New York: Random House.

————. 1976. *The History of Sexuality: Vol. 1. An Introduction* (Robert Hurley, Trans.). New York: Vintage Books.

————. 1977. *Discipline and Punish* (A. Sheridan, Trans.). New York: Pantheon Books.

————. 1978/1980. *Herculine Barbin* (Richard McDougall, Trans.). New York: Random House.

————. 1980. *Power/Knowledge, Selected Interviews and Other Writings, 1972–1977* (Colin Gordon, Ed.). Brighton, England: Harvester.

————. 1984a. *The Foucault Reader* (Paul Rabinow, Ed.). New York: Pantheon.

————. 1984b/1985. *The History of Sexuality: Vol. 2. The Use of Pleasure* (Robert Hurley, Trans.). New York: Vintage Books.

————. 1984c/1986. *The History of Sexuality: Vol. 3. The Care of the Self* (Robert Hurley, Trans.). New York: Pantheon.

————. 1988a. *Michel Foucault: Interviews and Other Writings* (A. Sheridan and others, Trans.). New York: Routledge.

————. 1988b. "'The Minimalist Self': Interview with Stephen Riggins." In Lawrence D. Kritzman (Ed.), *Michel Foucault: Politics, Philosophy, Culture* (pp. 3–16). New York: Routledge.

————. 1991. *Remarks on Marx, Conversations with Duccio Trombadori* (R. James Goldstein and James Cascaito, Trans.). New York: Semiotext(e).

————. 1997. *The Politics of Truth* (Sylvere Lotringer and Lysa Hochroth, Eds.). New York: Semiotext(e).

Fraser, Nancy. 1989. *Unruly Practices: Power, Discourse and Gender in Contemporary Social Theory*. Minneapolis: University of Minnesota Press.

Gane, Mike, and Terry Johnson (Eds.). 1993. *Foucault's New Domains*. London: Routledge.

Goldstein, Jan (Ed.). 1994. *Foucault and the Writing of History*. Oxford: Basil Blackwell.

Gordon, Colin (Ed.). 1980. *Power/Knowledge: Selected Interviews and Other Writings, 1872–1977.* Brighton, England: Harvester.

Grimshaw, Jean. 1993. "Practices of Freedom." In Caroline Ramazanoglu (Ed.), *Up Against Foucault* (pp. 51–71). London: Routledge.

Gutting, Gary (Ed.). 1994. *The Cambridge Companion to Foucault*. Cambridge: Cambridge University Press.

Hacking, Ian. 1986. "The Archaeology of Foucault." In David Couzens Hoy (Ed.), *Foucault: A Critical Reader*. Oxford: Basil Blackwell.

Hartsock, Nancy. 1990. "Foucault on Power: A Theory for Women?" In Linda J. Nicholson (Ed.), *Feminism/Postmodernism* (pp. 157–175). New York: Routledge.

Kritzman, Lawrence D. (Ed.). 1988. *Michel Foucault: Politics, Philosophy, Culture*. New York: Routledge.

Kuhn, Thomas. 1962. *The Structure of Scientific Revolutions*. Chicago: University of Chicago Press.

Lendermann, Patricia, and Jill Niebrugge-Brantley. 1990. "Feminist Sociological Theory: The Near-Future Prospects." In George Ritzer (Ed.), *Frontiers of Social Theory* (pp. 316–344). New York: Columbia University Press.

Lotringer, Sylvere. 1989. *Foucault Live*. New York: Semiotext(e).

Macey, David. 1993. *The Lives of Michel Foucault*. London: Vintage Books.

Martin, Biddy. 1988. "Feminism, Criticism, and Foucault." In Irene Diamond and Lee Quinby (Eds.), *Feminism and Foucault* (pp. 3–19). Boston: Northeastern University Press.

Merquior, J. G. 1985. *Foucault*. London: Fontana.

Miller, James. 1993. *The Passion of Michel Foucault*. New York: Simon & Schuster.

Morris, Meaghan. 1988. "The Pirate's Fiancée: Feminists and Philosophers, or Maybe Tonight It'll Happen." In Irene Diamond and Lee Quinby (Eds.), *Feminism and Foucault*. Boston: Northeastern University Press.

Poster, Mark. 1989. *Critical Theory and Poststructuralism*. Ithaca, NY: Cornell University Press.

Ramazanoglu, Caroline. 1993. *Up Against Foucault*. New York: Routledge.

Ricci, N. P. 1987. "The End/s of Woman." *Canadian Journal of Political and Social Theory, 11*(3), 11–27.

Rouse, Joseph. 1994. "Power/Knowledge." In Gary Gutting (Ed.), *The Cambridge Companion to Foucault* (pp. 92–114). Cambridge: Cambridge University Press.

Sawicki, Jana. 1991. *Disciplining Foucault*. New York: Routledge.

Sheridan, Alan. 1980. *Michel Foucault: The Will to Truth*. London: Tavistock.

Shumway, David. 1989. *Michel Foucault*. Boston: Twayne Publications.

Simons, Jon. 1995. *Foucault and the Political*. London: Routledge.

Soper, Kate. 1993. "Productive Contradictions." In Caroline Ramazanoglu (Ed.), *Up Against Foucault* (pp. 29–50). New York: Routledge.

Trombadori, Duccio. 1991. *Michel Foucault: Remarks on Marx* (R. James, Trans.). New York: Semiotext(e).

Wuthnow, Robert, James Davison Hunter, Albert Bergesen, and Edith Kurzweil (Eds.). 1984. *Cultural Analysis*. London: Routledge & Kegan Paul.

Yeatman, Anna. 1990. "A Feminist Theory of Social Differentiation." In Linda J. Nicholson, (Ed.), *Feminism/Postmodernism* (pp. 281–299). New York: Routledge.

Chapter 24

Final Thoughts on Sociological Theory

Ilya Prigogine in 1997 reminded us that humanity has gone through three major hurts to its pride: First, Copernicus demonstrated that the earth is not the center of the universe; second, Darwin showed that humans are an evolutionary species of animal; and, third, Freud explained human behavior as governed by biological drives and the unconscious, rather than by reason (Prigogine, 1997; Wallerstein, 1999:237). These "hurts," plus dramatic social and technological changes, have left humanity and its analysts with a high level of uncertainty.

We are not only uncertain about the present; we are uncertain about the past. We live in the era of cable television, e-mail, and the Internet. It is difficult for anyone—including those of us who are older—to project ourselves back a couple of generations, much less back over the 200 years that have been the focus of this text. In 1950, we had no computers, and many families listened to the radio in the evening. Fifty years before that, there were no airplanes or cars, no factory assembly lines, no automation (machines running machines), and no movies. Communication was not only not instantaneous, it was slow; what is now called "snail mail" was all there was, and it was considered fast. There had been no so-called "world wars." So, what important events occurred in the nineteenth century, and what theories were produced to explain them?

Nineteenth-Century Sociological Theory

If you look at this book's Timeline, you will find important late-nineteenth-century events that influenced the theories of society propounded at that time. For example, in 1885 the European countries agreed on how to divide up Africa into colonies. A few years later the Chinese leaders were subdued, so that Europe could keep alive its trade in opium. Several Latin American countries had become politically independent, but were still dominated economically by the United States and to a lesser extent by Great Britain. India was still under British rule, being the single most important element in the British Empire.

The second set of important events on the nineteenth-century Timeline pertains to technology. Although the computer and television were still far in the future, developments in the 1800s included the railroad, steamship and steam engine, steel converter, telephone, and telegraph. The Suez Canal was completed, giving Britain and France easier access to the Far East. In addition, numerous breakthroughs in medicine were altering health and life expectancy. Thus, technological change and European imperialism were two aspects of nineteenth-century history that greatly affected European and U.S. theories about society.

Dominant Theories

The dominant nineteenth-century theories—presented in the first eight chapters of this text—were those of Comte, Spencer, Durkheim, Weber, and Simmel. They included French postrevolutionary positivism, with its belief in the scientific study of society for its own sake, and differentiation of functions (division of labor) as the basis for an organically integrated society. The division of society into institutional subsystems explained why individuals were becoming, as has been said today, "more and more expert in less and less." It also explained why, as Simmel noted, people change their behavior as they move from setting to setting—grocery store, church, gambling casino, school, or bar. These theories also suggested that such differentiation continues to evolve, and that social facts are not reducible to either psychology or biology.

Another important factor in nineteenth-century theory was the legitimation or acceptability of "rational-legal" authority, resulting in the increasing strength of nation-states. Coupled with the positivist belief in science was a commitment to objectivity. Finally, the analysis of social forms and content was used to explain social interaction in various kinds of groups. Although many other theoretical issues were raised, these seem to be the most important ones. Most of them are related to capitalism and the increasing industrialization of the Western world.

Dominant Ideologies

These theories were intermingled with ideological elements. For the most part, the theorists offering these explanations were supportive of industrial capitalism. Increased productivity had resulted in worldwide economic progress. The division of labor, especially the development of bureaucracy, made for greater efficiency in accomplishing the tasks of life. The evolutionary survival of the fittest was considered good, even though it meant the nonsurvival of the less fit. Understanding for its own sake was seen as a sufficient goal. Even when improvements were needed, they could be made incrementally within the established, legislative means of change. In short, industrial capitalist competition was seen as a good thing, leading to a better world. The optimism of this dominant ideology at the beginning of the twentieth century was quite consistent with the Western theories being used to explain social life, and with the "goodness" of Western development.

Secondary and Reactive Theory and Ideology

Not all nineteenth-century theorists saw the growth of industrial capitalism as a good thing. Some, such as Karl Marx, viewed capitalism from the standpoint of the workers. The theoretical arguments included the exploitive, oppressive nature of capitalism; the meaningless nature of work in the capitalist world; the importance of economic classes in world history; the expansion of capitalism to worldwide oppression, or imperialism; and the expected eventual revolution of the world's working classes against the capitalist owners. Instead of resulting in a functioning organism, the division of labor resulted in alienation. Ideologically, the first- and second-generation radical anticapitalists argued that explanation and understanding must have change as their goal. They, too, were optimists, convinced that the revolutionary overthrow of capitalism was not only needed, but inevitable.

Early-Twentieth-Century Sociological Theory

The first quarter of the twentieth century brought dramatic changes in sociological theorizing. Some were a result of the First World War, others of the Russian Revolution, and still others of economic uncertainties and fluctuations.

Gender and Race

The nineteenth-century status quo included both gender and racial inequality. Perspectives on gender included patriarchy and women's inferiority; those on race were used to justify colonialism and slavery. But by the turn of the century social scientists such as C. P. Gilman and W. E. B. Du Bois were questioning the theories behind these inequities, arguing that the theories and ideologies of inferiority had actually followed and been used to justify the treatment of women and nonwhite races. In other words, oppression needed a justification, and it arose out of the ideology of inferiority. Both Gilman and Du Bois explained the bases for equality—equal abilities and even unique contributions of women and blacks—and then argued for its implementation.

Inequality, Progress, and Revolution

Capitalist optimism about evolutionary progress was severely shaken by World War I. Critical theorists of various sorts, from the Frankfurt School to Veblen, questioned the nature of capitalism. Economic domination led to many abuses, both of individuals and of categories or groups of individuals. Wars were seen as useful to capitalists, while costing common people their lives. Capitalism furthered individualistic competition or selfishness. This competition did *not* benefit society as a whole, but only a few.

At the same time, Pareto and others (recalling Machiavelli) argued that both capitalist and radical optimism were misguided. The "iron law of oligarchy" stated that there will always be a ruling class, and that capitalism's ills will not lead to its overthrow. The final revolution leading to equal sharing in the means of production is not only not inevitable, it is impossible. Combining the critical theorists with the ruling class theorists produced a theoretical position that was critical of capitalism, but saw little chance of dramatic change for the better.

The Self

An important micro-level theoretical issue that received attention in the early twentieth century concerned how the self develops in society. Freud's emphasis was on society's control over the individual's biological drives. Cooley and Mead focused on the influence of other people (looking-glass self, significant others), and on the importance of shared symbols in any given society. All of these theorists made it clear that the individual who adjusts to one culture may, with the same character and personality, be maladjusted in a different culture.

Sociological Theory Since 1930

At the beginning of this chapter we noted some of the technological changes that we now take for granted. In addition, as you have seen in the Timeline, the years since 1930 have seen the Great Depression; World War II and many smaller wars; the successful struggle for independence of many colonies, especially in Africa and Asia; increasing feminist and racial movements for equality, and their theoretical justification; and the rise and decline of ideologically Marxist societies. Let us look briefly at sociological theories responding to a few of these developments.

Functionalism

Most observers have stated that the dominance of functional thinking in sociology, led by Parsons and Merton, peaked in the middle third of the twentieth century. The functionalist approach sees society as a differentiated organism, based on consensus and on structures developed to meet human needs, and centered in politics or economics or both. Kingsley Davis went so far as to claim that the view that societies are integrated makes every sociologist a functionalist, and modernization theorists asserted that the world's societies are striving to be like those of Europe and the United States. At the turn of the twenty-first century, however, there are few true believing functionalists. Instead, former disciples of Parsons, such as Nicholas Luhmann, have explained modern society as consisting of semi-independent subsystems, with no institution—political or economic—dominant or in control. And although there is clearly a division of labor, this does not necessarily increase society's efficiency in accomplishing its tasks.

Marxism

The other major theoretical position regarding modern society is that it is held together by ruling-class exploitation and oppression. For much of the twentieth century, the Soviet Union was held up as the vanguard of a worldwide overthrow of capitalism. By the latter third of the century, Eastern Europe and a scattering of societies around the world had adopted a Marxist ideology, though to a much lesser extent the structural characteristics that Marxists believed were necessary. By midcentury, however, the Marxist Dunayevskaya had asserted that the Soviet Union was not an example of true socialism, but was in fact state capitalism. And by the end of the century, the Soviet bloc of nations had renounced its Marxist ideology. In the 1990s, many capitalist theoreticians and ideologues stated that Marxism is dead, and there is now a capitalist world order. At the beginning of the twenty-first century, few remaining Western Marxists are willing to argue that the revolutionary overthrow of capitalism is inevitable—despite their continuing negative assessment of the nature of capitalism.

Power

Not all the important theories of society are covered either by the chapter subheadings (such as class and gender) or by the major themes of this book (such as capitalist industrialization). Many of the theories we have studied have as an important element the explanation of power.

Marxism began by treating control of the means of production as the basis for power, while later Marxists have used false consciousness and hegemonic ideology to explain why the oppressed have accepted inequities as inevitable. Feminist theorists and writers on race show how the power of white males has been structured into society and then justified by ideology ("what is, should be"). Foucault, for example, notes how notions of racial "blood" and genetic inequalities have been built into both colonialism and racial oppression in Western societies. He and his feminist critics also explain the way power is expressed through sex and violence—two very popular topics in contemporary culture.

Luhmann, following Weber, explains power as both a system and a personal characteristic. To this he adds that power requires communication, though Luhmann also argues that the semi-independence of society's subsystems makes it difficult to be "all-powerful," or to have societywide—much less worldwide—power. Finally, one point on which Luhmann departs from his mentor Parsons is in emphasizing the potential misuse of power. Power, then, is explained by economic structures and propaganda-based hegemony and authority, and includes the factors of violence, communication, and misuse.

Views of Change

What do you believe is changing in your world, and why is it changing? Let us bring together some of the views of change encountered in this book.

A few theorists still believe that change is evolutionary and progressive. Even fewer believe that change will be brought about by a mass revolution that will result in economic and social equality. Non-Marxist theorists of revolution, such as Skocpol, suggest that structural strains and early signs of change, rather than total oppression, lead to revolution. Others, such as Wallerstein, believe that changes such as increased crowding and speed are negative, making the world a worse and more difficult place in which to live, with mass destruction a real possibility and danger. Many others, following Durkheim and Giddens, adopt the liberal view that change is incremental and takes place by means of society's established or administrative mechanisms. Finally, there are still those who claim, with Pareto, that except for technology, nothing important ever changes. Our motives and selfish desires are what they have always been, and humans are no more and no less rational than ever.

Theory and Ideology

Throughout the book we have tried to make clear the way theory or explanation and ideology or justification are intertwined. Those who theorize that capitalist society is a self-corrective organism that meets people's needs are usually overtly status quo conservatives, or supportive of the capitalist status quo. Even the positivists, who claim understanding as the goal, may be covert conservatives, since they are willing to accept what is, in the process of studying it. Those who explain society as based on exploitation and oppression are at the same time ideological radicals who see capitalist society as bad and its revolutionary overthrow as desirable.

As for human nature, some see it as good but corrupted by society, while others view it as aggressive and requiring control by civilization. Many theorists, however—from micro-theorists of the self to feminists to critical theorists—believe that humans are eminently malleable, adaptable to what the environment contains, what society expects, and what technology provides.

The Future of Society

One thing is clear: The future will include many more technological changes. Some may be as simple as the video-telephone, through which we can both see and hear another person; others may involve biotechnology, such as cloning.

Other far less certain but nonetheless interesting predictions can be made, based on what we believe we know and understand. One such prediction involves surveillance. Ever since George Orwell wrote *1984*, the notion of "Big Brother" in complete control has been of concern to some people. The risk of almost total lack of privacy comes from both satellite surveillance and business and government knowledge based on tax and credit card information. This development is seen as both dangerous and likely.

A column in the *Washington Post* by Neal Peirce (2000) raises two other future possibilities, each a change from the dominance of the nation-state in the year 2000. The first, the "citistate," refers to a prediction by Robert Kaplan and others. Urban corridors, such as that from Boston to Washington, DC, will become dominant worldwide, and will control their surrounding territory—a development that is already occurring in various parts of the world. Coupled with Luhmann's theory that claims no dominant politico-economic system, but semi-independent subsystems, this can be seen as portending the decline of the nation-state.

In the same article, Peirce refers to Daniel Kemmis's argument that global economy and global ecology will simply flow around and over existing structures of governmental sovereignty. When such globalism is combined with either the multinational corporation's quasi-state character, or the notion of regional and then world government, it gives a global politico-economic spin to the "new world order." Thus, Peirce's article looks in both directions from the nation-state: citistates and supranational—even global—politico-economic units.

Finally, Wallerstein's 1999 book, *The End of the World As We Know It*, in effect predicts, as Prigogine (1997) put it, "the end of certainty." But Wallerstein declares uncertainty in very strong terms: We are, he says, headed toward some sort of cataclysm—not the Marxist revolution, which in his early days he had espoused, but something unpredictable and terrifying. Such a prediction, while hardly of great help, is simply a way of saying that "things are out of hand," and perhaps headed toward chaos.

The Future of Sociological Theory

> All intellectual disciplines and institutions take for granted that not everything has been said, written, or recorded; that words already heard or pronounced are not the last words (Lyotard, 1984:37).

> We live in an imperfect world, one that will always be imperfect and therefore always harbor injustice. But we are far from helpless before this reality. We can make the world less unjust; we can make it more beautiful; we can increase our cognition of it. (Wallerstein, 1999:250)

In the first chapter of this book, we discussed the eighteenth- and nineteenth-century background to the development of sociology. An important part of that background, whatever the theorist's ideology, was the idea that sociology could contribute to a more perfect social world. For Enlightenment philosophers, and later for sociologists, the way to a more perfect social world lay in the use of critical reason and science. Many theorists believed that a new era, a "modern" era, was at hand that would produce the "emancipation of humanity from poverty, ignorance, prejudice, and the absence of enjoyment" (Lyotard, 1988:302). Modernity would bring the "victorious struggle of Reason against emotions or animal instincts, science against religion and magic, truth against prejudice, correct knowledge against superstition, reflection against uncritical existence" (Bauman, 1987:111).

From Comte on, many sociologists were confident in promising the truth about society. However, as you have seen, agreement about the specifics of that truth, and its explanation, have been sadly lacking. In fact, sociology has been a contentious exercise in theoretical and methodological multidimensionality (Ritzer, 1992).

The most recent critiques of sociological theorizing have focused on the categorizations that have characterized much of this volume: traditional/modern, male/female, conservative/radical, public/private, objective/subjective, and class divisions. Lyotard, in *The Postmodern Condition* (1984), claimed that transformations both in society and in the production of knowledge make such postmodern rethinking both inevitable and necessary.

But what do postmodernists claim, and what do they criticize? According to Bentz and Kenny (1997:83), they claim that the

> "order" theories of Spencer, Comte, Durkheim, Merton, Parsons, and Sumner have lulled us into belief that we are part of a "real" social order which protects, balances, and regulates our activities. "Conflict" theories from Marx, Simmel, and Mills to Marcuse and Habermas, while revealing that all was not right with this ordered world, have reaffirmed the possibility of a reordered and right world. Marxist and neo-Marxist theorists present the hope that some new group—the workers, the students, or the new professional class—may bring about a more just social order. And finally, symbolic interactionists have filled in the cracks of the social world with "selves" who are created and reproduce social order.

Postmodernism seeks not only to deconstruct the accepted social categories, but to depict a world produced by and producing multiple discourses. Its critical position points to the Eurocentric character of the "grand narratives," both in their meaning and in the way they support global power relations. As Seidman (1991a:139) puts it, the grand narratives of modernity,

> industrialization, bureaucratization, urbanization, secularization, democratization, those sweeping stories that presume to uncover a uniform social process in a multitude of different societies . . . repress important differences between (and within) societies; they perpetuate Western-world hegemonic aspirations and national chauvinistic wishes: they are, in short, little more than myths that aim to authorize certain social patterns.

Certainly in our sections on class, gender, and race, these male Eurocentric tendencies and thought patterns have been apparent.

In 1941, Pitirim Sorokin predicted that by 2000 a period of nihilism would occur and any genuine, authoritative, and binding public opinion would disappear to be replaced by the "pseudo consciences" of pressure groups so that the "magnificent contractual sociocultural house built by Western man during the preceding centuries will collapse" (4:776). This pessimistic prediction is echoed in the criticisms of postmodernists. The new subjects—feminists, gays and lesbians, a rainbow of ethnic and racial identities—and the resulting approaches to the sociological enterprise reject the sociologist's ability to be objective, or to stand apart from the data in order to reveal the truths about the social. Their question is "Whose truth?"

The end of the universal "Man" and the recognition of basic differences raises important issues for sociological theory. Seidman points out that Marxists, feminists, gay liberationists, and others continue to appeal to the agency (to use Giddens's term) or effective action of the working class, women, blacks, and homosexuals. Yet these categories are no more fixed or uniform in their meaning than the concept of "Man." Seidman's point is that "categories of identity are always multiple and intersect in highly idiosyncratic and diverse ways."

> There is no reason to believe that a middle-class southern heterosexual Methodist woman will share a common experience or even common gender interests with a northern working-class Jewish lesbian, [and it is] equally naive to assume that whatever gender commonalities they do share will override their divergent interests. (Seidman, 1991a:141–142)

Critics of postmodern discourse claim that postmodernism goes too far in the direction of giving up all attempts at the practical generalization and assuming that statements about social reality tell the reader only about the writer. The idea that today's conditions and diversity efface all differences between truth and falsehood, reality and illusion, serious and nonserious dialogue may simply be a reflection of current times.

One critic of postmodernism argues that the postmodern "willingness to jettison every last notion of truth, justice, or critical understanding" and to reduce "all philosophy to an undifferentiated 'kind of writing'" becomes simply an "escape-route from pressing political questions and a pretext for avoiding any serious engagement with real-world historical events" (Norris, 1990:44). It is too easy, critics of postmodernism say, in a society giving itself increasingly to amoral acquisition, to give up the search for truth and justice.

So, should we abandon all the theoretical arguments and insights summarized in the first part of this chapter? Must the student of sociology now throw out both the "modern" categories of Durkheim, Parsons, Giddens, and Goffman and the claim that this particular expertise can help us both understand and benefit society? Must sociology, in other words, give itself up to ever-changing subjectivity, discourse, and decategorization? To us, the answer is no. Though a sociological gospel of order and system may be overstated, if not misguided, sociology can still offer cultural resistance, critique, and understanding.

As Lyotard (1988:302) puts it, the task of sociology for the twenty-first century is still to uncover and expose—to further the questioning that thinking and writing offer "to established thought, to what has already been done, to what everybody thinks, to what is well known, to what is widely recognized, to what is 'readable,' to everything which can change its form and make itself acceptable to opinion in general." Sociological theory itself "must challenge the authority of all theories of the world" (Lemert, 1992:245). Seidman (1991b:190) adds that sociology's legitimacy in the future rests on its encouragement of "an open, reflexive, elaborated culture of public debate on the meaning and moral character of our social arrangements." Sociological theory remains an important resource as long as it continues to seek, as Merton puts it, finer distinctions and the insights not available to the untrained eye. The difference,

> between what we know without sociology and what we know after we have heard its comments is not the difference between error and truth (though, let us admit, sociology may happen to correct our opinions here

and there); it is, rather, the difference between believing that what we experience can be described and explained in one way and in one way only, and knowing that possible—and plausible—interpretations are plentiful. Sociology . . . is not the end of our search for understanding, but an inducement to go on searching. (Bauman, 1990:215)

Sociological theory is always an exciting but unfinished business as long as it registers a fascination with and skepticism about the complexity and messiness of the social world, as well as about the efforts to clear up, order, and control that messiness. It is an enterprise that, if it is true to its heritage, must be concerned with the promotion of ways and means to transform that world, in order to offer dignity, health, and security to all human beings.

References

Bauman, Zygmont. 1987. *Legislators and Interpreters: On Modernity, Post-Modernity, and Intellectuals*. Ithaca, NY: Cornell University Press.

———. 1990. *Thinking Sociologically*. Cambridge, MA: Blackwell Press.

Bentz, Valerie Malhotra, and Wade Kenny. 1997. "Body as World: Kenneth Burke's Answer to the Postmodernist Charges Against Sociology." *Sociological Theory*, 15, 81–96.

Lemert, Charles. 1992. "Sez Who?" *Sociological Theory*, 10(2), 244–246.

Lyotard, Jean-François. 1984. *The Postmodern Condition: A Report on Knowledge*. Manchester, England: Manchester University Press.

———. 1988. *The Differend: Phrases in Dispute*. Minneapolis: University of Minnesota Press.

Norris, Christopher. 1990. *What's Wrong with Postmodernism: Critical Theory and the Ends of Philosophy*. Baltimore: Johns Hopkins University Press.

Peirce, Neal. 2000, January 9. "Citistates: Their Time Ripens." *Washington Post*.

Prigogine, Ilya. 1997. *The End of Certainty*. New York: Free Press.

Ritzer, George (Ed.). 1992. *Metatheorizing*. Newbury Park, CA: Sage Publications.

Seidman, Steven. 1991a. "The End of Sociological Theory: The Postmodern Hope." *Sociological Theory*, 9, 131–146.

———. 1991b. "Postmodern Anxiety: The Politics of Epistemology." *Sociological Theory*, 9, 180–190.

Sorokin, Pitirim A. 1941/1962. *Social and Cultural Dynamics* (Vol. 4). New York: Bedminster Press.

Wallerstein, Immanuel. 1999. *The End of the World As We Know It*. Minneapolis: University of Minnesota Press.

Credits

Chapter 2

Comte, Auguste, *The Positive Philosophy of Auguste Comte*, freely translated and condensed by Harriet Martineau. Copyright © 1858 New York: Calvin Blanchard.

Martineau, Harriet, *How to Observe Manners and Morals*. Copyright © 1838 London: Charles Knight.

Chapter 3

Spencer, Herbert, *The Study of Sociology*. Copyright © 1891 New York: Appleton.

Spencer, Herbert, *The Principles of Sociology*, edited by Stanislav Andreski. Copyright © 1969 New York: Macmillan, Inc.

Spencer, Herbert, *Social Statics Together with Man versus the State*. Copyright © 1910 New York: D. Appleton & Co.

Chapter 4

Durkheim, Emile, *The Division of Labor in Society*, translated by W. D. Halls, with an introduction by Lewis Coser. Copyright © 1984 London: Macmillan, Ltd.

Durkheim, Emile, *The Elementary Forms of Religious Life*, translated by Joseph Ward Swain. Copyright © 1961 New York: Collier Books.

Durkheim, Emile, *Suicide: A Study in Sociology*, translated by John A. Spaulding and George Simpson, edited with an introduction by George Simpson. Copyright © 1951 New York: The Free Press, a division of Macmillan, Inc.

Chapter 5

Rubel, Maximilien, and Margaret Manale, *Marx Without Myth*. Copyright © 1975 Oxford: Basil Blackwell.

Chapter 7

Weber, Marianne, *Max Weber: A Bibliography*, translated and edited by Harry Zohn, New York: John Wiley & Sons. Copyright © 1975 by Harry Zohn.

Weber, Max, *Economy and Society*, 2 vols., edited by Guenther Roth and Claus Wittich. Copyright © 1978 Berkeley: University of California Press. Reprinted with permission of the publisher.

Weber, Max, *From Max Weber: Essays in Sociology*, translated, edited, and with an introduction by H. H. Gerth and C. Wright Mills. Copyright © 1946 New York: Oxford University Press.

Weber, Max, *The Protestant Ethic and the Spirit of Capitalism*, trans. by Talcott Parsons, forwarded by R. H. Tawney. Copyright © 1958 New York: Charles Scribner's Sons.

Chapter 8

Coser, Lewis A., *Masters of Sociological Thought*. Copyright © 1971 New York: Harcourt Brace Jovanovich.

Simmel, Georg, *The Philosophy of Money*, translated by Tom Bottomore and David Frisby. Copyright © 1978 London: Routledge & Kegan Paul.

Index

Boldface indicates key terms.

Herland (Gilman), 269
Higher education, 252–253
Higher Learning in America, The (Veblen), 252
Hippolite, Jean, 575
Historical analysis, 41
Historical materialism, 127
History and Class Consciousness (Lukacs), 402
History of Economic Analysis, The (Schumpeter), 255
History of Marxian Economics, A (Howard and King), 425
History of Sexuality (Foucault), 576, 580, 584, 585, 590
Hobbes, Thomas, 13–14, 119, 334
Hobhouse, L. T., 346
Hochschild, Arlie Russell, 478, 517–523
  biographical sketch of, 517–518
  central theories and methods of, 518–519
  class, gender, race issues and, 519–522
  critiques and conclusions on, 523
  theories and theorists relevant to, 523
Homans, George C., 484–485, 535–536, 541
Hook, Sidney, 232–233
Horkheimer, Max, 396, 397–398, 400, 404, 405, 406, 408, 409–411, 412n
Horney, Karen, 337n
Houdini, Harry, 359
Housework, 494, 521
How to Observe Manners and Morals (Martineau), 48, 49, 53, 55
Hudis, Peter, 428
Hughes, Everett C., 481, 498
Hull House, 270, 326
Human capital, 529
Human nature
  alterability of, 300
  Coleman's view of, 532
  Collins's view of, 566–567
  communication and, 315
  critical theorists on, 405–406
  duality of, 106–107, 378
  Foucault's view of, 582–587
  Freud's view of, 334
  Giddens's view of, 387–388
  Goffman's view of, 511–514
  Habermas's theories about, 417–419
  Luhmann's view of, 378–380
  Marxist view of, 435–436
  Merton's observation of, 364
  Pareto's cynicism about, 232

Parsons's view of, 354–355
  self-reflection and, 324–325
  Service's view of, 454–455
  Smith's view of, 556–557
Human Relations Area Files, 68, 81
Human Work (Gilman), 273
Humanism, 328
Huxley, Thomas, 80
Hysteria, 584

I

"**I,**" the, 325
Id, 330
Ideal speech community, 414, 422
Ideal types, 176–177, 201
Idealism, 7–8, 283
  German tradition of, 321
Identity, virtual vs. actual, 512–513
Ideological disputes, 479–480
Ideology, 5–6, 480, 605
  "end of ideology" thesis, 483n
  nineteenth-century, 601–602
Illustrations of Political Economy (Martineau), 47, 82
Immigration, restricting, 317
Imperialism, 149–151, 260
  basic features of, 150–151
  capitalist system and, 158–159, 295
  colonialism and, 149–150, 295–296
  economic, 260
Impression management, 511–512
Impressionism, 219
Indirect form of domination, 181
Indirectly experienced reality, 556
Individual Interests and Collective Action (Coleman), 527
Individualism, 93, 94, 95
  methodological, 435, 440–441
Inductive approach, 4, 68, 507
Industrial capitalism, 256
Industrial production, 211–212
Industrial revolution, 21–23
  inventions facilitating, 22, 23
Industrial societies, 72–73
Industrialism, 385
  logic of, 469
  social change and, 34, 88
Industry, 21, 36
Inspection stage, 505
Instincts, 332
Institute of Social Research, 395–412
  central theories and methods of, 399–403
  class, gender, race issues and, 407–411